Springer Proceedings in Business and Economics

Springer Proceedings in Business and Economics brings the most current research presented at conferences and workshops to a global readership. The series features volumes (in electronic and print formats) of selected contributions from conferences in all areas of economics, business, management, and finance. In addition to an overall evaluation by the publisher of the topical interest, scientific quality, and timeliness of each volume, each contribution is refereed to standards comparable to those of leading journals, resulting in authoritative contributions to the respective fields. Springer's production and distribution infrastructure ensures rapid publication and wide circulation of the latest developments in the most compelling and promising areas of research today.

The editorial development of volumes may be managed using Springer Nature's innovative EquinOCS, a proven online conference proceedings submission, management and review system. This system is designed to ensure an efficient timeline for your publication, making Springer Proceedings in Business and Economics the premier series to publish your workshop or conference volume.

This book series is indexed in SCOPUS.

David Procházka
Editor

Regulation of Finance and Accounting

21st and 22nd Virtual Annual Conference on Finance and Accounting (ACFA2020-21), Prague, Czech Republic

Springer

Editor
David Procházka
Faculty of Finance & Accounting
Prague University of Economics
and Business
Prague, Czech Republic

ISSN 2198-7246 ISSN 2198-7254 (electronic)
Springer Proceedings in Business and Economics
ISBN 978-3-030-99872-1 ISBN 978-3-030-99873-8 (eBook)
https://doi.org/10.1007/978-3-030-99873-8

This Springer imprint is published by the registered company Springer Nature Switzerland AG
The registered company address is: Gewerbestrasse 11, 6330 Cham, Switzerland

Preface

Dear readers,
We are glad to present to you the next edition of the papers presented at the Annual Conference of Finance and Accounting (ACFA). The Conference, organised by the Faculty of Finance and Accounting of Prague University of Economics and Business, provides a vital platform for the presentation of research that address up-to-date developments in the field.

Unexpected real and financial shocks occurring recently are bringing new challenges to global finance and accounting. As a result, traditional regulatory patterns as well market participants' behaviour are being reshaped in unprecedented ways. Being co-affected by ongoing globalisation, fiscal and monetary policy, public regulation and supervision, financial markets, corporate reporting, and auditing have to adapt to those shocks which are expected to persist in the long run. Shocks manifest themselves through many channels, requiring a variant approach to investigating their causes and consequences. ACFA therefore supports the use of a mix of research methods (including modelling, empirical testing, case studies or qualitative analysis) to gain a deeper understanding of the drivers of and responses to the recent events affecting the global financial and accounting systems.

The volume offers different research perspectives on not only economic but also non-economic impacts of global developments in financial regulation, monetary and fiscal measures, or sustainable development, with a tailored focus on specifics in emerging and transitioning countries. Contributing authors investigate emerging topics (e.g., economics of emissions and corporate social responsibility reporting) as well as traditional issues requiring new approaches (e.g., exchange rate mechanisms, investment strategies and the impact of corporate reporting on economic fundamentals). We believe that such a comprehensive view of contemporary economic phenomena makes the volume attractive not only to academia but also to regulators and policymakers, when deliberating on the potential outcomes of competing regulatory mechanisms.

Prague, Czech Republic David Procházka

Chapter 1
Financial Regulations, Supervision Structure and Banking Performance in CESEE

Karel Janda and Oleg Kravtsov

Abstract We examine the effects of supervision activities and structure on the risk-adjusted performance of banking institutions. For a data set of 450 banks from 20 economies of Central Eastern Southern Eastern Europe, we employ the moderation analysis framework and find that the supervision structure affects the supervision activities. Especially, this is relevant for bank units with a status "too-big-to-fail" on the national level. Seemingly, supervision scrutiny does not affect their performance, and it is associated with lower riskiness. On the contrary, such an effect is negligible for bank units with lower capitalization. The findings highlight the area of attention for regulators and policymakers and thus contribute to the designing of effective supervision mechanisms.

Keywords Supervision · Regulation · RAROC · Moderation analysis · Central Eastern Southern Eastern Europe (CESEE)

1.1 Introduction

While the academic literature has paid increasing attention to the impacts of financial regulations on the banking sector, for example (Demirgüç-Kunt et al., 2008; Laeven & Levine, 2009; Barth et al., 2010, 2013), few studies are dedicated to the analysis of supervision efforts in the monitoring and enforcement of established rules, which are often carried out by national regulators or on behalf of supranational banking authorities, e.g. in the case of cross-border banking activities. Supervision is rarely

K. Janda
Department of Banking and Insurance, Prague University of Economics and Business, Prague, Czech Republic

Institute of Economic Studies, Faculty of Social Sciences, Charles University, Praha, Czech Republic

O. Kravtsov (✉)
Department of Banking and Insurance, Prague University of Economics and Business, Prague, Czech Republic

D. Procházka (ed.), *Regulation of Finance and Accounting*, Springer Proceedings in Business and Economics, https://doi.org/10.1007/978-3-030-99873-8_1

examined separately from regulations for several reasons. In the practical world, it is difficult to explore regulation and supervision separately due to their overlapping nature as they can interact in a complex way (Ongena et al., 2013). Partly, it is attributable to the relative opacity of supervisory activities, which stems from supervisors' reliance on confidential information (Eisenbach et al., 2016). Relatively, little is known about the distinct impact of supervisory monitoring efforts on the performance of banks.

In this paper, we build upon the recent studies with the focus on broad concept of supervisory attention without limiting to the specific supervisory programme similar to Eisenbach et al. (2016) and Hirtle et al. (2019) and adapt it to the analysis of the banking sector in Central Eastern and Southern Eastern Europe (CESEE) (Janda & Kravtsov, 2021). We exploit a cross-country difference in supervisory activities and structure to analyze the effects of supervision scrutiny on the risk-adjusted performance of the banking sector. Our hypothesis is that supervisory monitoring is associated with the lower riskiness of banking institutions and simultaneously does not impact their economic performance. Specifically, we attempt to answer the following questions:

1. How the proposed proxies for enhanced supervisory: (i) too-big-to-fail (TBTF) status measured as top three highest-ranking banks on a country level and (ii) low quartile of capitalization relate to the risk-adjusted performance of the banking units in CESEE
2. Whether the structure of supervision, i.e. national or decentralized versus centralized or supranational, has an impact on monitoring efforts and supervision activities in the form of the Single Supervisory Mechanism (SSM)

These questions are especially relevant for the regulation of banks in the region of our interest, where cross-border banking activities are significant and supervisory structure plays a significant role in the financial stability of the national economies and, consequently, the European Union (EU). In this study, we are motivated also by the latest European Central Bank (ECB) discussions on the allocation of power and responsibilities for conduct and supervision policies for the economic and financial environment, in the context of integrated supervision and regulations (Schoenmaker et al., 2011; Ampudia et al., 2019; Carstens, 2019).

Our paper contributes to the latest literature dedicated to the investigation of the impact of regulations and supervision structure on the performance of banking institutions; for example, the studies of Ongena et al. (2013), with a focus on the Central Eastern Europe (CEE) region, indicate the presence of cross-border spillover effects of domestic regulation and supervision; Djalilov and Piesse (2019) suggest that banking regulations such as those concerning capital requirements, market discipline and supervisory power are not sufficiently effective to improve the banking efficiency in the region. Bisetti (2020) highlights a novel substitution effect between public monitoring by regulators and private monitoring by shareholders; Hirtle et al. (2019) find that more supervision adds value over and above the effects of regulation. As an example, when it comes to top US banks, ranked by size within supervisory districts, these bank units, which are subject to increased supervisory attention, tend to hold less risky loan portfolios, are less volatile and are less sensitive to industry downturns. However, they have slower growth and are less profitable.

According to Bisetti (2020), the agency theory predicts a positive role for regulation in reducing shareholder monitoring costs. His findings highlight a novel substitution effect between public monitoring by regulators and private monitoring by shareholders. The results of the studies by Djalilov and Piesse (2019) suggest that banking regulations such as those concerning capital requirements, market discipline and supervisory power are not sufficiently effective to improve banking efficiency in the transition countries. This suggests that policymakers and supervisors need to explore the weaknesses of existing banking regulations and improve their effectiveness. While doing so, they need to take account of the specifications of their institutions as well as the business and economic environment.

Kandrac and Schlusche (2019) find that financial institutions that witnessed a reduction in supervision took on much more risks than their counterparts, which were subject to identical regulations but unaffected by a change in supervisory attention. From a policy perspective, their findings underscore the importance of supervision per se as a companion to financial regulation in banking policies. They show that allocating sufficient supervisory resources has an important effect on bank behaviour and is crucial for optimal banking policy and financial stability. Additionally, our paper relates to the stream of theoretical literature with a focus on the analysis of the incentives of regulators in cross-border banking activities (Calzolari & Loranth, 2011; Beck et al., 2012) and the benefits and costs of centralized and decentralized banking supervision (Schoenmaker et al., 2011; Näther & Vollmer, 2019).

Following the conceptual framework (Laffont & Tirole, 1993; Dewatripont & Tirole, 1994; Eisenbach et al., 2016), we construct the proxies for higher supervisory attention on the country level. The identification strategy stems from the cross-country comparison of the supervision structure in relation to the strength of a signal to the enhanced supervision contingent on the individual bank characteristics and country macroeconomic conditions. We propose two proxies as a signal for enhanced supervisory attention from the point of view:

1. *Macroprudential*: "too-big-to-fail" (TBTF), which is represented by the three largest banks, i.e. the highest ranking by asset size, on a single country level. On an individual bank level, the TBTF status is aligned with the definition of a large bank according to the World Bank statistics. A large bank is defined as such when its total assets account for larger than 20% of the national gross domestic product (GDP).
2. *Microprudential*: the lowest quartile of the solvency ratio (CAP_low) among peers on a single country level.

The main findings indicate that the supervision structure (i.e. centralized or decentralized supervision) matters only for the segment of larger banks (TBTF) in the national economies in the CESEE region. Supervision scrutiny does not affect their performance and is associated with a decline in the riskiness of these banks. For bank units with lower capitalization (measured as the lowest quartile of solvency ratio on a country level), we do not find any statistical evidence that the supervisory structure affects supervisory efforts ultimately leading to improvement in risk-adjusted performance. This study provides important policy implications highlighting the area of attention on banking regulators and policymakers in the CESEE region.

1.2 Data and Variables

The sample consists of 450 commercial banks from 20 economies of the European Union (EU) and European non-EU member states.[1] The bank-level data are obtained from the database BankFocus. The data cover a 7-year period, from 2012 to 2018, which corresponds to the time after the financial crisis in 2008–2010. It allows us to consider the effect of changes in economic cycles, as in Stádník et al. (2016), on the results of the calculation. The data from BankFocus are presented in the form of annual results of banks, whose financial statements are available for at least 3 years during the period 2012–2018. We restrict our sample to bank units with total assets above 100 million EUR by the end of 2018. Furthermore, the sample is refined by manually checking and removing bank units that report an error and inconsistent data. To remove the outliers, we winsorize all financial data at lower 2.5% and upper 97.5%. We acquire the macroeconomic data for GDP growth, unemployment and inflation, as well as market power concentration, from the World Bank Development Indicators.

The dependent variables are the risk-adjusted performance metrics. We use several metrics that capture performance, taking into account risk and economic capital, and for robustness, we use mixed metrics, including the simple accounting metrics. The primary measure of performance is a risk-adjusted return on capital (RAROC). It is commonly employed to assess the profitability of a portfolio or financial institution, taking into account the risk that is being assumed. The ratio shows a risk traded off against a benefit. It is defined as the ratio of the expected rate of return to the risk-based required capital or economic capital (Klaassen & Eeghen, 2009):

$$\mathrm{RAROC}_{it} = \frac{ER_{it}}{EC_{it}} \tag{1.1}$$

where ER_{it} is the expected rate of return and EC_{it} is the economic capital of the bank unit i at the time period t. The expected rate of return ER_{it} for banking unit i at time

[1] List of countries in sample – EU members: Bulgaria, Croatia, Czech Republic, Estonia, Hungary, Latvia, Lithuania, Poland, Romania, Slovakia and Slovenia. Other are non-EU members: Albania, Bosnia and Herzegovina, Kosovo, Macedonia and Serbia, and former Soviet Union independent states: Belarus, Moldova, Russia and Ukraine.

t is its realized profit NI, plus profit fluctuations σ_i, which can vary across units and over the observation period.

The economic capital EC in the denominator is the amount of capital that is needed to secure survival in a worst-case scenario or potential unexpected losses. Thus, we work with a common benchmark of minimum capital requirements.[2] It is calculated as risk-weighted assets *(RWA)* of the banking unit divided by the minimum required regulatory capital *(CAR)* threshold:

$$EC_{it} = \frac{\mathrm{RWA}_{it}}{\mathrm{CAR}^{\mathrm{reg\ min}}} \tag{1.2}$$

For robustness, we employ other metrics with semi-risk adjusted and pure accounting measures. Semi-risk adjusted metrics are represented by the ratio of return on risk-weighted assets (RORWA). It is an indicator of accounting profit per unit of risk and is measured by profit before tax as a percentage of the total risk-weighted assets. These measures are complemented by the classic accounting metrics on the performance of investments, which is measured by the ratio of net income to average equity (ROAE).

1.2.1 Observable Characteristics

The proposed proxies of supervisory attention, such as the highest ranking and low capitalization, imply certain observable characteristics, which we ought to control in the selection of the relevant covariates. First of all, we control for the size, which is an important determinant of banks' risk and performance; for example, Demsetz and Strahan (1997) find evidence that size is an advantage due to the diversification effect. Size is represented by a logarithm of total assets (TAlog). The business model and efficiency are the determining factors of the performance and riskiness of banking operations. For this, we consider metrics such as net interest margin (NIM) and the ratio of the gross loan to total assets (LOANTA). These identify the portfolio and business mix and the proportion of standard banking activities, such as lending (Teplý et al., 2015; Kuc & Teplý, 2018). The funding and liquidity structure is represented by the ratio of customer deposits to total liabilities (DLR) and loan-to-deposit ratio (LDR). DLR is capturing the structure of funding with more safe deposits in comparison to other funding sources. LDR ratio is used to assess a bank's liquidity by comparing its total loans to its total deposits for the same period. If the ratio is too high, it means the bank may not have enough liquidity to cover any unforeseen fund requirements (Table 1.1).

[2] Note: the minimum capital requirements may vary slightly across the countries and the period 2011–2016. The exact data for calculation are obtained from the World Bank – Bank Regulation and Supervision Survey

Table 1.1 Descriptive statistics of variables

Variable	*n*	Mean	s.d.	Min	Median	Max
RAROC	1,603	0.08	0.28	−0.89	0.11	0.67
RORWA	1,603	0.01	0.03	−0.09	0.01	0.08
ROAE	2,610	0.05	0.18	−0.65	0.07	0.41
TBTF	2,759	0.41	0.49	0.00	0.00	1.00
CAP_low	2,325	0.19	0.40	0.00	0.00	1.00
SSM_ dummy	3,191	0.43	0.50	0.00	0.00	1.00
TAlog	2,736	6.82	1.50	4.70	6.55	10.39
DLR	2,758	0.87	0.24	0.00	0.95	0.99
LDR	2,596	0.77	0.27	0.16	0.79	1.47
LOANTA	2,614	0.61	0.19	0.12	0.64	0.96
NIM	1,351	3.38	1.59	0.00	3.25	7.64
GDP	3,219	1.98	2.29	−9.77	2.26	9.04
INF	3,219	4.20	6.28	−1.74	2.85	59.22
UNP	3,219	9.45	6.56	0.50	6.56	35.15
HHI	3,149	1,073	342	450	1,078	2,493

Source: BankFocus Bureau van Dijk and own calculation
Note: The reported data are after winsorizing the upper and lower 2.5% to mitigate the effect of outliers

1.3 Empirical Strategy and Methods

Noting the complexity of relationships and interlinks on various levels of policies, regulations and individual bank performance, primarily we attempt in our modelling approach to track evidence of statistical significance in the causal relationships among the model inputs, namely outcome variables of performance, supervision attention proxies, supervision structure and explanatory variables. With the goal of establishing a potential link between the effect of supervision structure and the bank risk-adjusted performance, we adopt the following empirical strategy.

First, since supervisory attention is endogenously related to the current and expected bank performance, we construct the relevant proxies for a signal to enhanced supervisory attention. Identification stems from a cross-country comparison of the supervision structure (mediator) in relation to the strength of a signal to the enhanced supervision (treatment effect). Simultaneously, we control the bank-specific and country macroeconomic conditions that potentially can influence the outcome of interest (bank performance). In modelling, we assume that the effectiveness of supervision activities is identical irrespective of the geography.

Second, we employ the conventional way of analyzing the causal interactions effects in moderation analysis (Judd & Kenny, 1981; Baron & Kenny, 1986) with a help of hierarchical multi-regression approach (Aiken & West, 1991) and adapted to the causal inference framework (Imai et al., 2010; Imai & Ratkovic, 2013). The advantage of such an approach is that it allows researchers to test competing theoretical explanations by identifying intermediate variables or moderators, which contribute to the outcome through the treatment effect. A moderation analysis implies a statistical interaction effect from the interaction between continuous or categorical variables, whereby the introduction of a moderating variable tends to change the direction or magnitude of the relationship between treatment and outcome variables (Hayes, 2013).

1.3.1 How Does a Signal for Higher Supervisory Attention Relate to the Risk-Adjusted Performance of Individual Banks?

We start with testing how the proxies for a signal to enhanced supervisory attention relate to the performance of the banking units in our sample. There are three types of performance metrics for the purpose of cross-examination and robustness, as described in Sect. 1.2. We employ the ordinary least square (OLS) unit and fixed effects regression to the panel data as a baseline model:

$$Y_{ict} = \alpha_{i0} + \beta_0 T_{ict} + \gamma' \text{Controls}_{it} + \delta' \text{Macro}_{ct} + \eta_{ct} + \varepsilon_{ict} \tag{1.3}$$

where i, c and t represent the bank, country and time period, respectively. Outcome variable Y_{ict} is a performance metric that is measured by the following indicators: (i) risk-adjusted return on capital (RAROC), in the definition of Klaassen and Eeghen (2009); (ii) alternatively, return on risk-weighted assets, which is the ratio of net income to risk-weighted assets (RORWA); and (iii) the standard accounting measure of return on average equity (ROAE). T_{ict} is a treatment indicator for the signal of enhanced supervision. It takes a value of 1 if the bank unit belongs to the treated group (e.g. status of TBTF on the national level or with the lowest quartile of the capitalization CAP_low), and 0 is assigned to the control group, i.e. other remaining units in the sample. $Controls_{it}$ denotes a set of specific characteristics of the bank units. $Macro_{ct}$ is a set of country-specific variables that capture macroeconomic conditions: GDP growth, inflation and unemployment. Following Vozková and Teplý (2018), we incorporate also market concentration metrics measured by the Herfindahl Hirschman Index (HHI). η_{ct} represents the dummy variables capturing, within the state, endogenous time-variant macroeconomic country conditions, such as economic growth. ε_{ict} is the idiosyncratic error.

The results of the specification are presented in Table 1.2 in the Appendix. As anticipated, we observe in the sample that the largest banks show a better risk-adjusted performance in all types of metrics (1–3), probably utilizing the economy of scale effect and benefits of diversification. On the other hand, the bank units with lower capitalization indicate poorer risk-adjusted performance (4–6), most likely due to less efficient operations or defaults in their portfolio.

1.3.2 Does the Centralized or Decentralized Supervision Structure (SSM) Have Any Contribution to the Total Effect of Supervision Scrutiny?

With an ambitious goal of drawing a conclusion on the nature of causal relationships between supervisory structure, proposed proxies and outcome, a finding of any statistical significance will help us confirm the existence (or absence) of a link between supervision structure and the effectiveness of supervision scrutiny. Ultimately, it should lead us to the assessment of the impact on the performance of individual banks and thus fulfilling the main goal of this analysis. To do so, we adopt the hierarchical multi-regression approach of Aiken and West (1991). A common approach to the moderator analysis is based on multiple regressions, where we test the impact of different variables alone and together with interactions by determining whether their coefficients differ significantly from 0 (Baron & Kenny, 1986). In our case, we are interested in the investigation of the effect of the treatment T (supervisory attention) on the final outcome Y (bank performance) through the intermediate variable or moderator M (supervision structure). The intermediate effect variable is a binary variable that equals 1 if the bank unit belongs to the country under the centralized supervisory regime (e.g. SSM) and 0 otherwise. The simple moderation model employed in the study is formally expressed as a series of regression equations:

$$Y_{ict} = \alpha_{i1} + \beta_1 T_{ict} + \xi^T X_{it} + \delta' Z_{ct} + \eta_{ct} + \varepsilon_{ict} \tag{1.4}$$

$$Y_{\text{ict}} = \alpha_{i2} + \beta_1 T_{ict} + \beta_2 M_{ict} + \xi^T X_{it} + \delta' Z_{ct} + \eta_{ct} + \varepsilon_{ict} \tag{1.5}$$

$$Y_{ict} = \alpha_{i3} + \beta_1 T_{ict} + \beta_2 M_{ict} + \beta_3 (T \cdot M)_{ict} + \xi^T X_{it} + \delta' Z_{ct} + \eta_{ct} + \varepsilon_{ict} \tag{1.6}$$

where X denotes a set of bank-specific characteristics related to the treatment effect (signal to supervisory attention) with the indexes unit i, time period t and country c. The specification includes macroeconomic and market controls all identical to the ones used in Eq. 1.3. If the β_1 and β_3 coefficients in Eqs. 1.4, 1.5, and 1.6 are non-zero and statistically significant, then the existence of the moderation effect can be confirmed. The interpretation of the β_1 and β_3 estimates hold greater relevance for the moderation model. In testing the size of the moderation effect, the aim is not just to confirm whether treatment T causes Y contingent on moderator M, controlling a set of confounders X, but also to determine whether β_3 deviates too far from 0 or not.

1.4 Results and Discussions

The results of hierarchical linear regressions on the outcome variable of risk-adjusted performance are reported in Table 1.3 in the Appendix. For the treatment indicator "too-big-too-fail" (TBTF) in the models (2–3), the β_1 and β_3 estimates are significant, and $\beta_3 \neq 0$. The results confirm the presence of a moderation effect of the supervision structure through a treatment effect (enhanced supervisory attention) on the outcome. Adding the interaction term in the regression model (3), the explanatory power of the regression model is strengthened negligibly, with a minor increase in the values of the adjusted R^2 from 0.274 to 0.276. For a treatment indicator of higher supervisory attention, such as a lower quartile of capitalization (CAP_low), we observe a weak association and an absence of the moderation effect. The estimate β_3 shows no statistical significance in the model (6), while the estimate β_1 in the model (4–5) indicates a significant statistical power (−0.052**) at a 95% confidence interval. No changes in the values of the adjusted R-squared in the models (4, 5 and 6) confirm the absence of such an effect too. These findings indicate that the supervision structure (i.e. centralized or decentralized supervision) matters only for the category of larger banks (TBTF) on the country level in the CESEE region. Supervision scrutiny does not affect their performance, while seemingly it is associated with lower risk in this category of bank institutions. For the bank units with lower capitalization, we find no statistical evidence that the supervisory structure contributes in any way to supervisory efforts ultimately leading to improving risk-adjusted performance. A more comprehensive analysis has to be performed to get more insights into this matter.

This analysis presents an initial view and is not intended to draw an explicit conclusion about the positive or negative nature of the causal relationships between supervisory structure, proposed proxies for supervisors' attention and outcome. Nevertheless, a finding of evidence with statistical significance helps us identify the existence of a link between the supervision structure and its impact through the scrutiny of banking supervision on the safety and soundness of the largest banking institutions in the CESEE region. Thus, it fulfils the ultimate goal of this specific study. These findings provide also important policy implications related to the banking regulation and supervisory mechanism of the larger banks in the region. Especially, it is important for ensuring the financial stability of the CESEE region, where the subsidiaries of large multinational banking groups constitute a large proportion of the systemically important banks in the national economies.

1.5 Conclusion

In this paper, we study the impact of the supervision structure and regulatory scrutiny on the risk-adjusted performance of banking institutions. To do so, we employ a novel empirical strategy with the application of the moderation analysis to study intermediary effects based on the data set of 450 banks from 20 economies of the CESEE region. Our findings suggest that the supervision structure (i.e. national or supranational of SSM) matters mostly for larger banks with a status "too-big-to-fail" (TBTF) in the region of our interest. Supervision scrutiny does not affect their performance, while it is associated with lower riskiness. On the contrary, we do not observe a similar effect for bank units with lower capitalization. These findings provide important policy implications related to the banking regulation and supervisory mechanism of the largest and systemic banks. In particular, it is relevant for the supervision of the largest subsidiaries of multinational banking groups, which constitute a major portion of the systemically important banks in the national economies of the CESEE region.

Acknowledgements This chapter is part of a project that has received funding from the European Union's Horizon 2020 Research and Innovation Staff Exchange programme under the Marie Sklodowska-Curie grant agreement No.870245. We also acknowledge financial support from the Czech Science Foundation (grant 22-19617S). Views expressed represent exclusively the authors' own opinions and do not necessarily reflect those of our institutions.

Appendix

Table 1.2 Proxies for the enhanced supervision attention and individual banks' performance

Variables	(1) RAROC	(2) RORWA	(3) ROAE	(4) RAROC	(5) RORWA	(6) ROAE
TBTF	0.076***	0.007***	0.032**			
	(0.026)	(0.003)	(0.014)			
CAP_low				−0.052**	−0.006**	−0.015
				(0.023)	(0.003)	(0.013)
TAlog	0.057***	0.007***	0.020***	0.062***	0.007***	0.024***
	(0.009)	(0.001)	(0.004)	(0.007)	(0.001)	(0.004)
DLR	0.235	0.027	0.085	0.199	0.022	0.073
	(0.202)	(0.021)	(0.065)	(0.196)	(0.020)	(0.081)
LDR	0.544**	0.069***	0.148*	0.457**	0.059***	0.154
	(0.225)	(0.022)	(0.076)	(0.226)	(0.022)	(0.099)
LOANTA	−0.883***	−0.111***	−0.358***	−0.782***	−0.099***	−0.335**
	(0.273)	(0.027)	(0.107)	(0.274)	(0.028)	(0.131)
NIM	0.043***	0.005***	0.021***	0.043***	0.005***	0.023***
	(0.010)	(0.001)	(0.004)	(0.010)	(0.001)	(0.004)
GDP	−0.005	−0.000	−0.000	−0.007	−0.000	0.000
	(0.009)	(0.001)	(0.003)	(0.009)	(0.001)	(0.003)
INF	−0.013	−0.002*	−0.014***	−0.013	−0.002*	−0.013***
	(0.011)	(0.001)	(0.005)	(0.011)	(0.001)	(0.005)
UNP	0.001	0.000	0.001	0.002	0.000	0.000
	(0.008)	(0.001)	(0.004)	(0.008)	(0.001)	(0.004)
HHI	−0.000**	−0.000*	−0.000*	−0.000*	−0.000	−0.000

(continued)

Table 1.2 (continued)

	(1)	(2)	(3)	(4)	(5)	(6)
Variables	RAROC	RORWA	ROAE	RAROC	RORWA	ROAE
	(0.000)	(0.000)	(0.000)	(0.000)	(0.000)	(0.000)
Constant	−0.482	−0.066**	−0.079	−0.467	−0.064**	−0.125
	(0.299)	(0.031)	(0.140)	(0.295)	(0.031)	(0.148)
Time FE	Yes	Yes	Yes	Yes	Yes	Yes
Country FE	Yes	Yes	Yes	Yes	Yes	Yes
Observations	881	881	1,209	872	872	1,123
R-squared	0.302	0.336	0.237	0.298	0.334	0.246
Adjusted R^2	0.274	0.309	0.215	0.270	0.307	0.222
F test	0.000	0.000	0.000	0.000	0.000	0.000

Note: Standard errors are shown in parenthesis FE stands for fixed effects. Stars indicate statistical significance levels: ***$p < 0.01$, **$p < 0.05$ and *$p < 0.10$

Table 1.3 Results for the outcome variable of risk-adjusted performance (RAROC)

	(1)	(2)	(3)	(4)	(5)	(6)
Variables	TBTF	TBTF_SSM	TBTF_SSM	CAP_low	CAP_low_ SSM	CAP_low_ SSM
TBTF (T)	0.076***	0.076***	0.144***			
	(0.026)	(0.026)	(0.045)			
TBTF (T x M)			−0.101*			
			(0.052)			
CAP_low (T)				−0.052**	−0.052**	−0.048
				(0.023)	(0.023)	(0.048)
CAP_low (T x M)						−0.004
						(0.055)
M		−0.179	−0.132		−0.143	−0.143
		(0.122)	(0.124)		(0.122)	(0.122)
Constant	−0.661***	−0.482	−0.539*	−0.611**	−0.467	−0.466
	(0.242)	(0.299)	(0.301)	(0.237)	(0.295)	(0.295)
Bank controls	Yes	Yes	Yes	Yes	Yes	Yes
Macro controls	Yes	Yes	Yes	Yes	Yes	Yes
Time FE	Yes	Yes	Yes	Yes	Yes	Yes
Country FE	Yes	Yes	Yes	Yes	Yes	Yes
Observations	881	881	881	872	872	872
R-squared	0.302	0.302	0.305	0.298	0.298	0.298
Adjusted R^2	0.274	0.274	0.276	0.270	0.270	0.269
F test	0.000	0.000	0.000	0.000	0.000	0.000

Note: Standard errors are shown in parenthesis robust to heteroscedasticity. FE stands for fixed effects. ***$p < 0.01$, **$p < 0.05$ and *$p < 0.10$

References

Aiken, L. S., & West, S. G. (1991). *Multiple regression: Testing and interpreting interactions*. Sage.

Ampudia, M., Beck, T., Beyer, A., et al. (2019). *The architecture of supervision*. Social Science Research Network.

Baron, R. M., & Kenny, D. A. (1986). The moderator-mediator variable distinction in social psychological research: conceptual, strategic, and statistical considerations. *Journal of Personality and Social Psychology, 51*, 1173–1182. https://doi.org/10.1037//0022-3514.51.6.1173

Barth, J. R., Lin, C., Ma, Y., et al. (2010). *Do bank regulation, supervision and monitoring enhance or Impede Bank efficiency?* Social Science Research Network.

Barth, J. R., Lin, C., Ma, Y., et al. (2013). Do bank regulation, supervision and monitoring enhance or impede bank efficiency? *Journal of Banking & Finance, 37*, 2879–2892. https://doi.org/10.1016/j.jbankfin.2013.04.030

Beck, T., Todorov, R., & Wagner, W. (2012). *Supervising cross-border banks: Theory, evidence and policy*. Social Science Research Network.

Bisetti, E. (2020). *The value of regulators as monitors: Evidence from banking*. Social Science Research Network.

Calzolari, G., & Loranth, G. (2011). Regulation of multinational banks: A theoretical inquiry. *Journal of Financial Intermediation, 20*, 178–198. https://doi.org/10.1016/j.jfi.2010.02.002

Carstens, A. (2019). The quest for financial integration in Europe and globally. Web page accessed: https://www.bis.org/speeches/sp190912.htm

Demirgüç-Kunt, A., Detragiache, E., & Tressel, T. (2008). Banking on the principles: Compliance with basel core principles and bank soundness. *Journal of Financial Intermediation, 17*, 511–542. https://doi.org/10.1016/j.jfi.2007.10.003

Demsetz, R. S., & Strahan, P. E. (1997). Diversification, Size, and Risk at Bank Holding Companies. *Journal of Money, Credit and Banking, 29*, 300–313. https://doi.org/10.2307/2953695

Dewatripont, M., & Tirole, J. (1994). *The prudential regulation of banks*. ULB—Universite Libre de Bruxelles.

Djalilov, K., & Piesse, J. (2019). Bank regulation and efficiency: Evidence from transition countries. *International Review of Economics & Finance, 64*, 308–322. https://doi.org/10.1016/j.iref.2019.07.003

Eisenbach, T., Townsend, R., & Lucca, D. (2016). *The economics of bank supervision*. Federal Reserve Bank of New York.

Hayes, A. F. (2013). *Introduction to mediation, moderation, and conditional process analysis: A regression-based approach*. Guilford Press.

Hirtle, B., Kovner, A., & Plosser, M. C. (2019). *The impact of supervision on Bank performance*. Social Science Research Network.

Imai, K., & Ratkovic, M. (2013). Estimating treatment effect heterogeneity in randomized program evaluation. *Ann Appl Stat, 7*, 443–470. https://doi.org/10.1214/12-AOAS593

Imai, K., Keele, L., & Tingley, D. (2010). A general approach to causal mediation analysis. *Psychological Methods, 15*, 309–334. https://doi.org/10.1037/a0020761

Janda, K., & Kravtsov, O. (2021). Banking Supervision and Risk-Adjusted Performance inthe Host Country Environment. FFA Working Papers, 3, Article 2021.001. https://doi.org/10.XXXX/xxx.2020.006

Judd, C. M., & Kenny, D. A. (1981). Process analysis: Estimating mediation in treatment evaluations. *Evaluation Review, 5*, 602–619. https://doi.org/10.1177/0193841X8100500502

Kandrac, J., & Schlusche, B. (2019). *The effect of bank supervision on risk taking: Evidence from a natural experiment*. Social Science Research Network.

Klaassen, P., & van Eeghen, I. (2009). *Economic capital: How it works, and what every manager needs to know*. Elsevier.

Kuc, M., & Teplý, P. (2018). A financial performance comparison of Czech Credit Unions and European Cooperative Banks. *Prague Economic Papers, 27*, 723–742. https://doi.org/10.18267/j.pep.682

Laeven, L., & Levine, R. (2009). Bank governance, regulation and risk taking. *Journal of Financial Economics, 93*, 259–275. https://doi.org/10.1016/j.jfineco.2008.09.003

Laffont, J.-J., & Tirole, J. (1993). *A theory of incentives in procurement and regulation*. MIT Press.

Näther, M., & Vollmer, U. (2019). National versus supranational bank regulation: Gains and losses of joining a banking union. *Economic Systems, 43*, 1–18. https://doi.org/10.1016/j.ecosys.2018.05.004

Ongena, S., Popov, A., & Udell, G. F. (2013). "When the cat's away the mice will play": Does regulation at home affect bank risk-taking abroad? *Journal of Financial Economics, 108*, 727–750. https://doi.org/10.1016/j.jfineco.2013.01.006

Schoenmaker, D., Allen, F., Beck, T., et al. (2011). *Cross-border banking in Europe: Implications for financial stability and macroeconomic policies*. Centre for Economic Policy Research.

Stádník, B., Raudeliūnienė, J., & Davidavičienė, V. (2016). Fourier analysis for stock price forecasting: Assumption and evidence. *Journal of Business Economics and Management, 17*, 365–380. https://doi.org/10.3846/16111699.2016.1184180

Teplý, P., Mejstřík, M., & Pečená, M. (2015). *Bankovnictví v teorii a praxi/Banking in theory and practice*. Knihkupectví Karolinum.

Vozková, K., & Teplý, P. (2018). Determinants of bank fee income in the EU Banking Industry – Does market concentration matter? *Prague Economic Papers, 27*, 3–20. https://doi.org/10.18267/j.pep.645

Chapter 2
The Income Velocity of Money – Determinants (Case of the Czech Republic)

Jan Bohacik

Abstract The income velocity of money expresses a unique relationship – what is the production that an economy can create with a given money stock or how much money is needed to create a given production. The aim of this chapter is to elaborate on the factors that are behind the money velocity. An overview of the potential determinants of money velocity will be presented together with a brief description of the determinants. Where available, data relevant for the Czech Republic are presented. The examined period is 2000–2018, when the money velocity experienced a gradual decline.

Keywords Velocity of money · Money supply · Household finance

2.1 Introduction

As one professor said, money velocity is like a goulash soup – too many different ingredients can be a part of it. Indeed, it is quite ambitious to express the relationship between money and production using a single variable. The velocity of money, however, historically had and still has its place in the economic theory (despite the fact that inflation targeting, which is a prevailing monetary policy today, does not rely on money much). The income velocity of money[1] expresses a unique relationship – what is the production that an economy can create with a given money stock or how much money is needed to create a given production. The remaining part of the template will introduce some basic requirements on the paper format.

This chapter is intended as a broad study of potential determinants of the money velocity. An overview of the potential determinants of money velocity will be

[1] To simplify, further only "money velocity" or "the velocity of money."

J. Bohacik (✉)
Department of Monetary Theory and Policy, Prague University of Economics and Business, Prague, Czech Republic
e-mail: xbohj17@vse.cz

D. Procházka (ed.), *Regulation of Finance and Accounting*, Springer Proceedings in Business and Economics, https://doi.org/10.1007/978-3-030-99873-8_2

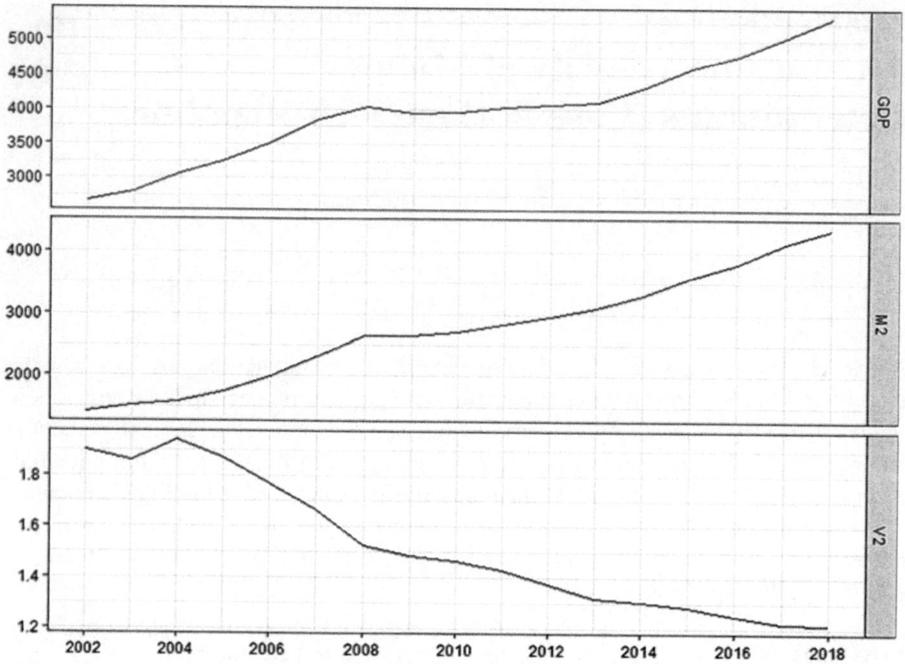

Fig. 2.1 GDP, M2 and V2 in the Czech Republic for the period 2002–2018. (Source: Czech National Bank, authorial computation)

presented together with a brief description of the determinants. Where available, data relevant for the Czech Republic will be presented. As for the money velocity determinants in general, a comprehensive historical overview can be found in (Humphrey, 1993). The velocity of broad money (M2, M3) in the Czech Republic was examined, for example, in (Jilek, 2015) or (Michl, 2019), where relationship with real GDP and inflation was examined.

2.2 Data and Methodology

The income velocity of money (V2[2]) in the Czech Republic, calculated as a ratio of 1-year GDP (measured in current prices) to the money stock (defined as M2) at the end of each year, was following (Fig. 2.1):

[2]V2 = Income velocity of money when money is defined as the monetary aggregate M2.

The income velocity of money had been showing a lasting decline since 2004. Each Czech koruna was used almost 2 times on average in 2004[3], but only 1.2 times in 2018. There is a real chance V2 is going to drop below 1 in a few years. The money stock would be lower than 1-year GDP. As time goes by, we need more and more money to achieve a certain level of GDP, that is, the productive capability of the money is worsening. This is an interesting phenomenon. The key question is: Which factors lie behind this drop?

2.3 Money Velocity Determinants

The potential determinants of money velocity may be split into:

1. Long-term structural:

Factors affecting components and structure of the economic system. These factors change over decades or even centuries. In the long run, economies experience evolution from barter (natural exchange) to monetized system, which is usually coupled with population shift from rural to urban areas and development of banking system and financial markets. Another factor that has an impact on the money balances is the degree of vertical integration of the economy.

2. Psychological:

Determinants that are subjective or personal and thus diverse among economic subjects. They are quite difficult to capture. The psychological determinants are: perception of uncertainty, mercantile confidence, tastes and preferences of the holders of money (especially liquidity preference), risk aversion or disposition to hoarding.

3. Financial:

Determinants connected to the financial situation of an individual or system as a whole. These are income (wealth), size of payments, frequency of income and payments, transaction costs and use of trade credit. Then there are factors like inflation expectations, domestic currency depreciation expectations and interest rate, which are heavily influenced by fiscal and monetary policy (Table 2.1).

Urbanization (population shift from rural areas to urban areas) leads to the decline of the natural exchange and the production for own consumption. It simultaneously leads to the expansion of the banking system and monetary sphere. Monetization of economic activity increases demand for money balances, which implicates the decline of the money velocity.

[3]In fact, each koruna was used more than 2 times on average if we talk about all economic transactions. However, when expressing the income velocity of money, we are concerned only about transactions that are used to calculate gross domestic product.

Table 2.1 Summary of money velocity determinants

Urbanization	–	Frequency of income	+
Banking development	–	Size of payments	–
Barter	+	Wealth	+
Trade credit	+	Distribution of income	+/–
Degree of vertical integration	–	Interest rate	+
Financial innovations	+	Inflation expectations	+
Uncertainty	–	Depreciation expectations	+
Hoarding	–		

Note: + means the rise of the determinant leads to the rise of money velocity; – vice versa
Source: Author

Table 2.2 Currency to M2

2002	2004	2006	2008	2010	2012	2014	2016	2018
14.03	15.00	14.88	13.88	13.20	13.18	13.09	13.49	13.06

Source: ARAD (Czech National Bank), authorial computation

The share of urban population in the Czech Republic increased from 70.6% to 73.4% during the period 2001–2011. In December 2018, the share of urban population was 73.3% (Czech Statistical Office).

Banking development (composition of the payment media) – only currency was considered money in the past[4]. This is equivalent to the situation when we define money as M0, which consists solely of the currency in circulation. The increased popularity of bank deposits relatively to currency causes M0 to fall and money velocity (calculated as GDP/M0) to increase. However, if we define money as M2, there should be no significant change to the money velocity when the economic subjects start to prefer bank deposits relatively more to currency. Nevertheless, this was not the case with the Czech Republic (Table 2.2):

In general, each payment medium (coins, banknotes, current deposits, etc.) can be attributed to its own velocity of circulation. The higher are the opportunity costs of holding a certain type of monetary asset, the higher is the motivation to pay with it. Therefore, for example, coins should circulate more than term deposits.

Barter (natural exchange) – economic subjects do not have to carry out trade by means of money. They may simply swap the goods. In practice, however, it is difficult to measure the volume of bartered trade.

Trade credit (non-interest, deferred payment) – if the popularity of trade credit rises, less money is needed. The ratio of trade credit (and advances) to GDP in the Czech Republic oscillated between 41% and 51% (Table 2.3).

Degree of vertical integration (number of production stages) – the longer it takes for the product to transform from raw material to the final product, respectively the

[4] Strictly speaking, only coins were considered money, not banknotes.

Table 2.3 Trade credits and advances to GDP

2002	2004	2006	2008	2010	2012	2014	2016	2018
50.9	46.8	45.1	41.3	46.5	49.7	48.4	49.0	46.1

Source: OECD – 720. Financial balance sheets – non-consolidated – SNA 2008, Total economy

Table 2.4 Financial derivatives and employee stock options to GDP (liabilities to GDP and total net position to GDP) in %

2002	2004	2006	2008	2010	2012	2014	2016	2018
0.85	1.16	1.27	4.12	2.50	2.77	2.16	1.57	2.71
0.32	0.27	0.48	−0.18	−0.10	−0.46	0.16	−0.12	−0.05

Note: Total net position is calculated as financial derivatives (assets) – Financial derivatives (liabilities)

Source: OECD – 710. Financial balance sheets – consolidated – SNA 2008, Total economy

more stages of production exist, the more money is needed to serve the production process. Integrated economy should therefore require less money balances.

The measurement of vertical integration is a rather demanding process. For instance, (Maddigan, 1981) or (Ponomarenko & Sergeev, 2016) measure the level of vertical integration for a group of companies, but the described procedures cannot be applied to an economy as a whole. Besides, there are not many studies of vertical integration relevant for the Czech Republic, and if any, they are focused on a specific sector or companies. Nevertheless, the observed drop in the money velocity in the period 2004–2018 would have to be caused by a massive de-integration of production, which is not very plausible.

Financial innovations usually act as accelerators of money velocity. Some examples of financial innovations are (a) clearing centers providing mutual settlements of receivables and liabilities; (b) new types of investment and savings accounts; (c) technical innovations like internet banking; (d) financial derivatives; etc. These innovations have the potential to lower transactions and precautionary money demand. For instance, if a bank uses a financial derivative to hedge against currency risk and closes its position in the currency, the risk is eliminated (or at least mitigated) and less precautionary money balances are needed. However, if used for speculative purposes, financial innovations may result in higher money demand. In the Czech Republic, the size of open derivatives is rather low (Table 2.4):

Uncertainty –economic agents cannot be certain about future development. They want their income to be at least as high as their expenses. To protect from unforeseen events, they hold (precautionary) money reserves. If the level of confidence in the business and financial system is high, economic subjects hold less precautionary balances. There are many measures that can be used as a proxy to estimate the level of uncertainty in an economy. For example, the European Commission issues the ESI index (economic sentiment indicator), which captures the market sentiment throughout the economy (Fig. 2.2).

Fig. 2.2 Economic sentiment indicator (CZ.ESI). (Source: European Commission, authorial computation)

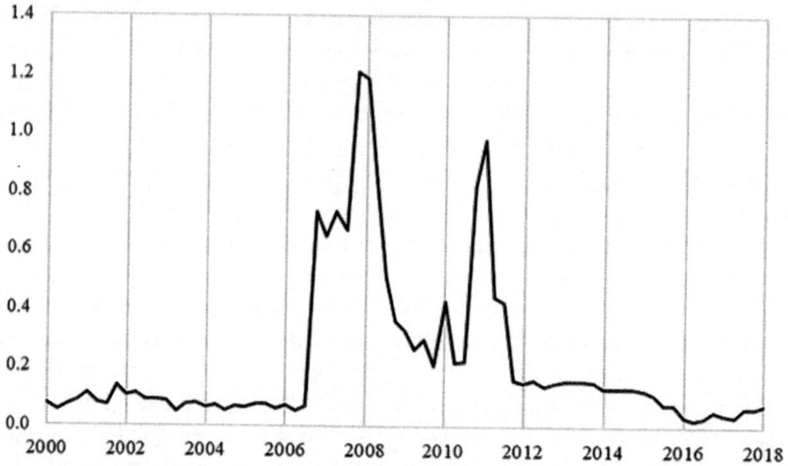

Fig. 2.3 3M EURIBOR – 3M EUR OIS. (Source: Refinitiv, authorial computation)

Another measure that aims more at the distress of financial markets is LIBOR-OIS spread. As the Czech Republic is closely linked to the eurozone, one can examine EURIBOR-OIS spread instead of PRIBOR-OIS spread, where shorter data history is available (Fig. 2.3).

Hoarding (money accumulation and its storage, without intention to use it). An example of hoarding from the past is gold buried in the ground. It is problematic to estimate the amount of hoarded money. In fact, observing money velocity is one of the methods to quantify the level of hoarding. However, (Cimburek & Rezabek, 2013) show that hoarding was present in 2008 in the Czech Republic.

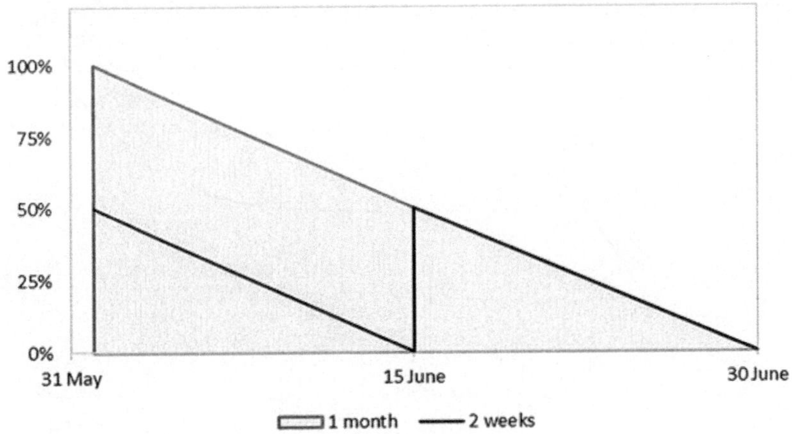

Fig. 2.4 2-week and 1-month income frequency. (Source: Author)

Frequency of income – if the economic subjects are paid more frequently, they hold lower money balances on average, as indicated on the graph (Fig. 2.4):

Let us assume that (a) the economic subjects are paid at the beginning of the period; (b) they keep their whole income in the form of money; (c) they spend the whole income linearly until the end of the income period; (d) the monthly income is 100%. Then:

- At monthly income frequency, the average money balance is 50%.
- At 2-week income frequency, the average money balance is 25%.

By shortening the income frequency by 50%, the average money balance fell by 50%. In reality, the assumptions do not hold, so the effect would be less than 50% (primarily due to savings creation). Additionally, households, corporations and governments have different income and outcome cycles.

Size of payment – the higher is the absolute value of the expense, the longer it takes to accumulate the targeted value (price). In the Czech Republic, the greatest concern is about real estate prices, which have been experiencing a significant increase over the last years (Fig. 2.5).

Distribution of income – socio-economic classes have various income cycles and transactions needs. Therefore, their money velocity may differ. The total income velocity of the money is then calculated as a weighted average of the individual velocities of various socio-economic classes, where the weights are the average money balances of the classes to the overall average money balances:

$$V = V1 * \frac{M1}{(M1 + M2)} + V2 * \frac{M2}{(M1 + M2)} \qquad (2.1)$$

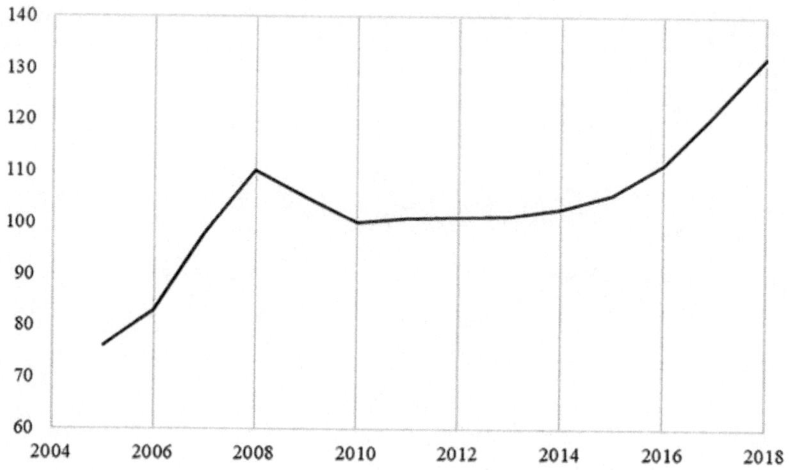

Fig. 2.5 Price indices of real estate – Czech Republic. (Note: Year of weighting scheme 2010, average 2010 = 2010. Source: Czech Statistical Office, authorial computation)

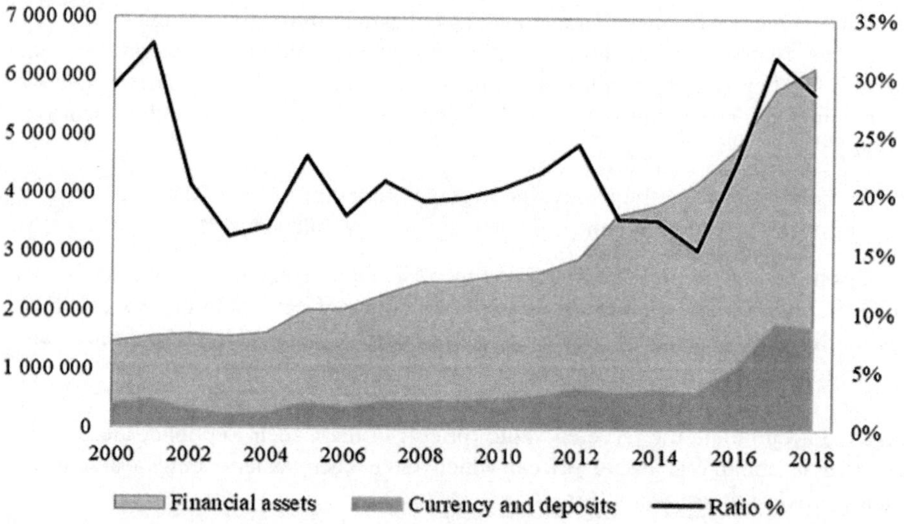

Fig. 2.6 Currency and deposits to financial assets. (Source: OECD – "710. Financial balance sheets – consolidated – SNA 2008", authorial computation)

Where V is the aggregate income velocity of money; V1 V2 are the income velocities of money of the socio-economic classes; M1, M2 express the average money balances of the socio-economic classes.

Wealth – it should be more rational for richer subjects to hold smaller cash balances relatively to the other assets, as money is a non-interest-bearing asset. However, if we look at the Czech Republic, the share of money to the financial assets does not show any discernible pattern (Fig. 2.6).

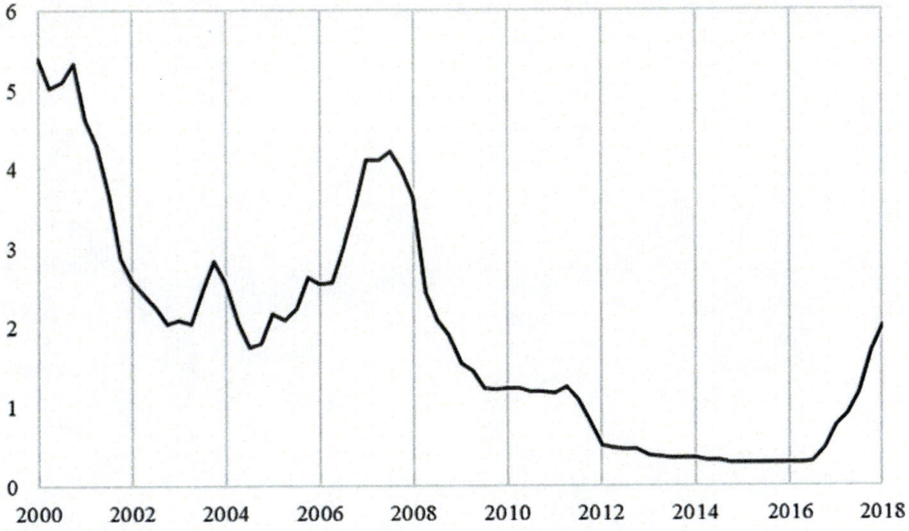

Fig. 2.7 3M PRIBOR (%). (Source: Refinitiv, authorial computation)

Interest rate – it is the opportunity cost of holding money. In case of interest rate decline, it is relatively cheaper to hold cash balances. The crucial point here is to define what money is – there are some interest-bearing deposits in M2 as well (Fig. 2.7).

Inflation expectations – high inflation expectations may lead to "run from cash" situation. If the future inflation is perceived to be high, the purchasing power of money is at risk and the expectations themselves (even if they are not eventually fulfilled) motivate economic subject to get rid of cash balances – either by increased consumption or by transformation of assets outside of M2. Moreover, inflation expectations may accelerate domestic currency depreciation.

The problem with the quantification of inflation expectations is there are many subjects in the economy and each of them has its own expectations. CNB currently publishes only the view of macro-financial analysts (employees of major financial institutions). Households' inflation expectations were published from 1999 to 2007. However, the measures became too volatile and difficult to interpret (CNB, 2007). The European Commission conducts some qualitative surveys on households' inflation expectations, and the discussion on its interpretation can be found in (Arioli et al., 2017).

Depreciation expectations – economic subjects may lose confidence in the domestic currency. Therefore, they are more inclined to get rid of it. Like inflation expectations, depreciation expectations vary across the economy. However, an estimate can be made comparing the forward and the spot CZK/EUR rate. As can be seen, the depreciation expectations were negligible (if any) (Fig. 2.8).

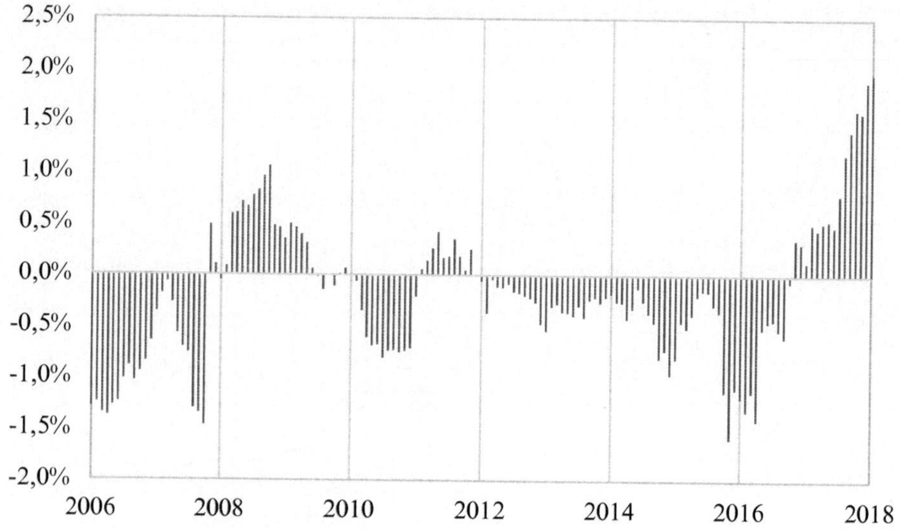

Fig. 2.8 CZK depreciation relative to EUR. (Note: Calculated as (1Y forward/spot rate – 1); + CZK depreciation; – CZK appreciation. Source: Refinitiv, authorial computation)

2.4 Conclusion

Potential determinants of the income velocity of money were discussed and their comprehensive overview was made. The determinants were classified into 3 groups: (a) structural; (b) psychological and (c) financial. Data for the Czech Republic were collected to analyze the determinants over the period 2002–2018, when the income velocity of money experienced a lasting decline.

Based on ratio analysis and graphical analysis, the major potential determinants of the velocity fall are: declining interest rates, increased real estate prices and shocks to economic sentiment. Other factors that should be also considered are: increased inflation and depreciation expectations, use of trade credit or the degree of vertical integration. More could be elaborated on the financial innovations, distribution of income or payment frequency.

Acknowledgments This paper has been prepared within the research project "Dynamika financnich a ekonomickych velicin v kontextu vnejsi rovnovahy," registered by the Grant Agency under the registration number F1/03/2020.

References

Arioli, R., Bates, C., Dieden, H., et al. (2017). *EU consumers' quantitative inflation perceptions and expectations: An evaluation* (Occasional Paper Series 186). European Central Bank.

Cimburek, J., & Rezabek, P. (2013). Currency in circulation: Reaction in crises [In Czech]. *Cesky financni a ucetni casopis, 3*, 62–72. https://doi.org/10.18267/j.cfuc.358

Czech National Bank. (2007). Novy pristup CNB ke sledovani inflacnich ocekavani domacnosti v Ceske republice. [seen 2020-02-22]. https://www.cnb.cz/cs/menova-politika/zpravy-o-inflaci/tematicke-prilohy-a-boxy/Novy-pristup-CNB-ke-sledovani-inflacnich-ocekavani-domacnosti-v-Ceske-republice/

Humphrey, T. M. (1993). The origins of velocity functions. *Federal Reserve Bank of Richmond Economic Quarterly, 79*(4), 1–17.

Jilek, J. (2015). Makroekonomicky dopad rustu sirokych menovych agregatu ve vybranych zemich v letech 1960–2007 [In Czech]. *Ekonomicky casopis/Journal of Economics, 63*(1), 3–18.

Maddigan, R. J. (1981). The measurement of vertical integration. *The Review of Economics and Statistics, 63*(3), 328–335. https://doi.org/10.2307/1924349

Michl, A. (2019). Money and inflation: Lost cointegration [In Czech]. *Politicka ekonomie, 67*(4), 385–405. https://doi.org/10.18267/j.polek.1255

Ponomarenko, T., & Sergeev, I. (2016). Quantitative methods for assessing levels of vertical integration as a basis for determining the economic and organizational sustainability of an Industrial Corporation. *Indian Journal of Science and Technology, 9*(20). https://doi.org/10.17485/ijst/2016/v9i20/94482

Woodford, M. (2008). How important is money in the conduct of Monetary Policy? *Journal of Money, Credit and Banking, 40*(8), 1561–1598. https://doi.org/10.3386/w13325

Chapter 3
The Impact of Central Bank Policy Rate on Financial Development: The Case of Europe

Korhan K. Gokmenoglu, Aysel Amir, and Mohamad Kaakeh

Abstract This study investigates the influence of central bank policy rate (CBPR) on financial development for a panel of fifteen European Union economies, utilizing annual data ranging from 2002 to 2017 inclusively. To this aim, an autoregressive distributive lag model was applied and Pooled Mean Group estimates were obtained. Economic growth, innovation, globalization index, and corruption perception index were incorporated within the empirical model as control variables to refrain from omitted variable bias. Our findings indicate that CBPR is a major driver of financial development alongside reduced corruption, increased economic growth, and increased globalization in the case of Europe. Based on the empirical findings we have obtained, we offer various policy recommendations such as; following the monetary policy which will support financial development, ensuring the central bank's independence, increasing trust in institutions, combating the informal economy, and encouraging innovations, especially in the financial sector. We discuss the policy implications of our findings in the conclusion section in more detail.

Key words Financial development · Central bank policy rate · Corruption · Innovation · ARDL-PMG

3.1 Introduction

The significance of financial development on a broad set of macroeconomic fundamentals, most notably economic growth (Calderón & Liu, 2003; Pradhan et al., 2018), has been predominately emphasized within the existing literature. The establishment of extensive literature devoted to the importance of financial development

K. K. Gokmenoglu (✉)
Department of Finance and Banking, Ankara HBV University, Ankara, Turkey
e-mail: korhan.gokmenoglu@hbv.edu.tr

A. Amir · M. Kaakeh
Department of Banking and Finance, Eastern Mediterranean University, Famagusta, North Cyprus via Mersin 10, Turkey
e-mail: aysel.amir@emu.edu.tr; mohamad.kaakeh@emu.edu.tr

D. Procházka (ed.), *Regulation of Finance and Accounting*, Springer Proceedings in Business and Economics, https://doi.org/10.1007/978-3-030-99873-8_3

has resulted in the construction of research that investigates the determinants of financial development. Although a wide range of potential determinants, such as inflation (Rousseau & Yilmazkuday, 2009), interest rates (Roubini & Sala-i-Martin, 1992; Odhiambo, 2009), human capital (Calderón & Liu, 2003), and liquidity (Pagano, 1993; Alfaro et al., 2004), have been examined to see their effect on financial development, central bank policy rate (CBPR) has been overlooked thus far. Our study aims to fulfill this gap by inspecting the role of the CBPR on financial development for the case of the top fifteen European Union countries in terms of their nominal GDP.

Institutions are responsible for the completion of financial sector activities and the implementation of procedures and regulations that advocate financial sector advancement (Beck et al., 2010); hence, they are essential for financial development. As the central bank is one of the most influential financial institutions, a central banking measure has been frequently incorporated within financial development studies (King & Levine, 1993; Neyapti, 2003; Tayssir & Feryel, 2018). Although many central bank institutional characteristics have been used to investigate their contribution to financial development, the role of monetary policy has been less elaborated. Monetary policy tools used to stabilize prices have consequences on the activities carried out by financial institutions, thus affecting financial development progression. The CBPR is the rate utilized by the central bank to signal or implement its' monetary policy stance (IMF, 2019). Tayssir and Feryel (2018) argued that central banks use the CBPR to supply banks with short-term loans and banks take the CBPR as a reference point to set the offered credit rates to customers. Thereby, the CBPR enables central banks to control loan amounts and rates of the banking system, which can affect financial development. For the abovementioned reason, there is a need to test the relationship between CBPR and financial development.

In order to refrain from committing omitted variable bias, we opt to include control variables largely reflected within the existing literature devoted to analyzing the determinants of financial development. The most widely repeating control variable is economic growth within financial development literature. In his early study, Robinson (1979) suggested that a greater economic growth level increases the request for financial services and hence supports financial development. There is an abundance of findings on the causal relationship between economic growth and financial development. The existing literature stresses both a bidirectional (King & Levine, 1993; Hsueh et al., 2013; Pradhan et al., 2018) and a unidirectional (Zang & Kim, 2007) causal relationship between economic growth and financial development. Given the extensive evidence to support a significant positive impact of economic growth on financial development (Kar et al., 2011; Hsueh et al., 2013; Pradhan et al., 2018), an economic growth proxy in the form of the logarithm of gross domestic product (GDP) is integrated within our model.

The effect of globalization has also been considered when investigating financial development. Studies have found that globalization contributes to trade liberalization, reduces transactional cost (Daisaka et al., 2014), brings forth institutional reform advancement (Mishkin, 2009), and advances the demand for financial goods and services, resulting in greater financial deepening and financial development. Law et al. (2014) found that globalization Granger causes financial development. Asongu (2014) suggested globalization forms financial liberalization, heightening financial development, in the case of Africa. Due to findings, which document the positive effect of globalization on financial development, a globalization measure—in the form of globalization index—is added to our model.

Especially recent research found evidence for the positive contribution of innovation to financial development (Pradhan et al., 2018; Zhu et al., 2020). Hsu et al. (2014) found innovation to be vital for the equity market and, therefore, financial development. Xiao and Zhao (2012) included an innovation measure when analyzing financial development from a banking perspective. They found innovation vital for increasing the inflow of resources, thus resulting in enhanced financial development. In this light, we incorporated an innovation measure in the form of research and development expenditure proportion of GDP within our empirical model. Corruption, considered to be an institutional quality proxy, has also been investigated as a hindering factor for financial development. Muye and Muye (2017) incorporated a corruption measure of institutional quality to analyze the causal relationship between globalization, institutions, and financial development. Naceur et al. (2014) indicated that corruption hinders financial development for MENA countries. This finding was also supported by Gazdar and Cherif (2015). Compatible with our interests, we find it fitting to incorporate corruption as an institutional quality measure within our model to prevent omitted variable bias. Following Gazdar and Cherif (2015) and Muye and Muye (2017), we chose to incorporate a corruption proxy in the form of a corruption perception index.

Our study analyzes the effect of CBPR on financial development for a panel of top 15 European Union countries according to nominal GDP (Austria, Czech Republic, Denmark, Finland, France, Germany, Hungary, Ireland, Italy, Netherlands, Poland, Portugal, Spain, Sweden, and United Kingdom). Due to data limitation, three countries were not included, namely, Belgium, Greece, and Romania. We considered the top 15 European Union countries as our sample given that they have financial system structures that are of a similar trait and share the same set of rules and regulations in terms of the monetary and fiscal policy framework; thus, we omit any possible sample bias by focusing on cross-sections that share similar characteristics. Our data set consists of annual observations for sixteen years spanning from 2002 to 2017 due to data availability. To investigate the determinants of financial development, we used the autoregressive distributive lag (ARDL) model (Pesaran et al., 1999), given the fact that the variables utilized within the model are of mixed integration order. The finding of our study provides important information that helps derive crucial policy implications necessary for improving financial development further within the European region.

3.2 Literature Review

Although many financial development studies have given importance primarily to macroeconomic variables, institutional measures have increasingly been given attention following Fry (1997), who argued that institutional features play a pivotal role in financial liberalization practices implemented on financial development. Institutional quality has been attributed to providing lucrative financial reforms (Acemoglu & Johnson, 2005). Institutional factors include a wide range of aspects such as legal origin (Beck et al., 2001), regulatory aspects, political conditions, bureaucracy, possible civil anarchy, governmental fundaments, political factors, democracy, taxation, and tax reformation (Fry, 1997). There is abundant evidence to show that institutional factors matter for financial development. For example, evidence suggests political instability diminishes financial development as investment opportunities are swindled (Roe & Siegel, 2011).

Financial institutions have a vital role in financial development. King and Levine (1993) extended the work of Schumpeter (1911) on financial intermediation by investigating the importance of financial institutions for both financial development and economic growth; for 80 countries. They found that central banks play a pivotal role in expanding financial depth, as the credits they provide to private firms enhance capital allocation efficiency. Due to the early supportive evidence and theoretical support that central banks have implications on the creation of financial development, studies started to elaborate on which central banking components matter the most in boosting financial development.

The literature devoted to investigating possible determinants of financial development has often incorporated some form of central bank measure. Most commonly, a central bank independence proxy is included within financial development models. Neyapti (2001) analyzed the role of independence of the central bank in the promotion of financial development for the case of Europe and found that it improves price stability and assists the maintenance of monetary policy fundamentals required to drive financial development. In continuation of this work, Neyapti (2003) found greater central bank independence brings forth heightened financial market development. The central bank assets variable is another frequently used central banking measure by researchers (Beck et al., 2010). Tayssir and Feryel (2018) explored how central bank aspects can influence financial development for various countries; by accounting for central banks' political role, transparency, inflation targeting, and monetary tools. Their findings indicate that central banking conditions can support financial sector development.

The existing literature on financial development emphasizes the importance of how monetary policies can expand financial development further. Past research has concluded that monetary policies and financial stability are closely linked (Yellen, 2014). Koenig (2013) reports that the close link between financial stability and monetary policy is crucial for price stability to mitigate risks associated with price volatility. Studies have also shown that financial intermediates are responsible for the creation of money and how this liquidity implicates monetary transmissions (Beck & Colciago, 2014). Research devoted to improving monetary targets in order to revamp the financial system notes that transparency is vital (Broaddus Jr, 2002). Ennis and Keister (2008) suggest it's of great importance to implement monetary policy efficiently. Thus, the literature supports the notion that monetary policies may affect financial development, as monetary tools strengthen financial market integration. Based on this information, we assess the potential impact of central banks' guiding the banking system through the CBPR on financial development for the

European region. Many important aspects of central banks have been incorporated when analyzing their role in driving financial development, and the role of the CBPR has been overlooked thus far.

3.3 Data

3.3.1 Definition of Data

This study utilizes a panel dataset of fifteen cross-sections (Austria, Czech Republic, Denmark, Finland, France, Germany, Hungary, Ireland, Italy, Netherlands, Poland, Portugal, Spain, Sweden, and United Kingdom), with a time span of 16 years ranging from 2002 to 2017 due to data availability. All of the data is of an annual frequency. Financial development, denoted as FD, the dependent variable within our model, is proxied by the financial development index sourced from the International Monetary Fund (IMF). The study's main contribution is to analyze the impact of CBPR on financial development for Europe; this measure was gathered from the Bank for International Settlements (BIS). Control variables, consistent with the existing literature, are incorporated into the model to refrain from committing omitted variable bias. Such variables include: corruption perception index, denoted as LCT as a measure of institutional quality in which a larger observation implies less corruption—supplied by Transparency International, innovation denoted as INN, measured as a proportion of GDP spent on research and development sourced from Worldbank database; globalization index, denoted as GI, collected from Swiss Economic Institute (KOF); and Gross Domestic Product (GDP), obtained from Worldbank database, in logarithmic form denoted by LGDP. We expect all the regressors to exhort a positive impact on FD in the case of Europe.

3.3.2 Descriptive Statistics

Descriptive statistics, displayed in Table 3.1, indicate that we have a strongly balanced panel. The number of observations is the same, 240, for all variables utilized within the study; thus, there is no missing observation. The mean, standard deviation, minimum, and maximum observations imply that the data don't suffer from any outliers/extreme values.

Table 3.2 reports the pairwise correlations between the regressand and all regressors of the model. The table provides evidence that no multicollinearity exists as all of the explanatory variables are correlated to a degree less than 0.80.

Table 3.1 Descriptive statistics

Variable	Obs	Mean	Std. dev.	Min	Max
FD	240	0.68	0.15	0.30	0.94
CBPR	240	1.91	2.03	−0.75	12.50
LCT	240	1.93	0.26	1.22	2.27
INN	240	1.91	0.86	0.54	3.91
GI	240	85.13	3.58	71.20	91.30
LGDP	240	27.14	1.05	25.48	28.99

Source: Authors' analysis of data

Table 3.2 Correlation matrix

Variables	CBPR	CT	INN	GI	GDP
CBPR	1.00				
CT	−0.27	1.00			
INN	−0.35	0.73	1.00		
GI	−0.37	0.76	0.71	1.00	
GDP	−0.24	0.12	0.55	0.19	1.00

Source: Authors' analysis of data

3.3.3 Unit Root Test Results

To check the integration order of variables used to construct the model, variables are investigated with the application of three different panel unit root tests, namely, Im et al. (2003), Breitung (1999), and Maddala and Wu (1999) Fisher ADF test, and the results are reported in Table 3.3. The results concerning the unit root tests are as follows: according to all three tests, the dependent variable (FD) is stationary at the first difference—I(1); majority of the tests imply that CBPR is stationary at level—I (0); LCT, INN, GI, and LGDP series are I(1) according to the majority of the results. Having stationary and nonstationary variables in the model makes the ARDL the most plausible estimation technique (Pesaran & Smith, 1995) to analyze cointegrating relationships. In addition, unit root tests confirm that none of our variables employed are I(2), which is a necessary condition to employ the ARDL method.

3.4 Econometric Method and Empirical Findings

3.4.1 Model and Methodology

This study investigates the link between financial development and CBPR in the case of Europe, while controlling for the impact of innovation, economic growth, globalization, and corruption. This model can be expressed by the following linear equation:

Table 3.3 Panel unit root test results

Level	FD	CBPR	LCT	INN	GI	LGDP
$\tau_{T\ \text{fisher ADF}}$	36.23	89.76*	42.82***	33.64	49.90**	35.19
$\tau_{\mu\ \text{fisher ADF}}$	45.58**	14.45	45.83**	22.18	39.04	19.64
$\tau_{\text{fisher ADF}}$	15.63	54.68*	30.02	8.88	1.16	2.14
$\tau_{T\ \text{IPS}}$	−1.31***	−5.92*	−1.15	−0.72	−2.29**	1.10
$\tau_{\mu\ \text{IPS}}$	−1.91**	1.03	−1.21	1.18	−0.74	0.91
$\tau_{T\ \text{BREITUNG}}$	−0.12	−5.89*	−0.16	−1.61***	−1.68**	−3.49*
First difference						
$\tau_{T\ \text{fisher ADF}}$	50.73**	88.09*	51.51*	37.07	70.23*	35.00
$\tau_{\mu\ \text{fisher ADF}}$	76.59*	132.80*	80.70*	61.46*	107.23*	63.97*
$\tau_{\text{fisher ADF}}$	144.88*	188.49*	133.62*	89.86*	123.80*	82.98*
$\tau_{T\ \text{IPS}}$	−2.50*	−5.76*	−2.53*	−1.17	−4.21*	−0.94
$\tau_{\mu\ \text{IPS}}$	−4.86*	−9.05*	−5.15*	−3.55*	−7.19*	−3.87*
$\tau_{T\ \text{BREITUNG}}$	−6.46*	−10.78*	−1.90**	−2.05**	−4.47*	−4.90*

Source: Authors' analysis of data
Note: ****p*-value < 0.10; ***p*-value < 0.05; **p*-value < 0.01

$$\begin{aligned}\text{FD}_{it} =& \beta_{0it} + \beta_{1it}\text{CBPR}_{it} + \beta_{2it}\text{LCT}_{it} + \beta_{3it}\text{INN}_{it} \\ &+ \beta_{4it}\text{GI}_{it} + \beta_{5it}\text{LGDP}_{it} + \varepsilon_{it}\end{aligned} \tag{3.1}$$

where i is the cross-sectional unit and t is the time element.

Our study focuses on investigating both the short- and long-run relationships between financial development and CBPR. Thus, conventional static panel estimations such as pooled OLS, fixed effects, and random effects are not applicable given that they are unable to distinguish between short- and long-run dynamics. Moreover, such estimations are only applicable to stationary variables, I(0). Since variables used within our model are of mixed integration order such estimations would provide spurious results. Likewise, panel cointegration methods such as Pedroni (1999) and Johansen-Fisher test), which requires all variables to be integrated in order of one, I(1), are not suitable given the dataset utilized within our study. The panel ARDL procedure is considered to be efficient and consistent within small samples (Haug, 2002). Thus, the empirical investigation is carried out with the use of the panel ARDL estimation framework, established by Pesaran et al. (1999), to analyze the short- and long-run relationships among the variables.

The ARDL model specification can be displayed as follows:

$$\Delta \mathrm{FD}_{i,t} = \delta_i + \beta_{1i}\mathrm{FD}_{i,t-1} + \beta_{2i}\mathrm{CBPR}_{i,t} + \beta_{3i}\mathrm{LCT}_{i,t} + \beta_{4i}\mathrm{INN}_{i,t} + \beta_{5i}\mathrm{GI}_{i,t} + \beta_{6i}\mathrm{LGDP}_{i,t} + \sum_{i=1}^{p-1}\alpha_{1i}\Delta \mathrm{FD}_{i,t-i} + \sum_{i=0}^{q-1}\alpha_{2i}\Delta \mathrm{CBPR}_{i,t-i} + \sum_{i=0}^{q}\alpha_{3i}\Delta \mathrm{LCT}_{i,t-i} + \sum_{i=0}^{q}\alpha_{4i}\Delta \mathrm{INN}_{i,t-i} + \sum_{i=0}^{q}\alpha_{5i}\Delta \mathrm{GI}_{i,t-i} + \sum_{i=0}^{q}\alpha_{6i}\Delta \mathrm{LGDP}_{i,t-i} + \varepsilon_{i,t} \quad (3.2)$$

Where Δ is the difference operator, β_1 is error correction coefficient, α_1 *to* α_6 are the short-run coefficients of the variables, while β_2 to β_6 indicate the long-run coefficients of the equation. δ_i is the constant and ε_{it} is the residual term. Cross-sectional and time dimensions are subscribed by *i* and *t*, respectively.

The optimal lag specification order chosen using Akaike Information Criterion (AIC) was (2, 1, 1, 1, 1, 1) for financial development, CBPR, corruption, innovation, globalization, and LGDP, respectively.

The presence of a significant and negative error correction term (ECT), −0.796, suggests that any short-run deviations from the equilibrium amongst the regressand and regressors will converge back to the long-run equilibrium in the future. ARDL pooled mean group (PMG) estimation (Pesaran et al., 1999) was conducted, which is applied in the case of heterogeneous panels. PMG allows intercepts, short-run coefficients, and error variances to vary across groups, providing average long-run coefficients for all groups within the sample, which is practical when the long-run relationships are expected to be similar for each cross-section.

3.4.2 Empirical Findings

The short- and long-run coefficients obtained from the PMG estimator are reported in Table 3.4. The long-run ARDL coefficients indicate the following: The coefficient of CBPR is positive and highly significant, suggesting that this variable is a long-run driver of financial development for the case of European countries. This might happen due to several channels. First, a higher CBPR rate is expected to cause an increase in deposits. Higher deposits will increase the capacity of banks in terms of providing funds and causes a deepening of financial markets. Moreover, Tayssir and Feryel (2018) mentioned that lower interest rates are associated with restricted financial markets and lower financial development. Moreover, the primary target of a central bank is price stability. Higher CBPR helps the monetary authority reach its primary target, which may support a well-functioning financial system and, ultimately financial development. Previously, researchers investigated several central bank features on financial development and found that improving the efficiency of regulations and instruments applied by the central bank would have a positive

Table 3.4 Pooled mean group ARDL estimation results

D.FD	Coefficient	Std. err.	t-statistic
Long-run coefficients			
L.CBPR	0.017*	0.001	10.171
L.LCT	0.059**	0.025	2.384
L.INN.	0.044*	0.014	3.087
GI	0.007*	0.002	2.675
LGDP	0.035	0.034	1.032
Short-run coefficients			
ECT	−0.796*	0.094	−8.437
Dl.FD	0.067	0.112	0.599
D1.CBPR	0.005	0.006	0.800
D1.LCT	0.036	0.097	0.375
D1.INN	−0.009	0.061	−0.142
D1.GI	−0.003	0.005	−0.719
D1.LGDP	−0.076	0.283	−0.269
Constant	−0.816*	0.100	−8.147
Trend	−0.002**	0.001	−1.979

Source: Authors' analysis of data
Note: ***p-value < 0.10; **p-value < 0.05; *p-value < 0.01

effect (King & Levine, 1993; Beck et al., 2000; Tayssir & Feryel, 2018). Our study contributes to the literature by providing evidence for another aspect of the central bank which might support financial development.

Corruption has a positive significant coefficient, implying reduced corruption also enhances financial development within Europe in the long run (based on the measure used, a positive association is desired). This finding is supported by the existing literature (Muye & Muye, 2017), suggesting less corruption diminishes the number of informal economy activities, which will boost the use of financial instruments provided by financial intermediates, thus heightening financial development further. The innovation coefficient is positive and highly significant. This finding implies that spurs in innovation contribute to financial development for the panel of countries we investigated. Literature provides strong evidence on the positive relationship between innovation and financial performance of companies (Govindarajan & Kopalle, 2006; Jansen et al., 2006; Walker, 2004). Increased financial performance offers extra income that companies tend to invest, which will boost financial development. The notion that innovation enhances financial development is also supported by previous studies (Ang & Kumar, 2014; Belazreg & Mtar, 2020).

Likewise, the coefficient of globalization variable is positive and highly significant, indicating that globalization positively contributes to financial development within Europe as a more borderless marketplace creates an ideal environment for investment opportunities to thrive; this result is in line with that of Mishkin (2009) and Muye and Muye (2017). Economic growth is found to be insignificant; therefore, it does not provide any evidence that supports the hypothesized relationship between economic growth and financial development, for the case of Europe in the long run. This result is compatible with the findings of Hsueh et al. (2013), where they found weak to no evidence on causality from economic growth to financial development. They claimed that financial development does not depend on economic growth but is enhanced by other indicators.

The error correction term is negative and highly significant. This finding indicates any short-run disequilibrium experienced is corrected within the long run. All short-run coefficients provided by ARDL are found to be insignificant; this suggests changes in any variable are unable to impact European financial development within the short run. Thus, said changes/adaptions will only be reflected by the European financial development in the long run.

3.5 Conclusion

Thus far, the financial development literature has overlooked how CBPR may affect the progression of financial development. Hence, to fulfill the mentioned gap, this study analyzes the short- and the long-run outcomes of CBPR on financial development enhancements for a panel of fifteen European Union countries from 2002 to 2017 inclusively due to data availability. To refrain from committing omitted variable bias, innovation, economic growth, globalization, and corruption were used as control variables. PMG estimators provide us with the long- and short-run cointegrating coefficients and error correction term. Obtained findings indicate that an increase in CBPR results in greater financial development for countries within the European region which is compatible with our a priori theoretical expectations. Results concerning control variables, in regards to long-run coefficients, are harmonious with that of the existing literature and indicate that a reduction in corruption perceptions, enhancements in globalization, and innovation induce greater financial development.

Based on our findings, we propose several policy implications. Matching the CBPR with the needs of the banking sector and the financial market would improve financial development, as it is a strong monetary policy tool. A higher CBPR rate is expected to result in more deposits in the banking system. If commercial banks can provide an integrated platform with multiple investment tools to link financial markets with the banking system and give depositors access to broader options, that will enhance financial development. Financial development is just one of many variables that corruption negatively affects. Therefore, fighting corruption is vital to building a sound financial infrastructure and contributing to financial development. Although there is a wide range of potential measures to mitigate corruption, increasing trust in institutions is particularly important (Sööt & Rootalu, 2012). In this context, reducing the informal economic activities by increasing the transparency of institutions; especially the transparency of the central bank; will be helpful (De Simone et al., 2017; Lopez, 2017). Globalization increases financial integration, which will result in higher resistance to possible shocks. This will ultimately help improve the financial system. To benefit from globalization, it is crucial to reduce trade barriers (Peters, 2017), increase technological innovation (Naz & Ahmad, 2018), provide better education (Sahlberg, 2004), and create a healthy macroeconomic environment. The promotion of innovation is considered to be a driving force behind financial development. Thus, advancements in financial reforms (Aksoy, 2019) and support in technological innovation (Maradana et al., 2017), especially financial technology, are crucial for fostering financial development as they will result in a more efficient allocation of financial resources (Pradhan et al., 2016).

References

Acemoglu, D., & Johnson, S. (2005). Unbundling institutions. *Journal of Political Economy, 113*(5), 949–995.

Aksoy, T. (2019). Structural reforms and growth in developing countries. *Journal of Economic Policy Reform, 22*(4), 325–350.

Alfaro, L., Chanda, A., Kalemli-Ozcan, S., & Sayek, S. (2004). FDI and economic growth: The role of local financial markets. *Journal of International Economics, 64*(1), 89–112.

Ang, J. B., & Kumar, S. (2014). Financial development and barriers to the cross-border diffusion of financial innovation. *Journal of Banking & Finance, 39*, 43–56.

Asongu, S. (2014). Financial development dynamic thresholds of financial globalization. *Journal of Economic Studies, 41*(2), 166–195.

Beck, T., & Colciago, P. D. (2014). The role of financial intermediaries in monetary policy transmission. *Journal of Economic Dynamics and Control, 43*, 1–11.

Beck, T., Demirgüç-Kunt, A., & Levine, R. (2000). A new database on the structure and development of the financial sector. *The World Bank Economic Review, 14*(3), 597–605.

Beck, T., Demirgüç-Kunt, A., & Levine, R. (2001). Legal theories of financial development. *Oxford Review of Economic Policy, 17*(4), 483–501.

Beck, T., Demirgüç-Kunt, A., & Levine, R. (2010). Financial institutions and markets across countries and over time: The updated financial development and structure database. *The World Bank Economic Review, 24*(1), 77–92.

Belazreg, W., & Mtar, K. (2020). Modelling the causal linkages between trade openness, innovation, financial development and economic growth in OECD Countries. *Applied Economics Letters, 27*(1), 5–8.

Breitung, J. (1999). Some nonparametric tests for unit roots and cointegration. *Journal of Econometrics, 108*, 343–363.

Broaddus, J. A., Jr. (2002). Transparency in the practice of monetary policy. (Panel discussion: Transparency in the practice of Monetary Policy). *Federal Reserve Bank of St. Louis Review, 84*(4), 161–166.

Calderón, C., & Liu, L. (2003). The direction of causality between financial development and economic growth. *Journal of Development Economics, 72*(1), 321–334.

Daisaka, H., Furusawa, T., & Yanagawa, N. (2014). Globalization, financial development and income inequality. *Pacific Economic Review, 19*(5), 612–633.

De Simone, E., Gaeta, G. L., & Mourão, P. R. (2017). The impact of Fiscal transparency on corruption: An empirical analysis based on longitudinal data. *The BE Journal of Economic Analysis & Policy, 17*(4), 1–17.

Ennis, H. M., & Keister, T. (2008). Understanding monetary policy implementation. *FRB Richmond Economic Quarterly, 94*(3), 235–263.

Fry, M. J. (1997). In favour of financial liberalisation. *The Economic Journal, 107*(442), 754–770.

Gazdar, K., & Cherif, M. (2015). Institutions and the finance–growth nexus: Empirical evidence from MENA countries. *Borsa Istanbul Review, 15*(3), 137–160.

Govindarajan, V., & Kopalle, P. K. (2006). The usefulness of measuring disruptiveness of innovations ex post in making ex ante predictions. *Journal of Product Innovation Management, 23*(1), 12–18.
Haug, A. A. (2002). Temporal aggregation and the power of cointegration tests: A Monte Carlo study. *Oxford Bulletin of Economics and statistics, 64*(4), 399–412.
Hsu, P. H., Tian, X., & Xu, Y. (2014). Financial development and innovation: Cross-country evidence. *Journal of Financial Economics, 112*(1), 116–135.
Hsueh, S. J., Hu, Y. H., & Tu, C. H. (2013). Economic growth and financial development in Asian countries: A bootstrap panel Granger causality analysis. *Economic Modelling, 32*, 294–301.
Im, K. S., Pesaran, M. H., & Shin, Y. (2003). Testing for unit roots in heterogeneous panels. *Journal of Econometrics, 115*(1), 53–74.
IMF. (2019). International Monetary Fund. http://www.imf.org/. Accessed 23 Feb 2020.
Jansen, J. J., Van Den Bosch, F. A., & Volberda, H. W. (2006). Exploratory innovation, exploitative innovation, and performance: Effects of organizational antecedents and environmental moderators. *Management Science, 52*(11), 1661–1674.
Kar, M., Nazlıoglu, Ş., & Agır, H. (2011). Financial development and economic growth nexus in the MENA countries: Bootstrap panel Granger causality analysis. *Economic Modelling, 28*(1-2), 685–693.
King, R. G., & Levine, R. (1993). Finance and growth: Schumpeter might be right. *The Quarterly Journal of Economics, 108*(3), 717–737.
Koenig, E. F. (2013). Like a good neighbor: Monetary policy, financial stability, and the distribution of risk. *International Journal of Central Banking, 9*(2), 57–82.
Law, S. H., Azman-Saini, W. N. W., & Tan, H. B. (2014). Economic globalization and financial development in East Asia: A panel cointegration and causality analysis. *Emerging Markets Finance and Trade, 50*(1), 210–225.
Lopez, S. (2017). Is transparency an effective way of reducing corruption? Evidence around the World. *International Journal of Economic Perspectives, 11*(2), 186–191.
Maddala, G. S., & Wu, S. (1999). A comparative study of unit root tests with panel data and a new simple test. *Oxford Bulletin of Economics and Statistics, 61*(S1), 631–652.
Maradana, R. P., Pradhan, R. P., Dash, S., Gaurav, K., Jayakumar, M., & Chatterjee, D. (2017). Does innovation promote economic growth? Evidence from European countries. *Journal of Innovation and Entrepreneurship, 6*(1), 1–23.
Mishkin, F. S. (2009). Globalization and financial development. *Journal of Development Economics, 89*(2), 164–169.
Muye, I. M., & Muye, I. Y. (2017). Testing for causality among globalization, institution and financial development: Further evidence from three economic blocs. *Borsa Istanbul Review, 17*(2), 117–132.
Naceur, S. B., Cherif, M., & Kandil, M. (2014). What drives the development of the MENA financial sector? *Borsa Istanbul Review, 14*(4), 212–223.
Naz, A., & Ahmad, E. (2018). Driving factors of globalization: An empirical analysis of the developed and developing countries. *Business and Economic Review, 10*(1), 133–157.
Neyapti, B. (2001). Central bank independence and economic performance in Eastern Europe. *Economic Systems, 25*(4), 381–399.
Neyapti, B. (2003). Budget deficits and inflation: The roles of central bank independence and financial market development. *Contemporary Economic Policy, 21*(4), 458–475.
Odhiambo, N. M. (2009). Interest rate reforms, financial deepening and economic growth in Kenya: An empirical investigation. *The Journal of Developing Areas, 43*, 295–313.
Pagano, M. (1993). The flotation of companies on the stock market: A coordination failure model. *European Economic Review, 37*(5), 1101–1125.
Pedroni, P. (1999). Critical values for cointegration tests in heterogeneous panels with multiple regressors. *Oxford Bulletin of Economics and Statistics, 61*(S1), 653–670.
Pesaran, M. H., & Smith, R. (1995). Estimating long-run relationships from dynamic heterogeneous panels. *Journal of Econometrics, 68*(1), 79–113.

Pesaran, M. H., Shin, Y., & Smith, R. P. (1999). Pooled mean group estimation of dynamic heterogeneous panels. *Journal of the American Statistical Association, 94*(446), 621–634.

Peters, M. E. (2017). *Trading barriers: Immigration and the remaking of globalization*. Princeton University Press.

Pradhan, R. P., Arvin, M. B., Hall, J. H., & Nair, M. (2016). Innovation, financial development and economic growth in Eurozone countries. *Applied Economics Letters, 23*(16), 1141–1144.

Pradhan, R. P., Arvin, M. B., & Bahmani, S. (2018). Are innovation and financial development causative factors in economic growth? Evidence from a panel Granger causality test. *Technological Forecasting and Social Change, 132*, 130–142.

Robinson, J. (1979). The rate of interest. In *The generalisation of the general theory and other essays* (pp. 135–164). Palgrave Macmillan.

Roe, M. J., & Siegel, J. I. (2011). Political instability: Effects on financial development, roots in the severity of economic inequality. *Journal of Comparative Economics, 39*(3), 279–309.

Roubini, N., & Sala-i-Martin, X. (1992). Financial repression and economic growth. *Journal of Development Economics, 39*(1), 5–30.

Rousseau, P. L., & Yilmazkuday, H. (2009). Inflation, financial development, and growth: A trilateral analysis. *Economic Systems, 33*(4), 310–324.

Sahlberg, P. (2004). Teaching and globalization. *Managing Global Transitions, 2*(1), 65–83.

Schumpeter, J. A. (1911). *The theory of economic development* (Vol. XLVI). Harvard Economic Studies.

Sööt, M. L., & Rootalu, K. (2012). Institutional trust and opinions of corruption. *Public Administration and Development, 32*(1), 82–95.

Tayssir, O., & Feryel, O. (2018). Does central banking promote financial development? *Borsa Istanbul Review, 18*(1), 52–75.

Walker, R. M. (2004). *Innovation and organizational performance: Evidence and a research agenda* (Advanced Institute of Management Research Paper, 002). AIM Research.

Xiao, S., & Zhao, S. (2012). Financial development, government ownership of banks and firm innovation. *Journal of International Money and Finance, 31*(4), 880–906.

Yellen, J. L. (2014). *Monetary policy and financial stability*. International Monetary Fund.

Zang, H., & Kim, Y. C. (2007). Does financial development precede growth? Robinson and Lucas might be right. *Applied Economics Letters, 14*(1), 15–19.

Zhu, X., Asimakopoulos, S., & Kim, J. (2020). Financial development and innovation-led growth: Is too much finance better? *Journal of International Money and Finance, 100*, 102083.

Chapter 4
Causes of Limitations of GDP Per Capita as an Indicator of Economic Development

Radek Dědeček and Viktar Dudzich

Abstract This chapter discusses the viability of gross domestic product (GDP) per capita in purchasing power parity as an indicator of economic development and well-being and estimates the factors which diminish its ability to represent the level of life. Firstly, we theoretically outline the factors that might be undermining GDP per capita's ability to serve as a measurement of well-being and debate other development indicators. Subsequently, we confront GDP per capita with the most well-known development indicator – Human Development Index (HDI) – and calculate the deviations between those two indicators. To empirically evaluate the potential limitations of GDP in measuring development, we regress the development-GDP gaps on an array of economic, social and political variables employing a broad panel dataset and modified fixed effects estimators. The results reveal that factors such as income inequality and level of economic freedom cause negative gap between development and GDP; the size of shadow economy has positive impact on deviation of HDI from GDP levels, while certain sociocultural factors such as higher fertility rates and alcohol consumption have negative effect on the dependent variable.

Key words Economic development · GDP per capita · Human development index

4.1 Introduction

In today's world, the macroeconomic policies are aimed primarily at the quantitative growth of the economy understood as the increase of the gross domestic product (GDP), which has long become a basic indicator of economic development and is often perceived as a measure of well-being. Among its pros are the simplicity, long history of usage (and, thus, long enough time series for the economic theorists to indulge in), elaborated methodology and calculation techniques (Stiglitz et al.,

R. Dědeček (✉) · V. Dudzich
Department of Monetary Theory and Policy, Prague University of Economics and Business, Prague, Czech Republic
e-mail: xdedr00@vse.cz; xdudv00@vse.cz

D. Procházka (ed.), *Regulation of Finance and Accounting*, Springer Proceedings in Business and Economics, https://doi.org/10.1007/978-3-030-99873-8_4

2009). Due to that, even less economically advanced countries possess the statisticians qualified enough for the computed numbers of GDP being embraced as relatively exact.

GDP as a gauge of economic size and productive capacities gave birth to the most popular approach to quantification of the people's level of life and overall economic welfare – GDP per capita[1] (Stiglitz et al., 2009; Atkinson & Marlier, 2015). It is commonly employed to compare the economic well-being between countries; the increase of GDP per capita is regarded as an outcome of successful economic policies (at the very least, by their authors – Syrovatka, 2008).

However, the ability of GDP per capita to serve as an appropriate measure of economic development has become a subject of criticism[2] (Costanza et al., 2009; Stiglitz et al., 2009; Dynan & Sheiner, 2018). The debates[3] concern both the methodological drawbacks of GDP and the fact that the quantitative increase of the economy (even in per capita terms) does not affect an array of individual components of human well-being, with social inequality, safety, health and civil rights being foremost among them (Costanza et al., 2009). These concerns stemmed from the opinion that GDP-oriented economic policies are often unable to augment the actual level of life and may be undermining the governments' ability to tend to the needs of the population (Sagar & Najam, 1998; Stiglitz et al., 2009). It spurred the genesis of a wide range of economic and institutional indexes and indicators that are meant to provide a clearer picture of what is perceived as economic development and capture its dynamics over time (Clapp & Sen, 1999). Enviable level of popularity among both the economists and general public has been attained by the so-called Human Development Index (HDI), which stands as one of the United Nations' centrepieces in regard to economic development since 1990 and encompasses measurements of income, length of life and educational standards (Klasen, 2018). Other indicators that concentrate on the real consumption, quality of institutions, depletion of natural resources and economic sustainability, albeit being quite accurate in their intentions, are lagging behind (besides being fairly complicated for calculation) in the general public's awareness, struggle with the lack of data and are only irregularly published (Stiglitz et al., 2009). Nevertheless, this calls for wider adoption of these indicators as aims of economic policy appear to be loudening (Sagar & Najam, 1998; Stiglitz et al., 2009).

---

[1] As a rule, in purchasing power parity.

[2] In this chapter, we use the terms "development," "well-being" and "level of life" as defined by the modern development economics: a multidimensional concept which embodies the aspects that are of direct or indirect impact on the quality of human life, such as health, income and education (Syrovatka, 2008). Therefore, for the purpose of simplicity, these terms may be viewed as synonymous.

[3] Which were started by one of the inventors of the GDP: Simon Kuznets often stated that the criticism stems from the fact that GDP became employed in a fashion it had never been meant to – according to him, GDP was developed to measure and compare the individual countries' productive capacities and cannot serve as a technique to evaluate economic development and well-being (Sagar and Najam, 1998).

The viability of such demands is amplified by the fact that GDP per capita exhibits only a limited degree of correlation with the most common development indexes (Hopkins, 1991; Deb, 2015). Clear illustration emerges from a simple operation: the order of the countries by GDP per capita (PPP) and HDI commonly diverges from each other by 30–80 rankings for both high- and low-income countries alike. The roots of this divergence (i.e. discrepancy between the mere per capita size of the economy and the level of life it facilitates) arose as a subject of this chapter's research.

Up to this time, the existent surveys inquired into either individual methodological drawbacks of GDP per capita or attempted to explain its inability to serve as a standard of well-being using common logic and conventional wisdom. This chapter takes a more general approach and seeks to construct a rigorous framework for identification of factors that cause so-called development-GDP gaps – situations in which the level of life captured by HDI deviates from the level implied by GDP per capita. To achieve this, we quantify these deviations and regress them on a wide selection of economic, political and sociocultural indicators that may represent the fundamental reasons for deviations between well-being and GDP while affecting either of them or both. The aim of this work lies in providing answers to the following questions: In what instances can the increase of GDP per capita not be associated with the rise of quality of life and what are the fundamentals accountable for it?

Firstly, we thoroughly explain the hindrances to the usage of GDP per capita as an indicator of economic well-being. Subsequently, we explain the advantages of HDI as a measurement of development and discuss its usability and potential limitations. Afterwards, we introduce the econometric framework employed to quantify the factors standing behind the deviations between GDP per capita and HDI using a range of multidimensional variables and panel dataset for 141 countries, which is followed by discussion of the results and the implications they provide.

4.2 Limitations of GDP Per Capita as an Indicator of Economic Development

Despite common preconceptions, the rise of GDP as the cornerstone indicator of economic power (together with GDP growth being a criterion of economic policies' success) occurred relatively recently – it has been in the scope of the economists' attention for less than 100 years (Clapp & Sen, 1999). The elaborated methodology resembling the one we possess today is no older than the American government's essays at evaluation of their productive capacities before entering the WW2 (Clapp & Sen, 1999). The subsequent global spread of GDP was spurred by the post-war reconstruction of Europe and, more importantly, the wave of decolonization, which generated a demand for an indicator enabling to compare the level of economic development in the newly emerged countries and, thus, evaluate the successfulness of economic policies produced by the international institutions (Clapp & Sen, 1999). GDP per capita in purchasing power parity arose as the most suitable: It resulted in developing countries being categorized according to their GDP per capita; it served as a benchmark for providing development aid, whereas its increase was perceived as the basic output of the development policies (Clapp & Sen, 1999; Costanza et al., 2009; Stiglitz et al., 2009). This approach had remained almost exclusive up to the end of the 1990s, albeit few concerns had already been expressed by those on the frontier of the development economics (Dasgupta, 1990; Hopkins, 1991; Clapp & Sen, 1999). The criticism was related to relatively evident but largely ignored issues: GDP per capita failed to reliably encompass an assortment of economic activities that may possess an immense impact on the population's life and living standards in less developed countries[4] (which may be labelled as GDP calculation drawback and include the outputs of shadow economy as well as non-monetary and non-market production – Giannetti et al., 2015), while also glossing over such aspects of well-being as inequalities, quality of institutions, public safety or the economic sustainability (Dasgupta, 1990; Syrovatka, 2008; Bala, 2013). It fuelled the academic discussions, which yielded the first development-oriented indicators – complex and multidimensional, but data-demanding and unnoticed by anyone outside the economists' community (Clapp & Sen, 1999; Syrovatka, 2008; Atkinson & Marlier, 2015). The change came when the policy-makers from both developed and developing worlds were confronted with the harsh reality of GDP per capita growth not being perceived as an increase in well-being by the population, which started to raise doubts about the rightness of conventional economic policies' direction (Osberg & Sharpe, 2001). This perception was only fortified by the individual authors' attempts to construct their own well-being indexes and compare their dynamics with the changes in GDP per capita (Hopkins, 1991; Osberg & Sharpe, 2001). However sharp was GDP per capita accretion, many countries neither experienced a decrease in poverty nor positive changes in unemployment (Clapp and Sen, 1999). It was especially evident in the countries with a high percentage of capital owned by foreigners as well as those with especially inegalitarian political systems often combined with the fact that the growth was primarily driven by the commodity prices' increase (Clapp & Sen, 1999; Lange et al., 2017). The limitations of GDP per capita drifted out of the shadows and arrived in the scope of the policymakers' and mainstream economics' attention (Syrovatka, 2008; Stiglitz et al., 2009; Giannetti et al., 2015). The rising popularity of the already-existent development indexes, such as HDI, went hand in hand with that (Klasen, 2018).

As for today, there is no longer a lack of explanations of GDP per capita inadequacy in regard to the economic policy as well as measuring the well-being, but the quantitative data to either support or disprove the statements criticizing this indicator or highlighting its deviation from the common development indexes are still scarce. Nevertheless, the previous research has enabled us to outline the basic

[4]With the exact computation of grey economy's size still posing a problem even for middle-income countries (Bala, 2013).

aspects held responsible for GDP per capita losing its position as the gauge of economic development and level of life[5].

Firstly, albeit being perceived as an indicator of material (or financial) well-being, it still falters to capture some of such well-being's significant components (Osberg & Sharpe, 2001). Constructed as a measurement of production, GDP per capita struggles with accurate depiction of the living standards due to the difference between production and private consumption, which may be a more precise view of the level of life in material terms (Osberg & Sharpe, 2001). Furthermore, it fails to encompass the issues that undermine its ability to speak for an average member of the population, such as the distribution of incomes and the production/consumption that remains unnoticed by the statisticians accountable for the GDP computation (Bala, 2013; Giannetti et al., 2015). Hence, inequality and informal economy were proclaimed GDP per capita's main adversaries and should not be left out if one is to explain the divergence between the quantitative size of the economy and the well-being it produces (Clapp & Sen, 1999; Giannetti et al., 2015). It brings forward more egalitarian indicators of median income or consumption, as well as the demands for more precise inclusion of the shadow economy (Nolan et al., 2018; Dynan & Sheiner, 2018).

Secondly, the changes of GDP per capita are often disconnected from the well-being of the less fortunate part of the population – that is GDP is often criticized for not taking into account the poorest share of the people, which (especially in the developing world – Clapp & Sen, 1999) often doesn't experience the effects of the economy's quantitative increase (Atkinson & Marlier, 2015). The solution has been attributed to the common development indexes such as HDI, which are more efficient at capturing the changes in the well-being due to their multidimensional nature (Clapp & Sen, 1999; Klasen, 2018).

The inadequacy of GDP per capita is relatively plain in cases of countries with a large share of foreign ownership: In such situations, GDP incorporates the rents and profits of the external asset holders and deviates from what can be understood as national well-being (Nolan et al., 2018). However, this drawback is easily dealt with a range of GDP-based indicators, such as gross national income (GNI) or gross national disposable income (GNDI), which are correcting GDP for the non-resident incomes, while including the resident incomes from abroad (Osberg & Sharpe, 2001). While those indicators are derived from the national accounting and balance of payments and are often computed by the same institutions that are entrusted with the GDP estimation, they remain less employed by the policymakers (Stiglitz et al., 2009).

More abstract discussions are related to the nature of well-being itself, which, according to popularizing claims, cannot be equalized to quantitative GDP-based indicators and should embody less straightforward and quantifiable concepts

[5] As simple as it gets, those limits may be approximately collapsed into two spheres: one deals with the quantitative issues that GDP per capita fails to include, while the other relates to the points that are of qualitative nature and cannot be included into the accounting monetary indicator.

(Stiglitz et al., 2009). Whereas well-being is synonymized with the quality of life, it is hard to avoid philosophic discourses[6] on the components of such construct; nevertheless, it's difficult to ignore the social fundamentals of the economic production, or, in other words, at what cost the GDP is produced (Stiglitz et al., 2009). This may relate to healthcare, education, social safety or employment, which are undoubtedly the constituents of what we generally understand as the living standards (Deb, 2015; Hudakova, 2017). Albeit there are certainly some linkages between the GDP growth and the aforementioned elements of life, the strength and causality of such linkages are still subjects of discussion (Deb, 2015). Furthermore, the quality of life may be linked to a handful of other factors that the GDP fails to embrace and struggles to influence – these may be of ecological or geographical nature, as well as based on social culture or religion even (Giannetti et al., 2015). Additionally, such non-economic traits may be perceived as not only drawbacks of GDP (and therefore, demands for a more informative indicator), but as the factors standing behind the deviations of GDP from already established development indexes[7] as well (Giannetti et al., 2015).

It is also evident that GDP per capita cannot be associated with the economic development in countries with poor institutional environment (Deb, 2015; Teker & Guner, 2016). The conventional explanation is twofold: firstly, the high-quality institutions themselves (including but not limited to the democratic political system, inviolability of basic rights, social and economic security, personal safety, etc.) form an inseparable part of the well-being and quality of life; secondly, the institutional imperfections (such as unequal distribution of national wealth or economic restrictions for certain groups of population) could be affecting the way GDP per capita is produced, calculated[8] and dispensed (Syrovatka, 2008). Moreover, certain displays of institutional deficiencies are stated to undermine the informative value of GDP per capita as an indicator of development due to their impact on the before-mentioned factors of development-GDP deviations (for example, corruption is negatively affecting the income distribution and inequalities, which are believed to produce discrepancies between well-being and GDP per capita – Syrovatka, 2008; Giannetti et al., 2015).

The discussions also arise in regard to the sustainability of the economic growth and the linkages between development and, for example, natural resources depletion or environmental damage (Costanza et al., 2009). When the production of GDP pours into the excessive deterioration of the ecology or the exhaustion of the non-renewable resources, the overall effect on the well-being and long-term development is stated to be debatable at best (Costanza et al., 2009). Furthermore, such

[6]Which are supported by a handful of relatively popular "happiness indexes" of too lax or too complicated methodology, which aim at quantifying the quality of life without turning to economic framework of GDP (Stiglitz et al., 2009).

[7]For example, those idiosyncrasies may be affecting the non-economic components of HDI and explain the well-known divergence between the countries' rankings in both GDP per capita and HDI (Hopkins, 1991; Deb, 2015).

[8]It refers to the inklings of undemocratic regimes deliberately overvaluing their economic indicators due to ideological or propagational needs (Syrovatka, 2008).

economic growth (together with the growth policies oriented at the quantitative increase of the GDP at any cost often present in resource-rich countries) bears clearly unsustainable nature and elicits questions about the future perspectives of such accretion (Costanza et al., 2009). The limited effects of the commodity-driven growth on the development are indirectly confirmed by the long-lasting and substantial divergence between HDI and GDP in resource-rich countries – while their GDP per capita makes them high-income nations, their level of well-being (captured by HDI) corresponds to much poorer countries (Hopkins, 1991; Syrovatka, 2008; Lange et al., 2017). This divergence reaches the extremes in those commodity producers where the substantial mineral stocks are accompanied by non-democratic and extractive institutions, which may be the reasons for the uneven distribution of the commodity revenues (Teker & Guner, 2016; Lange et al., 2017).

Generally, it poses an insidious task to distinguish between the limits of GDP per capita as such (i.e. something to be dealt with by the construction of a better indicator) and the factors standing behind the deviation between the GDP per capita and economic development captured by some of the already existent indexes (Sagar & Najam, 1998; Dynan & Sheiner, 2018). The twofold nature of those limits comes as little help: Both the GDP's methodological drawbacks and development's unquantifiable components may be perceived as the causes of deviations or the demands for switching GDP per capita for a more encompassing indicator (or, more realistically, supplementing GDP-oriented policies with an additional measure of well-being). Given that there still is no (and likely in the foreseeable future will not be) academic consensus on the latter, we incline to accept the former and view the factors reviewed in this section as the ones producing divergence between development and GDP.

4.3 Human Development Index as an Indicator of Well-Being

Whereas GDP per capita persists to play the role of the most well-known indicator for comparing living standards, the coherent depiction of development and well-being has been in scope of the development economists' attention for decades (Dasgupta, 1990; Hopkins, 1991; Clapp & Sen, 1999). The approaches corresponded with the GDP's drawbacks – the newly constructed approaches were either meant to correct GDP from the items irrelevant for development and level of life (such as non-resident incomes) or to embody non-economic and often non-measurable aspects such as institutions, safety or even happiness (Costanza et al., 2009; Stiglitz et al., 2009).

The most elaborate indicators, such as GNI[9], were not developed to measure well-being and appear to be another version of production indicators, but even they

[9] Or its most trendy iteration, adjusted net national income, which is the GNI minus natural resources depletion and fixed capital amortization (Lange et al., 2017).

perform better in evaluating actual well-being than the traditional GDP per capita (Osberg & Sharpe, 2001; Stiglitz et al., 2009; Nolan et al., 2018). Nevertheless, if one is to examine the nature of deviations between GDP and development, it certainly is not enough to define development as one of the GDP's corrected renditions (Stiglitz et al., 2009).

More sophisticated quantitative approaches encompassing the concepts of education, natural resources depletion and environmental damage have already been designed[10] – the indicators of net adjusted savings or net adjusted wealth may be a favourable future of development measurement, but they are still difficult to compute, lack statistical infrastructure for data collection together with historical time series of any substantive length (Lange et al., 2017). Given that the same problems are encountered when working with even more wide-ranging indexes of well-being incorporating tens of variables, the feasible options of well-being quantification are reduced to few (Stiglitz et al., 2009; Giannetti et al., 2015; Klasen, 2018).

Given the multidimensional nature of economic well-being and living standards, we ought to highlight the viability of complex indexes that combine income (usually GDP-based) and non-income indicators and produce means to evaluate and compare different iterations of development. The most widespread of such indexes is the already-mentioned HDI – Human Development Index, which is annually computed and published by the United Nations (Klasen, 2018). This index covers nearly all countries of the world and evaluates them according to three parameters that may be viewed as dimensions of development: gross national income per capita as an indicator of income; average life expectancy as a gauge of healthcare and living conditions; and the level of education[11], which is to capture the human capital development (Klasen, 2018). While its methodology is relatively straightforward, it quickly rose as the most well-known indicator of well-being due to its components being regarded as relatively accurate renderings of the level of life's different sides (Klasen, 2018). Furthermore, being computed from the beginning of the 1990s, it has relatively long time series enabling econometric estimations.

HDI harvests its portion of criticism for certain methodological drawbacks, such as the interchangeability of its individual components (Syrovatka, 2008). Besides that, the nature of its parts appears to be oriented towards developing countries; with the healthcare and educational constituents' depiction being less relevant for already developed countries (Syrovatka, 2008). Moreover, the smaller difference in those indicators common for economically advanced nations makes HDI less fit for comparing high-income countries (Klasen, 2018). Further reproaches are stated to lay in HDI's inability to capture the impact of institutional environment[12], episodic unreliability of the data sources (though the things are getting better with the increase

[10] See Lange et al. (2017) for the concrete methodology of these approaches.

[11] Which is calculated using mean years of schooling and expected years of schooling (Klasen, 2018).

[12] Albeit some may argue that its components are directly affected by the institutions and therefore may be viewed as fairly representative in terms of this matter (Syrovatka, 2008).

in HDI's popularity and usability – Stiglitz et al., 2009) and presumption of the high correlation to GDP per capita (Hopkins, 1991; Clapp & Sen, 1999). Notwithstanding, this correlation appears to be substantial only for the least developed countries, while those with middle and high income exhibit no such idiosyncrasy (Deb, 2015; Hudakova, 2017).

Despite the criticism, the value of HDI for academic research is hard to overestimate – it has long left the discussions of the development economists and became widespread amongst the general public, and while it is still a rough measure of what we perceive as development and well-being, HDI stands out as a relatively consistent and easy-to-understand mensuration. Our research intends to utilize that in order to clarify the roots of divergence between purely economical and production-based GDP per capita and burdensomely quantifiable development.

4.4 Data and Methodology

4.4.1 Data

For econometric analysis, an unbalanced panel dataset of 141 countries, across all stages of economic development, and yearly time series ranging from 2000 to 2017 was employed. The intention was to include an extensive and heterogenous selection of countries as possible, and the exclusions from the sample were primarily due to the lack of data on crucial variables. The same principle applied to the sample's time period.

All of the datasets[13] are accessible from publicly available sources. The main source for the wide array of variables was the World Bank (GDP per capita, net primary income, net secondary income, fertility rate, adolescent fertility rate). Other sources include the United Nations Development Programme database for HDI, the Heritage Foundation for the Index of Economic Freedom, the World Inequality Database for Gini index, the United Nations Office on Drugs and Crime for homicide rate, the World Health Organization for data on suicide rates and alcohol consumption and the Pew Research Center for data on religion and Medina and Schneider (2019) for the estimate of shadow economy extent.

4.4.2 Dependent Variable

To estimate the causes of deviations between economic development/well-being that is to be represented by the Human Development Index and GDP per capita (PPP), we

[13] List and description of all the variables, descriptive statistics and correlation table available upon request.

calculate those deviations (further referred to as development–GDP gaps) and regress them on a wide array of aforediscussed variables that may be understood as both the limitations of GDP per capita and factors affecting the development and quality of life without any direct relation to the economic capacities.

The results are meant to present a comprehensive view of the issues that stand behind the GDP–development gaps and empirically evaluate the numerous theoretical discussions regarding this topic. While the obvious drawback and a reasonable ground for criticism may be linked to the choice of the development indicator, we believe that there is no other viable option given the either one-dimensionality or lack of data for other indicators that were developed to assess well-being and living standards.

The development-GDP gap can be expressed as

$$\mathrm{GAP}_{i,t} = \mathrm{HDI}_{i,t} - \mathrm{GDPI}_{i,t}, \tag{4.1}$$

where $\mathrm{HDI}_{i,t}$ is Human Development Index and $\mathrm{GDPI}_{i,t}$ is GDP per capita index calculated as follows:

$$\mathrm{GDPI}_{i,t} = \frac{\ln\left(\text{GDP per capita}_{i,t}\right) - \ln(100)}{\ln(75{,}000) - \ln(100)}. \tag{4.2}$$

Adaptation of the UNDP (2020) methodology for calculation of HDI, specifically its GNP component, was employed to calculate the GDP per capita index. Consistently with GNP component calculation, the interval of 100 USD (minimum value which takes into account non-market production) to 75,000 USD (according to Kahneman & Deaton, 2010, boundary, above which the benefits of GDP per capita are negligible) was applied.

4.4.3 Model

Our dependent variable, development-GDP gap, on one hand contains $\mathrm{HDI}_{i,t}$, and on the other hand $\mathrm{GDPI}_{i,t}$. If we consider that

$$\mathrm{HDI}_{i,t} = c_i + \boldsymbol{ZZ}_{i,t}\boldsymbol{a} + \mathrm{GDPI}_{i,t}b + \omega_{i,t}, \tag{4.3}$$

where c_i is an intercept, $\boldsymbol{ZZ}_{i,t}$ is a vector of other factors affecting HDI other than GDP per capita, $\omega_{i,t}$ is an idiosyncratic error, $\boldsymbol{a}$ is a vector of parameters for respective factors in $\boldsymbol{ZZ}_{i,t}$ and b is a parameter for $\mathrm{GDPI}_{i,t}$ and

$$\boldsymbol{ZZ}_{i,t} = \boldsymbol{\alpha}_i + \boldsymbol{W}_{it}\boldsymbol{\beta} + \boldsymbol{S}_{it}\boldsymbol{\gamma} + \boldsymbol{u}_{i,t}, \tag{4.4}$$

$$\mathrm{GDPI}_{i,t} = \delta_i + \boldsymbol{S}_{it}\boldsymbol{\theta} + \boldsymbol{Z}_{it}\boldsymbol{\mu} + v_{i,t}, \tag{4.5}$$

where $\boldsymbol{W}_{it}$ is a vector of exogenous factors affecting solely $\mathrm{HDI}_{i,t}$ without an effect on $\mathrm{HDPI}_{i,t}$, $\boldsymbol{S}_{it}$ is a vector of exogenous factors affecting $\mathrm{GDPI}_{i,t}$ as well as $\mathrm{HDI}_{i,t}$, $\boldsymbol{Z}_{it}$ is a vector of exogenous factors affecting solely $\mathrm{GDPI}_{i,\ t}$, δ_i is an intercept for $\mathrm{GDPI}_{i,t}$, $\boldsymbol{\alpha_i}$ is a vector of intercepts for respective factors in $\boldsymbol{ZZ}_{i,t}$, $\boldsymbol{\beta}$, $\boldsymbol{\gamma}$, $\boldsymbol{\theta}$, $\boldsymbol{\mu}$ are vectors of respective parameters, $\boldsymbol{u}_{i,t}$ is a vector of respective idiosyncratic errors for $\boldsymbol{ZZ}_{i,t}$ and $v_{i,t}$ is an idiosyncratic error for $\mathrm{GDPI}_{i,t}$, then

$$\mathrm{HDI}_{i,t} = c_i + (\boldsymbol{\alpha_i} + \boldsymbol{W}_{it}\boldsymbol{\beta} + \boldsymbol{S}_{it}\boldsymbol{\gamma} + \boldsymbol{u}_{i,t})\boldsymbol{a} + (\delta_i + \boldsymbol{S}_{it}\boldsymbol{\theta} + \boldsymbol{Z}_{it}\boldsymbol{\mu} + v_{i,t})b + \omega_{i,t} \tag{4.6}$$

and

$$\begin{aligned}\mathrm{HDI}_{i,t} - \mathrm{GDPI}_{i,t} = c_i + \boldsymbol{\alpha}_i\boldsymbol{a} + (b-1)\delta_i + \boldsymbol{W}_{it}\boldsymbol{\beta}\boldsymbol{a} + \boldsymbol{S}_{it}(\boldsymbol{\gamma}\boldsymbol{a} + \boldsymbol{\theta}(b-1)) + \boldsymbol{Z}_{it}\boldsymbol{\mu}(b-1)\\ +\boldsymbol{u}_{i,t}\boldsymbol{a} + (b-1)v_{i,t} + \omega_{i,t}.\end{aligned} \tag{4.7}$$

In compact form, we can write[14]

$$\mathrm{HDI}_{i,t} - \mathrm{GDPI}_{i,t} = d_i + \boldsymbol{W}_{it}\boldsymbol{\pi} + \boldsymbol{S}_{it}(\boldsymbol{\rho} + \boldsymbol{\tau}) + \boldsymbol{Z}_{it}\boldsymbol{\varphi} + \varepsilon_{i,t}, \tag{4.8}$$

where

$$d_i = c_i + \boldsymbol{\alpha}_i\boldsymbol{a} + (b-1)\delta_i \tag{4.9}$$

$$\boldsymbol{\pi} = \boldsymbol{\beta}\boldsymbol{a}, \tag{4.10}$$

$$\boldsymbol{\rho} = \boldsymbol{\gamma}\boldsymbol{a}, \tag{4.11}$$

$$\boldsymbol{\tau} = \boldsymbol{\theta}(b-1), \tag{4.12}$$

$$\boldsymbol{\varphi} = \boldsymbol{\mu}(b-1), \tag{4.13}$$

$$\varepsilon_{i,t} = \boldsymbol{u}_{i,t}\boldsymbol{a} + (b-1)v_{i,t} + \omega_{i,t}. \tag{4.14}$$

If we, based on $\mathrm{HDI}_{i,t}$ calculation methodology, presume that parameter b, that is the effect of $\mathrm{GDPI}_{i,t}$ on $\mathrm{HDI}_{i,t}$, is greater than 0 and lower than 1, positive parameters of individual explanatory variables in our estimated models can be a result of one of the three scenarios – (1) positive impact ($\boldsymbol{\pi}$) of factors $\boldsymbol{W}_{it}$ through positive impact on $\mathrm{HDI}_{i,t}$, (2) positive impact ($\boldsymbol{\varphi}$) of factors $\boldsymbol{Z}_{it}$ through negative impact ($\boldsymbol{\mu}$) on $\mathrm{GDPI}_{i,t}$

[14] For idiosyncratic error $\varepsilon_{i,t}$ in fixed-effects and random-effects models, we consider assumptions $E(\varepsilon_{i,t}| d_{i,t}, \boldsymbol{W}_{it}, \boldsymbol{S}_{it}, \boldsymbol{Z}_{it}) = 0$, $Var(\varepsilon_{i,t}|d_{i,t}, \boldsymbol{W}_{it}, \boldsymbol{S}_{it}, \boldsymbol{Z}_{it}) = Var(\varepsilon_{i,t}) = \sigma_\varepsilon^2$ in all time periods t, $Cov(\varepsilon_{i,t}, \varepsilon_{i,s}| d_{i,t}, \boldsymbol{W}_{it}, \boldsymbol{S}_{it}, \boldsymbol{Z}_{it}) = 0$ for all $t \neq s$ and for fixed-effects ideally also $(\varepsilon_{i,t}|d_{i,t}, \boldsymbol{W}_{it}, \boldsymbol{S}_{it}, \boldsymbol{Z}_{it})\tilde{N}(0, \sigma_\varepsilon^2)$.

and (3) positive impact ($\rho + \tau$) of factors S_{it} due to (3a) positive impact (ρ) through $ZZ_{i,t}$ and positive impact (τ) from negative effect (θ) on $GDPI_{i,t}$ ($\rho > 0; \tau > 0; \theta < 0$), (3b) positive impact through $ZZ_{i,t}$ surpassing negative impact from positive effect on $GDPI_{i,t}$ ($\rho > 0; \tau < 0; \theta > 0; |\rho| > |\tau|$) and (3c) positive impact from negative effect on $GDPI_{i,t}$ surpassing negative impact through $ZZ_{i,t}$ ($\rho < 0; \tau > 0; \theta < 0; |\rho| < |\tau|$).

4.4.4 Explanatory Variables

The selection of independent variables which are meant to explain the development-GDP gaps is based on the theoretical underpinnings outlined in Sect. 4.2. We aim to include the variables correcting the methodological drawbacks of GDP, as well as those which might impact the well-being/development without any direct effect on the quantitative side of the economy. The theoretical background behind the below-described variables is summarized in the works of Hopkins (1991), Syrovatka (2008), Stiglitz et al. (2009) and Giannetti et al. (2015).

To capture the potential impact of the institutional environment, we used an index of economic freedom – a complex measure of socio-political and economic institutions in individual countries. It is reasonable to expect the institutional quality to be of impact not only on the level of life directly but on the creation and distribution of GDP as well (Syrovatka, 2008; Teker & Guner, 2016). An increase in the index represents an improvement in the institutional quality and vice versa. Higher economic freedom might have positive impact on development-GDP gap due to its positive impact on components of development other than GDP, which are of higher priority especially in more economically advanced countries, typically characterized by their more developed institutions and higher economic freedom. However, negative effect on the gap cannot be ruled out due to the potentially disproportionate beneficial effect of the economic freedom on the GDP versus other development components.

The extent of shadow economy[15] should not only account for discrepancies in national estimate methodologies (many countries underestimate the extent of shadow economy, which is especially prevalent in developing countries – Bala, 2013) but also act as a proxy partially representing ingrained crime culture, corruption, moral values and institutional quality, and thus evaluating their impact on development-GDP gap. Presumed underestimation of shadow economy is expected to have positive impact on development-GDP gap. Nonetheless, extensive shadow economy might have opposite effect due to its accompanying root causes.

Furthermore, we add the balance of payments items such as primary and secondary income flows in order to correct GDP for the non-resident transactions and

[15] In contrast with estimates included in GDP figures by the national statistical offices, proxy estimated by Medina and Schneider (2019) offers uniform methodology and thus universally comparable values.

control for development-sensible issues such as remittance flows and foreign asset ownership (Hopkins, 1991; Stiglitz et al., 2009). Higher foreign incomes are expected to have positive impact on the development-GDP gap due to the GNI component of development indicator.

Another crucial determinant of development-GDP gaps to be included in the estimations is the Gini index, which represents income inequality and impacts both the distribution of GDP and the potential social tensions in the case of highly inegalitarian societies (Giannetti et al., 2015; Nolan et al., 2018). It is reasonable to expect it to have negative impact on development-GDP gap due to a presumed ineffective utilization of aggregate income for securing basic development elements such as healthcare and education in a highly unequal economy.

We control for the upper boundary present in our GDP index calculation by the inclusion of so-called GDP excess variable[16] in econometric estimation, which reflects effects of GDP per capita exceeding the limit on development-GDP gap. It is assumed to have positive impact on the gap due to the index computation methodology.

In addition to the aforementioned explanatory variables which constitute the foundation of the baseline model, extended models were estimated. Extended models include additional, secondary explanatory variables encompassing societal, cultural and traditional idiosyncrasies – namely homicide rate, suicide rate, general and adolescent fertility rates, alcohol consumption and religion – the goal of extended estimates being the identification of potential additional factors with strong explanatory power from the chosen factor category.

The main potential downside of the explanatory variables selection is the inevitable arbitrariness – some relevant factors might be omitted, and chosen factor combinations might have explanatory power shortages.

4.4.5 *Methods*

Three most common model options come into consideration for an analysis of panel data – pooling OLS model, fixed-effects model and random-effects model. Pooling OLS and two-way (individual and time) fixed-effects models both utilize OLS estimation. Our one-way (individual) random-effects models utilize feasible generalized least squares, in order to take into account effects-induced correlation, with two-step estimation method of Swamy and Arora (1972), in our case, modified by Baltagi and Chang (1994) for use in unbalanced panels.

Baseline and extended models were estimated using all of the aforementioned methods where applicable (exception being models including time-invariant variable and consequential inapplicability of fixed-effects). The most suitable models were

[16] GDP excess is equal to zero in case of GDP per capita being below 75,000 dollars. Amount exceeding this limit value causes proportionately higher GDP excess variable.

selected by conducting appropriate tests – F-test for presence of fixed-effects, LM test for random-effects and Hausman test to evaluate random-effects consistency.

Constructed models were tested for cross-sectional dependence by using the Pesaran CD test, for multicollinearity utilizing variance inflation factor (VIF), serial correlation by performing the Breusch-Godfrey/Wooldridge test, stationarity by implementing the Augmented Dickey-Fuller test and heteroskedasticity by enacting the Breusch-Pagan test. Due to the test-indicated presence of serial correlation and heteroskedasticity and consequent potential invalidity of statistical tests of significance, t-statistics of all the models were estimated using Arellano (1987) robust covariance matrix and appropriate robust model statistics were produced.

4.5 Results and Discussion

In Table 4.1, baseline model estimates are displayed. Across all estimates, every explanatory variable except "Shadow economy" in the case of random-effects model exhibits an influence of the same sign, thus indicating at least elementary consistency of the results.

The Index of Economic Freedom (not significant in the pooled OLS and the random-effects models, while being significant in fixed-effects model) has negative effect on development-GDP gap, which most likely stems from having a positive impact on GDP with higher magnitude than it having a positive impact on other components of economic development.

Shadow economy variable (significant in all estimates) has positive effect on dependent variable in OLS and fixed-effects model but negative effect in random-effects model (we can assume that results given by fixed-effects model are more accurate based on the performed tests). As mentioned in Sect. 4.4.4, there are at least two possible explanations of either effect. Firstly, national statistical offices might underestimate the extent of shadow economy, thus underestimating actual GDP per capita leading to positive development-GDP gap. Nonetheless, higher extent of shadow economy can be expected in the countries with lower institutional development, higher corruption etc., that is in an economic environment less favourable for economic development.

Net primary and secondary incomes (primary being significant in fixed-effects and random-effects model and secondary being significant in pooled OLS) both have positive impact on the development-GDP gap – the expected results given that these variables directly impact disposable income of country inhabitants but are not included in GDP per capita calculation.

Income inequality in form of Gini index (significant in all estimates) has a negative effect on the development-GDP gap. First and foremost, income inequality might be strongly associated with inequality in education and healthcare. Additionally, unequally distributed GDP per capita increment will not be proportionally reflected in other main components of development indicators due to ineffective utilization.

Table 4.1 Baseline model estimates

	(1)	(2)	(3)
Intercept	0.084**		0.102***
	(0.039)		(0.033)
Index of Economic Freedom	−0.0004	−0.001**	−0.0004
	(0.0004)	(0.0003)	(0.0003)
Shadow economy	0.001*	0.002***	−0.001***
	(0.0004)	(0.001)	(0.0004)
Net primary income	0.027	0.075**	0.087**
	(0.089)	(0.033)	(0.035)
Net secondary income	0.288***	0.047	0.050
	(0.056)	(0.029)	(0.035)
Gini index	−0.191***	−0.080*	−0.113**
	(0.047)	(0.046)	(0.051)
GDP excess	−1.845***	0.520	0.677*
	(0.503)	(0.360)	(0.344)
Fixed effects	—	Country, year	—
Observations	2364	2364	2364
R^2	0.304	0.120	0.080
Adjusted R^2	0.302	0.055	0.078
F stat. (robust)	13.997*** (df = 6; 140)	6.1101*** (df = 6; 140)	4.1929*** (df = 6; 140)
χ^2	83.979*** (df = 6)	36.661*** (df = 6)	25.157*** (df = 6)

Source: Authors' analysis
Note: *$p < 0.1$; **$p < 0.05$; ***$p < 0.01$; (1) OLS (2) Fixed effects (3) Random Effects

The extended model, presented in Table 4.2, captures effects of selected societal, cultural and traditional factors. Offering, based on conducted tests, the most consistent and accurate results, fixed-effects models are the primary models presented, an exception being the use of random-effects model, in order to incorporate time-invariant variables.

Homicide rate and suicide rate variables are not significant – perhaps a little unanticipated result. Either one having similarly large negative effect on both economic development and economic activity is the most probable explanation.

Fertility rate and adolescent fertility rate (both significant) both have negative effect on development-GDP gap. General fertility rate supports labour force and economic activity but might not uplift other components of economic development to the same extent, and on top of that, higher fertility is often induced by higher infant mortality. General fertility rate and adolescent fertility rate both reflect socio-cultural environment of the country – especially adolescent fertility might be associated with gender inequality and as a result with lower economic development.

Alcohol consumption has significant negative effect on development-GDP gap – higher alcohol consumption having sizable adverse effect on other components of economic development other than economic activity is to be expected. Whether

Table 4.2 Extended model estimates

	(1)	(2)	(3)	(4)	(5)	(6)
Intercept						0.050
						(0.038)
The Index of Economic Freedom	−0.001***	−0.0005*	−0.0005	−0.001**	−0.001*	−0.0004
	(0.0003)	(0.0003)	(0.0003)	(0.0003)	(0.0003)	(0.0003)
Shadow economy	0.003***	0.002***	0.002***	0.002***	0.002***	-0.001***
	(0.001)	(0.001)	(0.001)	(0.001)	(0.001)	(0.0004)
Net primary income	0.017	0.061*	0.066**	0.069**	0.076**	0.093***
	(0.019)	(0.033)	(0.028)	(0.041)	(0.034)	(0.036)
Net secondary income	0.044	0.041*	0.021	0.045	0.042	0.050
	(0.033)	(0.024)	(0.024)	(0.028)	(0.030)	(0.035)
Gini index	−0.011	−0.072*	−0.074*	−0.080*	−0.073*	−0.116**
	(0.037)	(0.041)	(0.043)	(0.046)	(0.045)	(0.051)
GDP excess	0.571***	0.143	0.582	0.460	0.441	0.714**
	(0.174)	(0.619)	(0.410)	(0.342)	(0.324)	(0.343)
Homicide	−0.0001					
	(0.0001)					
Fertility rate		−0.020***				
		(0.004)				
Adolescent fertility rate			−0.001***			
			(0.0002)			
Suicide rate				−0.0002		
				(0.0003)		
Alcohol consumption					−0.002**	
					(0.001)	
Christians						0.001**
						(0.0003)
Muslims						0.0004
						(0.0003)
Buddhists						0.001**
						(0.0004)
Hindus						0.0005
						(0.0004)
Folk religions						0.002**
						(0.001)
Fixed effects	Country, year	Country, year	Country, year	Country, year	Country, year	—
Observations	1801	2364	2364	2346	2341	2328
R^2	0.176	0.209	0.243	0.123	0.137	0.094
Adjusted R^2	0.102	0.150	0.187	0.058	0.072	0.090
F stat. (robust)	10.216*** (df = 7; 125)	11.425*** (df = 7; 140)	12.43*** (df = 7; 140)	5.4293*** (df = 7; 139)	6.7984*** (df = 7; 139)	3.1066*** (df = 7; 138)

(continued)

Table 4.2 (continued)

	(1)	(2)	(3)	(4)	(5)	(6)
χ^2	71.512*** (df = 7)	79.972*** (df = 7)	87.008*** (df = 7)	38.005*** (df = 7)	47.589*** (df = 7)	34.173*** (df = 11)

Source: Authors' analysis
Note: *$p < 0.1$; **$p < 0.05$; ***$p < 0.01$; (1)–(5) fixed effects (6) random effects

alcohol consumption has negative effect on economic activity as well is up to discussion.

Lastly, various religions were included in the estimation – in substance, the religious group numeric representation is at the expense of the atheistic population. As can be seen, Christianity, Buddhism and folk religions have significant effects – all of them positive, in fact, looking at insignificant estimated parameters of other religious groups, every single one has positive impact. Thus, a possible inference is that religions have positive effect in contrast to atheism.

4.6 Conclusion

The limitations of GDP per capita as a well-being indicator are already in scope of economic discussions: it is evident that it is unable to capture a number of components crucial for what the academics view as a development. The reaction of the researchers spurred the birth of a range of so-called development indicators, which are gaining on popularity and highlighting the inadequacy of GDP per capita due to the noticeable deviations between the well-being indexes and GDP. In this chapter, we made a rigorous attempt at explaining the factors standing behind these deviations. To do so, we calculated the gaps between GDP and one of the most well-known and elaborated indexes of well-being – Human Development Index created and promoted by the United Nations. The causes of those gaps were examined using panel data and a selection of multidimensional indicators that may be of impact on deviations between purely production-based GDP and a more complex concept of economic development.

The results were found to be in accordance with the commonly-stated presumptions related to the divergence between GDP and well-being. First of all, the extent of shadow economy and positive net international incomes understate GDP compared to gross national income component of well-being. On the other hand, larger income inequality gives rise to negative development-GDP gap. Economic freedom contributes to well-being lagging behind economic activity indicator, perhaps due to asymmetrical nature of its positive impacts. Fertility rates have negative impact on development-GDP gap, possibly due to cultural environment and undue focus on economic activity. Additional expected negative impact on well-being is attributable to alcohol consumption. Finally, larger proportion of population professing Christianity, Buddhism or folk religions have positive effect on economic development.

Acknowledgments The work on this chapter was funded by the internal grant of Prague University of Economics and Business #F1/03/2020.

References

Arellano, M. (1987). Computing robust standard errors for within group estimators. *Oxford Bulletin of Economics and Statistics, 49*, 431–434. https://doi.org/10.1111/j.1468-0084.1987.mp49004006.x

Atkinson, G., & Marlier, A. C. (2015). *Monitoring the evolution of income poverty and real incomes over time* (CASE Papers, 2015(188)). Centre for Analysis of Social Exclusion. Available at: http://eprints.lse.ac.uk/103979. Accessed 1 Feb 2021.

Bala RM (2013) *Limits of gross domestic product in characterizing economic welfare*. EBEEC Conference Papers, 2013(5), Istanbul: 5th International Conference on the Economics of Balkan and Eastern Europe Countries in the Changed World (pp. 133–142). Available at: https://www.researchgate.net/publication/263652456_Limits_of_Gross_Domestic_Product_in_characterizing_economic_welfare. Accessed 27 Jan 2021.

Baltagi, B., & Chang, Y. J. (1994). Incomplete panels: A comparative study of alternative estimators for the unbalanced one-way error component regression model. *Journal of Econometrics, 62*(2), 67–89. https://doi.org/10.1016/0304-4076(94)90017-5

Clapp, J., & Sen, A. (1999). Development as freedom. *International Journal, 55*(1), 160–178. https://doi.org/10.2307/40203469

Costanza, R., Hart, M., Posner, S., & Talberth, J. (2009). *Beyond GDP: The need for new measures of progress* (The Pardee Papers, 2009(4)). Pardee Center for the Study of the Longer-Range Future. Available at: https://www.bu.edu/pardee/files/documents/PP-004-GDP.pdf. Accessed 2 Feb 2021.

Dasgupta, P. (1990). Well-being and the extent of its realisation in poor countries. *The Economic Journal, 100*(400), 1–32. https://doi.org/10.2307/2234181

Deb, S. (2015). *Gap between GDP and HDI: Are the rich country experiences different from the poor?* Paper for the IARIW-OECD Special Conference: "Whither the SNA", Paris: OECD Conference. Available at: http://old.iariw.org/papers/2015/deb.pdf. Accessed 27 Jan 2021.

Dynan, K., & Sheiner, L. (2018). *GDP as a measure of economic well-being* (Hutchins Center Working Paper 2018(43)). Hutchin Center on Fiscal and Monetary Policy. Available at: https://www.brookings.edu/research/gdp-as-a-measure-of-economic-well-being. Accessed 11 Feb 2021.

Giannetti, B. F., Agostinho, F., Almeida, C. M. V. B., & Huisingh, D. (2015). A review of limitations of GDP and alternative indices to monitor human wellbeing and to manage eco-system functionality. *Journal of Cleaner Production, 87*, 11–25. https://doi.org/10.1016/j.jclepro.2014.10.051

Hopkins, M. (1991). Human development revisited: A new UNDP report. *World Development, 19*(10), 1469–1473. https://doi.org/10.1016/0305-750x(91)90089-z

Hudakova, J. (2017). Relationship between gross domestic product and human development index. In *4th International Multidisciplinary Scientific Conference on Social Sciences and Arts SGEM2017*. Modern Science – Economics and Tourism (pp. 665–672). https://doi.org/10.5593/sgemsocial2017/14/s04.087

Kahneman, D., & Deaton, A. (2010). High income improves evaluation of life but not emotional well-being. *Proceedings of National Academy of Sciences, 107*(38), 16489–16493. https://doi.org/10.1073/pnas.1011492107

Klasen, S. (2018). *Human development indices and indicators: A critical evaluation* (UNDP Background Paper). UNDP Human Development Report Office. Available at: http://hdr.undp.

org/en/content/human-development-indices-and-indicators-critical-evaluation. Accessed 23 Feb 2021.

Lange, G. M., Wodon, Q., & Carey, K. (2017). *The changing wealth of nations 2018: Building a sustainable future*. World Bank. https://doi.org/10.1596/978-1-4648-1046-6

Medina L and Schneider FG (2019) *Shedding light on the shadow economy: A global database and the interaction with the official one*. CESifo Working Paper No. 7981. Available at: https://ssrn.com/abstract=3502028. Accessed 2 Mar 2021.

Nolan, B., Roser, M., & Thewissen, S. (2018). GDP per capita versus median household income: What gives rise to the divergence over time and how does this vary across OECD countries? *Review of Income and Wealth, 65*(3), 465–494. https://doi.org/10.1111/roiw.12362

Osberg, L., & Sharpe, A. A. (2001). *Comparisons of Trends in GDP and Economic Well-being – The Impact of Social Capital* (International Symposium Report, 2001) (pp. 310–351). Organization for Economic Co-operation and Development. Available at: https://www.oecd.org/innovation/research/1824740.pdf. Accessed 27 Jan 2021.

Sagar, A., & Najam, A. (1998). The human development index: A critical review. *Ecological Economics, 25*(3), 249–264. https://doi.org/10.1016/S0921-8009(97)00168-7

Stiglitz, J., Sen, A., & Fitoussi, J. P. (2009). *The measurement of economic performance and social progress revisited: Reflections and overview*. Sciences Po Publications 2009(33). Available at: https://ideas.repec.org/p/spo/wpmain/infohdl2441-5l6uh8ogmqildh09h4687h53k.html. Accessed 24 Jan 2021.

Swamy, P. A. V. B., & Arora, S. S. (1972). The exact finite sample properties of the estimators of coefficients in the error components regression models. *Econometrica, 40*(2), 261–275. https://doi.org/10.2307/1909405

Syrovatka, M. (2008). Jak (ne)měřit kvalitu života – kritické pohledy na index lidského rozvoje. *Mezinárodní vztahy, 43*(1), 9–37. Available at: https://www.development.upol.cz/uploads/dokumenty/Syrovatka_HDI.pdf. Accessed 3 Feb 2021).

Teker, S., & Guner, A. (2016). Whether development indices affect economic growth: A cross-country analysis. *Procedia Economics and Finance, 38*(2016), 340–346. https://doi.org/10.1016/S2212-5671(16)30206-4

UNDP (United Nations Development Programme). (2020). *HDR 2020 technical notes*. Available at: http://hdr.undp.org/sites/default/files/hdr2020_technical_notes.pdf. Accessed 19 Feb 2021.

Chapter 5
A Synergistic Forecasting Model for Techno-Fundamental Analysis of Gold Market Returns

Korhan K. Gokmenoglu and Saeed Ebrahimijam

Abstract This study presents a novel approach to financial market forecasting based on a synergistic forecasting model, a type of techno-fundamental analysis that combines technical analysis indicators with fundamental variables using the Kalman filter to improve the accuracy of predictions. We used this model to forecast daily market price returns on gold. The obtained results show that our synergistic model can significantly deduct the root-mean-square error (RMSE) of the predictions compared to a sole technical and/or fundamental analysis. Also, 67% of the time, the model significantly and correctly predicted directional changes in prices one day ahead of time, outperforming the benchmark models.

Key words Gold price · Synergistic forecasting · EGARCH · Support vector regression · Technical analysis indicator

5.1 Introduction

Gold is one of the most important precious metals for investment, as it maintains its value over time and can be used for hedging against risks (Khan, 2013; Shafiee & Topal, 2010). Many investment instruments such as accounts, stocks, derivative certificates, and contracts for differences have been created based on this precious metal. For this reason, the ability to forecast gold prices and gold price volatility has immense importance for the finance community. To this aim, we used a novel approach called synergistic forecasting modeling. This model expands upon previous methods by combining information obtained from technical analysis indicators and fundamental variables using Kalman filtering to improve forecasting accuracy.

K. K. Gokmenoglu (✉)
Department of Finance and Banking, Ankara HBV University, Ankara, Turkey
e-mail: korhan.gokmenoglu@hbv.edu.tr

S. Ebrahimijam
Department of Banking and Finance, Eastern Mediterranean University, Famagusta, North Cyprus via Mersin 10, Turkey
e-mail: saeed.ebrahimijam@emu.edu.tr

D. Procházka (ed.), *Regulation of Finance and Accounting*, Springer Proceedings in Business and Economics, https://doi.org/10.1007/978-3-030-99873-8_5

Most changes in gold prices are attributed to demand-side factors. In this respect, demand for gold is affected by many variables. First, changes in the gold demand result from changes in sentiments and speculation, which cause daily movement in gold prices. Sentiments can be measured by technical analysis indicators (Potoski, 2013). Also, several fundamental factors are influential: Intermarket variables such as the oil price (Zhang & Wei, 2010), financial stress, political uncertainty (Reboredo & Uddin, 2016), and interest rates (Ul Sami & Junejo, 2017) are considered to be the most important fundamental factors that affect gold prices (Das et al., 2018).

Following the 2008 economic crisis, gold was considered a safe haven for investment, and the role of the gold market in the economy increased. Accordingly, forecasting the price and volatility of gold broadly attracted the interest of researchers and led researchers to propose a variety of mathematical and hybrid prediction models (Shafiee & Topal, 2010). Parisi et al. (2008) proposed a recursive and rolling neural network model to predict the sign variation of gold prices one step ahead by considering lags in changes to gold prices as well as lags in the Dow Jones industrial production index. Their method captured 60.68% of true sign variation. Yazdani-Chamzini et al. (2012) developed an adaptive neuro-fuzzy network based on oil and silver prices to predict changes in the gold price; this method outperformed the ANN and ARIMA model, generating a lower root-mean-square error (RMSE) and higher R-square. Khan (2013) also found that the Box Jenkins ARIMA (0,1,1) method is suitable for forecasting gold prices. Meanwhile, Kristjanpoller and Minutolo (2015) applied a hybrid ANN-GARCH model to forecast gold price volatility using foreign exchanges, the oil price, the Dow Jones index, the London stock exchange index, and the oil price return as inputs. They found that their hybrid model improved the mean absolute percentage error in the model compared to the standalone GARCH and ANN models. Finally, Fang et al. (2018) investigated the impact of macroeconomic variables on the volatility of US gold futures using the GARCH-MIDAS model. Their empirical results confirmed that the consideration of macroeconomic variables significantly improves the ability to predict long-term volatility in the US gold market.

The present research describes a hybrid prediction method: a synergistic forecasting model. This model performs a techno-fundamental analysis that fuses a structural model of technical analysis indicators with the exponential GARCH (EGARCH) model of fundamental variables, both of which have a significant impact on the price return volatility of gold. The aim is to create a better forecasting model that can determine gold price returns one step ahead. The data fusion was performed by applying a modified, extended Kalman filter to the indicators, wherein the operational parameters of the Kalman filter were calculated by a support vector regression (SVR) neural network.

5.2 Data

We applied the proposed model to a sample consisting of daily observations of fundamental variables and technical analysis indicators from March 2014 to March 2018. The historical returns of gold spot prices in US dollars (XAUUSD) were used as the dependent variable of the model. Two types of independent variables were used in the synergistic forecasting model, namely fundamental analysis and technical analysis indicators. For the fundamental indicators, the Cleveland Financial Stress Index (CFSI) was used as a proxy of investor sentiment; this index is released by the Federal Reserve Bank of St. Louis. Three-month treasury bill (DTB3MS) interest rates were also used and are considered to be indicators of short-term interest rates. Two CBOE® volatility indexes, the Gold Volatility Index (GVZ) and the Crude Oil Volatility Index (OVX), were used as proxies of the implied volatility of gold and oil options on the Standard & Poor's depositary receipt (SPDR®) and the United States Oil Fund (USO®), respectively.

Technical analysis indicators contain rich information about market dynamics in terms of price and volume and are widely used as inputs in different models for predicting price turning points and price trends. The lagged values of these variables have significant forecasting power (Bekiros, 2015; Neely & Weller, 2012). Specifically, the Relative Strength Index (RSI), stochastic indicator (%K), on-balanced volume (OBV), and standard division indicator (STD) were used in this research. RSI shows the strength or weakness of trends by measuring the acceleration of price movement. %K measures the velocity of price by considering the tendency of close prices. OBV indicates whether the demand or supply side is increasing in the market. Finally, STD shows the volatility of the gold price.

The descriptive statistics of these variables are listed in Table 5.1[1]. According to the Jarque-Bera test, with the exception of LGVZ, the variables are not normally distributed. So, the modified version of the Kalman filter must be applied (Mirza, 2011). Figure 5.1 shows the actual gold price returns in XAUUSD for the forecasting period.

5.3 Methodology

The applied synergistic forecasting approach is a type of time-series forecasting model that combines technical and fundamental models for more accurate prediction (Ebrahimijam et al., 2018). Appendix shows the synergistic model. The first input is the EGARCH regression, a fundamental model that estimates the impact of economic and financial variables on the volatility of gold price returns. Before performing GARCH-type estimations, the presence of an ARCH effect (Engle, 1982) should be verified. As the logarithm of variance is modeled by EGARCH, there is no need to artificially impose nonnegativity constraints on the negative model parameter and asymmetries are allowed. In the following, Eq. 5.1 describes the EGARCH model (Nelson, 1991):

[1] According to ADF and Phillips-Perron unit root test all of the variables are stationary at level. However, because of the space constraint, results are not presented here. They can be submitted upon request.

Table 5.1 Descriptive statistics of the fundamental and technical analysis indicators

	retxauusd	lvol	lovx	lgvz	lcfsi	ltbill	Rsi	obv	stoch	std
Mean	−0.00005	16.10	3.32	2.93	−0.30	−3.15	49	−163033	51	23
Median	0.00037	16.09	3.38	2.94	−0.16	−2.99	49	64908	52	19
Maximum	0.041	18.35	4.23	3.54	0.75	−1.89	87	105526	100	95.2
Minimum	−0.088	14.67	2.72	2.48	−4.60	−6.90	15	−2691060	0.00	6.31
Std. Dev.	0.010	0.47	0.24	0.18	0.89	0.71	12.56	753938	29.84	13
Skewness	−1.152	0.36	−0.15	0.01	−1.27	−0.63	0.01	−1.20	−0.05	2.16
Kurtosis	10.71	3.74	2.41	2.70	5.08	3.21	2.61	4.10	1.66	9.13
Jarque-Bera	2212	36.93	14.89	2.91	370	55.90	10	503.06	128	4060
Prob. of J-B	0.00	0.00	0.00	0.23	0.00	0.00	0.00	0.00	0.00	0.00

Source: Authors' analysis of data

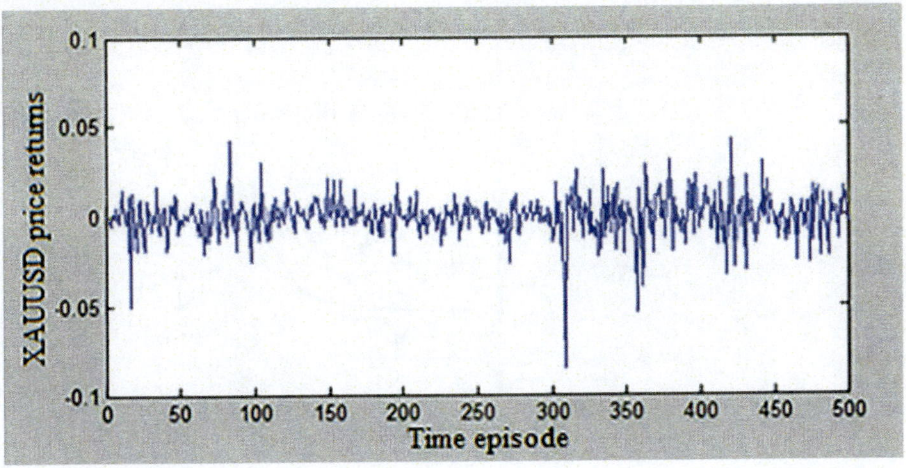

Fig. 5.1 Gold price (XAUUSD) returns

$$\ln\left(\sigma_t^2\right) = \omega + \beta \ln\left(\sigma_{t-1}^2\right) + \gamma \frac{u_{t-1}}{\sqrt{\sigma_{t-1}^2}} + \alpha\left[\frac{|u_{t-1}|}{\sqrt{\sigma_{t-1}^2}} - \sqrt{\frac{2}{\pi}}\right] \tag{5.1}$$

where σ_t^2 is the conditional variance and u_(t-1) is the error distribution.

The economic and financial variables, short-term T-bills, and the OVX, GVZ, and CFSI were utilized as exogenous variables by the model to investigate the impact of these variables on the volatility of XAUUSD. The second input of the synergistic forecasting model was the prediction of standard deviation obtained from the structural time-series model of technical analysis indicators, which indicates the impact of lags in the technical analysis indicators on gold market price volatility.

The third input was the estimated covariance of process noise (Q) for the Kalman (1961) filter at the center of the analysis. The Kalman filter is a two-step process of prediction and correction stages (Welch & Bishop, 2001). First, an estimation of the current state is generated based on uncertainties in the prediction stage; then, it is updated using a weighted average from the prediction and observation stages, with more weight being given to the more certain one.

Prediction stage:

$$\widehat{x_k^-} = f(\widehat{x}_{k-1}, u_{k-1}, w_{k-1}) \tag{5.2}$$

$$P_k^- = A_k P_{k-1} A_k^T + Q_{k-1} \tag{5.3}$$

$$\widehat{z}_k = h(x_k, v_k) \tag{5.4}$$

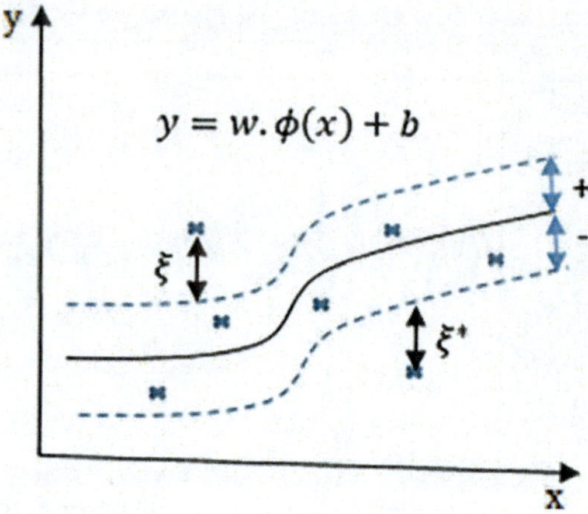

Fig. 5.2 Support vector regression

Update stage:

$$K_k = P_k{}^- H_k{}^T \left(H_k P_K^- H_k{}^T + R\right)^{-1} \tag{5.5}$$

$$\widehat{x}_k = \widehat{x}_k^- + K_k(z_k - \widehat{z}_k) \tag{5.6}$$

$$P_k = (I - K_k H_k) P_k^- \tag{5.7}$$

where *f* is the predicted state estimation function substituted by the EGARCH model as a predictor of fundamental variables, *h* is the prediction of the measurement function substituted by the structural model of the technical analysis indicators, $\widehat{x}_k^-$ is the prior estimate of the state variables, A_k is the state transition matrix, P_k^- is the prior estimate of the current covariance matrix, P_k^- is the previous covariance matrix, K_k is the Kalman gain, Q_{k-1} is the process noise covariance, and R is the measurement noise covariance.

An SVR neural network was applied to estimate gold market volatility as a time-varying parameter that changes based on market conditions and volatility (Q). In particular, SVR is a support vector machine (SVM) method based on supervised learning (machine learning) (Cortes & Vapnik, 1995) that can perform regression analysis and train sample data with target values. As shown in Fig. 5.2, the main characteristic of SVR is that it attempts to minimize the generalized bound instead of minimizing the observed training error. To develop a nonlinear SVR, sample data must be converted using kernel functions to perform linear separation.

The goal function and constraints are shown in Eqs. 5.8, 5.9, 5.10, and 5.11:

$$\text{Minimize } \frac{1}{2}\|w\|^2 + c\sum_{i=1}^{k} \xi_i + \xi_i^* \tag{5.8}$$

$$y_i - wx_i - b \le \varepsilon + \xi_i$$

$$wx_i + b - y_i \le \varepsilon + \xi_i^*$$

$$\xi_i, \xi_i^* \ge 0$$

where

$$y = \sum_{i=1}^{k} (\alpha_i - \alpha_i^*).K(x_i, x_j) + b \tag{5.9}$$

The Kernel function is a Gaussian nonlinear function, as shown below:

$$K(x_i, x_j) = \exp\left(-\frac{\|x_i - x_j\|^2}{2\sigma^2}\right) \tag{5.10}$$

For SVR, Cortes & Vapnik (1995) proposed that the loss function (L) in Eq. 5.11 should be used to penalize errors that are greater than the ε threshold.

$$L_\varepsilon(y, f(x, \omega)) = \begin{cases} 0 & if\ |y - f(x, \omega)| \leq \varepsilon \\ |y - f(x, \omega)| - \varepsilon & \text{otherwise} \end{cases} \tag{5.11}$$

At the end of the synergistic forecasting model, there is a lag operator (Z^{-1}) that generates the predicted gold price return for further use in the Kalman filter (Welch & Bishop, 2001).

5.4 Empirical Findings

The EGARCH model was first conducted on the financial variables. The results are presented in Table 5.2. The Engle heteroscedasticity test showed that an ARCH effect was present in the residuals. The significant α coefficients indicated that all of the fundamental variables had a significant impact on the volatility of gold prices. The highest impact was from GVZ. T-bill had the least negative impact (−0.009), and the CSFI had a slight negative impact (−0.028) on gold price volatility. 1% increase in oil price volatility increases gold price volatility by 0.048%.

Figure 5.3 shows the forecasting output for XAUUSD volatility based on the fundamental model (EGARCH), which can effectively forecast upcoming high volatilities.

Table 5.3 presents the estimation results of the structural model of technical analysis indicators, showing the effects of the technical analysis indicators on the standard deviation of gold prices. Most of the lags in the technical analysis indicators are significant. The highest impact is for one-day-ago RSI, which is 0.13% on next-day gold price volatility.

Figure 5.4 shows the forecasting output for XAUUSD volatility based on the structural model of the technical analysis indicators. Notably, some upcoming high volatility situations can be predicted by the model.

The SVR model predicted the process error covariance (Q) (an estimation of volatility in gold price returns) for the Kalman filter using the financial variables of

Table 5.2 Effects of the fundamental variables on gold price return and volatility calculated by the fundamental model (EGARCH)

Variable	Coefficient	z-Statistic	Prob.
C	−0.003146	−0.30552	0.7586
ln(Vol)	0.000257*	1.93244	0.0325
Variance equation			
C	−1.450085*	−940.0000	0.0000
γ_1	−0.133644	−1.226851	0.2199
γ_2	−0.093312	−0.855017	0.3925
β_1	−0.11534*	−3.877998	0.0001
β_2	0.923007*	400.0000	0.0000
α_1 *ln(T-Bill)*	−0.00928*	−3.382308	0.0007
α_2 *ln(OVX)*	0.048760*	7.996421	0.0000
α_3 *ln(GVZ)*	0.246481*	139.9340	0.0000
α_4 *ln(CSFI)*	−0.028428*	−3.832796	0.0001
ARCH heteroscedasticity test (Engle, 1982)	χ^2	P-value χ^2	H_0
	22.82	0.0000	No ARCH effect

Source: Authors' analysis of data
Note: * indicates significance at 1%

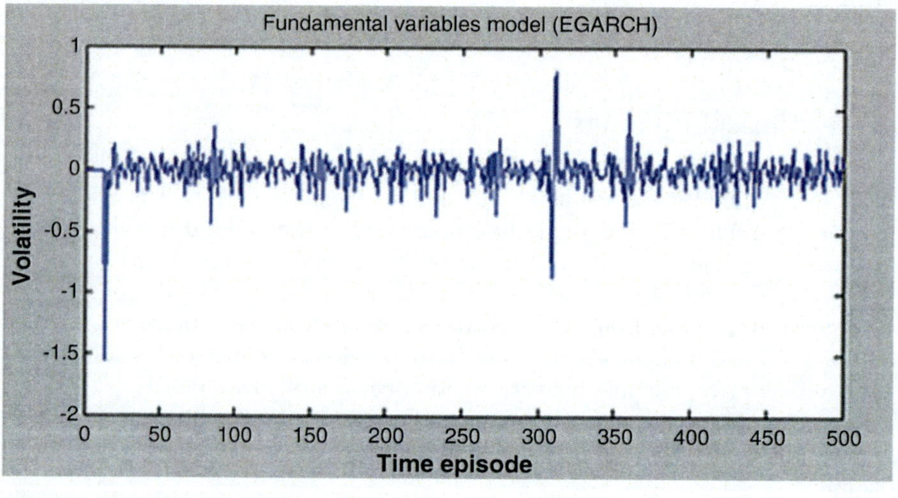

Fig. 5.3 Forecasting output of the fundamental model (EGARCH)

Table 5.3 Effects of the technical analysis indicators on gold price standard deviation calculated by the structural model

Variable	Coefficient	t-Statistic	Prob.
RSI(-1)	−0.14853*	−4.42130	0.0000
OBV(-1)	0.00003*	6.77096	0.0000
STOCH(-1)	0.05184*	3.74723	0.0002
C	28.5602*	20.0042	0.0000

Source: Authors' analysis of data
Note: * indicates significance at 1%

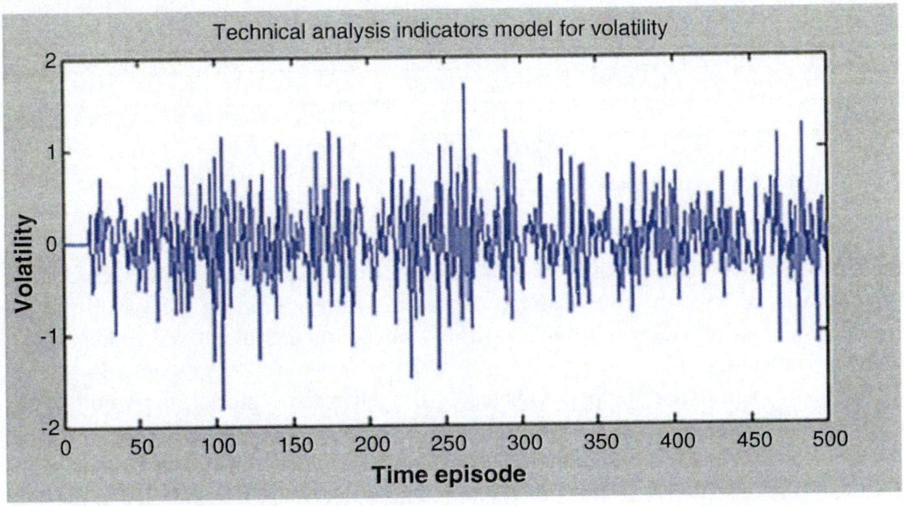

Fig. 5.4 Forecasting output of the structural model of the technical analysis indicators

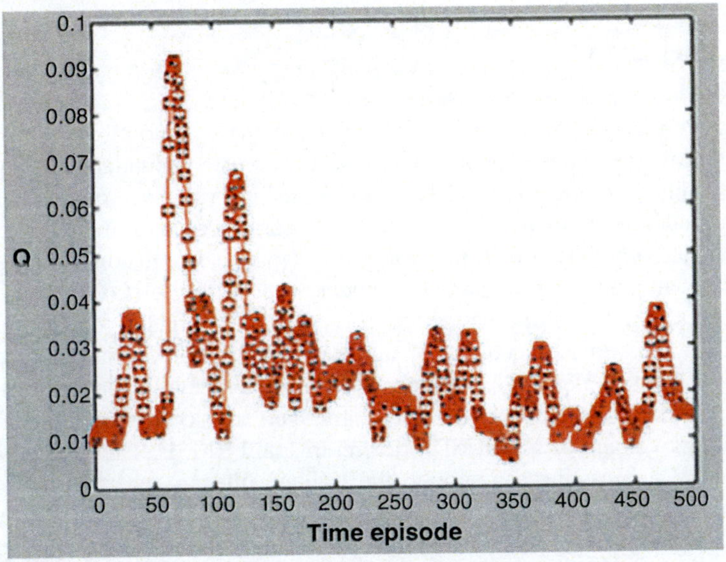

Fig. 5.5 Estimation output of process noise covariance (Q) using an SVR algorithm

OVX, CFSI, GVZ, and T-bills as inputs. According to Fig. 5.5, which shows the Q estimation for upcoming volatilities, the estimation model fitted very well to the actual data.

Table 5.4 presents the predictive power based on the RMSE and correct directional change performance (%CDCP). This type of direction-of-change forecasting is very popular in financial market studies (Bekiros & Georgoutsos, 2008). The synergistic model had a very small RMSE (0.0268) and a high % CDCP. Therefore,

Table 5.4 Forecasting accuracy measure for XAUUSD price with different models

XAUUSD volatility prediction				XAUUSD price return prediction		
Fundamental variables EGARCH		Technical indicators		Synergistic		
RMSE	%CDCP	RMSE	%CDCP	RMSE	%CDCP	%CDCP-50%
0.1442	51.4	0.4606	50.8	0.0268	67.0	0.17*

Source: Authors' analysis of data

the synergistic model was able to correctly predict the direction of the XAUUSD price returns 67% of the time through combining information on the volatilities of future gold market price returns from the models for technical and fundamental analysis indicators.

To confirm the superior performance of the synergistic model, the result of % CDCP must be greater than 50%, which would evidence that the model outperforms the random walk model (Hong et al., 2007). To confirm the statistical significance of %CDCP, the test statistic should be greater than the critical value defined at the 1% level (σ _ (0.01%)), which is approximately 0.083159 (Cai & Zhang, 2014).

5.5 Conclusion

This chapter presents a synergistic forecasting model that combines information from technical and fundamental analysis indicators (a techno-fundamental approach) to predict daily gold prices returns. Our model used information from the EGARCH model (a fundamental analysis) and from a time-series structural model of technical analysis indicators. This information was processed by a data fusion technique using the Kalman filter that can dynamically update process noise (Q) through support vector regression. The proposed new structure of the synergistic forecasting model effectively improved the accuracy of the prediction in comparison to forecasting solely based on technical and fundamental analysis and significantly outperformed the benchmark models in terms of its significant and correct prediction of the directional movement of XAUUSD price returns and RMSE. The results highlight how volatility forecasting can support the Kalman filter to generate superior gold price return predictions, which represents an important advantage of the proposed synergistic model. Also, these findings prove the efficiency of using publicly available data in forecasting and therefore have significant practical implications for the financial community.

Appendix

Flow Chart of the Proposed Synergistic Techno-Fundamental Model

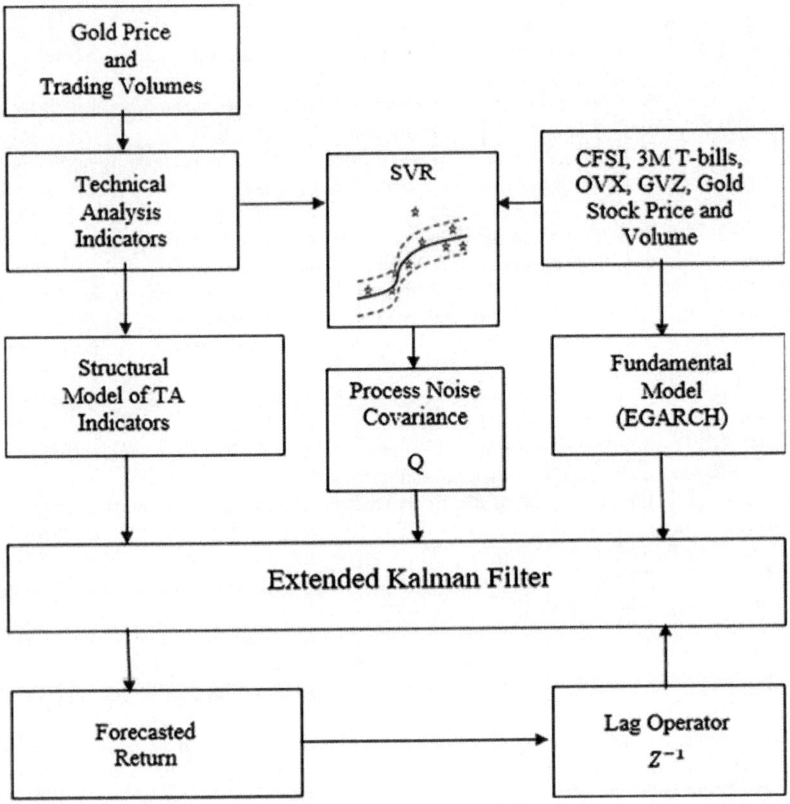

References

Bekiros, S. D. (2015). Heuristic learning in intraday trading under uncertainty. *Journal of Empirical Finance, 30*, 34–49.

Bekiros, S. D., & Georgoutsos, D. A. (2008). Direction-of-change forecasting using a volatility-based recurrent neural network. *Journal of Forecasting, 27*(5), 407–417.

Cai, C. X., & Zhang, Q. (2014). High-frequency exchange rate forecasting. *European Financial Management, 22*, 1–22.

Cortes, C., & Vapnik, V. N. (1995). Support-vector networks. *Machine Learning, 20*(3), 273–297.

Das, D., Kumar, S. B., Tiwari, A. K., Shahbaz, M., & Hasim, H. M. (2018). On the relationship of gold, crude oil, stocks with financial stress: A causality-in-quantiles approach. *Finance Research Letters, 27*, 169–174.

Ebrahimijam, S., Adaoglu, C., & Gokmenoglu, K. K. (2018). A synergistic forecasting model for high-frequency foreign exchange data. *Economic Computation and Economic Cybernetics Studies and Research, 52*(1), 293–312.

Engle, R. F. (1982). Autoregressive conditional heteroskedasticity with estimates of the variance of United Kingdom inflation. *Econometrica, 50*, 987–1007.

Fang, L., Chen, B., Yu, H., & Qian, Y. (2018). The importance of global economic policy uncertainty in predicting gold futures market volatility: A GARCH-MIDAS approach. *Journal of Futures Markets, 38*(3), 413–422.

Hong, Y., Li, H., Zhao, F., & Haitao, L. (2007). Can the random walk model be beaten in out-of-sample density forecasts? Evidence from intraday foreign exchange rates. *Journal of Econometrics, 141*, 736–776.

Kalman, R. (1961). A new approach to linear filtering and prediction problems. *Journal of Basic Engineering, 82*, 35–45.

Khan, M. M. A. (2013). Forecasting of gold prices (Box Jenkins approach). *International Journal of Emerging Technology and Advanced Engineering, 3*(3), 662–670.

Kristjanpoller, W., & Minutolo, M. C. (2015). Gold price volatility: A forecasting approach using the Artificial Neural Network–GARCH model. *Expert Systems with Applications, 42*(20), 7245–7251.

Mirza, M. J. (2011). A modified Kalman Filter for non-gaussian measurement noise. In *Communication systems and information technology* (pp. 401–409). Springer.

Neely, C. J., & Weller, P. A. (2012). Technical analysis in the foreign exchange market. In J. James, I. W. Marsh, & L. Sarno (Eds.), *Handbook of exchange rates*. Wiley.

Nelson, D. B. (1991). Conditional heteroskedasticity in asset return: A new approach. *Econometrica, 59*, 347–370.

Parisi, A., Parisi, F., & Díaz, D. (2008). Forecasting gold price changes: Rolling and recursive neural network models. *Journal of Multinational Financial Management, 18*(5), 477–487.

Potoski, M. (2013). *Predicting gold prices*. Computer Science CS229. Available at http://cs229.stanford.edu/proj2013/Potoski-PredictingGoldPrices.pdf

Reboredo, J. C., & Uddin, G. S. (2016). Do financial stress and policy uncertainty have an impact on the energy and metals markets? A quantile regression approach. *International Review of Economics & Finance, 43*, 284–298.

Shafiee, S., & Topal, E. (2010). An overview of global gold market and gold price forecasting. *Resources Policy, 35*(3), 178–189.

Ul Sami, I., & Junejo, K. N. (2017). Predicting future gold rates using machine learning approach. *International Journal of Advanced Computer Science and Applications, 8*(12), 92–99.

Welch, G., & Bishop, G. (2001). *An introduction to the Kalman filter (TR95-041)*. UNC-Chapel Hill/ACM, Inc.

Yazdani-Chamzini, A., Yakhchali, S. H., Volungevičienė, D., & Zavadskas, E. K. (2012). Forecasting gold price changes by using adaptive network fuzzy inference system. *Journal of Business Economics and Management, 13*(5), 994–1010.

Zhang, Y. J., & Wei, Y. M. (2010). The crude oil market and the gold market: Evidence for cointegration, causality and price discovery. *Resources Policy, 35*(3), 168–177.

Chapter 6
Inter-Market Sentiment Analysis Using Markov Switching Bayesian VAR Analysis

Saeed Ebrahimijam, Cahit Adaoglu, and Korhan K. Gokmenoglu

Abstract This study examines the nonlinear interdependency among the volatility indexes of gold, oil, and stock markets. The volatility indexes are used as proxies for market sentiment for the period from March 2010 to March 2017. The Markov switching Bayesian vector autoregressive (MS–BVAR) method is applied to measure the interdependency of the lags of these volatility indexes. The empirical results show three unidirectional causal relationships, lag dependencies, and positive impacts of the different market sentiments. There is always a moderate volatility period between every transition from recession to expansion of volatility situations which consistently last for 41 days; high-risk and low-risk periods last for one and three day(s), respectively. The greatest impact is from the first lag of the stock market volatility on the gold market volatility.

Keywords Market sentiment · Gold · Oil · Stock · MS Bayesian VAR

6.1 Introduction

Market sentiment is the general attitude of investors that affects price formation (Baker & Wurgler, 2007; Barberis et al., 1998; Brown & Cliff, 2004). This attitude is a result of a variety of factors, such as economic optimism or pessimism, investors' behavioral attitudes, financial reports, future cash flow, risk, historical prices, and news analytics (Baker & Wurgler, 2006; Chang et al., 2012). Based on market sentiment analysis, investors shift their portfolio positions among different interlinked stock, gold, and oil markets. They often diversify their portfolios by shifting their positions among these three markets (Soytas et al., 2009). Market

S. Ebrahimijam · C. Adaoglu
Department of Banking and Finance, Eastern Mediterranean University, Famagusta, North Cyprus via Mersin 10, Turkey
e-mail: saeed.ebrahimijam@emu.edu.tr; cahit.adaoglu@emu.edu.tr

K. K. Gokmenoglu (✉)
Department of Finance and Banking, HBV University, Ankara, Turkey
e-mail: korhan.gokmenoglu@hbv.edu.tr

D. Procházka (ed.), *Regulation of Finance and Accounting*, Springer Proceedings in Business and Economics, https://doi.org/10.1007/978-3-030-99873-8_6

sentiment analysis helps investors to determine periods of excessive optimism or pessimism in the market, and it is often used to develop a contrarian investment strategy. This research examines how market sentiments are interdependent on the volatility transmissions and how shocks to sentiment proxies in one market are reflected in the future sentiment of other markets; this helps investors to benefit from stock, oil, and gold market diversifications.

Since the 2008 global financial crisis, financial markets have become fragile, and the contagion of global macroeconomic shocks has dramatically increased (Liu et al., 2013). The increased interdependency of price and volatility transmission among financial markets has been a challenging issue for all investors. Many studies have investigated the volatility spillover of prices among the different financial markets (Akgül et al., 2015; Basher & Sadorsky, 2016; Bunnag, 2016; Creti et al., 2013; Kumar, 2014). Specifically, Arouri et al. (2011) studied the volatility spillovers between oil prices and stock markets in the Gulf Cooperation Council (GCC) countries. Malik and Ewing (2009) showed the volatility transmission among oil prices and returns in the five sectors of the US equity market. Jammazi (2012) showed the volatility and shock transmission between major crude oil markets and the equity markets in five developed countries.

These studies typically focus on the interdependency among different markets, using linear and nonlinear time series prices and GARCH–family volatility analysis methodologies. However, there is a lack of research on the interdependency of volatility indexes considering the nonlinear relationship among these indexes. Volatility indexes are used as measures to gauge market sentiment (Liu et al., 2013). The volatility indexes of the Chicago Board Options Exchange (CBOE), which include the Volatility Index (VIX), Gold Volatility Index (GVZ), and the Crude Oil Volatility Index (OVX) that measure the implied volatility of options on the S&P 500 Index, Standard & Poor's depositary receipt (SPDR) gold shares, and the United States Oil Fund (USO), respectively, have been suggested as potential sentiment proxies in the financial markets (Baker & Wurgler, 2007; Whaley, 2000). The daily volatility index data are collected from the CBOE. Due to the nonlinear behaviors and the different order of integrations of variables, the nonlinear Markov switching Bayesian vector autoregressive (MS–BVAR) model is used to detect interdependencies among the volatility indexes. Several studies use Markov switching models to successfully analyze price and volatility movement in the financial markets (Akgül et al., 2015; Casarin et al., 2017; Walid et al., 2011; Zhang & Zhang, 2015). Granger causality tests are also used to determine the direction of relationships (Jing–Tung, 2016).

This study contributes to the understanding of market sentiment variations in the stock, gold, and oil markets where investor sentiment shifts among these markets. The research also sheds light on the behavior of speculators in choosing their target markets. The results show the existence of a nonlinear relationship among the market sentiment indicators of the three markets. Also, many significant lag variables were found in the model that substantially proves the effects of the traders' changing enthusiasm for one market in the sentiment index of the other markets.

6.2 Data and Methodology

This research uses the daily time series data of 1769 observations for the three CBOE volatility indexes (VIX, GVZ, and OVX) from March 2010 to March 2017. The descriptive statistics are shown in Table 6.1.

In Table 6.1, the mean and median values are very close to each other, which indicates that the data is not affected by outliers. According to the skewness values, LVIX and LGVZ are positive (skewed to the right), but LOVX is negative (skewed to the left). In the models, we use the natural logarithm of the variables. As shown in Fig. 6.1, the data exhibit time-varying structural regime shifts.

Autoregressive Markov regime-switching models have been used in studies for modeling financial time series data that exhibit nonlinear behavior (Hamilton, 1989).

Table 6.1 Descriptive statistics

	LVIX	LGVZ	LOVX
Mean	1.227251	1.264160	1.509424
Median	1.203848	1.253338	1.517328
Maximum	1.681241	1.601517	1.897462
Minimum	1.013680	1.033424	1.161368
Standard Deviation	0.124065	0.090971	0.144990
Skewness	0.985358	0.645909	−0.187320
Kurtosis	3.664761	3.571729	2.506600
Observations	1769	1769	1769

Source: Authors' analysis

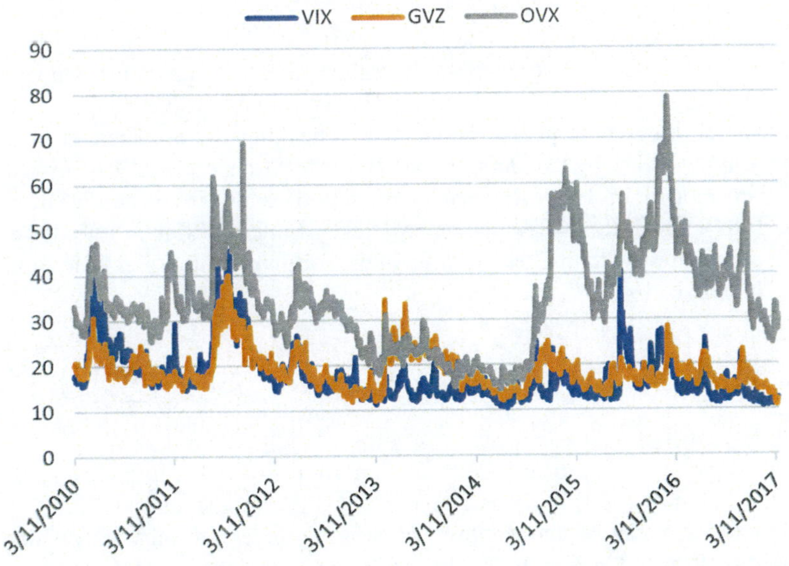

Fig. 6.1 CBOE financial market volatility indices from March 2010 to March 2017. (Source: Authors' analysis)

In 1997, Krolzig extended it to multivariate time series models and developed the MS–BVAR to overcome the presence of structural breaks and shifts in time series data (Krolzig, 2013). The Bayesian approach estimates the states considering the parameter of uncertainty by treating both model parameters and the unobserved state as random variables. This approach makes it possible to separately combine prior informative knowledge about state-specific parameters for each state to form the posterior distribution of the parameters (Sims & Zha, 1998).

More specifically, let LVIX, LGVZ, and LOVX denote the logarithms of daily stock price, crude oil price, and gold price volatility indexes, respectively. Let Y define the time–series vector including Y = [LVIX, LOVX, LGVZ]′. The MS–VAR model in which the stochastic process of Y matrices depend on time–series vector Y up to time t–i is shown in Eq. (6.1):

$$\begin{aligned} Y_t &= \mu_{st} + \sum\nolimits_{i=1}^{p} \Gamma_{st}^{(i)} Y_{t-1} + \varepsilon_t \\ \varepsilon_t &= i.i.N\left(0, \sum\nolimits_{st}\right) \end{aligned} \tag{6.1}$$

Where μ_{st} are the intercepts of the model conditional on state (regime) variable S; $\Gamma_{st}^{(i)}$ are the lag polynomial coefficient matrices, and Σ_{st} are the covariance matrices. Let s, the stochastic variable, follow a Markov (chain) process with q states. The transition probability matrix P is given as follows:

$$P = \begin{bmatrix} p_{11} & \cdots & p_{1q} \\ \vdots & \ddots & \vdots \\ p_{q1} & \cdots & p_{qq} \end{bmatrix}, \quad \sum_{i=1}^{q} p_{ij} = 1, \tag{6.2}$$

Where p_{ij} is the probability of being in regime j at time t, given that the volatility was in regime i at time $(t - 1)$, where i and j take possible values in $\{1, 2, \ldots, q\}$.

Firstly, the theoretical procedure starts by checking the nonlinear behavior of volatility time series by conducting the Broock, Dechert, and Scheinkman test (BDS), developed in 1987 (Broock et al., 1996) and Tsay's nonlinearity tests (Tsay, 1989). Then, the MS–Augmented Dickey-Fuller (MS–ADF) nonlinear unit root test, a regime-switching test, is done in the following form (Cevik & Dibooglu, 2013; Hall et al., 1999):

$$\Delta v_t = \mu(s_t) + \alpha(s_t) v_{t-1} + \sum_{j=1}^{p} \rho_j(s_t) \Delta v_{t-1} + \varepsilon_t, \quad \varepsilon_t \tilde{\text{NID}}\left(0, \sum(s_t)\right), \tag{6.3}$$

Where Δv_t is the first difference of the logarithms of volatility indexes; s_t is the regime; μ, α, and ρ are varying parameters, and ε is the innovation term.

Secondly, a model of the Markov switching Granger causality test, which was proposed by Psaradakis et al. in 2005 (Eqs. 6.4 and 6.5), is used to detect the causal direction of uncertainty and to identify the dynamic impact of the interrelated times series, which are the sentiment transmissions among the three markets (Jing–Tung, 2016; Psaradakis et al., 2005):

$$y_{1,t} = \mu_{1_{s_t}} + \sum\nolimits_{j=1}^{m_{11}} \gamma_{1j_{s_t}} y_{1,t-i} + \sum\nolimits_{j=1}^{m_{12}} \tau_{1j_{s_t}} y_{2,t-i} + \varepsilon_{1_{s_t}} \tag{6.4}$$

$$y_{2,t} = \mu_{2_{s_t}} + \sum\nolimits_{j=1}^{m_{12}} \gamma_{2j_{s_t}} y_{1,t-i} + \sum\nolimits_{j=1}^{m_{12}} \tau_{2j_{s_t}} y_{2,t-i} + \varepsilon_{1_{s_t}} \tag{6.5}$$

Thirdly, the MS–BVAR procedure is applied to model the interdependency of the lags of the volatility indexes and to investigate the respective market sentiment impact on each. Fourthly, the regime–dependent impulse response function is employed to illustrate the dynamic response to and influence of uncertainty shocks across the market sentiment proxies (Ehrmann et al., 2003).

6.3 Empirical Findings

In Table 6.2, the results of the Tsay nonlinearity test show that, for LVIX and LOVX, the null hypothesis of the linearity in the first delay (d = 1) is rejected, and that, for LGVZ, the null hypothesis of the linearity in the second *delay* (d = 2) is rejected. The time series of LVIX, LOVX, and LGVZ are all nonlinear. Additionally, BDS and Tsay results also prove the nonlinearity of the time series mentioned in this study. The stationarity test of the time series is conducted using the MS–ADF unit root test. Focusing on the linear ADF test results, Akaike criterion (AIC) lags of 5, 6, and 12 were chosen for the LVIX, LGVZ, and LOVX, respectively.

According to the α coefficients in Table 6.3, LVIX is stationary at level in the second regime, LGVZ is stationary in both regimes at level, and LOVX is stationary at level in the first regime.

In selecting the MS–VAR model, the first step is to choose the optimal lag length. According to the Schwartz Bayesian information criterion (SBIC), three lags are chosen based on the results in Table 6.4. The number of regimes is determined in the second stage.

According to the likelihood ratio (LR) test results shown in Table 6.5, three regimes are chosen which cover all the recessions in the volatility (low risk) regime, expansions in the volatility (high risk) regime, and the average volatility (moderate risk). Consequently, the appropriate MS–BVAR (3,3) is assigned for the model.

In Table 6.6, the Granger causality test results indicate that the stock market volatility Granger causes gold market volatility, the oil market volatility Granger causes stock market volatility, and, finally, the oil market volatility Granger causes gold market volatility. Thus, the gold market does not affect any other markets, according to the methodology applied in this study.

The estimated MS–BVAR (3, 3) model coefficients of the lags of the variables are given in Table 6.7. As shown in Table 6.7, in all regimes, most of the exogenous variables in the model are significant. The coefficients of the lags of the variables

Table 6.2 Nonlinearity test results

BDS test					
LVIX					
	190.2944	109.4390	86.3885	77.7092	
P–value	0	0	0	0	
	301.1997	130.1005	90.3563	76.5375	
P–value	0	0	0	0	
LGVZ					
	223.4735	125.7585	95.3932	84.8414	
P–value	0	0	0	0	
	370.8768	152.9791	100.4767	83.4881	
P–value	0	0	0	0	
LOVX					
	281.9317	281.9317	130.5958	126.9284	
P–value	0	0	0	0	
	522.5495	217.9790	140.6220	124.9500	
P–value	0	0	0	0	
Tsay					
	d = 1	d = 2	d = 3	d = 4	d = 5
LVIX					
	15.297*	21.904	47.950	84.917	117.59
P–value	0.0004	0.0026	4.8e–05	3.7e–07	2.2e–07
LGVZ					
	0.7658	24.643*	34.52	97.963	136.86
P–value	0.6819	0.0008	0.0046	3.83e–09	5.2e–10
LOVX					
	9.5668*	70.169	91.142	126.29	152.45
P–value	0.0083	1.3e–1	1.5e–12	8.8e–14	2.7e–12

Source: Authors' analysis

among all regimes differ in magnitude and sign. For the stock market (LVIX), the most positive significant variable is 0.88 in the gold market volatility at time *t*–2 ($LGVZ_{t-2}$) and the most negative significant impact is −0.80 in the oil market volatility at time *t*–2 ($LOVX_{t-2}$). For the gold market (LGVZ), the most positive significant variable is 1.90 in the stock market volatility at time *t*–1 (LVIX_{t-1}) and the most negative significant impact is −0.85 in the oil market volatility at time *t*–1 ($LOVX_{t-1}$). For the oil market volatility (LOVX), the most positive significant variable is 1.11 in the gold market volatility at time *t*–2 ($LGVZ_{t-2}$) and the most negative significant impact is −1.08 in the gold market volatility at time *t*–1 ($LGVZ_{t-1}$).

According to the intercept value shown in Table 6.7, regime 3 represents the recessions in the volatility (low risk) situation, regime 2 represents the expansions in the volatility (high risk) situation, and regime 1 represents the average volatility (moderate risk) situation.

Table 6.3 Stationarity test: Markov switching ADF unit root test results

	LVIX				LGVZ				LOVX			
	Reg 1	*P*–val	Reg 2	*P*–val	Reg 1	*P*–val	Reg 2	*P*–val	Reg 1	*P*–val	Reg 2	*P*–val
α	−0.04	0.358	−0.03	0.000	−0.01	0.000	0.075	0.038	−0.005	0.017	−0.000	0.987
μ	0.105	0.071	0.033	0.000	0.022	0.000	−0.16	0.008	0.007	0.039	0.048	0.017
ρ_1	0.345	0.006	−0.10	0.000	−0.08	0.000	1.180	0.000	0.016	0.476	−1.569	0.000
ρ_2	1.305	0.000	−0.12	0.000	−0.08	0.000	2.553	0.000	−0.025	0.270	−0.662	0.000
ρ_3	−0.00	0.977	−0.05	0.046	−0.07	0.000	1.117	0.000	−0.090	0.00	1.758	0.000
ρ_4	−0.65	0.000	−0.04	0.113	−0.02	0.116	1.729	0.000	−0.025	0.266	1.151	0.000
ρ_5	−0.24	0.217	−0.04	0.053	−0.02	0.206	−2.64	0.000	−0.041	0.060	−1.026	0.001
ρ_6					−0.04	0.009	0.713	0.003	−0.016	0.477	0.229	0.295
ρ_7									−0.039	0.087	0.102	0.597
ρ_8									−0.005	0.816	1.036	0.000
ρ_9									−0.021	0.344	−0.399	0.053
ρ_{10}									0.026	0.249	−0.475	0.039
ρ_{11}									−0.011	0.606	0.458	0.041
ρ_{12}									−0.053	0.018	−0.182	0.398
Σ	−3.60		0.000		−3.90		0.000		−4.065		0.000	
P11	−1.84		0.004		3.945		0.000		3.930		0.000	
P21	−3.04		0.000		0.994		0.007		0.727		0.042	

Source: Authors' analysis

Table 6.4 Lag length selection for MS–BVAR model

Lag	AIC	SBIC	H–Q[1]
1	−22.29291	−22.25554	−22.27910
2	−22.30385	−22.23846	−22.27968
3	−22.37732	−22.28390*	−22.34280*
4	−22.38765*	−22.26620	−22.34277
5	−22.38413	−22.23465	−22.32888
6	−22.38590	−22.20840	−22.32030
7	−22.38580	−22.18028	−22.30984
8	−22.38246	−22.14890	−22.29614
9	−22.37835	−22.11677	−22.28167
10	−22.37732	−22.08772	−22.27029
11	−22.37391	−22.05628	−22.25652
12	−22.37134	−22.02569	−22.24359

Source: Authors' analysis
Note: [1]Hannan–Quinn criterion was used
*The lag length with the smallest value was selected.

Table 6.5 LR test for number of regimes selection

	Regime	LR	H–Q[1]
MSBVAR (3,2)	2	12452.12	−14.0736
MSBVAR (3,3)	3*	12565.36	−14.1993*
MSBVAR (3,4)	4	12555.48	−14.1859
MSBVAR (3,5)	5	12541.31	−14.1676
MSBVAR (3,6)	6	12429.38	−14.0388

Source: Authors' analysis
Note: [1]Hannan–Quinn criterion was used
*The lag length with the smallest value was selected.

Table 6.6 Granger causality test for MS–BVAR

	Lag	*F*–statistic	*P*–Value
LVIX → LGVZ	2	12.07385***	6.194359e–06
LGVZ → LVIX	10	0.274483	9.867300e–01
LVIX → LOVX	10	1.300240	2.245800e–01
LOVX → LVIX	1	5.024555**	0.025114174
LGVZ → LOVX	10	0.913584	5.195424e–01
LOVX → LGVZ	3	5.643050***	7.576863e–04

Source: Authors' analysis
Note: *, **, *** represent for significant level at 10%, 5% and 1%, respectively

Table 6.8 presents the transition probability matrix. The probability of staying in the first regime is 97%, implying an average duration of 41 days. Thus, the market consistently has a moderate risk, but there might be a change in the regime after each 41-day period. The probability of staying in the second (high risk) and third regimes (low risk) are 33% and 67%, respectively, and the average durations are about one and three days, respectively. As a result, the high- and low-risk periods last less than

Table 6.7 Estimated MS–BVAR model coefficients

	LVIX			LGVZ			LOVX		
	Reg 1	Reg 2	Reg 3	Reg 1	Reg 2	Reg 3	Reg 1	Reg 2	Reg 3
Cons	0.900	1.190	0.515	0.053	−0.232	0.234	0.021	0.302	−0.170
LVIX_{t-1}	0.039	0.576***	−0.27***	0.869***	1.909***	0.522***	−0.015	0.861***	−0.014
t–stat	1.496	16.47	−12.24	33.11	54.59	23.53	−0.589	24.63	−0.659
LVIX_{t-2}	0.059***	−0.12***	−0.24***	0.057***	−0.20***	−0.14***	0.996***	−0.32***	0.905***
t–stat	2.268	−3.45	−11.1	2.189	−5.86	−6.65	37.94	−9.17	40.77
LVIX_{t-3}	−0.10***	0.562***	0.355***	−0.065***	−0.28***	0.037	−0.009	−0.034	0.061***
t–stat	−4.160	16.09	15.99	−2.481	−8.27	1.685	−0.373	−0.996	2.752
$LGVZ_{t-1}$	−0.06***	−0.62***	−0.022	0.035*	0.036	0.169***	0.003	−1.08***	0.031**
t–stat	−3.041	−14.5	−1.41	1.773	0.844	10.46	0.176	−25.24	1.942
$LGVZ_{t-2}$	0.266***	0.848***	0.887***	0.041**	1.013***	0.128***	−0.033	1.119***	0.056***
t–stat	13.28	19.78	54.84	2.054	23.64	7.921	−1.684	26.10	3.50
$LGVZ_{t-3}$	0.166***	−0.89***	−0.015	0.013	0.341***	−0.11***	−0.011	0.197***	0.001
t–stat	8.281	−20.82	−0.937	0.685	7.958	−7.24	−0.570	4.600	0.105
$LOVX_{t-1}$	0.024	0.253***	0.303***	0.058***	−0.85***	0.177***	0.006	0.094***	0.043
t–stat	1.410	8.373	12.47	3.374	−28.3	7.308	0.386	3.109	1.771
$LOVX_{t-2}$	−0.321	−0.80***	−0.55***	−0.374***	−0.72***	−0.01	−0.77***	−0.07***	0.040
t–stat	−0.099	−26.4	−22.69	−21.64	−24.0	−0.601	−45.02	−2.37	1.649
$LOVX_{t-3}$	0.039***	0.062**	0.079***	0.044***	0.025	0.029	0.015	0.042	0.072***
t–stat	2.279	2.068	3.254	2.565	0.850	1.230	0.867	1.405	2.996

Source: Authors' analysis
Note: *, **, *** represent for significant level at 10%, 5% and 1%, respectively

Table 6.8 Markov regime switch transitions probability matrix

Transition	Regime 1	Regime 2	Regime 3	Duration
Regime 1	0.9758	0.0149	0.0092	41.32
Regime 2	0.2977	0.3316	0.3705	1.496
Regime 3	0.3220	0.0001	0.6778	3.104

Source: Authors' analysis

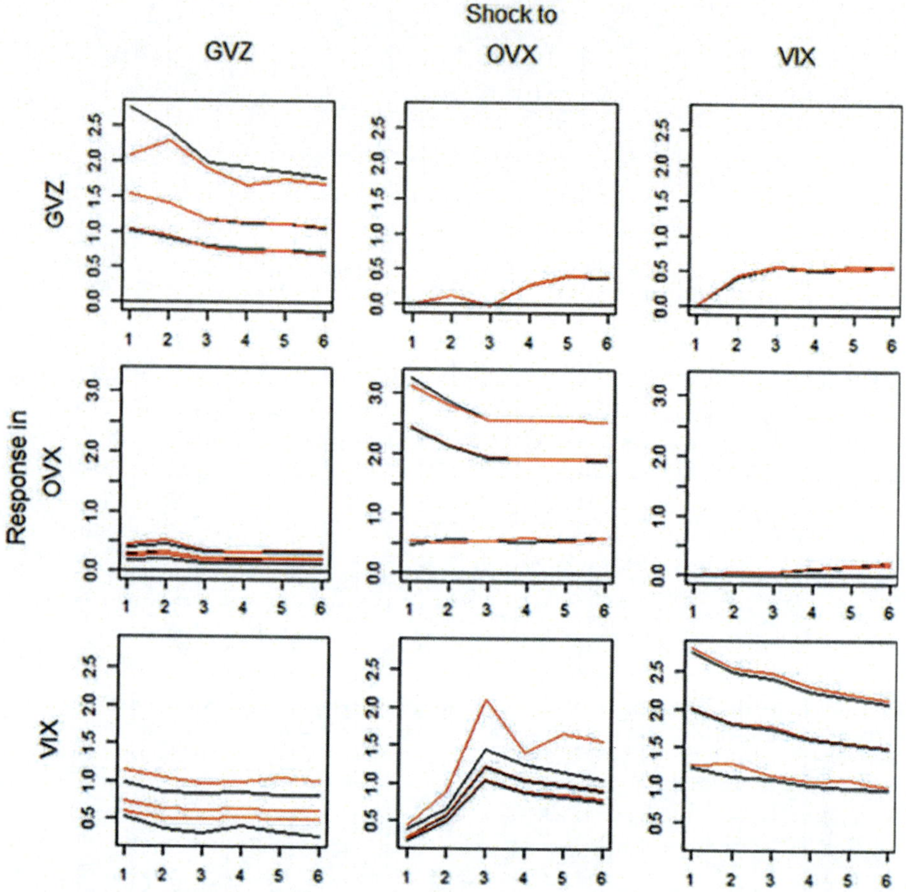

Fig. 6.2 Impulse responses of volatility indexes in MS–BVAR model. (Source: Authors' analysis)

three days in the markets. But the probability of low-risk days is twice that of high-risk days. The probability of transitions from regime 1 to 2 and from regime 2 to 3 is low. The probability of transitions from regime 3 to 2 and from 1 to 3 is about zero. This means that direct transition from a low- to high-risk market and from a moderate- to low-risk market may never happen.

To examine the transmission of shocks across different market sentiments, the regime–dependent impulse–response functions of the Bayesian Monte Carlo MS–VAR with Gibbs sampling employs 10,000 burn-in iterations; 50,000 posterior draws are shown in Fig. 6.2. Focusing on the signs of responses, the shock to gold market volatility (GVZ) always has a positive impact on stock market volatility and oil market volatility. In all regimes, the shock does not die even after six days. The shock to oil market volatility (OVX) has a positive impact on stock and gold market volatilities. However, the effect of the shock dies after three days in the gold market volatility. In all regimes, the shock to stock market volatility (VIX) always has a positive impact on gold and oil market volatilities and does not die.

6.4 Conclusion

This study uses the CBOE volatility indexes for stock, gold, and oil markets as proxies for measuring their market sentiments. By using the MS–BVAR, the interdependencies of the market sentiments of these three markets are investigated. The empirical results contribute to the effective implementation of volatility risk hedge strategies, especially for global asset portfolio managers. The empirical results indicate that the oil market sentiment Granger causes the gold market and stock market sentiments and the stock market sentiment Granger causes the gold market sentiment. The current volatility indexes are greatly affected by the lags of volatility indexes. We find that the stock market sentiment has the greatest impact on the gold market sentiment. Any shock in one market sentiment has a positive impact on the other two markets' sentiments. The empirical findings of this research are relevant for portfolio managers, as a policy implication, because findings denote that these markets are consistently on a moderate volatility level which lasts around 41 days, while high-risk and low-risk periods last for one and three day(s), respectively. There is no direct transition from a low-risk to a high-risk market, and there is always a moderate risk period in between them.

References

Akgül, I., Bildirici, M., & Özdemir, S. (2015). Evaluating the nonlinear linkage between gold prices and stock market index using Markov–switching Bayesian VAR models. *Procedia – Social and Behavioral Sciences, 210*, 408–415.

Arouri, M. E. H., Jouini, J., & Nguyen, D. K. (2011). Volatility spillovers between oil prices and stock sector returns: Implications for portfolio management. *Journal of International Money and Finance, 30*(7), 1387–1405.

Baker, M., & Wurgler, J. (2006). Investor sentiment and the cross-section of stock returns. *The Journal of Finance, 61*(4), 1645–1680.

Baker, M., & Wurgler, J. (2007). Investor sentiment in the stock market. *The Journal of Economic Perspectives, 21*(2), 129–151.

Barberis, N., Shleifer, A., & Vishny, R. (1998). A model of investor sentiment. *Journal of Financial Economics, 49*(3), 307–343.

Basher, S. A., & Sadorsky, P. (2016). Hedging emerging market stock prices with oil, gold, VIX, and bonds: A comparison between DCC, ADCC and GO–GARCH. *Energy Economics, 54*, 235–247.

Broock, W. A., Scheinkman, J. A., Dechert, W. D., & LeBaron, B. (1996). A test for independence based on the correlation dimension. *Econometric reviews, 15*(3), 197–235.

Brown, G. W., & Cliff, M. T. (2004). Investor sentiment and the near–term stock market. *Journal of Empirical Finance, 11*(1), 1–27.

Bunnag, T. (2016). Volatility transmission in crude oil, gold, S&P 500 and US Dollar Index Futures using VAR–MGARCH Model. *International Journal of Energy Economics and Policy, 6*(1), 39–52.

Casarin, R., Sartore, D., & Tronzano, M. (2017). A Bayesian Markov–switching correlation model for contagion analysis on exchange rate markets. *Journal of Business & Economic Statistics, 36*, 1–14.

Cevik, E. I., & Dibooglu, S. (2013). Persistence and non–linearity in US unemployment: A regime–switching approach. *Economic Systems, 37*(1), 61–68.

Chang, C., Faff, R. W., & Hwang, C. Y. (2012). *Local and global sentiment effects, and the role of legal, information and trading environments*. Available at SSRN 1800550.

Creti, A., Joëts, M., & Mignon, V. (2013). On the links between stock and commodity markets' volatility. *Energy Economics, 37*, 16–28.

Ehrmann, M., Ellison, M., & Valla, N. (2003). Regime–dependent impulse response functions in a Markov–switching vector auto regression model. *Economics Letters, 78*(3), 295–299.

Hall, S. G., Psaradakis, Z., & Sola, M. (1999). Detecting periodically collapsing bubbles: A Markov–switching unit root test. *Journal of Applied Econometrics, 14*, 143–154.

Hamilton, J. D. (1989). A new approach to the economic analysis of nonstationary time series and the business cycle. *Econometrica: Journal of the Econometric Society, 57*, 357–384.

Jammazi, R. (2012). Cross dynamics of oil–stock interactions: A redundant wavelet analysis. *Energy, 44*(1), 750–777.

Jing–Tung, W. U. (2016). The Markov–switching Granger causality of Asia–Pacific exchange rates. *Romanian Journal of Economic Forecasting, 19*(3), 94–115.

Krolzig, H. M. (2013). *Markov–switching vector autoregressions: Modelling, statistical inference, and application to business cycle analysis* (Vol. 454). Springer.

Kumar, D. (2014). Return and volatility transmission between gold and stock sectors: Application of portfolio management and hedging effectiveness. *IIMB Management Review, 26*(1), 5–16.

Liu, M. L., Ji, Q., & Fan, Y. (2013). How does oil market uncertainty interact with other markets? An empirical analysis of implied volatility index. *Energy, 55*, 860–868.

Malik, F., & Ewing, B. T. (2009). Volatility transmission between oil prices and equity sector returns. *International Review of Financial Analysis, 18*(3), 95–100.

Psaradakis, Z., Ravn, M. O., & Sola, M. (2005). Markov switching causality and the money–output relationship. *Journal of Applied Econometrics, 20*(5), 665–683.

Sims, C. A., & Zha, T. (1998). Bayesian methods for dynamic multivariate models. *International Economic Review, 39*, 949–968.

Soytas, U., Sari, R., Hammoudeh, S., & Hacihasanoglu, E. (2009). World oil prices, precious metal prices and macroeconomy in Turkey. *Energy Policy, 37*(12), 5557–5566.

Tsay, R. S. (1989). Testing and modeling threshold autoregressive processes. *Journal of the American Statistical Association, 84*(405), 231–240.

Walid, C., Chaker, A., Masood, O., & Fry, J. (2011). Stock market volatility and exchange rates in emerging countries: A Markov–state switching approach. *Emerging Markets Review, 12*(3), 272–292.

Whaley, R. E. (2000). The investor fear gauge. *The Journal of Portfolio Management, 26*(3), 12–17.

Zhang, Y. J., & Zhang, L. (2015). Interpreting the crude oil price movements: Evidence from the Markov regime switching model. *Applied Energy, 143*, 96–109.

Chapter 7
Heston-Hull-White Model

David Chval

Abstract This article analyzes the Heston stochastic volatility model with stochastic interest rates driven by the Hull-White process. We use call and put option prices on the Deutscher Aktien Index (DAX) and investigate whether the Heston-Hull-White (HHW) model can improve option pricing with negative interest rates. The prices obtained by the HHW model are compared with the pure Heston model and the Black-Scholes model.

Key words Calibration · Heston-Hull-White · Stochastic process

7.1 Introduction

The aim of this paper is twofold. Firstly, we present the full-scale Heston model with stochastic interest rates driven by the Hull-White process and describe the semi-analytic pricing formula. Secondly, we apply this model to real data and measure whether this model can forecast European option prices better than the pure Heston and Black-Scholes models.

The original Heston model was introduced by Heston (1993) and is based on the assumption that volatility is not constant, like in the Black-Scholes model (Black & Scholes, 1973), but stochastic. Both models also assume a constant risk-free interest rate, which is an unrealistic assumption. Therefore, we consider in our analysis stochastic interest rates following the Hull-White process (Hull & White, 1987), which is an extension of the Vasicek model (Vasicek, 1977). The Hull-White model allows interest rates to become negative, which has been considered a weakness of the model. However, since the last economic crisis, we can observe negative interest rates in the markets around the world.

This extended Heston-Hull-White (HHW) model has been studied in several works. Zhu (2000) introduced the hybrid model with stochastic but uncorrelated

D. Chval (✉)
Department of Banking and Insurance, Prague University of Economics and Business, Prague, Czech Republic
e-mail: qchvd00@vse.cz

D. Procházka (ed.), *Regulation of Finance and Accounting*, Springer Proceedings in Business and Economics, https://doi.org/10.1007/978-3-030-99873-8_7

interest rates. Andreasen (2006) presented a generalization by using the Heston model and an indirect correlation between equity and interest rates.

Grzelak and Oosterlee (2011) illustrated the full-scale hybrid Heston-Hull-White model with a full correlation matrix. The hybrid HHW model, which we use, has been presented by (Grzelak & Oosterlee, 2011). A modified version, with the Vasicek process, has been recently studied by Recchioni et al. (2017). They have studied the effect of negative interest rates on option pricing.

In our analysis, we have used the Fourier cosine method (COS method) described by Fang and Oosterlee (2009) to derive a semi-closed-form pricing formula. Haentjens and In't Hout (2012) investigates another possible approach based on the discretization of the corresponding partial differential equations (PDEs). They used alternating direction implicit (ADI) time discretization schemes to derive the values of the European options. Samimi et al. (2017) presented the least-square Monte Carlo method for pricing options under the HHW model.

The Fourier cosine method is faster than the other two methods. The efficiency of the computational technique is essential for model calibration. We use a similar calibration process as Wang (2011) and calibrate the Hull-White and Heston parts separately. The calibration of the Hull-White model is well known. One possible approach, based on swaptions, was presented by Russo and Torri (2019). In this article, we have used another method based on interest rate caps and floors (Brigo & Mercurio, 2007).

7.2 Data and Methodology

We assume a probability space (Ω, F, Q) and a finite time horizon $(0, T)$, with Ω being a sample space with outcome element ω, F being a σ-algebra, and Q being the risk-neutral probability measure on elements of F. The full-scale Heston-Hull-White model is defined, under the risk-neutral measure, by the following system of stochastic differential equations (SDEs):

$$dS(t) = r(t)S(t)dt + \sqrt{v(t)}S(t)dW_S^Q(t), \tag{7.1}$$

$$dv(t) = \kappa(\theta_v - v(t))dt + \nu \cdot \sqrt{(v(t))}dW_v^Q(t), \tag{7.2}$$

$$dr(t) = \lambda(\theta_r(t) - r(t))dt + \eta dW_r^Q(t), \tag{7.3}$$

where $S(t)$ is the stock price process, $v(t)$ is the instantaneous volatility, $r(t)$ is the short-term interest rate, parameters κ and λ control the speed of the mean reversion of the volatility and the interest rate, η is the interest rate volatility, ν is the volatility of the volatility, and θ_v and θ_r are the long-run mean of the volatility and the interest rate process, respectively. Meanwhile, $dW_S^Q(t), dW_v^Q(t)$, and $dW_r^Q(t)$ are three correlated standard Brownian motions, with the correlation structure given by

$$dW_S^Q(t)dW_v^Q(t) = \rho_{S,v}, \tag{7.4}$$

$$dW_S^Q(t)dW_r^Q(t) = \rho_{S,r}, \tag{7.5}$$

$$dW_v^Q(t)dW_r^Q(t) = \rho_{v,r}. \tag{7.6}$$

In our analysis, we assume that $\rho_{v,\ r} = 0$.[1] The model described above is not affine.[2] To make it affine, we reformulate the system of SDEs:

$$\begin{aligned} dS(t) = r(t)S(t)dt + \sqrt{v(t)}S(t)dW_S^Q(t) + \Omega(t)dW_r^Q(t) \\ + \delta \cdot \sqrt{(v(t))}dW_v^Q(t), \end{aligned} \tag{7.7}$$

$$dv(t) = \kappa(\theta_v - v(t))dt + \nu \cdot \sqrt{(v(t))}dW_v^Q(t), \tag{7.8}$$

$$dr(t) = \lambda(\theta_r(t) - r(t))dt + \eta dW_r^Q(t). \tag{7.9}$$

where $dW_S^Q(t)dW_v^Q(t) = \widetilde{\rho}_{S,v}, \quad dW_S^Q(t)dW_r^Q(t) = 0, \quad dW_v^Q(t)dW_r^Q(t) = 0, \widetilde{\rho^2}_{S,v} = \rho^2{}_{S,v} + \rho^2{}_{S,r}$, and $\Omega(t) = \rho_{S,r}\sqrt{(t)}$, $\delta = \rho_{S,v} - \dot{\rho}_{S,v}$.

We also use logarithmic transformation to the asset prices $x(t) = \ ln\ (S)$ and following approximation to $\Omega(t)$:

$$\Omega(t) \approx a + b\, e^{-ct} \tag{7.10}$$

where $a = \sqrt{\left(\theta_v - \frac{\nu^2}{8\kappa}\right)}$, $b = \sqrt{(v(0))} - a$, $c = -\, ln\left(\frac{F(1)-a}{b}\right)$, and $F(t)$ is defined as

$$F(t) := \sqrt{\left(c(t)(\lambda(t) - 1) + c(t)d + \frac{c(t)d}{2(d + \lambda(t))}\right.} \tag{7.11}$$

with $c(t) = \frac{1}{4\kappa}\nu^2(1 - e^{-\kappa t})$, $d = \frac{4\kappa\theta_v}{\nu^2}$, and $\lambda(t) = \frac{4\kappa v(0)e^{-\kappa t}}{\nu^2(1-e^{-\kappa t})}$.

---

[1] See Guo et al. (2013).

[2] Model would be affine if we set $\rho_{S,\ r} = \rho_{v,\ r} = 0$.

The value of the European option, under the risk-free measure Q, is

$$u(t,S,v,r) = B(t)E^{Q}\left(\frac{1}{B(t)}g(T,S)|F_t\right), \tag{7.12}$$

where $B(t)$ is the money-saving account defined as

$$B(t) = e^{\int_0^t r(s)ds}, \tag{7.13}$$

where $g(T,S)$ is the option payoff at maturity T:

$$g(T,S) = \max(S-K,0) \text{ for call option}, \tag{7.14}$$

$$g(T,S) = \max(K-S,0) \text{ for put option}, \tag{7.15}$$

where K is the strike price.

For the COS method, it is essential to have an appropriate characteristic function. We have used the approach described in (Grzelak & Oosterlee, 2011). For our model, the characteristic function is approximately given by

$$\Phi(u,x,\tau) = e^{(A(u,\tau)+B(u,\tau)x(\tau)+C(u,\tau)r(\tau)+D(u,\tau)v(\tau))} \tag{7.16}$$

with boundary conditions $A(u,0) = 0$, $B(u,0) = iu$, $C(u,0) = 0$, $D(u,0) = 0$, and $\tau = T - t$.

The functions $A(u,\tau)$, $B(u,\tau)$, $C(u,\tau)$, and $D(u,\tau)$ are the same as in Grzelak and Oosterlee (2011).

7.3 Calibration Process

We have used in-sample and out-sample analysis and calibration based on the least-square optimization method. We need to find a set of model parameter values that minimize the sum of the squared differences of the option prices generated by our model and the option prices observed in the market:

$$\sum_{i=1}^{N}\left(P_i^{\text{model}} - P_i^{\text{market}}\right)^2$$

7.4 Data

The data sample consists of three data sets.

The first data set contains daily observations of interest rate caps indexed on the 6 months Euro Interbank Offered Rate (EURIBOR). The interest rate cap prices are quoted for different maturities, ranging from 1 year to 10 years with different cap strike rates. All prices are quoted as closing mid prices.

The second data set consists of daily observations of zero-coupon interest rates based on money and swap market instruments. The zero-coupon rates are quoted for the maturities, ranging from 6 months to 10 years with 6-month intervals, corresponding to the maturities of the market-quoted interest rate caps and the intermediate dates.

The third data set consists of daily closing prices of the European call and put options on the DAX with different expiry dates and different strikes in the period from January 1, 2017, to December 20, 2019. Figure 7.1 shows the DAX in this period.

The options have been divided into several categories according to time to maturity and moneyness. The number of options in each category is shown in Table 7.1.

For all categories, the HHW parameters have been computed. We have used one set of parameters for one category. Then we have calculated the out-of-sample option price forecast and compared it with the market price.

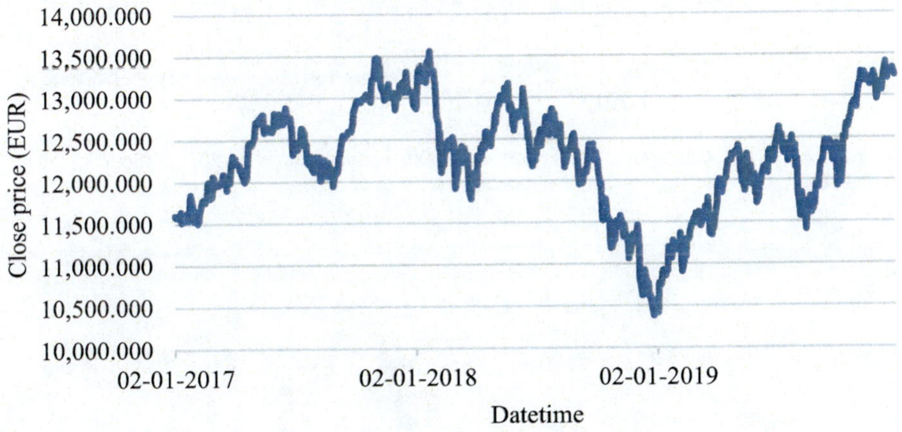

Fig. 7.1 DAX. (Source: Thomson Reuters)

Table 7.1 Option categories

Time to maturity	Deep ITM	ITM	ATM	OTM
< 60 days	103	167	164	103
> 60 days	129	195	204	130

Source: Own computation

7.5 Results and Discussion

We have applied the HHW, Heston, and BS models to out-of-sample options and compared the calculated prices with market prices. The results are shown in Figs. 7.2, 7.3, 7.4, 7.5, 7.6, 7.7, 7.8 and 7.9. Figures 7.2, 7.3, 7.4 and 7.5 show the options with more than 60 days to maturity, and Figs. 7.6, 7.7, 7.8 and 7.9 show the options with less than 60 days to maturity.

Table 7.2 shows the sums of mean square errors for all the options in each category.

The mean of the relative errors for all options using the HHW model is 14.13%, compared to 15.12% for the Heston model and 25.05% for the Black-Scholes model. HHW outperforms Heston and B-S models.

This result is consistent with the results in other works. However, the calibration process for HHW is much more complicated and time-consuming than for the Heston or Black-Scholes model.

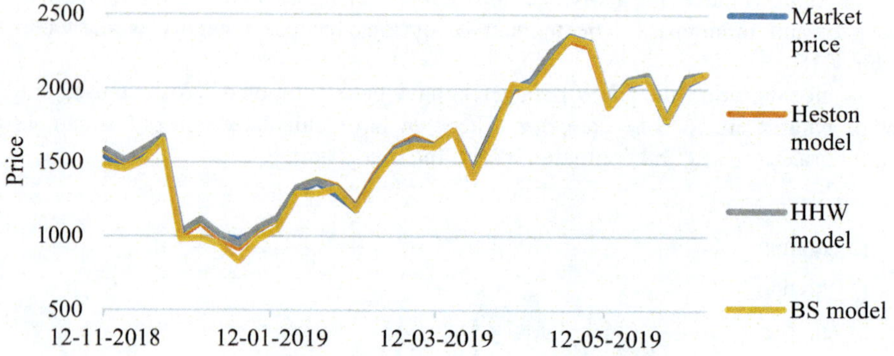

Fig. 7.2 Deep ITM call option (Strike price 10,000, maturity June 1, 2019). (Source: Own calculation)

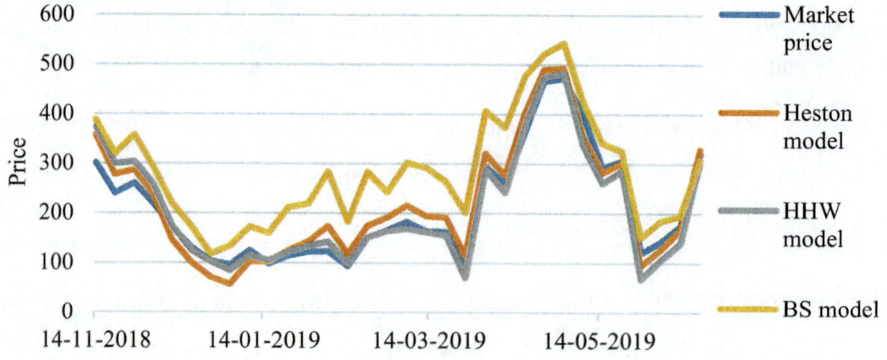

Fig. 7.3 ITM call option (Strike price 12,000, maturity June 19, 2019). (Source: Own calculation)

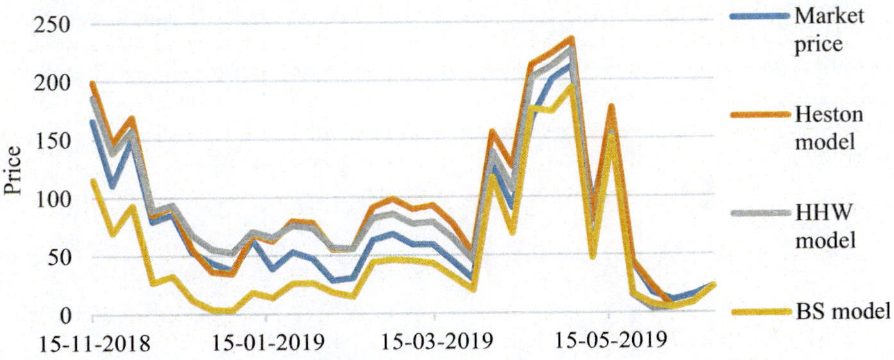

Fig. 7.4 ATM call option (Strike price 12,400, maturity June 19, 2019). (Source: Own calculation)

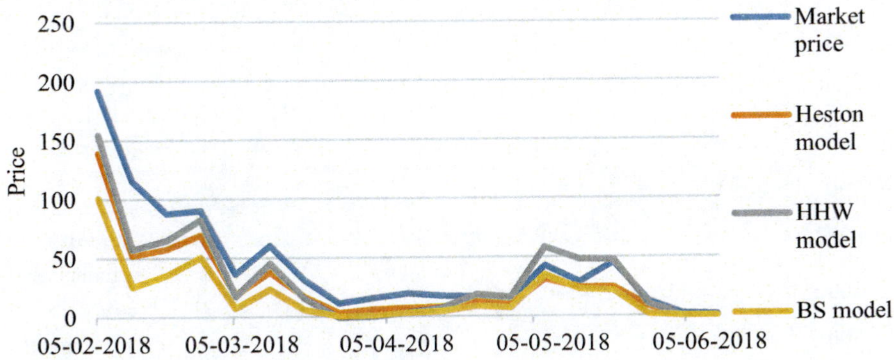

Fig. 7.5 OTM call option (strike price 13,400, maturity June 11, 2018. (Source: Own calculation)

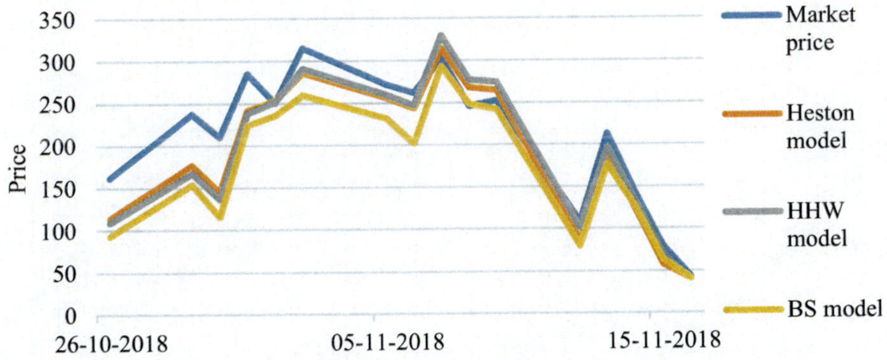

Fig. 7.6 ATM call option (Strike price 11,300, maturity November 16, 2018). (Source: Own calculation)

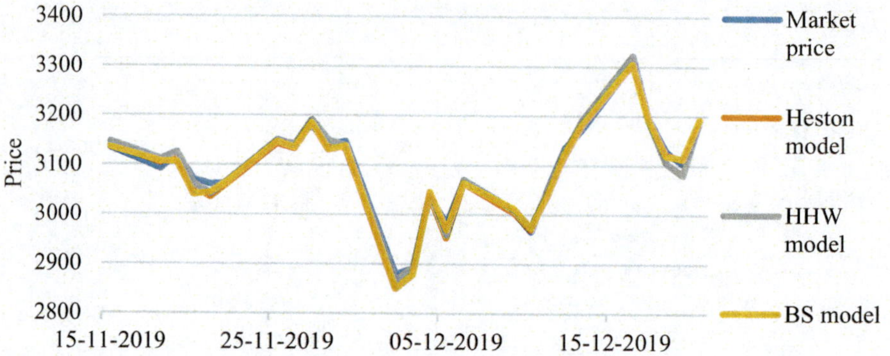

Fig. 7.7 Deep ITM call option (Strike price 10,000, maturity December 19, 2019). (Source: Own calculation)

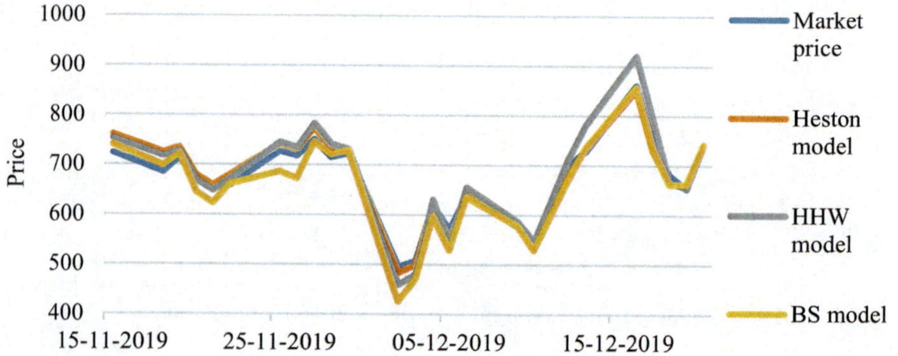

Fig. 7.8 ITM call option (Strike price 12,550, maturity December 19, 2019). (Source: Own calculation)

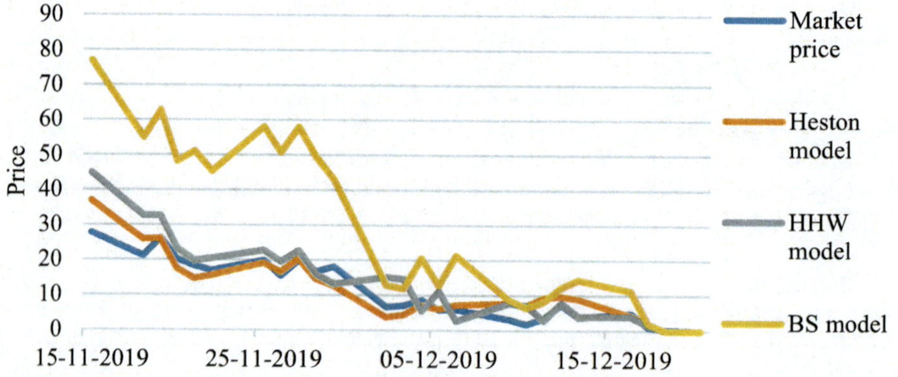

Fig. 7.9 OTM call option (Strike price 13,700, maturity December 19, 2019). (Source: Own calculation)

Table 7.2 Sum of mean square errors

(Time to maturity > 60 days)				
nnnn	**Deep ITM**	**ITM**	**ATM**	**OTM**
HHW	14,231.37	10,726.21	15,512.27	4700.70
Heston	17,069.47	18,788.20	19,061.48	5297.65
Black-Scholes	72,781.50	19,134.00	28,371.81	9103.88
(Time to maturity < 60 days)				
Model	**Deep ITM**	**ITM**	**ATM**	**OTM**
HHW	3842.95	6121.79	16,209.80	5347.38
Heston	6373.56	7114.76	16,466.69	5261.42
Black-Scholes	4692.94	16,260.73	35,653.38	6840.52

Source: own computation

7.6 Conclusion

This paper deals with a full-scale Heston-Hull-White model. We have shown the derivation of the semi-closed-form analytic formula for the European option based on the Fourier cosine method. We have also described the calibration process using the caps and floors to estimate the Hull-White parameters and the option prices observed in the market to estimate the Heston parameters and the correlations between the DAX, interest rates, and volatility.

The HHW model has been tested and compared with the pure Heston and Black-Scholes models. We have shown that in the negative interest rate environment, the HHW model outperforms both models.

On the other hand, the calibration of the HHW model is very time-consuming. Even with a two-step calibration process, the calibration is significantly slower than the calibration of the pure Heston model. Therefore, we focus on the optimization methods and different calibration approaches in our future research.

Acknowledgments The research has been supported by the internal grant VŠE IG102029 and the research project GAČR 18-05244S, Innovation Approaches to Credit Risk Management, which the author gratefully acknowledges.

References

Andreasen, J. (2006). Closed form pricing of FX options under stochastic rates and volatility. In *Presentation at global derivatives conference*.

Black, F., & Scholes, M. (1973). The pricing of options and corporate liabilities. *Journal of Political Economy, 81*(3), 637–654.

Brigo, D., & Mercurio, F. (2007). *Interest rate models-theory and practice: With smile, inflation and credit*. Springer Science & Business Media.

Fang, F., & Oosterlee, C. W. (2009). A novel pricing method for European options based on Fourier-cosine series expansions. *SIAM Journal on Scientific Computing, 31*(2), 826–848.

Grzelak, L. A., & Oosterlee, C. W. (2011). On the Heston model with stochastic interest rates. *SIAM Journal on Financial Mathematics, 2*(1), 255–286.

Guo, S., Grzelak, L. A., & Oosterlee, C. W. (2013). Analysis of an affine version of the Heston–Hull–White option pricing partial differential equation. *Applied Numerical Mathematics, 72*, 143–159.

Haentjens, T., & In't Hout, K. J. (2012). Alternating direction implicit finite difference schemes for the Heston-Hull-White partial differential equation. *The Journal of Computational Finance, 16*(1), 83.

Heston, S. L. (1993). A closed-form solution for options with stochastic volatility with applications to bond and currency options. *The Review of Financial Studies, 6*(2), 327–343.

Hull, J., & White, A. (1987). The pricing of options on assets with stochastic volatilities. *The Journal of Finance, 42*(2), 281–300.

Recchioni, M. C., Sun, Y., & Tedeschi, G. (2017). Can negative interest rates really affect option pricing? Empirical evidence from an explicitly solvable stochastic volatility model. *Quantitative Finance, 17*(8), 1257–1275.

Russo, V., & Torri, G. (2019). Calibration of one-factor and two-factor hull–white models using swaptions. *Computational Management Science, 16*(1–2), 275–295.

Samimi, O., et al. (2017). LSM algorithm for pricing American option under Heston–Hull–White's stochastic volatility model. *Computational Economics, 50*(2), 173–187.

Vasicek, O. (1977). An equilibrium characterization of the term structure. *Journal of Financial Economics, 5*(2), 177–188.

Wang, G. (2011). *An equity and foreign exchange Heston-Hull-White model for variable annuities*. Master's thesis, Delft University of Technology.

Zhu, J. (2000). *Modular pricing of options* (Vol. 493). Springer.

Chapter 8
The Implementation of Borrower-Based Measures: The Case of the Czech Republic

Lukáš Fiala

Abstract The article deals with the implementation of borrower-based measures within the framework of the macroprudential policy in the Czech Republic. The contribution is threefold. Firstly, we show the activation of instruments relating to mortgage market and house price development, which have gained strong growth during the last 5 years. Secondly, we discuss the Czech National Bank's reaction to the COVID-19 crisis in the form of active instruments targeted at borrowers, which led to the abolition of debt-to-income (DTI) and debt-service-to-income (DSTI) ratios. Finally, we provide a view on the effort to incorporate these instruments into the national legal framework.

Key words Czech National Bank · Macroprudential policy · Borrower-based measures

8.1 Introduction

The global financial crisis (GFC) of 2007–2009 has resulted in a greater focus on the stability of the financial system from both regulators and policymakers. Achieving financial stability became another important goal of central banks in order to safeguard the resilience of the financial sector. Lombardi and Schembri (2016) and Cao and Cholletec (2017) explain this target involving the utilization of new instruments to underpin the financial system. In line with this, macroprudential policy instruments became the toolkit used to achieve this objective. The maintenance of the stability of the financial system as an important goal safeguarding the main functions of the whole system amid the coronavirus crisis was explained by Restoy (2020).

The European Systemic Risk Board (ESRB) (2013) proposes that one of the goals of the macroprudential policy is to reduce the increasing systemic risk resulting from

L. Fiala (✉)
Faculty of Finance and Accounting, Department of Banking and Insurance, Prague University of Economics and Business, Prague, Czech Republic
e-mail: fial01@vse.cz

D. Procházka (ed.), *Regulation of Finance and Accounting*, Springer Proceedings in Business and Economics, https://doi.org/10.1007/978-3-030-99873-8_8

excessive credit growth, in order to keep the financial system stable. In this context, the ESRB (2013) has recommended the implementation of several instruments, including borrower-based measures.

Borio and Restoy (2020) demonstrate the importance of prudential regulation in the aftermath of the coronavirus crisis, which has made borrowers more vulnerable. The authors, in this context, emphasize the need for a prudential approach during the economic downturn.

The rapid increase in the Czech mortgage market has been discussed in recent years (Mandel & Teplý, 2018; Czech Banking Association, 2020). In this context, the Czech National Bank (CNB) has emphasized the need to focus on household debt development, which is mostly associated with mortgage debt. In line with the above-mentioned macroprudential objective, the central bank has implemented borrower-based measures covering limits on loan-to-value (LTV), debt-to-income (DTI), and debt-service-to-income ratios (DSTI).

Blahová (2019) explains that the instruments have a positive impact on the demand side, i.e. the borrowers, which are constrained when drawing loans. The use of these measures leads to an increase in the level of their resilience because of the lower level of their commitments resulting from exposures secured by real estate and their higher resilience to default. On the other hand, the implementation of the measures also favors the credit institutions because of the higher likelihood of debt repayment. The use of instruments aimed at borrowers, besides other measures, and their impact on the demand for financing were shown by Claessens (2014). In this context, the ESRB (2014) highlights the effects of these measures in light of the lower probability of borrowers' defaults and lower loss given default, which is a result of a more direct form of this regulation when compared to other macroprudential measures (for example, additional capital requirements).

Beneš et al. (2016) show LTV procyclicality and recommend the activation of other limits, such as DTI or DSTI, at the same time. Bierut et al. (2015) bring very similar findings and confirm the importance of the usage of LTV and DSTI together. Nier et al. (2019) present the positive influence of an active DSTI limit on the consumers' probability of default, i.e. lower default rates. This analysis is based on Romanian data set and shows the sensitivity of the probability of default to the DSTI limit for consumer loans and mortgage loans separately, which indicates different policy implications when setting up the limits. CNB (2020a) introduced the new methodology for household stress tests in 2020. The research showed that households with DSTI above 40% and DTI higher than 8 were highly influenced in a stress scenario and loans with DSTI and DTI above these thresholds can be treated as very risky.

In line with the literature review, the first aim of this contribution is to provide a view on the implementation of limits with respect to mortgage debt development and house price changes. The second objective of the article covers the CNB's reaction to the COVID-19 crisis in the form of borrower-based measures and its effort to set up those measures in accordance with legislation.

Table 8.1 Data used in the analysis

Variable	Period (frequency)	Source
Total household debt (outstanding) in billion CZK	2014–2020 (monthly)	Czech National Bank
Mortgage loans to households (outstanding) in billion CZK	2014–2020 (monthly)	Czech National Bank
Total housing loans to households (outstanding) in billion CZK	2014–2020 (monthly)	Czech National Bank
Newly issued mortgages to households (volume) in billion CZK	2014–2020 (monthly)	Czech National Bank

Source: Author

8.2 Data and Methodology

This paper contains a descriptive analysis used as a primary toolkit and based on data sets covering household debt (especially mortgage debt) and house prices. Table 8.1 provides more detailed information about the data used in the analysis and the sources.

8.3 Empirical Analysis

As Fig. 8.1 shows, mortgage loans to households make up the majority of household debt. The figure also shows that the outstanding part of the observed loan categories has increased during the last 6 years, and the cumulative change in the mortgage market from 2014 to the end of 2020 reached 68.5% when the total stock of household mortgage debt reached 1.34 trillion CZK. From the perspective of the changes in housing loans (covering mortgage loans and other consumer loans for house purchases), the year-on-year changes varied between 6% and 9%, with the lowest change occurring in 2019 (6.7%). The strong growth in household debt in the observed period has been evaluated as a potential risk to financial stability due to the level of indebtedness of the household sector. Due to the high demand for housing loans, the central bank decided to activate borrower-based measures in line with its objectives.

Table 8.2 presents the development of the number of implemented measures and their limits. The CNB (2015b) implemented the LTV ratio in 2015, recommending that the limit should not exceed the level of 100%. However, the central bank also pointed out that the share of loans with LTV exceeding the 90% threshold should not be higher than 10% of the total volume of loans granted in the previous quarter. The CNB (2015a) presented the reasons for the implementation of the LTV in its financial stability report.

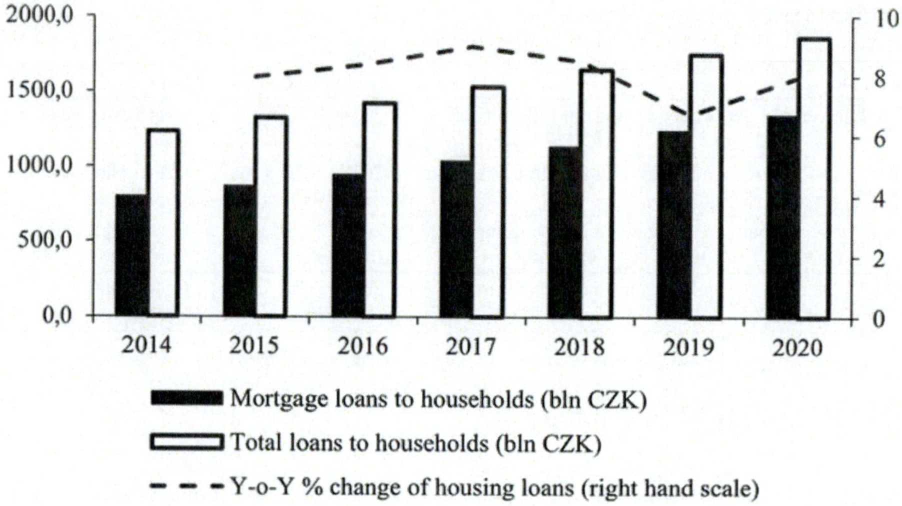

Fig. 8.1 Development of household debt. (Source: Author based on CNB, 2021)

These results confirmed the growing pace of housing loans to the household sector since 2013, which was caused particularly by the low level of interest rates. This evolution was also supported by the easing of lending standards, which made credit more accessible to borrowers. Moreover, the dynamics of credit recovery indicated a shift in the financial cycle, which was also encouraged by a moderate overvaluation of house prices (2.5% at the end of 2014). As a response, the CNB (2015a) introduced the LTV limit to serve as a preventive measure against the potential accumulation of systemic risks, in line with the ESRB recommendation.

The continuing period of low interest rates was considered by the CNB (2016a) as an indication for the banking sector to accept a higher credit risk in order to maintain profitability. This behavior of the banking sector led to a more noticeable declining tendency in credit standards in the case of housing loans.

The CNB (2016a) highlighted that the prudential approach to granting housing loans was crucial due to low interest rates and the easing of lending standards in combination with growing house prices and the optimistic future expectations of households. The central bank also emphasized the potential risk to financial stability resulting from households' vulnerability to potential income or interest rate shocks in the event of adverse scenarios.

Moreover, the results presented in the financial stability report confirmed that the limits for LTV values were not fully complied with by all banks because 4% of the total loan production exceeded the 100% LTV threshold in the third and fourth quarters of 2015. Some institutions did not adhere to the 10% exemption for loans with LTV higher than 90%. With regard to these findings, the CNB (2016b) decided to tighten the limits on LTV. This recommendation gradually lowered the threshold of the ratio and set the dates for the coming into force of the measures. The lowering of this cap was also a consequence of the house price development and the

Table 8.2 The activation of borrower-based measures in the Czech Republic

	Loan to value (LTV) (exceptions as a share of quarterly issued loans)	Debt to income (DTI) (exceptions as a share of quarterly issued loans)	Debt service to income (DSTI) (exceptions as a share of quarterly issued loans)
Recommendation from June 16, 2015	**100%** (10% for loans with LTV > 90%)	No active cap	No active cap
Recommendation from June 14, 2016	**LTV 100%** until September 30, 2016 (10% for loans with LTV > 90%) **LTV 95%** since October 1, 2016 (10% for loans with LTV 85–95%) **LTV 90%** since April 1, 2017 (15% for loans with LTV > 80%) **LTV 60%** for other real estate purchases	No active cap	No active cap
Recommendation from June 13, 2017	**LTV 90%** (15% for loans with LTV > 80%)	Loans with DTI > 8 prudentially assessed	Loans with DSTI > 40% prudentially assessed
Recommendation from June 12, 2018	**LTV 90%** (15% for loans with LTV > 80%)	**DTI 9** since October 1, 2018 (5% for loans with DTI > 9)	**DSTI 45%** since October 1, 2018 (5% for loans with DSTI > 45%)
Recommendation from June 11, 2019	Limits unchanged		
Recommendation from December 13, 2019	Limits unchanged		
Recommendation from April 1, 2020	**LTV 90%** (5% for loans with LTV > 90%)	No active cap	**DSTI 50%** (5% for loans with DSTI > 50%)
Recommendation from July 8, 2020	**LTV 90%** (5% for loans with LTV > 90%)	No active cap	No active cap

Source: CNB (2015b; 2016b; 2017b; 2018b; 2019b, c; 2020b, c)

continuing overvaluation of house prices. In addition, an LTV cap on other than residential real estate was introduced. The main objective of this activation was to reduce access to real estate purchased for investing purposes, i.e. for rent. The threshold was set at 60%. The recommendation also pointed out the need to focus on income ratios and set their internal limits to ensure a prudential approach to the granting of loans. On the other hand, no thresholds were activated.

In 2017, the CNB (2017a) stated that the overvaluation of residential real estate varied between 8% and 9% at the end of 2016. The growth in house prices and their estimated overvaluation are displayed in Fig. 8.3. In reaction to this result, the central bank stated that house prices were not in line with the fundamental factors determining the prices and that this was caused by a higher number of transactions with residential real estate financed by loans. These findings referred to the continuing risk of ratcheting up the spiral resulting from credit-fueled house prices. Although the recommended limits were adhered to until October 2016, the tightened caps since October 1, 2016, were not fully followed. The results presented in the Financial Stability Report in 2017 confirmed that the share of granted loans with LTV higher than 80% exceeded the allowed threshold (10%) by 10 percentage points.

The CNB (2017a) highlighted the potential risk to financial stability associated with DTI exceeding the level of 8 and DSTI surpassing 40% based on household stress test results. Moreover, there was not confirmed that higher risk associated with granted loans was not projected into the level of lending interest rates. The role of financial intermediaries was confirmed as another cause of risk because they provide unsecured loans to avoid the limits set by the recommendations. However, the CNB, in cooperation with the Ministry of Finance (MoF), prepared a legislative proposal to change the Act on the Czech National Bank,[1] which would allow the central bank to set the caps under the law and to help implement these measures. These consequences led the CNB (2017b) to scale up the recommendation in the case of income ratios with high risk values (DSTI 40%, DTI 8). The scope of this recommendation was also extended to all consumer loan providers.

The ongoing dynamic of loans to households stayed strong during 2017. The CNB (2018a) emphasized the fact that the recommended limits on these loans did not cause a decline in newly issued mortgages, as had been expected. In that year, the stock of newly issued mortgages reached nearly 174 billion CZK. The volume of newly issued mortgages and their year-on-year change are presented in Fig. 8.2. On the other hand, the overvaluation of residential real estate reached approximately 14% at the end of 2017. The central bank also indicated that market conditions could be considered very attractive despite the active LTV limit. This referred, for example, to the low level of interest rates and strong income growth, causing an increasing demand for housing loans. These factors led to a rise in the average loan amount. From the perspective of the implementation of the borrower-based measures, the CNB (2018a) confirmed that limits on LTV were, on an aggregate level, accomplished.

In this context, the central bank considered the LTV cap to be sufficient and decided not to change this limit. Indeed, the CNB highlighted the rapid growth in house prices, which exceeded the average increase in household income. This state was evaluated as very risky for potential loan applicants because of rising debt commitments resulting from higher loan amounts. The expectation as to the number of loans granted to riskier applicants was reflected in the context of the higher

[1] Act No. 6/1993 Coll., on Czech National Bank.

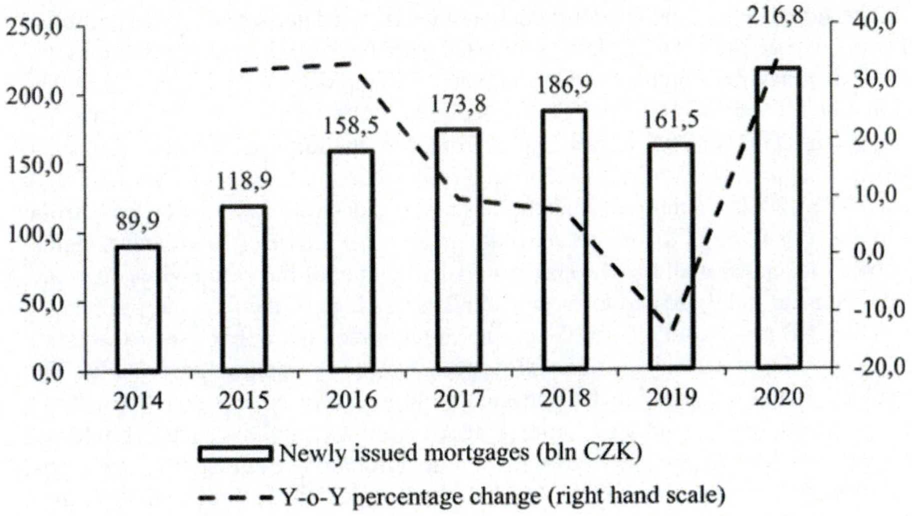

Fig. 8.2 The development of newly issued mortgages. (Source: Author based on CNB, 2021)

vulnerability of households under worsening market conditions. The potential deterioration of the ability to service the debts was the reason for the change in the CNB's recommendation, which implemented the caps on DTI and DSTI. The CNB (2018b) recommended that DTI should not be higher than 9 and that DSTI should not surpass the threshold of 45%. The central bank also mentioned the effort to incorporate the macroprudential objectives connected with excessive credit growth into national legislation, as mentioned above.

The CNB (2019a) stated that the activation of income ratios did not lead to a rapid decline in newly issued mortgages. On the contrary, the volume of these loans was 7 billion CZK higher in comparison to the averages since 2015 in the third quarter of 2018 and 8 billion CZK higher in the fourth quarter. The effect of the activation of the caps was evident in the first quarter of 2019 when the stock declined by 9 billion CZK. This development can be justified by the frontloading effect associated with households' decision to apply for a loan before the activation of the new regulation. The CNB (2019a) also clarified that it is necessary to examine this development from the perspective of time, and the declining tendency of new loans can be explained by the high level of loans in the previous time periods, which serves as the basis for calculation.

In addition to a certain drop in the number of loans at the beginning of 2019, the central bank continued to highlight those market conditions that increase the risk to financial stability associated with growing household debt and the rising prices of residential real estate. On the other hand, the limits set by the recommendation were not changed in 2019. However, a potential tightening of the caps was communicated in the financial stability report for the following periods due to continuing house price growth.

The adjustment of the macroprudential ratios targeted at borrowers was revised in the first half of 2020. These changes resulted from the shift in market conditions due to the coronavirus outbreak, which affected the approach to risk evaluation. The limit on LTV was increased to 90% (earlier, it was 80%, with some exemptions), and the cap on DSTI was set at 50%. Apart from that, the limit on DTI was abolished. The new adjustments to the levels of each ratio entered into force on April 1, 2020. The CNB (2020a) proposed that the easing of standards should not lead to the imprudent granting of loans because of the expected negative effects on households' income associated with the coronavirus crisis. In spite of the coronavirus outbreak, the volume of newly issued loans stayed relatively high in the first half of 2020.

The CNB (2020a) explained the easing of regulation not only by the expectation of the banking sector's prudential approach when granting new loans. The conducted analysis showed that the income limits were largely respected during the previous periods. In this context, there were exemptions to the prudential approach to loan applicants due to income deterioration resulting from the crisis. In line with this, the CNB (2020b) decided to remove the DSTI limit with effect from July 2020. The differentiation of interest rates caused by different LTVs in certain cases and the expected conservative approach to the granting of loans during the pandemic can serve as a supporting argument. Ever since, the only active limit has been the LTV ratio, which is in force because of the level of house prices and their indicated overvaluation, which was estimated at 17% at the end of June 2020 (Fig. 8.3).

The worsening economic outlook and labor market did not affect the mortgage market significantly in 2020 (CNB, 2020d). As Fig. 8.2 shows, the volume of newly issued loans reached the level of 217 billion CZK, which can be considered a new

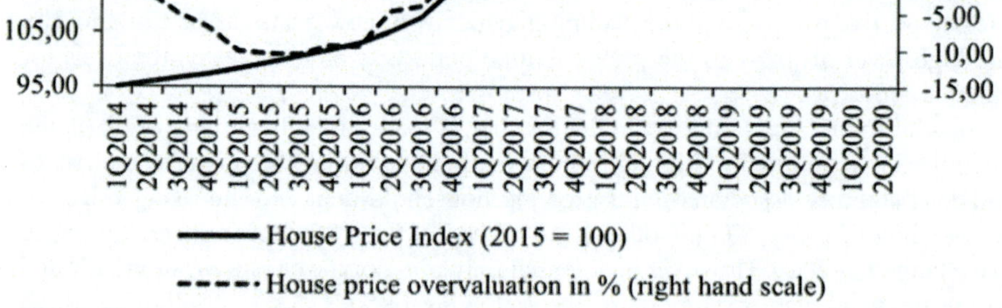

Fig. 8.3 The development of house prices and their overvaluation. (Source: Author in accordance with CNB, 2020d)

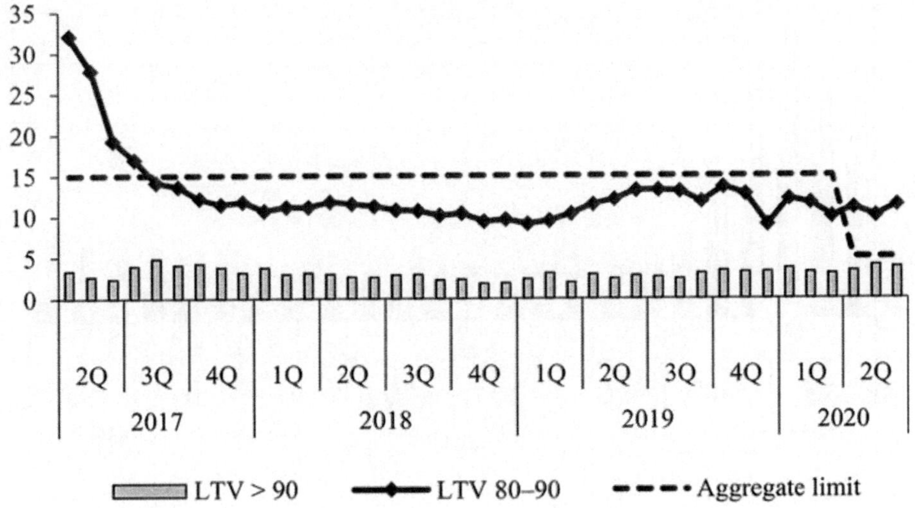

Fig. 8.4 Accomplishment of recommended loan-to-value limits. (Source: Author in accordance with CNB (2020d). Note: The data represents the share of loans of the total granted volume in each quarter)

historic maximum. This signals a very strong demand for home ownership, which was not weakened by the second wave of the coronavirus pandemic, which came in October 2020. On the other hand, the measures targeted at borrowers in order to reduce excessive credit growth have remained unchanged.

Figures 8.4 and 8.5 display the fulfilment of the recommended LTV and DSTI limits. It is obvious that the volume of newly issued mortgages with these characteristics was mostly meeting the recommended thresholds. However, the volume of newly issued loans secured by real estate continued in strong growth in 2021. The statistics showed more than 100% year-on-year growth of newly issued mortgages in March 2021, which indicates a still growing household demand for loans despite the continuing coronavirus crisis.

As mentioned above, the CNB, in cooperation with the MoF, was pressing for the incorporation of borrower-based measures into legislation. The main reasons for the incorporation of these instruments into law are associated with the scope of the institutions that would be obliged to adhere to the limits and the enforceability of adherence to the limits. At the current time, the CNB only recommends the levels that should not be exceeded when granting loans secured by residential real estate. As presented, the CNBs' findings confirmed that some institutions did not follow these limits, but the central bank did not possess any competence to make them meet the criteria.

With regard to a legal mandate, the central bank should have at its disposal an appropriate toolkit to safeguard financial stability, which can be disrupted by excessive credit growth. The incorporation of a borrower-based instrument into national legislation was emphasized in an ESRB warning to the Czech Republic in

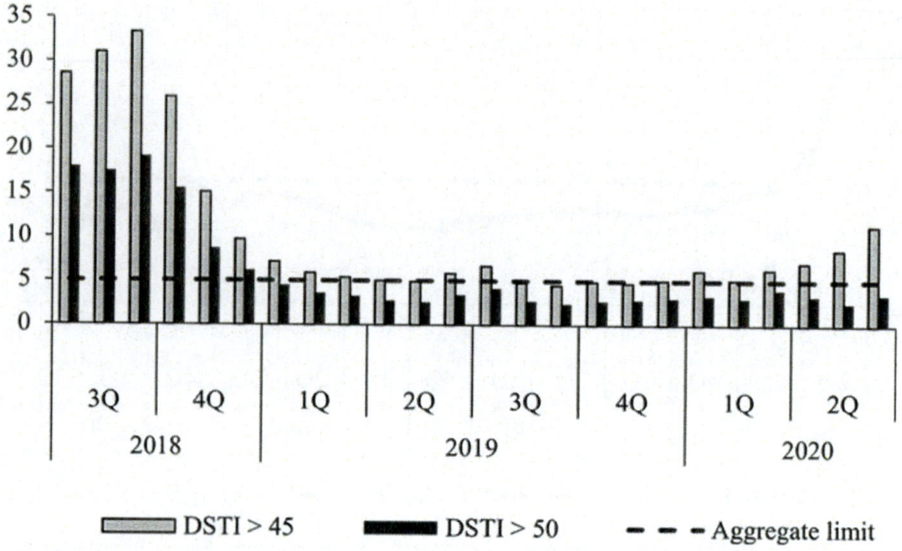

Fig. 8.5 Accomplishment of recommended debt-service-to-income limits. (Source: Author in accordance with CNB (2020d). Note: The data represents the share of loans of the granted volume in each quarter)

2019. The ESRB (2019) pointed out that a binding regulation is a more powerful tool for addressing vulnerabilities and covering all credit providers, thus ensuring aggregate adherence to the standards.

In this context, it is worth mentioning the current practice of using borrower-based measures in other jurisdictions. Based on ESRB (2021) data set, which was updated at the end of March, there were 23 countries with an active LTV limit (18 of them as a binding regulation). From an income ratio perspective, there were seven economies with an active DTI (or LTI)—five countries as a binding regulation. DSTI was active in 14 countries (recommended caps in five countries). Moreover, there were identified 22 countries of the European Economic Area that have incorporated these measures into national legislation (at least one cap). Nevertheless, the thresholds of each cap are activated as a response to country-specific situations, and the analysis of their developments in every single country is beyond this paper. However, the abovementioned information confirms the wide usage of these instruments in many countries under national law. These findings are in line with other research, for example, Fiala and Teplý (2021).

The abovementioned effort to incorporate borrower-based measures into national legislation (Act on the Czech National Bank) was already fulfilled due to the approval of Act No. 219/2021 Coll. amending Act No. 6/1993 Coll., on the Czech National Bank. The amendment was approved in June 2021 and has come into force since August 2021. At this moment, the CNB is justified to set up the LTV, DTI, and DSTI limits as a binding regulation.

8.4 Results and Discussion

The analysis showed that the Czech mortgage market has grown very strongly in the last 6 years, which the CNB considered to pose a potential risk to financial stability associated with excessive credit, which is accepted by the ESRB as a form of vulnerability of the financial system. The CNB has implemented several borrower-based measures in line with the ESRB's recommendation. The reaction of the central bank may be considered very active because of the yearly changes to the limits and revisions resulting from shifts in the market conditions.

One example of the CNB's active intervention is the revision of the thresholds and active caps in response to the COVID-19 outbreak. The central bank followed the change in market conditions in 2020 and abolished first the DTI and, finally, the DSTI cap as well. The only active instrument is the LTV limit, which reflects the level of house prices and their estimated overvaluation. However, it is possible to state that the activity of the mortgage market was not significantly affected by the crisis with regard to the supply of newly issued mortgages.

On the other hand, the CNB at present only recommends the thresholds of the instruments. The ESRB warned the Czech Republic about medium-term vulnerabilities in 2019 and showed the need to incorporate the instruments into the national legislative in order to safeguard the enforceability of adherence to the limits. The CNB, in cooperation with the MoF, has prepared a legislative proposal to implement this recommendation, and the legislative process has already been finished. At this moment, the central bank can implement the measures targeted at borrowers as a binding regulation, which should increase the efficiency of this regulation when fulfilling the goal of financial stability.

8.5 Conclusion

This article deals with the implementation of borrower-based measures in the Czech Republic in relation to household debt and house price development. The contribution of the article is threefold. Firstly, we show the development in the implementation of the caps used and their changes during the last five years and explain their activations in line with the shifts in market conditions. Secondly, we highlight the amendments in the field of borrower-based measures as a response to the coronavirus outbreak, which have resulted in a relaxation of standards, which is connected with the abolition of the DTI and DSTI limits. Thirdly, we provide a view on the effort to incorporate these measures into the national legal framework as a binding regulation, which could ensure more powerful instruments to enforce the active limits and safeguard a more prudential approach when granting secured loans.

Acknowledgments This paper has been prepared as an output of research projects registered by the Czech Science Foundation (Project. No. GA 20-00178S) and by the Prague University of Economics and Business (Project No. VSE IP100040 and No. IG102029).

References

Beneš, J., Laxton, D., & Mongardini, J. (2016). *Mitigating the deadly embrace in financial cycles: Countercyclical buffers and loan-to-values limits* (IMF working papers (87)). International Monetary Fund.

Bierut B, Chmielewski T, Glogowski A et al (2015) Implementing loan-to-value and debt-to-income ratios: Learning from country experiences. The case of Poland. NBP Working papers (212).

Blahová, N. (2019). Analysis of macroprudential policy approaches in the practice of the Czech Republic. *Český finanční a účetní časopis., 2019*, 31–55. https://doi.org/10.18267/j.cfuc.538

Borio, C., & Restoy, F. (2020). *Reflections on regulatory responses to the Covid-19 pandemic* (Financial Stability Institute Briefs 2020 April (1)). Bank for International Settlements.

Cao, J., & Cholletec, L. (2017). Monetary policy and financial stability in the long run: a simple gametheoretic approach. *Journal of Financial Stability, 28*, 125–142. https://doi.org/10.1016/j.jfs.2016.12.002

Claessens, S. (2014). *An overview of macroprudential policy tools* (IMF working papers (14)). International Monetary Fund.

Czech Banking Association. (2020). *Czechs and mortgages 2020*. Available via DIALOG. https://cbaonline.cz/cesi-a-hypoteky-2020. Accessed 20 Dec 2020.

Czech National Bank. (2015a). *Financial stability report 2014/2015*. ISBN 978-80-87225-58-5. Available via DIALOG. https://www.cnb.cz/cs/financni-stabilita/zpravy-fs/zprava-o-financni-stabilite-2014-2015/. Accessed 16 Jan 2021.

Czech National Bank. (2015b). *Recommendation of 16th June 2015 for managing the risk associated with granting the retail loans secured by residential real estate*. Available via DIALOG. https://www.cnb.cz/cs/financni-stabilita/makroobezretnostni-politika/doporuceni-limity-pro-poskytovani-hypotecnich-uveru/. Accessed 2 Feb 2021.

Czech National Bank. (2016a). *Financial stability report 2015/2016*. ISBN 978-80-87225-64-6. Available via DIALOG. https://www.cnb.cz/cs/financni-stabilita/zpravy-fs/zprava-o-financni-stabilite-2015-2016/. Accessed 16 Jan 2021.

Czech National Bank. (2016b). *Recommendation of 14th June 2016 for managing the risk associated with granting the retail loans secured by residential real estate*. Available via DIALOG. https://www.cnb.cz/cs/financni-stabilita/makroobezretnostni-politika/doporuceni-limity-pro-poskytovani-hypotecnich-uveru/. Accessed 2 Feb 2021.

Czech National Bank. (2017a). *Financial stability report 2016/2017*. ISBN 978-80-87225-71-4. Available via DIALOG. https://www.cnb.cz/cs/financni-stabilita/zpravy-fs/zprava-o-financni-stabilite-2016-2017/. Accessed 17 Jan 2021.

Czech National Bank. (2017b). *Recommendation of 13th June 2017 for managing the risk associated with granting the retail loans secured by residential real estate*. Available via DIALOG. https://www.cnb.cz/cs/financni-stabilita/makroobezretnostni-politika/doporuceni-limity-pro-poskytovani-hypotecnich-uveru/. Accessed 4 Feb 2021.

Czech National Bank. (2018a). *Financial stability report 2017/2018*. ISBN 978-80-87225-79-0. Available via DIALOG. https://www.cnb.cz/cs/financni-stabilita/zpravy-fs/zprava-o-financni-stabilite-2017-2018/. Accessed 17 Jan 2021.

Czech National Bank. (2018b). *Recommendation of 12th June 2018 for managing the risk associated with granting the retail loans secured by residential real estate*. Available via DIALOG. https://www.cnb.cz/cs/financni-stabilita/makroobezretnostni-politika/doporuceni-limity-pro-poskytovani-hypotecnich-uveru/. Accessed 4 Feb 2021.

Czech National Bank. (2019a). *Financial stability report 2018/2019*. ISBN 978-80-87225-86-8. Available via DIALOG. https://www.cnb.cz/cs/financni-stabilita/zpravy-fs/zprava-o-financni-stabilite-2018-2019/. Accessed 19 Jan 2021.

Czech National Bank. (2019b). *Recommendation of 11th June 2019 for managing the risk associated with granting the retail loans secured by residential real estate*. Available via DIALOG. https://www.cnb.cz/cs/financni-stabilita/makroobezretnostni-politika/doporuceni-limity-pro-poskytovani-hypotecnich-uveru/. Accessed 5 Feb 2021.

Czech National Bank. (2019c). *Recommendation of 12th December 2019 for managing the risk associated with granting the retail loans secured by residential real estate*. Available via DIALOG. https://www.cnb.cz/cs/financni-stabilita/makroobezretnostni-politika/doporuceni-limity-pro-poskytovani-hypotecnich-uveru/. Accessed 5 Feb 2021.

Czech National Bank. (2020a). *Financial stability report 2019/2020*. ISBN 978-80-87225-95-0. Available via DIALOG. https://www.cnb.cz/cs/financni-stabilita/zpravy-fs/zprava-o-financni-stabilite-2019-2020/. Accessed 19 Jan 2021.

Czech National Bank. (2020b). *Recommendation of 1st April 2020 for managing the risk associated with granting the retail loans secured by residential real estate*. Available via DIALOG. https://www.cnb.cz/cs/financni-stabilita/makroobezretnostni-politika/doporuceni-limity-pro-poskytovani-hypotecnich-uveru/. Accessed 7 Feb 2021.

Czech National Bank. (2020c). *Recommendation of 8th July 2020 for managing the risk associated with granting the retail loans secured by residential real estate*. Available via DIALOG. https://www.cnb.cz/cs/financni-stabilita/makroobezretnostni-politika/doporuceni-limity-pro-poskytovani-hypotecnich-uveru/. Accessed 7 Feb 2021.

Czech National Bank. (2020d). *Risks for financial stability and their indicators – December 2020*. Available via DIALOG. https://www.cnb.cz/export/sites/cnb/cs/financni-stabilita/.galleries/rizika_pro_fs/rizika_pro_financni_stabilitu_a_jejich_indikatory_prosinec_2020_cz.pdf. Accessed 2 Feb 2021.

Czech National Bank. (2021). Czech National Bank Database, *online*, 30.1., https://www.cnb.cz/docs/ARADY/HTML/index.htm.

European Systemic Risk Board. (2013). *Recommendation of the European Systemic Risk Board of 4 April 2013 on intermediate objectives and instruments of macro-prudential policy*. Available via DIALOG. https://op.europa.eu/en/publication-detail/-/publication/de25b43d-d5a1-11e2-bfa7-01aa75ed71a1. Accessed 7 Jan 2021.

European Systemic Risk Board. (2014). *Flagship report on macro-prudential policy in the Banking Sector*. Available via DIALOG. https://www.esrb.europa.eu/pub/pdf/other/140303_flagship_report.pdf. Accessed 7 Jan 2021.

European Systemic Risk Board. (2019). *Warning of the European Systemic Risk Board of 27 June 2019 on medium-term vulnerabilities in the residential real estate sector in the Czech Republic* (ESRB/2019/10). Available via DIALOG. https://www.esrb.europa.eu/mppa/warnings/html/index.en.html. Accessed 7 Jan 2021.

European Systemic Risk Board. (2021). *National measures of macroprudential interest in the EU/EEA*. Available via DIALOG. https://www.esrb.europa.eu/national_policy/html/index.en.html. Accessed 10 June 2021.

Fiala, L., & Teplý, P. (2021). The use of borrower-based measures within macroprudential policy: Evidence from the European Economic Area. *European Financial and Accounting Journal, 16*(1), 71–91. https://doi.org/10.18267/j.efaj.249

Lombardi, D., & Schembri, L. (2016). Reinvesting the role of central banks in financial stability. *Bank of Canada Review, 2016*, 1–11.

Mandel, M., Teplý, P. (2018). *Finanční chování domácností v teorii a praxi*. Available via DIALOG. https://cbaonline.cz/studie-pro-cba-financni-chovani-domacnosti. Accessed 11 Jan 2021.

Nier, E., Popa, R., Shamloo, M., et al. (2019). *Debt service and default: Calibrating macroprudential policy using micro data* (IMF working papers (182)). International Monetary Fund.

Restoy, F. (2020). *Central banks and financial stability: A reflection after the Covid-19 outbreak* (Financial Stability Institute – Occasional Paper 2020) (Vol. 16). Bank for International Settlements.

Chapter 9
Prepayment Risk in Banking: Empirical Evidence from the Czech Republic

Petr Hanzlík and Petr Teplý

Abstract This paper deals with prepayment risks in banking and provides empirical evidence from the Czech banking sector. The prepayment risk of a loan can be viewed as an embedded option for a client to refinance his mortgage with a lower interest rate. Conversely, it holds that the clients' profit means a loss to the bank as a mortgage provider. Our analysis quantifies the impact of early repayment of a mortgage on the balance sheets of three different types of banks, which differ in the structure of their financing. In particular, we examine the negative effects of prepaid mortgages on the interest margins of these banks. The results of models have shown that these prepayments risks not only were theoretical, but they were also reflected in the decreasing net interest margin of the Czech banking sector in the 2019–2020 period.

Key words Asset liability management · Bank · Interest rate · Mortgage · Prepayment risk

9.1 Introduction

Prepayment risk is an important type of risk to be considered by every bank. Choudhry (2018, p. 107) defines it as "the risk associated with the early unscheduled return of principal on an instrument. … This risk also extends to typical retail lending products (for instance unsecured loans, mortgages, and vehicle finance)." Therefore, it has to be considered especially by those banks whose assets consist, to a large extent, of long-term retail loans, particularly mortgages. The prepayment risk

P. Hanzlík (✉)
Institute of Economic Studies, Faculty of Social Sciences, Charles University, Prague 1, Czech Republic
e-mail: 96193552@fsv.cuni.cz

P. Teplý
Department of Banking and Insurance, Faculty of Finance and Accounting, Prague University of Economics and Business, Prague, Czech Republic
e-mail: petr.teply@vse.cz

D. Procházka (ed.), *Regulation of Finance and Accounting*, Springer Proceedings in Business and Economics, https://doi.org/10.1007/978-3-030-99873-8_9

may result in a decrease in banks' profitability in times of decreasing market interest rates. In such circumstances, bank clients have incentives to refinance their existing loans with higher interest rates by means of new loans with lower interest rates. In times of increasing rates, the prepayment risk may tend to decrease as, in such cases, clients would prefer to stick to previously contracted lower rates. However, the banks may experience higher default rates when the mortgages are repriced at the end of the fixation period to higher rates. Such increase in mortgage defaults caused by a combination of increasing interest rates and house price bubble occurred in the United States in 2007 and 2008 and contributed to the start of the global financial crisis (Mayer et al., 2009). The prepayment risk may be, to some extent, limited by contractual terms or legal provisions that specify the circumstances in which the loan can be prepaid. On the other hand, the legislation may be also designed in favor of the clients and thus contribute to the prepayment risk.

Our paper provides a case study of the mortgage market in the Czech Republic. The legislation in the Czech Republic effective since December 1, 2016 (Act No. 257/2016 Coll. on Consumer Loan, which transposed European Directive 2014/17/EU to Czech law) allowed for an interpretation by the Czech National Bank that the bank can charge the client only a very limited scope of the costs related to the prepayment of a loan. This interpretation leads to a higher probability of the materialization of prepayment risks in the Czech banking sector by lowering the costs of the prepayment option for the client.

Our analysis thus focuses on the impact of prepayment risk, defined as the risk of a fully repaid mortgage balance (but foregone interest) prior to the scheduled or contracted maturity, on the Czech banking sector. The remainder of the paper is organized as follows: in Sect. 9.2, we discuss key basic terms (embedded options of a bond and of a bank loan) needed for our research. Section 9.3 presents the methodology applied (case study on the interest rate risk of a bank and the net present value concept of a bank's total loss). In Sect. 9.4, we undertake an empirical analysis and compute the impact of early repayment of a mortgage on the balance sheets of three different types of banks. The last section concludes the paper.

9.2 Theoretical Part

9.2.1 Embedded Options of a Bond

In this section, we provide theoretical context, which will serve as the basis for our empirical research. In the financial markets, the problem of early repayment of a mortgage is similar to the problem of valuing callable bonds. Fabozzi (2015) defines *a callable bond as a bond in which the bondholder has sold the issuer a call option that allows the issuer to repurchase the contractual cash flows of the bond from the time the bond is first callable until the maturity date.* The call feature is a special feature of a bond or other financial instruments that give creditors and/or debtors the right to take action in the future against their counterparty. The embedded option is an integral part of a financial instrument and is generally not separately tradable. One financial instrument may include more embedded options. The value of a callable bond is then expressed as the difference between the value of a non-callable bond and the value of the call option.

The call option protects the borrower or lender from unexpected changes in market interest rates (i.e., against price loss, which may arise from a decrease/increase of the interest rate between the issue date and the maturity date). Fabozzi (2004) lists a call option as the most typical embedded option, which gives the right to the debtor to repay his debt before an agreed maturity at a preagreed upon price (serving as a de facto ceiling on the price of the bond). This fact favors the borrower in the event of a fall in market interest rates because it gives him the opportunity to refinance debt under more favorable conditions. On a related note, Fabozzi (2004) introduces a put option on the market as a typical option to protect the lender when interest rates go up. In the remainder of our paper, we will focus primarily on the impact of the call option, which favors the borrower during decreasing market interest rates and also results in the lender's (bank) loss. Recently, two embedded options have been examined in the Czech financial market: construction savings by Horváth and Teplý (2013) and savings accounts by Džmuráňová and Teplý (2016).

9.2.2 *Embedded Options of a Bank Loan*

The prepayment risk of a loan represents an embedded option for a client to refinance his bank loan (e.g., a mortgage) for a lower interest rate. When the client exercises his early repayment option, he can repay the remaining balance of the loan (and forego future interest payments) before its maturity, which is better for him because this represents a lower implied interest rate. Obviously, this client's profit means a loss (of foregone interest payments less the risk of a default of an outstanding loan) to the bank as a mortgage provider. Moreover, the early mortgage repayment will have an impact on the interest rate position of the bank, as will be discussed later.

Hayre and Young (2004) highlight five main causes of premature repayment of a mortgage: replacement of housing (prepayment rate depends on the replacement of existing homes), refinancing (full early repayment for a new loan for better conditions), default (full repayment of the house as a seized collateral), partial prepayment (the client prepays part of the loan and shortens the original maturity), and full payment (e.g., in the case of destruction of the house by a natural disaster). However, it is necessary to distinguish the different sensitivities of the client's willingness to prepay a mortgage. While interest rates are decreasing, sensitivity is high. In contrast, sensitivity can be quite minimal in the case of solving life situations, such as divorce or the settlement of inheritance.

9.2.3 Prepayment Risk

Prepayment or Early Redemption Risk: applies on fixed-rate loans and deposits, where customers have the right (or an option) to repay loans or redeem deposits ahead of the scheduled maturity date, on payment of an early repayment or redemption charge (Choudhry, 2018, p. 1015). Banks in different countries handle the prepayment risk on mortgages differently. In countries such as the United States or the United Kingdom, the risk is transferred, via a process known as securitization, to the investors buying mortgage-backed securities (MBS) issued by a special purpose entity, to which the mortgages are sold by the originating bank. On the other hand, in many European countries, including Germany or the Czech Republic, the prepayment risk remains on the banks' balance sheets and the mortgages are funded either by the issuance of covered bonds or by retail deposits.

The existing literature on prepayment risk focuses mainly on the prepayment risk securitized through MBS in the United States (Becketti, 1988) or option-adjusted valuation of MBS related to the prepayment risk (Levin & Davidson, 2005). Kau et al. (1992) provide a generalized valuation model for fixed-rate mortgages (FRM). A paper by Ambrose and LaCour-Little (2001) deals with prepayment risk in adjustable-rate mortgages (ARM) and its securitization through MBS and provides evidence that prepayment risk is much less important for ARM than for FRM. Chernov et al. (2018) developed a reduced-form modeling framework to observe the implied prepayment function in which the prepayment rates are influenced by, besides interest rates, other macroeconomic factors.

9.3 Methodology

Our paper uses two methodological approaches. First, we present a case study on the interest rate risk of a bank through the bank's ALM. Second, we apply a net present value concept for the calculation of the bank's losses that resulted from lower interest income.

9.3.1 Case Study on the Interest Rate Risk of a Bank

The impact of early repayment of a mortgage can be illustrated by a bank's asset-liability-department (ALM) problem. For example, for a mortgage with a 5-year fixed term, the bank would need to offset its risk by finding adequate resources, such as an interest rate swap with the same maturity (a 5-year bank liability). If a mortgage is terminated before its contractual maturity, the bank's ALM should ensure that such a situation is balanced in the bank's balance sheet by means of a substitute transaction (e.g., by replacing the original source of mortgage funding with a new instrument with a shorter maturity). This problem becomes significant in a low-interest-rate environment. For simplicity, let us assume that a bank has two parts of its portfolio: the first part is funded at recent low interest rates, and the second one is funded at past high interest rates. Figures 9.1 and 9.2 below illustrate this interest rate risk based on the development of real yield curves in the Czech Republic valid between December 31, 2000, and December 31, 2005, and between September

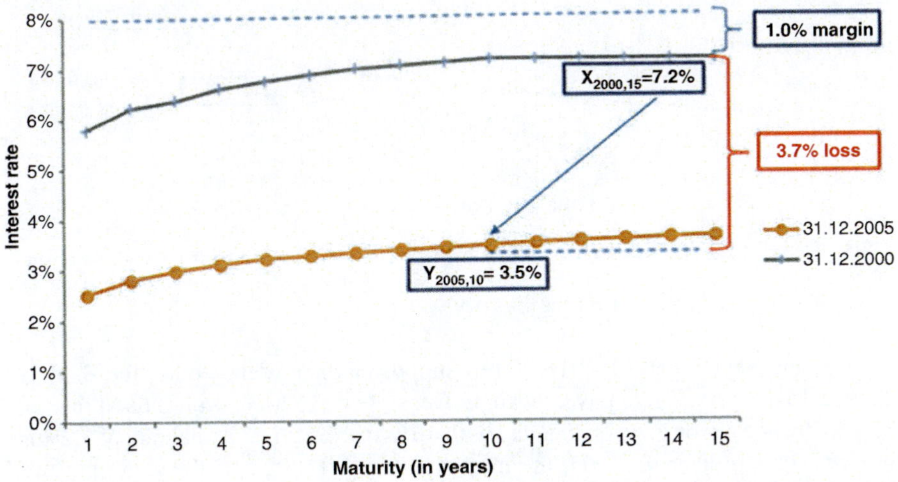

Fig. 9.1 Interest rate risk of the Bank as of 31 December 2005. (Source: Authors. Note: Loss from funding = $X_{(2000,15)} - Y_{(2005,10)}$ = 7.2% – 3.5% = 3.7%, where $X_{(2000,15)}$ = 15-year interest rate in 2000 and $Y_{(2005,10)}$ = 10-year interest rate in 2005)

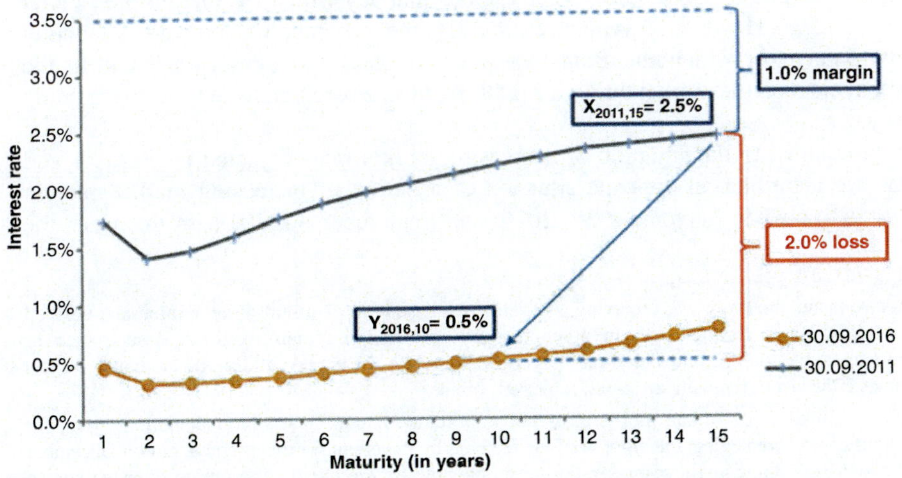

Fig. 9.2 Interest rate risk of the Bank as of September 30, 2011. (Source: Authors. Note: Loss on funding = $X_{(2011,15)} - Y_{(2016,10)}$ = 2.5% – 0.5% = 2.0%, where $X_{(2011,15)}$ = 15-year interest rate in 2011 and $Y_{(2016,10)}$ = 10-year interest rate in 2016)

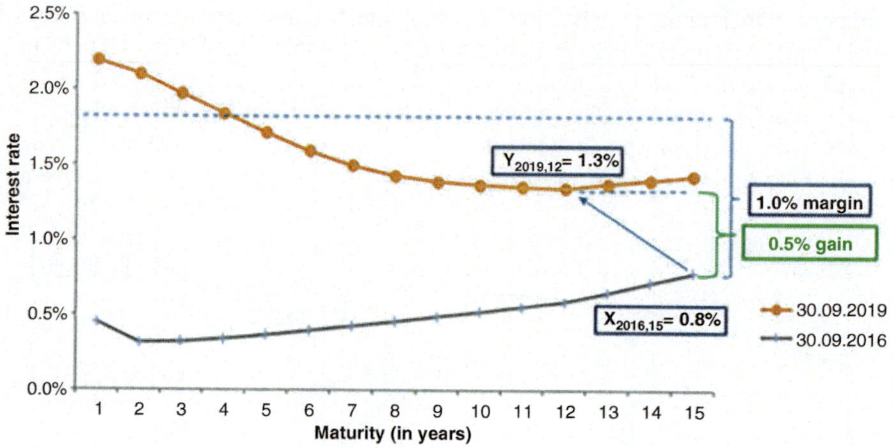

Fig. 9.3 Interest rate risk of the Bank as of September 30, 2016. (Source: Authors. Note: Gain from funding = $Y_{(2019,12)} - X_{(2016,15)} = 1.3\% - 0.8\% = 0.5\%$, where $X_{(2016,15)}$ = 15-year interest rate in 2016 and $Y_{(2019,12)}$ = 12-year interest rate in 2019)

30, 2011, and September 30, 2016. Let us suppose a bank (denoted as "the Bank") entered a 15-year fixed-rate payer swap on December 31, 2000, with a fixed rate of 7.2%[1] to finance a mortgage on that day with a 1% margin[2] (i.e., a total rate of 8.2%). However, 5 years later, in 2005, the mortgage was prepaid, and the Bank put the money raised from the mortgage prepayment on the market through a 3.5% fix rate receiver swap for the remaining 10 years, implying a loss of 3.7%[3] for the period 2006–2015, as displayed in Fig. 9.1. A similar situation is illustrated in Fig. 9.2, where the bank entered a 15-year fixed-rate payer swap on September 30, 2011, with a fixed rate of 2.5% to finance a mortgage on that day with a 1% margin (i.e., a total rate of 3.5%). However, 5 years later, in 2016, the mortgage was prepaid in a market environment in which the Bank was able to place the money raised from the prepayment on the market through a 0.5% fixed-rate receiver swap for the remaining 10 years.

In contrast to the situation of decreasing market rates depicted in Figs. 9.1 and 9.2, we identified an opposite situation of a period of increasing market rates in Fig. 9.3 between September 30, 2016, and September 30, 2019. In this case, the

---

[1] It means that the Bank was receiving a variable rate based on a 1-month Prague Interbank Offered Rate (PRIBOR), for instance. In practice, banks are hedging their fixed-rate assets, such as mortgages, by entering into fixed-rate payer swaps, while the actual funding of the balance sheet comes either from deposits or issued (covered) bonds.

[2] The nominal value of the mortgage is not important for our illustrative calculation. Also, for simplification, we neglect the amount of the fee paid by the client for this prepayment on December 31, 2015 (i.e., the Bank's compensation costs payable by the client—the option adjusted spread (OAS) rate—is equal to 0).

[3] 3.7% = 7.2% − 3.5% (loss on funding = funding costs − a new swap interest rate). In fact, the total loss for the bank is 4.7% = 3.7% + 1 % (loss on funding + margin).

prepayment is rather desirable for the Bank since it can put the money from prepayment into the fixed-rate receiver swap for a higher rate (1.3%) than at the time of the loan origination (0.8%). However, in such an event, the Bank still loses the 1% margin in case the money is placed on the market instead of being used for the provision of a new mortgage with the same margin.

9.3.2 The Net Present Value of a Bank's Total Loss

If we want to calculate the total loss for the whole 2006–2015 period, it is possible to use a standard formula for discounted cash flows:

$$PV = \sum_{t=1}^{T} \frac{CF_t}{(1 + r_t)^t}$$

where

$PV =$ present value of a loss
$CF_t =$ cash flow in a given year
$r_t =$ interest rate in a given year
$t =$ given year
$T =$ end of the period

Let us assume that the Bank will provide a mortgage of CZK 1,000,000, then an annual loss of CZK 37,000 (3.7% loss from funding) was generated over the entire period, with the interest rate corresponding to the yield curve as of December 31, 2005 (see also Fig. 9.1):

$$\begin{aligned} \text{Loss} &= \frac{CF_1}{(1 + r_1)^1} + \frac{CF_1}{(1 + r_1)^1} + \frac{CF_2}{(1 + r_2)^2} + \ldots + \frac{CF_{10}}{(1 + r_{10})^{10}} \\ &= \frac{37\ 000}{(1 + 2.5\%)^1} + \frac{37\ 000}{(1 + 2.8\%)^2} + \ldots + \frac{37\ 000}{(1 + 3.5\%)^{10}} = 310,900 \end{aligned}$$

The loss can be understood as a bank's cost in a situation when a counterparty (such as a corporate client or other banks) would terminate a swap contract. As a result, the Bank would have to conclude a new contract as of December 31, 2005, but at a lower rate (3.5% instead of the original 7.2% as of December 31, 2000). The total loss for the bank discounted as of December 31, 2015, arising from the swap contract termination amounted to CZK 310,900 over the 10-year period, which corresponds to a high volume since it is 31.09% of the nominal value of the loan.

9.4 Empirical Part

In this section, we provide the quantification of the impact of early repayment of a mortgage on three types of banks with different costs of funding. First, we provide a model of banks' portfolios without mortgage prepayment and then a model with mortgage prepayment. We distinguish three different periods of decreasing interest rates (2006–2011), low interest rates (2012–2017), and increasing interest rates (2017–2020).

9.4.1 Modeling Periods

9.4.1.1 Decreasing Interest Rates (2006–2011)

The period 2006–2011 is, in our paper, considered a time of decreasing interest rate, although during the years 2006–2008, the rates were in fact increasing, as shown in Fig. 9.4. However, in 2008, they started to drop quickly due to the global financial crisis. For a detailed analysis of the performance of the Czech banking sector in this period, we refer to Černohorská et al. (2017) or Palečková (2017).

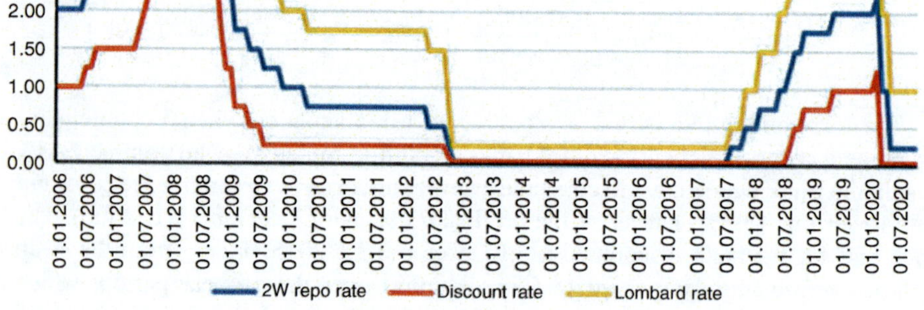

Fig. 9.4 CNB policy rates in 2006–2020. (Source: Authors based on CNB data)

9.4.1.2 Low Interest Rates (2012–2017)

The Czech banking sector is stable and well-capitalized and reports a liquidity surplus (CNB, 2017). In the years 2012–2017, the Czech National Bank (CNB) was keeping key interest rates technically at the zero level. The risk of early repayment of mortgages can be therefore significant, yet this risk is somewhat offset by long-term fixed mortgages granted before 2012, i.e., in periods of relatively higher interest rates. Moreover, this phenomenon can fully materialize in the next economic cycle.

CNB (2015) presented in its Financial Stability Report analysis of new mortgage loans, which distinguished between the totally new, refinanced, and refixed loans within the overall volume of new mortgage loans. It reported four groups of new mortgages as of March 1, 2015. First, 43% of the total volume was new loans. Second, 35% of the total loans were concluded with the new interest rate on the outstanding portion of the loan with the same financial service provider (refixed loans). Third, 14% of the total loans have been negotiated on the unpaid principal of the loan with the new provider (refinanced loans). Fourth, the remaining 8% share were mortgages with an increased principal. CNB (2015) further states that the largest increase in lending was recorded by small banks, namely, by more than 80%. It can be attributed to the fact that small banks most significantly compress the interest rate compared to other types of banks, and they were attracting clients to refinance their loans.

Moreover, CNB expected in 2017 that "Interest income can be expected to be adversely affected for some time to come by refixation and refinancing of mortgage loans, which will cause the average interest margin on the stock of such loans to move closer to that on new loans, which is significantly lower" (CNB, 2017).

9.4.1.3 Increasing Interest Rates (2017–2020)

The last considered period begins in 2017 when the CNB ended its unconventional monetary policy of exchange rate commitment and then started increasing its policy rates in a relatively fast way. This continued until the beginning of 2020 when CNB changed the course again due to the outbreak of the Covid-19 pandemic and decreased the policy rates in two steps to 0.25% from its peak of 2.25% in February 2020.

Due to the protracted Covid-19 pandemic situation continuing in 2021, the future development of monetary policy and market interest rates is rather uncertain. There are two main possible scenarios—that the rates will either remain low for a longer time (a situation resembling the period 2012–2017) or that the rates will start to go up similarly as in the period 2017–2020. Therefore, it is relevant to consider both periods as a model situation for both possible future scenarios.

9.4.2 *Results of Theoretical Modeling in the 2011–2016 Period*

9.4.2.1 Theoretical Modeling (Without Mortgage Prepayment)

Table 9.1 displays the banks' financing costs for the 2016–2021 period, assuming constant annual funding costs of 1.25% since 2016.[4] It is clear that the funding costs fall over time due to a decrease in market rates (from 1.73% at the end of 2016 to 1.25% at the end of 2021). In the calculations below, for simplicity, we assume a flat yield curve (for example, in 2012, the assumed interest rate for all maturities amounts to 2.0%, in 2013 to 1.75%, etc.). We also incorporate in the calculations a 5-year mortgage fixation, i.e., that only a portion of the banking portfolio is fixed each year. Specifically, 10% of mortgages are fixed in 2016, 20% of mortgages are fixed in 2017, and so on. Based on such an approximation, it is possible to obtain the average financing costs for the given years:

$$r_p = \sum_{t=1}^{T} r_t * w_t$$

where

r_p = average funding costs of the Bank in a given year
r_t = interest rate in a given year
w_t = weight in portfolio (share of fixed mortgages in a given year)
t = given year
T = end of the period

For the year rate r_p it holds that is equal to the weighted average of the applicable rate in the given year and its weight in the portfolio. After computations, the average rate $r_{2011-2016}$ for the 2011–2016 period reached 1.73%:

$$\begin{aligned} r_{2011-2016} &= r_{2011} * w_{2011} + r_{2012} * w_{2012} + \ldots + r_{2016} * w_{2016} \\ &= 2.00\% * 10\% + 2.00\% * 20\% + \ldots + 1.25\% * 10\% = 1.73\% \end{aligned}$$

9.4.3 *Theoretical Modeling (with Mortgage Prepayment)*

In our models, three types of banks have been created, each with a different funding structure.[5] The benchmark is Bank 1, which cuts its financing costs from 2% in 2011

[4]These are real-time expert estimates.

[5]This is an illustrative example of an analysis of different levels of risk from different banks, which is reflected in the cost of financing. Assuming the same risk, banks should theoretically have the same financing costs (i.e. the possibility of financing for the same market yield curve). The only difference is in the yield curve (riskier banks should pay more upward on the credit margin). The increase and fall in interest rates on the market would then be the same for all banks, it would be a parallel shift in the yield curve.

Table 9.1 Funding costs of the Bank for the 2016–2021 period

Year	Interest rate	2016	2017	2018	2019	2020	2021
2011	2.00%	10%					
2012	2.00%	20%	10%				
2013	1.75%	20%	20%	10%			
2014	1.75%	20%	20%	20%	10%		
2015	1.50%	20%	20%	20%	20%	10%	
2016	1.25%	10%	20%	20%	20%	20%	10%
2017	1.25%		10%	20%	20%	20%	20%
2018	1.25%			10%	20%	20%	20%
2019	1.25%				10%	20%	20%
2020	1.25%					10%	20%
2021	1.25%						10%
Funding costs		**1.73%**	**1.58%**	**1.45%**	**1.35%**	**1.28%**	**1.25%**

Source: Authors
Note: We assume that interest rates reached the minimum in 2016 and will not decrease afterward

Table 9.2 Funding costs of Bank 1, Bank 2, and Bank 3 for the 2011–2016 period

	Funding costs		
Year	Bank 1	Bank 2	Bank 3
2011	2.00%	3.00%	4.00%
2012	2.00%	3.00%	4.00%
2013	1.75%	2.63%	3.50%
2014	1.75%	2.63%	3.50%
2015	1.50%	2.25%	3.00%
2016	1.25%	1.88%	2.50%

Source: Authors

to 1.25% in 2016. Bank 2 in this period reports 1.5 times the rates of Bank 1, while Bank 3 has its funding at 2 times the rates of Bank 1 (Table 9.2).

Table 9.3 summarizes the results of modeling the impact of early repayment of mortgages on Bank 1 income and a 20% share of prepaid mortgages,[6] according to which the accumulated loss on the Bank's interest income would reach 0.27% at the end of 2021.

Table 9.4 shows the results of modeling the impact of early repayment of mortgages on Bank 3's income and a 20% share of prepaid mortgages. It displays that the cumulative loss on Bank 3's interest income would reach 0.53% at the end of 2021 (0.16% by 2017), which may be a significant loss for this type of bank.[7]

[6]The Czech consumer credit law approved in 2016 allows the client to prepay up to 25% of the mortgage a year free of charge. However, we do not expect that the 25% ratio would have materialized, so provide a robust scenario analysis for 10%, 20%, and 50% shares of prepaid mortgages.

[7]For comparison, Wüstenrot Mortgage Bank a.s., a small Czech bank, reported an overall interest margin of 1.79% as of December 31, 2014. The computed 0.53% loss would represent 29.6% of the 1.79% total margin. Overall, the net interest rate margin of the Czech banking sector fell down from 2.48% as of 31 December 2008 to 1.53% as of 30 September 2020 (i.e. a 37.3% decrease, see Fig. 9.5).

Table 9.3 Impact of early repayment of mortgages on the Bank's income (Bank 1, 20% share of prepaid mortgages)

Bank 1						Calculated loss					
Year	Interest rate	Structure of funding costs in 2016	Ratio of prepaid mortgages	Volume	Difference	2016	2017	2018	2019	2020	2021
2011	2.00%	10%	20%	2.00%	0.75%	0.02%					
2012	2.00%	20%	20%	4.00%	0.75%	0.03%	0.03%				
2013	1.75%	20%	20%	4.00%	0.50%	0.02%	0.02%	0.02%			
2014	1.75%	20%	20%	4.00%	0.50%	0.02%	0.02%	0.02%	0.02%		
2015	1.50%	20%	20%	4.00%	0.25%	0.01%	0.01%	0.01%	0.01%	0.01%	
2016	1.25%	10%	20%	2.00%	0.00%	0.00%	0.00%	0.00%	0.00%	0.00%	0.00%
Loss in a given year						**0.10%**	**0.08%**	**0.05%**	**0.03%**	**0.01%**	**0.00%**
Cumulative loss for the whole period						**0.10%**	**0.18%**	**0.23%**	**0.26%**	**0.27%**	**0.27%**

Source: Authors

Table 9.4 Impact of early repayment of mortgages on the Bank's income (Bank 3, 20% share of prepaid mortgages)

Bank 3						Calculated loss					
Year	Interest rate	Structure of funding costs in 2016	Ratio of prepaid mortgages	Volume	Difference	2016	2017	2018	2019	2020	2021
2011	4.00%	10%	20%	2.00%	1.50%	0.03%					
2012	4.00%	20%	20%	4.00%	1.50%	0.06%	0.06%				
2013	3.50%	20%	20%	4.00%	1.00%	0.04%	0.04%	0.04%			
2014	3.50%	20%	20%	4.00%	1.00%	0.04%	0.04%	0.04%	0.04%		
2015	3.00%	20%	20%	4.00%	0.50%	0.02%	0.02%	0.02%	0.02%	0.02%	
2016	2.50%	10%	20%	2.00%	0.00%	0.00%	0.00%	0.00%	0.00%	0.00%	0.00%
Loss in a given year						**0.19%**	**0.16%**	**0.10%**	**0.06%**	**0.02%**	**0.00%**
Cumulative loss for the whole period						**0.19%**	**0.35%**	**0.45%**	**0.51%**	**0.53%**	**0.53%**

Source: Authors

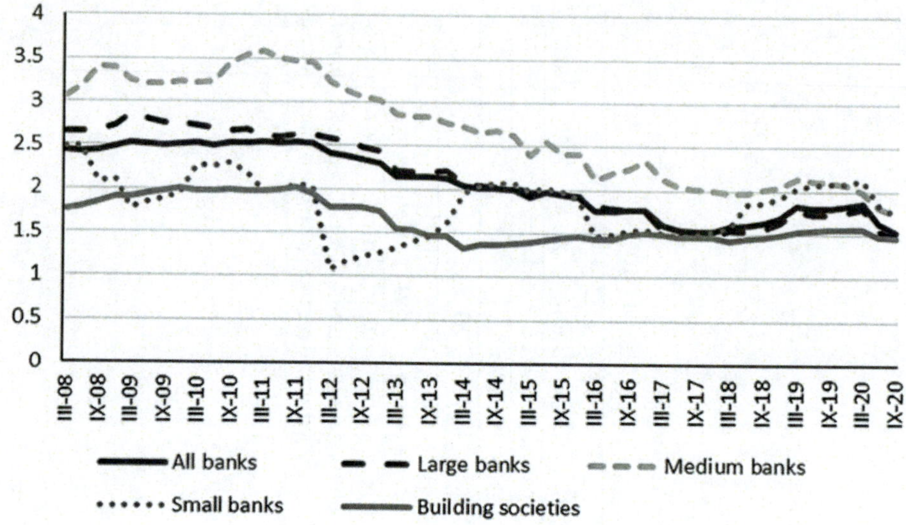

Fig. 9.5 Quarterly development of net interest margin of Czech banks (%). (Source: Authors based on CNB data)

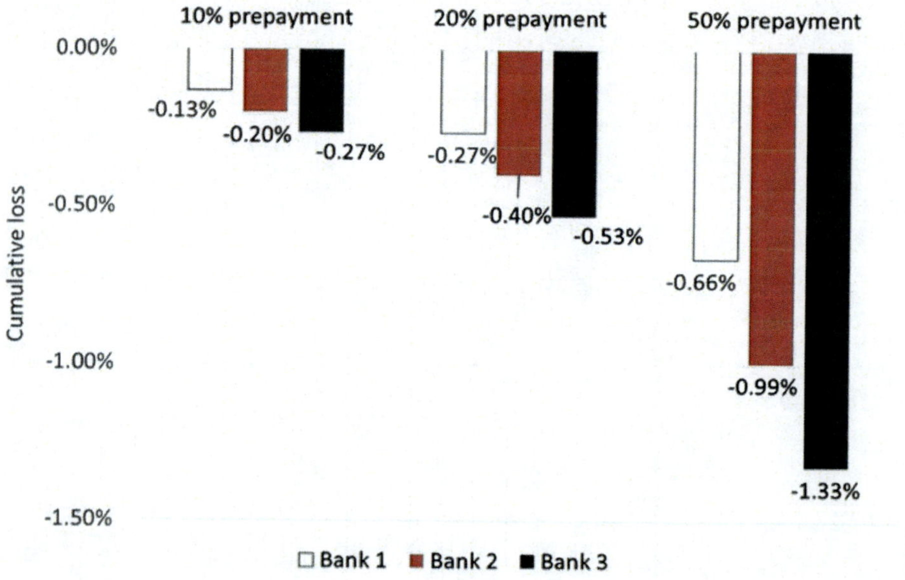

Fig. 9.6 The impact of early repayment of mortgages on the income of Banks 1, 2, and 3 for different ratios of early repayments (10%, 20%, 50%) in the period 2016–2021. (Source: Authors)

Figure 9.6 illustrates the impact of early repayment of mortgages on the returns of Banks 1, 2, and 3 for the various proportions of early repayment mortgages (10%, 20%, 50%) for the period 2016–2021. It is clear that different types of banks have different impacts, which are generally linear. The results show that, in the extreme case, Bank 3, at 50% early repayment, could accumulate a loss in interest rate margin of 1.33% in the period 2016–2021.

9.4.3.1 Empirical Modeling (Without Mortgage Prepayment)

The above theoretical modeling can be verified by empirical analysis. Looking at the history of interest rates in the Czech Republic over the period 2000–2020, we find that the largest drops in rates were recorded in the 2001–2006 period, when the 1-year Prague Interbank Offered Rate (PRIBOR) dropped from 5.85% to 2.55% (Table 9.5), and in 2008–2013, when the 1Y PRIBOR dropped from 4.24% to 0.87% (Table 9.6). On the other hand, in the period 2017–2020, the 1Y PRIBOR experienced a period of relatively fast increase (Table 9.8). In such a case, the banks could theoretically gain from prepayments by reinvesting the cash from prepaid mortgages into new mortgages with higher rates. On the other hand, these gains may be limited by lower incentives for the clients to repay their mortgages.

By applying the abovementioned market rates and assuming a 20% prepayment of mortgages, it can be calculated that the total cumulative expected loss would be 0.24% in the period 2001–2006 (Table 9.5) and, respectively, 0.78% in the 2008–2013 period (Table 9.6).

In Table 9.7, we present results for the period 2011–2016, i.e., a period in which the rates were already very low and decreased only modestly toward the zero lower bound. Finally, Table 9.8 shows results for the period 2016–2020, during which the rates started to rise. Assuming a constant rate of prepayment, we can see that in such a case, the cumulative expected loss becomes negative; that is, the bank experiences a gain in margin of 0.65 percentage points.

9.5 Conclusion

In this paper, we deal with prepayment risks in banking and provide empirical evidence from the Czech banking sector. The prepayment risk of a loan represents an embedded option for a client to refinance his mortgage for a lower interest rate. The client may have an incentive to repay the remaining amount of the loan before its maturity, especially in case he can refinance the loan with a new loan with a lower interest rate. Conversely, it holds that the client's profit means a loss to the bank as a mortgage provider. In the empirical part, our analysis quantifies the impact of early repayment of the mortgage on the balance sheets of different types of banks, which differ in the structure of their financing. In particular, the effect of prepaying mortgages on the interest margins of model banks was examined. Our results show that this effect could become significant, especially in the decreasing interest rate environment, when the clients have incentives to repay their existing mortgage with a higher rate with a new one with a lower rate. On the contrary, in the period of increasing interest rates, the bank could gain on the prepayments if they are able to

Table 9.5 Loss of bank income based on actual 1Y PRIBOR market rates in 2001–2006

						Calculated loss					
Year	Market interest rate (1Y PRIBOR)	Structure of funding costs in 2016	Ratio of prepaid mortgages	Volume	Difference	2006	2007	2008	2009	2010	2011
2001	5.85%	10%	20%	2.00%	3.30%	0.07%					
2002	4.47%	20%	20%	4.00%	1.92%	0.08%	0.08%				
2003	2.54%	20%	20%	4.00%	−0.01%	0.00%	0.00%	0.00%			
2004	2.35%	20%	20%	4.00%	−0.20%	−0.01%	−0.01%	−0.01%	−0.01%		
2005	2.81%	20%	20%	4.00%	0.26%	0.01%	0.01%	0.01%	0.01%	0.01%	
2006	2.55%	10%	20%	2.00%	0.00%	0.00%	0.00%	0.00%	0.00%	0.00%	0.00%
Loss in a given year						**0.14%**	**0.08%**	**0.00%**	**0.00%**	**0.01%**	**0.00%**
Cumulative loss for the whole period						**0.14%**	**0.22%**	**0.23%**	**0.23%**	**0.24%**	**0.24%**

Source: Authors

Table 9.6 Loss of bank income based on real 1Y PRIBOR market rates in 2008–2013

						Calculated loss					
Year	Market interest rate (1Y PRIBOR)	Structure of funding costs in 2016	Ratio of prepaid mortgages	Volume	Difference	2013	2014	2015	2016	2017	2018
2008	4.24%	10%	20%	2.00%	3.37%	0.07%					
2009	3.89%	20%	20%	4.00%	3.02%	0.12%	0.12%				
2010	2.13%	20%	20%	4.00%	1.26%	0.05%	0.05%	0.05%			
2011	1.80%	20%	20%	4.00%	0.93%	0.04%	0.04%	0.04%	0.04%		
2012	1.72%	20%	20%	4.00%	0.85%	0.03%	0.03%	0.03%	0.03%	0.03%	
2013	0.87%	10%	20%	2.00%	0.00%	0.00%	0.00%	0.00%	0.00%	0.00%	0.00%
Loss in a given year						**0.31%**	**0.24%**	**0.12%**	**0.07%**	**0.03%**	**0.00%**
Cumulative loss for the whole period						**0.31%**	**0.55%**	**0.67%**	**0.75%**	**0.78%**	**0.78%**

Source: Authors

Table 9.7 Loss of bank income based on real 1Y PRIBOR market rates in 2011–2016

						Calculated loss					
Year	Market interest rate (1Y PRIBOR)	Structure of funding costs in 2016	Ratio of prepaid mortgages	Volume	Difference	2016	2017	2018	2019	2020	2021
2011	1.80%	10%	20%	2.00%	1.34%	0.03%					
2012	1.72%	20%	20%	4.00%	1.26%	0.05%	0.05%				
2013	0.87%	20%	20%	4.00%	0.41%	0.02%	0.02%	0.02%			
2014	0.60%	20%	20%	4.00%	0.14%	0.01%	0.01%	0.01%	0.01%		
2015	0.51%	20%	20%	4.00%	0.05%	0.00%	0.00%	0.00%	0.00%	0.00%	
2016	0.46%	10%	20%	2.00%	0.00%	0.00%	0.00%	0.00%	0.00%	0.00%	0.00%
Loss in a given year						**0.10%**	**0.07%**	**0.02%**	**0.01%**	**0.00%**	**0.00%**
Cumulative loss for the whole period						**0.10%**	**0.18%**	**0.20%**	**0.21%**	**0.21%**	**0.21%**

Source: Authors

Table 9.8 Loss of bank income based on real 1Y PRIBOR market rates in 2015–2020

						Calculated loss					
Year	Market interest rate (1Y PRIBOR)	Structure of funding costs in 2016	Ratio of prepaid mortgages	Volume	Difference	2020	2021	2022	2023	2024	2025
2015	0.51%	10%	20%	2.00%	−1.76%	−0.04%					
2016	0.46%	20%	20%	4.00%	−1.81%	−0.07%	−0.07%				
2017	0.44%	20%	20%	4.00%	−1.83%	−0.07%	−0.07%	−0.07%			
2018	0.97%	20%	20%	4.00%	−1.30%	−0.05%	−0.05%	−0.05%	−0.05%		
2019	2.07%	20%	20%	4.00%	−0.21%	−0.01%	−0.01%	−0.01%	−0.01%	−0.01%	
2020	2.27%	10%	20%	2.00%	0.00%	0.00%	0.00%	0.00%	0.00%	0.00%	0.00%
Loss in a given year						**−0.24%**	**−0.21%**	**−0.13%**	**−0.06%**	**−0.01%**	**0.00%**
Cumulative loss for the whole period						**−0.24%**	**−0.45%**	**−0.58%**	**−0.64%**	**−0.65%**	**-0.65%**

Source: Authors

provide new loans for the higher rates, but at the same time, the prepayment risk decreases due to lower incentives for clients to prepay.

The prepayment risk was strengthened by the Czech consumer credit law approved in 2016, which allows the client to prepay up to 25% of the mortgage a year free of charge. Based on our model, we compute the impact of early repayment of the mortgage on the balance sheets of three different types of banks. The results of theoretical modeling have shown that these risks forced by banks might have a substantial effect, and they are likely to be one of the factors contributing to the decreasing net interest margin of the Czech banking sector in the 2019–2020 period. However, the prepayment risk in the Czech Republic decreased when interest rates started to rise in 2021.

Acknowledgments This research was supported by the Czech Science Foundation (Project No. 20-00178S) and Prague University of Economics and Business (Project No. VŠE IP100040).

References

Ambrose, B. W., & LaCour-Little, M. (2001). Prepayment risk in adjustable rate mortgages subject to initial year discounts: Some new evidence. *Real Estate Economics, 29*(2), 305–327.

Becketti, S. (1988). *The prepayment risk of mortgage-backed securities*. Federal Reserve.

Černohorská, L., Pilyavskyy, A., & Aaronson, W. (2017). Comparative performance of the Visegrad Group Banks For the Period 2009–2013. *E+M Ekonomie a Management, 2*, 175–187.

Chernov, M., Dunn, B. R., & Longstaff, F. A. (2018). Macroeconomic-driven prepayment risk and the valuation of mortgage-backed securities. *The Review of Financial Studies, 31*(3), 1132–1183.

Choudhry, M. (2018). *The Moorad Choudhry Anthology: Past, Present and Future Principles of Banking and Finance*. Wiley.

CNB. (2015). *Financial Stability Report 2014/2015*. The Czech National Bank. Available: http://www.cnb.cz/en/financial_stability/fs_reports/fsr_2014-2015/index.html

CNB. (2017). *Financial Stability Report 2016/2017*. The Czech National Bank. Available: http://www.cnb.cz/en/financial_stability/fs_reports/fsr_2016-2017/index.html

Džmuráňová, H., & Teplý, P. (2016). Why are savings accounts perceived as risky bank products? *Prague Economic Papers, 25*(5), 617–633.

Fabozzi, F. J. (2004). *Bond markets, analysis, and strategies* (5th ed.). Pearson Prentice Hall. ISBN: 0-13-049782-7.

Fabozzi, F. J. (2015). *Bond markets, analysis, and strategies* (9th ed.). Pearson Prentice Hall.

Hayre, L., & Young, R. (2004). Guide to mortgage-backed securities. *Citigroup White Paper*.

Horváth, R., & Teplý, P. (2013). Risk management of building societies in the Czech Republic. *Journal of Economics/Ekonomicky casopis, 61*(1), 24–46.

Kau, J. B., Keenan, D. C., Muller, W. J., & Epperson, J. F. (1992). A generalized valuation model for fixed-rate residential mortgages. *Journal of Money, Credit and Banking, 24*(3), 279–299.

Levin, A., & Davidson, A. (2005). Prepayment risk-and option-adjusted valuation of MBS. *The Journal of Portfolio Management, 31*(4), 73–85.

Mayer, C., Pence, K., & Sherlund, S. M. (2009). The rise in mortgage defaults. *Journal of Economic perspectives, 23*(1), 27–50.

Palečková, I. (2017). Efficiency change of banking sectors and banks in the financial conglomerates in Visegrad Group Countries. *Ekonomický časopis, 65*(1), 79–92.

Chapter 10
Determinants of Capital Structure: The Case of Chinese Technology Firms

Mohamad Kaakeh and Korhan K. Gokmenoglu

Abstract This research addresses the effects of firm-specific factors on the formation of capital structure in the case of the Chinese technology sector. Also, it aims to shed light on whether the key drivers of capital structure in China are different from those in western countries. To this aim, we analyzed the annual balanced panel data of 460 companies for the period 2007–2017 by means of the structural equation modeling approach. Empirical findings demonstrated that size, financial cost, liquidity, tangibility, profitability, and nondebt tax shields have a significant impact on the leverage structure of Chinese technology firms. Obtained results provide evidence of partial similarities between western countries and China in the determinants of capital structure. Besides, we detected that both trade-off and pecking order theories partially explain the leverage structure decisions of firms in the Chinese technology sector.

Key words Capital structure · Technology sector · Structural equation modeling · China

10.1 Introduction

The critical drivers of corporate capital structures have been studied extensively, both theoretically and empirically. Two competing financial models stand out in terms of theoretical explanation. The trade-off theory suggests that the company has to find the optimal mixture of debt and equity where benefits from tax shields on debts are equal to the financial distress faced when a company is under external financing, alongside agency costs (Jensen & Meckling, 1976). Alternatively, the

M. Kaakeh
Department of Banking and Finance, Eastern Mediterranean University, Famagusta, North Cyprus via Mersin 10, Turkey
e-mail: mohamad.kaakeh@emu.edu.tr

K. K. Gokmenoglu (✉)
Department of Finance and Banking, Ankara HBV University, Ankara, Turkey
e-mail: korhan.gokmenoglu@hbv.edu.tr

D. Procházka (ed.), *Regulation of Finance and Accounting*, Springer Proceedings in Business and Economics, https://doi.org/10.1007/978-3-030-99873-8_10

pecking order theory suggests that the choice of financing should start from retained earnings when possible. When retained earnings are not sufficient, external financing should be sought, first by increasing their debt and finally by issuing new equity (Myers & Majluf, 1984). Also, ever since the seminal article by Miller and Modigliani (MM) (1958), there has been a great deal of empirical research on the subject. However, empirical researchers examining the determinants of capital structure have reached mixed results (Sheikh & Wang, 2011); hence, a thorough understanding of the critical drivers of companies' capital structures is still elusive (Brealey et al., 2012). Moreover, prior research generally examined the case of developed countries, paying less attention to the case of developing and transition ones (Chang et al., 2014). For the reasons stated, this paper empirically explores the determinants of the capital structure of Chinese technology firms and evaluates the relevance of theoretical explanations.

Even though the bulk of capital structure literature has concentrated on developed economies, in recent years, capital structure research has become more internationalized. Literature provides evidence that there are differences between the determinants of capital structure in developing and developed countries, and various reasons have been put forward to explain them. First, accounting and auditing standards in developing countries are lax, suggesting that asymmetric information is a more prevalent problem for these countries compared to developed ones (Tong & Green, 2005). Second, numerous companies in developing countries are state-owned enterprises and have different financial goals and strategies. Finally, capital markets of developing and emerging economies are less developed, and commonly, these economies have more financial constraints and a more limited variety of financial instruments than developed ones.

To investigate the determinants of capital structure, we chose China as our sample country, given that it is one of the leading economies in the world. China currently is the world's second-largest economy and the largest emerging market (IMF, 2018). It has been the world's fastest-growing economy, with a growth rate averaging around 10% for the past 30 years (World Economic Outlook, 2018). The country has the world's fastest-growing consumer market and is the biggest exporter of goods (National Bureau of Statistics of China, 2018). Its rapidly developing capital market is progressively giving access to international investors and global companies. In addition, China has quite different characteristics in terms of its concentration of ownership and institutional structure. Generally, the biggest shareholder holds around 36% of a company share, while the other five biggest owners hold about 52% of shares (Guo et al., 2013). Moreover, 38.8% of the total assets of China belong to government-owned enterprises (China Statistical Yearbook, 2016). For the abovementioned reasons, China is an interesting case study to explore the drivers of capital structure.

In this study, in which we examine the corporate capital structures of companies, our focus on technology companies is based on several reasons. China's plan of "made in China 2025" aims to secure its position as a global powerhouse in high-tech industries and focuses on replacing China's dependency on foreign technology imports with domestically made products. Under the plan, China wants to supply

70% of the domestic robotics market and provide all the needs of the domestic mobile communication equipment market (UN Comtrade Database, 2019). The involvement of technology among Chinese businesses is proliferating. The majority of the companies are heavily investing in technology, increasing the growth of technology providers in China (Institute for Security and Development Policy, 2019). The value added of the high-tech industry increased by 11.7% in 2017 and 8.1% in 2018, while the technology hardware sector rose by 13.1% in 2018, which is higher than the overall manufacturing industry. Furthermore, technology-related companies are known to have the least tangible assets in their facilities compared to other sectors (Colombo & Grilli, 2007), which may offer different insights into the determinants of financial leverage.

The basic approach used in previous studies is to estimate models with proxies for theoretical determinants of capital structure by ordinary least squares (OLS) regression. This approach has several limitations. First, there might be more than one proxy to represent a variable. Thus, researchers might be tempted to use the proxy that gives the best results in terms of goodness of fit criteria. This practice causes the results to be misleading. Second, a proxy might measure more than one variable and not be specific to the variable that the researcher desires to measure. Third, a single proxy might not be sufficient to measure a theoretical determinant of capital structure. Finally, it is possible to encounter errors in variables when using these proxies (Maddala & Nimalendran, 1996). To overcome these problems in our research, we use the structural equation modeling (SEM) approach. SEM would help us tackle various issues, most importantly, the measurement of the latent variable. Additionally, SEM can manage several dependent variables. Regarding independent variables, SEM makes it possible for several observable variables to act as indicators of the latent variable while at the same time not causing multicollinearity issues. Although many empirical papers represent profitability using a single proxy, Joo and Hussanie (2017) mentioned that there is no consensus in the literature on the best measure of profitability. Consequently, we treat profitability as a latent variable and use three variables—return on sales (ROS), return on equity (ROE), and net income—to represent this variable in the present study.

10.2 Literature Review

Several pioneering papers set the theoretical framework for the determinants of capital structure (Jensen & Meckling, 1976; Miller & Modigliani, 1958). Among these theories, the trade-off theory and the pecking order theory are the ones that have been paid the most attention. The ongoing discussion on the relevancy of each theoretical framework triggered the interest to empirically examine the determinants of capital structure. While many empirical papers supported the trade-off theory (Banga & Gupta, 2017; Sardo & Serrasqueiro, 2017), others found evidence of the validity of the pecking order theory (Nunes & Serrasqueiro, 2017; Pacheco, 2016; Sardo & Serrasqueiro, 2017). However, despite the volume of empirical work done on the determinants of capital structure, the results of empirical studies are still away from reaching a consensus (Vo, 2017).

Empirical research on capital structure determinants concentrates on developed economies and reports mixed results (Drobetz et al., 2013; Guida & Sabato, 2017; Garcia-Rodriguez & Jegers, 2017; Li & Islam, 2019; Li & Singal, 2019; Macnamara, 2019; Michaelas et al., 1999; Moradi & Paulet, 2019). Michaelas et al. (1999) examined the capital structure of small and medium-sized enterprises in the United Kingdom. The authors showed that size, profitability, growth, asset structure, net debtors, and operational risk are key determinants of capital structure. Drobetz et al. (2013) found that tangibility, profitability, operating leverage, and asset risk are the main determinants of capital structure in the case of shipping firms in the G7 countries. Moradi and Paulet (2019) investigated the case of European firms before and after the euro crisis. They concluded that the main drivers of their choice of financial leverage are size, tangibility, nondebt tax shield, growth, profitability, and earnings volatility.

Developing economies have different structural characteristics from developed ones. This difference has been a source of motivation for researchers over the past two decades to examine the choice of capital structure in emerging economies (Alnori & Alqahtani, 2019; Belkhir et al., 2016; Fattouh et al., 2005; Gombola et al., 2019; Khémiri & Noubbigh, 2018; Sheikh & Wang, 2011). Fattouh et al. (2005) utilized the quantile regression analysis to examine the choice of capital leverage in the case of South Korean companies. Results showed that size, profitability, depreciation, tangibility, and growth have a significant relationship with the level of debt in the selected sample. Karadeniz et al. (2009) found that neither the pecking order theory nor the trade-off theory fully explains the capital structure of Turkish lodging companies. Belkhir et al. (2016) examined the firm and country factors influencing capital structure in the case of ten Middle East and North Africa (MENA) countries. The authors found that significant firm-level factors affecting corporations' capital structure are consistent with both the pecking order theory and the trade-off theory.

As China is the most important emerging market globally, researchers have been interested in examining the choice of capital structure of Chinese firms. Chen (2004) argued that neither the trade-off theory nor the pecking order theory could fully explain the debt levels in the selected sample. Huang (2006) noted that firm size and fixed assets are positively related to the level of leverage, while profitability, depreciation, and growth opportunities have a negative relationship with the debt levels of Chinese firms. Zezhong and Hong (2008) showed that the determinants of the choice of leverage of western firms, namely, profitability, size, tangibility, and growth, also affect the capital structure decisions of Chinese corporations. Chang et al. (2014) identified seven core determinants of capital structure in the case of A-share listed Chinese companies: profitability, state control, size, largest shareholder, industry leverage, and tangibility. Vijayakumaran and Vijayakumaran (2018) investigated the determinants of capital leverage for 1844 Chinese companies for the period 2003–2010. They found tangibility, volatility, profitability, firm age, and size as the main factors affecting the capital structure of these firms. Although the mentioned studies have contributed to academic knowledge significantly, their mixed results raise the need for additional research on the main drivers of capital structure for Chinese firms. In addition, Chinese technology companies deserve to be examined, specifically due to the unique structure of this sector.

10.3 Data

We analyzed a comprehensive data set of 460 Chinese companies. Our data set covers the 2007–2017 period. The sample was drawn from Thompson Reuters DataStream, and it includes publicly listed soft and hardware technology companies in China. Companies were chosen based on the size of their total assets, and the ones with missing observations were excluded. We measured leverage as the logarithmic form of total liabilities. The variables used in this study are summarized in Table 10.1.

10.3.1 Hypothesis Development

In the present study, we chose six potential determinants of capital structure based on the previous literature: size, profitability, liquidity, financial cost, tangibility, and nondebt tax shield.

According to the literature, firm size is one of the main factors affecting the firm's leverage policy. Many authors examined the effect of companies' size on their choice of debt-equity mixture and found a positive link between firm size and leverage (Bartoloni, 2013; Fattouh et al., 2005; Khémiri & Noubbigh, 2018; Lim, 2012; Michaelas et al., 1999; Ramli et al., 2019; Vijayakumaran & Vijayakumaran, 2018; Zezhong & Hong, 2008). According to the trade-off theory, sizable firms are expected to have higher debt capacity (Chen, 2004). Larger companies have the ability to attain economies of scale, undertake diversification, receive higher credit ratings, and have a lower probability of bankruptcy compared to smaller firms (Pinches & Mingo, 1973; Titman & Wessels, 1988). All these factors make it easier

Table 10.1 Description of variables

Variable	Proxy	Abbreviation
Leverage	Logarithmic form of total liabilities	LEV
Tangibility	Property, plant, and equipment/total assets	TAN
Liquidity	Current assets/current liabilities	LIQ
Financial cost	Interest expense/earnings before interest	FC
Profitability	Return on sales	ROS
	Return on equity	ROE
	Logarithmic form of net income	LNI
Size	Logarithmic form of total assets	S
Depreciation	Logarithmic form of depreciation, depletion, and amortization	DEP

for large companies to increase their debt levels. Therefore, we suggest the following hypothesis:

H1: Firm size positively influences the leverage choice of the firm.

The majority of researchers agree on the negative relationship between financial leverage and the profitability of corporations (Acaravci, 2014; Chang et al., 2014; Drobetz et al., 2013; Michaelas et al., 1999; Sheikh & Wang, 2011). Moradi and Paulet (2019) argued that profitable firms generate enough income to cover their financing needs; thus, they need a lower level of external debt. Moreover, less debt minimizes the financial distress and agency costs of the firms. Therefore, we hypothesize as follows:

H2: Higher profitability is associated with lower debt.

There is a considerable amount of empirical evidence that suggests a negative relationship between liquidity and the financial leverage of firms (Afza & Hussain, 2011; Sheikh & Wang, 2011). According to the pecking order theory, corporations with more liquidity decrease their external debt levels as their internal resources are sufficient to cover their financing needs (Deesomsak et al., 2004). Moreover, the agency cost increases if companies with high liquidity or free cash flow borrow heavily (Deesomsak et al., 2004). Also, high liquidity firms could minimize debt levels to decrease interest costs. Therefore, we expect a negative link between liquidity and leverage.

H3: Higher liquidity would induce lower leverage.

Financial cost is a crucial determinant of the choice of the amount of external financing. A higher interest rate is expected to cause firms to borrow less because of the increased cost of debt. Previous literature supported the negative relationship between financial cost and leverage (Lim, 2012; Sharma, 2018). However, China has a unique case as state-owned enterprises (SOEs) play a major role in the economy. It was estimated that 38.8% of the total industrial assets of China belong to state-owned enterprises (China Statistical Yearbook, 2016). The SOE sector, which is known to have less sensitivity to financial costs, has been the major driver of the increasing corporate debt, accounting for 88% of it in 2017 (Molnar & Lu, 2019). Although China has its peculiar conditions, following the existing literature, we form our a priori expectation through the following hypothesis:

H4: A negative relationship between financial costs and debt level is present.

Both the pecking order theory and the agency model predict a negative association between tangibility and the firms' debt level. Companies with fewer assets to be used as collateral suffer from higher agency costs (Grossman & Hart, 1982). Hence, the monitoring costs of managers are higher for the aforementioned firms. Therefore, these firms might voluntarily choose a higher leverage level to increase constraints on managers and limit agency costs (Drobetz & Fix, 2005). The pecking order theory suggests that companies with fewer tangible assets have a higher sensitivity to information asymmetry (Salawu & Agboola, 2008). Consequently, these companies would prefer to increase their debt levels rather than issue equity when in need of external financing (Harris & Raviv, 1991). In the light of these explanations, we hypothesize:

H5: Lower tangibility would imply higher leverage.

The trade-off theory suggests that interest expense can be used to gain tax benefits (Modigliani & Miller, 1958). Besides debt, the depreciation of fixed assets also offers tax deductions and, hence, can replace tax benefits from interest expense (DeAngelo & Masulis, 1980). Companies with high depreciation expenses often reduce debt levels because of the tax benefits offered by depreciation without any financial stress (Lim, 2012). Both Wald (1999) and Chen (2004) confirmed the significant negative effect of a nondebt tax shield (NTDS) on leverage levels. Our study hypothesizes a negative relationship between NTDS and leverage levels, as the constraints faced by Chinese firms when increasing external debt would motivate firms to choose NTDS over higher leverage:

H6: A higher nondebt tax shield would affect financial leverage negatively.

10.4 Model and Methodology

SEM is used to analyze the data in this study. SEM is an extension of the path analysis developed by Wright (1931). The model has two components, which are estimated simultaneously. The first part is the structural model, which can include both latent and observed variables to examine the link between these variables and the dependent variable. The second component is the measurement model, where unobserved (latent) variables are measured using observed measures. Joo and Hussanie (2017) claimed that there is no agreement on the best construct to represent profitability in academic research. Authors disagree on how to proxy profitability; some used return on assets (Ibrahim, 2017), while others used return on equity (Waleed et al., 2016). To overcome the problem mentioned above, we treat profitability as an unobserved variable. Profitability is measured by three components: return on equity, the logarithmic form of net income, and return on sales. Figure 10.1 represents measurement and structural models.

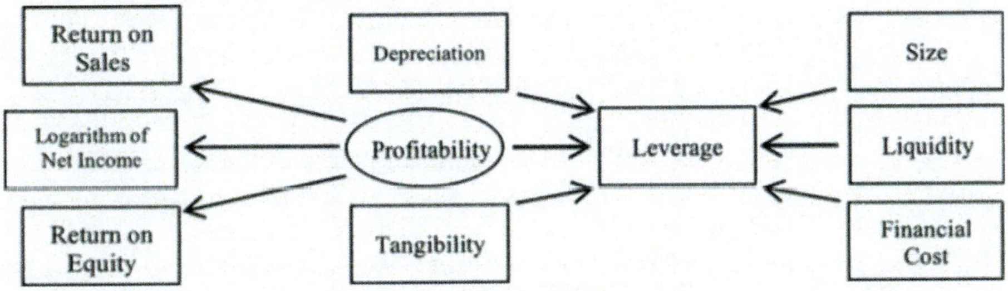

Fig. 10.1 Measurement and structural models

The choice of methodology was motivated by several reasons. First, SEM is a powerful multivariate technique that reveals all the possible relationships between variables (observed and/or latent), including both direct and indirect links. Second, SEM can accurately measure latent variables. Third, SEM can simultaneously estimate different models with different dependent variables.

10.5 Empirical Results and Discussion

Since we treat profitability as a latent variable in our model, the analysis has two stages. First, we measured the latent variable using three components: ROE, ROS, and the logarithmic form of net income. Table 10.2 presents the findings of the measurement model, which indicate that the three variables are measuring profitability efficiently as they have a 1% level of significance.

Second, to acquire the determinants of capital structure, we applied the structural model to the data set. Table 10.3 summarizes the unstandardized results for the second stage. Findings show that size has a highly significant positive coefficient, which is consistent with the notion of the trade-off theory. Large firms have more collateral, lower borrowing costs, and lower bankruptcy risk than small firms do. Thus, larger companies tend to acquire more leverage (Chen, 2004). This finding is compatible with those reported by Bartoloni (2013), Khémiri and Noubbigh (2018), Lim (2012), and Ramli et al. (2019), who also found a positive link between size and leverage. We detected a highly significant negative relationship between latent variable profitability and the leverage level of the firms in the sample. The result is in line with the predictions of the pecking order theory, which shows that

Table 10.2 Output of the measurement model

Variables	Coefficient	Z value
Log(net income) ← profitability	1	.
ROE ← profitability	.536*	10.66
ROS ← profitability	.460*	11.51

Source: Authors' analysis of data
Note: * denotes significance at 1% level

Table 10.3 Output of the structural model

Variables	Coefficient	Z value
Depreciation	−.097*	−19.69
Tangibility	−.127*	−9.27
Liquidity	−.088*	−52.84
Size	.983*	152.19
Financial cost	.126*	32.27
Profitability	−.043*	−4.12
Constant	−.149*	−7.63

Source: Authors' analysis of data
Note: * denotes significance at 1% level

higher profitability leads to higher retained earnings, a superior source of funding (Myers & Majluf, 1984). This finding is supported by many previous empirical research as well (Acaravci, 2014; Belkhir et al., 2016; Moradi & Paulet, 2019). Findings reveal that liquidity has a significant negative relationship with leverage. This result is compatible with the pecking order theory and is in line with the findings of previous literature (Afza & Hussain, 2011). According to the pecking order theory, firms with higher liquidity should use their own funds first instead of relying on external debt to lower agency costs. Moreover, these firms will require less external funding as they have less need to cover their finances due to the liquidity available in the firm.

The most interesting finding of our study is related to the financial cost for which we obtained a significant positive association with leverage. This unexpected finding also contradicts the findings of many existing studies. We can explain the positive relationship detected by considering the peculiar conditions of China and the characteristics of the analyzed period. Because many Chinese firms are established in the form of SOEs, some of their decisions can be different from those of the firms working under free-market conditions. In addition, the period covered by our sample is characterized by many large-scale financial events that put companies in a very difficult position. Chinese corporations and SOEs increased their debt levels to counteract the effects of the global financial crisis, the slackening in the economic performance of China, the worsening external conditions, and the slowing domestic demand in 2012 (Molnar & Lu, 2019). We can argue that debt costs were not a top priority for Chinese companies in this process.

Tangibility has a significant negative relationship with leverage, which is consistent with the predictions of the pecking order theory and agency model. Under the pecking order theory, information asymmetry increases with decreased tangibility, encouraging the management to accumulate debt (Harris & Raviv, 1991). In addition, the agency model suggests that firms with fewer assets are associated with higher agency costs. These firms might increase debt levels to increase constraints and control agency costs (Drobetz & Fix, 2005).

Depreciation measuring nondebt tax shields was found to have a negative relationship with the debt of the firm. When items other than interest expense on the income statement offer a tax shield, companies are less likely to borrow, and leverage would decrease. Doukas and Pantzalis (2003) suggested that more tax shields from sources other than interest expense would lower the need for external financing.

The robustness of the model was checked using the goodness of fit indicators, and the results are reported in Table 10.4. The root mean square error of approximation (RMSEA) is equal to 0.063. According to the criteria given by Hu and Bentler (1999), this value implies that the model is a reasonable fit. The comparative fit index (CFI) and the non-normed fit index (TLI) amount to the values of 0.993 and 0.985 for our model, respectively. Given the threshold of 0.95 (Hu & Bentler, 1999), these values indicate that the model is well fitted. The standardized root mean square residual (SRMR) is equal to 0.025, which is less than the 0.05 threshold value. This finding shows that the model is robust (Hu & Bentler, 1999).

Table 10.4 Goodness of fit measures

Name	Coefficient
Comparative fit index	0.993
Tucker-Lewis index	0.985
Coefficient of determination	0.997
Akaike's information criterion	32260.212
Bayesian information criterion	32393.145
RMSEA	0.063
SRMR	0.025

Source: Authors' analysis of data

10.6 Conclusion

This research investigates the determinants of capital structure in the case of the Chinese technology sector. In addition to its importance for the global economy, China has a unique institutional structure that affects firms' choices with regard to their capital structure. These factors make China an ideal environment for our research. We utilized SEM to analyze a new data set consisting of 460 Chinese technology companies over the period from 2007 to 2017. We considered six potential determinants of capital structure: size, profitability, tangibility, financial cost, liquidity, and nondebt tax shield. Since profitability has no agreed-upon proxy (Joo & Hussanie, 2017), the present study considered it a latent variable. The measurement model of SEM was used to determine the latent variable using three observed variables: return on equity, return on sales, and net income.

We obtained important empirical findings that imply relevant policy implications. First, we found that both the pecking order theory and the trade-off theory have a role in explaining the determinants of the capital structure of Chinese technology companies. Significant positive and negative coefficients of the firms' size and depreciation respectively provide support for the relevance of the trade-off theory. However, the negative link between liquidity and debt level offers evidence for the pecking order theory. However, the positive relationship between financial cost and leverage cannot be explained by any of these theories, and this unexpected finding reflects China's unique structural features and the conditions in the examined period. The positive relationship between debt levels and financial burden is due to the increased debt in SOEs to counteract the effects of the global financial crisis in 2009 and the decreased domestic demand and deterioration of external conditions in 2012. These findings reveal some important aspects of the Chinese technology sector and suggest some policy recommendations. The influencing factors of capital structure in China are mostly similar to that of western countries. This is because listed companies in China are the most successful practitioners of corporate governance in the country. This finding shows the profit-oriented tendency of Chinese companies, and regardless of state control over the companies, the firms mostly follow the market economy. For a better-functioning market mechanism, policymakers should provide suitable conditions to strengthen financial markets and limit government interventions in both financial intermediaries and firms. Moreover, financial constraints faced by Chinese corporations involving the issuance of new equity or the borrowing of external funding should be lifted for corporations to be able to choose the optimal capital structure.

References

Acaravci, S. K. (2014). The determinants of capital structure: Evidence from the Turkish manufacturing sector. *International Journal of Economics and Financial Issues, 5*(1), 158–171.

Afza, T., & Hussain, A. (2011). Determinants of capital structure across selected manufacturing sectors of Pakistan. *International Journal of Humanities and Social Science, 1*(12), 254–262.

Alnori, F., & Alqahtani, F. (2019). Capital structure and speed of adjustment in non-financial firms: Does sharia compliance matter? Evidence from Saudi Arabia. *Emerging Markets Review, 39*, 50–67.

Banga, C., & Gupta, A. (2017). Effect of firm characteristics on capital structure decisions of Indian SMEs. *International Journal of Applied Business and Economic Research, 15*(10), 281–301.

Bartoloni, E. (2013). Capital structure and innovation: Causality and determinants. *Empirica, 40*(1), 111–151.

Belkhir, M., Maghyereh, A., & Awartani, B. (2016). Institutions and corporate capital structure in the MENA region. *Emerging Markets Review, 26*, 99–129.

Brealey, R. A., Myers, S. C., Allen, F., & Mohanty, P. (2012). *Principles of corporate finance*. Tata McGraw-Hill Education.

Chang, C., Chen, X., & Liao, G. (2014). What are the reliably important determinants of capital structure in China? *Pacific-Basin Finance Journal, 30*, 87–113.

Chen, J. J. (2004). Determinants of capital structure of Chinese-listed companies. *Journal of Business Research, 57*(12), 1341–1351.

China Statistical Yearbook. (2016). Available via http://www.stats.gov.cn/tjsj/ndsj/2016/indexeh.htm. Accessed 15 Apr 2020.

Colombo, M. G., & Grilli, L. (2007). Funding gaps? Access to bank loans by high-tech start-ups. *Small Business Economics, 29*(1-2), 25–46.

DeAngelo, H., & Masulis, R. W. (1980). Optimal capital structure under corporate and personal taxation. *Journal of Financial Economics, 8*(1), 3–29.

Deesomsak, R., Paudyal, K., & Pescetto, G. (2004). The determinants of capital structure: Evidence from the Asia Pacific region. *Journal of Multinational Financial Management, 14*(4–5), 387–405.

Doukas, J. A., & Pantzalis, C. (2003). Geographic diversification and agency costs of debt of multinational firms. *Journal of Corporate Finance, 9*(1), 59–92.

Drobetz, W., & Fix, R. (2005). What are the determinants of the capital structure? Evidence from Switzerland. *Swiss Journal of Economics and Statistics (SJES), 141*(I), 71–113.

Drobetz, W., Gounopoulos, D., Merikas, A., & Schröder, H. (2013). Capital structure decisions of globally-listed shipping companies. *Transportation Research Part E: Logistics and Transportation Review, 52*, 49–76.

Fattouh, B., Scaramozzino, P., & Harris, L. (2005). Capital structure in South Korea: A quantile regression approach. *Journal of Development Economics, 76*(1), 231–250.

Garcia-Rodriguez, I., & Jegers, M. (2017). Capital structure of nongovernmental development organizations: First cross-country evidence. *Non-profit Management and Leadership, 28*(2), 175–194.

Gombola, M., Liu, F. Y., & Chou, D. W. (2019). Capital structure dynamics with restricted equity issuance: Evidence from Chinese post-IPO firms. *Asia Pacific Management Review, 24*(1), 72–85.

Grossman, S. J., & Hart, O. D. (1982). Corporate financial structure and managerial incentives. In *The economics of information and uncertainty*. University of Chicago Press.

Guida, R., & Sabato, V. (2017). Relationship lending and firms' leverage: Empirical evidence in Europe. *European Financial Management, 23*(4), 807–835.

Guo, L., Smallman, C., & Radford, J. (2013). A critique of corporate governance in China. *International Journal of Law and Management, 55*(4), 257–272.

Harris, M., & Raviv, A. (1991). The theory of capital structure. *The Journal of Finance, 46*(1), 297–355.

Hu, L. T., & Bentler, P. M. (1999). Cutoff criteria for fit indexes in covariance structure analysis: Conventional criteria versus new alternatives. *Structural Equation Modeling: A Multidisciplinary Journal, 6*(1), 1–55.

Huang, G. (2006). The determinants of capital structure: Evidence from China. *China Economic Review, 17*(1), 14–36.

Ibrahim, S. S. (2017). The impacts of liquidity on profitability in banking sectors of Iraq: A case of Iraqi commercial banks International. *Journal of Finance & Banking Studies, 6*(1), 113–121.

Institute for Security and Development Policy. (2019). Available via https://isdp.eu/content/uploads/2018/06/Made-in-China-Backgrounder.pdf. Accessed 15 Apr 2020.

International Monetary Funds. (2018). Available via https://www.imf.org/. Accessed 15 Apr 2020.

Jensen, M. C., & Meckling, W. H. (1976). Theory of the firm: Managerial behavior, agency costs and ownership structure. *Journal of Financial Economics, 3*(4), 305–360.

Joo, B. A., & Hussanie, I. (2017). Selecting the right variable as a proxy for profitability – A propitious beginning for researchers. *Journal of Arts, Science & Commerce, 8*(4), 80–95.

Karadeniz, E., Yilmaz Kandir, S., Balcilar, M., & Beyazit Onal, Y. (2009). Determinants of capital structure: Evidence from Turkish lodging companies. *International Journal of Contemporary Hospitality Management, 21*(5), 594–609.

Khémiri, W., & Noubbigh, H. (2018). Determinants of capital structure: Evidence from sub-Saharan African firms. *The Quarterly Review of Economics and Finance, 70*(4), 150–159.

Li, L., & Islam, S. Z. (2019). Firm and industry-specific determinants of capital structure: Evidence from the Australian Market International. *Review of Economics & Finance, 59*, 425–437.

Li, Y., & Singal, M. (2019). Capital structure in the hospitality industry: The role of the asset-light and fee-oriented strategy. *Tourism Management, 70*, 124–133.

Lim, T. C. (2012). Determinants of capital structure empirical evidence from financial services listed firms in China. *International Journal of Economics and Finance, 4*(3), 191–203.

Macnamara, P. (2019). Taxes and financial frictions: Implications for corporate capital structure. *Journal of Economic Dynamics and Control, 101*, 82–100.

Maddala, G. S., & Nimalendran, M. (1996). Errors-in-variables problems in financial models. *Handbook of Statistics, 14*, 507–528.

Michaelas, N., Chittenden, F., & Poutziouris, P. (1999). Financial policy and capital structure choice in UK SMEs: Empirical evidence from company panel data. *Small Business Economics, 12*(2), 113–130.

Miller, M., & Modigliani, F. (1958). The cost of capital corporate finance and the theory of investment. *American Economic Review, 48*, 261–297.

Modigliani, F., & Miller, M. H. (1958). The cost of capital, corporation finance and the theory of investment. *The American Economic Review, 48*(3), 261–297.

Molnar, M., & Lu, J. (2019). *State-owned firms behind China's corporate debt* (OECD Economic Department Working Papers (1536)) (pp. 1–49). OECD.

Moradi, A., & Paulet, E. (2019). The firm-specific determinants of capital structure – An empirical analysis of firms before and during the Euro crisis. *Research in International Business and Finance, 47*, 150–161.

Myers, S. C., & Majluf, N. S. (1984). Corporate financing and investment decisions when firms have information that investors do not have. *Journal of Financial Economics, 13*(2), 187–221.

National Bureau of Statistics of China. (2018). Available via http://www.stats.gov.cn/english/. Accessed 15 Apr 2020.

Nunes, P. M., & Serrasqueiro, Z. (2017). Short-term debt and long-term debt determinants in small and medium-sized hospitality firms. *Tourism Economics, 23*(3), 543–560.

Pacheco, L. (2016). Capital structure and internationalization: The case of Portuguese industrial SMEs. *Research in International Business and Finance, 38*, 531–545.

Pinches, G. E., & Mingo, K. A. (1973). A multivariate analysis of industrial bond ratings. *The Journal of Finance, 28*(1), 1–18.

Ramli, N. A., Latan, H., & Solovida, G. T. (2019). Determinants of capital structure and firm financial performance – A PLS-SEM approach: Evidence from Malaysia and Indonesia. *The Quarterly Review of Economics and Finance, 71*, 148–160.

Salawu, R. O., & Agboola, A. A. (2008). The determinants of capital structure of large non-financial listed firms in Nigeria. *The International Journal of Business and Finance Research, 2*(2), 75–84.

Sardo, F., & Serrasqueiro, Z. (2017). Does dynamic trade-off theory explain Portuguese SME capital structure decisions? *Journal of Small Business and Enterprise Development, 24*(3), 485–502.

Sharma, R. K. (2018). Factors affecting financial leveraging for BSE listed real estate development companies in India. *Journal of Financial Management of Property and Construction, 23*(3), 274–294.

Sheikh, A. N., & Wang, Z. (2011). Determinants of capital structure: An empirical study of firms in manufacturing industry of Pakistan. *Managerial Finance, 37*(2), 117–133.

Titman, S., & Wessels, R. (1988). The determinants of capital structure choice. *The Journal of Finance, 43*(1), 1–19.

Tong, G., & Green, C. J. (2005). Pecking order or trade-off hypothesis? Evidence on the capital structure of Chinese companies. *Applied economics, 37*(19), 2179–2189.

UN Comtrade Database. (2019). Available via https://comtrade.un.org/data/. Accessed 15 Apr 2020.

Vijayakumaran, S., & Vijayakumaran, R. (2018). The determinants of capital structure decisions: Evidence from Chinese listed companies. *Asian Journal of Finance and Accounting, 10*(2), 63–81.

Vo, X. V. (2017). Determinants of capital structure in emerging markets: Evidence from Vietnam. *Research in International Business and Finance, 40*, 105–113.

Wald, J. K. (1999). How firm characteristics affect capital structure: An international comparison. *Journal of Financial Research, 22*(2), 161–187.

Waleed, A., Pasha, A. T., & Akhtar, A. (2016). Exploring the impact of liquidity on profitability: Evidence from banking sector of Pakistan. *Journal of Internet Banking and Commerce, 21*(3), 1–12.

World Economic Outlook. (2018). Available via https://www.imf.org/external/pubs/ft/weo/2018/02/ weodata/indexaspx. Accessed 15 Apr 2020.

Wright, S. (1931). Evolution in Mendelian populations. *Genetics, 16*(2), 97–159.

Zezhong, X., & Hong, Z. (2008). The Determinants of capital structure and equity financing preference in listed Chinese companies. *[J] Economic Research Journal, 6*, 119–134.

Chapter 11
The Analysis of Share Repurchases in European Countries

Dániel Szládek

Abstract The way companies return cash to their shareholders has changed considerably in recent decades. After changes in the legislation, share repurchases or buybacks have gained prominence. Empirical research regarding share repurchases has mainly focused on the United States and the developed markets of Europe. In this paper, I extend the analysis of share repurchases to a broader set of European countries. I employ random-effect probit panel and dynamic panel models to explain what determines whether a European firm repurchases its shares or not and what influences the repurchased amount. My results suggest that the size and leverage ratio of the firm, as well as its dividend payments, influence both.

Key words Corporate finance · Payout policy · Share repurchases

11.1 Introduction

Corporate finance involves three questions that firms face: how to optimally invest their resources (investment policy), what the best way is to fund these investments (financing policy), and how much money should be returned to shareholders (payout policy). In this paper, I focus on the third element of corporate finance, highlighting the change in the way firms return cash to their shareholders.

Dividends were the primary means of transferring money back to shareholders for much of the twentieth century. However, Fama and French (2001) report that in 1973, approximately 52.8% of public firms in the United States (excluding utilities and financial services) paid dividends; the ratio peaked in 1978 (66.5%) then fell sharply: in 1999, only 20.8% of US public firms were dividend payers. This significant decline coincided with the emergence of share repurchases or stock buybacks. Farre-Mensa et al. (2014) show that the ratio of repurchasing firms has exceeded that of dividend-paying firms in the United States since 1997. A similar

---

D. Szládek (✉)
Faculty of Economics and Business Administration, University of Szeged, Szeged, Hungary
e-mail: szladek.daniel@eco.u-szeged.hu

D. Procházka (ed.), *Regulation of Finance and Accounting*, Springer Proceedings in Business and Economics, https://doi.org/10.1007/978-3-030-99873-8_11

pattern is observed in absolute terms: the aggregate dollar amount of share repurchases has overtaken the aggregate dividends paid since 1997; thus, buybacks have provided the greater part of the total payout of US public firms in the twenty-first century.

The shift in payout methods is quite apparent in the United States. Is it a universal phenomenon? In Europe, the ratio of dividend-paying firms has also decreased toward the end of the twentieth century, although not as drastically as in the US (von Eije & Megginson, 2008). Dividends remained the major form of payout for European firms at the start of the twenty-first century, although share repurchases have gained prominence in Europe as well. Most of the empirical studies concerning share repurchases analyzed the United States or the most developed markets in Europe (e.g., Lee et al., 2010; Andriosopoulos & Hoque, 2013; Andriosopoulos & Lasfer, 2015). The aim of this paper is to examine the determinants of the share repurchasing activity of firms in a broader set of European countries.

11.2 Data and Methodology

I analyze the share repurchases of European firms from 1995 to 2018. My sample includes firms from the twenty-eight countries (including the United Kingdom) of the European Union, plus firms from the members of the European Free Trade Association, which maintain strong economic ties with the Union. I collect yearly data from the Refinitiv Eikon database, a comprehensive source of financial data. Firms with positive total assets (TA) reported in at least one year of the observation period were included in my sample to avoid survivor bias. The sample excludes financial services and ulitity firms, as common in the literature. As my main focus is payout policy, I start by demonstrating the main metrics related to dividends and share repurchases from 1995 to 2018. I collected the cash dividends paid on common shares and the cash amount spent on the repurchases of common shares from the cash-flow statements. The Appendix summarizes the whole sample based on the number of firms, their dividend and/or repurchase data availability, and activity.

Table 11.3 of the Appendix lists the number of firms from 1995 to 2018 that have available data related to dividends or repurchases. Clearly, the number of firms with dividend data available is much more than those with repurchase data reported (38,705 vs. 12,399, respectively, through the whole observation period). Relative to the number of firms with dividend data available, approximately 90% of firms pay dividends, and the ratio is quite stable during the period analyzed. This ratio is approximately 72% for repurchasers, although there is a sharp increase from 39.39% in 1995 to 81.82% in 2018. Compared to the total number of firms, however, the ratio of dividend payers decreases from 65.73% (1995) to 42.90% (2018), while the relative number of repurchasers increases from 3.32% (1995) to 13.75% (2018).

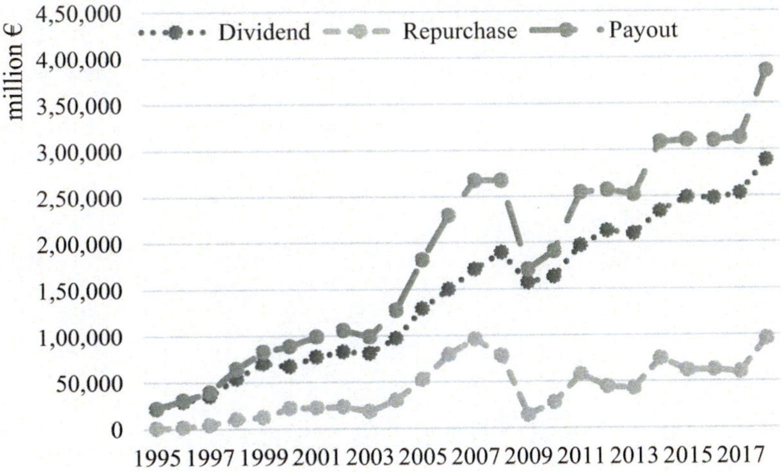

Fig. 11.1 Aggregated amount of dividends, share repurchases, and payouts in million euros (1995–2018). (Source: Author's calculations based on data from Refinitiv Eikon)

Table 11.4 of the Appendix contains the yearly number of firms that have both dividend and repurchase data available. Approximately 70% of such firms pay dividends and also repurchase shares in the whole observation period, although their relative ratio also increases from 39.19% (1995) to 82.92% (2018). This phenomenon also coincides with the reduction of dividend-only firms (52.17% to 13.93%). The ratio of firms that report both data but do not return cash to shareholders either way is unsubstantial (3.31% for 24 years and decreasing).

However, not only the number of dividend-paying or repurchasing firms matter but the aggregate amount of payouts as well. Figure 11.1 shows the development of the aggregated amount spent by firms in the sample on dividend payments, share repurchases, and payouts (the sum of dividends and repurchases).

Based on Fig. 11.1, it is clear that dividends still remain the dominant form of payout in European countries. There was a steep rise in the amount spent on share repurchases in the middle of the 2000s; the financial crisis, however, broke that momentum. Since then, a moderate increase is observed, which resulted in reaching the precrisis repurchase level. Dividends also took a hit during the crisis but were more resilient than repurchases (similar to what was observed in the United States; see Floyd, Li, and Skinner 2015). Still, almost 100 billion euros spent on share repurchases in 2018 is a huge amount of money, and the upward trajectory may propel repurchases to new heights.

The aggregate amount spent on dividends and share repurchases does not show the whole picture of the payout policy. It is common to compare the money returned to shareholders with the earnings of the firm. Figure 11.2 depicts the dividend, repurchase, and payout ratio, where the denominator was the net income of the previous year. I aggregated the payouts of every firm in a given year and divided it by the aggregated net income of every firm in the previous year.

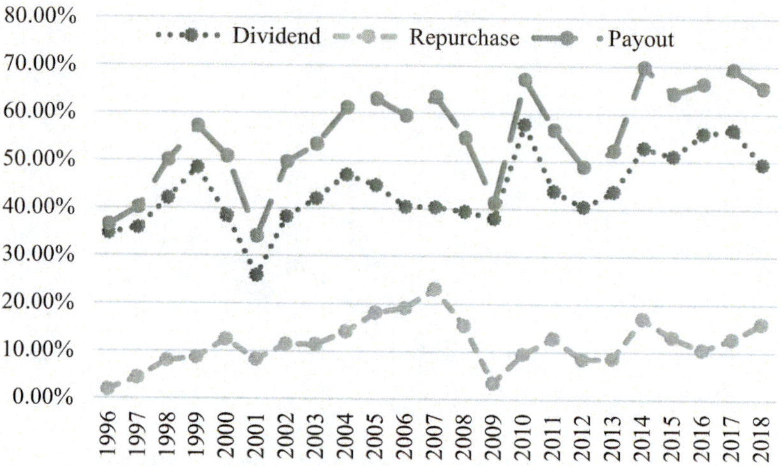

Fig. 11.2 Dividend, repurchase, and payout ratio (1996–2018). (Source: Author's calculations based on data from Refinitiv Eikon. Note: Relative to the previous year's net income)

The dividend, repurchase, and payout ratios are somewhat volatile during the observation period, as shown in Fig. 11.2. This is not surprising because earnings can be volatile as well. Generally, European firms return much of their earnings to shareholders; the payout ratio is above 50% in the last 20 years except during crisis years. The share repurchase ratio peaked above 20% in 2007 before the financial crisis; in the 2010s, it remained between 10% and 20%. Again, Fig. 11.2 highlights the fact that European firms have not yet followed the American ones in shifting their payout method from dividends to repurchases.

The next section of the paper will discuss the results of my econometric analysis of European share repurchases. I examine two questions: what influences a firm to repurchase its shares, and what affects the amount spent on share repurchases. To answer the first question, I apply random-effect probit models, where the dependent variable is a dummy variable, *REPP*, which takes the value of 1 if the firm repurchases its shares in a given year and 0 if otherwise. The second question is answered with dynamic panel models, utilizing the GMM-in-system estimation technique, which gives consistent estimates for panel data with a relatively short time series (24 years) and a relatively high number of groups (424 firms) (Andres et al. (2015) cite Bundell and Bond (1998)). In the dynamic panel models, the dependent variable is the natural logarithm of the amount spent on share repurchases, *LREP*.

The independent variables included in the models are the following: *ROA*—return on assets—and *NITA*—the net income divided by the total assets measures the profitability of the firm. Generally, higher profitability may incur higher payout to shareholders, thus share repurchases. *LTA* means the natural logarithm of total assets, which is a proxy for the size of the firm. *LC* is the natural logarithm of the cash balance of the firm—again, a higher cash balance should allow greater payouts.

PBV is the price-to-book value of the equity of the firm. A low price-to-book value may suggest undervaluation, and managers tend to signal appropriate operation with payouts (Miller & Rock, 1985; Ofer & Thakor, 1987) or simply favor exploiting undervaluation (Brav et al., 2005). *LEV* is the leverage ratio of the firm, calculated by dividing the book value of the total debt by the book value of the total assets. A higher leverage ratio may help control agency costs, thus decreasing the amount of cash returned to shareholders to mitigate agency costs (Easterbrook, 1984; Jensen, 1986). Finally, a dividend payer dummy (*DIVP*) and the natural logarithm of dividends paid (*LDIV*) are included in the probit and dynamic panel models, respectively. These variables test the substitution hypothesis, which states that share repurchases replace dividends in the payout of firms (Grullon & Michaely, 2002).

11.3 Results and Discussion

First, I analyze the determinants of becoming a share repurchasing firm. Table 11.1 details the results of the random-effect probit models, estimating the coefficients for the factors that may influence repurchasing activity.

Table 11.1 Random-effect probit models explaining whether a firm repurchases its shares or not

	(1)	(2)	(3)	(4)
const	−0.7769***	−1.2220***	−1.1590***	−1.5520***
	(0.1490)	(0.1540)	(0.1940)	(0.1969)
ROA_1	0.4325***	0.4649***	1.3280*	1.5110**
	(0.0975)	(0.0976)	(0.7577)	(0.7697)
PBV_1	−0.0003	−0.0003	−0.0000	−0.0001
	(0.0002)	(0.0002)	(0.0003)	(0.0003)
LEV_1	−0.0540	−0.0572	−0.2334*	−0.2029*
	(0.0618)	(0.0612)	(0.1225)	(0.1217)
LTA_1	0.0283**	0.0312**	0.0697***	0.0715***
	(0.0143)	(0.0142)	(0.0191)	(0.0189)
LC_1	0.0489***	0.0414***	0.0151	0.0061
	(0.0130)	(0.0129)	(0.0168)	(0.0167)
NITA_1	−0.0264	−0.0262	−0.0490	−0.1768
	(0.0183)	(0.0182)	(0.6991)	(0.7134)
T		0.0311***		0.0310***
		(0.0030)		(0.0035)
DIVP_1			0.1384**	0.1329**
			(0.0626)	(0.0625)
Observations	10,687	10,687	8095	8095

Source: Author's calculations based on data from Refinitiv Eikon

Note: _1 indicates lagged variables; ***, **, and * denote significance at the 1%, 5%, 10% level, respectively

Table 11.1 summarizes the random-effect panel probit estimations to capture the determinants of being a share repurchase firm. The independent variables are described in the previous section, and their lagged versions are included in the model, except *T*, which denotes the time variable. In column 4 of Table 11.1, the results of the most comprehensive model are shown; this model includes the time variable and the *DIVP* dummy variable. According to this model, whether a firm repurchases its shares or not is determined by its profitability (measured by return on assets), its leverage ratio, its size (proxied by total assets), and whether the firm is a dividend payer or not. The other variables are not significant even at the 10% level. The signs of the coefficients of the lagged values of *ROA* and *LTA* are positive and negative for the lagged leverage variable (*LEV*), as expected. Greater profitability and size are the characteristics of repurchasing firms, while a higher leverage ratio discourages repurchasing activity. The coefficient of *DIVP* is positive as well, which means that the substitution hypothesis is not valid for European firms, at least related to their choice whether to repurchase their shares or pay dividends. The time variable *T* is also significant and has a positive coefficient, which signals that more and more firms repurchase their shares, as we have seen in the data in the Appendix.

I also ran dynamic panel data models to determine what influences the amount of money spent on share repurchases. For brevity, I only report the results and diagnostics of the last specification, which includes the variables described at the end of the previous section, plus the time variable *T*. The estimation results are summarized in Table 11.2.

Table 11.2 Dynamic panel model explaining the amount of money spent on share repurchases

	Coefficient	Std. error	*z*	*p* value	
LREP_1	0.2603	0.0400	6.5040	<0.0001	***
const	−3.7864	0.5456	−6.9400	<0.0001	***
ROA_1	2.8088	3.9149	0.7175	0.4731	
PBV_1	−0.0000	0.0000	−1.7180	0.0857	*
LEV_1	−0.7049	0.3555	−1.9830	0.0474	**
LTA_1	0.5732	0.0683	8.3940	<0.0001	***
LC_1	0.1270	0.0380	3.3400	0.0008	***
NITA_1	−0.6800	3.7353	−0.1820	0.8556	
T	−0.0251	0.0074	−3.3690	0.0008	***
LDIV_1	0.0917	0.0413	2.2180	0.0265	**
Test for AR(1) errors: $z = -7.5098$ [0.0000]					
Test for AR(2) errors: $z = -0.7659$ [0.4437]					
Sargan overidentification test: chi-square(255) = 279.3020 [0.1416]					
Wald (joint) test: chi-square(9) = 2413.8300 [0.0000]					

Source: Author's calculations based on data from Refinitiv Eikon
Note: _1 indicates lagged variables; ***, **, and * denote significance at the 1%, 5%, 10% level, respectively

The test diagnostics show that the estimation is appropriate: there is no second-order autocorrelation and overidentification. According to the results of the dynamic panel model estimation presented in Table 11.2, the amount spent on repurchases is significantly influenced by the level of repurchase in the previous year. The positive sign of the coefficient implies that the more cash is returned to shareholders via share repurchases, the more the firm will spend on them the following year. Size (*LTA*) is again significant and has a positive sign. Cash balance (*LC*) is also significant and has a positive coefficient, as expected. Price-to-book value (*PBV*) and leverage (*LEV*) have a negative coefficient, as suggested by the literature, underlining the undervaluation and the agency theory. The dividend payment variable (*LDIV*) influences positively the amount spent on repurchases; thus, this result also counters the substitution hypothesis.

11.4 Conclusion

Payout policy is one of the major decisions of corporate finance. The way firms return cash to their shareholders has changed significantly in the last decades. Share repurchases or buybacks have gradually replaced dividends as the major form of payout in the United States and have gained prominence in other capital markets of the world as well. In Europe, as I have shown above, dividends remain the dominant form of payout; however, share repurchases are also significant, totaling almost 100 billion euros in 2018.

The empirical analysis of this paper focused on the determinants of whether a firm repurchases its shares or not and those of the cash spent on share repurchases. Random-effect probit panel models imply that, in Europe, repurchasing shares is influenced by the size of the firm, profitability, leverage ratio, and whether the firm is a dividend payer or not. The dynamic panel model presented explains the amount spent on share repurchases by the size and cash balance of the firm, its price-to-book value, and leverage ratio, as well as by its paid dividends and repurchased amounts in the previous year.

This paper extended existing research regarding share repurchases by looking at a broader set of European countries than what has been analyzed in already published research articles. The examination could be continued by assessing the differences within Europe related to the share repurchase activity within the payout policy of firms. Sectoral analysis could be an interesting theme as well, e.g., the determinants of the share repurchase activity of financial service firms, which were excluded from this research. All in all, share repurchasing is a current topic for academic and finance professionals as well, which means there is a great amount of interest in this subject of corporate finance.

Appendix

Table 11.3 Dividend and share repurchase data separately

Year	Positive TA reported	Dividend data available	Dividend paid	Dividend not paid	Repurchase data available	Repurchase conducted	No repurchase
1995	391	271	257	14	33	13	20
1996	682	433	414	19	51	27	24
1997	919	569	537	32	86	45	41
1998	1619	931	877	54	158	90	68
1999	1846	1078	1007	71	230	140	90
2000	2021	1161	1078	83	292	195	97
2001	2209	1226	1120	106	353	234	119
2002	2541	1284	1106	178	367	237	130
2003	2768	1319	1161	158	376	241	135
2004	3010	1575	1425	150	435	309	126
2005	3169	1735	1560	175	489	337	152
2006	3314	1843	1667	176	600	390	210
2007	3430	1929	1711	218	732	504	228
2008	3526	1978	1800	178	776	621	155
2009	3587	1974	1637	337	723	443	280
2010	3725	1997	1663	334	712	435	277
2011	3915	2001	1770	231	689	524	165
2012	4157	2058	1844	214	700	540	160
2013	4354	2115	1933	182	700	531	169
2014	4606	2187	1959	228	735	566	169
2015	4799	2229	2035	194	756	585	171
2016	4969	2263	2082	181	781	624	157
2017	5021	2274	2108	166	789	620	169
2018	4974	2275	2134	141	836	684	152
1995–2018	75,552	38,705	34,885	3820	12,399	8935	3464

Source: Author's calculations based on data from Refinitiv Eikon

Table 11.4 Dividend and share repurchase data both available

Year	Both available	Did both	Only dividend paid	Only re-purchased	Did neither
1995	23	9	12	0	2
1996	39	21	15	2	1
1997	66	32	31	1	2
1998	120	68	44	3	5
1999	186	112	67	3	4
2000	229	154	63	7	5
2001	276	174	88	8	6
2002	276	163	80	19	14
2003	285	173	85	12	15
2004	337	234	80	16	7
2005	388	257	98	19	14
2006	481	303	143	15	20
2007	576	389	138	23	26
2008	603	469	102	21	11
2009	554	296	176	43	39
2010	540	311	165	30	34
2011	514	370	94	31	19
2012	515	385	87	25	18
2013	517	373	121	13	10
2014	531	399	95	23	14
2015	554	418	106	19	11
2016	567	432	100	24	11
2017	573	441	108	13	11
2018	603	500	84	8	11
1995–2018	9353	6483	2182	378	310

Source: Author's calculations based on data from Refinitiv Eikon

References

Andres, C., Doumet, M., Fernau, E., & Theissen, E. (2015). The Lintner model revisited: Dividends versus total payouts. *Journal of Banking & Finance, 55*, 56–69.

Andriosopoulos, D., & Hoque, H. (2013). The determinants of share repurchases in Europe. *International Review of Financial Analysis, 27*(C), 65–76.

Andriosopoulos, D., & Lasfer, M. (2015). The market valuation of share repurchases in Europe. *Journal of Banking & Finance, 55*(C), 327–339.

Brav, A., Graham, J. R., Harvey, C., & Michaely, R. (2005). Payout policy in the 21st century. *Journal of Financial Economics, 77*(3), 483–527.

Bundell, R., & Bond, S. (1998). Initial conditions and moment restrictions in dynamic panel data models. *Journal of Econometrics, 87*(1), 115–143.

Easterbrook, F. H. (1984). Two agency-cost explanations of dividends. *The American Economic Review, 74*(4), 650–659.

Fama, E., & French, K. (2001). Disappearing dividends: Changing firm characteristics or lower propensity to pay? *Journal of Financial Economics, 60*(1), 3–43.
Farre-Mensa, J., Michaely, R., & Schmalz, M. (2014). Payout Policy. *Annual Review of Financial Economics, 6*(1), 75–134.
Floyd, E., Li, N., & Skinner, D. J. (2015). Payout policy through the financial crisis: The growth of repurchases and the resilience of dividends. *Journal of Financial Economics, 118*(2), 299–316.
Grullon, G., & Michaely, R. (2002). Dividends, share repurchases, and the substitution hypothesis. *Journal of Finance, 57*(4), 1649–1684.
Jensen, M. (1986). Agency costs of free cash flow, corporate finance, and takeovers. *The American Economic Review, 76*(2), 323–329.
Lee, C. I., Ejara, D. D., & Gleason, K. C. (2010). An empirical analysis of European stock repurchases. *Journal of Multinational Financial Management, 20*(2–3), 114–125.
Miller, M., & Rock, K. (1985). Dividend policy under asymmetric information. *Journal of Finance, 40*(4), 1031–1051.
Ofer, A. R., & Thakor, A. (1987). A theory of stock price responses to alternative corporate cash disbursement methods: Stock repurchases and dividends. *Journal of Finance, 42*(2), 365–394.
von Eije, H., & Megginson, W. L. (2008). Dividends and share repurchases in the European Union. *Journal of Financial Economics, 89*(2), 347–374.

Chapter 12
Split Payment Mechanism in the European Union – Comparative Analysis

Dawid Obrzeżgiewicz

Abstract The purpose of the article is to compare the rules of the split payment mechanism in individual European Union (EU) countries. The split payment mechanism is one of the methods recommended by the European Commission in the fight against value-added tax (VAT) fraud. The article presents the functioning of the split payment mechanism in the following European Union countries: Poland, the Czech Republic, the Netherlands, Italy and Romania. The article uses the comparative analysis method and the critical literature analysis method. The comparative analysis showed that the rules of the split payment mechanism are very similar in the presented countries. However, delving into the details of the solutions in force in individual countries, they differ significantly. The research confirmed that EU countries adjust the split payment mechanism to their needs.

Key words Split payment · Taxation · Value-added tax · European Union

12.1 Introduction

Value-added tax (VAT) revenues are a very important part of public budgets; on average, they represent 7% of the gross domestic product (GDP) in the European Union (EU) member states (European Commission, 2018). Tax theory prefers consumption taxes, including value-added tax (VAT), to income taxation due to the economic distortions caused mainly by the latter on the labour market. This approach is confirmed by many research studies (Weisbach & Bankman, 2006, 2007). The efficient collection of value-added tax has been one of the topical tax policy issues in the EU for several recent years due to widespread carousel fraud (Cejkova & Zidkova, 2019).

Split payment is a mechanism to counteract tax fraud by excluding the possibility of fraudulent VAT payer being misappropriated. As a rule, the model only applies to

D. Obrzeżgiewicz (✉)
Department of Accounting and Financial Audit, Poznań University of Economics and Business, Poznań, Poland
e-mail: dawid.obrzezgiewicz@ue.poznan.pl

D. Procházka (ed.), *Regulation of Finance and Accounting*, Springer Proceedings in Business and Economics, https://doi.org/10.1007/978-3-030-99873-8_12

payments made by electronic means. This mechanism is one of the solutions recommended by the European Commission in a feasibility study on the alternative methods for improving and simplifying the collection of VAT (European Commission, 2017).

The use of the split payment mechanism divides the gross amount into two payment streams. The net amount remains on the seller's account, whereas the amount of VAT is transferred directly to a special bank account, the so-called VAT account. A VAT account is an individual bank account created for each VAT payer. The taxpayer is not free to dispose of funds that are accumulated on his VAT account. It may be used only for the purpose of paying this tax to another taxpayer or for paying VAT, personal income tax (PIT), corporate income tax (CIT) and social security contributions. In this case, when the amount remaining on the taxpayer's VAT account is insufficient to settle input VAT, it is charged from the buyer's ordinary bank account. VAT accounts can be created in individual commercial banks or, depending on the adopted solution, only in one bank, competent for the tax authority.

In the split payment model, tax authorities can control the amount of VAT due already at the stage of the transaction itself, from the time the payment is made by the buyer. This is done by obtaining insights into the payments made by taxpayers through their VAT accounts, where transactions are registered in real time. In the assumptions of the model, the tax authority should be able to constantly monitor payments made by the taxpayers, as well as block them.

The split payment model assumes that for a given accounting period, after the declaration is submitted by the taxpayer, the taxpayer and the tax authority make mutual VAT settlements based on the submitted declaration and the current state of the taxpayer's VAT account. Consequently, the amount of VAT payable or refundable is shown on the taxpayer's side. It should be emphasized that the introduction of the split payment model in no way affects the taxpayer's right to deduct input VAT. Each taxpayer retains the right to deduct VAT on his purchased goods and services.

The main effect of applying split payment is to remove the tax amount from the taxpayer's control. In this way, the split payment model guarantees that the tax authorities receive the entire amount of VAT, which should be paid to the Treasury. It also provides the possibility of monitoring the course of payments among taxpayers.

There are two basic split payment models: automated and manual. The automated model involves the automatic division of the gross payment amount into the net amount and VAT when a buyer makes payments for a given good or service. The buyer then issues one transfer order or makes a one-off payment with the card. Then the cash flow is divided into the net amount, which goes to the seller, and the amount of VAT, transferred to the VAT account. The instruction to make a transfer or card payment contains additional information: gross amount, VAT amount, recipient's tax identification number and invoice number.

In contrast to the automated system, manual split payment requires the buyer to separate the payment himself into two separate transfer orders – a transfer of the net amount, directed to the seller, and separate transfer of the VAT amount, which should be paid to the VAT account, over which custody is exercised by the Tax Office. Regardless of the split payment option used, the seller remains the entity responsible for issuing a correct invoice and determining the amount of input VAT.

The next part of the article will present the functioning of the split payment mechanism in the individual European Union countries that have already been able to use this mechanism. The split payment mechanism differs depending on the country; they differ in their structure and the way of settling payments. The following subsections aim to present the split payment mechanism in a given country.

12.2 Split Payment in Poland

VAT is one of the most commonly targeted taxes by fraudsters in Poland. The activities of criminal organizations specializing in VAT are the result of a specific structure and regulation of the European Union Directive in the field of VAT. State authorities wanting to protect themselves from fraud involving goods and service tax establish mechanisms to safeguard them against it. The first of these mechanisms is the so-called reverse charge mechanism. The design of this mechanism targets instances where the seller of a good or service issued a VAT invoice without calculating the tax due. As a result, the VAT declaration of the buyer of the good or service covered by this mechanism shows both the due tax and the input tax on this acquisition. This mechanism unfortunately did not work in practice in Poland because fraudsters also used this mechanism to commit tax scams. The latest idea to combat VAT scams in Poland is the split payment mechanism (Tratkiewicz, 2017).

The Polish split payment model is a specific payment mechanism for invoices. The application of this mechanism causes the VAT amount to affect the VAT account, while the net amount, the current settlement account of the transfer recipient. Especially for this purpose, the enterprise bank creates a separate VAT bank account for each settlement account. The amount of VAT is collected on it. Currently, the transferor decides whether to pay in a split payment. On July 1, 2018, a mandatory split payment mechanism was introduced in Poland.

However, from November 1, 2019, mandatory split payment was introduced for some goods and services. This solution covered a total of 150 groups of goods and services for transactions exceeding 15,000 PLN. Goods and services covered by this obligation are listed in the new Annex 15 to the VAT Act (including construction services, electronic goods, scrap, steel products, all sensitive goods, car parts, motorcycle parts and tires). This means that only a selected group of enterprises trading in goods or providing services listed in Annex 15 to the Polish Act on tax on goods and services is covered by the split payment mechanism. This results in a deterioration in the financial liquidity of these companies. Research conducted in Poland confirms the negative impact of the split payment mechanism on the financial liquidity of companies (Guziejewska & Zajączkowski, 2019).

There are other disadvantages of this mechanism. The main disadvantages include a larger amount of data required in the transfer message (e.g. NIP of the contractor, the invoice number, two amounts to be entered: net amount and VAT), no possibility of payment with one transfer for several invoices and, above all, limited access to funds on the VAT account. In order to use the funds from the VAT account for purposes other than those specified in the Act, the consent of the head of the Tax Office authorized for a given enterprise is required. Currently, without the consent of the head of the Tax Office, funds can be allocated for the following purposes only:

- Payment of VAT, CIT and PIT to the Tax Office
- Payment of social security contributions to the State Social Insurance Institution
- Settlement of VAT to your contractor on his VAT account

However, there are advantages of the Polish split payment mechanism, including the following: no joint and several liability with the supplier (Annex 13 to the VAT Act) and no additional tax liability charged by the Tax Office. In addition, you can get a bonus for paying ahead of schedule, and you can also apply for an accelerated VAT refund.

Research conducted by the National Bank of Poland (2019) shows that with the optional split payment mechanism, only about 1–10% of total payments, depending on the industry, were made using this mechanism. It was a very small portion of the total financial transfers made by enterprises in the business to business (B2B) market. The introduction of the obligatory split payment mechanism for about 150 goods and services with payment in excess of PLN 15,000 from November 1, 2019, may result in the deterioration of the financial liquidity of enterprises operating in these industries, as above mentioned, and increase the share of transactions in the split payment mechanism in general to over a dozen or several dozen percent. The most beneficial solution in terms of the financial liquidity of enterprises would be the introduction of a universal payment obligation in the split payment mechanism. Such actions could even improve liquidity in some industries, in particular those most exposed to payment bottlenecks.

12.3 Split Payment in Czech Republic

The Czech legislator has introduced a manual split payment, which is treated only as an optional settlement model. It finds application as an alternative system to the joint and several liability of the buyer for the VAT not paid by his supplier.

In the Czech Republic, there is a rule of joint and several liability in VAT obligations analogous to the one introduced by the Polish VAT Act. The buyer is jointly and severally liable with the seller in those situations in which he knew or should have known that the VAT due on a given transaction will not be paid by the seller. However, joint and several liability does not apply if the buyer opts to pay the VAT due on a given delivery/service on behalf of the seller. Along with making payment, the buyer in this case also provides the tax authority with information identifying the transaction, i.e. own and seller's data, the value of VAT due, and the date of sale or the date of receipt of payment by the seller. The buyer pays VAT directly to the bank account of the tax authority that has jurisdiction over the seller's registered office (Kassel et al., 2015).

In principle, the Czech model cannot be considered a typical example of the implementation of the split payment mechanism. Due to the limited scope of application and optionality, it does not bring all the benefits of sharing payments. Nevertheless, its existence indicates that it is justified to treat the split payment as an alternative model to existing mechanisms, whose purpose is to fight against VAT fraud, in particular those arising from the joint and several liability of buyers and suppliers, which is criticized by taxpayers. At present, the Czech Republic does not provide for the introduction of mandatory split payment into the system (Kassel et al., 2015).

The key difference between the Polish solution and the Czech split payment mechanism is that in the Czech Republic, the buyer under the split payment pays VAT to the sales office. Importantly, to use split payment safely in the Czech Republic, you must include this solution in the contract between the seller and the buyer. Without such a provision in the contract, the seller may claim from the buyer the amount of VAT (as part of the price), even if the buyer has already paid it to the seller's office (Wilk i Wróblewska, 2019).

12.4 Split Payment in the Netherlands

The second example of a solution, which is partly a model of the split VAT payment, is the Dutch solution. It has been operating in the Netherlands for a long time and concerns the secondment of personnel services provided by temporary work agencies and similar entities. Because these types of services cause many settlement problems, not only in the field of PIT (determination of the payer of social security contributions and advance payments for personal income tax) but also in the field of VAT, the following solutions have been applied in the Netherlands (Andrzejak, 2018):

1. In the case of employees made available for construction and assembly works and in the field of ship construction, a reverse VAT system has been introduced, in which the amount of input and output tax is calculated and declared by the recipient.
2. In the case of employees designated for other types of work, the recipient entity has the obligation to correctly settle the VAT charged by the service provider. Here, reverse payment is not applicable. However, such a service recipient has the

option to exclude its liability for the service provider's VAT settlement by using a specific split payment method. The exclusion of the recipient's liability requires, in particular, the following:

- Payment of VAT to a special blocked account of the service provider (G-account)
- Receiving a correctly issued VAT invoice
- Inclusion of the VAT invoice number and other invoice identification data in the transfer description
- Keeping of VAT records, enabling the easy identification of VAT invoices issued to personnel
- Demonstrating a lack of knowledge, or the possibility of obtaining knowledge, about the service provider's allocation of funds transferred to a blocked account for purposes other than settling his tax liabilities.

It is worth noting that in the Dutch system, as in Poland's, funds accumulated on a blocked account should be spent on tax settlements and for social security payments of the service provider. At the same time, unlike in Poland, the possibility of disposing funds from a blocked account (G-account) is limited by law not through provisions regulating VAT and banking law (imposing obligations to introduce appropriate restrictions on banking procedures) but in a different way; namely, the disposal of funds from such an account is subject to monitoring by an external accountant (auditor) (Andrzejak, 2018).

At the same time, the service provider has no legal obligation to have a blocked account (G-account). This is its right, not its duty. However, if such a bill is not created by the service provider and the recipient wants to avoid its own responsibility for the service provider's tax settlements, the recipient of the service may pay VAT directly to the tax authorities, indicating (Andrzejak, 2018) the following:

- Name
- Address
- Service provider's VAT number
- The VAT invoice number to which the payment relates
- The period for which the VAT invoice was issued

Therefore, the Dutch solution leaves the choice to the recipient. Avoiding liability for the service provider's tax settlement obligation in the case of providing personnel is possible either by directing the amount of VAT to a blocked account supervised by an independent auditor or by paying directly to the account of tax authorities.

12.5 Split Payment in Italy

The split payment model has been in operation in Italy since January 1, 2015. It has been implemented to curb VAT fraud by sellers who make deliveries and provide services to public law entities. Italy has obtained the consent of the EU Council to use the mechanism as a specific measure to prevent tax evasion or avoidance. The latest estimates of the European Commission for 2013 show that the VAT tax gap for Italy is around 33.6%. In the opinion of the Italian tax authorities, the split payment model, on the one hand, will allow the state budget to be secured against the risk of the supplier not paying VAT. On the other hand, it will also free public law entities from the risk of becoming entangled in schemes designed to extort VAT. Italy predicts that the introduction of a split payment mechanism will increase VAT tax revenues by around EUR 1 million per year (Kassel et al., 2015).

The variant introduced in Italy is a manual version of split payment. The obligation to apply the mechanism applies to all supplies of goods and services to public law entities, with the exception of those supplies or services that, under Italian law, are subject to exemption from VAT or to 0% VAT, and is documented solely through the issuance of a ticket or receipt. Goods and services covered by the reverse charge mechanism are also excluded from the split payment application. In practice, according to Italian regulations, the supplier issues a standard VAT invoice (providing the net amount and amount of VAT). The buyer, being a body governed by public law, transfers to the supplier only the net amount due to be paid for the delivery or service performed. In turn, the tax is transferred directly to the Treasury (Kassel et al., 2015).

The introduction of the split payment model in Italy has been criticized by entrepreneurs, in particular representatives of the construction industry. In their opinion, due to the fact that, in Italy, construction services are taxed at a reduced VAT rate, the introduction of the mechanism leads to a situation in which construction companies whose main clients are public law entities will have to pay their contractors the gross value (including tax) when making purchases. As a rule, the VAT in force in Italy is at a standard rate (i.e. 22%), but it is not received from the buyer. This will increase the value of VAT on which construction companies will be able to apply for a refund. It should be noted here that claiming a VAT refund in Italy is particularly complicated due to the long refund periods, which can reach up to 3 years. In order to limit the effects of split payments for taxpayers operating in sectors covered by it, Italy has significantly shortened the deadlines for refunds. Companies can apply for a VAT refund either quarterly or annually (Kassel et al., 2015).

12.6 Split Payment in Romania

Romanian regulations on mandatory split payment, introduced on January 1, 2018, require taxpayers using this method of settlement to divide payments for the purchase of goods or services into two parts, similar to Poland: the tax base and the amount of VAT transferred to a dedicated VAT account. In contrast to the Polish solution, however, only certain categories of taxpayers in Romania are obliged to use the split payment mechanism (Wilk i Wróblewska, 2019):

- Taxpayers with tax arrears (from 1000 to 3200 euros, depending on the size of the taxpayer)
- Taxpayers that do not settle their VAT obligations within 60 days from the expiry of the deadline of payment
- Taxpayers undergoing bankruptcy proceedings
- Taxpayers that voluntarily undertake to use the split payment procedure for a period of not less than a year

A special advantage encouraging the use of this model is a 5% CIT tax relief for those taxpayers that, without being obliged, decide to use split payment.

At the same time, it should be remembered that in November 2018, the European Commission expressed a negative opinion on the introduction by Romanian tax authorities of the mechanism of divisible VAT payments. One of the main reasons was the excessive administrative burden placed on "honest companies" and the introduction of provisions in contracts that would be contrary to EU VAT rules as well as the freedom to provide services. After this negative opinion by the European Commission, Romania gave up the mandatory model of split payment, replacing it with an optional model (Wilk i Wróblewska, 2019).

12.7 Conclusion

The conducted research has shown that the split payment solutions are very similar in different EU countries. However, delving into the details of the solutions available in various network services get significantly apart. Studies have confirmed that EU countries adapt it to their individual needs in terms of payment distribution.

Table 12.1 shows a comparison of split payment models in EU countries that use it. A comparison of the types of split payment (optional or obligatory) and the beneficiaries that receive VAT under the split payment mechanism is presented.

The mandatory split payment model only works in Italy and Poland and applies only to selected situations. In Poland, it covers a group of 150 goods and services (e.g. steel, construction services, electronics) whose transaction amounts to over PLN 15,000. On the other hand, the mandatory Italian split payment mechanism concerns the supply of goods and the provision of services to public law bodies. In other European Union countries, the split payment mechanism is optional. In the Netherlands, it has been limited to services provided by temporary employment agencies and similar entities.

As for the actual beneficiary of the split payment mechanism, in Poland, the Netherlands and Romania, VAT affects a special account maintained by the company's bank – the VAT account. In contrast, in the Czech Republic and Italy, VAT under the split payment mechanism is paid to the tax authority's account. In my

Table 12.1 Comparison of split payment mechanisms in the European Union

EU country	Kind of split payment	Beneficiary of VAT payments
Poland	Obligatory (150 groups of goods and services for transactions exceeding 15,000 PLN) and optional (other goods and services)	Bank where the company has an account
Czech Republic	Optional (exemption of VAT taxpayers from joint and several liability)	Tax authority
Netherlands	Optional (applies to services provided by temporary employment agencies and similar entities)	Bank where the company has an account
Italy	Obligatory (goods and services provided to public law bodies)	Tax authority
Romania	Optional (all goods and services)	Bank where the company has an account

Source: Own study

opinion, the solution used in Italy and the Czech Republic is much better because it allows faster inflow of cash to the state budget. It also promotes the primary purpose of the split payment mechanism, i.e. counteracting VAT frauds.

References

Andrzejak, P. (2018). *Split payment in VAT: Where in Europe split payment is used, Rzeczpospolita,* https://www.rp.pl/VAT/307169993-Split-payment-w-VAT-gdzie-w-Europie-stosuje-sie-podzielona-platnosc.html. Available from: 28 Feb 2020.

Cejkova, E., & Zidkova, H. (2019). The impact of specific reverse charge on waste and scrap on tax revenues in the Czech Republic. *European Financial and Accounting Journal, 14*(1), 65–83.

European Commission. (2017). *Analysis of the impact of the split payment mechanism as an alternative VAT collection method* (Final report), https://ec.europa.eu/taxation_customs/sites/taxation/files/split_payment_report2017_en.pdf. Available from: 22 Feb 2020.

European Commission. (2018). *Taxation Trends in the EU, Luxembourg*. Available from: 19 Feb 2020.

Guziejewska, B., & Zajączkowski, W. (2019). VAT split payment as a new tool of sealing of the tax system in Poland. *Research Papers of Wrocław University of Economics, 532*, 135–143.

Kassel, T., Tokarski, J., Walewski, M., & Gede, W. (2015). *Split payment Raport PwC*. https://www.pwc.pl/pl/pdf/split-payment-raport-pwc.pdf. Available from: 29 Feb 2020.

National Bank of Poland (NBP). (2019). https://www.money.pl/gielda/nbp-78-duzych-firm-nie-widzi-wplywu-split-payment-na-zmiany-w-ich-plynnosci-6402810612549762a.html. Available from: 29 Feb 2020.

Tratkiewicz, T. (2017). Split payment model – The remedy for VAT frauds? *Annales Universitatis Marie Curie-Sklodowska, 6*, 475–484.

Weisbach, D. A., & Bankman, J. (2006). *The superiority of an ideal consumption tax over an ideal income tax* (58 Stanford Law Review 1413). Law School, University of Chicago.

Weisbach, D. A., & Bankman, J. (2007). *Consumption taxation is still superior to income taxation* (John M. Olin Program in Law and Economics Working Paper No.358, 2007). Available from: 19 Feb 2020.

Wilk, K., & Wróblewska, K. (2019). *Obligatory split payment from September 1, 2019. How do Polish solutions compare with other EU countries?*, Alert podatkowy 24/2019, Available from: 28 Feb 2020.

Chapter 13
Investment in the Business Operations of Polish Listed Companies

Marzena Remlein

Abstract Investing is one of the basic ways to increase the capital of a company. It is also a basic factor for economic growth and development, a prerequisite for conducting profitable operations in the long run. The research problem of this paper is the importance of investment in business operations and the relationship between investment and the value of assets on one hand and the results achieved by companies on the other. Its objective is to quantify the investments made by companies listed on the Warsaw Stock Exchange. The article hypothesizes that investments are an important asset of an enterprise, influencing the company's financial results. The source of data for the research is the financial statements of companies listed on the Warsaw Stock Exchange, operating as part of the RESPECT Index project framework.

Key words Investment · Investment income · Investment costs · Investment inflows · Investment expenditure

13.1 Introduction

We are used to considering survival, continued growth and qualitative development as the universally accepted objectives of an enterprise. For many years, the basis used to describe the growth and development of an enterprise was its profit. It is now assumed that the objective of the company's operations is to create and multiply value for its owners, and profit can be one of the categories affecting this value. Investments form another important category, contributing to an increase in capital and the development of the enterprise while also increasing its value.

Investments are the conditions to be met in the economic operations of every entity, which means that investing is one of the basic ways to increase capital. A well-planned, justified and timely investment can contribute to the company's

M. Remlein (✉)
Department of Accounting and Financial Audit, Poznan University of Economics and Business, Poznań, Poland
e-mail: marzena.remlein@ue.poznan.pl

D. Procházka (ed.), *Regulation of Finance and Accounting*, Springer Proceedings in Business and Economics, https://doi.org/10.1007/978-3-030-99873-8_13

development, while a wrong decision can lead to a reduction in liquidity and flexibility of operations, and with a significant value of invested capital can cause a financial crisis and even bankruptcy (Remlein, 2019, p. 91).

The research problem of this paper is the relationship between investment and the value of assets of companies on one hand and the economic results.

Its objective is to quantify the investments made by companies listed on the Warsaw Stock Exchange.

The article hypothesizes that investments are an important asset of an enterprise, influencing the company's financial results.

13.2 Literature Review

The subject literature considers investments in both the financial aspect, as a monetary expenditure made in order to earn income (Gitman & Joehnk, 2003, p. 3), and the material aspect, a process in which cash is transformed into other goods (Różański, 2006, p. 13).

Investing as a term in the economic context is defined in connection with another category, i.e. capital. According to W.J. Baumol and A.S. Blinder (1991, p. 744), investing is a stream of resources intended for the production of new capital. According to these authors, the relationship between investing and capital is analogous to filling a bathtub with water. The water accumulated in the bathtub is compared to the capital resources, while the stream of tap water that supplies water in the bathtub to the stream of investments. Just as the tap needs to be opened to increase the amount of accumulated water, so does the capital increase only when the investment process is taking place. If investing is stopped, then the stock of capital will cease to grow.

R.J. Wonnacott and P. Wonncott (1990, p. 26) define investing in a similar way, stating that it is a process of creating and accumulating capital. They also emphasize that the current capital is the result of past investments, and the investments currently implemented – after their completion – will result in an increase in the current capital stock.

Investing in financial terms is determined from a narrower perspective than in economic terms, and it focuses on the allocation of monetary resources, mainly in financial instruments, to obtain financial benefits. The general definition of investment is formulated by L.J. Gitman and M.D. Joehnk (2003, p. 3), who state that an investment is a component of every asset, which can be used to allocate funds, in the hope that it will generate income and/or preserve or increase its value. A more elaborate definition of investing is proposed by F.K. Relly and E.A. Norton (2006, p. 5), who define investing as the current allocation of cash for a certain period in anticipation of future funds that will compensate the investor time, inflation rate and risk.

As techniques and technology continue to develop, there is an increase in investment in intangible assets, and the development of capital markets stimulated the increase in capital investments. Currently, when defining the concept of investment, emphasis is put on the financial side. The adoption of the monetary (financial) aspect in the concept of investment results from the inherent, natural relationship between finance and investment. In accounting, investments are equated to assets that the enterprise does not use for its own needs but from which it derives economic benefits just from the very fact of holding them. Pursuant to the Polish Accounting Act, the criteria for qualifying an asset as an investment are as follows:

- The purpose for holding the respective asset.
- The type of acquired economic benefits.
- Its exclusion from use to cover the internal needs of the enterprise.

In addition to the semantic issues, attention should be paid to the diversity of investment valuation principles and the presentation of investments in the financial statements.

The valuation of investments is not subject to our consideration; however, it should be noted that if the solutions included in the International Financial Reporting Standards (IFRS) are adopted, the company is obliged to assign a financial investment to the appropriate category and to apply the valuation model corresponding to this category. However, if the enterprise only applies the provisions of the Polish Accounting Act, then it has the option of applying a simplified approach to the valuation of financial investments. The consequence of adopting such a solution is the lack of an obligation to qualify financial investments in the appropriate categories, with the sole diversification in the form of short- and long-term investments.

The consequences of the adopted investment accounting policy (legal basis, classification, valuation) are reflected in the financial statements because they affect both the value of the assets on the balance sheet and the overall financial result.

13.3 Data and Methodology

Addressing the research problem boils down to examining the investments of companies, as presented in their financial statements.

The source of data for the research is the financial statements of companies listed on the Warsaw Stock Exchange, operating as part of the RESPECT Index project framework.

In order to select the research sample, the following considerations were made:

1. The time range of the research covers the years 2010–2018.
2. The survey included companies listed on the RESPECT Index as at 27 December 2018.
3. Due to the specifics of operations and the different accounting and financial reporting principles, we excluded from the search sample banks, insurance

companies, and entities operating on the basis of securities trading regulations and regulations on investment funds and investment fund management.
4. Also excluded from the sample were companies that did not publish financial statements for all the years covered by our research.

All RESPECT Index listed companies accepted for the study are presented in Table 13.1.

Out of 31 listed companies, 15 companies were excluded due to the following reasons:

- Specifics of their operations and different accounting and financial reporting principles.
- Lack of financial statements for all years covered by our survey.

Considering the 9-year time span, 144 financial statements, published by companies, were subject to observation.

Of the 16 companies accepted for the research, we included six companies listed in the WIG20 index, seven companies that were part of the mWIG40 index, and further three that were part of the mWIG80 index.

13.4 Results and Discussion

A preliminary analysis of the individual financial statements of the analyzed companies allowed us to conclude that in the period 2010–2018, all of the surveyed companies invested their free funds. This proves how important an asset group the investments are for the companies. The results of the study on the share of the value of long-term investments in the total value of all assets of the surveyed companies in the audited period are presented in Table 13.2.

From the data contained in the table, we see that Tauron had the largest share of total long-term investments in its assets. This share oscillates around 90%, with the lowest value in 2014 (87.6%) and the highest in 2015 (93.8%). This demonstrates the company's high investment commitment and the reduction of business activity – to a large extent – to investment activities. In turn, the lowest results were recorded for the Bogdanka company (from 1.7% in 2014 to 2.6% in 2010). A detailed analysis of the balance sheet and additional notes demonstrates, owing to the type of its business, that the vast majority of assets are components of its property, plant and equipment (fixed assets). It is also noteworthy that the number of companies whose long-term investments accounted for more than half of their assets is increasing over the period considered (in 2011, there were just two such companies, three in 2012 and 2013, four in 2014 and 2015, and five companies in 2016, 2017 and 2018). This confirms the thesis on the significant role of investments in the business operations of enterprises.

The current classification of investments allows for the assessment of which type (subject) of investments enjoys the greatest recognition among the surveyed

Table 13.1 RESPECT Index listed companies – selection of the research sample

Abbreviation	Name	Index	Industry	Available reports	Accepted in sample
CCC	CCC	WIG20	Retail	2011–2018	NO
ENG	Energa	WIG20	Energy industry	2014–2018	NO
KGH	KGHM Polska Miedź	WIG20	Raw materials	2010–2018	YES
LTS	LOTOS Group	WIG20	Fuel industry	2010–2018	YES
MBK	mBank	WIG20	Banks	2010–2018	NO
OPL	Orange Polska	WIG20	Telecommunication	2010–2017	NO
PEO	Bank Polska Kasa Opieki	WIG20	Banks	2010–2018	NO
PGE	PGE Polska Grupa Energetyczna	WIG20	Energy industry	2010–2018	YES
PKN	PKN ORLEN	WIG20	Fuel industry	2010–2018	YES
PGN	Polskie Górnictwo Naftowe i Gazownictwo	WIG20	Fuel industry	2010–2018	YES
PZU	Powszechny Zakład Ubezpieczeń	WIG20	Insurance	2010–2018	NO
SPL	Santander Bank Polska	WIG20	Banks	2010–2018	NO
TPE	TAURON Polska Energia	WIG20	Energy industry	2010–2018	YES
EAT	AmRest Holdings SE	mWIG40	Hotels and restaurants	2010–2017	NO
APT	APATOR	mWIG40	Electrical machinery industry	2010–2018	YES
ATT	GRUPA AZOTY	mWIG40	Chemical industry	2010–2018	YES
BDX	Budimex	mWIG40	Construction industry	2010–2018	YES
BHW	Bank Handlowy w Warszawie Spółka Akcyjna	mWIG40	Banks	2010–2018	NO
CAR	Inter Cars	mWIG40	Wholesale	2010–2018	YES
FTE	FABRYKI MEBLI "FORTE"	mWIG40	Timber industry	2010–2018	YES
GPW	Giełda pap. Wart. w Warszawie	mWIG40	Capital market	2010–2018	NO
ING	ING Bank Śląski	mWIG40	Banks	2010–2018	NO
JSW	Jastrzębska Spółka Węglowa	mWIG40	Raw materials	2011–2018	NO
LWB	Lubelski Węgiel BOGDANKA	mWIG40	Raw materials	2010–2018	YES
MIL	Bank Millennium	mWIG40	Banks	2010–2018	NO

(continued)

Table 13.1 (continued)

Abbreviation	Name	Index	Industry	Available reports	Accepted in sample
TRK	Trakcja PRKiI	mWIG40	Construction industry	2010–2018	YES
KGN	Zesp. Elektrociepłowni Wrocł. KOGENERACJA	sWIG80	Energy industry	2010–2018	YES
ELB	ELEKTROBUDOWA	sWIG80	Construction industry	2010–2018	YES
AGO	Agora	sWIG80	Media	2010–2018	YES
PCR	PCC Rokita	sWIG80	Chemical industry	2011–2018	**NO**
BOS	Bank Ochrony Środowiska	sWIG80	Banks	2010–2018	**NO**

Source: Author's own elaboration based on http://respectindex.pl

Table 13.2 Share of total long-term investments in total assets for the years 2010–2018 (in %)

Company	2010	2011	2012	2013	2014	2015	2016	2017	2018
KGH	25.4	13.7	47.7	45.1	40.6	44.1	34.7	29.2	32.0
LTS	7.2	7.3	6.3	7.1	8.5	12.0	13.6	15.0	16.3
PGE	71.6	68.6	76.2	77.7	77.8	74.6	67.3	66.2	62.8
PKN	29.0	19.8	21.8	23.0	17.8	20.9	20.8	19.8	27.8
PGN	33.8	32.7	35.5	34.6	36.2	33.6	35.4	33.9	35.0
TPE	93.3	93.4	89.0	91.6	87.6	93.8	93.4	90.4	91.5
APT	57.5	49.3	46.7	45.0	59.8	58.0	53.4	50.8	55.3
ATT	16.4	41.6	44.9	71.5	71.1	69.6	64.3	60.2	61.8
BDX	21.0	25.8	26.4	22.5	22.6	20.4	17.6	17.9	19.1
CAR	3.6	4.0	7.7	11.0	10.8	15.1	15.3	13.9	12.2
FTE	8.2	8.8	8.5	7.5	6.4	9.4	25.6	26.4	30.2
LWB	2.6	2.4	2.1	2.0	1.7	2.1	2.0	1.8	1.9
TRK	19.9	46.4	62.9	36.4	38.3	46.9	45.2	41.4	35.6
KGN	20.5	16.9	15.4	14.4	11.5	10.4	10.6	10.7	10.6
ELB	18.5	11.2	10.6	9.4	8.3	8.4	7.6	7.6	7.5
AGO	33.6	35.2	39.2	42.6	47.8	46.7	51.8	54.1	55.1

Source: Own elaboration, based on the financial statements of the surveyed companies

companies. A preliminary analysis allowed us to conclude that investments in the form of stocks and shares of other companies were very popular among the surveyed companies. Therefore, during the subsequent stage of our study, we analyzed the share of this type of investment in the value of long-term investments. The results of this analysis are presented in Table 13.3.

The results of the conducted analysis indicate that out of the 144 cases (16 companies, 9 years) considered, only in two cases did this share amount to less than 20%, and in the remaining cases, the ratio of the value of investments in the form of stocks and shares of other companies in the total long-term investments is high. The results testify to the large (and in some cases very large) investment commitment of the surveyed companies, and to locating their own resources in stock and shares of other companies. Table 13.4 presents a list of the surveyed companies that recorded a high (over 80%) share of investment in the form of stocks and shares of other companies in their total investments.

The results listed in the table indicate that the number of companies surveyed that had sole long-term investments in the form of investments in stocks and shares of other companies fluctuates between one company in 2010 and four companies in 2014. For the last year covered by our analysis, there were two companies that had their investment portfolios filled exclusively with stocks and shares of other companies. It is noteworthy that more than half of the surveyed companies had a share of 90% or more of the value of investments in the form of stocks and shares of other companies in their total long-term investments.

Subsequently, we conducted an analysis of the result categories of the investment activities presented in the income statement within the section devoted to financial

Table 13.3 Share of value of investments in stock and shares of other companies in total long-term investments in 2010–2018 (in %)

Company	2010	2011	2012	2013	2014	2015	2016	2017	2018
KGH	90.3	74.8	93.4	96.0	97.0	47.0	19.2	33.3	32.0
LTS	74.6	70.9	90.8	82.8	100.0	100.0	88.5	96.5	99.9
PGE	97.9	99.7	100.0	100.0	100.0	99.8	98.8	99.3	99.6
PKN	99.7	99.6	99.6	99.6	99.4	97.7	99.3	98.1	99.2
PGN	73.4	68.6	55.9	63.6	67.2	73.4	75.0	86.3	76.1
TPE	95.1	94.7	88.1	79.0	78.3	64.2	57.5	76.5	78.1
APT	98.1	98.6	98.5	98.7	99.5	98.2	99.5	99.5	99.6
ATT	89.9	97.7	98.5	99.6	99.7	94.3	93.7	93.6	94.3
BDX	98.3	99.2	99.0	98.9	98.7	98.7	97.5	91.5	90.6
CAR	94.0	96.6	97.9	98.7	98.8	99.3	99.4	99.5	99.9
FTE	83.7	19.8	20.1	19.9	20.2	92.4	71.7	68.5	92.4
LWB	100.0	100.0	100.0	100.0	100.0	100.0	100.0	100.0	100.0
TRK	96.3	99.2	95.0	91.9	93.4	94.9	95.2	95.1	95.1
KGN	79.6	86.2	91.3	91.3	90.5	90.6	91.0	91.3	91.5
ELB	69.1	100.0	100.0	100.0	100.0	100.0	100.0	100.0	100.0
AGO	99.8	99.6	99.6	96.3	97.3	98.7	99.1	100.0	99.6

Source: Own elaboration, based on the financial statements of the surveyed companies

Table 13.4 Number of companies with a high share of investments in stock and shares of other companies in total long-term investments

Share	2010	2011	2012	2013	2014	2015	2016	2017	2018
100%	1	2	3	3	4	3	2	3	2
90–99.9%	8	8	9	8	8	9	8	8	11
80–89.9%	2	1	1	1	0	0	1	2	0
Total	**11**	**11**	**13**	**12**	**12**	**12**	**11**	**13**	**13**

Source: Author's own elaboration, based on the data from Table 13.3

activities. For the purposes of this research, values corresponding to the income obtained from owned or disposed investments were separated from financial income and designated as "investment income." In the analyzed profit and loss accounts, investment income was presented in the following order:

- Dividends and profit shares.
- Profit from the sale of financial fixed assets.
- Interest on granted loans.
- Long-term investment write-offs.

Then the ratio of investment income to financial income (Ii/Fi) was calculated. Table 13.5 presents results testifying to the share of investment income in the financial income.

As the results in Table 13.5 show, investment income constitutes a significant percentage of the total financial income. In some companies (Elektrobudowa), the total financial income equaled the investment income over the entire period subject to our study. In others, this is the case for some of the years in the period considered (e.g. Budimex, Lotos, PGE). In addition, we observe a large group of companies where the investment income accounted for over 90% of their financial income (e.g. Kogeneracja, Tauron, PGE). The results show a large (and in some cases very large) impact of investment income on financial income and, as a result, on the result on financial activities and the financial result of the company. The number of surveyed companies with a high (over 80%) share of investment income in financial income is presented in Table 13.6.

The data in the table above demonstrate the following:

1. A large proportion (from 56.25% in 2011 to 87.5% in 2018) of the companies subject to our consideration had a high (over 80%) share of investment income in their financial income.
2. The number of companies with such a high share has the tendency to grow.

Table 13.5 Share of investment income in financial income (in %)

Company	2010	2011	2012	2013	2014	2015	2016	2017	2018
KGH	29.0	61.3	14.9	13.7	13.4	38.0	32.8	15.6	0.0
LTS	58.7	100.0	77.5	92.1	95.5	91.5	88.9	82.2	99.3
PGE	100.0	99.0	92.9	98.5	99.8	99.9	99.0	100.0	100.0
PKN	91.1	99.5	22.6	59.9	97.7	92.2	94.9	81.6	94.4
PGN	91.2	76.7	85.6	63.6	90.1	90.5	98.2	93.3	91.7
TPE	99.9	99.7	99.8	99.8	99.9	98.9	100.0	90.4	99.9
APT	88.9	85.1	96.4	96.7	98.5	98.3	99.3	98.7	99.8
ATT	39.4	45.9	93.3	94.8	99.8	97.9	98.5	97.1	85.2
BDX	99.7	44.7	100.0	100.0	4.0	37.0	53.5	72.3	87.4
CAR	83.6	96.0	96.7	99.2	97.1	98.3	98.3	94.5	98.6
FTE	22.8	35.1	89.9	87.2	77.2	74.0	99.0	100.0	100.0
LWB	0.0	0.0	0.0	0.0	34.2	36.0	12.5	58.5	6.9
TRK	90.9	98.4	90.7	55.8	89.3	91.0	97.7	91.1	95.9
KGN	99.0	98.6	99.5	99.4	99.8	99.7	100.0	96.2	95.7
ELB	100.0	100.0	100.0	100.0	100.0	100.0	100.0	100.0	100.0
AGO	42.8	27.3	23.7	79.4	83.3	91.8	94.4	97.5	97.7

Source: Own elaboration, based on the financial statements of the surveyed companies

Table 13.6 Number of companies with a high share of investment income in financial income

Ii/Fi	2010	2011	2012	2013	2014	2015	2016	2017	2018
100%	3	2	2	2	2	2	4	4	3
90–99.9%	5	6	8	8	8	10	8	8	9
80–89.9%	2	1	2	1	2	0	1	1	2
Total	**10**	**9**	**12**	**11**	**12**	**12**	**13**	**13**	**14**

Source: Author's own elaboration, based on the data from Table 13.5

Similarly, as in the case of financial revenues, this was done with the category of financial costs, from which "investment costs" were separated and the ratio of investment costs to financial costs was calculated (Ic/Fc). Among the cost items presented as part of financing activities, investment costs include the following:

- Loss on the sale of financial fixed assets.
- Long-term investment write-offs.

The indicators of the share of investment costs in financial costs are presented in Table 13.7.

As it results from the data presented in Table 13.7, the share of investment costs in financial costs is relatively small. Nevertheless, there are a few exceptions to that rule. Considering the large and very large share of investment income in financial income and the low and very low share of investment cost in financial costs, it can be stated that the result (profit) on investment activities has a high share in the total result of financial activities. However, due to the negative results on financial activities, it became impossible to calculate the ratio of the result on investment activities to the result on financial activities.

The subsequent stage of our research concerned the result of investment activities, as presented in the cash flow statement. The fact that cash flows from investing activities include inflows and expenses from the sale and purchase of fixed assets and intangible assets, we considered it appropriate to analyze the share of the inflows and expenses from investment activities that the inflows and expenses from investments understood in accordance to Polish Accountancy Law accounted for (Table 13.8).

Table 13.7 Share of investment costs in financial costs (in %)

Company	2010	2011	2012	2013	2014	2015	2016	2017	2018
KGH	0.0	0.0	0.0	0.0	4.1	83.5	84.1	32.3	0.0
LTS	30.0	22.2	0.0	0.0	42.8	0.0	4.1	0.0	0.0
PGE	0.0	0.0	0.0	1.3	81.5	6.7	3.8	43.2	0.0
PKN	7.4	49.1	54.9	27.1	86.8	60.0	4.3	83.8	48.4
PGN	2.2	1.9	5.4	40.4	13.3	12.3	16.2	36.7	23.0
TPE	0.0	0,4	0,3	0.3	3.1	92.9	80.7	28.7	84.6
APT	0.0	0.0	0.0	0.0	0.0	0.0	0.0	0.0	0.0
ATT	26.1	3.0	6.5	0.0	1.1	0.0	12.5	34.0	2.3
BDX	35.5	36.9	85.6	76.6	0.0	15.5	0.5	0.0	1.9
CAR	0.0	0.0	0.0	0.0	0.0	0.0	0.0	0.0	0.0
FTE	0.0	0.0	0.0	0.0	0.6	0.0	0.0	0.0	0.0
LWB	0.0	0.0	0.0	0.0	0.0	0.0	0.0	0.0	0.0
TRK	0.0	3.3	4.0	2.2	1.8	2.5	0.0	0.0	54.0
KGN	0.0	0.0	1.4	63.4	17.8	0.0	0.0	0.0	0.0
ELB	0,0	0,0	64.6	14.9	4.1	10.5	0.0	63.0	82.4
AGO	46.1	22.3	12.6	15.4	0.0	0.0	88.6	93.8	85.4

Source: Own elaboration, based on the financial statements of the surveyed companies

Table 13.8 The share of investment inflows in inflows from investment activities

Company	2010	2011	2012	2013	2014	2015	2016	2017	2018
KGH	99.1	99.9	80.2	75.0	80.0	100.0	100.0	100.0	87.2
LTS	97.5	23.6	96.6	99.2	85.1	60.5	28.5	71.3	73.2
PGE	100.0	100.0	99.7	99.9	84.8	100.0	100.0	63.5	100.0
PKN	63.8	87.5	88.2	32.5	71.9	65.9	92.6	82.2	59.7
PGN	97.5	47.3	59.9	90.9	86.0	75.7	98.9	94.9	98.2
TPE	98.1	100.0	100.0	99.6	99.2	100.0	100.0	100.0	100.0
APT	99.0	83.0	51.1	98.8	99.7	99.8	99.9	99.3	99.5
ATT	18.9	67.0	96.0	98.0	98.9	98.2	99.9	99.8	64.9
BDX	55.4	77.0	88.0	96.1	99.2	91.1	97.2	99.8	95.7
CAR	84.2	93.4	87.6	99.1	82.8	93.9	98.5	99.4	97.7
FTE	87.7	95.8	73.0	83.9	89.6	80.9	99.5	94.5	2.4
LWB	99.5	85.5	96.5	92.2	39.3	68.3	99.6	47.8	5.7
TRK	99.7	99.9	98.5	67.8	94.7	89.0	70.2	85.3	97.8
KGN	84.9	96.8	98.1	97.6	98.7	97.6	98.9	79.3	93.0
ELB	92.6	98.4	93.1	43.5	96.5	47.2	91.0	93.5	95.8
AGO	58.4	8.4	24.0	18.0	12.1	53.0	24.6	43.9	52.6

Source: Own elaboration, based on the financial statements of the surveyed companies

The analysis of investment inflows demonstrates that, depending on the company and its investment policy, they are at different levels. Therefore, it is difficult to draw clear conclusions without a detailed analysis of the sources of these inflows. When we calculate the average share of investment inflows in investment activity inflows, we see that it fluctuates around 90% over the entire period under review, which largely means that investment activity inflows are largely determined by inflows from investments that are understood as non-operating assets. When analyzing the share of investment expenditure in the total investment activity expenditure (Ie/Iae), we come to completely different results (Table 13.9).

The results presented in Table 13.9 demonstrate that, in the vast majority of the surveyed companies, investment expenditure accounts for less than 50% of the investment activity expenditure, which in turn means that the remainder is expenditure covering operating assets. This proves that the inflows and expenses from the sale and purchase of property, plant and equipment, and also intangible assets, are incorrectly accounted as cash flows from investing activities. The number of surveyed companies with a low share of investment expenditure in investment activity expenditure is shown in Table 13.10.

The data contained in the table above show that within the examined group of companies

1. Most companies (the exception is 2012 and 2018 – seven companies, i.e. 43.75% of the surveyed group) had a low (below 50%) ratio of investment expenditure to investment activity expenditure.
2. The number of companies with a share of 0% has a tendency to grow.

Table 13.9 The share of expenditure on long-term investments in expenditure on investment activities (%)

Company	2010	2011	2012	2013	2014	2015	2016	2017	2018
KGH	66.0	59.7	84.7	15.2	42.5	61.3	23.7	19.1	25.6
LTS	4.9	42.1	56.7	15.4	31.7	48.4	39.5	63.7	71.0
PGE	99.3	99.9	100.0	100.0	85.1	99.9	68.1	99.2	100.0
PKN	13.1	30.5	6.3	12.9	35.0	49.9	4.9	16.0	72.5
PGN	59.5	23.3	70.8	49.0	36.6	34.1	56.3	60.9	44.8
TPE	99.3	99.7	98.7	99.5	99.8	100.0	100.0	100.0	100.0
APT	9.9	13.3	0.0	26.3	90.4	40.8	17.4	59.8	74.0
ATT	69.4	80.5	53.8	80.7	0.0	52.0	23.7	31.3	79.8
BDX	15.2	96.1	81.8	59.3	79.5	72.9	18.6	97.4	82.3
CAR	43.2	39.3	100.7	64.7	57.2	85.7	62.1	24.7	17.6
FTE	1.4	5.1	0.2	9.3	0.0	25.9	82.6	66.0	70.3
LWB	0.0	0.0	0.0	0.0	0.2	0.0	0.0	0.0	0.0
TRK	71.0	98.8	86.2	75.2	28.9	69.0	57.0	52.7	30.9
KGN	5.9	12.4	4.9	0.0	0.0	0.0	0.0	0.0	0.0
ELB	47.3	0.0	0.0	0.0	0.0	0.0	0.0	0.0	0.0
AGO	72.3	9.2	0.6	20.7	24.0	7.6	27.9	0.0	18.4

Source: Own elaboration, based on the financial statements of the surveyed companies

Table 13.10 Number of companies with a low ratio of investment expenditure in investment activity expenditure

Ie/Iae	2010	2011	2012	2013	2014	2015	2016	2017	2018
0%	2	2	3	3	4	4	4	4	3
0.1–10%	4	3	4	2	2	1	0	1	0
10.1–50%	3	5	0	5	5	4	6	3	4
Total	**9**	**10**	**7**	**10**	**11**	**9**	**10**	**8**	**7**

Source: Author's own elaboration, based on the data from Table 13.9

The results of our research allows us to make a conclusion on the shortcoming of the cash flow statement in the area of investment activities, which comes down to accounting cash flows from transactions on non-investment assets, i.e. tangible fixed assets and intangible assets, in that category.

13.5 Conclusion

The analysis of the financial statements of Polish listed companies allowed us to draw the following conclusions:

- In the period 2010–2018, all analyzed companies invested their free funds.
- The number of companies whose long-term investments accounted for more than half of their assets is increasing over the period considered (in 2011, there were

just two such companies, three in 2012 and 2013, four in 2014 and 2015, and five companies in 2016, 2017 and 2018).
- The ratio of the value of investments in the form of stocks and shares of other companies in the total long-term investments is high. Over half of the analyzed companies had a share of 90% or more of the value of investments in the form of stocks and shares of other companies in their total long-term investments.
- The investment income constitutes a significant percentage of the total financial income. Over half of the companies had a high (over 80%) share of investment income in financial income.
- The share of investment costs in financial costs is relatively small.
- The analysis of investment inflows shows that, depending on the company and its investment policy, they are at different levels.
- In the vast majority of the analyzed companies, investment expenditure accounts for less than 50% of investment activity expenditure.

An analysis of the obtained results allows us to state that the research hypothesis – that is, that investments are an important element of a company's assets, which has an impact on its financial results – was positively verified.

The results show the large (in some cases very large) investment commitment of the analyzed companies, and investing their own resources in stock and shares of other companies.

Considering the large and very large share of investment income in financial income and the low and very low share of investment cost in financial costs, it can be stated that the result (profit) on investment activities has a high share in the total result of financial activities.

References

Baumol, W. J., & Blinder, A. S. (1991). *Economics. Principles and policy*. Harcourt Brace Jovanovich Publishers.

Gitman, L. J., & Joehnk, M. D. (2003). *Fundamentals of investing*. Pearson.

Relly, F. K., & Norton, E. A. (2006). *Investments*. Thomson South-Western.

Remlein, M. (2019). *Społecznie odpowiedzialne inwestycje w sprawozdawczości przedsiębiorstw*. Wydawnictwo UEP.

RESPECT Index. http://respectindex.pl

Różański, J. (Ed.). (2006). *Inwestycje rzeczowe i kapitałowe*. Difin.

Wonnacott, R. J., & Wonncott, P. (1990). *Economics*. Wiley.

Chapter 14
The Impact of Renewable Energy and Technology Innovation on Chinese Carbon Dioxide Emissions

Karel Janda and Binyi Zhang

Abstract Understanding the influencing factors of carbon dioxide emissions is an essential prerequisite for policy makers to maintain sustainable low-carbon economic growth. Based on the autoregressive distributed lag model (ARDL) and error correction model (ECM), this paper investigates the causal relationships between economic growth, carbon emission, financial development, renewable energy consumption, and technology innovation in the case of China for the period 1965–2018. Our empirical results confirm the presence of a long-run relationship among the underlying variables. Our long-run estimates show that financial development has negative significant impacts on carbon emissions, whereas renewable energy and technology innovation have limited impacts on carbon mitigations. In addition, the short-run Granger causality analysis reveals that renewable energy consumption has a bidirectional Granger causality with carbon emissions and technology innovations. In the short run, we find that financial development can positively affect China's carbon mitigation efforts indirectly via the channels of renewable energy sources and technology innovations. Our results have three following policy implications for Chinese policy makers to maintain sustainable low carbon economic development: (i) establish a green finance market to mobilize the social capital into green industry; (ii) continue the environmental law enforcement to control for carbon emissions among energy intensive industries; (iii) provide government fiscal incentives to promote renewable energy sources on both supply and demand sides of the market.

Key words China carbon emissions · Financial development · Renewable energy · China

K. Janda
Institute of Economic Studies, Faculty of Social Sciences, Charles University, Prague, Czech Republic

Department of Banking and Insurance, Faculty of Finance and Accounting, Prague University of Economics and Business, Prague, Czech Republic

B. Zhang (✉)
Institute of Economic Studies, Faculty of Social Sciences, Charles University, Prague, Czech Republic

D. Procházka (ed.), *Regulation of Finance and Accounting*, Springer Proceedings in Business and Economics, https://doi.org/10.1007/978-3-030-99873-8_14

14.1 Introduction

Along with tremendous energy consumption, China is facing serious challenges of energy scarcity and environmental degradation mainly resulting from its high reliance on fossil-fuel-based productions. According to British Petroleum (BP) Energy Outlook (2019), China is the largest carbon emitter in the world and accounted for 27.8% of the global total carbon emissions in 2018. Data published by the National Bureau of Statistics of China (NBSC) (2018) show that CO_2 emissions in China were 1.35 metric tons per capita (mtpc) in 1978, when China's economic reform plan entered into force. The figure increased to 2.41 mtpc in 2000 and further reached 6.12 mtpc in 2018, implying almost a 353% rise in carbon emissions since the reform of the Chinese economy. In order to control air pollution, China proposed to change the economic development strategy from conventional manufacturing driven to a service-oriented structure based on a clean energy supply system. Along with the transition to low-carbon economic development, China has a target to reduce carbon intensity to 60–65% of its 2005 levels by 2030 (Jiao et al., 2018). In addition, China introduced the Energy Production and Consumption Revolution Strategy (2016–2019) in 2016 and listed the renewable energy sector as one of the key industries to achieve a sustainable low carbon economy (National Development and Reformation Commission (NRDC) 2018). The accomplishment of the low-carbon economic development in China requires the government to consume significantly fewer fossil fuels. Therefore, an important dilemma arises about how China can achieve a balance between environmental degradation and economic growth, given the present massive market demand for fossil fuel energy consumption.

In this context, this paper aims to investigate the growth-pollution nexus for China by accommodating the roles of financial development, renewable energy, and technology innovation as additional control variables. Note that this paper is an expanded version of Janda and Zhang (2020). By doing it, we apply the autoregressive distributed lag model (ARDL) and the error correction model (ECM) as the main estimation approach for our empirical analysis. The present research contributes to the literature in the two aspects. First, we review the growth-pollution nexus for China with a considerably extended database. Second, we add empirical knowledge about influential factors toward carbon mitigation, emphasizing the roles of renewable energy sources and technology innovation.

A large number of existing studies have examined an inverted U-shaped nexus (known as the environmental Kuznets curve (EKC) hypothesis) between economic growth and carbon emissions. However, there is no consensus among researchers regarding the sign, magnitude, and significance of the relationship. Among these, the EKC hypothesis is more likely to be a country- or region-specific issue. For instance, the EKC hypothesis is empirically supported by Singapore, Thailand, China, Pakistan, Turkey, and the European Union (EU) countries (Cetin et al., 2018; Javid & Sharif, 2016; Kasman & Duman, 2015; Li et al., 2016; Saboori & Sulaiman, 2013). In contrast, the EKC hypothesis is invalidated for Russia, the Middle East countries, and the Organisation for Economic Co-operation and Development (OECD) countries (Dogan & Seker, 2016; Ozcan, 2013; Pao et al., 2011). We could see that some of the regions with different EKC results overlap. The study of Dogan and Seker (2016) indicates that economic growth is not the only indicator of carbon emissions in a country; financial development, energy consumption structure, production structure, and technology development may also be relevant sources of carbon mitigations.

The literature on the linkages between financial development and carbon emission has been extensively studied in both theoretical and empirical research (Tamazian & Rao, 2010; Zhang, 2011; Saboori & Sulaiman, 2013; Javid & Sharif, 2016). However, the previous findings regarding the impact of financial development on environmental performance are inconsistent and inconclusive. For instance, Sadorsky (2010) and Javid and Sharif (2016) note that a well-established financial system could provide listed companies with a significant advantage in achieving low financing costs, which leads to an increase in economic activities and, therefore, exacerbates environmental degradation. Moreover, Zhang (2011) highlights that financial liberalization may stimulate personal loan activities, which spurs the consumption of high-energy-consuming appliances and eventually produces more carbon emissions.

On the contrary, various studies have documented the positive impact of financial development on environmental performance. Saboori and Sulaiman (2013) and Dogan and Seker (2016) claim that the development of the financial sector allows firms to enhance the capital structure and, therefore, mobilize funds required for developing environmental-friendly production processes. Thus, firms can require less energy input for production and emit fewer greenhouse gases (GHG). Tamazian and Rao (2010) opine that since environmental projects are considered public responsibilities, financial intermediaries may mobilize public resources effectively for investments in green-economy-related projects. For bank-dominated financial systems, Shahbaz et al. (2013) indicate the significant role of financial development in combatting carbon emissions as stronger financial development can support green projects with more financing resources at lower transactional costs. Kim and Park (2016) emphasize that the dependency of renewable energy sectors on debt and equity financing raises disproportionately faster in countries with solid and matured financial markets. More recently, Nasreen et al. (2017) note the import role of financial stability in improving carbon emission mitigation in South Asian countries.

In terms of the relationship between technology innovation and carbon emission, Ang (2009) argues that technological innovation and progress in research and development (R&D) could be effective for improving environmental performance when there is a significant proportion of research effort that focuses on pollution abatement and the development of clean technology. Tang and Tan (2013) claim that technology innovation in areas of renewable energy and energy efficient products could reduce the usage of fossil fuels, which in turn leads to environmental improvement.

Renewable energy sources are expected to replace fossil fuels, leading to diminishing environmental degradation (Chen et al., 2019; Irandoust, 2016). By studying a panel of four Nordic countries, Irandoust (2016) finds a significant Granger causality between renewable energy consumption and carbon migrations. Based on the vector error correction model (VECM), Chen et al. (2019) reveal that renewable energy consumption was one of the significant contributors to carbon reductions in China over the period 1980–2014. Nevertheless, Bhattacharya et al. (2017) opine that the impact of renewable energy on carbon mitigations could be limited if it is not accomplished within solid institutional governance.

The remaining sections of this paper are structured as follows. Section 14.2 details data sources and empirical methodology. Section 14.3 discusses the main empirical results and their policy implications. Section 14.4 concludes the study.

14.2 Data and Methodology

Annual data over the period 1965–2018 was collected from BP, the World Bank Development Indicators (WDI) online databases, the National Bureau of Statistics of China (NBSC), and the Chinese Wind databases. Seven variables were included in this study to examine the impact of renewable energy consumption, technology innovation, and financial development on carbon emissions in the case of China. These variables include the following: (1) $CO_{2,\ t}$, employed to measure carbon emissions per capita; (2) gross domestic product (GDP) per capita; (3) the scale of the stock market represented by the ratio of market canalization to GDP; (4) the scale of financial intermediation measured by the ratio of domestic credit to GDP; (5) the share of net foreign direct investment (FDI) inflows to GDP; (6) renewable energy consumption measured in million tons of oil equivalent; and (7) technology innovation proxied by China's annual spending on R&D as percentage to GDP. All these variables were transformed into natural logarithms to avoid any unwanted non-normality and heteroscedasticity. A summary of descriptions of variables, measures, and data sources is reported in Table 14.1.

Table 14.2 details the descriptive statistics of the variables that have been employed in the empirical analysis of this paper. Note that our sample contains missing observations due to unavailable information. We use the iterative Markov chain Monte Carlo (MCMC) simulation method to fill in the missing information. The procedure of the MCMC approach imputes missing data by assuming a tractable parametric multivariate normal model for the data and simulating a continuous time series based on the characteristics of given sample observations. Thus, the main advantage of using the MCMC is that it results in better estimates by preserving the sample size and statistical power of given observations. The results of the Jarque-Bera (JB) normality test suggest that each of these variables is normally distributed. For the unit root tests, we perform the augmented Dicky-Fuller (ADF) and the Phillips-Perron (PP) tests. Note that the null hypothesis of both ADF and PP tests assumes that the underlying data contain unit roots. Table 14.3 reports the unit root

Table 14.1 Summary of variables, measures, and data sources

·	Description	Period	Source
$CO_{2,t}$	China's carbon emissions per capita in million tons of oil equivalent (Mtoe)	1965–2018	NBSC
GDP_t	China's GDP per capita measured in Chinese yuan	1965–2018	NBSC
SS_t	Stock market scale, represented by the ratio of market capitalization to GDP	1991–2018	WIND
FS_t	Financial intermediation scale, represented as the ratio of domestic credit provided by financial sector to GDP	1977–2018	World Bank
FDI_t	Foreign direct investment, represented as the ratio of FDI net inflows to GDP	1982–2018	World bank
REC_t	Renewable energy consumption, measured in million tons of oil equivalent (Mtoe)	1990–2018	BP
TI_t	Technology innovation, proxied by China's annual spending on research and development as percentage to GDP	1996–2017	World Bank

NBSC National Bureau of Statistics of China, *WIND* a data provider in China with a specific focus on China's economy, *BP* British Petroleum

Table 14.2 Summary of statistics

	Mean	SD	Skewness	Kurtosis	Normality
$\text{Ln}(CO_2)_t$	0.732	0.721	0.040	2.028	2.14(0.343)
$\text{Ln}(GDP)_t$	7.907	1.923	0.193	1.568	4.951(0.084)
$\text{Ln}(SS)_t$	−4.065	3.103	−0.127	1.381	6.041(0.049)
$\text{Ln}(FS)_t$	−0.135	0.488	0.154	1.863	3.121(0.210)
$\text{Ln}(FDI)_t$	−4.060	0.840	−0.442	2.298	2.866(0.239)
$\text{Ln}(REC)_t$	−5.331	0.994	0.124	1.575	4.708(0.095)
$\text{Ln}(TI)_t$	−2.689	4.304	0.276	1.653	4.765(0.092)

Note: The value in parentheses denotes the *p*-value for the test significance of Jarque-Bera (JB) normality

Table 14.3 Unit root tests

	Augmented Dicky-Fuller		Phillips-Perron	
Variables	Level	First difference	Level	First difference
$\text{Ln}(CO_2)_t$	−1.585	−3.918***	−9.818	−23.892***
$\text{Ln}(GDP)_t$	−3.472	−3.214*	−6.572	−18.279*
$\text{Ln}(SS)_t$	−2.215	−8.385***	−6.825	−61.058***
$\text{Ln}(FS)_t$	−2.656	−7.986***	−10.198	−55.158***
$\text{Ln}(FDI)_t$	−2.058	−7.206***	−8.148	−49.486***
$\text{Ln}(REC)_t$	−2.892	−7.472***	−11.444	−51.427***
$\text{Ln}(TI)_t$	−2.532	−7.856***	−7.447	−63.145***

Note: ***, **, and * represent statistical significance levels at 1%, 5%, and 10%, respectively test statistics and indicates that, all variables are nonstationary at their level and are stationary at their first difference, that is I (1).

To examine the presence of a long-run relationship between carbon emission and its determinants, we perform the autoregressive distributed lag (ARDL) bound testing approach (Pesaran et al., 2001; Pesaran & Shin, 1998) to test the cointegration among the variables of the model. The ARDL model has several advantages over other cointegration approaches. First, the ARDL has proved to be efficient, and it performs unbiased estimates with valid *t*-statistics for a small sample size. Second, ARDL estimation can be carried out regardless of the order of integration among underlying variables. Third, the error correction model (ECM) can be established straightforwardly through a simple linear transformation. Following bounds testing procedure of Pesaran et al. (2001), ARDL estimation is formulated as follows:

$$\begin{aligned}\Delta Ln(CO_2)_t = \beta_0 &+ \sum_{i=1}^{n}\beta_{1,i}\Delta Ln(CO_2)_{t-i} + \sum_{i=1}^{n}\beta_{2,i}\Delta Ln(GDP)_{t-i} + \sum_{i=1}^{n}\beta_{3,i}\Delta Ln(SS)_{t-i}\\ &+ \sum_{i=1}^{n}\beta_{4,i}\Delta Ln(FS)_{t-i} + \sum_{i=1}^{n}\beta_{5,i}\Delta Ln(FDI)_{t-i} + \sum_{i=1}^{n}\beta_{6,i}\Delta Ln(REC)_{t-i}\\ &+ \sum_{i=1}^{n}\beta_{7,i}\Delta Ln(TI)_{t-i} + \lambda_1 Ln(CO_2)_{t-1} + \lambda_2 Ln(GDP)_{t-1}\\ &+\lambda_3 Ln(SS)_{t-1} + \lambda_4 Ln(FS)_{t-1} + \lambda_5 Ln(FDI)_{t-1} + \lambda_6 Ln(TI)_{t-1}\\ &+\lambda_7 Ln(REC)_{t-1} + \varepsilon_t\end{aligned} \tag{14.1}$$

where β_i and λ_i refer to short-run and long-run parameters. Respectively and n is the optimal lag orders determined by the Schwarz-Bayesian Criteria (SBC). The error term ε_t is the white noise disturbance with 0 mean and constant variance. To identify the cointegration between the variables in the model, we perform the joint significance test (*F*-test) on the explanatory variables with the null hypothesis of no cointegration in Eq. 14.1 ($H_0 : \lambda_1 = \lambda_2 = \lambda_3 = \lambda_4 = \lambda_5 = \lambda_6 = \lambda_7 = 0$), against the alternative hypothesis of the presence of cointegration ($H_1 : \lambda_1 \neq \lambda_2 \neq \lambda_3 \neq \lambda_4 \neq \lambda_5 \neq \lambda_6 \neq \lambda_7 \neq 0$). The test result is based on a comparison between the model-produced *F*-statistics and the bounds critical values of Pesaran et al. (2001). We can reject the null hypothesis of no cointegration if the model-computed *F*-statistic is higher than the upper bound critical values (F – statistics > $I(1)_{critical}$). On the other hand, if the computed *F*-statistic is less than the upper bound critical values (F – statisctis < $I(1)_{critical}$), we would have insufficient evidence to reject the null hypothesis. However, if the *F*-statistics lie between the upper and lower critical values, our test result will remain inconclusive. In the case of the presence of a cointegration relationship, we can establish an error correction model (ECM) straightforwardly from the ARDL model through a simple linear transformation. Eq. 14.2 presents the specifications of our ECM model:

$$\begin{aligned}\Delta \mathrm{Ln}(\mathrm{CO_2})_t = \beta_0 + \sum_{i=1}^{n} \beta_{1,i} \Delta \mathrm{Ln}(\mathrm{CO_2})_{t-i} + \sum_{i=1}^{n} \beta_{2,i} \Delta \mathrm{Ln}(\mathrm{GDP})_{t-i} + \sum_{i=1}^{n} \beta_{3,i} \Delta \mathrm{Ln}(\mathrm{SS})_{t-i} \\ + \sum_{i=1}^{n} \beta_{4,i} \Delta \mathrm{Ln}(\mathrm{FS})_{t-i} + \sum_{i=1}^{n} \beta_{5,i} \Delta \mathrm{Ln}(\mathrm{FDI})_{t-i} \\ + \sum_{i=1}^{n} \beta_{6,i} \Delta \mathrm{Ln}(\mathrm{TI})_{t-i} + \sum_{i=1}^{n} \beta_{7,i} \Delta \mathrm{Ln}(\mathrm{REC})_{t-i} + \alpha \mathrm{ECM}_{t-1} + \varepsilon_t\end{aligned} \tag{14.2}$$

where ECM_{t-1} refers to the error correction term. For the presence of cointegration, the coefficient of ECM_{t-1} must be negatively significant. The value of α indicates the speed of adjustment back to the long-run equilibrium after unexpected short-term shocks. In order to ensure the robustness of our model estimates, we conduct diagnostic tests, including the Breusch-Godfrey test for serial correlation, White's test for heteroscedasticity, the Jarque-Bera test for normality, and the portmanteau test for white noise. Furthermore, model stability is examined by employing the cumulative sum of squares (CUSUMQ) and cumulative sum developed by Brown et al. (1975).

14.3 Results and Discussion

Table 14.4 below reports the bounds test results for our ARDL model. Since the calculated *F*-statistic exceeds the upper bounds critical value at 1% significance level, we have enough statistical evidence to reject the null hypothesis of no cointegration among variables. This result indicates the presence of a long-run relationship among the variables in Eq. 1.

The estimated short-run and long-run results are reported in Table 14.5. The estimated short-run and long-run elasticities of per capita carbon emissions with respect to economic growth are positive and significant. The coefficient of economic growth is 0.5483 in the short run and 0.4645 in the long run, respectively. This

Table 14.4 Bounds test result

Estimated equation	$CO_2 = f(GDP_t, SS_t, FS_t, FDI_t, TI_t, REC_t)$	
Lag structure	(2 2 1 0 1 0 2)	
F-statistics	4.704***	
Significance level	Lower bounds ⇒ I (0)	Upper bounds ⇒ I (1)
1%	3.15	4.43
5%	2.75	3.99
10%	2.45	3.61

Note: ***, **, and * represent statistical significance levels at 1%, 5%, and 10%, respectively. The optimal lag structure is selected by the Schwart-Bayesian Criteria (SBC). The critical values for the bounds test are obtained from Pesaranet et al. (2001)

Table 14.5 Estimated long-run and short-run coefficients

Variable	Coefficient	Std. errors	*t*-statistics
Long-run relationships			
Ln(GDP)_{t-1}	0.5483	0.2503	2.19**
Ln(SS)_{t-1}	−0.1504	0.0365	−4.12 ***
Ln(FS)_{t-1}	−0.3065	0.1352	−2.27**
Ln(FDI)_{t-1}	0.1190	0.0653	1.82*
Ln(TI)_{t-1}	0.4995	0.2171	2.30**
Ln(REC)_{t-1}	−0.0792	0.0698	−1.13
Short-run relationships			
$\Delta\text{ln(CO}_2)_{t-1}$	0.4619	0.097	4.769***
$\Delta\text{ln(GDP)}_t$	0.4645	0.112	4.14***
$\Delta\text{ln(GDP)}_{t-1}$	−0.6316	0.105	−6.02***
$\Delta\text{ln(SS)}_t$	0.0397	0.013	3.03***
$\Delta\text{ln(FDI)}_t$	−0.6917	0.206	−3.36***
$\Delta\text{ln(REC)}_t$	0.0217	0.023	0.95
$\Delta\text{ln(REC)}_{t-1}$	0.0368	0.172	2.14**
ECM_{t-1}	−0.4211	0.085	−4.97***

Note: ***, **, and * indicate statistical significance at the 1% level, 5% level, and 10% level, respectively. The maximum lag to be used is two, and the optimal lag length is chosen through the Schwartz information criterion

indicates that a 1% increase in GDP per capita in China will lead to a 0.5483% increase in carbon emissions per capita in the short run and a 0.4645% increase in the long run. The results of a positive relationship between economic growth and carbon emissions in the case of China are in line with existing literature.

The estimated coefficients of financial development indicators Ln(SS)_t and Ln(FS)_t show negative and statistically significant impacts on carbon emissions in the long run. This finding of the negative effect of financial development on carbon emission in the long run is consistent with the study of Jalil and Feridun (2011) in the case of China. Given that the estimated coefficient of Ln(FDI)_t is 0.119 in the long run, it implies a positive relationship between foreign direct investment and environmental pollution.

An interesting finding is that the coefficient of technology innovation in the long-run equation is significant with a positive sign. The positive coefficient of Ln(TI)_t indicates that a 1% increase in national expenditures on technology innovation will lead to a 0.5% increase in carbon emissions in the case of China. The result of the positive technology-pollution relationship is controversial in the literature, as discussed by Blanford (2009) and Irandoust (2016). This is mainly because the share of green technology innovation in China is relatively small in comparison with other strategic emerging sectors. As stated by Ang (2009) and Tang and Tan (2013), the impact of technology innovation on carbon emissions would be statistically observable only if there is a significant proportion of research focused on green-related projects. In addition, Zhang and Du (2017) emphasize that most of the core technologies in China's clean energy development are imported from the US and EU markets. Hence, the statistical impact of technology innovation on China's carbon emissions in our model went against expectations.

The estimated long-run coefficient of renewable energy consumption is negative with a lack of statistical significance, revealing that an increase in renewable consumption has a limited impact on emission management in China. This is mainly because the proportion of renewable energy consumption in China's energy supply mix is low with respect to other conventional energy sources (Chen et al., 2019). Although China has achieved remarkable progress in clean energy development, fossil fuels continue to dominate (85.4% of the total primary energy consumption) China's energy consumption mix (BP, 2019). Thus, the impact of renewable energy consumption on carbon mitigation in China is likely to remain limited. The insignificant clean energy-pollution nexus also reveals that despite the efforts of the Chinese central government to promote renewable energy adoption in the energy supply system, the target for reducing emissions is far below expectation.

As shown in the lower part of Table 14.5, the coefficient of $\Delta Ln(SS)_t$ is 0.0397, suggesting a positive correlation between financial development and carbon emissions in the short run. This effect has been observed because the Chinese stock market may support public listed enterprises by offering larger financing channels to implement new projects within a relatively short time period. Consequently, this would lead to an increase in energy consumption and exacerbate carbon emissions. According to the arguments of Sadorsky (2010) and Zhang (2011), a well-developed financial market may benefit consumers for personal loan activities, which encourages individual usage of high-energy-consuming products and eventually leads to carbon deterioration in the short run. In summary, in the case of China, an increase in financial development will lead to an increase in carbon emissions in the short run and improve environmental conditions in the long run. The negatively significant coefficient of $\Delta ln(FDI)_t$ indicates that a temporary increase in FDI drives carbon reductions in China. It is also noted that renewable energy consumption and technology innovation have limited impacts on the management of emissions in China in the short run.

The estimated coefficient of the error correction term ECM_{t-1} is -0.4211 with statistical significance at the 1% level, implying a convergence from the short-run dynamics to the long-run equilibrium. Given the negative sign of the error correction term, the short-run deviations are being corrected by 42.11% each year with respect to the long-run equilibrium.

The statistical results of the diagnostic tests are summarized in Table 14.6, and they suggest that our ARDL estimation is correctly specified with the absence of serial correlation and heteroscedasticity. Moreover, the Jarque-Bera normality test reveals that our model disturbances are normally distributed with the presence of the white noise process. Figure 14.1 below displays the plots of CUSUM and CUSUMQ tests for testing the parameter stability of our model estimation over the sample period. Since all CUSUM and CUSUMQ statistics lie between the upper and lower critical bounds, our model estimation satisfies the stability condition.

Table 14.6 Diagnostic tests

Test	Statistics	Test	Statistics
R^2	0.811	Adj R^2	0.7395
Serial correlation	0.049(0.824)	Heteroscedasticity	52.00(0.4347)
Jarque-bear normality	2.284(0.319)	Portmanteau test	30.580(0.1657)

Note: This table provides test results for different diagnostic tests. The Breusch-Godfrey test for serial correlation, White's test for heteroscedasticity, the Jarque-Bera test for normality, and the portmanteau test for white noise. The value in parentheses denotes the p-value for test significance

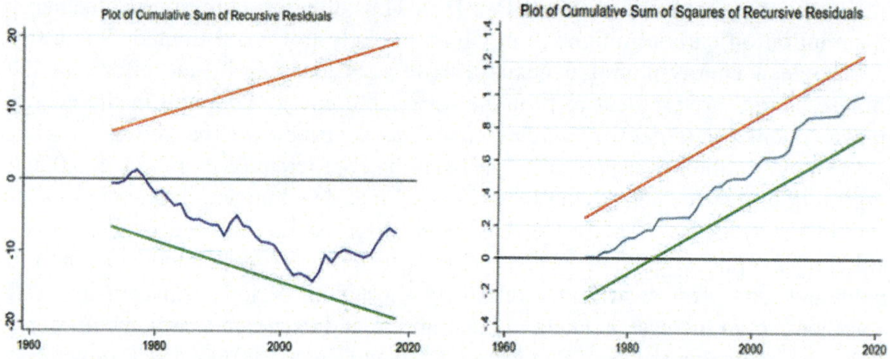

A: Cumulative Sum of Recursive Residuals

B: Cumulative Sum of Squares of Recursive Residuals

Fig. 14.1 Plots of model stability tests (CUSUM and CUSUMQ). (**a**) Cumulative sum of recursive residuals; (**b**) Cumulative sum of squares of recursive residuals

14.4 Conclusion

Understanding the influencing factors of carbon dioxide emission is an essential prerequisite for Chinese policy makers to maintain sustainable low-carbon economic growth in China. Although previous research programs have extensively studied the emission-growth nexus, those studies did not incorporate the impact of renewable energy development and technology innovations on carbon emissions. Therefore, we perform the ARDL bounds test and error correction model to explore the causal influence of China's financial development, renewable energy consumption, and technology innovation on carbon emissions over the period from 1965 to 2018. The ARDL bounds test confirms the presence of a long-run relationship between carbon emissions, economic growth, financial development, renewable energy consumptions, and technology innovations.

The empirical results reveal that both short-run and long-run coefficients of economic growth are positive and significant, suggesting that past economic developments had led to an increase in environmental pollutions in China. In contrast, financial development in China is found to contribute to a significant decrease in carbon emissions in the long run. In terms of the short-run effect, a sudden improvement of financial development exacerbates carbon emissions via additional economic activities and individual consumptions.

It is concluded that carbon emissions are mainly determined by economic growth, foreign direct investment, and technological progress in the long run. Moreover, the impact of renewable energy consumption on carbon emissions is found to be weak and insignificant in China, mainly because the proportion of renewable energy consumption is relatively insignificant with regard to the total energy consumption level.

Our empirical results have following three policy implications for Chinese policymakers regarding sustainable low-carbon economic development in China. First, givn significant impact of financial development on carbon emission reducation in China, the Chinese government should further progress the market scale and operational efficiency in the financial sector. Moreover, establishing a systematic and effective green finance market may allow the market to mobilize private capital and social funds into green industries through the channel of financial derivatives. In this respect, the establishment of a green finance market will encourage private green investors, banks, securities, insurance, funds, and other financial institutions to actively participate in low-carbon economic development. Second, given the insignificant effect of renewable energy consumption on environmental improvement, the government should pay more attention to the promotion of renewable energy sources from both supply and demand sides of China's economy. On the supply side, the government may support green enterprises by providing fiscal incentives, technology consultancy, and favorable policy implementations. Since the energy sector is mainly owned and operated by state-owned companies, government direct interventions remain one of the most effective strategies to increase the proportion of renewable energy sources in China's energy supply portfolio (Reboredo & Wen, 2015). In terms of the demand side, positive price discrimination of clean energy electricity encourages the public adoption of clean energy sources effectively among households. In addition, the government should continue to enforce environmental laws. Jalil and Feridun (2011) state that the government's proactive laws have not been beneficial to environmental protection over the past two decades due to an ineffective supervisory monitoring system and inefficient compliance measures. Therefore, the government should introduce more stringent legislation and an efficient compliance measuring scheme for controlling carbon emissions among energy-intensive industries. Furthermore, a carbon credit rating scheme and carbon allowance trading may also be effective strategies to accelerate the process of energy transformations among energy-intensive industries as enterprises are expected to be eco-friendly with regard to the impacts of price signaling and policy enforcement. Last but not least, our results show a positive relationship between technology innovation and carbon emission, principally because the percentage of clean energy science research is relatively small compared to other strategic emerging sectors. Considering the potential impacts of the US--China trade wars, we strongly recommend the Chinese government to undertake an aggressive investment strategy in cultivating talents to enhance science research in green technologies in order to achieve successful technology innovations in renewable energy sources and energy efficiency.

Acknowledgments This paper is part of a project that has received funding from the European Union's Horizon 2020 research and innovation program under Marie Sklodowska-Curie grant agreement No. 870245. Binyi Zhang acknowledges support from the Charles University Grant Agency (GAUK) under grant No. 862119. Karel Janda acknowledges support from the Czech Science Foundation (grant No.22-19617S). The views expressed here are those of the authors and not necessarily those of our institutions. All remaining errors are solely our responsibility. (I changed there the numbers both for EU grant and GACR grant).

References

Ang, J. B. (2009). CO_2 emissions, research and technology transfer in China. *Ecological Economics, 68*(10), 2658–2665.

Bhattacharya, M., Churchill, S. A., & Paramati, S. R. (2017). The dynamic impact of renewable energy and institutions on economic output and CO_2 emissions across regions. *Renewable Energy, 111*, 157–167.

Blanford, G. J. (2009). R&D investment strategy for climate change. *Energy Economics, 31*, S27–S36.

BP. (2019). BP Energy Outlook 2019 Edition. BP.

Brown, R. L., Durbin, J., & Evans, J. M. (1975). Techniques for testing the constancy of regression relationships over time. *Journal of the Royal Statistical Society: Series B: Methodological, 37*(2), 149–163.

Cetin, M., Ecevit, E., & Yucel, A. G. (2018). The impact of economic growth, energy consumption, trade openness, and financial development on carbon emissions: Empirical evidence from Turkey. *Environmental Science and Pollution Research, 25*(36), 36589–36603.

Chen, Y., Wang, Z., & Zhong, Z. (2019). CO_2 emissions, economic growth, renewable and non-renewable energy production and foreign trade in China. *Renewable Energy, 131*, 208–216.

Dogan, E., & Seker, F. (2016). The influence of real output, renewable and non-renewable energy, trade and financial development on carbon emissions in the top renewable energy countries. *Renewable and Sustainable Energy Reviews, 60*, 1074–1085.

Irandoust, M. (2016). The renewable energy-growth nexus with carbon emissions and technological innovation: Evidence from the Nordic countries. *Ecological Indicators, 69*, 118–125.

Jalil, A., & Feridun, M. (2011). The impact of growth, energy and financial development on the environment in China: A cointegration analysis. *Energy Economics, 33*(2), 284–291.

Janda, K., & Zhang, B. (2020). *The impact of renewable energy and technology innovation on Chinese carbon dioxide emissions*. FFA Working Paper 3/2020, FFA, University of Economics.

Javid, M., & Sharif, F. (2016). Environmental Kuznets curve and financial development in Pakistan. *Renewable and Sustainable Energy Reviews, 54*, 406–414.

Jiao, J., Jiang, G., & Yang, R. (2018). Impact of R&D technology spillovers on carbon emissions between China's regions. *Structural Change and Economic Dynamics, 47*, 35–45.

Kasman, A., & Duman, Y. S. (2015). CO_2 emissions, economic growth, energy consumption, trade and urbanization in new EU member and candidate countries: A panel data analysis. *Economic Modelling, 44*, 97–103.

Kim, J., & Park, K. (2016). Financial development and deployment of renewable energy technologies. *Energy Economics, 59*, 238–250.

Li, T., Wang, Y., & Zhao, D. (2016). Environmental Kuznets curve in China: New evidence from dynamic panel analysis. *Energy Policy, 91*, 138–147.

Nasreen, S., Anwar, S., & Ozturk, I. (2017). Financial stability, energy consumption and environmental quality: Evidence from South Asian economies. *Renewable and Sustainable Energy Reviews, 67*, 1105–1122.

National Bureau of Statistics of China (NBSC). (2019). *China energy statistical yearbook 2018*. China Statistics Press.

National Development and Reformation Commission (NRDC). (2018). *Energy production and consumption revolution strategy (2016–2030)*. NRDC.

Ozcan, B. (2013). The nexus between carbon emissions, energy consumption and economic growth in Middle East countries: A panel data analysis. *Energy Policy, 62*, 1138–1147.

Pao, H.-T., Yu, H.-C., & Yang, Y.-H. (2011). Modeling the CO_2 emissions, energy use, and economic growth in Russia. *Energy, 36*(8), 5094–5100.

Pesaran, M. H., & Shin, Y. (1998). An autoregressive distributed-lag modelling approach to cointegration analysis. *Econometric Society Monographs, 31*, 371–413.

Pesaran, M. H., Shin, Y., & Smith, R. J. (2001). Bounds testing approaches to the analysis of level relationships. *Journal of Applied Econometrics, 16*(3), 289–326.

Reboredo, J. C., & Wen, X. (2015). Are China's new energy stock prices driven by new energy policies? *Renewable and Sustainable Energy Reviews, 45*, 624–636.

Saboori, B., & Sulaiman, J. (2013). CO_2 emissions, energy consumption and economic growth in Association of Southeast Asian Nations (ASEAN) countries: A cointegration approach. *Energy, 55*, 813–822.

Sadorsky, P. (2010). The impact of financial development on energy consumption in emerging economies. *Energy Policy, 38*(5), 2528–2535.

Shahbaz, M., Solarin, S. A., Mahmood, H., & Arouri, M. (2013). Does financial development reduce CO_2 emissions in Malaysian economy? A time series analysis. *Economic Modelling, 35*, 145–152.

Tamazian, A., Rao, B.B (2010). Do economic, financial and institutional developments matter for environmental degradation? Evidence from transitional economies. Energy Economics 32(1), 137–145.

Tang, C. F., & Tan, E. C. (2013). Exploring the nexus of electricity consumption, economic growth, energy prices and technology innovation in Malaysia. *Applied Energy, 104*, 297–305.

Zhang, Y.-J. (2011). The impact of financial development on carbon emissions: An empirical analysis in China. *Energy Policy, 39*(4), 2197–2203.

Zhang, G., & Du, Z. (2017). Co-movements among the stock prices of new energy, high-technology and fossil fuel companies in China. *Energy, 135*, 249–256.

Chapter 15
Green Bond Pricing and Its Determinant: Evidence from Chinese Secondary Market

Karel Janda and Binyi Zhang

Abstract This paper investigates whether green bonds offer investors in China an attractive yield compared to other equivalent conventional bonds. By applying a matching method and, subsequently, fixed-effect estimation, our empirical results reveal a significant negative yield premium of green bonds on average—1.8 bps lower than that of their conventional counterparts in the Chinese secondary market. Furthermore, we find that green bond premiums vary across issuers' business sectors, mainly due to the public reputation of bond issuers. We also show that bond credit rating and corporate ESG rating have a significant impact on green bond premiums. Our results point to some practical implications for policymakers and investors.

Key words Green bonds · Green bond premium · ESG trading · China

15.1 Introduction

Climate change has become an increasing global concern, which exacerbates the need for scaling up the transition to a low-carbon and climate-resilient economy. Following this increase in public interest, the market for sustainable finance has grown remarkably in recent years, which opens new investment opportunities for individual and institutional investors (Reboredo & Ugolini, 2020). Within the framework of sustainable investment, green bonds represent a promising tool in fixed-income markets whose proceeds are exclusively earmarked for eligible green

---

K. Janda (✉)
Institute of Economic Studies, Faculty of Social Sciences, Charles University, Prague, Czech Republic

Department of Banking and Insurance, Faculty of Finance and Accounting, University of Economics, Prague, Czech Republic

B. Zhang
Institute of Economic Studies, Faculty of Social Sciences, Charles University, Prague, Czech Republic

D. Procházka (ed.), *Regulation of Finance and Accounting*, Springer Proceedings in Business and Economics, https://doi.org/10.1007/978-3-030-99873-8_15

projects, such as renewable energy, energy efficiency, carbon mitigation, clean transportation, sustainable waste management and land use, biodiversity conservation, and clean water management (International Capital Market Association (ICMA), 2018). Following the first green bond introduced by the European Investment Bank (EIB) in 2007, the green bond market has experienced remarkable growth over the last decade. According to data published by Climate Bond Initiative (CBI), the global issuance volume of green bonds has grown from $11 billion in 2013 to $258.9 billion in 2019 (CBI, 2020). For the future green bond market expansion, Fatin (2019) estimates that the volume of global green bond issuances may exceed $1 trillion per year in 2030.

As for the flourishing literature on green bond pricing, Maltais and Nykvist (2020) declare that both pecuniary and nonpecuniary motives can attract investors toward green bond investments. In terms of pecuniary motives, green bonds may provide investors opportunities to hedge against environmental financial risks (Elhers & Packer, 2017; Reboredo, 2018; Banga, 2019; Nanyakkara & Colombage, 2019). Alternatively, investors with nonpecuniary motives care less about financial returns and therefore derive proenvironmental preferences by paying a yield premium to acquire a green bond (Zerbib, 2019; Bachelet et al., 2019; Larcker & Watts, 2020; Maltais & Nykvist, 2020).

Previous studies investigating the dynamics of green bond pricing (Preclaw and Baksh 2015; Hachenberg & Schiereck, 2018; Zerbib, 2019; Gianfrate & Peri, 2019; Hyun et al., 2020) have focused on measuring the credit spread between a green bond and its corresponding conventional counterpart, which is known as the green bond premium. However, due to the wide methodological heterogeneity in study designs (e.g., sample selection, matching process, control variables, and empirical analysis), no consensus has been reached on the significance and magnitude of the green premium, and empirical results remain mixed and inconclusive.

Using a sample of bonds from the Bloomberg Global Green Bond Index, Preclaw and Bakshi (2015) perform an ordinary least square regression (OLS) analysis to evaluate the yield difference between green and conventional bonds. Their empirical result suggests a significant negative green bond premium of 17 basis points (bps) on the global secondary market. Nanayakkara and Colombage (2019) use the option-adjusted spread (OAS) to measure the green premium and to document the fact that green bonds are traded at a negative premium of 63 bps compared with other comparable corporate bonds. Based on a matching method that consists of 21 selected bond-specific characteristics, Zerbib (2019) creates 110 triplets of one green bond and two conventional bonds to quantify the magnitude of the effect of proenvironmental risk preferences on the dynamics of green bond pricing. Using a two-step regression analysis, Zerbib (2019) reveals a significant negative green bond premium of −2 bps in the secondary market. Likewise, based on a data set of 121 European green bonds, Gianfrate and Peri (2019) perform a propensity score matching technique and declare the existence of green premiums of −20 bps for the primary market and −5 bps for the secondary market. Moreover, Gianfrate and Peri (2019) point out that a significant negative green premium provides a financial incentive to bond issuers to become more willing to raise funds by issuing green bonds rather than conventional bonds. Reboredo (2018) and Reboredo and Ugolini (2020) conclude that price changes in the green bond market comove with other financial markets, and specifically, the green bond market receives significant spillover effects from price changes in the treasury, USD currency, and the corporate debt market. In a systematic review in the literature of green bond markets, MacAskill et al. (2021) observe an average level of green premium in the range of −1 bp to −9 bps across different secondary markets.

Based on the World Bank's Emerging Market Green Bond Report 2018, East Asia and the Pacific is the largest green bond market among other geographical regions. Among Asian countries, China represents the largest market for the future development of sustainable finance and investment. Given the commitments under the Paris Climate Agreement, China has prioritized the environmental and energy transitions in its governance principles for mitigating climate change. In 2015, China's 13th Five Year Plan for Energy Development emphasized the need to establish a green finance system including the development of green bonds to support the transition to a lower-carbon economy. In September 2020, China further announced at the United Nations General Assembly that it will peak its carbon emissions before 2030 and achieve carbon neutrality to attain net-zero emissions by 2060 (known as the dual carbon goals) (Janda et.al, 2022). As facilitated by the government's promise to maintain sustainable economic growth, the Chinese green bond market has experienced extraordinary growth since 2016. With a total volume of US$ 44 billion in green bonds issued in 2020, China remains the second-largest green bond issuing country in the world (Climate Bond Initiative (CBI), 2021). Since then, green bonds have become a top priority for the Chinese authorities (Wang & Zhang, 2017) with regard to the target of reaching carbon neutrality by 2060. Along with preferential policies and bullish markets for sustainable finance, green bonds have become a crucial financial instrument for China's capital market to finance low-carbon sustainable development. Despite the remarkable growth in issuance volumes over the past few years, the green bond market in China remains relatively nascent and substantially smaller than conventional bond markets.

The examination of previous green bond literature reveals that the evidence of green premium in the green bond market remains mixed and inconclusive. Besides, it is yet to be determined whether this newly developed financial instrument offers investors attractive yields as compared to conventional bonds in the Chinese secondary market. Given that so far only limited attention has been paid to the Chinese green bond market, this paper aims to quantify the magnitude of the yield difference between green bonds and equivalent conventional bonds with the use of the most up-to-date data from the Chinese secondary market. Particularly, this paper aims to address the following two research questions:

- Do bond prices reflect the environmental awareness of financial investors in the Chinese secondary market?
- If there exists a significant green premium in the Chinese bond market, what are the potential factors that have an impact on the premium?

This paper, in investigating the green premium in the Chinese secondary market, contributes to the extant green bond literature in three ways. First, given China's special national conditions in banking and financial sectors, the bond market is mainly dominated by the interbank bond and exchange bond markets. The disconnectedness among the submarkets may restrict investors and policy makers from exploring and understanding the potential influential factors of green bond pricing. Hence, our analysis contributes to the understanding of investors' preference in the choice of green bonds in the Chinese secondary market. Second, in contrast to Wang et al. (2019), who conclude the presence of a positive green bond risk premium in the Chinese market, our empirical analysis provides significant statistical evidence of the existence of a negative green bond premium. Although green bonds are a newly emerging financial instrument in the Chinese market, our results confirm the presence of proenvironmental preferences among the Chinese financial investors that are willing to pay a premium to acquire a green bond in their portfolio management. Third, our empirical results reveal a mixed conclusion regarding the statistical impact of external auditing on the variation in green bond premiums. Typically, CBI climate certification is found to have no significant impact on green premiums, while environmental, social, and governance (ESG)-rated bond issuers are expected to enjoy a lower cost of capital. These findings reflect an inconsistent definition of green bond standards in the Chinese market. Therefore, the ongoing work to improve the consistency of definition standards would be important for the further development of green finance in China.

The remainder of this paper is structured as follows. Section 15.2 outlines the research question and the testable research hypothesis of this paper. Section 15.3 details data sources and the matching process. Section 15.4 reports the empirical methodology we use to identify green bond premiums in the Chinese secondary market. Section 15.5 reports and discusses our main empirical results. Finally, Sect. 15.6 summarizes our empirical findings and concludes the paper with policy implications.

15.2 Research Hypothesis Formulation

Several studies have shown that the green premium is driven by the presence of information asymmetries between investors and bond issuers in the bond market. Thus, investors tend to take independent information enhancers (e.g., bond issuer types, credit rating classes, third-party certifications) as key indicators to minimize the risks associated with information asymmetry (Bachelet et al., 2019; Hyun et al., 2020; Stádník, 2022). In order to address our research questions, we provide the following testable hypotheses:

- **Hypothesis 1** (H1): There does not exist a yield premium on green bonds in comparison with equivalent conventional bonds in the Chinese secondary market.

Except for the use of proceeds, green bonds are almost identical to conventional fixed-income securities. Tolliver et al. (2020) argue that green bonds pricing should be affected by many of the same factors that affect conventional bonds, and investors should not observe any systematic significant pricing differences between the two in both primary and secondary markets. Meanwhile, Stádník (2021) claims that investors should have similar trading strategies and take interest rates sensitivity arbitrage in their green and conventional bond portfolio management.

Hence, like other conventional bonds, the green bond should be traded at its face value, and investors should perceive no price difference between the two. However, the green bond premium has been widely documented in previous studies (Bachelet et al., 2019; Zerbib, 2019; Toilliver et al., 2020; MacAskill et al., 2021). As discussed by Zerbib (2019) and Tolliver et al. (2020), investors with proenvironmental preferences and nonpecuniary motives are encouraged to incorporate—besides financial values—social and environmental values into their portfolio management. Under the condition of similar bond characteristics, the nonpecuniary-motivated investors are willing to accept a lower return on green bond investment, thus causing a negative credit spread between a green bond and a conventional bond and supporting the significance of a negative bond premium in the market. In order to quantify the significance and magnitude of the green bond premium, we hypothesize that there is no difference in the ask yields of green and conventional bonds with identical characteristics in the Chinese secondary market.

- **Hypothesis 2** (H2): A third-party credit rating does not affect the magnitude of the green premium.

Previous literature has documented that the factors affecting the risk premium of green bonds are mainly categorized into macroeconomic conditions, bond characteristics, and the firm-specific characteristics of bond issuers. Moreover, Wang et al. (2019) declare that credit rating, time to maturity, and bond issue size are the three major factors influencing the green premium in the Chinese secondary market. On the basis that bond pricing is closely determined to its credit ratings (Stádník, 2018), Agliardi and Agliardi (2019) conduct a set of numerical computations and their empirical results reveal that credit rating upgrade may lead to a lower cost of capital for green bond issuers. Using the Pearson correlation analysis, MacAskill et al. (2021) demonstrate that bond with credit ratings and investment-grade tend to provide the most predictable existence of a green premium in the range of −2 to −6 bps. Based on the analysis of green bonds in the US municipal bond market, Karpf and Mandel (2018) find that the green premium negatively correlates with bond crediting rating classes. Likewise, Zerbib (2019) finds that the yield premium increases by 2.43 bps for A- and AA-rated bonds in comparison to AAA-rated green bonds. On the other hand, Hachenberg and Schiereck (2018) suggest an insignificant relationship between the green premium and bond credit rating classes. Based on the above examinations, we hypothesize that credit rating classes do not have a statistically significant impact on the green bond premium in the Chinese secondary market.

- **Hypothesis 3** (H3): The green bond premium does not differ across business sectors in the Chinese secondary bond market.

The research conducted by Kapraun and Scheins (2019) and Zerbib (2019) declares that, apart from bond characteristics, the magnitude of green premium varies across issuer types and business sectors. Given the presence of a negative green premium in the US and European bond markets, Kapraun and Scheins (2019) find that the magnitude of the yield premium of green bonds issued by governments or supranational bodies is much larger than those issued by corporations. Meanwhile, Zerbib (2019) reveals that green bonds issued by business sectors associated with consumer products, industrials, and utilities are traded at a higher premium level compared to those issued by finance and material sectors. Based on this notion, we hypothesize that the green bond premium does not vary across business sectors in the Chinese secondary bond market.

- **Hypothesis 4** (H4): A third green bond certification and an external EGS revision do not affect the magnitude of the green bond premium in the Chinese secondary bond market.

Due to the presence of asymmetric information in the bond market, green bonds with third-party green bond certifications and external reviews of corporate environmental, social, and governance (ESG) performance may allow financial investors to reduce the suspicion of a greenwashing behavior (Bachelet et al., 2019; Wang et al., 2019). As Ehlers and Packer (2017) stated, from the issuer's point of view, external green certification enables asset managers to prove to investors that the proceeds from green bonds are truly earmarked for environmentally friendly projects. Given the notice of the certification, investors might become more willing to pay a premium for acquiring a green bond. For instance, Larcker and Watts (2019), Bachelet et al. (2019), Wang et al. (2019), and Hyun et al. (2020) conclude that green bonds with third-party certification enjoy a certain amount of pricing benefits. Since green bonds are newly developed financial instruments in the Chinese market, the statistical impact of third-party green certification on the bond premium remains undetermined. Accordingly, our last hypothesis in this research assumes that third-party green bond certification and an external ESG rating do not have a statistical impact on the magnitude of the green bond premium in the Chinese secondary bond market.

15.3 Data

In order to study the green premium in the Chinese secondary market, our first step in data collection is to create a green bond database that contains all bond-specific characteristics. We collect our data from two sources, Thomson Reuters Datastream and the Chinese iFind database, on November 27, 2020. As of that date, there are 179 active green bonds available in the market with issue dates between the years

Table 15.1 Matching Criteria

Bond characteristics	Matching criteria
Issuer	Exact match
Issuer type	Exact match
Bond instrument type	Exact match
Maturity date	±2 years
Issue date	±4 years
Bond issuance volume	25–400% of the green bond
Coupon type	Exact match
Coupon frequency	Exact match
Bond rating	Exact match
Seniority	Exact match
Tenor	±2 years
Executable	Exact match
Callable	Exact match
Puttable	Exact match
Extendible	Exact match
Has sinking fund	Exact match
Partly paid	Exact match
Paid in kind	Exact match
Perpetual	Exact match

2016 and 2020. Since 2016 was the first year of green bond issuance in China, we do not include any bonds issued before 2016 in our sample observation. By considering only straight and senior green bonds with a plain-vanilla-fixed coupon payment, we exclude 66 bonds from our sample data. Therefore, only 113 green bonds are available in the next step of the matching process.

Following previous literature on green bond pricing, we use econometric specifications to investigate the differences between the yield term structures of green and conventional bonds in the Chinese bond market. As discussed by Bachelet et al. (2019) and Zerbib (2019), the ideal methodological approach to assess the yield premium of green bonds in comparison with that of conventional bonds would be the use of a one-to-one exact matching method. However, such a one-to-one exact matching can result in a significant level of sample reduction and therefore increase our estimation bias. By considering the above suggestions and in line with previous literature, we adopt a matching method that consists of 19 matching criteria to investigate the yield difference between green bonds and their corresponding conventional bonds (Table 15.1). For each green bond in our matching procedure, we search for two conventional bonds that are the nearest neighbor in terms of the selected bond characteristics. In the case that a green bond is identified to have either none or only one matched conventional bond in our matching process, we would exclude it from our sample data. Since it is impossible to find two bonds with exactly the same characteristics in terms of the issue date, maturity, amount issued, and tenor, we adjust our matching procedure by allowing a reasonable variation in these four bond characteristics. For the issue dates, we consider a maximum of 4-year difference between green and conventional bonds. Besides, we match conventional bonds with a maturity that is neither more than 2 years shorter nor more than 2 years longer than the green bond's maturity. The issue amount of a conventional bond is allowed to lie within the range of 25% as the minimum to four times the matched green bond as the maximum. In terms of tenor, the difference is controlled within 2 years. Based on these principles, we create 64 matched triplets composed of one green bond and two matched conventional bonds.

Once the matching is completed, we use linear interpolation and extrapolation to combine the ask yields of matched conventional bonds into a synthetic bond. In doing so, we retrieve the ask yields of each triplet of bonds (the green bond and the corresponding conventional bonds) from Thomson Reuters Datastream, from the issue date of the matched green bond up to October 22, 2020. For any missing values on each of the three matched bonds, we remove the entire line out of our panel. The ask yield of the synthetic conventional bond is estimated by a linear function between the two conventional bonds at the time of maturity of the green bond. For each triplet of matched bonds, with α as the intercept and β as the slope coefficient of a linear function passing through $\left(\text{Maturity}_{i,t}^{\text{CB1}}, Y_{i,t}^{\text{CB1}}\right)$ and $\left(\text{Maturity}_{i,t}^{\text{CB2}}, Y_{i,t}^{\text{CB2}}\right)$, the daily ask yield of a synthetic conventional bond is estimated through the following equation:

$$Y_{i,t}^{\text{SB}} = \alpha + \beta \cdot M_{i,t}^{\text{GB}} \tag{15.1}$$

where $Y_{i,t}^{\text{SB}}$ represents the daily ask yield of the synthetic bond and $M_{i,t}^{\text{GB}}$ refers to the number of days to maturity with respect to the green bond maturity date. In addition to that, we take the difference in the ask yield of a green bond and a corresponding synthetic bond to measure the yield spread among matched green bonds and the corresponding synthetic bonds (See Eq. 15.2)

$$\Delta Y_{i,t} = Y_{i,t}^{\text{GB}} - Y_{i,t}^{\text{SB}} \tag{15.2}$$

In order to ensure the robustness of our matching result, we keep the estimated yield spread within the interval from the 2.5th to the 97.5th percentile based on the general distribution of the average of $\Delta Y_{i,\ t}$, which we obtained from Eq. 15.2. This approach allows us to avoid unwanted high or low unrealistic values of the ask yield difference in our data sample and therefore to minimize the impact of outliers on our estimation.

Based on the matching criteria presented in Table 15.1, we apply the Wilcoxon signed-rank test to assess the quality of our matching result by testing whether the sample distribution of the matched green bond differs from the conventional bonds. The test results reported in Table 15.2 reveal that, at the median level, the coupon rate, time to maturity, and the issue price between the two sample groups are not statistically different. Figure 15.1 shows how the ask yields and the yield differences

Table 15.2 Comparison of bond characteristics using Wilcoxon signed-rank test

Bond characteristics	GB	CBs	Mean difference	*P*-value
Coupon (%)	4.263	4.202	0.06	0.556
Time to maturity (year)	3.875	4.094	−0.218	0.459
Issue price	100	100	0.000	1.00
Amount issue	4.246	9.054	−4.806	0.0198

Note: The null hypothesis suggests an identical distribution between two pairs of observations

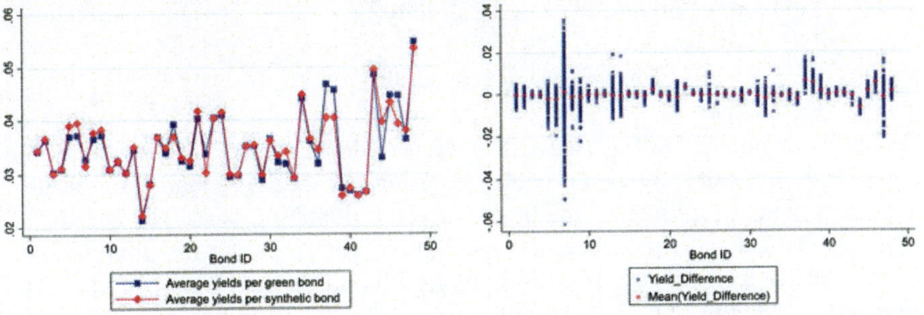

(a) (b)

Fig. 15.1 Distribution of the yield differences and the ask yields between green and synthetic bonds. (**a**) Average daily yields of green and synthetic bonds. (**b**) Yield difference between green and synthetic bonds

Table 15.3 Steps for sample construction

Search criteria	Number of bonds
Number of active bonds labeled as "green" on Thomson Reuters Eikon/ Datastream and the Chinese iFind database	179
Straight and senior green bonds with plain-vanilla-fixed coupon payment	113
Green bonds available for the matching process	64
Matched green with sufficient time-series length	48

Note: We removed three green bonds from our sample observation due to the limited time series available for the matching. Additionally, three matched triplets were excluded from the sample to avoid unwanted high and low synthetic ask yields. The number of bond trading days available for each pair of group ranges from a minimum of 41 days to a maximum of 684 days.

vary across matched pairs of green and synthetic bonds, and it indicates a good quality control of our matching process.

Table 15.3 summarizes the steps we undertake to construct our final database for empirical analysis. Our sample data constitute an unbalanced panel of 48 triplets of green bonds and synthetic bonds from 33 bond issuers with a total number of 14088 daily observations. The number of bond trading days available for each pair of group ranges from a minimum of 41 days to a maximum of 684 days. The earliest observation of yield difference ($\Delta Y_{i,\ t}$) is available from May 17, 2017; the latest is dated October 22, 2020.

15.4 Methodology

We take the ask yield spreads of green bonds and their corresponding synthetic bonds to determine if there exists a green premium in the Chinese secondary market. Since the matched bond pairs are designed to be consistent as far as possible, the green premium is defined by controlling the residual differences in liquidity between matched conventional bonds and their corresponding green counterparts (Zerbib, 2019; Hyun et al., 2020). Hence, we apply a one-way individual fixed-effect panel regression model to estimate $\Delta Y_{i,\,t}$ on $\Delta \text{Liquidity}_{i,\,t}$:

$$\Delta Y_{i,t} = \alpha_i + \beta\, \Delta\, \text{Liquidity}_{i,t} + \varepsilon_{i,t} \tag{15.3}$$

From the parameters in Eq. 15.3, $\Delta Y_{i,\,t}$ refers to the daily yield difference for the ith bond pair on the day t, which is computed using Eq. 15.2. The main parameter of our interest, which captures a time-invariant green premium, is α_i. The significant negative α_i indicates the presence of a green premium, revealing that investors are willing to accept a lower yield for acquiring green bonds in the Chinese market. The parameter $\varepsilon_{i,\,t}$ denotes the idiosyncratic error term. $\Delta \text{Liquidity}_{i,\,t}$ represents the liquidity difference between a green bond and its synthetic counterpart, which is defined as

$$\Delta\, \text{Liquidity}_{i,t} = \text{Liquidity}_{i,t}^{\text{GB}} - \text{Liquidity}_{i,t}^{\text{CB}} \tag{15.4}$$

Since the intraday transactional quote data are not available for infrequently traded bonds, we cannot apply conventional liquidity benchmarks, such as the intraday effective bid-ask spreads, to estimate the liquidity of the Chinese green bond market. Among the existing low-frequency proxies for the measurement of liquidity, one strand of previous literature based on global research has suggested that the daily version of the closing percent quoted spread (CPQS) is superior to all other low-frequency percent-cost proxies (Chuang & Zhang, 2014; Fong et al., 2017; Zerbib, 2019; Będowska-Sójka & Echaust, 2020). In this paper, we comply with previous research and use the closing percent quoted spread (CPQS) as our liquidity proxy, which is expressed as follows:

$$\text{Liquidity}_{i,t} = \text{CPQS}_{i,t} = \frac{(P_{A,t} - P_{B,t})}{M_{i,t}} \tag{15.5}$$

where $P_{A,\,t}$ and $P_{B,\,t}$ are the closing ask and bid price, respectively, observed at the end of each available trading day t. $M_{i,\,t}$ refers to the average of $P_{A,\,t}$ and $P_{B,\,t}$. For the purpose of computing liquidity difference, a liquidity proxy for the matched synthetic bonds is also estimated using the distance-weighted average of the CPQS based on the maturity of conventional bonds in relation to the maturity of green bonds:

Table 15.4 Descriptive statistics of the estimated bond liquidity

	Min	1st quartile	Mean	Median	3rd quartile	Max	SD	N
$CPQS_{GB}$(%)	0.00	0.16	0.23	0.25	0.33	0.98	0.13	14088
$CPQS_{CB}$(%)	0.000	0.001	0.002	0.002	0.003	0.007	0.001	28176
ΔCPQS (%)	−0.53	−0.05	0.03	0.00	0.09	0.92	0.12	14088

Note: This table reports the descriptive statistics of the difference in bond liquidity between green bonds and their synthetic conventional counterparts using the closing percent quoted spread (CPQS). GB and CB refer to green bond and conventional bond, respectively

$$\mathrm{CPQS}_{i,t}^{\mathrm{SB}} = \frac{d_2}{d_1 + d_2}\mathrm{CPQS}_{i,t}^{\mathrm{CB}_1} + \frac{\mathrm{d}_1}{\mathrm{d}_1 + \mathrm{d}_2}\mathrm{CPQS}_{i,t}^{\mathrm{CB}_2} \tag{15.6}$$

where $d_1 = |\mathrm{Maturity}_{\mathrm{GB}} - \mathrm{Maturity}_{\mathrm{CB1}}|$ and $d_2 = |\mathrm{Maturity}_{\mathrm{GB}} - \mathrm{Maturity}_{\mathrm{CB2}}|$.

Table 15.4 provides the descriptive statistics of the estimated CPQS of green bonds and their synthetic bond counterparts. Given that $\Delta\mathrm{CPQS}_{i,\ t}$ is centered around zero with a low level of standard deviation, our matching process has well managed to have control of the liquidity differentials between the matched green and conventional bonds.

15.5 Determinants of the Green Premium

Besides green premium identification, we investigate the potential determinants of the green premium as our second research question. Based on both theoretical and empirical evidence from previous literature on green bond pricing, we consider third-party credit rating, external verification, and bond issuers' sector as the potential factors influencing the green premium in the Chinese bond market. Table 15.5 reports detailed descriptions of the variables we used for our investigation.

It is worth noting that our second step in the analysis is based on a strict assumption that all time-invariant green effects are fully captured by estimating Eq. 15.3. Based on that prior assumption, we perform OLS model specifications with robust standard errors to test our hypotheses 2–4. Consistent with other research, we take the variables issue amount and maturity as our control variables for the purpose of robustness control. Given that small bond issuance may result in a small investor base in the market, the trading activities and bond liquidities are expected to be relatively low (Stádník, 2014). In contrast, bonds with higher issue amounts are more likely to experience price volatility by having a higher volume of trading activities in the market. In this paper, we take the natural logarithm of the issuance amount to avoid any unwanted heteroskedasticity. The variable Maturity is calculated as the number of years to green bond maturity. To test our second hypothesis (H2), the possible impact of credit rating on the green bond premium, we include a categorical variable representing the third-party credit rating into our model specification based on information retrieved from Chinese domestic rating agencies. Based on the Thomson Reuters Business Classification (TRBC), we create a

Table 15.5 Descriptions of variables

Variable	Description
Yield difference $\Delta\text{Yield}_{i,t}$	Calculated as the yield difference between a green bond and the corresponding synthetic bond. The ask yield of synthetic is calculated using Eq. 15.1.
Green premium ($\widehat{\alpha}$)	Green premium is calculated using the one-way individual fixed-effect estimation, Eq. 15.3.
Time to maturity (years)	The time to maturity of each green bond, measured in number of years.
Credit rating	The bond credit rating of our matched green bond (AAA, AA+, AA), set as a categorical variable, with a corresponding value from 1 to 3, respectively. The rating is issued by Chinese domestic rating agencies, and we retrieved the credit rating data from the Chinese iFind database.
CBI certificate	A dummy variable indicating whether a green bond is certified by the Climate Bond Initiative. The variable is equal to 1 if the bond is certified by CBI and 0 otherwise.
ESG rating	The ESG rating of our green bonds (B, C, C−, D, D+, and not rated), set as a categorical variable, with a corresponding value from 1 to 6, respectively. Data source from Thomson Reuters Eikon/Datastream.
Sector	We use the Thomson Reuters Business Classification (TRBC) to determine the bond issuers' business sector, which leaves us, in the case of the present sample, with eight categories: (i) agency; (ii) bank; (iii) financials, which encompass nonpublic banks and financial services; (iv) chemicals; (v) consumer; (vi) industrials; (vii) transportation; and (viii) utility-electricity. The base value in our case is agency.
Issues amount	The total amount of green bond issuance. We take the natural logarithm to avoid unwanted heteroscedasticity.

categorical variable, "Sector," to investigate whether green premiums can vary across bond issuers' sectors (H3). In addition to that, we use dummy variables "CBI certified" and "EGS rating" to investigate the impact of third-party certification on the green premium in the Chinese secondary market. Overall, we perform our second step of the analysis using the following model specification:

$$\widehat{\alpha}_i = \beta_0 + \beta_1 \text{Maturity}_i + \beta_2 \log(\text{Issue amount}) + \beta_3(\text{CBI certified}) + \beta_4(\text{ESG rating}) + \sum_{i=1}^{N\ \text{Sector}} \beta_{\text{sector}}(i) \times \text{Sector}_i + \sum_{i=1}^{N\ \text{rating}} \beta_{\text{rating}}(j) \times (\text{rating})_j + \varepsilon_i \tag{15.7}$$

15.6 Empirical Results and Discussion

We identify the presence of individual effects in our sample observation through the Breusch-Pagan Lagrange multiplier (LM) test. Furthermore, based on the result of the Hausman test (Table 15.7), we expect the fixed-effect estimator to be more efficient than the random-effect estimator. Therefore, we specify a within-fixed-

Table 15.6 Within-fixed-effect estimation results

	Dependent variable: $\Delta Y_{i,t}$			
	Fixed effects	Fixed effects with robust standard errors	Fixed effects with one-way cluster standard errors	Fixed effects with two-way cluster standard errors
$\Delta \text{Liquidity}_{i,t}$	−1.009***	−1.009**	−1.009**	−1.009***
	(0.0965)	(0.390)	(0.390)	(0.339)
Constant	0.000436***	0.000436***	0.000436***	0.000436***
	(4.54e–05)	(0.000127)	(0.000127)	(0.000108)
No. obs	14,088	14,088	14,088	14,088
No. pair	48	48	48	48
R^2	0.008	0.008	0.008	0.008
F-statistic	109.16***	6.67***	6.67***	8.85***

Note: ***, **, and * refer to statistical significance at 1%, 5%, and 10% levels, respectively. The number in parentheses represents standard errors

Table 15.7 Diagnostic tests

Tests	Test statistic	*P*-value	Conclusion
Breusch and Pagan LM test	63944.55	0.000	Presence of individual effects
Hausman test	10.05	0.001	Fixed estimator is better than random effect
Modified Wald test	1.0e + 07	0.000	Presence of heteroscedasticity
Wooldridge serial correlation	2.448	0.1243	Absence serial correlation
Pesaran cross-sectional dependence test	35.954	0.000	Presence of cross-sectional dependence

effect regression model to estimate the sign, significance, and magnitude of the green bond premium in the Chinese secondary market. Table 15.6 reports the results of the within-fixed-effect estimation of Eq. 15.3 based on an unbalanced panel of 14088 daily observations. The negative coefficient of ΔLiquidity is highly significant at the 5% level. Specifically, the estimated coefficient implies that an increase of 1 bp in ΔLiquidity leads to a decrease in green bond premium of 1.009 bps in the Chinese secondary market, controlling green-bond-specific time-invariant characteristics. This finding is consistent with the findings of Zerbib (2019) and Gianfrate and Peri (2019), who declare a significant negative relationship between liquidity differentials and yield spread in the green bond market.

Although the Woolridge test suggests the absence of a serial correlation, the diagnostic test results from Pesaran and Modified Wald tests reveal the presence of cross-sectional dependence and heteroscedasticity in the model's residual (Table 15.7). In order to account for heteroscedasticity and cross-sectional dependence, we specify robust standard errors and one-way and two-way cluster standard errors in our model estimations to combat the presence of these effects. The model estimations in Table 15.6 report a low level of R^2, which is around 1%, indicating a low explanatory power of our model specification. The low level of R^2 is

Table 15.8 Distribution of the green bond premium estimates

$\widehat{\alpha}_i$(bps)					
Min	1st quart	Median	Mean	3rd quart	Max
−70.1	−11.9	−5.2***	−1.8***	2.4	65.8

Note: The green bond premium α_i is defined as the fixed-effect model of Eq. 15.3. We apply the Student t-test and the Wilcoxon matched-pair signed-rank test to determine whether the mean and median values of the estimated green premium are statistically different from 0. ***, **, and * represent the significance at 1%, 5%, and 10% levels of significance, respectively

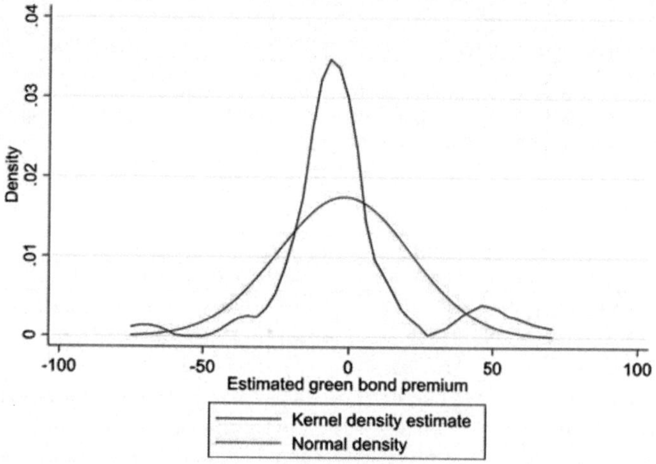

Fig. 15.2 Distribution of estimated green bond premiums in the Chinese secondary market

acceptable for within-fixed-effect estimation since the model setup discards individual effects in the estimation procedure (Bachelet et al., 2019). Moreover, the highly significant estimated coefficient of $\Delta \text{Liquidity}_{i,\ t}$ suggests the importance of using CPQS as the proxy for liquidity control in our model specification.

The distribution of the green bond premium ranges from –70 bps to 65 bps, and the average and median values of the premium are –5.2 bps and –1.8 bps, respectively (Table 15.8). Especially, a total of 71% of the premium are negative, as presented by the kernel density plot of the estimated green bond yield premium in Fig. 15.2. To test our first hypothesis (H1) on the presence of a green premium in the Chinese secondary market, we apply the Student t-test and the nonparametric Wilcoxon signed-rank test with continuity correction to access whether the mean and median values of the estimated green premium are statistically different from 0. Based on the P-values of these two tests, we do have enough statistical evidence to reject the null hypotheses, revealing that the green premium does exist in the Chinese secondary market.

The negative green bond premium in the Chinese market is consistent with the findings from previous green bond literature, which also documents that financial investors are willing to accept a lower financial return for a green bond investment (Gianfrate & Peri, 2019; Zerbib, 2019; MacAskill et al., 2021). The presence of the green premium confirms the intention of the Chinese financial investors to be driven by nonpecuniary motives and thereby be willing to pay for a premium to green their investment portfolio. Although the estimated magnitude of the green premium in our empirical analysis is relatively small, it does significantly reflect Chinese investors' willingness to incorporate proenvironmental preferences into their portfolio design and risk management.

However, our finding is in contrast with that of Wang et al. (2019), who reveal a positive risk premium on an average of 1.73% in the Chinese green bond market. Notice that Wang et al. (2019) have not adopted a matching process; neither have they included liquidity as the control variable in their model specifications. Alternatively, Wang et al. (2019) perform their empirical analysis on green bond premium based on an extended version of the capital asset pricing model (CPAM) and compute the premium by taking the difference between the yield to maturity of green bonds and risk-free interest rates. Thus, our result adds to the green bond literature by providing significant evidence to argue for the presence of a negative green bond premium in the Chinese secondary market.

Besides green bond premium identification, we further explore premium variation in several subsamples according to the main characteristics of the selected green bond sample: its rating, business sector, CBI certificate, and ESG rating. By doing this, we calculate the average and median premiums of each subsample and test whether they are significantly different from 0. Table 15.10 reports the average and median green premiums per subsample. The −8.194 bps average yield premium on the green bonds issued by financials is significantly different from 0 at a 99% confidence level. AAA-rated green bonds show an average level of −5.445 bps premium with the same degree of significance. Additionally, ESG-rated green bonds show a significant negative green premium of −12.583 bps at a 95% confidence level. Although the average and median values of CBI-certificated green bonds are negative, they are not statistically significantly different from 0 (Table 15.9).

Regarding the determinants of the green premium, we apply a cross-section linear regression of $\widehat{\alpha}_i$ on the bond-specific characteristics. Table 15.10 represents four model specifications, which we undertake to address hypotheses 2–4. The variance inflation factor (VIF) test results indicate the absence of multicollinearity of underlying variables in each of these model specifications. By choosing maturity and log (issue amount) as the control variables, the model specification (a) evaluates the impact of bond crediting on the green bond premium, and model specification (b) captures green bond premium variation across different business sectors. Likewise, model specifications (c) and (d) assess the impacts of external green certification and verification on the green bond premium. In terms of robustness control, we perform our OLS specifications with the use of robust standard errors.

Table 15.10 summarizes our OLS estimation results of Eq. 15.7. With regard to control variables, we do not find that bond issue amount has a significant impact on the magnitude of green premiums. Hence, the green bond premium does not seem to be determined by the bond issue amount in the Chinese market. In terms of maturity

Table 15.9 Green bond premium in several market segments

		Median	Mean	No. Green bond
Total		−1.775***	−5.235***	48
Sector	Agency	−5.859	−5.859	1
	Bank	−6.142**	−3.765	16
	Financials	−5.364**	−8.194**	10
	Chemicals	−6.340	−6.340	2
	Consumer	22.622	22.622	2
	Industrials	17.058	24.984*	5
	Transportation	2.350	0.4356	6
	Utility	−7.759	−16.190	6
Credit rating	AAA	−5.445***	−5.887***	41
	AA+	22.891	23.183*	6
	AA	17.059	17.059	1
CBI bond	Certificated green bond	−3.778	−1.120	35
	Self-labelled green bond	−5.798**	−3.537	13
ESG rating	ESG rated	−12.136***	−12.583**	15
	Not rated	−3.340	3.138	33

Note: We apply the paired Student *t*-test and Wilcoxon signed-rank test to determine whether the mean and median values are statistically different from 0. ***, **, and * refer to statistical significance at 1%, 5%, and 10% levels, respectively

between different green bonds, a generally positive relationship is found, suggesting that the green bond premium increases with the number of years to bond maturity. However, the estimated coefficient on maturity is only significant in model specifications (a) and (d). To test our Hypothesis 2, the model specification (a) indicates that the third-party credit rating has a significant impact on the magnitude of the green bond premium in the Chinese secondary market. Specifically, the statistical impact of a credit rating is significant for AAA-rated green bonds with a magnitude of −16.76 bps with respect to the reference group of AA-rated bonds. In terms of the AA+-rated green bond, we do not find a significant difference in comparison to the reference group. Based on the model specification (b), we find out that the green premium varies between different business sectors, and we thus have enough statistical evidence to reject Hypothesis 3. Furthermore, our estimated results suggest that the green bonds issued by agencies, financials, and transportation- and utility-related sectors have a negative effect of 27.88 bps, 25.84 bps, 22.39 bps, and 32.02 bps, respectively, on the green premium in comparison with industrial-related sectors. In terms of the green bonds issued by banks, we do not find any statistical significance to support the negative effect on green bond premiums. This finding is consistent with previous literature, which suggests that the green bond premium varies among business sectors and it is closely related to the public reputation of the bond issuers (e.g., Hanenberg & Schiereck, 2018; Bachelet et al., 2019; Fatica et al., 2019; Gianfrate & Peri, 2019; Kapraun & Scheins, 2019; Zerbib, 2019).

Surprisingly, contrary to previous studies (e.g., Bachelet et al., 2019; Flammer, 2020), we do not observe any statistical evidence to support a significant relationship

Table 15.10 Determinants of green bond premium in the Chinese secondary market

	Variable	(a)	(b)	(c)	(d)
Control variables	Maturity	4.940*	5.232	3.071	5.394*
		(2.805)	(4.054)	(2.999)	(2.810)
	Log (issue amount)	−0.460	−0.471	−0.469	−3.961
		(2.065)	(2.275)	(2.126)	(2.672)
TRBC sector	Agency		−27.88**		
			(12.53)		
	Bank		−17.78		
			(13.33)		
	Financials		−25.84**		
			(11.50)		
	Transportation		−22.39*		
			(11.26)		
	Utility		−32.02*		
			(16.79)		
Credit rating	AA+	12.91			
		(13.16)			
	AAA	−16.76***			
		(4.953)			
External verification	ESG rating			−13.62*	
				(7.492)	
Green bond certification	CBI certificate				9.465
					(6.387)
	Constant	1.546	6.633	0.554	54.72
		(39.79)	(46.21)	(47.13)	(56.92)
	Observations	48	48	48	48
	R-squared	0.243	0.248	0.122	0.091
	VIF	3.37	1.65	1.23	1.16

Note: This table summarizes the empirical results of step 2 regression based on a sample of 48 green bonds. Robust standard errors are reported in parentheses; ***, **, and * represent the individual test significance at 1%, 5%, and 10%, respectively. VIF tests are applied to examine the presence of multicollinearity. The sector refers to a categorical variable based on the Thomson Reuters Business Classifications (TRBC), and we use the industrials as the reference group in our regression analysis. Credit ratings are retrieved by Chinese domestic credit rating agencies, where AA is equal to 1 and AAA is equal to 3 in the common credit rating scale, and we use AA credit rating as the reference variable in our analysis. CBI certificate and ESG rating represent the third-party certificate and external certification, respectively

between green certification and the yield premium. However, our result is in line with the finding of Larcker and Watts (2020), who document that CBI climate certification does not have an economically significant impact on the green premium in the global secondary market. The insignificant label effect on the green premium may be due to the inconsistent definition of green bond standards in the Chinese market. Since there is no global definition of green bond, Ehlers and Packer (2017) point out that various organizations have developed their own customized measuring standard green bond definition. Given the country-specific characteristics, agencies may modify the measuring standards accordingly to develop their own customized taxonomies. Hence, practitioners have raised concerns that green bonds could be merely a form of greenwashing (Flammer, 2020) and the credibility of the CBI green certificate remains questionable in the Chinese market. Since there is no global definition of green bonds, various organizations have customized their green labelling standards and have gained popularity and acceptance among investors and regulators in China. Having definitional divergence in green bond eligibility between the Chinese and international standards, the impact of CBI green certification on the green premium remains limited and questionable in the Chinese market. Therefore, the regulatory development on labelling standards for green bonds is crucial for the future expansion of the green bond market in China. The estimated coeffcient on variable is negative and significant at a 10% level, suggesting that ESG policies can benefit green bond issuers from lower cost of capital. Thus, as long as external ESG auditing is concerned with green bond pricing, our results support a partial rejection of Hypothesis 4.

15.7 Conclusion

Green bonds, as an innovative fixed-income financial instrument, represent a promising channel for mobilizing financial resources to scale up the transition to a carbon-neutral economy. Along with supporting policies and bullish market development, the green bond market has experienced remarkable growth in China in recent years. In this paper, we study the green bond premium in the Chinese secondary market by addressing the following two research questions: first, is there a green bond premium in the Chinese market? Second, what factors influence the magnitude of the green premium? To do so, we apply a matching method that consists of 19 bond-specific characteristics to create a data set of 48 matched pairs of green and conventional bonds. Using CPQS as a proxy variable for liquidity control, we perform fixed-effect panel regression on our unbalanced panel of 14088 bond-day observations to estimate the sign, magnitude, and significance of the green premium in the Chinese secondary market.

Overall, our empirical results reveal a significant negative green bond premium of −1.8 bps in the Chinese secondary market, suggesting that nonpecuniary-motivated investors are willing to accept lower financial returns for green bond investments rather than those for conventional bonds. Besides the presence of pro-environmental preferences among investors, our paper adds to the extant green bond literature by examining how the estimated negative green bond premium varies with bond-specific characteristics in the Chinese secondary market.

Based on a two-step regression analysis, our findings suggest that the green bond premium varies across issuers' business sectors, where green bonds issued by agencies, financials, and transportation- and utility-related sectors are traded at lower yields compared to the green bonds issued by industrials. According to our estimates, investors are willing to pay a higher price for green bonds with AAA credit ratings in comparison with other lower-rated green bonds. Consistent with Larcker and Watts (2020), our estimates conclude that the CBI climate certification has no significant impact on the green premium, which leads us to question the credibility of the CBI green certificate in the Chinese markets. Although ICMA's Green Bond Principles and CBI Climate Bond Standards are being applied as the main reference standards for defining green bond in China (Wang & Zhang, 2017), many other customized certification mechanisms are available to any bond issuers on the market. Given the lack of consistent green bond standards, investors' willingness to venture into green bond investments is limited because of information asymmetry and suspicions of greenwashing behaviors (Hyun et al., 2020). For policy makers, as highlighted by Ehlers and Packer (2017), the ongoing legal improvement to the consistency of green bond standards would be especially important for the future development of sustainable green finance in the Chinese secondary market.

Lastly, we find that external bond issuers with ESG ratings enjoy a 13.62-bps discount at green bond issuance, as compared with bond issuers that do not have such verification. With the global trend of integrating ESG considerations into corporate policies, Tang and Zhang (2020) show that the ESG policy and green bond issuance could raise a company's public reputation and hence improve stock valuation and liquidity. Furthermore, Slimane et al. (2020) argue that ESG rating has had a larger and increasing part in determining the yield premium in bond pricing. Our empirical results have the following policy implications with respect to the future development of sustainable finance market in China. Under the current regulatory regime in China, the transparency requirement for disclosure of information on green bond is relatively loose compared to the international standards. Investors are not capable to fully process all information from the market and therefore lack objective evaluation of underlying financial and environmental values of green projects. Greater information transparency is needed to remove information asymmetry among the market participants. While having a large domestic market, the green bond market in China is also progressively promoted to attract more international investors. Prevailing inconsistencies between the local and international green bond standards present a significant barrier for the Chinese green bond market when it comes to its attractiveness to international investors. Hence, a regulatory development that would minimize the gap between the Chinese and international green bond standards is critical for China to attract investors from the international market.

Acknowledgment This paper is part of a project that has received funding from the European Union's Horizon 2020 research and innovation program under Marie Sklodowska-Curie grant agreement No. 870245. Binyi Zhang acknowledges support from the Charles University Grant Agency (GAUK) under grant No. 862119. Karel Janda acknowledges support from the Czech Science Foundation (grant No.22-19617S). The views expressed here are those of the authors and not necessarily those of our institutions. All remaining errors are solely our responsibility.

References

Agliardi, E., & Agliardi, R. (2019). Financing environmentally sustainable projects with green bonds. *Environment and Development Economics, 24*(6), 608–623.

Bachelet, M. J., Becchetti, L., & Manfredonia, S. (2019). The green bond premium puzzle: The role of issuer characteristics and third-party verification. *Sustainability, 11*(4), 1098.

Będowska-Sójka, B., & Echaust, K. (2020). What is the best proxy for liquidity in the presence of extreme illiquidity? *Emerging Markets Review, 43*, 100695.

Banga, J. (2019). The green bond market: A potential source of climate finance for developing countries. *Journal of Sustainable Finance & Investment, 9*(1), 17–32.

Chung, K. H., & Zhang, H. (2014). A simple approximation of intraday spreads using daily data. *Journal of Financial Markets, 17*, 94–120.

Climate Bonds Initiative (CBI). (2020). *Green bonds global state of the market 2019*. Available at https://www.climatebonds.net/resources/reports/green-bonds-global-state-market-2019

Climate Bonds Initiative (CBI). (2021). *China Green Bond Market Report 2020*. Available at https://www.climatebonds.net/resources/reports/china-state-market-2020-report

Ehlers, T., & Packer, F. (2017). *Green Bond Finance and Certification*. BIS Quarterly Review.

Fatica, S., Panzica, R., & Rancan, M. (2019). *The pricing of green bonds: Are financial institutions special?* (No. 2019/7). JRC Working Papers in Economics and Finance.

Fatin, L. (2019). *Green bond issuance tops $200bn milestone – New global record in green Finance*. September 18th, 2020. Retrieved October 1, 2020. Available from. https://www.climatebonds.net/2019/10/green-bond-issuance-tops-200bn-milestone-new-global-record-green-finance-latest-climate

Flammer, C. (2020). Green bonds: effectiveness and implications for public policy. *Environmental and Energy Policy and the Economy, 1*(1), 95–128.

Fong, K. Y., Holden, C. W., & Trzcinka, C. A. (2017). What are the best liquidity proxies for global research? *Review of Finance, 21*(4), 1355–1401.

Gianfrate, G., & Peri, M. (2019). The green advantage: Exploring the convenience of issuing green bonds. *Journal of cleaner production, 219*, 127–135.

Hachenberg, B., & Schiereck, D. (2018). Are green bonds priced differently from conventional bonds? *Journal of Asset Management, 19*, 371–383.

Hyun, S., Park, D., & Tian, S. (2020). The price of going green: The role of greenness in green bond markets. *Accounting & Finance, 60*(1), 73–95.

International Capital Market Association (ICMA). (2018). *Green bond principles: Voluntary process guidelines for issuing green bonds*. ICMA.

Janda, K., Kristoufek, L., & Zhang, B. (2022). Return and volatility spillovers between Chinese and US clean energy related stocks. Energy Economics, 105911.

Kapraun, J., & Scheins, C. (2019). (In)-credibly green: Which bonds trade at a green bond premium? In *Proceedings of Paris December 2019 Finance Meeting EUROFIDAI-ESSEC*.

Karpf, A., & Mandel, A. (2018). The changing value of the 'green' label on the US municipal bond market. *Nature Climate Change, 8*(2), 161–165.

Larcker, D., & Watts, M. (2019). *Where's the Greenium?* Rock Center for Corporate Governance at Stanford University.

Larcker, D. F., & Watts, E. M. (2020). Where's the greenium?. *Journal of Accounting and Economics, 69*(2–3), 101312.

MacAskill, S., et al. (2021). Is there a green premium in the Green Bond market? Systematic literature review revealing premium determinants. *Journal of Cleaner Production, 280*, 124491.

Maltais, A., & Nykvist, B. (2020). Understanding the role of green bonds in advancing sustainability. *Journal of Sustainable Finance & Investment, 1*, 1–20.

Nanayakkara, M., & Colombage, S. (2019). Do investors in Green Bond market pay a premium? Global evidence. *Applied Economics, 51*(40), 4425–4437.

Preclaw, R., & Baksh, A. (2015). *The cost of being green*. Barclays Research. Retrieved November 1, 2020. Available from: https://www.environmental-finance.com/assets/files/US_Credit_Focus_The_Cost_of_Being_Green.pdf

Reboredo, J. C., & Ugolini, A. (2020). Price connectedness between green bond and financial markets. *Economic Modelling, 88*(C), 25–38.

Reboredo, J. C. (2018). Green bond and financial markets: Co-movement, diversification, and price spillover effects. *Energy Economics, 74*(C), 38–50.

Slimane, M. B., Fonseca, D. D., & Mahtani, V. (2020). *Facts and fantasies about the green bond premium* (Working paper 102–2020). Publications.

Stádník, B. (2014). Spring oscillations within financial markets. *Procedia-Social and Behavioral Sciences, 110*, 1176–1184.

Stádník, B. (2018). Behaviour of bond's embedded option with regard to credit rating. *Verslas: teorija ir praktika, 19*(1), 261–270.

Stádník, B. (2021). Interest rates sensitivity arbitrage–theory and practical assessment for financial market trading. *Business, Management and Economics Engineering, 19*(1), 12–23.

Stádník, B. (2022). Convexity arbitrage–the idea which does not work. *Cogent Economics & Finance, 10*(1), 2019361.

Tang, D. Y., & Zhang, Y. (2020). Do shareholders benefit from green bonds? *Journal of Corporate Finance, 61*(C), 101427.

Tolliver, C., Keeley, A. R., & Managi, S. (2020). Drivers of green bond market growth: The importance of Nationally Determined Contributions to the Paris Agreement and implications for sustainability. *Journal of Cleaner Production, 244*, 118643.

Wang, Q., Zhou, Y., Luo, L., & Ji, J. (2019). Research on the factors affecting the risk premium of China's green bond issuance. *Sustainability, 11*(22), 6394.

Wang, Y., & Zhang, R. (2017). China's green bond market. *International Capital Market Features, 44*, 16–17.

Zerbib, O. D. (2019). The effect of pro-environmental preferences on bond prices: Evidence from green bonds. *Journal of Banking & Finance, 98*, 39–60.

Chapter 16
The Use of Sustainable Archetypes in Financial Entities: A Comparison of Developed and Emerging Economies

Mariusz Karwowski

Abstract The aim of this article is to examine how sustainable archetypes are reflected in the business activity of financial entities in both developed and emerging economies, as delineated in their integrated reports. The paper shows that sustainable archetypes are better reflected in the business activity of financial entities in developed economies, although the difference between developed and emerging economies is slight. The most common archetype among financial entities in both types of economies is "substitution with digital processes," which includes digitalization, virtual reality, and artificial intelligence. This not only facilitates transactions but also encourages customers to make more frequent use of digital platforms.

Keywords Corporate social responsibility · Integrated reports · Sustainable development · Sustainable archetypes

16.1 Introduction

Sustainable development for an organization means caring for its various stakeholders as well as the triple bottom line. In terms of financial activity, it also refers to meeting the needs of clients and protecting the environment while generating profit—not just doing no harm but actively using finance to do good. Financial entities hold a distinct intermediary role within sustainable development, as they do in the public domain, commerce, and industry. For example, banks assess and price risks during the credit approval process. Through such differentiation in prices, banks can support sustainability (Yip & Bocken, 2018) (cf. Adeel-Farooq et al., 2020; Gerasimov et al., 2020). Sustainable development in financial entities involves a variety of sustainable archetypes (cf. Karwowski, 2018). The aim of the research underlying the results presented in this article is to identify which of these archetypes are reflected in the business activity of financial entities in developed and emerging

M. Karwowski (✉)
Department of Management Accounting, Warsaw School of Economics, Warsaw, Poland
e-mail: mkarwo@sgh.waw.pl

D. Procházka (ed.), *Regulation of Finance and Accounting*, Springer Proceedings in Business and Economics, https://doi.org/10.1007/978-3-030-99873-8_16

economies, as presented in their integrated reports. For this purpose, the scope of the information disclosed in the integrated reports of each of the subject financial entities was examined.

This paper contributes to the accounting literature by illuminating the disclosure of sustainable archetypes by financial entities, thus raising the usefulness of accounting, primarily by increasing its relevance. It also demonstrates that each archetype is reflected in the business activities of financial entities to varying degrees.

16.2 Data and Methodology

The empirical study was based on a content analysis of the integrated reports. Initially, the integrated reports of financial entities were downloaded from http://examples.integratedreporting.org/. The final sample included 27 reports of financial entities, as shown in Table 16.1.

The integrated reports were produced by companies from a range of financial entities—primarily banks (16 companies) and insurance institutions (six)—and from various regions—Africa (12 companies), Europe (nine), and Asia (three).

Then relevant data were collected—revenues, assets, and number of employees. Table 16.2 presents a summary of the research sample divided between developed and emerging economies.

Finally, a content analysis was conducted relating to the eight sustainable archetypes illustrated in Table 16.3 (Yip & Bocken, 2018) (cf. Bocken et al., 2014).

The foregoing information can typically be found in chapters with titles containing wording such as "business model" or "value creation."

16.3 Results

Table 16.4 illustrates the percentages of companies from the research sample that disclose the adoption of each of the sustainable archetypes—calculated separately by the type of economy and the weighted average of the subject entities.

The overall combined mean of the archetypes is 51.4%—i.e., overall, 51.4% of the 27 subject reports disclosed the use of one or more of the archetypes. The mean is slightly higher among just the integrated reports of the financial entities from developed economies (52.5%), compared to those from emerging economies (50.7%).

The archetypes that are the most common among the ten financial entities in developed economies are "maximizing material and energy efficiency" and "substitution with digital processes" at 70.0%, while "encouraging sufficiency" and "creation of inclusive value" appear in 60% of the reports. The least common are "adopting a stewardship role" and "repurpose for society/environment" at 30%.

Table 16.1 Research sample

Company	Region	Year
ABSA	Africa	2019
Aegon	Europe	2017
Bankmecu	Australasia	2012
Barclays Africa	Africa	2017
Capricorn Group	Africa	2017
DBS	Asia	2019
DBSA	Africa	2016
Eurazeo	Europe	2016
FMO	Europe	2019
FNB Namibia	Africa	2017
Garanti	Europe	2019
Generali	Europe	2019
Hammerson	Europe	2014
IDLC Finance	Asia	2016
ING	Europe	2016
Itaú Unibanco	S. America	2017
Lloyds Banking Group	Europe	2017
Liberty	Africa	2016
Nedbank	Africa	2019
People's Leasing & Finance	Asia	2019
Road Accident Fund	Africa	2015
Sanlam	Africa	2015
Standard Bank	Africa	2019
Sasria	Africa	2017
Stockland	Australasia	2013
Strate	Africa	2017
TSKB	Europe	2016

Source: Own study based on analyzed reports

Table 16.2 Summary of the research sample

		Median		
Type of economy	Number of entities	Revenues (USD mln)	Assets (USD mln)	Employees
Developed	10	20,827	290,386	25,954
Emerging	17	1514	45,782	18,486
Total	27	8757	136,376	21,252

Source: Own study based on analyzed reports

In the emerging economies, the most frequently disclosed archetypes among the 17 financial entities are "substitution with digital processes," mentioned in 79.6% of the reports, followed at 64.7% by "encouraging sufficiency" and "adopting a stewardship role"—the latter being the least employed in developed economies at 30%. The least common are "resilience in establishing cooperation" at 29.4% and

Table 16.3 List of sustainable archetypes employed in financial entities

Archetype	Characteristics of the archetype
Maximizing material and energy efficiency	Optimizes the use of resources (doing more with fewer resources) and tries to generate less waste, emissions, and pollution
Substitution with digital processes	Focuses on service innovation by using digital means
Encouraging sufficiency	Concentrates on the effective utilization of services and avoiding their overprovision in order to increase loyalty and reputation
Adopting a stewardship role	Engages with all stakeholders to ensure their long-term health and well-being
Creation of inclusive value	Focuses on providing and/or improving access to innovative services to underserved and vulnerable customers
Repurpose for society/the environment	Centers on prioritizing the delivery of social and environmental benefits instead of profit maximization
Resilience in establishing cooperation	Focuses on cooperating with those parties that do not negatively impact the environment and/or society
Providing sustainable financial products	Allows more customers to participate in the potential growth opportunities of sustainable businesses

Source: Based on Yip and Bocken (2018)

Table 16.4 Percentages of companies disclosing the adoption of sustainable archetypes—divided between developed and emerging economies

Archetype	Developed (%)	Emerging (%)	Combined (%)
Maximizing material and energy efficiency	70.0	35.3	48.1
Substitution with digital processes	70.0	70.6	70.4
Encouraging sufficiency	60.0	64.7	63.0
Adopting a stewardship role	30.0	64.7	51.9
Creation of inclusive value	60.0	47.1	51.9
Repurpose for society/the environment	30.0	52.9	44.4
Resilience in establishing cooperation	50.0	29.4	37.0
Providing sustainable financial products	50.0	41.2	44.4
Total	52.5	50.7	51.4

Source: Own study based on analyzed reports

"maximizing material and energy efficiency" at 35.3%—the latter being the most common at 70% among the sample from developed economies.

When considering the total sample, "substitution with digital processes" is the most common archetype at 70.4%. This refers to digitalization, virtual reality, artificial intelligence, and all related elements. Digitalization means delivering secure, personalized, and relevant experiences, plus a full range of solutions—continuously and in real time. This is ensured by establishing a digital strategy within the financial entity developed to identify and create the appropriate capacity to build a channel of continuous and innovative solutions. Such strategy allows the entity to be much closer to customers and helps it better understand them, respond to their needs, and build lasting customer loyalty while still providing clients the option of conducting transactions by telephone or face to face.

The core of a digital strategy is appropriate infrastructure, including Wi-Fi, loyalty apps, and social media channels, providing connection with customers to ensure their visits are tailored to their individual needs. Digital technology involves the frequent use of devices, emphasizing communication via a private social network. These digital possibilities have the power to transform experiences, improve people-to-people connectivity and knowledge sharing, create access, and improve customers' experiences.

Digital transformation is helpful in measuring progress in the following:

- Developing meaningful relationships with ecosystem partners and generating results from these partnerships
- Using digital channels to acquire new customers and increase the entity's share of digital channels
- Eliminating paper and driving automation to ensure immediate delivery
- Driving customer engagement, conversion, and contextual marketing cross-buy across digital assets

E-solutions, process solutions, and mobile solutions not only drive internal efficiency but also enable customers to increase their wealth by helping them improve their own lives. A dedicated staff is available to inform customers about the possibilities of e-channels. Digital platforms are particularly extended by launching applications specifically designed for customers to address their individual needs. Adopting a digital platform ensures the secure management of customer database and provides employees with customer information at their fingertips.

By serving clients predominantly online, processing in the cloud, and leveraging open innovation driven by data and insights, financial entities provide services, solutions, and capabilities that clients and employees need to achieve growth, prosperity, and fulfilment.

"Encouraging sufficiency" is the second-ranking archetype, important in both types of economies at 63.0% combined. Remuneration for employees, including the executive team, is divided into fixed and variable components, together with short-term incentive schemes, which motivate and reward the achievement of annually agreed individual, business unit, and group performance objectives and strategic priorities. Specific quantitative performance measures include but are not limited to the following:

- Return on equity
- Earnings in increase and net income after capital charge
- Performance within overall group risk appetite
- Quality of earnings
- Audit findings
- Operational losses

The remuneration policy is fully aligned to ensure similar salary scales for investment and risk functions and to avoid bonus structures that encourage excessive risk taking. Consequently, the balance between guaranteed and variable remuneration is appropriately structured and should not reward risk taking beyond management-approved risk mandates.

A higher weighting toward financial outcomes is applied primarily to the most senior individuals who are able to influence these outcomes. Junior individuals with limited ability to influence such outcomes have little or no weighting assigned to financial achievements.

The two other archetypes above the overall mean are "adopting a stewardship role" and "creation of inclusive value," both at 51.9%.

"Adopting a stewardship role" addresses issues focused on women, students, and persons with disabilities among both employees and customers. A diverse workforce broadens prospects and enhances resilience and performance. Such diversity includes gender, race, age, disability, experience, religion, values, and beliefs. Points are given for recruitment and the retention of females at senior, middle, and junior management levels and for attracting individuals with disabilities. Employees are encouraged toward personal giving and volunteering. In such situations, a personal volunteering leave allowance is possible.

Efforts are undertaken to provide employees with disabilities the best possible resources in terms of accessibility and minimizing constraints on the performance of their job functions. The aim is to offer conditions for personal development and equal opportunities to utilize their competencies fully. As health conditions or disabilities can make getting to a branch difficult for some customers, digital access has transformed the nature of customer services.

There are also benefits in programs aimed at recognizing new entrepreneurs as attracting and investing in the country's young and upcoming future leaders is considered worthwhile. Scholarships are awarded to promising and talented students studying in various specialized fields, providing full financial support and covering expenses such as accommodation, books, travel, and monthly allowances. The support of financial entities helps millions of low- and middle-income individuals attend university.

Financial entities also contribute to meeting the national and regional demands for energy generation capacity, including renewable energy, as well as for the construction of schools and residences and the maintenance of health facilities. Each strategic imperative is supported by a series of strategies centered on acting as a socially responsible corporate citizen in addressing national priorities as well as those of the local communities and the environment.

One goal underlying the sustainable archetype "creation of inclusive value" is to help small and medium-sized enterprises (SMEs) develop and grow, particularly by reinventing and expanding the boundaries of their activities through the long-term investments of both operational knowledge and financial resources. Thanks to such partnerships, many small businesses are expected to receive loan approvals. Such loans provide support to female entrepreneurs, renewable energy projects, and small companies located in regions that are less developed and most affected by refugee migration. The main goal of such projects is twofold. The first is to increase access to finance in underdeveloped regions and for the most underserved segments of the economy, SMEs in the least developed regions that are most affected by the refugee influx. The second is to increase the economic activity of vulnerable groups in these areas that are most impacted by migration and the resulting increased social and economic challenges.

Financial entities are particularly interested in the SME value proposition in the form of a dedicated fund targeted at future SMEs that have business ideas but lack sufficient collateral or capital to set up businesses. The purpose of such financing is to support, develop, and expand the SME sector by providing necessary funding while continuing partnerships with external contractors to provide technical assistance and education on a sustainable basis.

The other four archetypes fall below the overall mean.

"Maximizing material and energy efficiency" (48.1%) involves the responsible use of natural resources, including energy sources (electricity, solar, and gas), air, water, paper, and fuel, and the management of impacts, including carbon emissions and waste. Financial entities consume energy, paper, and water and are required to reduce their environmental impact over time. Although they are not significant consumers of natural resources, they try to minimize their direct or indirect impact and adapt investment criteria to assess the responsible use of these resources when investing both shareholder and customer capital. Initiatives are implemented to make branches more environmentally friendly and reduce their carbon footprints. They also invest in increasing the energy efficiency of their premises.

Among other aspects, the reduction of environmental impact may focus on water, energy, CO^2, waste, air, and fuel consumption in a variety of ways, as illustrated in Table 16.5.

The "repurpose for society/environment" archetype (44.4%) contributes toward community resilience, housing, and international development, as well as the environment by supporting the renewable energy sector and offering other climate-related solutions through research into opportunities such as financing water and energy infrastructure development projects. Financial entities intensify their strategy to support renewable energy projects that are economically, environmentally, and socially viable and play a key role in the diversification of electricity supply, as

Table 16.5 Ways of reducing environmental impact

Focus	Ways of reducing environmental impact
Water	Installation of flow restrictor devices, rainwater collection, campaigns for conscious use of water, careful selection of fixtures and fittings, and ensuring the best possible use of each drop of water
Energy	Reduction of energy consumption for lighting, installation of LED bulbs, replacement of high-energy-consuming equipment, as well as thermal insulation and glazing, thanks to which it is cooler in summer and warmer in winter
CO^2	Direct emissions mainly arising from diesel oil combustion, indirect emissions from electricity consumption, and emissions arising from employees' transport and business trips
Waste	Minimizing the amount of waste destined for landfills and the generation of solid waste
Air	Continuous monitoring of air quality, optimization of natural light, reduction of toxins from materials
Transport	Providing cycling facilities for employees, residents, and visitors to help reduce transport emissions and support an active lifestyle

Source: Own study based on analyzed reports

expressed in the national development plans of many of the economies in which they operate. This archetype constitutes a value proposition for companies developing energy-efficient products and fights against climate change by prioritizing renewable investments, applying detailed environmental and social due diligence, promoting energy-efficient buildings and electric and hybrid cars, as well as raising awareness among stakeholders.

The main thrust of this archetype is to finance various ventures, such as renewable energy and energy-efficient projects, green buildings, and waste management development initiatives that ensure the safety and protection of workers. This also includes organic farming, renewable energy generation, sustainable construction, and the reuse of waste materials.

As part of “providing sustainable financial products” (44.4%) and the growing global awareness of the negative impact of fossil fuels and other conventional energy sources, green business should be identified as one of its major priority sectors and be recognized as one of the market leaders in promoting this concept. Financial entities sell their investments in coal and invest more in green bonds and new, cleaner technologies. They provide customers with green loans or bonds, as well as loans related to renewable and clean energy, offering support in improving environmental performance. In particular, they provide the following:

- Loans linked to sustainability, which are structured to allow customers to pay less interest when they achieve a set of preagreed environmental, social, and governance (ESG) performance targets, which are validated by an independent ESG rating agency or other verification party
- Green loans or bonds that exclusively finance eligible green projects in areas such as energy efficiency and pollution prevention
- Renewable and clean energy loans that finance renewable and clean energy projects (e.g., solar and wind), rooftop solar systems, and energy-efficient buildings

“Resilience in establishing cooperation” (37.0%) considers strict social, ethical, and environmental risk criteria in order to finance activities that have a positive impact on the environment and society. While this influence initially focused on the positive environmental impact of financing, a structured approach was later developed to allow the positive social impact of funded projects to be considered as well.

Financial entities are committed to adhering to the principles of responsibility as a global guide in the projects they finance. They evaluate projects against nonfinancial criteria relating to environmental and social risks or impact, as well as financial parameters regarding these principles.

Under this archetype, financial entities acknowledge the growing local and international pressure on them to withdraw their lending from resource-intensive sectors, in particular the coal mining sector. They try to avoid any negative social or environmental consequences as a result of investing their clients’ money. Financial entities also do not invest customer savings in an unethical or socially and environmentally disruptive manner.

Financial entities also help their commercial clients understand and manage their sustainability risks and conduct an environmental risk assessment at the beginning of each new client relationship. Including sustainability factors in investment decisions demonstrates commitment to responsible environmental stewardship.

16.4 Conclusion

This study explored the disclosure of sustainable archetypes of financial entities, whose products are both intangible and inseparably linked to the customer interface (Yip & Bocken, 2018). To investigate this, a content analysis of the integrated reports of 27 financial entities was conducted.

At the aggregate level, the sustainable archetypes are better reflected in the business activity of financial entities in developed economies, although the difference between developed and emerging economies is slight. An interesting insight comes from the analysis at a disaggregate level in terms of the disclosure of sustainable archetypes. This analysis shows the sustainable archetype "substitution with digital processes" to be the most common, followed by "encouraging sufficiency," "adopting a stewardship role," and "creation of inclusive value." These archetypes fall above the overall mean value. At the lower end of the scale, archetypes "resilience in establishing cooperation," "repurpose for society/environment," and "providing sustainable financial products" attract the least interest among the subject financial entities.

All the interrelated archetypes have the potential to and do actually change the value proposition toward the environment and society, either by creating new value or by significantly reducing negative impacts on the environment or society.

References

Adeel-Farooq, R. M., Abu Bakar, N. A., & Raji, J. O. (2020). Financial sector development and economic growth: A co-integration analysis for ASEAN countries. *International Journal of Economic Policy in Emerging Economies, 13*(3), 195–208. https://doi.org/10.1504/IJEPEE.2020.109056

Bocken, N. M. P., Short, S. W., Rana, P., & Evans, S. (2014). A literature and practice review to develop sustainable business model archetypes. *Journal of Cleaner Production, 65*, 42–56. https://doi.org/10.1016/j.jclepro.2013.11.039

Gerasimov, A. N., Azhieva, I. A., Kurbatov, V. I., Kartashevich, E. V., & Salogub, A. M. (2020). Management efficiencies in Russian banking: Specificity of the transition to socially-oriented management. *International Journal of Economic Policy in Emerging Economies, 13*(5), 471–482. https://doi.org/10.1504/IJEPEE.2020.110435

Karwowski, M. (2018). Wpływ modelu zrównoważonego biznesu na kształt raportu biznesowego. *Studia i Materiały. Miscellanea Oeconomicae, 22*(4/2), 125–136.

Yip, A. W. H., & Bocken, N. M. P. (2018). Sustainable business model archetypes for the banking industry. *Journal of Cleaner Production, 174*, 150–169. https://doi.org/10.1016/j.jclepro.2017.10.190

Chapter 17
The Role of IAS 38 in the Evaluation of the Effects of Business Model Innovation

Mariusz Karwowski

Abstract IAS 38 "Intangible Assets" forces companies in which business model innovation (BMI) occurs to recognize expenditures in the research stage aimed at formulating and designing alternatives for new or improved processes, systems, or additional services, as well as expenditures during the development stage at the moment of incurring such costs, before meeting the criteria for capitalizing expenses in profit or loss. This requirement is important as BMI is driven by internally generated intangible assets that often cannot be recognized in the statement of financial position, resulting in the need for nonfinancial information in regard to these expenses.

Key words Business model innovation · Research and development · IAS 38

17.1 Introduction

Business model innovation (BMI) has emerged as a potential path to growth and value creation (Wirtz & Daiser, 2017; Sinfield et al., 2012). CEO-level surveys also identify it as a key source of sustained value creation (Foss & Saebi, 2017). Schneider and Spieth (2013) believe there is a need for a deeper and more reliable understanding of the impact of BMI on financial performance because, interestingly, little is known about this issue.

An important input in the process of evaluating the success of BMI is information about internally generated intangibles (e.g., research and development (R&D)), the recognition of such assets in the statement of financial position demonstrating the indirect impact of BMI on financial performance. The objective of the research underlying this article is to determine the role of IAS 38 "Intangible Assets" in explaining this impact.

M. Karwowski (✉)
Department of Management Accounting, Warsaw School of Economics, Warsaw, Poland
e-mail: mkarwo@sgh.waw.pl

D. Procházka (ed.), *Regulation of Finance and Accounting*, Springer Proceedings in Business and Economics, https://doi.org/10.1007/978-3-030-99873-8_17

A review of pertinent literature was conducted, as well as empirical analysis, based on the financial statements of companies from the following sectors: biotechnology, gaming, information technology (IT), and pharmaceuticals.

In the field of accounting research, this article may be treated as an attempt to examine BMI from the perspective of financial statements.

17.2 Data and Methodology

The literature review was based on six databases containing publications related to accounting: EBSCO, Emerald, JSTOR, ProQuest, Scopus, and Wiley Online Library. The search was limited to abstracts in scholarly journals with the primary filter aimed at identifying articles related to the topic of this text. Table 17.1 presents the preliminary results of the literature review.

The identified articles were then analyzed to pinpoint those that focus strictly on the topic of this article. The literature review was supplemented by a critical analysis of the International Financial Reporting Standards (IFRS).

The empirical study was based on a content analysis of the 2017 financial statements of 52 Polish companies in terms of research and development. Table 17.2 presents the research sample divided according to sector.

The financial statements were produced by companies in four industrial sectors in which BMI is a frequent occurrence: biotechnology (five companies), gaming (seven), IT (31), and pharmaceuticals (nine). The building blocks for such companies are their research and development activities (IAS 38) creating enormous potential for creating value (Govindarajan et al., 2018a; Maniora, 2017) and

Table 17.1 Preliminary results of the literature review

Name of database	EBSCO	Emerald	JSTOR	ProQuest	Scopus	Wiley
Number of articles	27	11	0	44	46	17

Source: Own study

Table 17.2 Research sample

Sector	Number of entities	Median				
		Return on sales (%)	Return on assets (%)	Intangible assets to total assets (%)	Capitalized development costs to assets (%)	Expensed R&D costs to assets (%)
Biotechnology	5	0.6	0.5	40	31	5
Gaming	7	17.8	7.0	27	27	0
IT	31	3.8	3.4	12	1	0
Pharmaceuticals	9	1.9	0.5	6	0	1
Total	52	4.0	3.3	12	2	0

Source: Own study

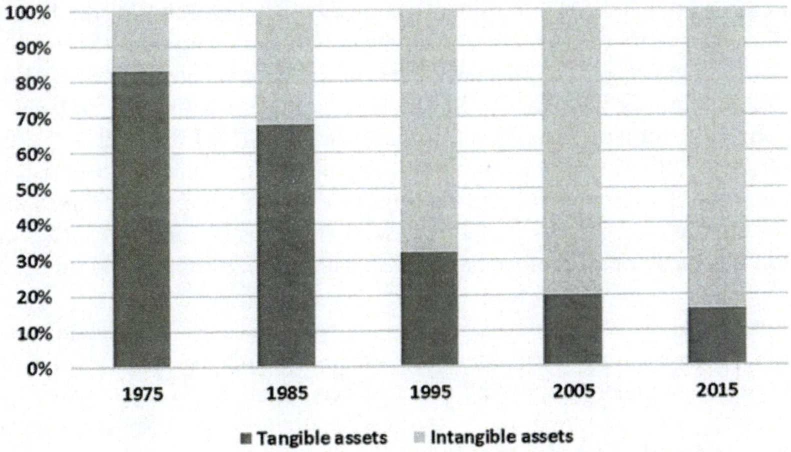

Fig. 17.1 The change in proportion of the components of the S&P 500. (Source: SEG, 2016)

contributing to explaining the indirect impact of BMI on financial performance. According to SEG (2016), the significant change in current business models is confirmed by the varying proportions of asset types in the S&P 500 over four decades (Fig. 17.1).

In 1975, tangible assets amounted to 83% of the S&P 500 index, while these assets represented only 16% of the index in 2015. The resulting challenge for accounting is the reporting of intangible assets, which today requires a qualitatively different approach (SEG, 2016).

17.3 Results and Discussion

17.3.1 The Literature Study

BMI can be defined as a process of finding a novel way of doing business, which results in the reconfiguration of value creation and value capturing mechanisms (Bashir & Verma, 2017; Björkdahl & Holmén, 2013). It is consistent with Foss and Saebi (2017), who describe BMI as designed, novel, and nontrivial changes to the key elements of a firm's business model and/or the architecture linking these elements (Bashir & Verma, 2017; Demil & Lecocq, 2010).

According to Amit and Zott (2012), BMI is of greatest importance to managers because it represents an often underutilized source of value. Researchers, scholars, and top executives also concur that BMI is a new form of innovation that is distinct from product innovation (Bashir & Verma, 2017; Björkdahl & Holmén, 2013). One of the major advantages associated with BMI is that it is much more difficult for companies to replicate a novel system than to imitate a product. The returns of product innovation are often relatively easier to undermine and can be eroded over time. On the other hand, BMI aims at consciously renewing a firm's core business logic rather than restricting its scope of innovation to single products (Schneider & Spieth, 2013), and it can be translated into a competitive advantage (Bashir & Verma, 2017; Amit & Zott, 2012). So the benefits linked with BMI undoubtedly outstrip any other form of innovation (Bashir & Verma, 2017; Lindgardt et al., 2009; Snihur & Zott, 2013). Product innovation emphasizes the status quo of a firm's current business model and focuses on adjustments and incremental innovations within the established business model framework, whereas BMI removes itself from the status quo and focuses on opportunities within the external environment of a firm.

BMI may be undertaken for a number of reasons, such as reducing costs, optimizing processes, introducing new additional services, accessing new markets, and, of course, ultimately improving financial performance (Foss & Saebi, 2017). However, once invoked as part of the motivation, attention to those consequences often fades. In fact, few articles explain how BMI improves competitive advantage, profitability, or other areas of innovation (Foss & Saebi, 2017; Aspara et al., 2010; Giesen et al., 2007).

One reason for this is that BMI research is a relatively recent development. In comparison with the huge volume of research on business models, the number of published papers that address BMI is still comparatively low. The literature on the topic exhibits many of the characteristics of an emerging research stream—notably, a lack of construct clarity (Foss & Saebi, 2017) and a resulting absence of a comprehensive framework (Di Fabio & Avallone, 2018; Beattie & Smith, 2013; Bini et al., 2016).

Relative to accounting, BMI may affect a firm's financial performance both directly and indirectly (c.f. Karwowski, 2019). Firstly, it enhances the prospect of additional revenues from new products or services and superior business models. This logic assumes a relatively direct link between BMI and financial performance through revenue growth and higher margins (Lichtenthaler, 2018).

Secondly, it also affects financial performance indirectly (Salman & Saives, 2005). In particular, innovation activities may strengthen the image and reputation of both the firm and its solutions (Chiang & Hung, 2010). In turn, this bolstered market position may enable the company to achieve superior financial results—for example, arising from a higher brand value than that of competitors (Lichtenthaler, 2018).

17.3.2 The Empirical Study

According to the Conceptual Framework for Financial Reporting (2018), financial statements represent economic phenomena in words and numbers. In preparing useful information, entities must consider recognition, measurement, presentation, and disclosure issues. In the case of internally generated intangibles, which are crucial for BMI, IAS 38 introduces strict recognition and measurement criteria

Table 17.3 The recognition criteria of capitalizing development work

1	2	3	4	5	6
The technical feasibility of completing the asset so that it would be available for use or sale	The intention to complete the construction of the asset	The ability to use or sell the asset	The ability to generate probable future economic benefits	The availability of technical, financial, and other resources to complete the asset and make it ready for use or sale	The ability to reliably measure the expenditure for the asset

Source: Own study based on IAS 38

Table 17.4 Expenditures included and excluded in the cost of an internally generated intangible asset

The cost of an internally generated intangible asset	
Includes	Excludes
Employee benefits directly incurred in the generation of an asset	Selling expenditures
Legal title registration fees	Administrative expenditures
Amortization of patents and licenses that are used to generate an asset	Other general overhead expenditures
Materials and services that are used or consumed directly in generating an asset	Work inefficiencies incurred before an asset achieves planned performance
Depreciation of equipment utilized by the work team	Initial operating losses
Rental of office space utilized by the work team	Expenditures on training staff

Source: Own study based on IAS 38

(c.f. Karwowski, 2017). All research expenditures are to be recognized as expenses when they are incurred. An intangible asset generated internally as a result of development work is recognized if, and only if, the six recognition criteria illustrated in Table 17.3 can be demonstrated.

The cost of an internally generated intangible asset is the sum of expenditures incurred from the date when the intangible asset first meets the abovementioned recognition criteria. Expenditures previously recognized as expenses cannot be capitalized. The cost of an internally generated intangible asset comprises directly attributable costs necessary to create, produce, and prepare that asset to be capable of operating in the manner intended by management. Table 17.4 illustrates expenditures included and not included in the cost of an internally generated intangible asset.

Upon the completion of development work, such internally generated intangibles are amortized over the estimated period in which the entity is expected to generate revenues (c.f. Karwowski, 2017).

The form of presentation of internally generated intangible assets is not specified in IAS 38. Of the 52 studied financial statements, 38 (73%) present development costs in the statement of financial position and/or research expenditures in the statement of profit or loss. One company recognized all expenditures referring to research and development works as expenses in profit or loss. Fourteen companies (27%) do not present development expenditures in the statement of financial position

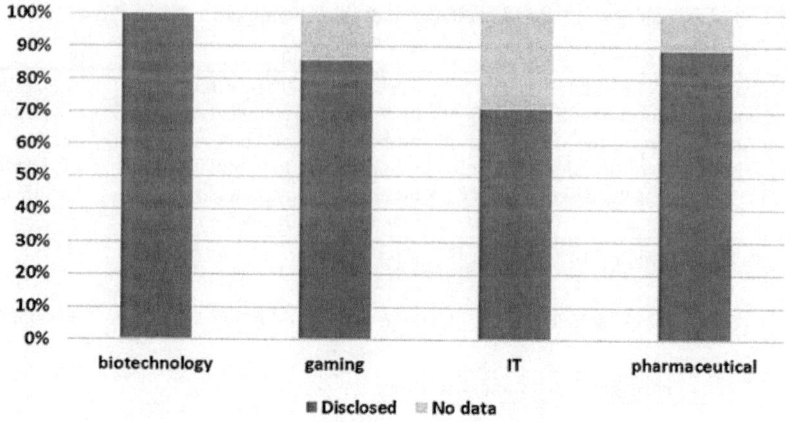

Fig. 17.2 Disclosing information about accounting policy concerning R&D expenditures. (Source: Own study)

and/or as research expenses in the statement of profit or loss. Of the 14 financial statements, two provide information that research expenses amount to zero, while 12 offer no information about research and development expenses. Based on the analysis of the financial statements in which such information is disclosed, it can be concluded that the most suitable solution for companies in which BMI occurs is to present completed development projects as a separate category in the statement of financial position, such as "internally generated intangibles," and development projects that are still incomplete as, for instance, "costs of development projects in progress."

The final issue to consider in preparing useful information is disclosure. Figure 17.2 illustrates if the companies from the research sample divided by sector disclose information on accounting policy concerning R&D expenditures.

The 52 financial statements examined provide the following data:

- Forty-one (79%) companies disclose information about accounting policies concerning research and development expenditures—among them are all the companies in the biotechnology sector. Thirty-five of these companies present development costs in the statement of financial position and/or as research expenses in the statement of profit or loss, while six of these companies present neither development costs in the statement of financial position nor research expenses in the statement of profit or loss.
- Eleven companies (21%) do not disclose information about accounting policies concerning research and development expenditures—among them are seven companies from the IT sector. Three of these companies present development costs in the statement of financial position and/or research expenses in the statement of profit or loss—but as the amount is not material, it need not be treated as a deviation from the requirements of financial accounting. Eight of these companies present neither development costs in the statement of financial position nor research expenses in the statement of profit or loss.

IAS 38 "Intangible Assets" forces companies in which BMI occurs to recognize expenditures in the research stage aimed at formulating and designing alternatives for new or improved processes, systems, or additional services, as well as expenditures during the development stage at the moment of incurring such costs, before meeting the criteria for capitalizing expenses in profit or loss. This requirement is important as BMI is driven by internally generated intangible assets that cannot be recognized in the statement of financial position. For this reason, nonfinancial information about these expenses must be part of the company's overall value creation story (Maniora, 2017). Unfortunately, only 13 of the 52 studied financial statements (25%) disclose information regarding research expenses. Nine of these 13 subjects (75%) disclose information that research expenses amount to zero, while four others (25%) disclose information that research expenses exceeded zero. For these four entities, research expenses amounted to 0.5%, 1%, 11%, and 52% of the total assets. Thirty-nine of the 52 studied financial statements (75%) do not disclose any information regarding research expenses, which can be considered a shortcoming of their financial statements.

17.4 Conclusion

Recent research claims that financial statements are practically irrelevant for companies in which BMI often occurs (Govindarajan et al., 2018a, b). The main reason for this is that the value of some potentially significant assets, such as brands, data, domain names, customer relationships, and employees, often are not recognized in the statement of financial position. In particular, according to IAS 38, the expenditures for building idea-based platforms that have enormous potential to create value in such companies are reported as expenses in the initial years when they have little, if any, revenue (ICAEW, 2018).

ICAEW (2018) noted that the International Accounting Standards Board's (IASB's) research program before 2015 included intangible assets and the activities of the extractive sector, but little progress was made on the first topic. In view of the growing debate about the financial reporting of climate change and other environmental issues, the IASB has included a project on extractive activities, but any reference to intangible assets was removed based on the belief that any attempt to address the recognition and measurement of intangible assets would require significant resources with very uncertain prospects for any significant improvement in financial reporting. A separate IASB research project will consider just one aspect of accounting in this area: the extent to which intangible assets should be separated from goodwill.

It was acknowledged that previous attempts at progress in the area of standard-setting have not been very successful, and it is undoubtedly a difficult and complex issue where investor views vary. Few intangibles meet the criteria for recognition in a company's statement of financial position, except in the context of the acquisition of a business. This weakens the extent to which financial reporting can provide a clear picture of a company's resources to investors and other users of financial reports (ICAEW, 2018).

This concern is only likely to increase as BMI is driven by internally generated intangible assets that cannot be recognized in the statement of financial position. For this reason, nonfinancial information about these assets has to be a part of the company's overall value creation story (Maniora, 2017). With far-reaching changes to IFRS unlikely, the focus should be firmly on ensuring that companies disclose clear, consistent, and relevant information to investors seeking alternative means of understanding how BMI creates value over time. In terms of disclosing information, it is worth mentioning the guidance in the strategic report published by the Financial Reporting Council, which calls for information on an entity's intangible resources, including items that are not reflected in the financial statements, and the International Integrated Reporting Framework, which calls for information on the business model, clarifying how a firm's business activities create or destroy value by processing input—the six forms of capital, including the intellectual capital of knowledge and innovation—into output (ICAEW, 2018; IIRC, 2013).

References

Amit, R., & Zott, C. (2012). Creating value through business model innovation. *Sloan Management Review, 53*(3), 41–49.

Aspara, J., Hietanen, J., & Tikkanen, H. (2010). Business model innovation vs. replication: Financial performance implications of strategic emphases. *Journal of Strategic Marketing, 18*(1), 39–56.

Bashir, M., & Verma, R. (2017). Why business model innovation is the new competitive advantage. *The IUP Journal of Business Strategy, XIV*(1), 7–17.

Beattie, V., & Smith, S. J. (2013). Value creation and business models: Refocusing the intellectual capital debate. *The British Accounting Review, 45*(4), 243–254.

Bini, L., Dainelli, F., & Giunta, F. (2016). Business model disclosure in the strategic report: Entangling intellectual capital in value creation process. *Journal of Intellectual Capital, 17*(1), 83–102.

Björkdahl, J., & Holmén, M. (2013). Editorial: Business model innovation: The challenges ahead. *International Journal of Product Development, 18*(3–4), 213–225.

Chiang, Y. H., & Hung, K. P. (2010). Exploring open search strategies and perceived innovation performance from the perspective of inter-organizational knowledge flows. *R&D Management, 40*(3), 292–299.

Conceptual Framework for Financial Reporting. (2018). IFRS Foundation.

Demil, B., & Lecocq, X. (2010). Business model evolution: In search of dynamic consistency. *Long Range Planning, 43*(2–3), 227–246.

Di Fabio, C., & Avallone, F. (2018). Business model in accounting: An overview. *Journal of Business Models, 6*(2), 25–31.

Foss, N. J., & Saebi, T. (2017). Fifteen years of research on business model innovation: How far have we come, and where should we go? *Journal of Management, 43*(1), 200–227. https://doi.org/10.1177/0149206316675927

Giesen, E., Berman, S. J., Bell, R., & Blitz, A. (2007). Three ways to successfully innovate your business model. *Strategy & Leadership, 35*(6), 27–33.

Govindarajan, V., Rajgopal, S., Srivastava, A. (2018a, February 26). Why financial statements don't work for digital companies? *Harvard Business Review*, hbr.org/2018/02/why-financial-statements-dont-work-for-digital-companies. Access: 12 Nov 2018.

Govindarajan, V., Rajgopal, S., Srivastava, A. (2018b, June 8). Why we need to update financial reporting for the digital era? *Harvard Business Review*, hbr.org/2018/06/why-we-need-to-update-financial-reporting-for-the-digital-era. Access: 10 May 2019.

ICAEW. (2018). *What's next for corporate reporting: Time to decide?* icaew.com/-/media/corporate/archive/files/technical/financial-reporting/information-for-better-markets/whats-next-for-corporate-reporting.ashx. Access: 10 May 2019.

IIRC. (2013). *The international integrated reporting framework*. International Integrated Reporting Council.

Karwowski, M. (2017). Innowacje w modelach biznesu w rachunkowości. *Ekonomika i Organizacja Przedsiębiorstwa, 5*, 53–64.

Karwowski, M. (2019). *The role of IFRS 15 in the evaluation of the effects of business model innovation*. In European financial systems 2019: Proceedings of the 16th international scientific conference (pp. 247–254).

Lichtenthaler, U. (2018). The world's most innovative companies: A meta-ranking. *Journal of Strategy and Management, 11*(4), 497–511. https://doi.org/10.1108/JSMA-07-2018-0065

Lindgardt, Z., Reeves, M., Stalk, G., & Deimler, M. S. (2009). Business model innovation. When the game gets tough. In *change the game*. The Boston Consulting Group.

Maniora, J. (2017). Is integrated reporting really the superior mechanism for the integration of ethics into the core business model? An empirical analysis. *Journal of Business Ethics, 140*, 755–786. https://doi.org/10.1007/s10551-015-2874-z

Salman, N., & Saives, A. L. (2005). Indirect networks: An intangible resource for biotechnology innovation. *R&D Management, 35*(2), 203–215.

Schneider, S., & Spieth, P. (2013). Business model innovation: Towards an integrated future research agenda. *International Journal of Innovation Management, 17*(1), 7–34. https://doi.org/10.1142/S136391961340001X

SEG. (2016). Raportowanie niefinansowe. Wartość dla spółek i inwestorów, publication prepared by Polish Association of Listed Companies, GES Global Ethical Standard and EY, https://seg.org.pl/sites/seg13.message-asp.com/files/seg_esg-2016_www_5.pdf. Access: 13 Feb 2020.

Sinfield, J. V., Calder, E., McConnell, B., & Colson, S. (2012). How to identify new business models? *MIT Sloan Management Review, 53*(2), 85–90.

Snihur, Y., & Zott, C. (2013). *Legitimacy without imitation: How to achieve robust business model innovation*. In 35th DRUID celebration conference, June (pp. 1–35).

Wirtz, B. W., & Daiser, P. (2017). Business model innovation: An integrative conceptual framework. *Journal of Business Models, 5*(1), 14–34.

Chapter 18
How Czech Companies Comply with IAS 36 Disclosure Requirements

Pavel Huňáček

Abstract This article examines the extent to which the disclosure requirements of IAS 36 Impairment of Assets are fulfilled. Apart from the mandatory disclosure, the analysis also includes an assessment of the potential impact on market liquidity and investment decisions of mainly smaller investors. The analysed data relate to publicly traded companies on the Prague Stock Exchange during the period 2015–2017 and cover impairment information on goodwill, property, plant, equipment and investments in subsidiaries. The results of the investigation confirmed the continuing historically observed non-compliance with information obligations and identified this deficiency as one of the causes of the underdevelopment of the securities market.

Key words IAS 36 · Impairment of assets · Prague Stock Exchange

18.1 Introduction

International Accounting Standard (IAS) 36 Impairment of Assets was accepted by the International Accounting Standards Board (IASB) in April 2001. However, it was created already in June 1998 by the International Accounting Standards Committee (IASC) and revised several times over the years. In 2004, intangible assets were added. It was revised, and several amendments were integrated into it in 2008, 2009 and 2013. The principle of impairment is to ensure that assets are not shown in the balance sheet in excess of the recoverable amount (IASB, 2013).

The disclosure of quality, transparent and comparable information is one of the several main objectives of financial statements prepared in accordance with International Financial Reporting Standards (hereinafter "IFRS" or "Standards"). Financial statements under these Standards have been required for companies that issue securities on the regulated capital markets of the European Union since 2005.

P. Huňáček (✉)
Department of Corporate Finance, Prague University of Economics and Business, Prague, Czech Republic
e-mail: xmasp00@vse.cz

D. Procházka (ed.), *Regulation of Finance and Accounting*, Springer Proceedings in Business and Economics, https://doi.org/10.1007/978-3-030-99873-8_18

They are primarily intended for profit-making companies and are based on the needs of their users, in particular current and potential investors. Thanks to the Standards, investors can get high-quality information, especially about the financial situation of companies that will assist them in their investment decision-making (Dvořáková, 2017).

This brief introduction is followed by a review of literature that addresses an objective which is similar to this article, namely to determine whether publicly traded companies on the Prague Stock Exchange (PSE) comply with the disclosure requirements imposed on them by IFRS. Subsequently are briefly explained the basic issues of IAS 36 that are specifically addressed in this article. Four information requirements are in turn selected and subsequently tested within the published financial statements. In the conclusion are presented the results of the analysis and the reasoning why this information is not disclosed. Finally, the consequences of the absence of this information are drawn.

18.2 Literature Review

IAS 36 has been effective for many years, and much has been written about it. The same applies to the verification of the disclosure of mandatory information. However, reference to the direct impact of the violations of this obligation of disclosures is missing in the tests carried out under Czech conditions. In addition, the tests were performed on older data, so it is also intended to analyse whether the situation has improved.

Ašenbrenerová (2016) deals with IFRS 12 Disclosure of Interests in Other Entities and analyses the minimum required information that an investor should disclose about entities in which he has an interest. This article, unlike those that follow, had proven a relatively high percentage of compliance with disclosure obligations, 96–97%. Ašenbrenerová (2016) analyses mainly basic information presented on face of the balance sheet and profit and loss statements, distinguishing the financial and non-financial companies. The year examined is 2014.

Pospíšil (2017) focuses on the information required by IFRS 3 Business Combinations. According to the results of the tests performed using the D-score model, compliance with disclosure ranged between 47 and 86%, which represents a relatively large variance. Unlike other articles, the rate of disclosure has slightly improved during the reporting period, 2011–2014.

Another author, Dvořák (2017), focuses on IFRS 13 Fair Value Measurement. The author tests whether Czech companies publish the information required by the Standard. The research initially shows good results, when only a quarter of the companies correctly distinguish fair value with respect to the fair value hierarchy. Eventually, the results of the investigation deteriorated and resulted in the concluding finding that almost 50% of the companies in the test sample did not report changes between the hierarchy levels and more than 60% of the companies did not describe the valuation techniques used in the fair value measurement.

The last covered author is Červený (2017), who focused on IFRS 2 Share-Based Payment in 2013–2015. Like the previous authors, he monitors the quality of published information. In this case, he compares them to randomly selected companies from the German Deutscher Aktien Index (DAX). According to empirical evidence, some Czech companies fail to comply with the disclosures required by IFRS 2. On the other hand, according to the article, companies from the German market publish an exhaustive volume of information beyond the minimum obligations.

All these articles were based mainly on data from Czech companies, which are from the Prague Stock Exchange. With the exception of Ašenbrenerová (2016) and Červený (2017), these articles prove the unequivocal failure to comply with the disclosure requirements of IFRS.

18.3 Theoretical Basis

The cornerstone of IAS 36 is the cautionary principle of not overestimating assets and not underestimating liabilities. The condition is also a presumption of continuity, i.e. the continuation of the company in the future, which will allow the use of long-term asset benefits (Dvořáková, 2017).

The impairment of assets applies to most fixed assets. Their definition is so extensive that the Standard rather states to which assets it does not relate:

- Inventories (see IAS 2)
- Contract assets and assets arising from costs to obtain or fulfil a contract that are recognised in accordance with IFRS 15
- Deferred tax assets (see IAS 12)
- Assets arising from employee benefits (see IAS 19)
- Financial assets within the scope of IFRS 9
- Investment property measured at fair value (see IAS 40)
- Biological assets related to agricultural activity within the scope of IAS 41
- Deferred acquisition costs, and intangible assets, arising from an insurer's contractual rights under insurance contracts within the scope of IFRS 4
- Non-current assets (or disposal groups) classified as held for sale in accordance with IFRS 5 (IASB, 2013)

So IAS 36 mainly deals with the following:

- Property, plant and equipment
- Intangible assets
- Goodwill
- Investments valued by equivalence
- Investments in subsidiaries and
- Investments in property in initial costs (IASB, 2013)

The objective of this Standard is to determine the procedures to be applied by an entity to ensure that its assets are carried at up to the maximum of the recoverable amount, that is to say, do not exceed the recoverable amount (IASB, 2013),

The recoverable amount is determined as the higher of the value in use or fair value less the costs of disposal. The value in use reflects the present value of future net cash flows that will be generated by the use of the asset, including the potential revenue from its sale. If the recoverable amount is less than the carrying amount, an impairment loss for the asset is recognised and it is included in the profit and loss statement. The value of the asset being analysed is reduced (Dvořáková, 2017).

If the recoverable amount of an individual asset cannot be determined, it is determined for the so-called cash-generating unit. This represents the smallest possible group of assets that separately generates divisible cash flows (Dvořáková, 2017).

Asset impairment testing shall be performed at least once a year for intangible assets with indefinite useful lives, intangible assets at the acquisition stage and goodwill from a business combination. Other assets are tested at the instigation of external or internal indicators. The main external indicators are as follows:

- Reduction in the price of an asset is faster than expected when determining its depreciation.
- Change in the market interest rate.
- The carrying amount of the entity's net assets is greater than its market capitalisation.
- Changes in the market, economic, legislative or technological environment (IASB, 2013).

Internal indicators may be as follows:

- Evidence of obsolescence or physical damage to the asset.
- Negative changes affecting the entity to the extent to which or the manner in which the asset is used.
- Internal statements contain signals that indicate that the asset's economic performance is, or will be, worse (IASB, 2013).

If the effect of these indicators ceases, the impairment loss of the asset may be reversed and the value of the asset may increase. The exception is goodwill, for which this loss must not be reversed.

The disclosure requirements of this standard are quite extensive, so only those that will be examined are noted below:

1. Amount of an impairment loss.
2. If the recoverable amount of the cash-generating unit is based on the value in use, disclosed are the discount rate used to estimate the value in use and the rate of growth used to extrapolate cash-flow plans.
3. Events and circumstances that led to the recognition of an impairment loss.
4. If the recoverable amount is based on the value in use, an entity shall disclose the description of each key assumption on which the cash flow plans are based.

18.4 Testing of Mandatory Disclosed Information

The Prague Stock Exchange, more precisely the companies from the stock and bond market, was chosen for the survey on disclosed information. Initially, the sample contained 62 companies, but it was clear that it was necessary to sort some companies out because they did not correspond to the subject of the analysis. The first condition was that the companies were listed on the public market for the entire period of 2015–2017 and they were not just short-term "participants". Furthermore, there had to be traceable annual reports prepared under IFRS. At least one of the annual reports of each company had to allow for electronic extraction of data; that is, the report could not be, e.g., only optically scanned. This requirement allowed the annual reports to be text-based searched since the information for this survey has been scattered across entire documents. Duplicities have been eliminated. The final condition was compliance with the assumption of going-concern (see the previous chapter).

A relatively large number of companies that did not meet the selection conditions were excluded from the survey (see the left-hand part of Table 18.1). The right-hand part of the table shows the distribution of the final sample of companies, which is unfortunately not even on the part of the stock market. The sample ended up with 32 companies.

Due to their unevenness, the observed values will be presented in tables as percentages. In the left-hand side table, there will always be a share of the companies with at least one positive finding in the total number of companies. The right-hand side table will show the ratio of the number of positive findings to the total possible number of findings (this is three times the number of companies given the three-year reporting period).

18.4.1 Mandatory Disclosed Information for Positive Impairment Testing of Goodwill

As already mentioned towards the end of the third chapter, in positive goodwill impairment testing, the annual report should include, inter alia, the amount by which the value is impaired. In cases when the value in use is adopted, the discount rate and the rate of growth used to extrapolate cash flow plans should also be provided.

Table 18.1 Selection of companies

	Companies on the stock market	Companies on the bond market		Companies on the stock market	Companies on the bond market
Original number of companies	27	35	Financial companies	4	7
Number of selected companies	17	15	Non- financial companies	13	8

Source: PSE (2019) and authorial computation

Table 18.2 Observed impairment of goodwill

	Companies on the stock market (%)	Companies on the bond market (%)		Companies on the stock market (%)	Companies on the bond market (%)
Financial companies	75.0	14.3	Financial companies	41.7	9.5
Non-financial companies	23.1	12.5	Non-financial companies	7.7	8.3

Source: Annual reports and authorial computation
Note: Left-hand: share of the companies with a positive finding. Right-hand: share of positive findings for the entire reporting period

Out of the 32 examined companies, eight did not show goodwill in their balance sheets at all during the observed period. Of the remaining companies, there were only eight that reported a total of 12 goodwill impairments during the observed period (see Table 18.2). Six companies used the value in use for testing, only one adopted fair value less the costs of disposal and one used both of these methods.

The amount was reported for all impairments. There were no significant differences in the distribution of impairments between individual years and the financial and non-financial companies. Significant is the absence of the discount rate in two cases, representing about 17% of the positive occurrences. The growth rate for subsequent extrapolation (about 33%) was also missing for these two companies and two other firms. In addition to the numerical values for these impairments, accepted were also statements that no growth rate for the second phase was considered.

The focus on this information was mainly due to the investors' own efforts to determine the discount rate. The reported discount rate may serve as a guide for determining the investors' own discount rate for their valuation of the company and their subsequent decision on a possible investment. However, it should be borne in mind that the discount rate under IAS 36 is reported as a pre-tax quantity.

18.4.2 Mandatory Disclosed Information for Positive Impairment Testing of Property, Plant and Equipment

The selection of this group was also influenced by the importance of the information that the annual report could provide in the case of positive testing. For some companies, property, plant and equipment play a crucial role, and reasons for their impairment may have a decisive impact on the valuation of the company itself.

There were many more positive tests in this category, with a total of 14 impaired companies reporting 32 impairments, one third of the possible observations (see Table 18.3 for more details). As in the previous chapter, there were no trends in individual markets, year-on-year development or the types of companies.

Table 18.3 Observed impairment of property, plant and equipment

	Companies on the stock market (%)	Companies on the bond market (%)		Companies on the stock market (%)	Companies on the bond market (%)
Financial companies	75.0	28.6	Financial companies	75.0	28.6
Non-financial companies	46.2	37.5	Non-financial companies	30.8	20.8

Source: Annual reports and authorial computation
Note: Left-hand: share of the companies with a positive finding. Right-hand: share of positive findings for the entire reporting period

Admittedly, the problem is that in 23 cases, i.e. in about 72% of the positive findings, the reasons for the impairment were missing, which is a diametrical difference from the previous chapter. Just to clarify, in some cases, it has been explained that the recoverable amount is higher than the book value, but this is not considered an acceptable explanation. The most common reason for the impairment was the fall in the prices of manufactured products, as well as increased regulation, reference to the result of the expert opinion, lower economic performance than expected and doubts about the future use of assets. Interestingly, Unipetrol, which did not detect any indicators of possible impairment, carried out tests with a subsequent impairment.

18.4.3 Mandatory Disclosed Information for Positive Impairment Testing of Investments in Subsidiaries

The next information under test was the reason that led to impairments in the value of investments in subsidiaries. This information is important because subsidiaries in many cases represent foreign branches or a related, though not the same, production or service. Some publicly traded companies have dozens of subsidiaries, while five companies from the sample did not have any; four of these fall under the non-financial type from the bond market.

In this category, there were ten companies with a positive test for impairment of investments in subsidiaries (see Table 18.4). Again, no clear trend or deviation was observed. In total, 16 impairments were reported, but only three of them were reported together with a reason; that is, approximately 81% of cases were without a reason. There were only two kinds of reasons: decrease in profitability and negative development of the geopolitical and economic situation.

Table 18.4 Observed impairment of investments in subsidiaries

	Companies on the stock market (%)	Companies on the bond market (%)		Companies on the stock market (%)	Companies on the bond market (%)
Financial companies	0.0	42.9	Financial companies	0.0	23.8
Non-financial companies	38.5	25.0	Non-financial companies	23.1	8.3

Source: Annual reports and authorial computation

Note: Left-hand: share of the companies with a positive finding. Right-hand: share of positive findings for the entire reporting period

18.4.4 Key Assumptions upon Which Cash Flow Plans Are Based

The key assumptions upon which the cash flow plans are based when using the value in use to determine recoverable amounts are also required to be disclosed. These assumptions may complement the risks that a potential investor can include in his/her valuation of or comparison with other companies and in determining whether they are subjected to the same risks. Although from the previous three tests there were 21 companies that showed positive results from impairment tests (see Sects. 18.4.1, 18.4.2, and 18.4.3), only two of them had disclosed these assumptions. In addition to these subjects, there was one more company that has reported assumptions. For several companies, the key stated assumption was that the rate of return should not fall below the discount rate, which is nevertheless obvious and not meaningful, so it was not considered a sufficient argument. Among the accepted reasons were the assumptions of a stable excise tax and stable costs of raw materials, followed by stable inflation and others.

18.5 Conclusion

This paper examined compliance with information obligations under IAS 36 Impairment of Assets in the annual reports of companies traded on the Prague Stock Exchange in the Czech Republic. The analyses carried out confirmed long-term non-compliance with these obligations.

Within the scope of the undertaken analysis, as an author, I can say that, generally, better prepared and more comprehensible were the annual reports of companies from the stock market. Among the best, I would rate the annual reports of ČEZ, a.s.; this company has reported all the categories of impairment losses and also included almost all the mandatory data. On the other hand, financial companies from the bond market fared rather badly, mainly because of the impossibility to distinguish among impairments. The reason was their inclusion in the accumulated depreciation of property, plant and equipment or their inclusion in financial assets, which are dealt with in IFRS 9.

Annual reports should be a comprehensive source of neutral information. Although it is understandable why companies try to provide information in a better light than they actually are, it is not admissible not to give information at all or not to justify them more precisely. The fact is – as demonstrated by the literature review – that the situation has been unsatisfactory for a long time, and no positive shift can be seen.

If the Prague Stock Exchange is to catch up with the developed markets in the future, the situation has to improve in many ways. Low liquidity leads to expensive trading and large real spreads. It does not make sense to trade on PSE for small investors. In addition, if these small investors do not closely monitor the development of companies and some information behind the numbers is missing, they must look for additional resources. This increases the time required and makes investment decisions more difficult. The result is a further reduction in market liquidity. Therefore, the currently traded companies can contribute to market quality improvement "simply" by improving their annual reports.

Acknowledgements The article is processed as an output of the research project "Nové výzvy Corporate Finance v České republice" by the Grant Agency under registration number F1/42/2019.

References

Ašenbrenerová, P. (2016). Disclosure of joint ventures and associates in financial statement under IFRS. *European Financial and Accounting Journal, 2011*(3), 85–94. https://doi.org/10.18267/j.efaj.164

Červený, M. (2017). Fulfillment of IFRS 2 disclosure requirements by companies listed on the Prague Stock Exchange. *European Financial and Accounting Journal, 2012*(3), 53–64. https://doi.org/10.18267/j.efaj.187

Dvořák, J. (2017). How do Czech companies report fair value measurement under IFRS 13? *European Financial and Accounting Journal., 2012*(3), 117–128. https://doi.org/10.18267/j.efaj.191

Dvořáková, D. (2017). *Finanční účetnictví a výkaznictví podle mezinárodních standardů IFRS.* BizBooks.

IASB [International Accounting Standards Board]. (2013). *IAS Standard 36 Impairment of Assets.* IFRS Foundation.

Pospíšil, J. (2017). IFRS 3 compliance research at Czech Capital Market. *Acta academica karviniensia, 2017*(1), 76–86. https://doi.org/10.25142/aak.2017.007

PSE [Prague Stock Exchange]. (2019). *Prague Stock Exchange* [online]. [vid. 18. 8. 2019]. Available from: https://www.pse.cz/

Chapter 19
Does IFRS 9 Increase Volatility of Loan Loss Provisions?

Oľga Pastiranová and Jiří Witzany

Abstract This paper presents the main principles of the IFRS 9 accounting standard, which requires banks to estimate expected credit losses since 2018. The new standard is expected to change the flow of loan loss provisions, which are expected to be unstable, more volatile, and much more unpredictable than under the previous standard IAS 39, empirically tested on a sample of eight largest Czech banks according to their balance sheet volume. The hypothesis that the implementation of IFRS 9 causes increased volatility of loan loss provisions is confirmed in the case of five banks and within the whole sample of banks at a 5% probability level.

Key words Expected credit loss · Loan loss provisions · IFRS 9

19.1 Introduction

Due to the higher interest of regulators in the topic concerning the stability of the financial sector, especially the largest banks, there have been discussions on the recognition of the impairment of financial assets since the great financial crisis in 2008. According to International Accounting Standard (IAS) 39, banks created provisions after they had evidence that the financial asset was defaulted. Such rules were considered procyclical, stimulating the volume of provided loans during the good times and subsequently triggering the substantial creation of provisions during the recession and thus deepening the consequences of recession. There was a huge call for a necessity to update the rules on the creation of loan provisions. As a result, the new International Financial Reporting Standard (IFRS) 9 financial instrument (hereinafter referred to as "IFRS 9") was adopted, effective since January 1, 2018, replacing IAS 39.

IFRS 9 requires banks to recognize expected credit losses (ECLs), considering not only past events but also forward-looking information, including

O. Pastiranová (✉) · J. Witzany
Faculty of Finance and Accounting, Prague University of Economics and Business, Prague, Czech Republic
e-mail: olga.pastiranova@vse.cz; jiri.witzany@vse.cz

D. Procházka (ed.), *Regulation of Finance and Accounting*, Springer Proceedings in Business and Economics, https://doi.org/10.1007/978-3-030-99873-8_19

macroeconomic predictions and available information about the debtor (BCBS, 2015; Bischof & Daske, 2016).

Due to the increased complexity of models and their dependence on vast data and due to changing predictions, the flow of provisions is expected to be more volatile. Finally, through profit and loss, the banks are expected to be of lower stability. As observed by comparing year-end 2017 and 2018 data from the Czech banking sector, the implementation of IFRS 9 caused a decrease in the value of financial assets in Czech banks by 0.8% (Lukeš, 2019). Further research focuses on the behavior of banks during the cycle. Results show that provisioning procyclicality tested on pre-2018 data is strongest in the later contractionary phase; in contrast, there is no evidence of procyclicality in the early contractionary phase. Therefore, the banks with higher credit risk behave more procyclically, and such behavior might, under IFRS 9, delay transfers between stages and overstate the fluctuations (Malovaná & Tesařová, 2019).

The aim of this paper is to examine the flow of loan loss provisions under the new standard and to test the hypothesis that the implementation of IFRS 9 gives rise to the increased volatility of loan loss provisions, tested on a sample of the largest Czech banks. Volatility is tested by a comparison of the quarterly data on the cost of risk for two periods: the pre-IFRS 9 period (data from 2017) and the IFRS 9 period (data from 2018 and 2019).

19.2 Provisioning Rules Under IFRS 9

According to the new standard, banks are obliged to categorize their financial assets into three stages based on the level of the credit risk of the debtor. ECL is then estimated according to the corresponding phase.

In case the exposure to credit risk is considered low, banks should report 12-month ECL, defined as the portion of lifetime ECL representing ECL resulting from default of financial asset within the next 12 months after the reporting date (IFRS 9: Appendix A). Such exposure is categorized as stage 1. The standard requires the recognition of lifetime ECLs in case there is a significant increase in the credit risk of financial assets. ECL is defined as the expected credit loss that might arise in the event of a default over the lifetime of an asset (IFRS 9: Appendix A). Financial assets with a significant increase in credit risk are categorized as stage 2. The recognition of defaulted financial asset when the repayment of the receivable is not probable is the same as within stage 2 – bank creates lifetime ECL. For the main principles and stages under the IFRS 9 provisioning model, see the table below (Table 19.1).

The crucial part in the recognition of loan loss provisions is the estimation of the 12-month ECL and lifetime ECL. Usually, the 12-month ECL is decomposed into the probability of default (PD), loss given default (LGD), and exposure at default (EAD):

Table 19.1 The principles of the impairment model under IFRS 9

	Stage 1	Stage 2	Stage 3	Stage 1
Level of credit risk	Low credit risk	Significant increase in credit risk	Significant increase in credit risk	Low credit risk
Trigger	Initial recognition	Significant increase in credit risk	Default of asset	Initial recognition
Loan loss provision	12-month ECL	Lifetime ECL	Lifetime ECL	12-month ECL
Interest revenue	Effective interest rate applied on gross carrying value	Effective interest rate applied on gross carrying value	Effective interest rate applied on net carrying value	Effective interest rate applied on gross carrying value

Source: Authorial preparation

$$\mathrm{ECL}_{12\mathrm{M}} = \mathrm{PD} * \mathrm{LGD} * \mathrm{EAD} \tag{19.1}$$

When estimating lifetime ECL, the probability of default in each year until the maturity of the exposure needs to be estimated, and lifetime ECL is then expressed as

$$\mathrm{ECL}_{\mathrm{lifetime}} = \sum_{i=1}^{n} \mathrm{PD} * \mathrm{LGD}_i * \mathrm{EAD}_i \tag{19.2}$$

where PD_i denotes the probability of default in year i, LGD_i the loss given default in year i, EAD_i the exposure at default in year i, and n the maturity of the exposure (Witzany, 2017). In case the financial asset is already defaulted, PD does not need to be estimated, and forward-looking recovery rates of cash flows are used instead.

19.3 Data and Methodology

For the testing of the volatility of loan loss provisions, we selected eight Czech banks with the biggest balance sheet volume as of September 30, 2019 (the latest data available). The total balance sheet of the whole Czech banking sector at this date is 8.038 trillion CZK (ČNB, 2019), out of which 76% is represented by the balance sheet of eight banks in the sample. The table below presents the banks selected in the sample and the volume of their individual balance sheet at the end of the third quarter of 2019 (Table 19.2).

To test the volatility of loan loss provisions, data from the quarterly reporting of banks in the sample were extracted and divided into two periods: data within the period 1Q 2017 to 4Q 2017, representing the pre-IFRS 9 period, and data from 1Q 2018 to 3Q 2019 (latest available), representing the IFRS 9 period. Quarterly data on the cost of risk were available for almost all banks in the sample (with the exception

Table 19.2 List of biggest banks in the Czech Republic as of September 30, 2019, according to balance sheet volume

Bank	Balance sheet as of September 30, 2019 (million CZK)	Proportion on balance sheet of banking sector
Česká spořitelna, a.s.	1,512,602	19%
Československá obchodní banka, a. s.	1,542,169	19%
J&T BANKA, a.s.	148,885	2%
Komerční banka, a.s.	1,168,252	15%
MONETA Money Bank, a.s.	227,411	3%
PPF banka a.s.	221,257	3%
Raiffeisenbank a.s.	373,002	5%
UniCredit Bank Czech Republic and Slovakia, a.s.	876,573	11%

Source: Authorial computation, data extracted from quarterly reporting of banks
Note: Česká spořitelna (2019), ČSOB (2019), J&T BANKA (2019), Komerční banka (2019), MONETA Money Bank (2019), PPF banka (2019), Raiffeisen bank (2019), UniCredit bank (2019)

of PPF Banka, Raiffeisenbank, and UniCredit Bank, where the quarterly change in the provisions was used as a proxy). Furthermore, quarterly data on loan receivables from customers were extracted for all the banks. Subsequently, the ratio of loan provisions (cost of risk) to loan receivables was calculated, resulting in 32 observations for the pre-IFRS 9 period and 56 observations for the IFRS 9 period. Standard deviation for the cost of risk ratio was calculated separately for both tested periods at the level of individual banks and for the whole sample. To test the validity of the hypothesis, the F-test of equality of variances was used, with the null hypothesis that two normal populations have the same variance.

19.4 Results and Discussion

The development of the quarterly cost of risk ratio for the total sample of banks during the whole tested period is depicted in the figure below. Positive figures represent the release of provisions, and negative figures denote the creation of provisions (Fig. 19.1).

It is apparent from the figure that the quarterly cost of risk ratio is more volatile in the IFRS 9 period (in years 2018 and 2019) after the new standard was implemented than in the pre-IFRS 9 period (year 2017). The first quarter of 2018 reflects the initial impact of the implementation of the new standard when banks obviously had to create more provisions for their loan exposures.

Similarly, the quarterly development of the cost of risk on the level of individual banks is presented in the figure below (Fig. 19.2).

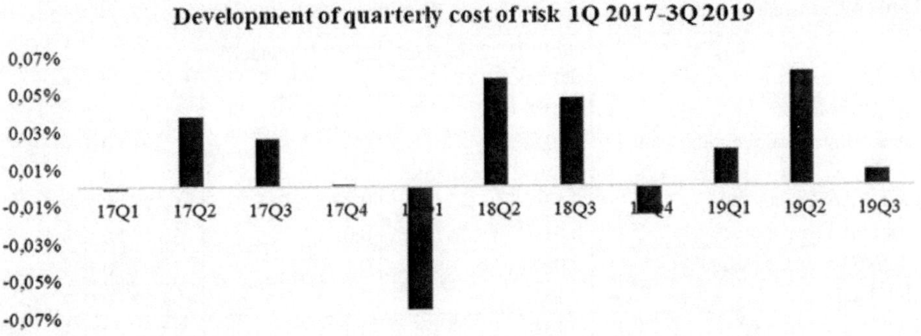

Fig. 19.1 Development of quarterly cost of risk on total sample. (Source: authorial computation, data extracted from quarterly reporting of banks)

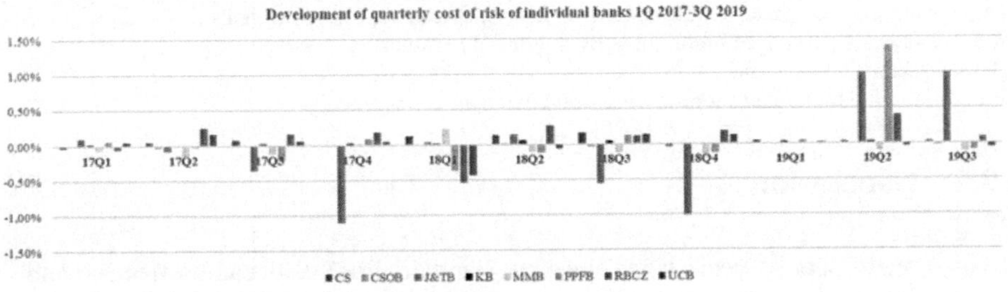

Fig. 19.2 Development of quarterly cost of risk of individual banks. (Source: Authorial computation, data extracted from quarterly reporting of banks)

Despite a relatively stable cost of risk ratio in the first quarter of 2019, it is visible that its development, in the case of most banks, is more volatile in the IFRS 9 period in comparison to the pre-IFRS 9 period.

The following table presents the standard deviation of the cost of risk ratio, *F*-test statistics, and *p*-values in the pre-IFRS 9 period and the IFRS 9 period, calculated for individual banks and the whole sample as well (Table 19.3).

The standard deviation of the series of the cost of risk is higher in the IFRS 9 period in the case of seven out of eight banks in the sample, while in the case of one bank (CSOB), the standard deviation is equal. A higher standard deviation in the IFRS 9 period was also confirmed for the whole sample in total in comparison with the pre-IFRS 9 period. *F*-test is larger than 1 in the case of seven banks where the standard deviation of the cost of risk was higher in the IFRS 9 period. For CSOB, where the standard deviation was equal in both periods, the *F*-test is very close to 1 (0,991). The null hypothesis on the equality of variances can be rejected at a 5% probability level in the case of three banks and at a 10% probability level in the case of two banks. For the whole sample, the null hypothesis was rejected, and the increase in the volatility of loan loss provisions was proved at a 5% probability level.

The hypothesis that IFRS 9 causes the increased volatility of loan loss provisions as compared to IAS 39 was confirmed despite a relatively short data series available.

Table 19.3 Volatility of loan loss provision in pre-IFRS 9 and IFRS 9 periods

Bank	Pre-IFRS 9 standard deviation	IFRS 9 standard deviation	*F*-test	*p*-value
Česká spořitelna, a.s.[a]	0.05%	0.07%	2,226	0,186
Československá obchodní banka, a. s.[a]	0.02%	0.02%	0,991	0,458
J&T BANKA, a.s.[a]	0.53%	0.74%	1,973	0,219
Komerční banka, a.s.[a]	0,01%	0.02%	3,913	0,073
MONETA Money Bank, a.s.[a]	0.08%	0.14%	3,397	0,094
PPF banka a.s.[b]	0.13%	0.58%	19,057	0,002
Raiffeisenbank a.s.[b]	0.13%	0.30%	4,922	0,047
UniCredit Bank Czech Republic and Slovakia, a.s.[b]	0.06%	0.19%	11,642	0,007
Total – Whole sample	0.02%	0.05%	5,735	0,034

Source: authorial computation, data extracted from quarterly reporting of banks
Note: statistical significance highlighted by boldfaced *p*-values
[a]Based on consolidated data
[b]Based on individual data as a proxy (consolidated data not available)

19.5 Conclusion

It has already been 2 years since the new standard IFRS 9 became effective and Czech banks had to cope with its requirements. The main idea behind the change of provisioning rules was to eliminate the procyclicality of loan loss provisions by adopting the model of expected credit losses instead of the model of incurred credit losses under IAS 39.

The new model is much more sophisticated and demanding and requires the use of noisy data sets and forward-looking predictions in order to comply with the complexity of the new methodology. With respect to the complexity of the model and the variability of predicted data, the paper assumes that the estimated expected losses of banks would be less stable and that the flow of provisions would be more volatile in comparison with provisioning under IAS 39. The paper therefore hypothesizes that the implementation of IFRS 9 leads to the increased volatility of loan loss provisions with an immediate impact on the result of banks.

For the testing of the hypothesis, quarterly data from 1Q 2017 to 3Q 2019 on the cost of risk and loan receivables from customers of the eight biggest Czech banks as of September 30, 2019, were extracted. Data were divided into two periods: the pre-IFRS 9 period and the IFRS 9 period. The standard deviation of relative change of loan loss provisions to loan receivables balances was calculated for both periods separately on the level of individual banks and for the whole sample as total. The standard deviation of the cost of risk series in the IFRS 9 period was higher for seven out of eight banks in the sample, while in the case of three banks, it was statistically significant at a 5% probability level and in the case of two banks at a 10% probability level. Increased standard deviation in the IFRS 9 period was also proven within the whole sample of banks, with statistical significance at a 5% level. Therefore, the null hypothesis on the equality of variances was rejected, and the hypothesis that the implementation of IFRS 9 gives rise to the increased volatility of loan loss provisions was confirmed with statistical significance. Due to the short data series available after the adoption of IFRS 9, new empirical testing should be performed with more data series to confirm the findings of this paper.

Acknowledgments This paper has been prepared under the financial support of grant "Development trends in financial markets" IG102029 and GAČR 18-05244S, which the authors gratefully acknowledge.

References

BCBS. (2015). *Guidance on accounting for expected credit losses Basel Committee on Banking Supervision*. http://bis.org/bcbs/publ/d311.pdf

Bischof, J., & Daske, H. (2016). Interpreting the European Union's IFRS endorsement criteria: The case of IFRS 9 Accounting in Europe. Roč. 13 č. 2 s. 129–168. https://doi.org/10.1080/17449480.2016.1210181.

Česká národní banka. (2019). ARAD. Systém časových řad.

Česká spořitelna. (2019). *Dokumenty ke stažení*. https://www.csas.cz/cs/dokumenty-ke-stazeni#/

ČSOB. (2019). Povinně uveřejňované informace.

J&T BANKA. (2019). *Informační povinnost*. https://www.jtbank.cz/informacni-povinnost/

Komerční banka. (2019). *Pro investory*. https://www.kb.cz/cs/o-bance/pro-investory-rozcestnik

Lukeš, J. (2019). Analýza dopadů IFRS 9 na bankovní sektor v České republice. Český finanční a účetní časopis roč. 14 č. 3 s. 17–31.

Malovaná and Tesařová. (2019). *Banks' credit losses and provisioning over the business cycle: Implications for IFRS 9*. CNB WORKING PAPER SERIES 4/2019.

MONETA Money Bank. (2019). *Hospodářské výsledky*. https://investors.moneta.cz/financni-vysledky

PPF banka. (2019). *Povinně uveřejňované informace*. https://www.ppfbanka.cz/cs/dulezite-dokumenty

Raiffeisen bank. (2019). *Výsledky hospodaření*. https://www.rb.cz/o-nas/kdo-jsme/vysledky-hospodareni

UniCredit bank. (2019). *Výsledky*. https://www.unicreditbank.cz/cs/o-bance.html#Banka

Witzany, J. (2017). *Credit risk management: Pricing, measurement, and modeling*. Springer.

Chapter 20
IFRS 9 – Implications on Procyclicality

Oľga Pastiranová and Jiří Witzany

Abstract The aim of this study is to analyze the cyclical behavior of loan loss provisions under IFRS 9 provisioning rules as compared to the previous standard IAS 39. Provisioning rules under IAS 39 were considered procyclical, and there has been an appeal to replace the incurred credit loss model with the expected credit loss model, which was assumed to have a countercyclical impact. However, recent development indicates the opposite. The hypothesis that loan loss provisions under IFRS 9 provisioning rules have procyclical effects was empirically tested and confirmed by the panel regression analysis of quarterly GDP growth and impairment ratio on the sample of EU member countries for the period 1Q 2015–3Q 2020.

Key words Procyclicality · Loan loss provisions · IFRS 9

20.1 Introduction

One of the topics widely discussed after the global financial crisis was the procyclicality of the financial system. Generally, procyclicality is perceived as positive interactions between the financial sector and the real sector of the economy, intensifying the fluctuations in the economic cycle. During the contractionary phases of the cycle, procyclicality might have a vastly negative impact on financial stability because of the deepening recession. In the context of the credit cycle of the banking industry, the procyclicality of credit cycle might contribute to the deepening of economic cycle fluctuations caused by activities within the financial system. The procyclicality of the credit cycle might be induced by factors inherent to lending, such as information asymmetry, expectations, and forecasts of economic development (too optimistic or pessimistic) or financial innovations. However, an important role might be also assigned to financial regulation and accounting rules. Procyclical behavior might have severe impact, especially during the phase of economic

O. Pastiranová (✉) · J. Witzany
Faculty of Finance and Accounting, Prague University of Economics and Business, Prague 3, Czech Republic
e-mail: olga.pastiranova@vse.cz; jiri.witzany@vse.cz

D. Procházka (ed.), *Regulation of Finance and Accounting*, Springer Proceedings in Business and Economics, https://doi.org/10.1007/978-3-030-99873-8_20

downturn, as it might contribute to an extension and the deepening of the financial recession. A high level of procyclicality within the financial system is undesirable for financial stability as it affects the ability of banks to absorb potential credit losses and provide necessary liquidity for the financial system, while a weakened financial system cannot absorb its losses and obtain necessary funding. The procyclicality of the provisioning might be especially undesirable within a monetary union, such as the Economic and Monetary Union within the European Union (EU), as the common monetary policy cannot adequately respond to different financial and economic cycles of individual countries within the union.

Since the global financial crisis in 2008, the financial and regulatory authorities have been trying to discuss procyclicality and take actions in order to eliminate the potential deepening of recession through new rules on provisioning and regulatory requirements for capital adequacy. One of the results of the actions taken was the implementation of a new international accounting standard, International Financial Reporting Standards (IFRS) 9, financial instruments effective for all financial institutions reporting under IFRS since January 1, 2018. In contrast to the previous standard International Accounting Standards (IAS) 39, based on which the incurred credit loss model has been applied, IFRS 9 requires the implementation of the expected credit loss (ECL) model, including forward-looking information.

The aim of this paper is an empirical analysis of the cyclical implications of forward-looking provisioning rules under IFRS 9 within the first years after its adoption, focused on the EU banking sector. In other words, the goal is to give an indication whether the provisioning rules under IFRS 9 actually lead to countercyclical behavior and thus to contribute to the discussion on generally observed impacts of the IFRS 9 standard. The empirical analysis is based on data on impairment to assets ratio and gross domestic product (GDP) growth for 28 EU member countries within the period 1Q 2015–3Q 2020, put together as a comprehensive panel data set. Panel regression analyses have been performed for the period before IFRS 9 (1Q 2015–4Q 2017) and the IFRS 9 period (1Q 2018–3Q 2020) to evaluate the procyclical behavior of loan loss provisions under both standards.

The paper is organized as follows: the existing empirical research on the procyclicality of loan loss provisioning and hypothesis development is described within the first section, followed by the section describing the credit cycle and the role of provisioning rules within this cycle. The next section explains the data and methodology used for the empirical analysis, followed by the core empirical analysis presented in Sect. 20.5, describing results and discussion. The findings of the paper are summarized in the conclusion.

20.2 On the Way to Countercyclicality of Loan Loss Provisioning

The cyclicality of provisioning has been the object of research for decades. The research published prior to the effectiveness of IFRS 9 often indicated that the rules for the creation of provisions under the previous standard IAS 39 have had a procyclical effect. Interdependence between provisioning behavior and the business cycle has been discussed, and a negative relationship between the stock of provisions and macroeconomic variables during the economic downturn has been observed (Leaven & Majnoni, 2003; Bikker & Metzemakers, 2004).

After the great financial crisis in 2008, the need for a reform of the regulatory and accounting standards, eliminating procyclicality, has been emphasized by the financial and regulatory authorities and standard-setting bodies. The International Monetary Fund (2009) stressed the need for a switch from incurred loss provisioning to dynamic, forward-looking provisioning rules, which were expected to mitigate the procyclical effect of provisioning during downward economic trends. The Financial Stability Forum (2009) appealed for the earlier identification of credit losses and reconsidering using the incurred loss models within accounting standards and capital adequacy requirements.

The recent research conducted in the period after the implementation of IFRS 9 indicates various findings on the procyclical behavior of the new standard. Huizinga and Leaven (2019) observed that estimated loan loss provisions in the euro area are negatively related to GDP growth, concluding on the procyclicality of provisioning, which was proved to be more significant in the case of larger banks with a higher volume of capital. Moreover, the procyclicality within the euro area is estimated to be twice as large as in other advanced economies, suggesting a stronger effect for monetary unions. The cyclical effect of IFRS 9 is questioned by Buesa et al. (2020), who compare the cyclical behavior of provisioning rules under IFRS 9, IAS 39, and the US Generally Accepted Accounting Principles (GAAP) by modeling the impact of loan loss provisions on profit and loss (P&L). The results of their research indicate that IFRS 9 is less procyclical than IAS 39, however, still being procyclical (and more procyclical than US GAAP). IFRS 9 provisioning rules influence P&L during the contractionary phase of the business cycle (using forward-looking information for the following 12 months within Stage 1). Abad and Suarez (2018) reach the conclusion that at the beginning of the contractionary phase, the loan loss provisions under a forward-looking standard amplify this phase of the cycle.

Recent research indicates interesting conclusions on the procyclicality of provisioning rules under IFRS 9. However, most of this research was performed on estimated data. The added value of this paper would be to contribute to the debate on the cyclical implications of IFRS 9 based on the actual data available after the implementation of IFRS 9 (since January 1, 2018). Because there are relevant indications suggesting that IFRS 9 might not necessarily cause countercyclical behavior, the following hypothesis is formulated: loan loss provisions under IFRS 9 have a procyclical effect.

20.3 Credit Cycle and the Role of Provisioning Rules

This section describes the link between the economic cycle, credit cycle, and the effect of provisioning rules during the cycles in order to understand the role of provisioning within particular phases of the cycles. The description addresses the financial sector, specifically the banking sector.

Historically, there has been evidence of an existing credit cycle, empirically observed across developed countries, suggesting that excessive lending might be one of the causes of financial crises. The positive relationship between credit growth and financial crisis has been examined long ago (Minsky, 1972). Growth in the ratio of bank lending to GDP has been observed to be correlated with banking crises. This finding suggests that credit cycle has an impact on the condition of the financial industry and economy as a whole (Aikman et al., 2015).

Credit cycle coexists with the economic cycle, and each of them functions with different depths and magnitudes. During economic expansion, banks tend to provide funding excessively, the risk appetite of banks is higher, they usually accept riskier debtors, the value of collateral is favorable, and the price of funding for debtors is convenient, so there is usually no problem obtaining the funding for the demanded volume. In addition, macroprudential policies set by regulators might be loosened as well, contributing to excessive lending observed by increasing volumes of credit. Under the incurred credit loss model, there was no need to record the possible decrease of the real value of assets as losses usually do not incur in the phase of economic booms, and there is no evidence of a credit event. In other words, during the expansion, banks were not obliged to create reserves for expected losses that could occur in the future, and the recognition of change in the value of banks' assets were not considered. By contrast, the expected credit loss model considers forward-looking information not only related to the debtor but also related to the expected development of macroeconomic variables up to the maturity of the asset. Therefore, it is anticipated that under the ECL model, banks need to create loan loss provisions for expected credit losses, which are probable to occur in the future. In other words, banks record loan loss provisions during good times for all the expected credit events in the future (and thus correct the value of the assets).

On the contrary, during the contractional phase of the economic cycle, the risk assessment of the debtors is stricter, the funding is accessible to a lesser extent, the value of collateral might decrease, and the price of lending increases due to the higher risk of the borrower defaulting. The credit is, in general, much less available, and the volume of credit in the economy tends to decline. The macroprudential policies might be tightened, reflecting the environment in the economy. The provisioning under incurred loss model during downturn was following; there was usually evidence of the credit default events, so banks created loan loss provisions (decreasing the value of the assets do that they reflect their real value). A significant portion of the provisions booked might significantly affect banks' results (and the value of banks' stocks), decreasing the value of assets of other economic subjects owning particular stocks. Moreover, the effect of the decrease in the value of assets might accumulate, and the whole banking industry might collapse, which might be a threat to financial stability and might destabilize the global economy. The expected credit loss model is believed to play a significant role within this phase of credit and economic cycle. The provisions are presumed to already have been created in the previous periods during the good times, and there are no huge volumes of provisions decreasing the value of assets unexpectedly, causing the deterioration of banks' results and destabilizing the financial system. The excessive lending boom connected with the overvaluation of assets and the interconnection of the financial system has been generally considered one of the causes of the latest financial recession, which happened in 2008.

It is important to note that the economic cycle itself is not destabilizing nor avoidable as it is an inherent part of an economy. Similarly, the credit cycle is long observed to be a part of the banking industry, and it is not possible to fully eliminate the interdependency between these cycles. However, at the same time, high fluctuations in credit might exacerbate the economic cycle to the extent that is destabilizing for the global economy, and its consequences might be severe. It is important to perceive this aspect and to prevent the mutual intensification of a destabilizing behavior. Therefore, the point is to reduce the procyclical behavior so that it is not disruptive during fluctuations.

It is the macroprudential policies, the risk assessment approach of banks, the valuation techniques of the assets and the architecture of the regulations of the financial system corresponding to the globalized and interconnected financial institutions that are considered to be the means through which extensive credit fluctuations can be reduced. And provisioning rules are part of those means.

The importance of credit cycle within the banking industry is especially apparent within the member countries of the EU. European households and companies use banking products (loans and deposits) as a main source of funding (or saving) in comparison with the rest of the world. Thus, it is particularly important to monitor the stability of the banking sector in the EU.

20.4 Data and Methodology

The empirical testing of the hypothesis is based on the data obtained from Statistical Data Warehouse – European Central Bank's official statistics (ECB, 2021) and the Eurostat Statistics Database (Eurostat, 2021). Data on the quarterly GDP volumes of EU member countries for the period 1Q 2015–3Q 2020 were obtained from the Eurostat database, and the quarterly GDP growth was calculated for each country, which gives 644 observations on GDP growth in total (336 observations for the IAS 39 period and 308 observations for the IFRS 9 period). Quarterly data on impairment as percentages of the total assets of banks were downloaded from ECB's database for 28 EU member countries for the same period, 1Q 2015–3Q 2020 (the maximum possible period with quarterly data available for all the countries), obtaining 644 observations on impairment ratio (336 observations for the IAS 39 period and

308 observations for the IFRS 9 period). Source data on quarterly impairments were available as cumulative yearly net impairments (cost of risk); therefore, quarterly impairments were calculated as differences between the quarters.

To check the accuracy of data from the ECB database, we reconciled them by comparing the volume of provisions in P/L and the total assets of the banking sector for the period 3Q 2020 for the Czech Republic to the data from ARAD, the statistical warehouse of the Czech National Bank (CNB, 2021).

The data were put together as a comprehensive cross-sectional time-series data set, and panel regression analysis was performed on two separate data sets – IAS period (1Q 2015–4Q 2017) and IFRS 9 period (1Q 2018–3Q 2020). The analysis works with relative measures – GDP growth (as an independent variable) and the ratio of impairment to total assets (as a dependent variable), which eliminate the potential issue of the nonstationarity of data.

The panel data regression model with random effects was estimated as

$$imp_{it} = \alpha + \beta gdp_{it} + \mu_{it} + \varepsilon_{it} \tag{20.1}$$

where imp_{it} represents the dependent variable, α is a constant, βgdp_{it} represents the independent variable, μ_{it} is an unobserved idiosyncratic error, and ε_{it} is an unobserved random error.

The development of GDP growth and impairment ratio on the total data for all the EU member countries (EU28) is depicted in the following graph. The vertical axis on the right depicts the scale for GDP growth, and the vertical axis on the left depicts the scale for impairment ratio (Fig. 20.1).

It is apparent that prior to 2018, there was no strong relation between GDP growth and impairment ratio, with a slightly positive correlation (0.13) within the observed period (2015–2017). It is important to mention that the global economy was in the phase of economic expansion in general, and there was no significant recession during this period. Therefore, the relationship between the variables does not include the impact of the contractionary phase. Surprisingly, the correlation in this period is

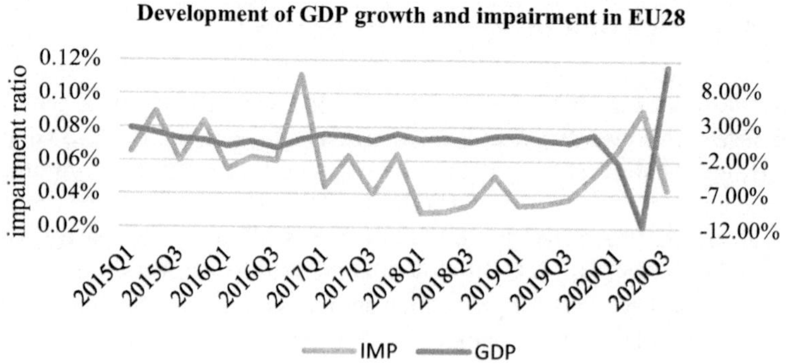

Fig. 20.1 Development of GDP growth and impairment in EU28. (Source: ECB, Eurostat, 2021 + authorial computation)

in contrast with the general conviction on the procyclicality of provisioning rules under IAS 39. On the other hand, due to the recent economic downturn in 2Q 2020 related to COVID-19, there is a visible substantial decrease in GDP growth. The development of impairment ratio is inverse, demonstrating a negative correlation (-0.66) between the variables, suggesting that the provisioning rules under IFRS 9 are indicating procyclicality.

20.5 Results and Discussion

The panel regression analysis has been performed with both the fixed-effect model and the random-effect model for both periods – IAS 39 period (1Q 2015–4Q 2017) and IFRS 9 period (1Q 2015–3Q 2020). To confirm whether the estimated effects are random effects (uncorrelated with the explanatory variable), the Hausman test was carried out for both periods (H0: there is no correlation between unique errors and the regressors in the model; the preferred model is the model with random effects). In both cases, *P*-value was higher than 0.05; therefore, the null hypothesis was accepted, and the model with random effects was used for panel regression for both periods. A model with random effects may give a better fit than the fixed-effect model. The result of the Hausman test also indicates that there is no correlation between the unique errors and the regressors in the model.

To comment on the cyclical effects of provisioning rules under both standards, the following text interprets the results of panel regressions carried out for both periods separately.

The following table presents the results of the panel regression analysis for the IAS 39 period (1Q 2015–4Q 2017) (Table 20.1).

Based on the results of regression for the IAS 39 period, it is noticeable that the value coefficient for GDP growth indicates that there is a negative impact of GDP growth development on impairment ratio. In other words, a 1% increase in GDP leads to a 0.150701 basis point decrease in impairment ratio and vice versa. Such a result is in favor of the procyclicality of IAS 39, which has been a generally perceived belief after 2008 and confirms the previous opinions on IAS 39 provisioning rules. However, the *P*-value does not confirm the statistical significance of such a relation.

The results of the panel regression analysis for the IFRS 9 period (1Q 2018–3Q 2020) are presented in the Table 20.2 below.

Table 20.1 Panel regression results – procyclicality for IAS 39 period

Variable	Coefficient	Std. error	*t*-statistic	*P*-value
C	0.001177	0.000286	4.113816	0.0000
GDP	−0.001507	0.004382	−0.343927	0.7311
Hausman test	N/A	N/A	N/A	0.3351

Source: Authorial computation

Table 20.2 Panel regression results – procyclicality for IFRS 9 period

Variable	Coefficient	Std. error	*t*-statistic	*P*-value
C	0.000730	0.000119	6.127879	0.0000
GDP	−0.005565	0.000776	−7.171748	0.0000
Hausman test	N/A	N/A	N/A	0.1072

Source: Authorial computation

The results of regression for the IFRS 9 period are noteworthy. The coefficient for GDP growth also indicates the negative relation between the dependent and independent variables. A 1% increase in GDP leads to a 0.556496 basis point decrease in impairment ratio and vice versa. Moreover, the *P*-value confirms that the results are statistically significant at a 0.1% significance level, which is in favor of the hypothesis of this paper that loan loss provisions under IFRS 9 have a procyclical effect. The results also confirm the correlation coefficient (-0.66) calculated for GDP growth and impairment ratio for all the EU member countries. The obtained results for the IFRS 9 period are in contradiction to the intention of creating a new standard that would require the creation of expected credit losses that would have a countercyclical impact.

It is important to mention that there is a restriction on data availability possibly limiting the conclusions of this empirical analysis. There are no quarterly data on impairment ratio in the ECB database prior to 1Q 2015 (the time series is discontinued), and the IAS 39 period unfortunately does not capture the economic recession in 2008. It would certainly be interesting to observe the development of the impairment under IAS 39 rules during the recession. On the other hand, the IFRS 9 period captures the current economic downturn due to the COVID-19 restrictions (visible on significant GDP decrease in 2Q 2020), unfortunately. The advantage of available data periods, however, lies in the fact that both tested periods are about the same length (336 observations for the IAS 39 period and 308 observations for the IFRS 9 period).

20.6 Conclusion

The procyclicality of the financial system, including the credit cycle within the banking industry, has been discussed since the great financial crisis in 2008. Positive interactions between the financial system and macroeconomic variables have been observed for a long time. Such a positive relation might be extremely harmful and might be exacerbating the fluctuations. The credit cycle and provisioning rules play an important role and have a direct impact, especially during the economic downturn. Therefore, the importance of replacing the incurred credit loss model under IAS 39 with the expected credit loss model has been stressed. As a result, the new standard IFRS 9 has been adopted. The standard requires considering forward-looking information on exposure level as well as macroeconomic predictions. The provisioning rules were, therefore, believed to have a countercyclical effect.

The hypothesis that IFRS 9 provisioning rules have a procyclical impact was tested on the panel of 28 EU member countries. Regression analysis was performed with impairment ratio as a dependent variable and GDP growth as an independent variable for two separate periods: IAS 39 period (1Q 2015–4Q 2017) and IFRS 9 period (1Q 2018–3Q 2002). In both periods, a negative relation between the variables has been observed. This relation was not statistically significant in the IAS 39 period; however, in the IFRS 9 period, the results were confirmed at a 1% significance level. Such findings contrast the intended countercyclical influence of the new standard.

To sustain the stability of the banking sector and the financial system as a whole, it is of course not sufficient to only consider the impact of provisioning rules. Relevant macroprudential policies, capital adequacy requirements, accounting standards, architecture of regulatory supervision, and the cautious behavior of economic subjects need to function mutually to secure the stability of the financial system.

The findings of this paper also support the existing estimates on the procyclical effects of IFRS 9.

The following research would be necessary to assess whether the procyclical effect is lesser than that under IAS 39, even though it is still present. Furthermore, after more data observations for the IFRS 9 period have been made available, a new empirical study should be carried out to confirm (or reject) the findings of this paper.

Acknowledgments This paper has been prepared with the financial support of a grant entitled "Development trends in financial markets" IG102029, which the authors gratefully acknowledge.

References

Abad, J., & Suarez, J. (2018). *The procyclicality of expected credit loss provisions* (CEPR Discussion Paper No. DP13135), https://www.cemfi.es/~suarez/Abad-Suarez_August_2018.pdf

Aikman, D., Haldane, A. G., & Nelson, B. D. (2015). Curbing the credit cycle. *The Economic Journal, 125*(585), 1072–1109. https://doi.org/10.1111/ecoj.12113

Bikker, J., & Metzemakers, P. (2004). Bank provisioning behaviour and procyclicality. *International Financial Markets, Institutions and Money, 15*, 141–157. https://doi.org/10.1016/j.intfin.2004.03.004

Buesa, A., García, F. J., & Tarancón, J. (2020). *Measuring the procyclicality of impairment accounting regimes: A comparison between IFRS 9 and US GAAP* (Documentos de Trabajo N.° 2003), https://www.bde.es/f/webbde/SES/Secciones/Publicaciones/PublicacionesSeriadas/DocumentosTrabajo/20/Files/dt2003e.pdf

Česká Národní Banka. (2021). *Databáze časových řad ARAD*. https://www.cnb.cz/cnb/STAT.ARADY_PKG.STROM_DRILL?p_strid=BA&p_lang=CS

European Central Bank. (2021). *Statistical Data Warehouse – Consolidated Banking* Data. https://sdw.ecb.europa.eu/browse.do?node=9691533

Eurostat. (2021). *Data Browser – GDP and main components*. https://ec.europa.eu/eurostat/databrowser/view/NAMQ_10_GDP__custom_589020/default/table?lang=en

Financial Stability Forum. (2009). *Report of the financial stability forum on addressing procyclicality in the financial system*. https://www.fsb.org/wp-content/uploads/r_0904a.pdf

Huizinga, H., & Leaven, L. (2019). The procyclicality of banking: Evidence from the Euro Area. *IMF Economic Review, 67*, 496–527. https://doi.org/10.1057/s41308-019-00081-5
International Monetary Fund. (2009). *Policies to Mitigate Procyclicality* (Staff Position Note No. 2009/09), https://www.imf.org/en/Publications/IMF-Staff-Position-Notes/Issues/2016/12/31/Policies-to-Mitigate-Procyclicality-22827
Leaven, L., & Majnoni, G. (2003). Loan loss provisions and economic slowdowns: Too much too late? *Journal of Financial Intermediation, 12*(2), 178–197.
Minsky, H. (1972). *Financial instability revisited: The economics of disaster* (Fundamental Reappraisal of the Discount Mechanism). Board of Governors of the Federal Reserve System. https://digitalcommons.bard.edu/cgi/viewcontent.cgi?article=1079&context=hm_archive

Chapter 21
Financial Highlights on Corporate Websites: Empirical Evidence from Poland

Marek Masztalerz

Abstract The main purpose of this paper is to identify the scope of the voluntary disclosures of the financial highlights (FH) on the websites of public companies in Poland. All the companies listed on the Warsaw Stock Exchange (excluding banks and financial institutions) and reporting FH on their websites were analyzed. The content of the FH sections of the websites of 225 selected companies was analyzed in order to identify the scope of the FH disclosure and to assess the frequency of the reported measures: the absolute numbers (figures from financial statements) and relative indicators (profitability, liquidity, activity, leverage, and capital market ratios). As a result of the conducted research, it was found that nearly three quarters of the companies listed on the WSE present FH on their website. However, companies make different choices regarding their selected financial measures. Almost all of the surveyed companies present absolute numbers (mostly from the profit and loss statement), and only 72% enhance their FH with relative financial ratios (mostly profitability and capital market ratios). Unfortunately, only a quarter of the companies reporting relative ratios present calculation formulas.

Key words Accounting communication · Investor relations · Financial performance indicators · Financial highlights

21.1 Introduction

Public companies have to communicate their financial results to the shareholders. They are obliged to publish their financial statements; however, many of them voluntarily report their accounting numbers and financial performance ratios not only in the required (by national law or a stock exchange regulation) documents but also in a shortened form on their websites as "financial highlights" (FH).

M. Masztalerz (✉)
Department of Accounting and Financial Audit, Poznan University of Economics and Business, Poznań, Poland
e-mail: marek.masztalerz@ue.poznan.pl

D. Procházka (ed.), *Regulation of Finance and Accounting*, Springer Proceedings in Business and Economics, https://doi.org/10.1007/978-3-030-99873-8_21

Financial highlights are a subjective selection of absolute and relative measures that can be used to assess the financial performance of a company. They are also referred to as "key/basic/selected financial data/figures/information/results" or "key performance indicators." They may be included in the financial statements, annual report, chairman's letter to the shareholders, management commentary, or presentation for investors or be published (as tables and graphs) on the corporate websites in HTML or XBRL format or in separate PDF or XLS files.

The research area of this paper is the voluntary disclosure of financial highlights by public companies on their websites. Considering the fact that reporting FH is not mandatory, it is interesting to check if, how, and to what extent public companies present relevant information on these key performance indicators.

The subject of reporting selected financial numbers is not new. A review of the Polish scientific literature from recent years is presented in Table 21.1.

The main purpose of this paper is to identify the scope of the voluntary disclosures of the FH on the websites of public companies in Poland. In other words, it is aimed to assess which measures are used by companies to present their financial performance directly on their websites and how frequently. The study differs from the previous research because of the large research sample (over 300 companies) and

Table 21.1 Recent research on the voluntary reporting of financial indicators

Authors	Description and results of the study
Krasodomska (2013)	Content analysis of the annual reports of 17 companies listed on the WIG20 Index (Warsaw Stock Exchange (WSE)) in order to identify the number and type of key financial and nonfinancial performance indicators
Skoczylas and Waśniewski (2014)	Content analysis of the auditors' reports on the audit of consolidated financial statements of 21 listed companies on the WIG30 Index (WSE) in order to determine the number, type, and applied formulas of the financial indicators (ratios) used by the auditors.
Andrzejewski et al. (2016)	Content analysis of the auditors' reports on the audit of financial statements of 20 listed companies (WSE) from the construction sector in order to determine the type and frequency of financial ratios and to compare the applied formulas.
Masztalerz (2019a)	Content analysis of the various corporate announcements (annual reports, financial statements, corporate websites, presentations for investors, chairman's letters to the shareholders) of 14 listed companies on the WIG20 Index in order to identify the scope and assess the quality of the disclosures of specific profit levels and profitability ratios.
Masztalerz (2019b)	Content analysis of the various corporate announcements (annual reports, financial statements, corporate websites, spreadsheets, presentations for investors, chairman's letters to the shareholders, auditor's reports) of 14 listed companies on the WIG20 Index in order to identify the scope and frequency of the disclosures of profitability, liquidity, activity, and leverage ratios in different messages and compare the ratios' calculation formulas.

Source: Own analysis

the type of researched sources (FH on the corporate websites in HTML or XBRL format, or in separate PDF or XLS files).

The structure of the further part of the paper is as follows. Section 2 presents the data and methodology of the empirical research. Section 3 includes the analysis and discussion of the results of the study. Section 4 presents the conclusion from the study and its limitations as well as further research directions.

21.2 Data and Methodology

The paper deals with the reporting of FH on the corporate websites by the public companies in Poland. At the time of writing, there were over 400 companies listed on the main market of the Warsaw Stock Exchange (WSE); however, financial institutions like banks or insurance companies (due to the specificity of their operations and the financial performance measures incomparable with other nonfinancial businesses) were excluded from the study, so the final research sample counts 304 companies.

For the next step, the websites of 304 companies were visited to find out whether the companies publish any financial highlights and to collect relevant data for the study. The following sections of the websites were visited to find relevant data: "About us"/"About the company," "Results center," and "Investor relations"/"For investors." Table 21.2 presents the results of the preliminary research. As shown, only 237 companies (78% of the total sample) included FH on their websites, either in HTML format directly on the website or as downloadable XLS or PDF files.

Further analysis encompasses 225 companies reporting FH on their websites directly. The downloadable XLS or PDF files have been excluded from the study because they usually include detailed financial statements, so they are not useful for the identification of the companies' choices on the measures reported as financial highlights. The content of the FH sections of the selected 225 companies' websites was analyzed in order to identify the scope of FH disclosure and to assess the

Table 21.2 Forms of financial highlights reporting

Form of financial highlights reporting	Number of companies reporting financial highlights	Percentage of the total sample of companies ($n = 304$)	Percentage of the reporting companies ($n = 237$)
Any form	237	78.0%	100.0%
Website directly:	225	74.0%	94.9%
Tables	225	74.0%	94.9%
Graphs	43	14.1%	18.1%
Interactive data	25	8.2%	10.5%
XLS file	97	31.9%	40.9%
PDF file	16	5.3%	6.8%

Source: Own analysis

frequency of the reported measures: the absolute numbers (figures from financial statements) and relative indicators (profitability, liquidity, activity, leverage, and capital market ratios) used by the surveyed public companies to communicate their financial performance.

21.3 Results and Discussion

As was mentioned above, only 225 companies (out of the total sample of 304 entities) reported FH on their websites directly. Almost all of these 225 companies (with one exception) reported selected absolute numbers from their financial statements, especially from their profit and loss statement, whereas only 72% of them presented relative indicators on their websites directly. The scope and frequency of the sources of financial numbers and the group of financial ratios are presented in Table 21.3.

It is worth noting that there were no significant differences between companies operating in different branches (industries), nor was there a strong statistical correlation between the scope of disclosure (number of financial performance indicators presented on websites) and the company market value; nevertheless, smaller companies have reported FH slightly more eagerly than the big ones. Only 46 companies

Table 21.3 Frequency of the financial performance measures on websites

Financial performance measures	Number of companies reporting financial measures	Percentage of the total sample of companies ($n = 304$)	Percentage of the reporting companies ($n = 225$)
Absolute numbers:	224	73.7%	99.6%
Income statement	224	73.7%	99.6%
Balance sheet	185	60.9%	82.2%
Cash flow statement	70	23.0%	31.1%
Relative indicators:	163	53.6%	72.4%
Profitability ratios	111	36.5%	49.3%
Liquidity ratios	65	21.4%	28.9%
Activity ratios	7	2.3%	3.1%
Leverage ratios	69	22.7%	30.7%
Capital market ratios	106	34.9%	47.1%

Source: Own analysis

provided information about the formulas used to calculate financial ratios, although some ratios do not have a single generally accepted formula, and in order to effectively communicate financial performance, one should include the formulas in the message to the audience (Masztalerz 2019b).

The surveyed companies presented 1–24 absolute financial numbers (with the mean, the median, and the dominant of ten figures) and 1–16 relative financial indicators (with the mean of four ratios, the median of three ratios, and the dominant of two ratios). The frequency of the distribution of absolute and relative financial performance indicators is presented in Figs. 21.1 and 21.2.

The most frequently reported absolute numbers were revenue (99%), net profit (96%), and operating profit (89%). The most frequently presented relative financial ratios were profitability ratios as return on sales (ROS) (41%) and return on assets (ROA) (33%). The frequency of measures reported in the FH on the websites is presented in Tables 21.4 and 21.5.

What is surprising is the fact that 35 companies (or over 20% out of the companies reporting relative financial ratios) use the same set of four measures, namely, ROS, ROA, current ratio (CR), and debt/assets (D/A). They probably do not select indicators but rather copy the FH reporting rules of other entities because all of these companies make the same grammar error in the Polish term of the ROA ratio (inexplicable in English).

As mentioned above, profitability ratios are the most popular indicators reported by the surveyed companies in their FH on the websites. Nine different ratios were identified (Table 21.6 and Fig. 21.3).

Liquidity ratios were presented less frequently (Table 21.7). The current ratio was presented by all 65 companies reporting on liquidity in the FH on the website.

Only seven companies presented activity ratios (Table 21.8) in their FH on the website; however, once a company decided to report on working capital ratios, it reported all three key indicators, i.e., the inventory holding period, the receivables collection period, and the payables period.

Eleven different leverage ratios were reported by 57 companies in their FH on the website (Table 21.9). Some companies presented indicators not listed in the table, i.e., equity/assets, net debt/equity, equity/fixed assets, capital employed/fixed assets, and operating cash flow/financial debts. It is clear that companies perceive leverage as a far more important issue than activity.

Over 100 companies included capital market ratios in their FH on the website. Eleven different indicators were reported (Table 21.10), including also (in addition to the ratios listed below) the following measures: price/revenue; price/cash flow; earnings before interest and taxes (EBIT) per share; earnings before interest, taxes, depreciation, and amortization (EBITDA) per share; revenue per share; and net cash flow per share.

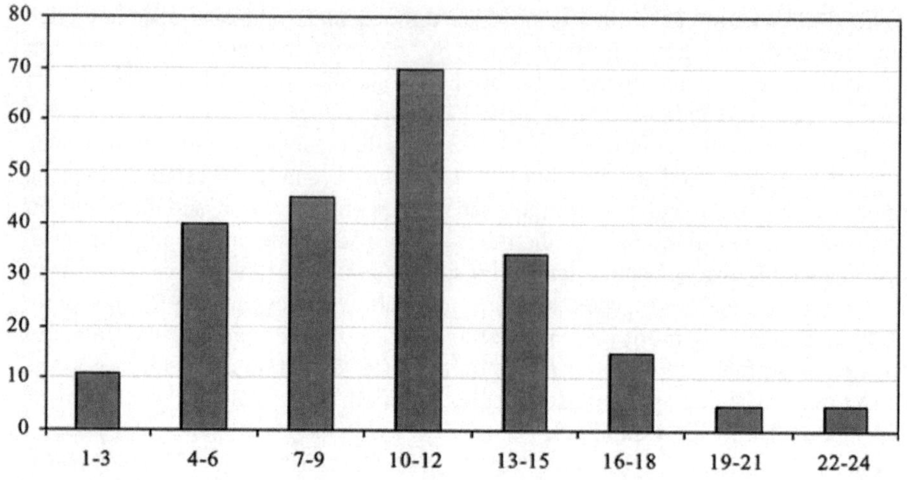

Fig. 21.1 Frequency distribution of absolute numbers in financial highlights. (Source: Own analysis)

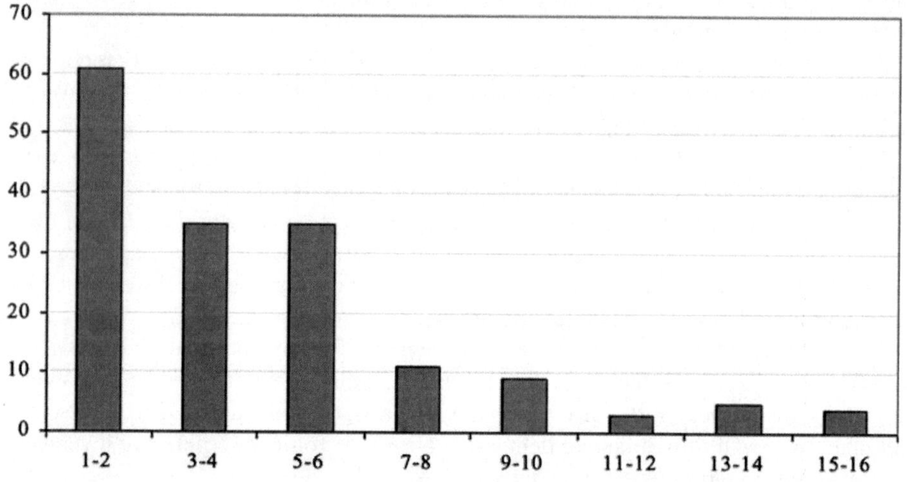

Fig. 21.2 Frequency distribution of relative indicators in financial highlights. (Source: Own analysis)

21.4 Conclusion

As a result of the conducted research, it was found that nearly three quarters of the companies listed on the Warsaw Stock Exchange present FH on their website. However, the content analysis showed that companies make different choices regarding their selected financial measures. Almost all of the surveyed companies

Table 21.4 Most frequent absolute financial numbers on websites

Absolute financial figures	Number of companies reporting absolute financial figures	Percentage of the total sample of companies ($n = 304$)	Percentage of the firms reporting FH on the website ($n = 225$)
Revenue	222	73.0%	98.7%
Net profit	215	70.7%	95.6%
EBIT	200	65.8%	88.9%
Equity	173	56.9%	76.9%
Assets (total)	165	54.3%	73.3%
Profit before tax	153	50.3%	68.0%
Short-term debts	130	42.8%	57.8%
Long-term debts	126	41.4%	56.0%
EBITDA	115	37.8%	51.1%
Debts (total)	97	31.9%	43.1%
Share capital	94	30.9%	41.8%
Operating cash flows	66	21.7%	29.3%
Current assets	66	21.7%	29.3%
Fixed assets	62	20.4%	27.6%
Investing cash flows	59	19.4%	26.2%
Financing cash flows	59	19.4%	26.2%
Cash flows (total)	48	15.8%	21.3%
Gross profit	47	15.5%	20.9%
Cash	37	12.2%	16.4%
Profit from sales	24	7.9%	10.7%
Receivables	16	5.3%	7.1%
Inventory	15	4.9%	6.7%
Net debts	14	4.6%	6.2%

Source: Own analysis

present absolute numbers (mostly from their profit and loss statement), and only 72% enhance their FH with relative financial ratios (mostly profitability and capital market ratios). Unfortunately, only a quarter of the companies reporting relative ratios present the calculation formulas. No significant correlation between the scope of the FH reporting and the company size or industry was found, so it was not discussed.

Table 21.5 Most frequent relative financial performance indicators on websites

Relative financial performance indicators	Number of companies reporting absolute financial figures	Percentage of the total sample of companies ($n = 304$)	Percentage of firms reporting FH on the website ($n = 225$)
Return on sales	93	30.6%	41.3%
Return on assets	75	24.7%	33.3%
Current ratio	65	21.4%	28.9%
Earnings per share	59	19.4%	26.2%
Debt/assets	57	18.8%	25.3%
Dividend per share	52	17.1%	23.1%
Return on equity	47	15.5%	20.9%
EBITDA margin	46	15.1%	20.4%
EBIT margin	38	12.5%	16.9%
Book value per share	37	12.2%	16.4%
Gross profit margin	28	9.2%	12.4%
Quick ratio	18	5.9%	8.0%
Debt/Equity	13	4.3%	5.8%
Net debt/ EBITDA	13	4.3%	5.8%

Source: Own analysis

Table 21.6 Frequency of the profitability ratios on websites

Profitability ratios	Number of companies reporting profitability ratios	Percentage of firms reporting relative indicators ($n = 163$)	Percentage of firms reporting profitability ratios ($n = 111$)
ROS	93	57.1%	83.8%
ROA	75	46.0%	67.6%
ROE	47	28.8%	42.3%
EBITDA margin	46	28.2%	41.4%
EBIT margin	38	23.3%	34.2%
GP margin	28	17.2%	25.2%
PBT margin	7	4.3%	6.3%
PFS margin	7	4.3%	6.3%
ROACE	1	0.6%	0.9%

Source: Own analysis

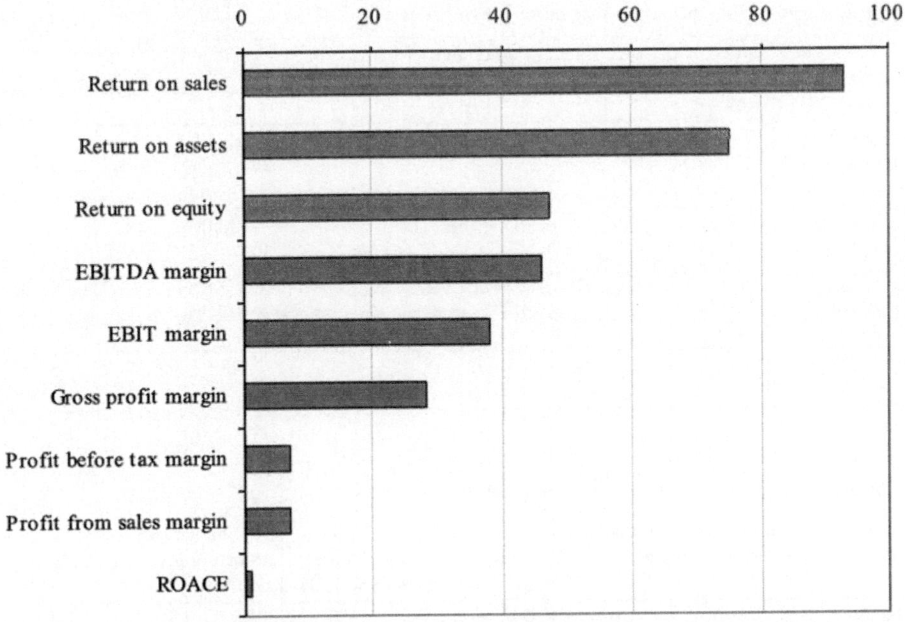

Fig. 21.3 Frequency of the profitability ratios on websites. (Source: Own analysis)

Table 21.7 Frequency of the liquidity ratios on websites

Liquidity ratios	Number of companies reporting liquidity ratios	Percentage of firms reporting relative indicators ($n = 163$)	Percentage of firms reporting liquidity ratios ($n = 65$)
Current ratio	65	39.9%	100.0%
Quick ratio	18	11.0%	27.7%
Cash ratio	4	2.5%	6.2%

Source: Own analysis

There are some limitations in the conducted research that set out potential further research directions. Firstly, the study is limited to the public companies listed on the Warsaw Stock Exchange. It would be interesting to compare the results in an international dimension. Secondly, the determinants of placing specific indicators in the FH on the website were not analyzed. A survey of the companies reporting FH on the websites could give a deeper insight into this issue. It was also not examined whether the selection of FH measures is not linked to the creation of a desired image or impression management. Finally, the issue of the interactive presentation of the FH was not discussed, although 25 companies allow the users of their websites to choose what (figures and ratios) and how (table or graph) they want to see them.

Table 21.8 Frequency of the activity ratios on websites

Activity ratios	Number of companies reporting activity ratios	Percentage of firms reporting relative indicators ($n = 163$)	Percentage of firms reporting activity ratios ($n = 7$)
Inventory holding period	7	4.3%	100.0%
Receivables collection period	7	4.3%	100.0%
Payables period	7	4.3%	100.0%
Cash conversion period	2	1.2%	28.6%

Source: Own analysis

Table 21.9 Frequency of the leverage ratios on websites

Leverage ratios	Number of companies reporting leverage ratios	Percentage of firms reporting relative indicators ($n = 163$)	Percentage of firms reporting leverage ratios ($n = 69$)
Debt/assets	57	35.0%	82.6%
Debt/equity	13	8.0%	18.8%
Net debt/EBITDA	13	8.0%	18.8%
Long-term debts	4	2.5%	5.8%
Short-term debts	2	1.2%	2.9%
Interest cover	1	0.6%	1.4%
Other	8	4.9%	11.6%

Source: Own analysis

Table 21.10 Frequency of capital market ratios on websites

Capital market ratios	Number of companies reporting capital market ratios	Percentage of firms reporting relative indicators ($n = 163$)	Percentage of firms reporting capital market ratios ($n = 106$)
EPS	59	36.2%	55.7%
DPS	52	31.9%	49.1%
BVPS	37	22.7%	34.9%
P/BV	7	4.3%	6.6%
P/E	7	4.3%	6.6%
Others	3	1.8%	2.8%

Source: Own analysis

References

Andrzejewski, M., Maślanka, T., & Mazur-Maślanka, I. (2016, September 30). International Financial Reporting Standards (IFRS) and an issue of comparability of assessments of financial standing of the companies listed on the Warsaw Stock Exchange made by the auditors in the reports on the audit of the financial statements. In I. Jindřichovská & D. Kubíčková (Eds.), *Proceedings of the 4th International Scientific Conference IFRS: Global Rules and Local Use*. Anglo-American University.

Krasodomska, J. (2013). Kluczowe wskaźniki efektywności w praktyce spółek notowanych na Giełdzie Papierów Wartościowych w Warszawie. *Zeszyty Teoretyczne Rachunkowości, 73*, 75–87.

Masztalerz, M. (2019a). Profit levels and profitability ratios reported in the communications of public companies. *Prace Naukowe Uniwersytetu Ekonomicznego we Wrocławiu, 63*(4), 19–28. https://doi.org/10.15611/pn.2019.4.02

Masztalerz, M. (2019b). Raportowanie wskaźników finansowych przez spółki publiczne. *Zeszyty Teoretyczne Rachunkowości, 103*, 99–118. https://doi.org/10.5604/01.3001.0013.3077

Skoczylas, W., & Waśniewski, P. (2014). Wskaźniki finansowe w raporcie z badania sprawozdania finansowego przez biegłego rewidenta. Zeszyty Naukowe Uniwersytetu Szczecińskiego. *Finanse, Rynki Finansowe i Ubezpieczenia, 69*, 243–252.

Chapter 22
International Financial Reporting Standards and Earnings Quality: The Case of Listed Firms in Saudi Arabia

Sarah Chehade

Abstract This chapter aims at testing empirically the impact of the IFRS adoption on the earnings quality in, one of the MENA region countries, the emerging market of Saudi Arabia. For this end, three models were developed each representing an earning quality metric: (a) earnings smoothing, (b) management earnings toward targets, and (c) timely loss recognition. After setting the descriptive statistics of the dependent and control variables, performing a Pearson correlation matrix, and estimating regression equations, results indicated that earnings smoothing was the only significant metric and that has increased after the IFRS adoption. This increase implies a decrease in earnings quality. However, our results failed to find any supporting evidence concerning the improvement of neither managing earnings toward a target nor timely loss recognition. Consequently, it can be concluded that the overall earnings quality of listed firms in Saudi Arabia was not found to have improved after the introduction of the International Financial Reporting Standards.

Key words Accounting quality · Earnings management · International Financial Reporting Standards (IFRS) · Saudi Arabia

22.1 Introduction

The history of accounting principles and standards began in early 1971 with the issuance of the first set of International Accounting Standards (IAS) that was reshaped in 2001 to create the International Financial Reporting Standards (IFRS). The quality of financial information is highly important for investors who basically rely on for an effective investment decision (Toumeh & Yahya, 2019); accounting standards are said to directly affect the reporting quality (Soderstrom & Sun, 2007); for this reason, it was found inevitable to explore and attempt to understand the impact of IFRS adoption on financial statements as a whole and on reporting quality

S. Chehade (✉)
Department of Financial Accounting and Auditing, Prague University of Economics and Business, Prague, Czech Republic
e-mail: ches06@vse.cz

D. Procházka (ed.), *Regulation of Finance and Accounting*, Springer Proceedings in Business and Economics, https://doi.org/10.1007/978-3-030-99873-8_22

in precision. According to Dechow et al. (2010), there is no single set of proxy for earnings quality, and the reason behind this is that the term quality is "contingent on the decision context" (Dechow et al., 2010 p. 1). However, researchers have identified various indicators to measure earnings quality such as accruals, asymmetric timeliness, and timely loss recognition (Dechow et al., 2010). Earnings are the core of the financial statements that represents the financial position and performance of an entity. According to Beneish (2001), three attempts are explored defining earnings management:

1. According to Schipper (1989), management of earnings is "the process of taking deliberate steps within the constraints of generally accepted accounting principles to bring about a desired level of reported earnings" (Schipper, 1989 p. 92.)
2. According to Schipper (1989), earnings management is an intentionally intrusion of management in the process of financial statements preparation seeking at acquiring some private gain.
3. According to Healy and Wahlen (1999), the core of earnings management is the involvement of managers' personal judgment in the external financial reporting process with the intent of misleading stakeholders about the actual financial position of the firm.

Timely loss recognition is an important attribute for financial reporting quality as the usefulness of financial statements in terms of corporate governance and all debt agreements are increased when the recognition of losses is performed in a timely manner.

The remaining of this section is devoted to the literature review; Section 22.2 is allocated for the hypothesis development. Section 22.3 will present all the data used and methodology implemented, while Sect. 22.4 will include the results and discussion from the empirical models. Finally, Sect. 22.5 is devoted to the conclusion.

22.2 Literature Review

The question that was addressed after the first issuance of International Accounting Standards (IAS) and that is still ongoing with the International Financial Reporting Standards (IFRS) is whether the adoption of these standards does lead to higher accounting and reporting quality (Healy & Wahlen, 1999; Dechow et al., 1995, 2010). Consequently, plenty of studies were prepared trying to investigate the association between IFRS and earnings quality with conflicting results documented; some researchers have found that IFRS adoption improved earnings quality (e.g., Chen et al., 2010; Barth et al., 2008) while others did not (e.g., Cameran et al., 2014; Paglietti, 2010; Sellami & Fakhfakh, 2013; Van Tendeloo & Vanstraelen, 2005).

Starting with single-country studies documenting no association between IFRS adoption and accounting quality metrics, Cameran et al. (2014) have analyzed the impact of IFRS adoption on the reporting quality, more precisely the level of abnormal accruals and timely loss recognition, between IFRS adopters and local

GAAP adopters in the case of Italian private companies. No improvement of the adoption of IFRS on the quality of financial reporting measured through earnings management and timely loss recognition. On the contrary, results revealed that the introduction of IFRS has increased earnings management and by return time loss recognition was worsened in private Italian firms. In the same direction, Paglietti (2010) has examined the accounting quality represented by earnings smoothing, managing earnings toward a target, and timely loss recognition. The data extracted from Italian nonfinancial firms demonstrated that IFRS adoption has worsen accounting quality. Along the same line, Sellami and Fakhfakh (2013) have investigated the impact of the mandatory IFRS adoption on earnings management through two different angles: the real earnings management approach and the accrual-based earnings management approach. The regression results indicated that the real earnings management is not significantly connected with the mandatory IFRS adoption and by then higher earnings quality. As well, the study of Van Tendeloo and Vanstraelen (2005) did not reveal any improvement in the behavior of earnings management in the case of voluntary listed adopters in Germany.

Moving to panel studies with unfound or negative association of IFRS adoption and earnings management, the results of Capkun et al. (2016) recorded an increase in earnings smoothing when comparing the period pre- and post-IFRS adoption. On the same track, Jeanjean and Stolowy (2008) have conducted a comparative study pre- and post-IFRS adoption on Australia, France, and the UK where results did not indicate any decrease in the extensiveness of earnings management post-IFRS adoption. Mongrut and Winkelried (2019) have employed a panel model for 871 firms operating in the emerging markets in the region of Latin America; it was concluded that the sole adoption of IFRS is insufficient to improve accounting quality. In addition, Zhou et al. (2009) have conducted a study using the variance of the change in net income, the frequency of small positive net income, and the frequency of large negative income in an attempt to discover whether the adoption of IFRS in Chinese market has led to higher accounting quality. It was concluded that IFRS adopters were less likely to engage in earnings smoothing, but no supporting evidence was found for either management earnings toward target or timely loss recognition.

Moving the attention to studies where IFRS was found to be associated with higher accounting quality, Chen et al. (2010) have found that the improvement of the accounting quality and, in return, the decrease in earnings management arw attributable to the IFRS adoption in EU firms and countries. The two measures of accounting quality used are earnings management and timely loss recognition. The study covered four different aspects of earnings management and one for timely loss recognition, and the results from the regression results indicate that accounting standards have a significant impact on accounting quality. Along the same side, Barth et al. (2008) have employed an estimation of four earnings management measures and one timely loss recognition metric to reveal whether IAS adoption leads to higher accounting quality. It was documented based on a large worldwide sample that firms' voluntary applying IAS have shown higher earnings quality which in return evidence less earnings management and higher timely loss recognition than non-IAS adopters.

The literature includes plenty of studies assessing the impact of IFRS on earnings management in developed countries. The contribution of this chapter lies in dealing with the uniqueness of investigating the accounting quality and more precisely the area of earnings management in the case of Saudi Arabia. A limited number of papers are found examining countries located in the MENA region which are emerging economies. Emerging economies are economies of developing nations around the world that are on the path of fast growth and integration within the global markets' economy. On one side, the adoption of IFRS is a need for emerging economies that will bring about many benefits, such as larger expansion of services into worldwide markets and lower cost associated with the preparation of financial statements. Unlike the developed countries, the implementation of IFRS in emerging economies and more precisely in the MENA region will face multiple milestones due to the corruption mindset, weak regulatory infrastructure, low financial transparency, and lack of compliance with rules and regulations (Irvine & Lucas, 2006; Trabelsi, 2016).

22.3 Hypothesis Development

This chapter will study the effect of IFRS adoption on earnings management in Saudi Arabia, a country located in the MENA region with an economy being the largest in the Arab world and the Middle East (nominal GDP of $680 billion in 2020) and among the top 20 economies in the world. In addition, Saudi Arabia is ranked first among MENA countries and second worldwide in terms of oil reserves.

While the quality of accounting information is highly important for investors in order to make effective decisions, accounting standards are said to have a significant impact on earnings quality. For this end, there is a need to empirically assess the impact of IFRS adoption on the earnings quality pre- and post-adoption. Previous literatures have identified different measures relating to earnings quality; in this chapter, three metrics will be employed, namely, (1) earnings smoothing, (2) managing earnings toward targets, and (3) timely loss recognition. Therefore, it is hypothesized that:

- Hypothesis 1: Earnings smoothing in Saudi Arabia is lower in the IFRS adoption period (2017–2019) than in the pre-adoption period (2014–2016).
- Hypothesis 2: Managing earnings toward a target in Saudi Arabia is less frequent in the post-IFRS adoption period than in the pre-adoption period.
- Hypothesis 3: Public firms in Saudi Arabia tend to timely recognize large losses in the post-IFRS adoption period more than they do in the pre-adoption period.

22.4 Data and Methodology

This section is allocated for the presentation of the sample used and data collected for the objective of determining the impact of IFRS adoption on earnings quality and more precisely on earnings management in the case of listed companies in Saudi Arabia.

22.4.1 Sample and Data

The Kingdom of Saudi Arabia requires listed firms to report using IFRS starting January 01, 2017. For this reason, the sample period for this study stands from 2014 to 2019, defining years 2014–2016 as the pre-adoption period, and years 2017–2019 as the adoption period. The audited financial statements for the publicly listed firms on the Saudi Stock Exchange were extracted from both platforms: Tadawul and Argaam. Similar to Cohen et al. (2008), Zang (2012), and Sellami and Fakhfakh (2013), all banks, financial institutions, real estate, and insurance firms are excluded from the sample as these firms are not always comparable with those industrial and commercial ones. After meeting the requirement for the availability of data, the final sample constituted of 56 listed firms and 336 observations for a period of 6 years covering 8 different market categories as shown in Table 22.1.

22.4.2 Empirical Models and Control Variables

The previous empirical literature on earnings management is highly rich and has produced multiple models to test earnings quality. In this chapter, three measures will be adopted representing earnings quality, namely, earnings management

Table 22.1 Final sample distribution by market category

Industry	Number of firms per year	Percentage of firms	Firm year observations
Materials	24	42.8%	144
Capital goods	8	14.3%	48
Food and beverages, food and staples retailing	6	10.7%	36
Consumer services	4	7.1%	24
Consumer durables and apparel	4	7.1%	24
Energy	3	5.5%	18
Commercial and professional services	2	3.6%	12
Other services	5	8.9%	30
Total	**56**	**100%**	**336**

Source: Own work

(smoothing), managing earnings toward targets, and timely loss recognition (Dechow et al., 1995; Chen et al., 2010; Sellami & Fakhfakh, 2013; Paglietti, 2009; Barth et al., 2007, 2008; Cameran et al., 2014; Chen et al., 2010).

22.4.2.1 Control Variables

Previous studies have identified several factors that are said to affect earnings management and that need to be controlled for higher validity results. Below are the control variables considered in our empirical models:

1. *SIZE:* This variable represents the size of the firm measured as the natural logarithm of the total firm's assets.
2. *GROWTH:* This variable represents the growth opportunities measured by the annual percentage change in sales.
3. *EISSUE:* This variable represents the increase in equity measured by the annual percentage change in total equity.
4. *LEV:* The leverage is measure as total liabilities over total assets for each firm.
5. *DISSUE*: This variable represents the increase in debt and is calculated as the annual percentage change in firm's total liabilities.
6. *TURN*: The turnover variable is the percentage of sales over total assets.
7. *CFO:* The cash flow from operations variable represents the operating cash flow scaled by lagged total assets.
8. *AUD:* This is a dummy variable that takes the value of 1 if the firm's auditor is at least one of the big four auditing companies, that is, PwC, KPMG, E&Y, or Deloitte, and zero otherwise.
9. *Year:* Year dummies.

22.4.2.2 Earnings Management

The first earnings quality metrics used in this study is earnings management, which, by definition, is the fact of misleading the company's stakeholders about the current economic and financial position of the firm (Healy & Wahlen, 1999). Results showing higher earnings management mean in other words a worsened earnings quality.

One special case of earnings management is the earnings smoothing where managers use accounting methods and standards to level out fluctuations in net income by reporting earnings that are either higher or lower than the economic earnings and consequently the reported earnings don't represent the actual economic earnings of the firm at every point in time (Bouwman, 2014; Goel & Thakor, 2003). This model includes two metrics: the first represented by Eq. (22.1) is the variability of the change in net income; and the second represented by Eq. (22.2) is the variability of the change in net income over the variability of change in cash flow from operations (following Capkun et al., 2016; Chen et al., 2010).

$$\Delta NI_{i,t} = \alpha_0 + \alpha_1 \text{SIZE}_{i,t} + \alpha_2 \text{GROWTH}_{i,t} + \alpha_3 \text{EISSUE}_{i,t} + \alpha_4 \text{LEV}_{i,t} + \alpha_5 \text{DISSUE}_{i,t} + \alpha_6 \text{TURN}_{i,t} + \alpha_7 \text{CFO}_{i,t} + \alpha_8 \text{AUD}_{i,t} + \sum_t \text{year}_t + \varepsilon_{i,t} \tag{22.1}$$

$$\Delta \text{NI}_{i,t}/\Delta \text{CFO}_{i,t} = \alpha_0 + \alpha_1 \text{SIZE}_{i,t} + \alpha_2 \text{GROWTH}_{i,t} + \alpha_3 \text{EISSUE}_{i,t} + \alpha_4 \text{LEV}_{i,t} + \alpha_5 \text{DISSUE}_{i,t} + \alpha_6 \text{TURN}_{i,t} + \alpha_7 \text{CFO}_{i,t} + \alpha_8 \text{AUD}_{i,t} + \sum_t \text{year}_t + \varepsilon_{i,t} \tag{22.2}$$

where

$\Delta \text{NI}_{i,\,t}$ = the change in net income before extraordinary items scaled by lagged total assets for firm i year t

$\Delta \text{CFO}_{i,\,t}$ = the change in cash flows from operations scaled by lagged total assets for firm i year t

The prediction of the univariate analysis from Eq. (22.1), consistent with IFRS objectives, is to record an increase in the variability of change in net incomes (ΔNI*) in the adoption period; in other words, larger variances are consistent with lower earnings smoothing and vice versa. For this end and for lower earnings smoothing after IFRS adoption, we expect the following two relations to hold:

$$\sigma^2(\Delta \text{NI}*_{\text{post}}) > \sigma^2(\Delta \text{NI}*_{\text{pre}}) \tag{22.1a}$$

$$\sigma^2(\Delta \text{NI}*_{\text{post}})/\sigma^2(\Delta \text{CFO}*_{\text{post}}) > \sigma^2(\Delta \text{NI}*_{\text{pre}})/\sigma^2(\Delta \text{CFO}*_{\text{pre}}) \tag{22.2a}$$

Managing earnings toward a target is another type of earnings management where managers tend to report small positive earnings instead of having negative earnings (Zhou et al., 2009; Chen et al., 2010; Leuz et al., 2003). Equation (22.3) is estimated in order to investigate the potential incentives for managing earnings toward a target after the IFRS adoption in Saudi Arabia.

$$\text{SPOS}_{i,t} = \alpha_0 + \alpha_1 \text{POST}_{i,t} + \beta_1 \text{SIZE}_{i,t} + \beta_2 \text{GROWTH}_{i,t} + \beta_3 \text{EISSUE}_{i,t} + \beta_4 \text{LEV}_{i,t} + \beta_5 \text{DISSUE}_{i,t} + \beta_6 \text{TURN}_{i,t} + \beta_7 \text{CFO}_{i,t} + \beta_8 \text{AUD}_{i,t} + \sum_t \text{year}_t + \varepsilon_{i,t} \tag{22.3}$$

where

$\text{SPOS}_{i,\,t}$ = indicator variable that equals 1 for observations of firms with annual net incomes scaled by lagged total assets between 0 and 0.01 for firm i year t

$\text{POST}_{i,\,t}$ = indicator variable that equals 1 for observations in the adoption period and 0 otherwise for firm i year t

The prediction of the regression analysis of Eq. (22.3), in consistency with IFRS objectives, is to have a significant negative coefficient on POST ($\alpha_1 < 0$) which demonstrates that in the post-adoption period, firms managed earnings toward small positive amounts less frequently than they did in the pre-adoption period; in other words, IFRS have improved earnings quality.

Moving to timely loss recognition, as suggested by previous literature (Barth et al., 2007, 2008; Chen et al., 2010, Paglietti, 2010), timely loss recognition is the aptitude of earnings to reflect losses in a timely manner. Equation (22.4) is estimated in order to reveal whether the public firms in Saudi Arabia tend to have a more-timely recognition of large losses in the post-adoption period more than they had in the pre-adoption period.

$$\begin{aligned}\mathrm{LNEG}_{i,t} = {} & \alpha_0 + \alpha_1\mathrm{POST}_{i,t} + \beta_1\mathrm{SIZE}_{i,t} + \beta_2\mathrm{GROWTH}_{i,t} + \beta_3\mathrm{EISSUE}_{i,t} \\ & + \beta_4\mathrm{LEV}_{i,t} + \beta_5\mathrm{DISSUE}_{i,t} + \beta_6\mathrm{TURN}_{i,t} + \beta_7\mathrm{CFO}_{i,t} \\ & + \beta_8\mathrm{AUD}_{i,t} + \sum_t \mathrm{year}_t + \varepsilon_{i,t}\end{aligned} \tag{22.4}$$

where

$\mathrm{LNEG}_{i,\,t}$ = indicator variable that equals 1 for observations of firms with annual net incomes scaled by lagged total assets less than −0.20 (<0.20), and zero otherwise for firm *i* year *t*.

The prediction of the regression analysis of Eq. (22.4), in consistency with the IASB objectives, is to have a significant positive coefficient on POST ($\alpha_1 > 0$) which reveals that firm's losses are timely recognized in post-adoption period than they did in the pre-adoption period, consequently indicating a higher earnings quality.

22.5 Empirical Results

22.5.1 Descriptive Statistics

Starting with the dependent variables, the results shown in Table 22.2 reveal that the means of the change in net income (ΔNI), change in operating cash flow (ΔCFO), management earnings toward a target (SPOS) and timely loss recognition (LNEG) represent, respectively, −1.1%, 0.4%, 9%, and 0.4% in the pre-adoption period and 0%, −0.7%, 1.1%, and 0.6% in period after the IFRS adoption.

A higher growth in profits is documented due to the significant increase in the change of net income (ΔNI) between the two periods under study; However, the change in operating cash flow (ΔCFO) recorded a significant decrease comparing between the pre-and the post-adoption period. Both the management earnings toward a target and the timely loss recognition increased in the period after the adoption of IFRS which means that in Saudi Arabia firms engaged more in earnings toward a target (inconsistent with the set hypothesis) but losses are more frequently recognized in a timely manner in the adoption period (consistent with the set hypothesis).

Moving to the control variables, descriptive statistics disclose a decrease in the means of company size (SIZE), annual percentage change in sales (GROWTH), annual percentage change in equity (EISSUE), turnover (TURN), cash flow from operations lagged by total assets (CFO), and an increase in annual percentage change in total liabilities (DISSUE) and leverage (LEV).

22.5.2 Univariate Analysis

The Pearson correlation matrix for the whole sample of 336 observations over the period 2014–2019 is illustrated in Table 22.3 between IFRS adoption from one side and earnings smoothing, managing earnings toward a target and timely loss recognition on the other side. The below can be noted:

- There exists a significant positive correlation between ΔNI and ΔCFO (coefficient of 0.1579 and p-value of 0.004 less than 5%).
- There exists a significant positive correlation between POST and ΔNI at the 10% significance level (coefficient of 0.1054 and p-value of 0.0575).
- POST has no significant association with ΔCFO, neither SPOS, nor LNEG.
- For SPOS and control variables, only two negative significant associations are found with TURN (coefficient of −0.1121 and p-value of 0.0418) and CFO (coefficient of −0.1161 and p-value 0.0349).
- Regarding LNEG and control variables, EISSUE is found to be negatively correlated with LNEG (coefficient of −0.6479 and p-value of 0.000), and LEV is found to be positively and significantly correlated with LNEG (coefficients of 0.3015 and p-value of 0.000).

Overall, it can be deduced that the variables used in this study are mainly independent, and there exists no serious problem of multicollinearity since the correlation value, in the case of significant correlation, is below 0.7.

22.5.3 Empirical Results

Table 22.4 is devoted to the results of the univariate analysis of IFRS adoption on earnings smoothing represented by ΔNI* and ΔCFO*. Both predicted relations previously set were not hold, and the variance of the change in net incomes decreased after the adoption of the international financial reporting standards. This implies that the two earnings smoothing increased post-IFRS adoption, and by return, it is suggested that the earnings quality is not improved after the introduction of IFRS.

Table 22.2 Descriptive statistics for dependent and control variables Pre- and Post- IFRS adoption

				Pre-IFRS adoption (number of obs. = 256)			Post- IFRS adoption (number of obs. = 164)			
Variables	Mean	Median	Std. Dev.	Mia	Max	Mean	Median	Std. Dev.	Min	Max
Dependent variables										
ΔNI	−0.011	−0.004	0.082	−0.665	0.49	0.000	0.000	0.081	−0.243	0.610
Δ*CFO*	0.004	0.000	0.096	−0.345	0.61	−0.007	0.000	0.105	−0.741	0.617
SPOS	0.090	0.000	0.287	0	1	0.110	0	0.314	0	1
LNEG	0.004	0.000	0.063	0	1	0.006	0	0.078	0	1
Control variables										
SIZE	8.060	8.601	1.304	5.260	10.90	8.036	8.653	1.834	−8.334	10.99
GROWTH	0.056	0.003	0.757	−1.125	11.30	0.052	−0.013	0.910	−0.683	11.29
EISSUE	0.013	0.016	0.171	−0.724	1.060	−0.040	−0.003	0.354	−3.942	0.949
DISSUE	0.075	0.004	0.637	−0.723	9.250	0.110	0.000	0.840	−0.723	10.03
LEV	0.423	0.424	0.261	0.001	1.580	0.455	0.484	0.297	0.012	2.199
TURN	0.592	0.444	0.831	−0.027	9.870	0.521	0.416	0.668	0.016	7.456
CFO	0.094	0.071	0.176	−0.224	2.410	0.061	0.051	0.093	−0.398	0.685
AUD	0.557	1	0.498	0	1	0.393	0	0.490	0	1

Table 22.3 Pearson correlation for independent and control variables

Variables	ΔNI	ΔCFO	SPOS	LNEG	POST	SIZE	GROWTH	EISSUE	DISSUE	LEV	TURN	CFO	AUD
_ΔNI	1												
p-value	—												
ΔCFO	0.158	1											
p-value	0.004	—											
SPOS	0.002	−0.164	1										
p-value	0.975	0.003	—										
LNEG	0.120	0.006	−0.026	1									
p-value	0.029	0.914	0.638	—									
POST	0.105	−0.072	0.036	0.001	1								
p-value	0.058	0.193	0.510	0.979	—								
SIZE	−0.017	0.094	0.077	−0.024	−0.016	1							
p-value	0.761	0.089	0.165	0.669	0.777	—							
GROWTH	0.073	0.087	−0.007	−0.046	0.037	0.053	1						
p-value	0.185	0.114	0.895	0.402	0.505	0.334	—						
EISSUE	−0.176	0.046	0.000	−0.648	−0.105	0.109	0.107	1					
p-value	0.001	0.403	0.993	0.000	0.058	0.046	0.051	—					
DISSUE	−0.047	0.050	−0.018	−0.007	0.001	−0.018	0.032	−0.019	1				
p-value	0.399	0.364	0.749	0.894	0.983	0.750	0.552	0.732	—				
LEV	0.201	0.051	0.057	0.301	0.024	−0.112	−0.080	−0.381	0.098	1			
p-value	0.000	0.354	0.306	0.000	0.666	0.040	0.144	0.000	0.075	—			
TURN	−0.023	0.032	−0.112	−0.039	−0.033	0.027	−0.012	0.068	0.053	0.100	1		
p-value	0.675	0.558	0.041	0.485	0.132	0.622	0.827	0.214	0.334	0.069	—		
CFO	0.090	0.548	−0.116	−0.046	−0.156	0.158	0.042	0.197	0.032	−0.053	0.128	1	
p-value	0.102	0.000	0.035	0.409	0.005	0.003	0.442	0.000	0.563	0.329	0.019	—	
AUD	0.029	0.043	−0.016	−0.079	−0.236	0.070	−0.013	0.137	0.038	0.129	0.141	0.215	1
p-value	0.601	0.433	0.770	0.149	0.000	0.202	0.811	0.012	0.486	0.018	0.010	0.000	—

Table 22.4 Univariate analysis of IFRS adoption and earnings smoothing

		Earnings smoothing pre-adoption		Earnings smoothing post-adoption	
Measure	Predicted relation to hold	Mean	Variance	Mean	Variance
Variability of ΔNI^*	$\sigma^2\ \Delta NI^*$ post > $\sigma^2 \Delta NI^*$ pre	−0.0111	0.0067	0.00006	0.0066
Variability of ΔNI^* over ΔCFO^*	$\sigma^2\ (\Delta NI^*)/\sigma^2(\Delta CFO^*)$ post>$\sigma^2\ (\Delta NI^*)/\sigma^2(\Delta CFO^*)$ pre	2.8174	0.7131	−0.0083	0.5976

Source: Own work

The results of the OLS regression testing the relationship between managing earnings toward a target (SPOS) and IFRS adoption reflected in Eq. 22.3 are presented in Table 22.5. Starting with the results of SPOS and POST, a positive but insignificant coefficient is shown on POST (p-value of 0.7910) which is consistent with the results shown in Tables 22.1 and 22.2 showing a positive insignificant association between SPOS and POST. This means that the behavior of reporting small positive earnings has not significantly changed in the post-adoption period in the case of public Saudi Arabian firms. Consequently, it is suggested that this measure of earnings quality was not improved after the introduction of IFRS. Moving to the relationship between SPOS and control variables, the firm's size (SIZE) is found to be significant and positive at the 10% significance level which is found to be quite different from the results shown in Tables 22.2 and 22.3. This result means that larger firms tend to engage in managing earnings toward targets more often than small firms do. However, both the coefficients of firm's turnover (TURN) and operating cash flow (CFO) are found to be significant and negative at the 5% significance level which is consistent with the results of the univariate analysis and descriptive statistics in Tables 22.2 and 22.3. No other significant results are found for other variables.

Table 22.6 presented reveals the results of the regression estimate from Equation 22.4, and as results show, the coefficient of POST is negative but insignificant (p-value of 0.1707) which is consistent with the results shown in Tables 22.2 and 22.3. It can be said that timely loss recognition was not significantly affected by the introduction of the international financial reporting standards into Saudi Arabia. As for other control variables, timely loss recognition (LNEG) was found to have a significant positive relationship on both the firm's leverage (LEV) and the cash flow from operating activities (CFO) at the 10% significance level. The association between LNEG and EISSUE was found negatively significant at the 1% significance level. No other significant results are found for other variables.

Table 22.5 Regression results of IFRS adoption on managing earnings toward target

$$SPOS_{i,t} = \alpha_0 + \alpha_1 POST_{i,t} + \beta_1 SIZE_{i,t} + \beta_2 GROWTH_{i,t} + \beta_3 EISSUE_{i,t} + \beta_4 LEV_{i,t} + \beta_5 DISSUE_{i,t} + \beta_6 TURN_{i,t} + \beta_7 CFO_{i,t} + \beta_8 AUD_{i,t} + \sum_t year_t + \varepsilon_{i,t}$$

Variables	Coefficients	t-statistic	P-value
Intercept	−0.0654	−0.6867	0.4928
POST	0.0090	0.2651	0.7910
SIZE	**0.0198**	1.8666*	0.0629
GROWTH	−0.00334	−0.1384	0.8900
EISSUE	0.0640	0.9719	0.3318
LEV	0.1043	1.5549	0.1210
DISSUE	−0.0053	−0.2568	0.7975
TURN	**−0.0439**	−1.9900**	0.0474
CFO	**−0.2223**	−2.1129**	0.0354
AUD	0.0016	0.0044	0.9647
Number of observations	336		
R-squared	0.0142		

Source: Own work

Note: *,**,*** significance level of 10%, 5% and 1%, respectively

Bold coefficients are found significant

Table 22.6 Regression results of IFRS adoption on timely loss recognition

$$LNEG_{i,t} = \alpha_0 + \alpha_1 POST_{i,t} + \beta_1 SIZE_{i,t} + \beta_2 GROWTH_{i,t} + \beta_3 EISSUE_{i,t} + \beta_4 LEV_{i,t} + \beta_5 DISSUE_{i,t} + \beta_6 TURN_{i,t} + \beta_7 CFO_{i,t} + \beta_8 AUD_{i,t} + \sum_t year_t + \varepsilon_{i,t}$$

Variables	Coefficients	t-statistic (P-value)
Intercept	−0.0200	−1.0584 (0.2907)
POST	−0.0093	−1.3732 (0.1707)
SIZE	0.0023	1.0996 (0.2723)
GROWTH	0.0030	0.6165 (0.5380)
EISSUE	**−0.1769**	−13.512*** (0.000)
LEV	**0.02188**	1.6394* (0.1021)
DISSUE	−0.0027	−0.6630 (0.5078)
TURN	−0.0014	−0.3140 (0.7537)
CFO	**0.0358**	1.7113* (0.0880)
AUD	−0.0044	−0.6340 (0.5265)
Number of observations	336	
R-squared	0.4175	

Source: Own work

Note: *,**,*** significance level of 10%, 5% and 1% respectively

Bold values emphasize the significance of test variables

22.6 Conclusion

This chapter aims to empirically test the impact of the IFRS adoption on the earnings quality in, one of the MENA region countries, the emerging market of Saudi Arabia. The sample was based on listed firms for a period of 6 years covering the pre- and post-adoption era. Based on previous literatures in this area of interest, three models were developed each representing an earnings quality metric: (a) earnings smoothing, (b) management earnings toward targets, and (c) timely loss recognition.

After showing the descriptive statistics of the dependent and control variables, performing a Pearson correlation matrix, and estimating regression equations using E-views, it was found that the earnings smoothing increased after the IFRS adoption. However, our results failed to find any supporting evidence concerning the improvement of neither the second metric, managing earnings toward a target nor the third which is timely loss recognition metrics. Consequently, it can be said that the earnings quality was not found to have improved after the introduction of the International Financial Reporting Standards into the Saudi Arabia market.

These conclusions are aligned with previous studies stating that the adoption of IFRS in emerging economies needs special implementation as these countries may lack the required infrastructure and monitoring system for such adoption.

Acknowledgments The chapter has been prepared within the research project "The determinants of accounting quality in emerging and transitioning economies" (OP RDE IGA/A, CZ.02.2.69/0.0/0.0/19_073/0016936, project no. 15/2021).

References

Barth, M. E., Landsman, W. R., Lang, M., & Williams, C. (2007). *Accounting quality: International accounting standards and US GAAP*. Manuscript, Stanford University.

Barth, M. E., Landsman, W. R., & Lang, M. H. (2008). International accounting standards and accounting quality. *Journal of Accounting Research, 46*(3), 467–498. https://doi.org/10.1111/j.1475-679X.2008.00287.x

Beneish, M. D. (2001). Earnings management: A perspective. *Managerial Finance, 27*, 3–17.

Bouwman, C. H. (2014). Managerial optimism and earnings smoothing. *Journal of Banking & Finance, 41*, 283–303.

Cameran, M., Campa, D., & Pettinicchio, A. (2014). IFRS adoption among private companies: Impact on earnings quality. *Journal of Accounting, Auditing & Finance, 29*(3), 278–305. https://doi.org/10.1177/0148558X14534260

Capkun, V., Collins, D., & Jeanjean, T. (2016). The effect of IAS/IFRS adoption on earnings management (smoothing): A closer look at competing explanations. *Journal of Accounting and Public Policy, 35*(4), 352–394. https://doi.org/10.1016/j.jaccpubpol.2016.04.002

Chen, H., Tang, Q., Jiang, Y., & Lin, Z. (2010). The role of international financial reporting standards in accounting quality: Evidence from the European Union. *Journal of International Financial Management & Accounting, 21*(3), 220–278.

Cohen, D. A., Dey, A., & Lys, T. Z. (2008). Real and accrual-based earnings management in the pre-and post-Sarbanes-Oxley periods. *The Accounting Review, 83*(3), 757–787.

Dechow, P. M., Sloan, R. G., & Sweeney, A. P. (1995). Detecting earnings management. *Accounting Review*, 193–225.

Dechow, P., Ge, W., & Schrand, C. (2010). Understanding earnings quality: A review of the proxies, their determinants and their consequences. *Journal of Accounting and Economics, 50*(2-3), 344–401. https://doi.org/10.1016/j.jacceco.2010.09.001

Goel, A. M., & Thakor, A. V. (2003). Why do firms smooth earnings? *The Journal of Business, 76*(1), 151–192.

Healy, P. M., & Wahlen, J. M. (1999). A review of the earnings management literature and its implications for standard setting. *Accounting Horizons, 13*(4), 365–383.

Irvine, H., & Lucas, N., 2006. Globalized accounting standards: The case of the United Arab Emirates. In *Proceedings, 3th international conference on contemporary business, Leura, New South Wales, Charles Sturt University, Australia*, ro.uow.edu.au/cgi/viewcontent.cgi

Jeanjean, T., & Stolowy, H. (2008). Do accounting standards matter? An exploratory analysis of earnings management before and after IFRS adoption. *Journal of Accounting and Public Policy, 27*(6), 480–494.

Leuz, C., Nanda, D., & Wysocki, P. D. (2003). Earnings management and investor protection: An international comparison. *Journal of Financial Economics, 69*(3), 505–527. https://doi.org/10.1016/S0304-405X(03)00121-1

Mongrut, S., & Winkelried, D. (2019). Unintended effects of IFRS adoption on earnings management: The case of Latin America. *Emerging Markets Review, 38*, 377–388. https://doi.org/10.1016/j.ememar.2018.11.004

Paglietti, P. (2010). Earnings management, timely loss recognition and value relevance in Europe following the IFRS mandatory adoption: Evidence from Italian listed companies. *Economia Aziendale Online, 1*(4), 97–117.

Paglietti, P. (2009). Exploring the role of accounting history following the adoption of IFRS in Europe. The case of Italy. *De Computis: Revista Española de Historia de la Contabilidad, 6* (11), 83–115.

Schipper, K. (1989). Earnings management. *Accounting Horizons, 3*(4), 91.

Sellami, M., & Fakhfakh, H. (2013). Effect of the mandatory adoption of IFRS on real and accruals-based earnings management: Empirical evidence from France. *International Journal of Accounting and Economics Studies, 2*(1), 22–33. https://doi.org/10.14419/ijaes.v2i1.1485

Soderstrom, N. S., & Sun, K. J. (2007). IFRS adoption and accounting quality: A review. *European Accounting Review, 16*(4), 675–702. https://doi.org/10.1080/09638180701706732

Toumeh, A. A., & Yahya, S. (2019). A review of earnings management techniques: An IFRS perspective. *Global Business & Management Research, 11*(3).

Trabelsi, R. (2016). Are IFRS harder to implement for emerging economies compared to developed countries? A literature review. *Journal of Modern Accounting and Auditing, 12*(1), 1–16. https://doi.org/10.17265/1548-6583/2016.01.001

Van Tendeloo, B., & Vanstraelen, A. (2005). Earnings management under German GAAP versus IFRS. *European Accounting Review, 14*(1), 155–180. https://doi.org/10.1080/0963818042000338988

Zang, A. Y. (2012). Evidence on the trade-off between real activities manipulation and accrual-based earnings management. *The Accounting Review, 87*(2), 675–703. https://doi.org/10.2308/accr-10196

Zhou, H., Xiong, Y., & Ganguli, G. (2009). Does the adoption of international financial reporting standards restrain earnings management? Evidence from an emerging market. *Academy of Accounting and Financial Studies Journal, 13*, 43.

Chapter 23
Deferred Tax Reporting in Czech Limited Partnerships

Richard Stiebal

Abstract This chapter discusses the role of deferred tax in pass-through entities and examines how Czech limited partnerships, which can be classified as partly pass-through, approach deferred tax reporting. It is found that Czech partnerships mostly acknowledge their tax position for deferred tax purposes and comply with basic deferred tax accounting principles, with desirable outcomes being more frequent among partnerships audited by any of the Big Four accounting firms. This chapter also presents a proposed method of deferred tax computation for partly pass-through entities which is formulated on the background of interperiod income tax allocation.

Keywords Deferred tax · Limited partnership · Pass-through entity

23.1 Introduction

A pass-through entity (PTE), also known as flow-through or fiscally transparent entity, is a business structure whose income is not taxed at the company level, but instead at the owner level. Because PTEs allow their owners to avoid double taxation of the income, such entities are sometimes referred to as tax-advantaged entities. They may exist in various legal forms depending on each country's tax laws, although the most common ones are partnerships.

From the financial reporting perspective, not many significant differences arise in comparison to ordinary taxable entities. One difference might be that in the case of a PTE, its current income tax expense would generally equal to zero. From a purely tax perspective, however, PTEs are closely observed, mainly due to tax revenue analyses. Cooper et al. (2016) find that an increasing number of PTEs in the USA leads to lower tax revenues. The specific tax position of PTEs shall be taken into consideration when accounting for deferred income taxes. This issue can be split into two levels: (a) the owner level and the temporary differences arising on an

R. Stiebal (✉)
Department of Financial Accounting and Auditing, Prague University of Economics and Business, Prague, Czech Republic
e-mail: stir00@vse.cz

D. Procházka (ed.), *Regulation of Finance and Accounting*, Springer Proceedings in Business and Economics, https://doi.org/10.1007/978-3-030-99873-8_23

investment in a PTE (outside basis differences) and (b) the PTE level and the temporary differences arising on assets and liabilities of the PTE itself (inside basis differences). This chapter focuses solely on the latter level.

IAS 12 currently does not provide any guidance for deferred tax reporting in PTEs. According to Deloitte (2009), upon revision of IAS 12, one of the planned additions to disclosures was to newly disclose the differences between tax and book bases for PTEs. However, this intended change to disclosures never made it into IAS 12, along with some other planned changes such as the revision of initial recognition exemption. ASC 740-10-50-16 under US GAAP prescribes that public entities which are not subject to income tax should disclose the net temporary difference. The expected future tax effects may then be computed using appropriate tax rates which may differ between investors due to the taxation at the investor level.

Despite no explicit information provided by the standards, it is apparent that deferred tax should equal to zero in PTEs, just like current income tax. Supporting evidence can be found in every of the Big Four firms' handbooks dedicated to income taxes, e.g., PwC (2020), according to which reporting of deferred taxes in a PTE would be inconsistent with the nature of such an entity. Another piece of supporting evidence is provided in Hodder et al. (2003), where US banks would write off all their deferred taxes at conversion from taxable C-corporations to nontaxable S-corporations. Deferred tax accounting in broader scope is interperiod allocation of corporate income taxes as described by Black (1966). It would make little sense to allocate income taxes into their respective periods if there are no income taxes at the company level in the first place.

More information can be found on a local, national level, mainly because countries' tax laws may give rise to unique situations. In Germany, corporations are liable for trade tax based on taxable income as calculated for corporate income tax purposes. This applies even to PTEs. Dennerlein (2018a) and Lange and Wolz (n.d.) state that deferred taxes on the company level can only be formed in the amount of trade tax effects, while no deferred tax related to corporate income tax is reported. Dennerlein (2018b) and Kastrup and Middendorf (2010) point out some problems associated with German accounting standards that may in certain cases require PTEs to account for deferred tax liability (DTL) from income tax, essentially violating the basic principles of interperiod income tax allocation. Stückler (2017) covers the situation for Austria, where the partner of a partnership accounts for deferred taxes with regard to his participation in the partnership, not the partnership itself.

In the Czech Republic, a unique type of otherwise widespread legal form limited partnership exists.[1] The Czech limited partnership can be perceived as partly pass-through, meaning that some portion of its income is taxed at the partner level, while the rest is taxed at the partnership level. The text above governed only those cases

[1]The unique aspect is that the Czech limited partnership has only partial pass-through character (as described further in the main text) unlike, for example, German limited partnership which is pass-through entirely.

where an entity is entirely pass-through. This unusual allocation requires specific deferred tax treatment. Czech accounting rules provide only limited guidance for deferred taxes. As criticized by Žárová (2010), this undesirable state is a result of incomplete implementation of IAS 12 into the Czech accounting system.[2] Czech limited partnerships therefore need to seek guidance from other sources. Moreover, IAS 12 – otherwise commonly used for situations where the Czech accounting system is insufficient – would provide no exact solution to this local issue.

Further text describes the legal form of the Czech limited partnership in more detail. Afterward, a proposed method is presented alongside some of the practical difficulties. Possible consequences of improper deferred tax reporting are discussed. Finally, financial statements of the audited Czech limited partnerships are examined, and the findings summarized. Besides, a link between useful provided information and being audited by a Big Four firm is observed.

23.2 Tax Position of the Czech Limited Partnership

In the Czech Republic, only two legal forms are generally perceived as pass-through. They are the general partnership (also known as the unlimited partnership) and the limited partnership. According to Czech Statistical Office (2018), the data for the first quarter of 2018 show that only less than 2% of all registered business corporations in the Czech Republic were partnerships. This differs immensely from the situation in the USA, where in 2011 there were almost 1.5 times more partnerships than taxable C-corporations. When combined with pass-through S-corporations, the total number of PTEs (excluding sole proprietorships) was almost four times greater than the number of C-corporations (Pomerleau, 2015).

The general partnership is an ordinary, entirely PTE where all of its income is taxed at the partner level. Therefore, no reported deferred tax is expected. On the other hand, the Czech limited partnership would be hardly ever entirely pass-through. In the majority of cases, the limited partnership would be considered partly pass-through. The reason for this is that from the total partnership's taxable income, only a portion attributable to general partners (partners with unlimited liability) is "passed-through" onto them without being taxed at the company level first. The rest of the taxable income belonging to limited partners (partners with limited liability) is first taxed at the company level. The net income is then either distributed to the limited partners (which is subject to a second layer of tax, this time at the partner level) or retained in the company.

Business Corporations Act No. 90/2012 Coll. allows partners to choose the portion of profit or loss attributable to general and limited partners. Information

[2]Czech accounting system (further also referred to as Czech accounting rules) for business entities consists of Accounting Act No. 563/1991 Coll., Decree on Accounting No. 500/2002 Coll. and Czech Accounting Standards Nos. 001–023.

about the allocation ratio must be included in a partnership agreement. If this ratio is not specified, a default ratio of 50:50 then applies. The same ratio used for allocating book income is also used for allocating tax income. Generally speaking, the bigger the portion allocated to general partners, ceteris paribus, the lower the corporate income tax of the limited partnership.

According to Schuster (2019), taking a role of limited partner in a Czech limited partnership can be more attractive to German investors than owning a Czech limited liability company (LLC). Schuster states that income from the Czech limited partnership is from a German point of view perceived as an income from a permanent establishment and is therefore not subject to the 25% taxation which would otherwise apply to income distribution from the LLC (through credit method), but only to the initial 15% tax rate.

23.3 Proposed Method for Deferred Tax Accounting in Czech Limited Partnerships

Applying the basic principles of deferred tax accounting, only the corporate income tax at the company level may be subject to interperiod income tax allocation. Therefore, deferred tax shall be recorded only on the portion attributable to limited partners. Practically speaking, the limited partnership would first identify all temporary differences in their full extent. These temporary differences would be generally similar to those usually arising in taxable corporations, simply because the Czech accounting system does not differentiate between legal forms in terms of applicable accounting methods. After identifying the total taxable (deductible) temporary difference, a DTL (deferred tax asset; DTA) would be computed using the corporate income tax rate for limited partnerships.[3] This DTL (DTA) would then be reduced accordingly to only reflect the portion attributable to the limited partners. Naturally, the process can be altered by already reducing the total taxable (deductible) temporary difference. This adjustment to deferred tax should be explained in the notes to financial statements. Ideally, the information about a total net temporary difference should also be provided.

In the case of a DTA, its recoverability would have to be tested. If this test was carried out on an already reduced DTA attributable to limited partners, the future comparable taxable profits would also need to be reduced accordingly, taking into account only limited partners' share.

The allocation ratios used in practice are rather polarized (as confirmed by the data presented below), meaning the vast majority of income is allocated either to general partners or to limited partners. The partnerships where general partners are allocated more than 95% of income may arguably be – for the purpose of deferred

[3] Since year 2010, the corporate income tax rate for business corporations in the Czech Republic has been 19%.

tax reporting – perceived as entirely pass-through and consequently would not have to report any deferred tax. On the other end, the partnerships where limited partners are allocated more than 95% of income may omit the reduction of deferred tax. This of course would not apply to current income tax. The distortion caused by different portions at which current and deferred tax are computed would mostly be negligible.

In partnerships where the allocation to general partners is a fixed amount or where it is derived from other bases (such as percentage of general partner's equity), the reduction used for deferred tax calculation can be derived from the share of current income tax relative to profit before tax in previous years. However, allocations determined in this way would mostly not exceed 5% of profit before tax and therefore – applying the assumption mentioned above – such partnership may be treated as entirely pass-through for deferred tax purposes.

The proposed options presented above could be violated in two ways: (a) a limited partnership that allocates significant portion of income to limited partners does not record any deferred tax or (b) a limited partnership that allocates a significant portion of income to general partners records deferred tax in its full extent.[4] Situations where no temporary differences arise or where a DTA is not reported due to its uncertain recoverability are excluded.

The first violation applies even to ordinary taxable entities, where deferred tax is intentionally or unintentionally overlooked by the reporting entity and information is provided neither in the financial statements nor in the notes. Consequently, financial position of an entity cannot be assessed in its entirety as a critical piece of information might be missing. This also applies to limited partnerships.

The second violation is unique to PTEs and generally leads to distortion of income tax expense item. Since general partners are allocated profit before tax, the whole deferred tax expense (along their portion of profit before tax) is decided upon by limited partners. In an extreme case where everything would be allocated to general partners, limited partners would be deciding upon distribution of deferred tax expense caused by a year-on-year change of deferred tax that is, however, borne as a whole by general partners.

The current deferred tax model is built on an assumption that all temporary differences ultimately reverse. If an ownership structure of a limited partnership never changed until all temporary differences reversed, the total income attributed to limited partners over the course of years would equal the same whether or not the right reduction in deferred tax computation was used. However, the timing of income attributed to limited partners in respective years would be altered. Due to the different timing, partnership's reported financial position might be different in each of the years.

Assuming that a limited partnership has been recording deferred tax only on the portion attributable to limited partners and the allocation ratio changes due to

[4]The remaining cases where deferred tax is not zero but its portion does not correspond with the portion allocated to limited partners are unlikely to occur, although the consequences would be analogical and would only differ in severity.

changes in a partnership agreement, the change in deferred tax shall be reported in profit and loss, as required by ASC 740-10-45-19 in situations where a tax status of an entity changes. On the contrary, if a limited partnership has been allocating a wrong portion of deferred tax to limited partners and wishes to correct the mistake by adjusting the deferred tax amount, the change in deferred tax shall be treated as a correction of an error. If a partnership decides to change its legal form and convert to taxable entity, removing the reduction of deferred tax shall be recorded in profit and loss and vice versa.

23.4 Data and Methodology

Under the Czech accounting rules, only mandatorily audited entities are obliged to account for deferred taxes. Examining financial statements of partnerships which are not audited would likely not provide relevant results. Therefore, this chapter targets Czech limited partnerships with statutory audit obligation. Financial statements of those are examined, and an extent at which deferred tax is reported is evaluated. The extent is rather independent of the year for which financial statements were prepared, provided that the partnership had undergone an audit in the analyzed year. A period of years between 2016 and 2019 was chosen. The process of obtaining the data is split into three stages: (a) identifying all audited limited partnerships between 2016 and 2019; (b) obtaining partnership agreements of the identified partnerships for information about profit or loss allocation between general and limited partners; and (c) obtaining partnerships' financial statements including the notes for details about deferred tax reporting.

A list of limited partnerships was obtained from Bisnode MagnusWeb database. Since the database does not provide an option to filter solely for audited financial statements, an alternative method was used. This required filtering for partnerships that – according to their financial statements – exceeded at least one of the following criteria: CZK 40 m total assets, CZK 80 m annual turnover, and/or 50 employees in any of the years between 2015 and 2019. This procedure should have ensured that no partnership with statutory audit was missing. On the other hand, such list included several partnerships without statutory audit. Each identified partnership was therefore manually checked in the Czech public register. Only the partnerships whose annual report included an auditor's report were subject to examination. If the partnership was audited in multiple years between 2016 and 2019, the most recent audited year was picked. If the partnership changed its legal form from limited partnership to another legal form, the most recent audited year before the legal form change was picked. This led to a total number of 74 limited partnerships. No sampling was performed for further analysis, and all the 74 partnerships had their partnership agreements and financial statements examined in detail. The allocation ratios were often heavily polarized, as shown in Table 23.1.

Table 23.1 Allocation ratios

Share of income attributable to limited partners in percent	Number of partnerships	Percentage of partnerships
≥ 99	32	43.24
≥ 95 and < 99	7	9.46
> 5 and < 95	2	2.70
> 1 and ≤ 5	3	4.06
≤ 1	30	40.54
Total	74	100.00

Source: Czech public register + authorial computation
Note: In partnerships where general partners are allocated a fixed amount or their amount is derived from other sources, the percentage was calculated as a share of an amount attributable to general partners in the examined year to a total profit before tax in that year

For the purpose of examination and due to tendencies to allocate almost all of the income to either general or limited partners, the partnerships were split into two categories. The first category comprises all partnerships (a total of 40) where the vast majority of income is allocated to limited partners, further referred to as "taxable partnerships." The second category contains the rest of the partnerships (a total of 34) where allocations to general partners prevail, further referred to as "pass-through partnerships."[5] Each category is then evaluated separately. Table 23.2 presents descriptive statistics for each category.

The partnerships were evaluated according to the following rules. For taxable partnerships, acceptable situations include deferred tax recorded in its full extent or in an extent it belongs to limited partners. Naturally, a DTA not reported due to uncertain recoverability is also acceptable, although this must be explicitly stated in notes. No deferred tax reported with no explanation in notes is insufficient.

For pass-through partnerships, deferred tax reduced to limited partners' portion or no deferred tax recorded is further acceptable. No explanation in notes given is still accepted, although not ideal. Information about total net temporary difference provided is desirable. Deferred tax recognized in its full extent is incorrect.

The author adopted own methodology with regard to basic interperiod income tax allocation principles as the Czech accounting rules require entities to report the total value of DTL or DTA and its year-on-year change at most. In addition to relatively insufficient requirements, the second mentioned requirement also leads to divergent interpretations in practice (e.g., whether temporary differences shall be presented individually). Table 23.3 summarizes the abovementioned criteria on disclosures for each category.

[5] For the sake of completeness, the two partnerships in Table 23.1 from the group "> 5 and < 95" were placed into their corresponding categories. In these two cases, the allocations to limited partners were 90 and 20 percent of income.

Table 23.2 Descriptive statistics relating to limited partnerships

	Number of taxable partnerships	Percentage of taxable partnerships	Number of pass-through partnerships	Percentage of pass-through partnerships
Year breakdown				
2016	1	2.50	2	5.88
2017	2	5.00	1	2.94
2018	7	17.50	6	17.65
2019	30	75.00	25	73.53
Total	40	100.00	34	100.00
Auditor breakdown				
Big four	5	12.50	17	50.00
Other audit firms	31	77.50	15	44.12
Self-employed	4	10.00	2	5.88
Total	40	100.00	34	100.00
Limited partner country breakdown				
Czech Republic	3	6.98	19	54.29
Germany	37	86.05	6	17.14
Luxembourg	0	–	3	8.57
Netherlands	2	4.65	1	2.86
Sweden	0	–	2	5.71
Other	1	2.32	4	11.43
Total	43	100.00	35	100.00
General partner country breakdown				
Cyprus	0	–	1	2.86
Czech Republic	37	92.50	25	71.43
Germany	3	7.50	4	11.43
Malta	0	–	5	14.28
Total	40	100.00	35	100.00

Source: Czech public register + authorial computation

Table 23.3 Disclosure requirements

Category	Disclosures
Taxable partnerships	Not recoverable DTA, information about reduction if it is applied, net temporary difference if reduction is applied
Pass-through partnerships	Not recoverable DTA, information about reduction, net temporary difference

Source: Authorial computation

23.5 Results and Discussion

The main findings relating to reported deferred taxes are presented in Table 23.4. Among the taxable partnerships, there were more DTAs than DTLs. However, one-third of these DTAs were not recognized due to uncertain recoverability. Deferred tax was either reported in its full extent or not at all, and no partial reductions occurred. In the total of seven cases, no deferred tax was reported, while no information was provided in notes either. Whether this was intentional or due to an oversight remains unclear. Nevertheless, most of the taxable partnerships acknowledged their tax position and reported deferred taxes in accordance with the proposed solution.

The pass-through partnerships showed more diversity. Overall, 29 partnerships reported deferred tax in an acceptable manner. In nine cases, deferred tax was reduced to limited partners' portion, which resulted only in minor amounts of deferred tax. In seven cases, no deferred tax was reported, while the reason that the partnership is "basically pass-through" was given. Another 13 partnerships did not report any deferred tax, but unlike in the previous case, no supplementary information was provided, meaning deferred tax was omitted entirely in the financial

Table 23.4 Reported deferred taxes in partnerships

	Number of taxable partnerships	Percentage of taxable partnerships	Number of pass-through partnerships	Percentage of pass-through partnerships
Deferred tax liability				
DTL full extent	15		5	
DTL limited partners' portion	0		5	
Total DTL	15	37.50	10	29.41
Deferred tax asset				
DTA full extent	12		0	
DTA limited partners' portion	0		4	
Total DTA	12	30.00	4	11.77
No deferred tax				
DTA not recoverable	6		0	
Pass-through reason given in notes	0		7	
No information	7		13	
Total no deferred tax	13	32.50	20	58.82
Total	40	100.00	34	100.00

Source: Czech public register + authorial computation

statements as well as in the notes. The partnerships with no deferred tax reported generally did not provide information about existing temporary differences, including total net temporary difference. In the remaining five cases, deferred tax was reported in its full extent. All these five cases represented DTL that naturally worsens partnership's presented financial situation; therefore, an intentional full-extent recognition is unlikely.

In total, taking results from both categories, 12 partnerships did not meet the minimum requirements on deferred tax recognition and/or presentation, while none of those 12 partnerships were audited by the Big Four firms. Looking at the data in Table 23.2, however, nearly one-third of the partnerships were audited by the Big Four firms. Although it cannot be stated for certain, it seems that partnerships audited by any of the Big Four firms are more likely to present deferred tax-related information in an acceptable manner. As it was the whole population of previously identified partnerships that had their financial statements examined, no chi-square test was conducted.

The shortcomings detected among taxable partnerships are similar to those found by Buzková (2014) among Czech joint-stock companies. The absolute disregard for deferred tax accounting which sometimes appears in the Czech Republic seems to be rather independent of the legal form of the reporting entity. Even though the currently applied deferred tax model is a subject of criticism, e.g., by Brouwer and Naarding (2018), it is not up to entities to decide whether they will pay attention to deferred tax or not.

The second category consisting of pass-through partnerships has brought more insight into how deferred tax is treated in practice by PTEs. In spite of no explicit guidance provided by IAS 12 and neither by Czech accounting rules, nine pass-through partnerships applied the reduction method proposed in this chapter. Another seven partnerships also implicitly took into account the reduction but in the end found the limited partners' share of deferred tax immaterial. On the other hand, the five partnerships that reported deferred tax in its full extent clearly misunderstood the purpose of deferred tax. To obtain a broader overview of this particular issue, brief research that targeted Czech general partnerships was carried out by the author. The results showed that two out of total 18 analyzed mandatorily audited general partnerships reported deferred tax that did not equal to zero.[6] This issue – in essence, same for both general and limited partnerships – could have been potentially avoided if the Czech accounting rules addressed this issue.

Properly calculated and recorded deferred tax of a partnership may be particularly helpful when comparing financial position either with another partnership or with an ordinary taxable entity. If comparing two partnerships, it should be assured that both partnerships follow the same rules when accounting for deferred taxes. If comparing a partnership with ordinary taxable entity, the actual tax advantages of a partnership shall be taken into account and projected into deferred tax computation.

[6] The methodology used was similar to that used for limited partnerships, although only year 2016 was analyzed.

Table 23.5 Analyzed partnerships' disclosures

Category and criterion	Number of partnerships which disclosed such information
Taxable partnerships (total of 40)	
DTA not recoverable	6
Information about DTA/DTL reduction and net temporary difference if reduction is applied	n/a – No reductions occurred in this category
Pass-through partnerships (total of 34)	
DTA not recoverable	0
Information about DTA/DTL reduction	13
Net temporary difference if reduction is applied	7[a]

Source: Czech public register + authorial computation
[a]Note: The seven cases also include situations where the net temporary difference is computable using the DTA/DTL and an applicable tax rate

Table 23.5 summarizes the information regarding deferred tax disclosed by the partnerships according to Table 23.3.

23.6 Conclusion

The nature of deferred tax primarily depends on reporting entity's tax position. While there are a lot of resources for deferred tax reporting in taxable entities, the same is not true for pass-through entities. The current version of IAS 12 does not address pass-through entities either. On top of that, local tax laws may give rise to even more uncommon types of entities in terms of corporate income taxation, as is the case with the Czech Republic. Treatment of deferred taxes in these entities should be consistent with the basic principles of interperiod income tax allocation. This chapter focused on the Czech limited partnership legal form which is in essence a partly pass-through entity. A general rule was established, that "only the company-level income tax can be subject to interperiod income tax allocation." Applying this rule on the Czech limited partnership means to report deferred tax only to an extent it is attributable to limited partners.

Afterward, a total of 74 audited Czech limited partnerships were examined to find how deferred tax is treated in practice. This included checking partnership agreements, financial statements and notes, as well as auditor's reports. The results showed that a majority of the partnerships (84%) complied with the basic deferred tax accounting principles, despite the fact that Czech accounting rules do not touch upon this issue at all. Additionally, it was also found that partnerships audited by any of the Big Four accounting firms were less likely to record deferred tax in an insufficient way. In general, the partnerships mostly acknowledged their tax position and projected it accordingly into the way deferred tax was recorded.

Although the research targeted exclusively Czech limited partnerships that used local accounting standards for their financial reporting, the proposed method is applicable to entirely or partly pass-through entities in general. The method can be further developed and adjusted to target similar deferred tax complexities which may exist due to varying tax laws among countries.

Acknowledgments This chapter is processed as an output of a research project IGA VŠE F1/25/2019 (Market failures and their impact on audit quality in the Czech Republic).

References

Black, H. A. (1966). Interperiod allocation of corporate income taxes. *Financial Analysts Journal, 22*, 41–47. https://doi.org/10.2469/faj.v22.n5.41

Brouwer, A., & Naarding, E. (2018). Making deferred taxes relevant. *Accounting in Europe, 15*, 200–230. https://doi.org/10.1080/17449480.2018.1451903

Buzková, V. (2014). *Problematika odložené daně a jejího vykazování*. Master's thesis, Prague University of Economics and Business.

Cooper, M., McClelland, J., Pearce, J., et al. (2016). Business in the United States: Who owns it, and how much tax do they pay? *Tax Policy and the Economy, 30*, 91–128. https://doi.org/10.1086/685594

Czech Statistical Office. (2018). V tuzemsku působí necelých 900 tisíc podnikatelů. In: *Český Statistický Úřad*. https://www.czso.cz/csu/czso/v-tuzemsku-pusobi-necelych-900-tisic-podnikatelu. Accessed 27 Feb 2021.

Deloitte. (2009). *Changes proposed for income tax accounting*. https://www.iasplus.com/en/binary/iasplus/0904incometaxed.pdf. Accessed 26 Feb 2021.

Dennerlein, B. (2018a). Latente Steuern bei Personengesellschaften im Einzelabsc … / 4 Besonderheiten bei der Ermittlung latenter Steuern im Einzelabschluss von Personengesellschaften. In: *Haufe.de News und Fachwissen*. https://www.haufe.de/finance/haufe-finance-office-premium/latente-steuern-bei-personengesellschaften-im-einzelabsc-4-besonderheiten-bei-der-ermittlung-latenter-steuern-im-einzelabschluss-von-personengesellschaften_idesk_PI20354_HI2861869.html. Accessed 26 Feb 2021.

Dennerlein, B. (2018b). Latente Steuern bei Personengesellschaften im Einzelabsc … / 2 Anwendung/Größenabhängige Erleichterungen. In: *Haufe.de News und Fachwissen*. https://www.haufe.de/finance/haufe-finance-office-premium/latente-steuern-bei-personengesellschaften-im-einzelabsc-2-anwendunggroessenabhaengige-erleichterungen_idesk_PI20354_HI2861867.html. Accessed 26 Feb 2021.

Hodder, L., McAnally, M. L., & Weaver, C. D. (2003). The influence of tax and nontax factors on banks' choice of organizational form. *The Accounting Review, 78*, 297–325. https://doi.org/10.2308/accr.2003.78.1.297

Kastrup, B., & Middendorf, O. (2010). Latente Steuern bei Personengesellschaften im handelsrechtlichen Jahresabschluss nach BilMoG. *Betriebs-Berater, 65*, 815–820.

Lange, B., & Wolz, C. (n.d.). Latente Steuern bei Personengesellschaften. In: *COMPLIANCEdigital*. https://www.compliancedigital.de/ce/latente-steuern-bei-personengesellschaften-1/detail.html. Accessed 26 Feb 2021.

Pomerleau, K. (2015). An overview of pass-through businesses in the United States. In: *Tax Foundation*. https://taxfoundation.org/overview-pass-through-businesses-united-states/. Accessed 27 Feb 2021.

PwC. (2020). *Income taxes*. https://www.pwc.com/us/en/cfodirect/assets/pdf/accounting-guides/pwc-income-taxes-guide.pdf. Accessed 26 Feb 2021.

Schuster, P. (2019). *Rechtsformwahl in der Tschechischen Republik*. Dissertation, Universität Regensburg.

Stückler, K. (2017). Bilanzierung latenter Steuern bei Personengesellschaften. In: *Deloitte Österreich Tax & Legal News*. https://www.deloittetax.at/2017/09/13/bilanzierung-latenter-steuern-bei-personengesellschaften/. Accessed 26 Feb 2021.

Žárová, M. (2010). Impact of IAS 12 on deferred taxes regulation in the Czech Republic. *European Financial and Accounting Journal, 5*, 6–27. https://doi.org/10.18267/j.efaj.42

Chapter 24
The Effect of the Deferred Tax on Business Combinations in the Czech Republic

Jiří Pospíšil

Abstract This chapter is a starting point of a research project which aims to analyze and evaluate various approaches to financial reporting of deferred tax during business combinations currently used in the Czech Republic. Since the current Czech national regulation offers only limited guidance on deferred tax reporting, practitioners apply diverse approaches which lead to the decreased comparability of the financial statements and might lead the users of the financial statements to misinterpretation of the data presented. This chapter describes the concept of the research work – the data gathering, analytic procedures, and some of the intended evaluation methods. The aim of this research is to describe the current practice using the descriptive analysis of the whole population of business combinations like legal mergers, spin-offs, etc. which occurred in the Czech Republic in the period of 2015–2019.

Key words Deferred tax · Business combinations · Equity

24.1 Introduction

Deferred tax is often considered a difficult topic of financial reporting – especially for practitioners who often face numerous challenges in their attempts to identify all the temporary differences which might give rise to a deferred tax asset or to a deferred tax liability. Unfortunately, this issue brings a whole new level of complexity when set in the context of business combination. The regulation of financial reporting in the Czech Republic is carried out mostly through the Accounting Act no. 563/1991 Sb. and decrees of the Ministry of Finance which are closely tied to the tax and business law (Pospíšil & Strojek-Filus, 2017). Such regulation provides rather rigid rules for financial reporting which often does not allow entities to report business combinations in a way that would best depict their nature. Moreover, the

J. Pospíšil (✉)
Department of Financial Accounting and Auditing, Prague University of Economics and Business, Prague, Czech Republic
e-mail: jiri.pospisil@vse.cz

D. Procházka (ed.), *Regulation of Finance and Accounting*, Springer Proceedings in Business and Economics, https://doi.org/10.1007/978-3-030-99873-8_24

current Czech national regulation offers only limited guidance on deferred tax reporting. As a result, practitioners apply diverse approaches which lead to the decreased comparability of the financial statements and might lead the users of the financial statements to misinterpretation of the data presented.

This chapter is a starting point of a research project which aims to analyze and evaluate various approaches to financial reporting of deferred tax during business combinations currently used in the Czech Republic. The research team is going to gather the data of business combinations which were carried out according to the Act no. 125/2008 Sb. on company transformations during the 5 years period and evaluate:

- How do the entities report their deferred tax?
- How does the deferred tax influences goodwill recognized as a result of the business combination?
- Whether the deferred tax recognition impacts equity.

This chapter describes the concept of this research. The main purpose of this research project is to contribute to the harmonization of reporting methods when dealing with the deferred tax during the business combinations, which shall lead to increased understandability and comparability of the financial statements of Czech entities, and also to assist in reaching just taxation in some cases since some of the aspects a transformation project deals with have direct impact on corporate income tax of Czech entities as well.

24.2 Data and Methodology

Deferred tax is reported either as a deferred tax liability or a deferred tax asset. According to IAS 21, the deferred tax liability is an amount of income taxes payable in future periods in respect of taxable temporary differences, while the deferred tax asset is the amount of income taxes recoverable in future periods in respect of deductible temporary differences and tax losses and tax credits deductible in the future periods. The focal point of our research is the temporary differences which arise during the business combinations. According to IAS 21, temporary differences are differences between the carrying amount of an asset or liability and its tax base. Business combinations (as defined below) give rise to new temporary differences, usually due to the revaluation of asset during the purchase price allocation process.

The object of this research is deferred tax measurement and recognition during business combinations which occurred in the Czech Republic in the 5-year period from 2015 to 2019. For the purpose of our research, we define business combinations as those transactions with corporations and their net assets that meet the definitions of the Act no. 89/2012 Sb. and Act no. 125/2008 Sb. of the Czech Republic which outlines general types of company transformations available for companies in the Czech Republic. It is important to note that our definition of the term "business combination" does not comply with general understanding of this term, which is defined by International Financial Reporting Standards (specifically: IFRS 3 Business Combinations). While the definition of the term "business combination" set by IFRS 3 comprises of transactions in which an acquirer obtains control of one or more businesses and includes transactions like share deals or asset deals (acquisition of business), our definition of this term does not include these transactions. Act no. 125/2008 Sb. deals mostly with legal merges ("fúze") and separations ("rozdělení"). These are formal legal procedures which do not distinguish between real acquisition and mere reorganizations.

For the purposes of this research, we adopt merger classification as described by Pospíšil and Vomáčková:

> True merger (in Czech: "fúze splynutím") is defined as a transaction in which at least two companies cease to exist, and their net assets are transferred to at least one new company which emerges from the transaction as their successor. Acquisition merger (in Czech: "fúze sloučením") is defined as a transaction in which one or more companies cease to exist and their net assets are transferred to another existing company which absorbs the net assets transferred and continues its existence. (Pospíšil & Vomáčková, 2017, 1908)

For the purposes of this research, we adopt separations classification as described by Pospíšil and Vomáčková:

> Spin-off (in Czech: "odštěpení") is defined as a transaction where an existing company detach a part of its business which forms a new company while the original company continues its existence. Merger spin-off (in Czech: "odštěpení sloučením") is defined as a transaction in which an existing company detach a part of its business and transfer the respective net assets to another existing company which incorporates the net assets into its own structures, while the original company continues its existence. Split (in Czech: "rozštěpení") is defined as a transaction in which a company ceases to exist, and its nets assets are used to form at least two new companies. Merger split (in Czech: "rozštěpení sloučením") is defined as a transaction in which a company ceases to exist, and its net assets are transferred to at least two other existing companies which incorporate the net assets into their own structures. (Pospíšil & Vomáčková 2017, 1908)

Another important difference between our definition of the term "business combination" and the definition included in IFRS 3 is the fact that we do not exclude transactions with businesses or corporations taking place between (among) parties under common control. Moreover, while IFRS 3 requires that business combination must be a transaction with a business, Act no. 125/2008 Sb. does not require that the characteristics of business are met – the same accounting method applies to any transaction with a corporation and its net assets as long as it is legally structured and carried out in accordance with the Act no. 125/2008 Sb.

To gather the data necessary for the analysis and evaluation, we are data-mining two major databases administrated by the Czech government, namely, the Corporate Register which is administrated by the Czech Ministry of Justice and the Business Bulletin which is administrated by the Czech Ministry Interior. According to the Act no. 125/2008 Sb., all corporations undergoing the transformation process are required to publicly announce this transaction in the Business Bulletin and to publish the relevant documentation (the financial statements and the transformation project) in the Corporate Register.

The number of transformations which occur every year amount to approximately 900. We are going to analyze the whole population.

The data extraction is mostly manual. Except for the financial statements, the source documents are not well structured. Nevertheless, we are taking advantage of some external databases like Amadeus, Albertina, or MagnusWeb to gain basic descriptive data about the corporations undergoing the transformation. These data include net assets, equity, debt, revenue, industry sector, and information about auditor.

The first component of our analysis is the measurement of the deferred tax. We are looking to verify whether the successor company reported an increase or a decrease in the deferred tax asset or the deferred tax liability. Then we cluster the transactions which resulted in the goodwill recognition (referred to as “GW cluster”) and the transactions which resulted in OCER recognition (referred to as “OCER cluster”). OCER (i.e., “Oceňovací rozdíl k nabytému majetku”) is a Czech specific item similar to goodwill which consists of goodwill and a revaluation surplus which should be otherwise allocated to the net assets as part of the purchase-price allocation process. On each cluster, a series of calculations is performed in order to verify the amount of goodwill, OCER, and deferred tax recognized.

There are several methods for deferred tax measurement during the business combinations in the Czech practice. The additional deferred tax is sometimes calculated as a product of the corporate income tax rate and the OCER or goodwill (Skálová, 2019). This approach leads to the recognition of the deferred tax from temporary differences on goodwill which is prohibited, for example, by IAS 12 or NÚR I-1. Another approach, usually referred to as “gross-up method,” assumes that the value of the net assets acquired is a “post-tax value” and needs to be adjusted (usually increased) by the deferred tax in order to obtain the gross value (Bajgerová, 2016). The difference between the “post-tax value” and the grossed-up value is then recognized as the deferred tax and an increase (in the case of deferred tax liability) or decrease (in the case of the deferred tax asset) of goodwill or OCER. Lastly, there is another method applicable for goodwill only, where the amount of the deferred tax equals to the product of the corporate tax rate and the difference of the net asset value and the goodwill (Pelák, 2016). In our research, we are going to verify the calculation of the deferred tax in the opening balance sheet of the entities participating in the business combination by:

- Comparing the total value of deferred tax recognized in the financial statements of the participating entities to the deferred tax recognized in the opening balance sheet of the successor entity.
- Comparing the equity increase in the successor’s opening balance sheet to the net assets value of the participating companies.

Revaluation of net assets during the business combination usually results in an increase of the deferred tax liability. Current regulation is not clear as to which item should absorb the change in the deferred tax. In the case of the acquisition method, as described in the IFRS 3, the deferred tax is considered part of the net assets acquired and as such is included in the goodwill calculation. Czech accounting regulation (specifically Decree no. 500/2002 Sb.) stipulates a different approach where the change in the deferred tax is either recognized as a gain/loss in the income statement or recognized as part of the balance sheet item. Other retained earnings ("Jiný výsledek hospodaření minulých let") which is a special component of retained earnings designated for restatements of accounting errors and impacts of changes in accounting policies. Some authors point out that this treatment is not appropriate for business combinations and argue that the change in the deferred tax should be recognized as an increase or decrease of equity, more specifically at the account group 41 which represents registered capital, contributions, and other paid-in capital (Pospíšil, 2020). In our research, we examine how entities report these changes in the deferred tax in their business combinations by:

- Comparing the total value of other retained earnings recognized in the financial statements of the participating entities to the other retained earnings recognized in the opening balance sheet of the successor entity.
- Testing whether the increase (or decrease) in the total deferred tax recognized equals to the product of tax rate and OCER (or goodwill).

Some of the business combinations require valuation (fair value) of the net assets acquired by court-appointed valuation expert. This valuation serves as a proxy for market price of the business (corporation) as a whole. The accounting treatment prescribed by the Czech regulation of financial reporting introduces a fiction of law that such business combination is in fact an exchange (an acquisition) because the essence of the prescribed accounting procedures is in fact a purchase method for business combinations. Therefore a "fair value" of net asset is necessary in order to calculate goodwill or OCER according to one of the following formulae:

$$GW = V - \left(\sum A_{FV} - \sum L_{BV}\right) \tag{24.1}$$

$$\mathrm{OCER} = V - \left(\sum A_{BV} - \sum L_{BV}\right) \tag{24.2}$$

where *GW* stands for goodwill; OCER stands for "Oceňovací rozdíl k nabytému majetku"; *V* is net assets valuation (business/corporation as a whole); *A* means assets acquired; *L* means liabilities assumed; *FV* stands for fair value; and *BV* stands for book value.

The calculation of goodwill or OCER might be influenced by the deferred tax asset or a deferred tax liability. According to IFRS 3, the deferred tax should be included in the value of the net assets which in the Eqs. 24.1 and 24.2 is represented by the expression in brackets (Maruszewska et al., 2019). Czech regulation chose different approach, where the deferred tax is recognized through other retained earnings, independently on goodwill or OCER calculation. Still there is an anecdotal evidence that some entities opt for IFRS approach instead of the approach prescribed by the Czech national regulation of financial reporting. In our research, we will examine whether the calculation of goodwill or OCER was influenced by the deferred tax through goodwill or OCER calculation simulation on data gathered from the financial statements of the entities participating in the transaction.

The calculation of the change of deferred tax as a result of a business combination is usually a difficult task due to the fact that it is often unclear how the net asset valuation (the "*V*" variable in the equations above) was determined. Valuation experts employ various valuation models, for example, DCF method, multipliers derived from the market stock prices, yield methods, or cost methods. While some of these methods are in fact able to take into account the temporary differences which give rise to deferred tax, other methods are not. Unfortunately, many valuation experts in the Czech Republic are not well acquainted with the deferred tax concept and thus pay little regard to this phenomenon (Jindra, 2012). For financial reporting professionals, it is then very difficult to understand whether the value of the net assets (business/corporation as a whole) provided by the valuation expert is a post-tax value or pre-tax value and whether the respective tax effects in the valuation model acknowledges the fact that the successor entity in the business combination is required by Czech tax law to adopt tax values of all assets acquired and liabilities assumed (Pelák, 2010). In our research, we examine whether the valuation experts address the issue of the deferred tax in their valuation reports explicitly and how do they include the deferred tax in their valuation models. Especially in the case of the cost valuation methods, we will analyze whether the resulting valuation was adjusted for the deferred tax liability or deferred tax asset. We expect to encounter three most common scenarios:

1. The valuation is not adjusted for the deferred tax at all.
2. The valuation is adjusted only for the deferred tax reported by the entity in its financial statements prior to the business combination.
3. The valuation is adjusted for the deferred tax which is calculated by the valuation expert based on the resulting valuation of the net assets.

For scenario 2, we check for the situations where there was no deferred tax recognized in the entity's financial statements prior to the business combination. There is an exception in the Czech accounting regulation for small entities which are not required to recognize deferred tax in their financial statements. Moreover, some entities might not report their deferred tax asset due to the prudence principle.

Our research pays special attention to the mergers following share deals in which the acquirer purchased 100% share in the target. Large portion of mergers takes place shortly after the share deal to finalize the acquisition process (Pospíšil & Vomáčková, 2018). Rather distinctive group of these "follow-up mergers" is represented by property transactions in the real estate sector. Until 2020, all property purchase transactions were subject to special property-transfer tax. To avoid this taxation, some corporations structured their property acquisitions through the business combinations. The seller first spin off the property to a special purpose entity which was then sold to the acquirer who carried out a merger shortly after in which the special purpose entity ceased to exist and its net assets (i.e., the property) transferred to the acquirer. These transactions are in fact the acquisition transaction even though they are carried out as a spin-off followed by a share deal and merger. Nevertheless, these transactions still do not meet the definition of business combination according to IFRS 3 as the goal here is to purchase a property rather than business. On the other hand, the calculation of the temporary differences and the deferred tax should be rather straightforward compared to the transactions with businesses.

The literature review shows that there is a controversy regarding the option to use the business combination to achieve fair value valuation of assets, especially in situations where the transactions take place between the parent entity and its subsidiary or related parties in general. Some claim that such accounting treatment should be allowed only for business combinations between (among) non-related parties, where true acquisition happens. Enabling this method for transaction under common control makes possible to recognize an unrealized gain in equity of the acquirer as a result of a mere reorganization (Vomáčková, 2013). Others claim that in the case of the follow-up mergers, the valuation of assets acquired at their fair value is legitimate as the follow-up merger simply completes the acquisition which in fact occurred at the preceding share deal.

Apart from the quantification of portion of all the transactions that can be considered as follow-up mergers, we examine whether the merger was structured in a way that allowed valuation of net assets at their fair value. Then we use this data to assess how frequent the revaluation of net asset helped the successor company to overcome the threshold set by Act no. 586/1992 Sb. for tax deductibility of loan interests. This rule limits the amount of tax-deductible interest from loans provided by a related party to the maximum of interest calculated from principal four times higher than the debtor's equity (Lukeš, 2020a, b).

Together with the aspect of the tax deductibility of the interest on the intra-group loan, we analyze how many entities taking part in the business combination took advantage of the option to extend their accounting period. By the means of extending accounting period (up to 24 months), entities also extend the period for tax returns and thus defer the actual tax payment day. This option might be misused by overlaying/linking more business combinations in a row (Lukeš, 2020a, b). In our research, we measure the length of the accounting period which corresponds to the periods for tax returns to find out whether some companies exploited this option.

In some cases, the revaluation of net assets might be necessary to finalize the business combination. This is often the case of mergers between parent and its subsidiary in which case the amount of the investment disclosed in the financial statements of the parent must be eliminated against the value of subsidiary's equity, fair value of subsidiary's net assets, respectively (Mikyska & Skálová, 2019). We identify all business combinations in the specified period of 2015–2019 which would not be possible without revaluation of the net assets which were transferred to the successor company. Then, we confront this information with our findings regarding the follow-up mergers, where revaluation might have economic substance and might increase the informative potential of the financial statements as opposed to business combinations under common control which are not considered follow-up mergers, where employing the revaluation option lacks economic substance, because in such cases there are no real acquisitions.

From our previous research work, we have gathered evidence that the accounting treatment used in some business combinations between parent and subsidiary does not comply with certain provisions of Act no. 125/2008 Sb. which require valuation experts to adjust their valuation by the value of the investment recognized in the financial statements of the parent entity. In our research, we also examine the frequency of cases where the valuation expert omits this adjustment.

Specifically, for spin-offs (from subsidiary to parent), we do have anecdotal evidence that in some cases the parent does not adjust the value of their investment in a subsidiary even though they have performed the spin-off through which a portion of the subsidiary's equity was transferred to the parent. In our research, we are going to verify this anecdotal evidence and quantify the share of transactions where such misstatement occurred.

24.3 Conclusion

This chapter discussed the current unclear practice of financial reporting for the effects of additional temporary differences arising during the business combinations like legal mergers and spin-offs in the Czech Republic. It has described the data gathering and research process for the research project in progress which aims to describe the current practice of deferred tax reporting in the context of business combinations using the descriptive analysis of the whole population of business combinations which occurred in the Czech Republic in the time span of 5 years (from 2015 to 2019). Since the amount of the deferred tax arising on the additional temporary differences can be rather significant in some transactions, various accounting treatments which currently remain without proper harmonization may often lead to creative accounting, window dressing, misstatements, and potential distortions in goodwill or equity valuation and recognition in the successor's financial statements. Successively, such misstatement could potentially lead to retained earning overestimation thus create opportunities to wrongful dividend payouts or to contribute to stock market bubbles forming.

At this point, there are no particular conclusions to be drawn since the research itself is still in progress. However, even at such an early stage, we have found and described several cases of mergers and spin-offs which were reported in the financial statements in the wrong way, even though the respective financial statements were audited. In some instances, such erroneous reporting enabled finalizing mergers which were badly structured and should have never been successfully finalized. We have also identified cases where mergers between parties under common control led to recognizing unrealized gain in the balance sheet of the "acquirer" which were distributed to the owners shortly after the finalization of the merger using the debt financing. Last but not least, we have found many transactions which either disregarded the deferred tax completely or, on the other hand, used the recognition of the deferred tax in a wrong way, which allowed the company to meet the debt-to-equity ratio of interest deductibility for income tax purposes.

I do expect that this research project will contribute significantly to the harmonization of reporting methods when dealing with the deferred tax during the business combinations, which shall lead to increased understandability and comparability of the financial statements of Czech entities. Hopefully, it will also assist in reaching a just tax regime in some problematic cases where the amount of deferred tax is significant, and the incorrect reporting might allow for favorable (and in some instances unjustified) corporate income tax regime.

Acknowledgments This chapter has been prepared within the research project "Empirická analýza účetního řešení podnikových kombinací a dopad na vypovídací schopnost účetních závěrek nástupnických společností" (supported by the Internal Grant Agency of Prague University of Economics and Business, No. F1/41/2021).

References

Bajgerová, P. (2016). Odložená daň podle IFRS a českých předpisů pro oblast nemovitostí. *Auditor, 19*(4), 20–22.

Jindra, M. (2012). Rychlý exkurz do problematiky odložené daně při různých metodách ocenění aktiv. *Auditor, 19*(4), 22–24.

Lukeš, J. (2020a). Řádné ekonomické důvody realizace fúzí z pohledu daňového práva a ekonomie. *Český finanční a účetní časopis, 15*(2), 27–42.

Lukeš, J. (2020b). Řetězení přeměn. *Bulletin Komory daňových poradců ČR, 51*(4), 51–54.

Maruszewska, E. W., Strojek-Filus, M., & Pospíšil, J. (2019). An empirical examination of accounting comparability: Goodwill recognition and disclosure in selected Central European countries. *Acta Universitatis Agriculturae et Silviculturae Mendelianae Brunensis, 67*(5), 1309–1323.

Mikyska, P., & Skálová, J. (2019). An analysis of the influence of mergers on the economic situation of a successor company in the finance and the insurance sectors. In *Global versus local perspectives on finance and accounting – 19th annual conference on finance and accounting (ACFA 2018)* (pp. 265–278). Springer.

Pelák, J. (2010). Problematika odložené daně ve fúzích z pohledu oceňování a účetnictví. *Český finanční a účetní časopis, 5*(4), 101–107.

Pelák, J. (2016). Odložená daň v konsolidaci. *Auditor, 23*(4), 12–15.

Pospíšil, J. (2020). Odložená daň při přeměnách a nepeněžitých vkladech. *Auditor, 27*(10), 14–26.

Pospíšil, J., & Strojek-Filus, M. (2017). Comparison of accounting for mergers in the Czech Republic and Poland. In *New trends in finance and accounting – Proceedings of the 17th annual conference on finance and accounting* (pp. 419–431). Springer International Publishing.

Pospíšil, J., & Vomáčková, H. (2017). Net assets valuation in transformations of Czech companies. *Journal of Applied Economic Sciences, 12*(7), 1906–1917.

Pospíšil, J., & Vomáčková, H. (2018). Business combinations of Czech companies: Empirical analysis of their typology. *Acta Universitatis Agriculturae et Silviculturae Mendelianae Brunensis, 66*(1), 313–323.

Skálová, J. (2019). *Účetní a daňové souvislosti přeměn obchodních společností.* Wolters Kluwer ČR.

Vomáčková, H. (2013). Oceňování a přeceňování při přeměnách (fúzích a rozdělování) obchodní společnosti a družstev v účetnictví v České republice. *Český finanční a účetní časopis, 8*(8), 110–113.

Chapter 25
The Specificity of the Accounting and Tax System and the Importance of a Limited Partnership on the Example of the Economy of the Republic of Poland

Artur Jastrzębowski and Marek Wierzbiński

Abstract This chapter aims to present the specifics of the operation of limited partnerships in Poland in terms of tax and accounting and to determine the attractiveness of this form of business for entrepreneurs.

At the beginning, the history of creation and contemporary understanding of the essence of a limited partnership are presented. Then, the authors focus on the conditions for the functioning of this legal form in the context of the specificity of the accounting system, with particular emphasis on concerns related to the recognition of the company's capital. The last part analyzes the actual level of use of a limited partnership form in Poland. The conducted analysis showed that the number of companies organized in this way is systematically growing in Polish conditions as well as capital-information gap.

The work is prepared with the use of literature analysis methods and Polish regulations regarding the functioning of companies. A detailed analysis of statistical data is made in the empirical part.

Key words Limited partnership company · Joint stock limited partnership company · Accounting of limited partnership company

A. Jastrzębowski (✉)
Department of Accounting and Financial Audit, Poznań University of Economics and Business, Poznań, Poland
e-mail: artur.jastrzebowski@ue.poznan.pl

M. Wierzbiński
Department of Management Accounting, Poznań University of Economics and Business, Poznań, Poland
e-mail: marek.wierzbinski@ue.poznan.pl

D. Procházka (ed.), *Regulation of Finance and Accounting*, Springer Proceedings in Business and Economics, https://doi.org/10.1007/978-3-030-99873-8_25

25.1 Introduction

Economic development began long before the invention of handwriting. As archaeological research shows, the first forms of economic records which confirm this date back to the fifteenth-century BC (Dobija, 1996). In turn, the first discovered regulations devoted to companies appeared in the Hammurabi Code (Lutz, 1917; Borden, 2008).

Social and technological changes have led to an increase in trade intensity, first locally and then globally. One of the stages of this process was associated with the creation of a characteristic form of cooperation – a limited partnership (Hendriksen et al., 2002).

Today, after nearly ten centuries, this structure is still used for business operations. And although such a long period of its use would suggest full knowledge of its specifics, changing regulatory conditions result in a periodic increase in the importance of this form of business organization. One of the geographical areas in which the advantages of using the company's personal form are being rediscovered is Eastern Europe, where entrepreneurs after liberation from the socialist system and stimulating their entrepreneurship still (despite the passage of over 30 years since the political transformation) are looking for the optimal legal form for their activities.

To get to know the specifics of how a business operates in the form of a limited partnership, it can be seen that so far research conducted researches focuses mainly on approximating the tax conditions of operation in limited partnership companies. The expression of this statement is the observations of B. Wells (Pass-Through 2013) or Ch. Trump and M. Graham (in search 2015), who said that in the world literature on corporate taxation, more and more attention is paid to limited partnership form, while pointing out that this is one of the most difficult areas of tax law for regulation.

This problem is due to the fact that taxation of partnerships is not uniform in individual countries (Easson & Thuronyi, 1998). In many countries, partnerships have been recognized as legal entities, as a consequence of becoming corporation taxpayers with corporate tax (Blanchard, 2015). For example, partnerships in countries such as Brazil, Mexico, France, and the Scandinavian countries are recognized as companies with legal personality, but in Germany or Poland, they are no legal entities (Easson & Thuronyi, 1998).

The approach represented by the second of the mentioned groups of states assumes that the company should be treated as a group of individual entrepreneurs (aggregate theory), which results in taxation of income from participation in the company at the level of partners, and that is why taxation of partners is one of the main advantages offered by tax law for this type of business (McKee et al., 1977).

It should be noted that tax issues also naturally affect the aspects of managing an entity's assets. For example, research carried out in previous years (Guenther, 1992; Shaw & Weir, 1993; Gentry, 1994) showed that limited partnerships have a smaller percentage share of debt in capital compared to capital units. The reasons for this are seen in the more favorable impact of debt in the tax aspect of capital companies (Jaffe, 1991; Scholes & Wolfson, 1991).

Also other areas of the organization of the company's operations are modified as a result of the impact of the legal and economic characteristics of the limited partnership. From the point of view of this study, changes in the company's accounting system are most interesting. The analysis of literature allows to identifying key areas of the interaction of the limited partnership structure, which includes problems with (Weygandt et al., 2010):

- Contribution of fund.
- Contribution of other than funds.
- Withdrawal of funds.
- Withdrawal of assets.
- Allocation of profit or loss.
- Tax reporting and booking.

Problems with the correct representation of the specificity of limited partnerships in the accounting system can be observed by analyzing the interest of the accounting practitioners in Poland to gain knowledge on this subject. The Chart 25.1 below presents a summary of the total number of participants in accounting training of limited partnerships in 2015–2019 years, carried out by one of the authors of this chapter on behalf of the Accountants Association in Poland.[1]

As shown, interest in the subject of the correct recognition of economic events in the books of accounts is steadily growing. Nevertheless, question should be asked whether this trend is a consequence of the growing number of companies operating in the form of a limited partnership.

As a result, the purpose of the chapter is to present the specifics of the operation of limited partnerships in Poland in terms of tax and accounting and to determine the

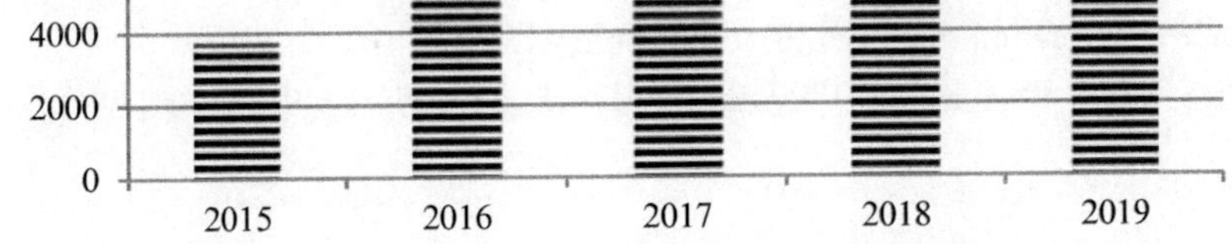

Chart 25.1 Number of persons trained in accounting of limited partnerships in AAP centers. (Source: Own study)

[1] Also known as AAP.

attractiveness of this form of business for entrepreneurs by quoting national statistics on the shares of this legal form in general for enterprises operating in the territory of the Republic of Poland.

Finally, the work is divided into three parts covering the presentation of the essence of a limited partnership, the term accounting, and tax issues related to this legal form and determining its attractiveness to investors.

The first part presents the current state of regulations regarding the operation of limited partnerships in Poland. It was determined that, similar to the research cited above, the main focus of interest in partnerships in Poland is on the tax area. Neither entrepreneurs nor the legislator pay due attention to the impact of the legal form of a limited partnership company on other aspects of business, including the accounting system.

A detailed analysis of accounting and tax law in Poland has shown in the next part that problems identified in international literature regarding limited partnerships are also present in the Polish legal system. In particular, the authors drew attention to the doubts regarding the correct presentation of owner's contributions, especially in the event of a discrepancy at the time of establishment of the company. Further discussed is the issue of payments from the company already made during the financial year, without having information on the value of annual profit. In such a situation, often these payments are not proportional to the share in the profits of the shareholders specified in the company contract. Another aspect that distinguishes the accounting of partnerships from capital companies is the need to record payments of taxes and social security liabilities regarding owners paid directly from the company's account. By analogy, there is the problem of regulating other private liabilities from owners from the company's account. It was finally determined that the identified problems in the accounting system arising in limited partnerships are analogous as in other entities of this type operating outside Poland.

As part of the empirical study, the increase in the interest of accounting departments in the problems associated with the recognition of selected economic operations in limited partnerships with the number of limited partnerships operating in Poland was confronted. The presented data shows that the number of companies operating on the basis of a limited partnership is systematically growing in Poland; thus, it has been shown that despite the existing vulnerabilities in the area of accounting, the benefits of using this form of conducting business are more important for entrepreneurs than identifiable problems.

The chapter uses the method of analyzing literature and critical analysis of primary study data.

25.2 The Essence of a Limited Partnership

The conquest of Jerusalem by the Turkish army and (consequently) the organization of the Crusades increased interest in maritime trade in the region of the Mediterranean. On the one hand, war expedition participants from Europe needed means of transport and supply channels; on the other hand (parallel to the ongoing warfare), trade between Italian cities and the Middle East developed (Hendriksen et al., 2002).

The growing scale of business ventures was associated with the need to raise additional capital. A single merchant was not able to cover all costs of the expedition. Moreover, high profits were closely connected with increasing risk. The result of the abovementioned situation was the creation of first capital companies – *commenda*. In character, they corresponded to modern limited partnerships (Hendriksen et al., 2002).

Originally, a limited partnership was a tool enabling the cooperation of people with various interests: persons, who are willing to invest specific capital in the venture, but not interested in incurring own work and risk, as well as persons, who do not have their own capital (or who do not have adequate capital to undertake the project) but willing to engage their work in the venture and take the risk in the event of its failure. The former are referred to as limited partners, and the latter are general partners.

The asymmetry of liability is the most characteristic feature of a limited partnership – one of the partnerships with operating principles determined in the Polish Commercial Companies Code (Journal of Laws of 2019, item 505).[2] As already mentioned, a limited partnership includes (at least) two entities with different scopes of competences and also responsibilities. However, the role of a limited partnership has changed over the centuries. Nowadays, this form of business activity is popular primarily due to the possibility of optimizing the risk of the business and the level of its taxation. However, entrepreneurs deciding on this form of business forget about its impact also on other aspects of the entity's area, including the accounting system.

According to entrepreneurs, economic activity should be characterized by two features: low risk and low taxation. Low risk is ensured by capital companies, in which the liability of shareholders is limited to the amount of invested funds. Unfortunately, limited companies require double taxation of income. On the other hand, single taxation of income is possible in partnerships – however, it is usually connected with the full liability of partners for the partnership's obligations. A hybrid of advantages observed in a limited company and a partnership is a limited partnership, in which the general partner is a limited company – usually a limited liability company. It is a general partner with assets (and also risk level) limited by setting the share capital at a level acceptable to shareholders. Simultaneously, the PCCC (Journal of Laws of 2019, item 505) makes it possible to determine the proportion of profit distribution among partners in any way – hence, an adversely taxed partner (twice taxed), i.e., a limited liability company, can receive a marginal share in profits, and in the case of natural persons, who are favorably taxed (once), share in profits is higher.

[2] Also as PCCC.

As mentioned, the growing popularity of this structure brings many application problems for accountants, both in terms of taxes and accounting. Analysis of the content of legal acts regulating accounting issues leads to the conclusion that they mainly focus on capital companies, without paying sufficient attention to partnerships.

For example, the Polish Code of Commercial Companies characterizes capital of a limited partnership in a very reserved way, while issues related to capitals of limited liability companies and joint stock companies are extensively regulated in this legal act. In the entire section III, title II of the Polish Code of Commercial Companies (Journal of Laws of 2019, item 505, chapter III), dedicated to limited partnerships; the phrase "capital" is not mentioned even once. In matters not covered in this party, the CCC refers to the provisions of a general partnership. Section I stipulates that the partner's equity interest corresponds to the value of the actually contributed funds (Journal of Laws of 2019, item 505, Article 50 section 1). In the face of such limited regulations in business practice, many doubts arise around the principles for recognizing and creating equity of limited partnerships. There is a question whether this lack of regulation gives partners a broad spectrum of actions in the area of creating individual capitals or on the contrary – it limits their possibilities.

The Polish Accounting Act (Journal of Laws of 2019, item 351)[3] notes the fact of the existence of partnerships (including limited partnerships) in regulations concerning registration obligations but in no way refers to their specificity by regulating specific issues connected with the recording of assets and liabilities, revenues, and costs. No national (or international) accounting standard dedicated to partnerships has been developed yet.

In Poland, tax law acts seem to pay the most attention to partnerships, but it is worth nothing that the majority of provisions in income tax acts refer to the partners of these companies rather than to the companies themselves. Act on tax from civil legal actions (Journal of Laws of 2019, item 1519) regulates the issues of taxation of partnerships in a special way. It sets out for them a wide range of activities "change of articles of association," which translates into, for example, the application of 0.5% rate to a loan granted to a partnership by its partner, with standard taxation of loan agreements at a rate of 2% or the exemption from such a tax in the case of a loan granted to a capital company by its shareholder.

In the rest of the chapter, the authors' attention will be focused on issues related to the specificity of accounting in limited partnerships.

[3] Also as AA.

25.3 Accounting System of Limited Partnerships

As has been mentioned, the following problem areas of limited partnership accounting are identified in international literature (Weygandt et al., 2010):

- Contribution of fund.
- Contribution of other than funds.
- Withdrawal of funds.
- Withdrawal of assets.
- Allocation of profit or loss.
- Tax reporting and booking.

In Polish business reality, limited partnership company is obliged to keep accounting books, regardless of the volume of its turnover; it is not covered by the limit of 1.200,000 EUR provided for (inter alia) general partnerships and limited liability partnerships (Journal of Laws of 2019, item 351). However, the status of a limited partnership does not exclude it from the possibility of being classified as micro entities (Journal of Laws of 2019, item 351, Article 3, section 1a) or a small unit (Journal of Laws of 2019, item 451, Article 3, section 1c), provided that the restriction determined for such units is met: sales revenues, total assets, and average annual employment. The possibility of treating a limited partnership as a micro or small unit gives it the opportunity to take advantage of certain simplifications, including the possibility of preparing financial statements according to the formulas determined in Annexes No. 4 and 5 to the Act (Journal of Laws of 2019, item 351).

It is also worth indicating that until the end of 2015, limited partnerships were exempted from the obligation to prepare an activity report. From 2016, such a report must be prepared by, among others, general partnerships and limited partnerships with partners (having unlimited liability) in the form of capital companies. If a limited liability company is a general partner in a limited partnership (currently this is a common procedure), limited partnerships must also draw up a report about their activities. However, if such a company is classified as micro or small entity, it may benefit from the exemption pursuant to Article 49, Section 4 or 5 (Journal of Laws of 2019, item 351).

Pursuant to the PCCC (Journal of Laws of 2019, item 505), a limited partnership is established only upon entry in the register. In the case of using the option of creating a limited partnership electronically, this is a shorter period of time – however, in the case of establishing a company in a traditional manner, in the notary's office, at least a few weeks pass from the moment of signing the association to obtaining the entry in the National Court Register. There is not a limited partnership in the process of formation. Therefore, accounting books of a limited partnership are opened on the date of its entry in the register, and not on the date of the articles of association.

The limited partnership agreement specifies the amount of the commandite sum and the amount of partners' contributions. The commandite sum is the limit of material liability of limited partners for the company's obligations – it is not included in the company's accounting books, because it does not (at least until the company's insolvency) bring real cash flows. The matter of contributions to a limited partnership looks different. In the company's agreement, partners specify contributions, but there is no need to pay them at the time of conclusion of the articles of association. In practice, it turns out that the coverage of contributions is often deferred. This situation is anticipated by the CCC (Journal of Law od 2019, item 505), indicating in Article 123 section 2 that the profit attributable to a limited partner for a given financial year is allocated primarily to supplement his contribution to the value of the agreed contribution. In the event of a coincidence in the moment of establishment of the company and making contributions, contributions are recorded as share capital in correspondence with an adequate asset. However, booking of contributions to share capital is not indicated in legal provisions (the CCC does not regulate this situation – it was mentioned earlier), but it helps to fulfill the principles of a faithful and reliable picture: share capital constitutes a "founding" source of financing.

The problem in terms of presentation arises in the event of discrepancies in the moments of company's establishment and making contributions. Content of Article 123 section 1 of the CCC (Journal of Laws of 2019, item 505), according to which "a limited partner participates in the company's profit in proportion to his actual contribution to the company (. . .)" suggests that greater importance is attributable to actually made contributions than contractual contributions. Adopting this assumption would result in disclosing the value of contributions in share capital only at the time of making contributions. In these circumstances, until the total contributions have been made, the value of share capitals indicated in the balance sheet would be lower than the value of the agreed contributions. This is a rather conservative approach.

However, when looking for analogies to capital companies during the analysis of the content of AA (Journal of Laws of 2019, item 1519), attention should be paid to Article 36 section 2, according to which "the share capital of capital companies (. . .) is presented in the amount specified in the agreement or statute and entered in the court register. Declared, but unpaid capital contributions are recognized as due contributions to capital." Pursuant to this provision, the value of contributions (agreed in full as share capital) should be recognized, while the unpaid part of contributions should be understood as due contributions to the share capital. However, this provision applies directly to capital companies – not partnerships. Therefore, there is no obligation to use it in limited partnerships.

In these circumstances, the accounting policy is an essential that enables to keep accounting books. It is an internal document, in which the company regulates its accounting principles (in areas not regulated by law) or in which its right to choose is left. According to the authors, in the case of entities such as partnerships (specific in terms of accounting, and simultaneously marginally treated by the balance sheet law), the accounting policy plays a special role.

When it comes to choosing between the options for the presentation of contributions shown in Table 25.1, the authors are (rather) inclined to the second method – i.e., a separate recognition of contributions agreed in share capital and unpaid contributions as due contributions to share capital. However, the final decision is made by units.

Table 25.1 Variants of the presentation of contributions in a limited partnership

Variant I			
Assets		Liabilities	
		Share capital	8.000
Variant II			
Assets		Liabilities	
Due contributions for share capital	7.000	Share capital	15.000

Source: Own research
Explanations:
8.000 – contributions actually made
15.000 – agreed contributions

Another specific feature of a limited partnership is the method of settlement with partners. A limited partnership makes a profit. It is not an income taxpayer – partners in a limited partnership are taxpayers. Therefore, regardless of the fact of transferring profits to partners, they must deduct from the company's profit an appropriate income tax: from natural persons or legal persons. Furthermore, natural persons, who are partners in a limited partnership, are subject to the obligation to pay social security and health insurance contributions (just like natural persons conducting non-agricultural economic activity). This is connected with the creation of demand for cash enabling (at least) the realization of these public law obligations. Moreover, partners usually expect cash flows that ensure current functioning. Pursuant to Article 52 section 1 of the CCC (Journal of Laws of 2019, item 505) (relating directly to a general partnership), a partner may request the distribution and payment of the total profit at the end of each financial year. However, the CCC does not exclude the possibility of making advance payments for profit – it remains a discretionary issue whether the payment of an advance is an activity that reaches beyond the scope of the ordinary activities of the company and requires a resolution of partners – pursuant to Article 121 section 2 of the CCC (Journal of Laws of 2019, item 505).

The most desirable action (taking into account the opinion of accountants) would be to adopt a resolution about the distribution of the generated profit and to make its payment after approval of the annual financial statements. However, in business practice, it is most often a fiction – partners usually pay out money from the company during the financial year – often (unfortunately) these payments are not proportional to the share in profits of partners specified in the articles of association, and (what is worse) in many cases, they are paid despite the lack of profit in the company. Furthermore, many partners pay taxes and liabilities to the National Healthcare Fund (ZUS) directly from the company's account. This is inappropriate action, because the company has no title to be a payer in these relations. Despite the fact that the Tax Code (Journal of Laws of 2009, item 900) provides in Article 62b section 1 the possibility of paying tax by another entity, the amount of tax (in this case) is limited to 1.000,00 PLN. However, it is worth nothing that funds paid by another entity should constate taxpayer's funds. If a company makes payments, we can say about this situation (at the earliest) when it has made a profit and the agreed contributions have been fully paid up – i.e., when the partner has the right to any claims against the company. In extreme cases, despite the payment to the tax office's account, the partner's tax liability may be considered as unregulated.

Disbursement of funds or payment of private obligations by partners is another type of operations specific to a partnership. Their accounting method requires special attention. In this case, several variants should be considered:

- Treating disbursed funds as a write-off from net profit during the financial year.
- Treating disbursed funds (until the resolution on distribution of profit) as receivables from partners.

It is worth nothing that the partner, who keeps accounting books, must solve a similar dilemma (this problem usually concerns a limited liability company acting as a general partner) – when it is necessary to recognize income from participation in profits – at the time of receipt of cash or at the time of adopting the resolution (and until that time the received funds should be treated as a liability). Due to the fact that, according to the authors, the behavior of both parties should be convergent in this respect – the aspect of a partner will also be included in considerations.

The Polish Accounting Act (Journal of Laws of 2019, item 351) does not regulate the above issue in detail, but in unregulated matters, it gives the possibility to use the content of the regulations of the International Financial Reporting Standards. IAS 18 "Revenue" (Iasplus.com, 2020, point 30c) indicates that dividends are recognized at the time of determining the rights of shareholders to receive them. The use of the content of the provision in relation to a limited partnership and partners would lead to the adoption of variant II. However, it is worth paying attention to the definition of revenue presented in the AA, according to which the revenue constitutes a "probable emergence of economic benefits of a reliably determined value, in the form of an increase in the value of assets within a certain period" (Journal of Laws of 2019, item 351, Article 3, section 1, point 30). Special attention should be paid to the word "probable." According to the authors, when deciding about the fact of recognition of revenue during the receipt of cash, we should indicate the probability, with which the disbursed funds will actually remain at the partner's disposal. This (in turn) depends, among others, on:

- Making a profit in the company.
- Profit disbursement policy in the company.
- Ratio of disbursed and achieved profits.
- Profits expected until the end of the financial year.
- Coverage of agreed contributions.

Therefore, it should be determined by the entity. In the event that the partner will be entitled to a profit in the amount at least corresponding to the disbursed profit and the partner will not be obliged to return the collected funds, recognition of income already at the time of receiving funds seems justified. Similar arguments should be used in order to determine the disbursed funds by a limited partnership as "write-offs from profit during the financial year."

If the above conditions do not apply, a limited partnership should determine the disbursed funds as "other receivables" and the partner as "other liabilities."

If the recognition of financial revenues (for the partner) already at the moment of receiving funds (not at the moment of adopting a resolution about the disbursement of profit) may be questioned with a more radical interpretation of the precautionary principle, determination of the disbursed funds in a limited partnership as "write-offs" is more in line with the precautionary regulations than their recognition as "other receivables." "Write-offs from profit" are an item indicating that funds have been disbursed from the company and their return is not expected. On the other hand, the item called "other receivables" suggests that cash flows for the company should be expected in the near future. Determination of the method of presentation of disbursements from profit is another issue that requires clarification in the entity's accounting policy.

Due to the specifics of tax settlement in a limited partnership, according to which different income tax is calculated for different partners, the chart of accounts should be properly designed in order to organize income and expense data in a manner that enables to determine the tax base for partners. In a limited partnership, we need to talk about adjustments to accounting results at two levels: limited partnership and partners. The majority of revenues and costs included in accounting books of a limited partnership will constitute tax revenues and costs for all partners. However, next to them – there are also revenues and costs that will not constitute tax for any of the partners (e.g., costs of representation of unpaid remuneration connected with civil law contracts). The third group of accounting revenues and costs of a limited partnership will include revenues and costs, which are taxable only for some partners (e.g., interest paid to the partner, costs of the partner's remuneration). Adequate preparation of the chart of accounts enables to separate result categories from each group.

To sum up the above considerations, it can be stated that despite the specifics of the Polish tax system, accounting problems related to the recognition of economic operations occurring in limited partnerships are analogous to those identified in international literature. The final solutions largely depend on national tax regulations.

25.4 Data and Methodology

As mentioned above, the construction of limited partnerships has been known since the beginning of shaping joint economic ventures. This form has its own specific procedures and recording schemes within the framework of the accounting system, which cause reasonable doubts as to their correct listing in the books of accounts. Therefore, the question arises whether the benefits identified outweigh the problems and translate into interest in this form on the part of investors.

The purpose of the study conducted for the needs of this chapter is to determine the attractiveness of the legal form of a limited partnership for the purposes of conducting business activity under the conditions of the Polish legal system.

The study was divided into two stages:

- Determination of the change in the attractiveness of this form of business activity among Polish entrepreneurs.
- Presentation of characteristic features of entities deciding to select this form of business activity.

The following analysis is based on source data collected and prepared by the Central Statistical Office in Poland within the framework of the primary research called "Structural changes in groups of entities of the national economy in the REGON register, 2018," published in 2019.

This study presents an analysis of entities from the national economy in the REGON register[4] with the specification of the number of newly registered entities and removed entities (according to selected characteristics), including legal forms – in the years 2009–2018.

25.5 Results and Discussion

Determination of the attractiveness of a limited partnership form for investors was examined by determining the changes in the number of limited partnerships and limited joint-stock partnerships (Chart 25.2).

According to the obtained information, over the decade, there has been no significant change in the number of entities operating within the Polish economic area. However, the number of entities systematically increased – from approx. 3.7 million entities at the end of 2009 to approx. 4.3 million on the last day of 2018. This tendency is consistent with changes observed in the national economy, expressed in changes in the gross domestic product (presented in the Chart 25.3 below).

Therefore, it can be assumed that the increase in the number of partnerships is a response to beneficial internal and external factors stimulating economic development in Poland.

However, it should be emphasized that investors deciding to start a new business activity are not limited to only one type of organization. Chart 25.4 presents the division into basic categories – including personal, commercial, and other forms.

As indicated in the above data, although (in Polish conditions) the economic activity in terms of the adopted legal form is dominated by entities, who are natural persons conducting business activity, it can be seen that the share of companies subject to the regulations indicated in the Code of Commercial Companies increases.

[4]Register of Polish enterprises.

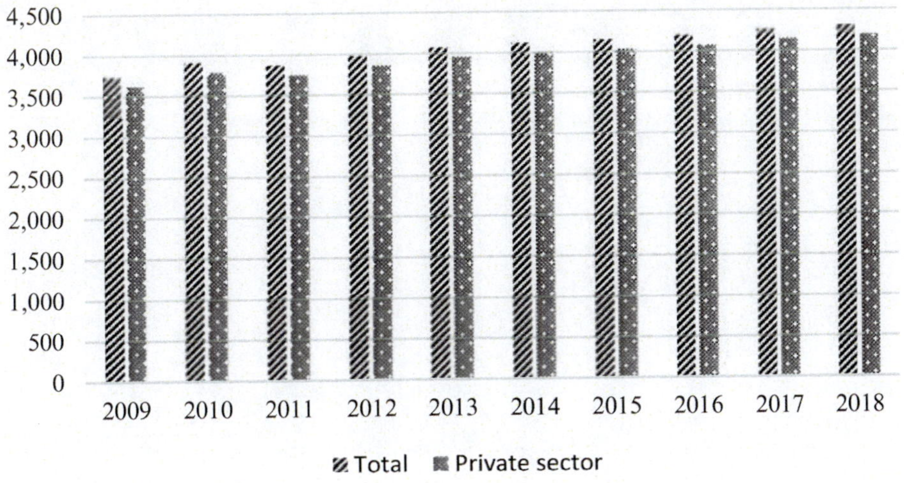

Chart 25.2 Number of entities registered in Poland (in thousands). (Source: Own research based on GUS, 2019)

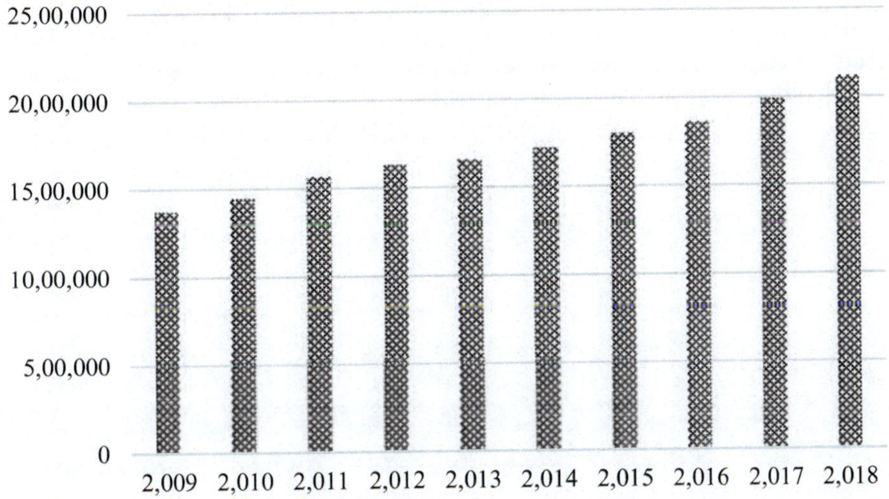

Chart 25.3 Gross domestic product in Poland (in million PLN). (Source: Own research based on GUS, 2020)

The discussed limited partnerships and limited joint-stock partnerships are included in the category of commercial companies. What is important is their share within this group is successively increasing (as shown below) (Chart 25.5).

The total number of limited partnerships and limited joint-stock partnerships increased from approx. 6000 entities at the end of 2009 to 40,000 on the last day of 2018. In other words, due to the attractiveness of this form of business activity in Poland, the increase in this type of companies amounted to over 65% in the years 2009–2018.

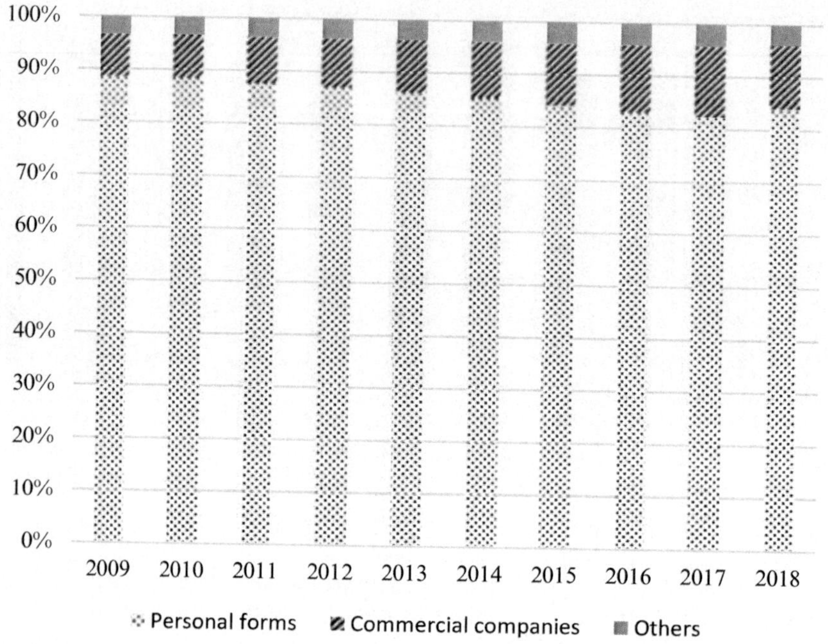

Chart 25.4 Share of organization forms for enterprises in Poland. (Source: Own research based on GUS, 2019)

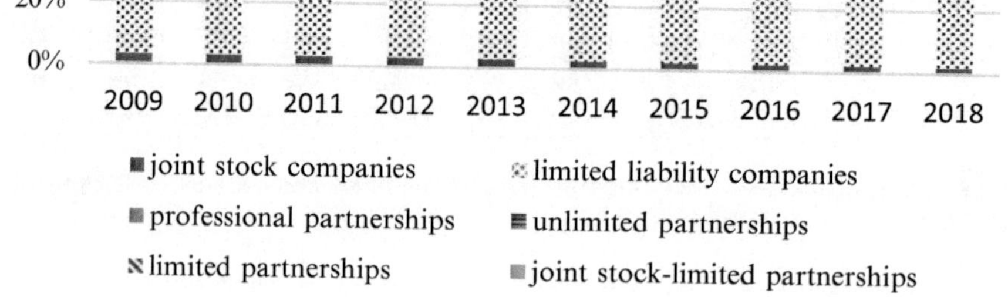

Chart 25.5 Share of partnership forms in the structure of Polish companies. (Source: Own research based on GUS, 2019)

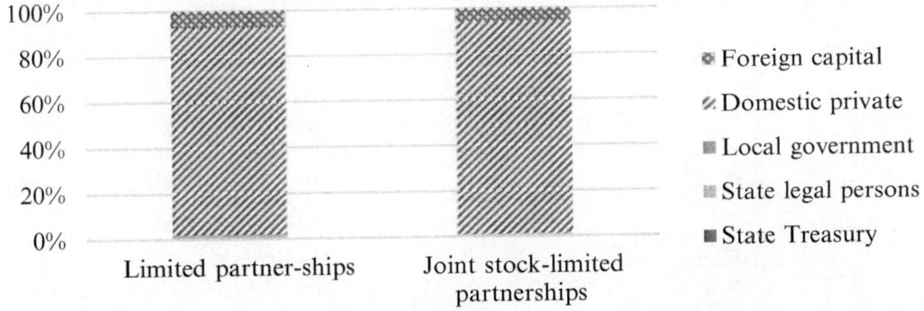

Chart 25.6 Structure of shareholders in limited partnerships in Poland. (Source: Own research based on GUS, 2019)

The next stage of the research is to determine the type of investors interested in being involved in this form of business activity. The data collected as of December 31, 2018 by the Central Statistical Office (CSO) presents that both the case of limited partnerships and limited joint-stock partnerships, the main type of capital providers, are domestic private entities (see Chart 25.6). It should be mentioned that this shape of the ownership structure is a logical consequence of the benefits mentioned in the previous points, with particular emphasis on tax benefits.

The last element in the analysis is to determine whether the polarization is equally strong in relation to branches of the Polish economy (Chart 25.7).

Data analysis does not enable to (clearly) indicate the area of activity that would dominate among units operating as limited partnerships or limited joint-stock partnerships. Two largest groups are units from the building and trade industries. This information can be connected with the overall industry structure of Polish enterprises presented in Chart 25.8. As can be seen, the division into areas of the national economy of all enterprises is similar to the structure within the framework of limited partnership and limited joint-stock partnership structures. In other words, the choice of this form of business activity is not dependent on the industry, in which the company operates.

The conducted empirical research indicates that the interest of entities to implement business plans as a part of limited partnerships and limited joint-stock partnerships systematically grows on the Polish market. Additionally, an in-depth analysis shows that this legal form is preferred by private entities, which can realize specific benefits, including tax optimizations. However, it should be noted that there is a lack of connection between the industry, in which the entity operates, and the usefulness of solutions functioning within the framework of limited partnerships and limited joint-stock partnerships.

In other words, the benefits presented in this chapter (in particular tax benefits) in the eyes of Polish entrepreneurs outweigh the problems appearing in the accounting records and arising from the adopted form of conducting business as a limited partnership.

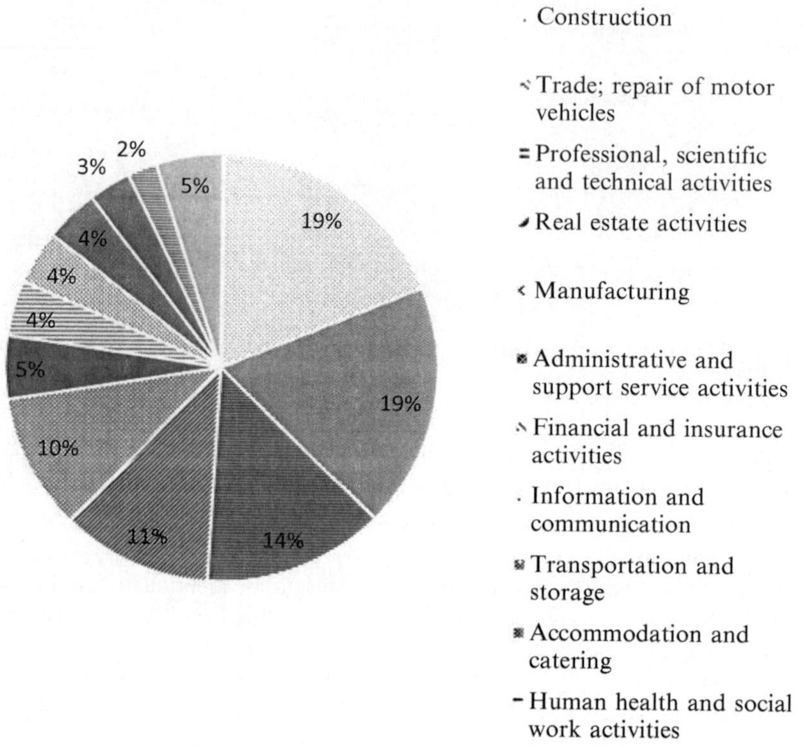

Chart 25.7 Division of Polish limited partnerships according to the criterion of economic areas. (Source: Own research based on GUS, 2019)

25.6 Conclusion

The purpose of the chapter was to present the specifics of the operation of limited partnerships in Poland in terms of tax and accounting and to determine the attractiveness of this form of business for entrepreneurs.

A limited partnership is a form of business activity rapidly developed in the Middle Ages. It naturally combines the involvement of one partner with the financial capabilities of the other partner.

In the sphere of accounting, doubts primarily arise in terms of the recognition of the partnership's capital. However, possible problems in the case of entities operating in the territory of Poland are compensated by attractive relations between business security and tax burdens.

Attractiveness of this form of business activity was confirmed at the stage of empirical research. The conducted analysis showed that the number of companies organized in this way is systematically growing in Polish conditions.

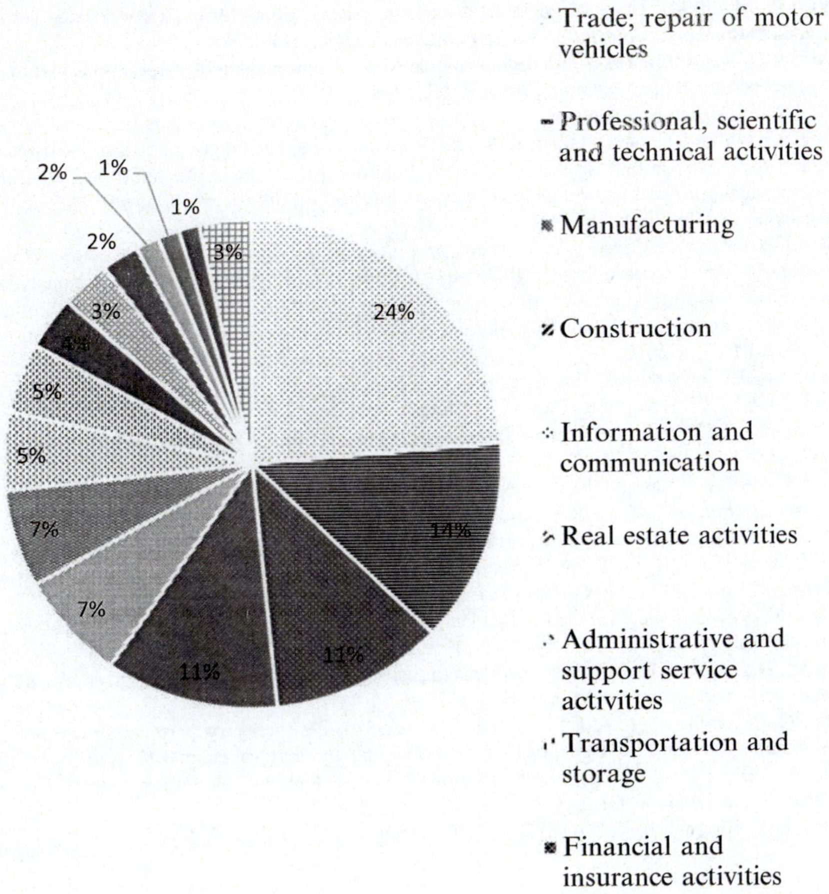

Chart 25.8 Division of Polish companies according to the criterion of economy's areas. (Source: Own research based on GUS, 2019)

References

Act of 15.09.2000 – Code of Commercial Companies, Journal of Laws of 2019, item 505.

Act of 29.08.1997 – Tax Code, Journal of Laws of 2019, item 900.

Act of 29.09.1994 – Accounting Act, Journal of Laws of 2019, item 351.

Act of 9.09.2000 – Tax on civil law transaction, Journal of Laws of 2019, item 1519.

Blanchard, K. (2015). *The tax significance of legal personality* [online]. Available at https://www.law.nyu.edu/sites/default/files/upload_documents/Kimberly%20S.%20Blanchard2.pdf. Accessed 23 Apr 2020.

Borden, B. T. (2008). Aggregate-plus theory of partnership taxation. *Georgia Law Review, 43*, 717.

Dobija, M. (1996). Postępowe idee rachunkowości w cywilizacji sumeryjskiej. *Zeszyty Naukowe/Akademia Ekonomiczna w Krakowie, 467*, 5–18.

Easson, A., & Thuronyi, V. (1998). Fiscal transparency. *Tax Law Design and Drafting, 2*, 949.

Gentry, W. M. (1994). Taxes, financial decisions and organizational form: Evidence from publicly traded partnerships. *Journal of Public Economics, 53*(2), 223–244.

Guenther, D. A. (1992). Taxes and organizational form: A comparison of corporations and master limited partnerships. *Accounting Review, 67*, 17–45.

GUS. (2019). *Structural changes in groups of entities of the national economy in the REGON register* [online]. Central Statistical Office. Available at https://stat.gov.pl/obszary-tematyczne/podmioty-gospodarcze-wyniki-finansowe/zmiany-strukturalne-grup-podmiotow/zmiany-strukturalne-grup-podmiotow-gospodarki-narodowej-w-rejestrze-regon-2018-rok,1,23.html. Accessed 23 Feb 2020.

GUS. (2020). *Structural changes in groups of entities of the national economy in the REGON register [online]*. Central Statistical Office. Available at https://stat.gov.pl/obszary-tematyczne/podmioty-gospodarcze-wynikifinansowe/zmiany-strukturalne-grup-podmiotow/zmiany-strukturalne-grup-podmiotow-gospodarki-narodowej-wrejestrze-regon-2019-r-,1,24.html. Accessed 16 Mar 2020.

Hendriksen, E., Idzikowska, G., Jarugowa, A., & Van Breda, M. (2002). *Accounting theory* (pp. 59–60). PWN Scientific Publishing House.

Iasplus.com. (2020). *IAS 18 – Revenue* [online]. Available at http://www.iasplus.com/en/standards/ias/ias18. Accessed 23 Feb 2020.

Jaffe, J. F. (1991). Taxes and the capital structure of partnerships, REIT's, and related entities. *The Journal of Finance, 46*(1), 401–407.

Lutz, H. F. (Ed.). (1917). *Early Babylonian letters from Larsa* (Vol. 2). Yale University Press.

McKee, W. S., Nelson, W. F., & Whitmire, R. L. (1977). *Federal taxation of partnerships and partners* (Vol. 1). Warren, Gorham & Lamont.

Scholes, M., & Wolfson, M. (1991). *Taxes and business strategy: A global planning approach*. PrenticeHall.

Shaw, W. H., & Wier, H. A. (1993). Organizational form choice and the valuation of oil and gas producers. *Accounting Review, 68*, 657–667.

Trump, C., & Graham, M. (2015). In search of a normative theory of partnership taxation for international tax (or how we learned to stop worrying and love subchapter K). *Taxes, 93*, 123.

Wells, B. (2013). Pass-through entity taxation: A tempest in the tax reform teapot. *Houston Business and Tax Law Journal, 14*, 1.

Weygandt, J., Kimmel, P., & Kieso, D. (2010). *Accounting principles*. Wiley.

Chapter 26
The Origin of True and Fair View in the Czech Accounting

Marcela Zárybnická Žárová

Abstract True and fair view (TFV) has been introduced into the Czech accounting and reported only in 90s of last century, after changes in 1989. At the early 90s, debates concerning which of the basic accounting philosophies should be adopted and have been opened. Debates on strategies in accounting were primarily oriented on the introduction of accounting concepts from the 4th EC Directive as the Czech Republic focused on becoming a member of the EU. This chapter targets on the origin of TFV in the Czech accounting and brings overview of TFV understanding represented by different users of accounting information including the opinion of the Ministry of Finance in the Czech Republic.

Key words True and fair view · 4th EC Directive · Accounting regulation

26.1 Introduction

True and fair view (TFV) is traditionally associated with the UK accounting and accounting profession. TFV discussion is from time to time open in the UK, mostly against the background of the court case. In the 1980s, true and fair were seen to be relevant to the debate on creative accounting. More intensive debate has been open since 1990 not only in the UK but also in Continental Europe.

As this chapter concentrates on the origin of TFV in the Czech Republic, it is useful to divide the overview of literature concerning TFV into two separate parts: overview of TFV essential research in Europe, mainly in 90s of last century, and overview of TFV essential research in Czechoslovakia/Czech Republic after 1989 when accounting reform has been discussed.

M. Z. Žárová (✉)
Department of Financial Accounting and Auditing, Prague University of Economics and Business, Prague, Czech Republic
e-mail: zarova@vse.cz

D. Procházka (ed.), *Regulation of Finance and Accounting*, Springer Proceedings in Business and Economics, https://doi.org/10.1007/978-3-030-99873-8_26

26.1.1 Overview of TFV Essential Research in Europe

Application of TFV in the European Union has been extensively debated by leading researchers. Walton (1993) suggested that there may be possible to discuss TFV either as a legal residual clause: independent concept or general accepted accounting principle. Walton assesses the above-mentioned aspects of TFV separately and not in the mutual context. If TFV is a legal residuary, it will probably have little practical individual meaning. If TFV is an independent concept, then it may override all other aspects of the 4th EC Directive as incorporated into individual member state laws. As such it could have a vague, but powerful, independent meaning. If TFV is a principle, then users will keep within the generally accepted framework of their national law.

Another research that belongs under research in the 90s of the twentieth century is Nobes (1993) and Alexander (1993) debates on TFV. Nobes deals with the development of TFV requirement in the 4th EC Directive, and then the relevant effects of this element of the Directive on the laws and practices in EC member states. Alexander explores differences and nuances from language and translation viewpoint and also related to pre-Fourth Directive requirements and culture. The direct comments on Alexander contribution to TFV, whether TFV is or isn't the only overriding UK principle is written by Karel Van Hulle (1993), with a special stress on the fact that because TFV is incorporated into the accounting lay of all member states of the EC, it is a concept of the Community Law because of its inclusion in the EC Accounting Directive.

Abovementioned leading researchers are crucial for understanding the developments of TFV in Europe in 90s, but the discussion on TFV has suffered from the lack of empirical research.

Later research on TFV is prepared by Alexander and Jermakowicz (2006), which examines the implementation of the true and fair view requirement into the laws of Austria, Finland, Norway, and Sweden. It is found that three of the four countries depart from the wording of the appropriate language versions of the Fourth Directive. Alexander is the author of another discussion of the paper, where Eva Eberhartinger is co-author (2009). The authors of this chapter explored the issue of the TFV as an overriding principle within the European Union, via a legally based analysis of the relationship between EU and national laws. The true and fair override remains central to European Union Directives, and its importance was confirmed by the IASB in its 2007 revision of IAS 1 (see paras. BC 23–30). They (authors) applied the supremacy of European law to methods of incorporating TFV into national legislation, using Austria as a detailed case study.

26.1.2 Overview of TFV Essential Research in Czechoslovakia/Czech Republic

Research concerning TFV in Czechoslovakia or the Czech Republic was rather unique. One of the early notes concerning TFV can be found in the article of Schroll (1995), who described the newly organized accounting system in the Czech Republic, and TFV was mentioned as a basic feature of the new accounting system. As a part of academic systematic research on audit profession in the Czech Republic, TFV was examined by Sucher et al. (1996). Specific research papers, where TFV is subject to research, are only found in Sucher et al. (1996). This research paper concentrated upon incorporating the Fourth Directive into the local law, where there is requirement for financial statements to show TFV. Findings indicate that TFV varies in its significance in preparing and using financial statements in the Czech Republic.

In the comment on Alexander and Eberhartinger (2009) research study on TFV, prepared by Zelenková (2010), part of her comments concerning the previous article is done by Czech leading researcher Kovanicová (1996). Kovanicová published her explanation of TFV in one of the Czech economic newspapers to help the accounting profession to understand and apply TFV in practice.

26.2 True and Fair View in the EC 4th Directive and Methodology

26.2.1 True and Fair View in the EC 4th Directive

The origin of the TFV in the 4EC Directive may be traced in the UK. Rutherford (1985) summarized that in the UK, in 1900, the requirement to "exhibit a true and correct view of the state of the company's affairs" appeared in the UK Companies Act, and this requirement lasted until the Second World War. Later, the Committee on Company Law Amendment (The Cohen Committee) in its report (1945) recommended that Company Law should require a true and fair view rather than a true and correct view. TFV wording was suggested to the committee in a memorandum from the Institute of Chartered Accountants in England and Wales (ICAEW). Nobody objected. Very important is to note that TFV is undefined in the law.

The EC Directive on Accounting has appeared in three drafts 1972, 1974, and 1978. The first draft was published in OJ in January 1972.[1] There is no English version as the UK hasn't been an EC member state yet. Therefore, the original text in German is used in this chapter, as it was published in "Journal officiel des

[1] https://eur-lex.europa.eu/legal-content/DE/TXT/PDF/?uri=OJ:C:1972:007:FULL&from=EN

Communautés européennes," C 7, 28 Janvier 1972,[2] followed by short explanation in English. The draft EC 4th Directive was based on the 1965 German Aktiengesetz (Company Law).

The following text is the original one from the Official Journal. "ABSCHNITT ALLGEMEINE VORSCHRIFTEN Artikel 2 (1) Der Jahresabschluß besteht aus der Bilanz, der Gewinn- und Verlustrechnung und dem Anhang zum Jahresabschluß. Diese Unterlagen bilden eine Einheit. (2) Der Jahresabschluß hat den Grundsätzen ordnungsmäßiger Buchführung zu entsprechen. (3) Der Jahresabschluß ist klar und übersichtlich aufzustellen. Er hat im Rahmen der Bewertungsund Gliederungsvorschriften einen möglichst sicheren Einblick in die Vermögens-, Finanz- und Ertragslage der Gesellschaft zu geben." From the original draft EC 4th Directive from 1972, which was based on the 1965 German Aktiengesetz (Company Law), it is evident that TFV was not included.

The second draft EC 4th Directive from 1974 was issued after the UK joined the EC. In an explanatory memorandum,[3] it is said that: "The new wording has been drafted in response to the wishes of 'both the European Parliament and the Economic and Social Committee'." It brings out more clearly the essential principle that the annual accounts should be drawn up in such a way as to give a true and fair view of the position of the company. This principle implies that should the specific provisions of the Directive be of themselves insufficient to ensure that this objective is attained; the company will be legally obliged to provide further information. It has been possible to delete the reference to the principles of regular and proper accounting since the requirement of a true and fair view necessarily implies that such principles must be observed." The principle of regular and proper accounting in this draft that was based on the German Company Law was replaced by TFV.

This draft included TFV:

1. The annual accounts shall comprise the balance sheet, the profit and loss account, and the notes on the accounts. These documents shall constitute a composite whole.
2. The annual accounts shall give a true and fair view of the company's assets, liabilities, financial position, and results.
3. They shall be drawn up clearly and in accordance with the provisions of this Directive.

In the explanatory memorandum, it is said that TFV "brings out more clearly the essential principle that the annual accounts should be drawn up in such a way as to give a true and fair view of the position of the company."

My comment concerning two aspects: Firstly, majority of EC member states in 1974 were states from Continental Europe, where there is no tradition of using TFV. Secondly, the statement in the explanatory memorandum that says that this change is

[2] https://eur-lex.europa.eu/legal-content/EN/TXT/?uri=OJ:C:1972:007:TOC

[3] https://eur-lex.europa.eu/legal-content/EN/TXT/?qid=1582476009388&uri=CELEX:51974PC0191

in response to the wishes of "both the European Parliament and the Economic and Social Committee" seems to be a rather weak explanation of this radical change in using fundamental principles in accounting in community mostly based on regular and proper accounting.

As an explanation of TFV, introduction into the Directive on accounting is to strengthen the influence of the UK accounting profession, profession from the new EC member. The reason for export of TFV from Britain into the Continental Europe and British interest in true and fair is clarified by Nobes (1993). He notes that accounting establishment in the UK is seen interest in true and fair as a way of preserving British practice despite the detailed regulatory approach of the European Directives.

Final draft EC 4th Directive from 1978 included TFV in the Section 1 General provisions in Article 2:

1. The annual accounts shall comprise the balance sheet, the profit and loss account, and the notes on the accounts. These documents shall constitute a composite whole.
2. They shall be drawn up clearly and in accordance with the provisions of this Directive.
3. The annual accounts shall give a true and fair view of the company's assets, liabilities, financial position, and profit or loss.
4. Where the application of the provisions of this Directive would not be sufficient to give a true and fair view within the meaning of paragraph 3, additional information must be given.
5. Where in exceptional cases the application of a provision of this Directive is incompatible with the obligation laid down in paragraph 3, that provision must be departed in order to give a true and fair view within the meaning of paragraph (3). Any such departure must be disclosed in the notes on the accounts together with an explanation of the reasons for it and a statement of its effect on the assets, liabilities, financial position, and profit or loss. The member states may define the exceptional cases in question and lay down the relevant special rules.
6. The member states may authorize or require the disclosure in the annual accounts of other information as well as that which must be disclosed in accordance with this Directive.

Is the TFV in the EC 4th Directive only export of the UK accounting profession into the European Community? Among academic interpretation of TFV, the interpretation of TFV in Europe by Karel Van Hulle, a lawyer by training, and the Head of Unit at the European Commission (Directorate-General "Internal Market and Services"), is the most relevant. He contributed the debate concerning TFV not only as a DG at the European Commission but also as an academic. He published his opinion on TFV in the academic journal European Accounting Review (Van Hulle, 1993), where he stresses on the fact that TFV principle is a concept of Community Law because of its inclusion in the EC Accounting Directive.

The concept of TFV principle and its implications lies therefore with the European Court of Justice. Even though it is evident that the UK very much insisted on having this principle included in the 4th Directive, the acceptance of TFV by the other member states and its inclusion in a Community legal instrument, the interpretation of this principle can no longer come exclusively from UK law and practice. Van Hulle (1993) points out that although there are many similarities, between UK TFV and TFV in the 4th Directive, the context in which this principle is situated in the Community is different. Comparability and equivalence are the main objectives of the harmonization of accounting standards in the EC in 80s of the twentieth century. In order to achieve these objectives, the accounting directives combine rigidity (e.g., formats) with flexibility (e.g., options), and TFV principle adds an element of flexibility. This is highly desirable in an international context because of the socioeconomic, cultural, and legal differences between member states. Here it is pointed out that it is possible that annual accounts which are regarded as true and fair in one member state would not be interpreted as such in another member state. They would still be true and fair because of the environment in which they originate, but in order to be true and fair for the readers in another member state, some further explanations are no doubt required. This is the reason why the accounting directives require in many instances further information in the notes to the accounts. Van Hulle (1993) specifies that all legal systems in the EC contain general concepts of a similar nature which allow and indeed require an individual to adapt his behavior in certain cases and to derogate from a mechanical application of the law.

There is another threat, and that is abusing the TFV. In order to prevent from abusing the TFV override as a justification for bad forms of creative accounting, some restrictions were included in the accounting directive. In Section 1 General Provisions in Article 2 (4) EC 4th Directive, it is said that "Where the application of the provisions of this Directive would not be sufficient to give a true and fair view within the meaning of paragraph 3, additional information must be given." Therefore, derogations can be made only from specific provisions and only in exceptional case. In order to stress on the fact that it concerns only exceptional situations, it was understood that the mere application of the provision would normally bring about the true and fair view. Unfortunately, what is not pointed out directly in the Directive is that disclosure in the notes is required with justification and its effects. This could simplify the situation.

26.2.2 Methodology

The topic of this chapter is to investigate the origin of TFV in accounting system in the Czech Republic. TFV has no tradition in states of Continental Europe, where accounting systems are more or less connected with tax system. TFV, as a principle with origin in the UK, was then transferred into Continental Europe and as a part of Directive became requirement of Community Law. As this chapter analyzed legal requirements of drafts of accounting Directives published in Official Journal in 1972, 1974, and 1978, then information was compared. Therefore, the method of content analysis was used to analyze draft directives first, followed by the method of comparison in order to compare information from three accounting directives. The second part of the chapter on origin of TFV in the Czech accounting concerned interviews of six different groups of users of accounting information on two questions. Answers on questions were organized in the form of table where the method of content analyses was used.

26.3 True and Fair View in the Czech Accounting

26.3.1 True and Fair View Before 1989

Accounting and financial reporting, prior to fundamental political change in 1989, were subordinated to the requirements of the central planning system and reflected the diminished scope of financial management in centrally planned economy. The principal function of accounting became the provision of factual data to assess plan and to generate statistics for other planning-related purposes. Accounting generally required adherence to a prescribed chart of accounts and did not involve taking a view on the financial position of an enterprise. Therefore, financial reporting providing a true and fair view on financial performance of enterprises to the general public did not exist in the former Czechoslovakia before 1989 (Zarova, 2011). On the other hand, it is to be said that until 1953, the Czechoslovak accounting was influenced by the German accounting rules. This situation began to change after 1989 as the change to a market economy and privatization of enterprises proceeded.

26.3.2 True and Fair View After 1989

In the period of 2 years (1990–1992), the new Accounting Act was discussed and submitted to the Parliament. A complete reform of Czechoslovak accounting was undertaken, through the Accounting Act that came into effect on January 1, 1992. In common with other areas of institutional reforms, government was seeking, as far as possible, to ensure that new laws were consistent with those of the European Community (EC), so as to facilitate transition to full membership. New legislation was therefore influenced by EC accounting practices, particularly the Fourth and Seventh Directives on Company Law (Žárová, 2011). As both Directives include TFV, requirement as for TFV were incorporated into the Act on Accounting.

Newly structured accounting regulatory system in Czechoslovakia/Czech Republic was built under the characteristic features of the codified Roman law system. A characteristic feature of this accounting regulatory system is that financial reporting is regulated by law, which is too detailed on one hand, and on the other hand most legislators are not well informed about accounting concepts and technicalities of financial reporting. The Ministry of Finance remained the only regulator of accounting without the influence of accounting profession. The stock exchange is less important; companies obtain majority of their funds from banks and other financial institutions. Naturally, this regulatory system of accounting, the system where the Accounting Act is on the top of the regulatory hierarchy, is supplemented and completed by a number of other rules (Žárová, 2006), in the case of the Czech Republic, issued by the same institution of the government that provides the Act. Moreover, rules used to compute taxable profit were introduced directly into the accounting rules in order to simplify the consequent process of revising accounting data by financial authorities.

During the short period of preparation of the new accounting system (1990–1992), the following fundamental question was asked: which of the basic accounting philosophies should be adopted (Schroll, 1995)?

1. The Anglo-Saxon accounting system embracing the principle of the "true and fair view"
2. The German accounting system based on fulfilling legal requirements, in particular with respect to the taxation regulations (especially those for income tax)
3. The French accounting system representing a compromise between the Anglo-Saxon and German system

As Scholl mentioned (1995), the accounting academics supported the first approach. While there has been some experience with the German system as the Czech accounting system has been influenced by the German system until 1953, the German system was not chosen as a basis for accounting reform. The Ministry of Finance selected the French system. The argument for selecting of the French system was that a relatively high proportion of the French economy has been nationalized, and for this reason, the "Plan Comptable general" had been introduced. And therefore, it seemed to be the most acceptable approach for the Ministry of Finance to realize the accounting reform in Czechoslovakia based on the French system.

The dissolution of the Czech-Slovak Federation on December 31, 1992, and the successful completion of the first wave of "voucher" privatization were the most significant political and economic events in Czechoslovakia during 1992 (Zarova, 1999). A complete reform of Czechoslovak accounting was undertaken, through the Accounting Act that came into effect on January 1, 1992.

In change to a market economy and privatization of enterprises, providing a true and fair view on financial performance of enterprises to the general public increase in its importance. During the year 1992, the most significant political and economic events in the prior Czechoslovakia affected the accounting legislation and started to be first step of successful completion. A complete reform of Czechoslovak accounting was undertaken as government came with the Accounting Act on January 1, 1992.

New Act on Accounting applies to all legal entities and individual entrepreneurs engaged in business. It was modeled on Fourth Directive, and the Act tries to incorporate the concept of TFV. There were two research questions:

First question: What is the literal translation into English?
Second question: What do the words TFV signify for those implementing and using the Act on Accounting?

Official translation of article concerning TFV in Accounting Act from one of the leading Czech translation agencies is: "Accounting entities shall keep their books fully, conclusively and correctly to give true and fair view of the objects of accounting."

Conclusion from the research done by Sucher et al. (1996) is summarized in Table 26.1. Interviews took place between July 1992 and March 1995. Interviewers: directors in five industrial enterprises, partners in the "Big Six" audit firms, individuals in three investment funds, individual in one large bank, individuals at the Prague Stock Exchange, individual in a small accounting practice, a manager in a medium-sized accountancy firm, and the ministers responsible for drafting the legislation.

Table 26.1 Overview of answers to research questions

Interviewers	What they understand by TFV	How TFV will be interpreted in practice
Representatives of Accounting department at the MF	It is unlikely that the financial statements will show a TFV view, though they will be prepared in accordance with the Act	TFV allows a certain flexibility in financial reporting, but not at the expense of overriding other parts of the accounting legislation
Big Six	They were qualified to interpret TFV for their clients in such a matter as valuation of assets	They do not believe that Czech accountants and auditors would be able to interpret TFV properly Any of the Big Six audit firms will go beyond the law
Investment funds and a bank	They believe that the "Big Six" are uniquely qualified in ensuring accounts were TFV	The individuals concerned saw TFV as meaning "in compliance with law and the assets were fairly stated"
Czech accountants/ smaller firms of Czech accountants and auditors	Simplification so that the financial accounts agreed with the tax accounts	In some cases, it was unlikely that they will make any provisions against assets, and therefore they will ignore TFV. Taxation is considered as a much bigger issue than whether the accounts are TFV
Individual small companies	Different approaches: (a)to ignore the need to value assets to reflect their TFV as the provisions were not allowable for tax (small company); (b) TFV mean making proper valuation of assets and liabilities and that such provisions will be made (large company)	Different approaches: from ignorance of TFV to respecting TFV depending on the size of enterprise
Prague Stock Exchange	Accounts are correct and meet legal requirements in all aspects	TFV is meeting legal requirements in all aspects

Source: Own elaboration based on research (Sucher et al., 1996)

Important is to note that interviews took place between July 1992 and March 1995. Therefore, there was a short time to practice how to publish accounts under circumstances of inconsistencies in the legislation as to how accounts should be published. As Sucher said, "interpreting the significance of TFV for preparers and users of accounts in the Czech Republic, in a manner suggested by Walton (1991), is fraught with difficulty."

The development of the Czech Accounting system has been finalized before the Czech Republic joined the European Union (EU) in May 2004, where TFV is even defined as a separate article of the Act. Since January 2004, legislation framework was enhanced into three separate regulatory levels: Accounting Act, Decrees to Accounting Act, and Czech Accounting Standards (CAS). Accounting Act is prepared by the Ministry of Finance and approved by the Parliament; Decrees to Accounting Act and CAS are issued by the Ministry of Finance. On the other hand, the Ministry of Finance admits the possibility of the existence of a rule-making body since 2004 (Žárová, 2011), but not once was any professional body asked to do it. The last amendment of the Act on Accounting is a consequence of the Directive 2013/34/EU, which aims at designing and delivering regulation of the highest quality while respecting that the administrative burdens are proportionate to the benefits they bring. The Amended Act on Accounting came into force on January 1, 2017. There was not any revision of TFV position either in this amended Act or public debate on accounting reform prepared and published by the Ministry of Finance on the new concept of Accounting Act in the Czech Republic in 2020.

26.4 Conclusion

TFV has been incorporated into European accounting regulation, represented by EC Directives, namely, 4th and 7th EC Directive, only after the UK became the EC member state. Incorporation of TFV brought debate not only on the meaning of this principle into Community Law but also the debate of EC member states on how to translate the principle from English to the languages of EC member states. In the UK, TFV is part of the conceptual framework of accounting represented by accounting standards issued by FRC (Financial Reporting Council). Despite the similarities, there is one essential difference between principles within the conceptual framework and the true and fair requirements (Cook 1997). The latter is an explicit legal requirement and the former is not. Countries in which accounting regulation operates within legal structure need a fundamental principle, such as the obligation to give TFV as an explicit requirement of the law. An explanation of understanding the TFV within the Community accounting regulation was provided by the Head of Directorate-General for Internal market and services, K. Van Hulle, who published that the concept of TFV principle is a concept of the Community Law because of its inclusion in the EC Accounting Directive. As a Community Law, the interpretation of the TFV principle can no longer come exclusively from UK law and practice. Czech accounting as an example of a newly accessed EC member state who has obligation to transpose requirements of EC Directives into their law, among other things, had to cope with the requirements of introduction TFV in the Czech accounting in 90s of last century. This chapter brings information on origin of TFV in the Czech accounting and overview of representatives of practice how TFV was understood and how different groups of users of accounting translate principle from English. Five groups of representatives of practice were interviewed. From the overview research results, it is evident that research shows that there are differences in understanding of TFV between groups of users but even within the same group of users. The most serious differences in understanding TFV are from total ignorance of TFV through compliance with Act and mostly with tax law to respecting TFV as accounting principle mostly concerning valuation of assets.

Acknowledgments This chapter has been prepared within the research project: Institutional Support of Research Activities IP100040.

References

Alexander, D. (1993). A European true and fair view? *European Accounting Review, 2*(1), 17–46. https://doi.org/10.1080/09638189300000002

Alexander, D., & Eberhartinger, E. (2009). The true and fair view in the European Union. *European Accounting Review, 18*(3), 571–594.

Alexander, D., & Jermakowicz, E. (2006). A true and fair view of the principles/rules debate. *Abacus*, roč. 42, č. 2, s. 132–164.

Cook, A. (1997). Requirement for a true and fair view—A UK standard-setter's perspective. *European Accounting Review, 6*(4), 693–704. https://doi.org/10.1080/09638189700000010

https://eur-lex.europa.eu/legal-content/DE/TXT/PDF/?uri=OJ:C:1972:007:FULL&from=EN [online]. [cit. 28.2.2020].

https://eur-lex.europa.eu/legal-content/EN/TXT/?qid=1582476009388&uri=CELEX:51974PC0191 [online]. [cit. 28.2.2020].

https://eur-lex.europa.eu/legal-content/EN/TXT/?uri=OJ:C:1972:007:TOC [online]. [cit. 28.2.2020].

Kovanicová, D. (1996). Věrný a poctivý obraz. *Ekonom*, 1996, č. 51, s. 63.

Nobes, C. (1993). The true and fair view requirements: Impact on and of the fourth directive. *Accounting and Business Research, 24*(93), 35–48.

Rutherford, B. A. (1985). The true and fair view doctrine: a search for explication. Journal of Business Finance & Accounting, 12(4), 483–494.

Sucher, P., Seal, W., & Zelenka, I. (1996). True and fair in the Czech Republic: A note on local perceptions. *European Accounting Review, 5*(3), 545–557. https://doi.org/10.1080/09638189600000034

Schroll, R. (1995). The new accounting system in the Czech Republic. European Accounting Review, 4(4), 827–832.

Van Hulle, K., & K. U. Leuven. (1993). Truth and untruth about true and fair: A commentary on 'A European true and fair view' comment. *European Accounting Review, 2*(1), 99–104. https://doi.org/10.1080/09638189300000008

Walton, P. (1993). Introduction: The true and fair vies in British accounting. *European Accounting Review, 2*(1), 49–58. https://doi.org/10.1080/09638189300000003

Zarova, M. (1999). International accounting from the perspective of European development. *Acta Oeconomica Pragensia, 7*(8), 213–224.

Žárová, M. (2006). *Regulace evropského účetnictví*. Transl. Regulation of European Accounting. Nakladatelství Oeconomica, Praha 2006, pp. 185.

Žárová, M. (2011). Impact of international financial reporting standards on development of accounting regulatory system in the Czech Republic. In *Trends in international business* (Vol. 2011, pp. 253–261). IAE Lyon.

Zelenková, M. (2010). Věrný a poctivý obraz v Evropské unii. *Český finanční a účetní časopis, 2010*(3), 101–110. https://doi.org/10.18267/j.cfuc.79

Chapter 27
Role of Independent Professional Body in Accounting Regulation in the Czech Republic

Marcela Zárybnická Žárová

Abstract This chapter illustrates and comments on the role and position of an independent professional body in accounting regulation in the Czech Republic not only because of a change in political regime and a change in the application of IFRS but also as a result of the response of professional chambers in accounting and taxes to participate in the standard setting process. Accounting is regulated in the Czech Republic, which corresponds to the continental legal environment, The analysis provides evidence that professional accounting chambers did not influence the legal regulation of accounting and also did not have an influence on the development of accounting standards till the late 1990s. The negligible role of the accounting profession resulted from the traditional system of accounting regulation in the Czech Republic, grounded in the continental legal environment. The impact of the establishment of the independent professional body and its decision to provide expert advice to practice on accounting regulation are discussed in detail.

Key words Independent professional body · National Accounting Board · Accounting Interpretation

27.1 Introduction

The role of professional accounting bodies in accounting regulation is a subject of ongoing research, which usually intensifies in the periods of major changes in economic and political environments. The reasons are either connected to changes in the political regime or when a crucial and fundamental change in using a set of accounting regulations or accounting standards has been introduced, like the IFRS for consolidated financial statements since 2005 for registered companies on European stock exchanges or other essential cultural or economic events.

M. Z. Žárová (✉)
Department of Financial Accounting and Auditing, Prague University of Economics and Business, Prague, Czech Republic
e-mail: zarova@vse.cz

D. Procházka (ed.), *Regulation of Finance and Accounting*, Springer Proceedings in Business and Economics, https://doi.org/10.1007/978-3-030-99873-8_27

Changes in the political regime do not happen very often, but change of rules is a more frequent reason for change in regulation. In the last two decades, discussion concerning accounting regulation in Europe intensified during the period when IFRS has become mandatory for companies listed on European stock exchanges. As Véron (2007) notes, "The regulation which went into effect in 2005 mandates consolidated group reporting by companies with securities traded on a stock exchange to adhere IFRS as issued by IASB and endorsed by the EU." Moreover, Žárová (2016) highlights the new phenomenon in regulatory accounting systems, i.e., "hybrid accounting systems." As she introduced in her article, this new phenomenon was presented by Schmidt and Kirschner (2005), explaining what do accounting standards play in continental European systems. Authors started to call this special organization of accounting regulation in Europe, where there are two different standard setters, governmental and private ones, as the "hybrid regulatory system." These situations, where several public entities are involved in the development of accounting standards in addition to private sector standard setters, are described later by Königsgruber (2014). He also points out that "accounting standard setters are often criticized for having excessive influence over individual, mostly corporate entities and being subject to regulatory capture."

Topics on accounting regulation in research began to appear more often in the late 1980s. Research from this period was mainly concerned with modeling and finding a standard model of accounting regulation at both national and international levels. In modeling, research has focused on assessing the nature and quality of accounting information that different models produce and exist within different regulatory frameworks. Research on accounting regulation, as Žárová (2016) notes, has been conducted by world-respected authors: the first group represented by Watts and Zimmerman (1978), Bromwich (1985), Horngren (1985), and Robson (1993) dealt with theories on the evolution of accounting rules; the second group represented by Benston (1980), Johnson (1991), and Mitchell and Sikka (1993) investigated the role of institutions that represent interests gained through regulatory privileges and also regulatory instruments that enable the enforcement of accounting rules; and the third group represented by Walker and Robinson (1993, 1994) and Klumpes (1994) focused on political lobbying and similar forms of influence including topics concerning political pressure on bodies issuing the accounting rules.

Research on accounting regulation was later organized and described by Dennis (2014) and Di Pietra et al. (2014). Research of these authors offers two approaches on how to understand accounting regulation. Their first research approach understands the accounting regulation as regulation that affects management behavior. In this context, they deal with behavior at strategic and operational levels under the specific characteristics of corporate governance in individual firms. Under the second approach study, the study aims to improve "the efficacy and efficiency of the regulation at the national and international levels."

A new wave of topics on the relation between politics and accounting appears in recent research like Camfferman (2020), who refers to "return to geopolitics" as a movement away from an organized global order based on multilateral cooperation, international institutions, and economic liberalization to the assertion of national interests and adversarial competition among nations. Another inspirational research concerning legitimacy of private accounting standard setters is written by Sanada (2020). A very personal view on accounting and politics in Europe brings paper by Walton (2020). In this chapter, he explains how despite the extensive open lobbying process organized through the due process, there are also other fewer overt channels that are used to attempt to influence outcomes.

Among recent research that brings a study evidence of the complexities of national settings in relation to policy formulation is research prepared by Hartmann et al. (2020). This study illustrates and comments implementing and enforcing IFRS in Sweden, where there is a long tradition of orienting national regulation toward IFRS. This study is explained based on the example of two financial institutions. The authors said that: "It is important to study complexities of national settings in relation to policy formulation, implementation, and enforcement, because the effects on organizational accounting behavior are 'filtered' through a complex system of different regulating, endorsing, and assuring bodies that ate bound to their national context with a specific accounting history and culture."

Research that has been done directly toward the Czech regulation in accounting is represented by the article written by Žárová and Mejzlík (2018). This research includes besides analytical data also historical overview of development from regulation of accounting procedures toward financial accounting and financial reporting regulation. Czech research studies mainly focused on influence of IFRS on financial reporting (Mejzlík et al., 2015). Specific research that overviewed research studies in transitive economies and confirm that majority of research studies concentrate on IFRS implementation was prepared by Procházka (2015).

In contrast to the research mentioned above, this chapter illustrates and comments on the role and position of an independent professional body in accounting regulation in the Czech Republic not only because of a change in political regime and a change in the application of IFRS but also as a result of the response of professional chambers in accounting and taxes to participate in the standard setting process.

27.2 Data and Methodology

This chapter illustrates and comments on the role of an independent professional body in accounting regulation in the Czech Republic based on the development of regulatory accounting system. There was a process of transition from a centrally planned economy to a market economy after 1989. Accounting in the Czech Republic was regulated by the Ministry of Finance before 1989 and remained after 1989. During the short period of preparation of the new accounting system (1990–1992), the following fundamental question was asked: which of the basic accounting philosophies should be adopted (Schroll, 1995).

1. The Anglo-Saxon accounting system embracing the principle of the "true and fair view".

2. The German accounting system based on fulfilling legal requirements, in particular with respect to the taxation regulations (especially those for income tax).
3. The French accounting system representing a compromise between the Anglo-Saxon and German system.

As Scholl mentioned (1995), the accounting academics supported the first approach. While there has been some experience with the German system as the Czech accounting system has been influenced by the German system until 1953, the German system was not chosen as a basis for accounting reform. The Ministry of Finance selected the French system. The argument for selecting the French system was that a relatively high proportion of the French economy has been nationalized, and for this reason, the "Plan Comptable general" had been introduced. And therefore, it seemed to be the most acceptable approach for the Ministry of Finance to realize the accounting reform in Czechoslovakia based on the French system. A complete reform of Czechoslovak accounting was undertaken, through the Accounting Act that came into effect on January 1, 1992 (although certain provisions were delayed until January 1, 1993). New legislation was therefore influenced by EC accounting practices, particularly the Fourth and Seventh Directives on Company Law (Žárová, 2011).

The Czech Republic became a member of the European Union (EU) in May 2004. The accession of the Czech Republic to the EU has accelerated its reform in the field of accounting to bring accounting regulation in compliance with the Accounting Regulation and Directives. EU membership has resulted in a particular obligation for listed companies in the Czech Republic. Listed companies must comply with IFRS at least in their consolidated financial statements since 2005 at the latest. The example of accounting regulation in the Czech Republic shows the consequences of the European Commission's decision to apply IFRS at the national level. Thus, in the Czech Republic, since May 1, 2004, there has been an obligation to prepare at least consolidated financial statements in accordance with IFRS.

As IFRS has been introduced into the Continental European regulatory systems, the influence of professional accounting bodies was expected to increase into the process of standard settings. This expectation is even included in the Preface to IFRS where there it is said that "within each country, local regulations govern, to a greater or lesser degree, the issue of financial statements. Such local regulations include accounting standards which are promulgated by the regulatory bodies and/or the professional accounting bodies in the countries concerned." The natural consequence of IFRS introduction as obligatory rules for publicly traded companies in Europe would be the strengthening the influence of professional institutions in accounting. The expectation, which was even part of the Preface to IFRS, was not realized in the Czech Republic because professional accounting organizations and academics had no influence on the legal regulation of accounting. The Ministry of Finance, the only regulator of accounting in the Czech Republic, did not allow any cooperation with the professional accounting chambers or academics. The accounting profession's involvement in the development of standards for practical accounting practices was virtually nonexistent.

The research on the role of an independent professional body in accounting regulation in the Czech Republic is designed as a single country study with descriptive analysis. As the chapter illustrates and comments on the role and position of an independent professional body in accounting regulation in the Czech Republic, the method of content analysis is used here. Then information on development of the professional body itself and information on the constitution of interpretations of the professional body are separately determined and deeply analyzed for better understanding of the increasing position of NAB in the Czech Republic for practice.

27.3 Results and Discussion

The basis for the current discussion is the historical fact, stated by Žárová (2016), that the Ministry of Finance issued the so-called Czech Accounting Standards in 2004. Czech Accounting Standards are basically called decrees of the Ministry of Finance, which do not represent "best practice." Accounting standards usually refer to best practices developed by a professional accounting institution. The above characteristics of an accounting standard imply that the standard should contain a description of accounting methods or practices, with the provision that the standard should not contradict or circumvent the provisions of the Accounting Act and other statutory provisions. In order to understand the whole strange situation where a ministerial decree is called an accounting standard, it is important to point out that until the end of 2003, the Ministry of Finance did not launch a public tender for a professional body to become the mandated accounting standard setter. This is the only reason why professional institutions in the Czech Republic, like accounting chambers, do not issue accounting standards or participate in their preparation.

Comparison of standard due process with the process of issuing standards by the governmental agency brings us to the extremely opposite view that is represented by Königsgruber (2007), where he argues that "managers generally do not wish to express their preferences in full view of the investing public." The exposure draft is not published and accessible for public comments at all in the Czech Republic. Public and managers generally in the Czech Republic do not have any access to the exposure draft, but they are even not informed about upcoming changes of rules. Analyzing the standard setting process the following conclusion is to be made. Standard due process consists of three steps realized by the Ministry of Finance, while process realized by professional independent rule-making body consists of seven steps as a minimum and ten steps usually, where realization of one step of the due process is dependent on the particular situation and topic discussed.

As the research on accounting regulation and modeling illustrates, there is a fundamental difference between the influence of professional institutions and the accounting academic environment on the form of regulation in the Anglo-American system and the continental system. An overview of international differences in accounting regulation" and practice can be found in Nobes and Parker (2012) or Flower and Ebbers (2002). Zeff stated (2005) that whereas "the US has a long tradition of standard setting by an organism belonging to the private sector, Continental European countries are characterized by a larger role given to legislation in accounting regulation." The fact that private standard setters have a long tradition in the USA brings companies to participate in the process of standard setting. Königsgruber (2007) also deals with the participation of academics in the standard setting process. He cites research by McLeay et al. (2000) who note that there is traditionally high involvement by accounting academics in Germany, while few academics participate in the standard setting process in the USA by submitting comment letters (Tandy & Wilburn, 1996). The situation in the Czech Republic was completely different. The question is not how strong the participation of academics in the standard setting process is because academics in the Czech Republic could not participate at all. Mejzlík (2008) criticized the mechanism of making comments on the legal accounting regulations prepared by the Ministry of Finance. The mechanism of comments is considered redundant and ineffective due to the fragmentation of the addressing of comments by the Ministry to professional organizations and academics from the University of Economics in Prague during the preparation of the first amendment to the Act on Accounting. As a result of dissatisfaction, the National Accounting Board (hereinafter the "NAB") as a special-interest association of legal entities was established. However, the development of the role and the position of the independent professional accounting body, the NAB, in the Czech Republic differ from the expectation one would have based on the experience from other countries.

27.3.1 Organizing NAB

The idea of professional chambers in the Czech Republic leads to establishing NAB with the unique role to prepare the accounting legislation, commentary procedure, as well as other standards related to accounting, taxes, and audit and to become an official commentary legislative institution. The original ambitious intention of the Board that the NAB will be appointed by the Ministry of Finance in the Czech Republic with creating the Czech accounting standards as permitted by the Accounting Act has not been fulfilled yet (Žárová, 2016).

The role of the NAB is generally defined in the preamble of the statutes: "The National Accounting Board is an independent professional institution to promote professional qualification and professional ethics in the development of accounting professions and in the area of accounting and finance methodology."

The members of the National Accounting Board include the following parties to the memorandum of association by which the National Accounting Board was established, more specifically the Chamber of Auditors of the Czech Republic, the Chamber of Tax Advisors of the Czech Republic, the Union of Accountants of the Czech Republic, and the University of Economics represented by the Faculty of Finance and Accounting (NAB, 2012).

Establishment, activity, and powers of the NAB are not defined by any legal regulation. The position of the NAB relies upon the professional background of the professions it associates and membership base and experts the individual CNAB members associate and represent. In this respect, the Board is quite undoubtedly the most representative nongovernmental organization representing professions engaged in the area of accounting and taxes in the Czech Republic.

The NAB meets regularly, always once a month, and it addresses current aspects from the area of accounting and taxes at its meetings. In 2003, there were significant changes in the Czech accounting legislation (change in the system functioning from 1993 to 2002, introduction of regulation where decrees and the Czech accounting standards are subordinate to the Accounting Act). Introduction of the Czech Accounting Standards into practice was the reason why the NAB members started to elaborate on the interpretations of the Czech accounting regulations as professional help to the accounting public 1 year later.

27.3.2 The NAB Interpretations

The NAB Interpretations take into consideration the Accounting Act and decrees, as well as other laws and regulations. Where these regulations do not provide unambiguous guidance, it takes into account the true and fair view on the accounts, and it proceeds independently and objectively while respecting the public interests (Müllerová, 2012).

The individual Interpretations (Foreword, Art. 5 and 6) are concerned with expressing a professional opinion on practical application of the Czech accounting policies that will respond to:

- Accounting aspects which have not been addressed by the Czech accounting regulations or the way they have been addressed is insufficient for practice.
- Issues that newly arose in applying the Czech accounting regulations in practice.
- Issues that have been addressed by the accounting regulations but their application is not uniform in practice.

If the NAB determines not to deal with the proposed problem, it is followed by a formal procedure consisting in entrusting any of the members with preparation of a working draft of the interpretation, the process of its internal discussion, public commentary procedure, and final issue and publication of the approved text of the interpretation. The key element of preparation of an interpretation consists in public commentary procedure, which is open to anyone. The approved text also includes a progress report of the interpretation setter who sums up comments have been sent, which comments have been processed, and how and which comments have not been accepted and reasons for (Mejzlík, 2008).

The text of each interpretation has a fixed structure, the core of which consists of three main chapters:

- "Description of the problem′ which is dealt with by the Interpretation, including wording of the question to which the Interpretation responds
- "Solution of the problem" in the form of an answer to the question formulated in the "Description of the problem"
- "Basis for conclusions" with references to accounting regulations that have been used as arguments in formulating the solution of the problem and that the solution relies upon.

The specified structure of the text of interpretation and its commentary and approval procedure are similar to IFRS interpretations (SIC and IFRIC), and the entire project of NAB interpretations is noncommercial, and the published proposals for comments as well as the approved texts of interpretations are available free of charge at the website of NAB (Mejzlík, 2008).

NAB recorded cases when Interpretations had been used as supporting arguments during the work of accountants and auditors, and they are cited in professional academic works. Some Interpretations had been used when resolving tax disputes at the Supreme Administrative Court. It can thus be stated that Interpretations gradually create what is known in the Anglo-Saxon environment as "best practice" (Mejzlík, 2011).

Moreover, the NAB, a private professional accounting body, serves as an advisory group for the Ministry of Finance on legislative issues. The NAB advised with the transposition of the Directive 2013/34/EU of the European Parliament and of the Council of 26 June 2013 on the annual financial statements, consolidated financial statements, and related reports of certain types of undertakings into Czech legislation, where member states should transpose Directive into the laws, regulations, and administrative provisions by 20 July 2015. Another several years cooperation and advisory work concern the preparation of accounting reform with the proposal of a new Act on accounting that was finalized at the beginning of 2020.

Regular help of the NAB to practice is represented by Interpretations of NAB. The list of NAB Interpretations is in Table 27.1.

27.4 Conclusion

Based on the historical overview of the development of regulation of accounting in the Czech Republic over the last 31 years, this chapter illustrates and comments on the role and position of an independent professional body in the accounting profession. The chapter illustrates that accounting regulation in the Czech Republic has been changed not only because of a change in political regime and a change in the application of IFRS but also as a result of the response of professional chambers in accounting and taxes to participate in the standard setting process.

After 2000, it became common in Europe for accounting to be regulated not only by governmental regulatory body but also by private professional accounting ones. But the Ministry of Finance in the Czech Republic, the supreme accounting

Table 27.1 NAB's Interpretations

Interpretation number	Title of Interpretations
I – 1	Temporary differences upon initial recognition of assets
I – 2	Temporary differences upon company transformations and equity investments
I – 3	Provision for current tax payable
I – 4	Deferred tax arising from temporary differences upon the valuation of equity investments using the equity method of accounting
I – 5	Determination of the date at which the costs related to the acquisition of fixed assets start to be reported
I – 6	Compliance with the conditions for putting long-term tangible assets into use
I – 7	Commissionaire agreements
I – 8	Social fund and accounting for funds from profit
I – 9	Deferred tax – Initial recognition
I – 10	Date of accounting for receivables arising from accrued interest and fees on receivables by the creditor
I – 11	Superseded by I – 30 Comparability of information for the current and previous reporting period presented in the individual financial statements of entrepreneurs
I – 12	Factoring
I – 13	STA6ENA Accounting for lump-sum amounts paid as liability compensations for the quality of supplies
I – 14	Reporting date of the entitlement to accept or the obligation to return a subsidy
I – 15	Settlement of nonpaid awarded profit shares
I – 16	Reporting of a stand-alone easement acquired for consideration
I – 17	Incentives related to lease relationships
I – 18	Estimated receivables and payables denominated in foreign currencies
I – 19	Settlement of payables arising from distribution of equity
I – 20	Accounting treatment of contingent capital expenditures
I – 21	Write-off of receivables and/or payables denominated in foreign currencies
I – 22	Subsidies denominated in foreign currencies
I – 23	Valuation of acquired receivables denominated in foreign currencies
I – 24	Events after the balance sheet date
I – 25	Valuation after predecessor
I – 26	Discounts on acquisition cost of long-term assets in subsequent accounting periods after putting into use
I – 27	Receipt of government grants
I – 28	Repayment of government grants related to noncurrent assets
I – 29	Changes in accounting estimates and errors
I – 30	Comparability of accounting information for current accounting period and past one in financial statements
I – 31	Interim reporting
I – 32	Statement of changes in owner's equity; structure and content

(continued)

Table 27.1 (continued)

Interpretation number	Title of Interpretations
I – 33	Determination of the moment when acquired assets are included into tangible fixed assets section
I – 34	Provisions for liquidation
I – 35	Inventory of own production measurement
I – 36	Additional procedure of calculation of consolidation differences
I – 37	Deferrals and accruals and foreign currency translation
I – 38	Sale of the share in subsidiary in consolidated financial statements
I – 39	Inventory-taking differences in inventories and fixed assets
I – 40	Reporting and disclosure of research and development costs
I – 41	Customer loyalty program
I – 42	Accounts receivables in foreign currency with adjustments
I – 43	Provided advances in foreign currency

Source: Own elaboration based on https://nur.cz/interpretace/schvalene-interpretace/

regulator, hasn't allowed Czech professional institutions to participate in the development of standards. In the Czech Republic, the process of standard setting is concentrated into the governmental regulatory body, where there is a usual effect of this approach to the standard setting process, and that is the trend to respond to the solution of economic operations in accounting with a delay in time and often with the lack of feedback from real economic life. Separating the standard-setting process from practical processes in the real life of companies is a natural consequence.

In the situation where professional institutions and professional chambers haven't been allowed to participate in the development of standards, professional chambers in the Czech Republic decided to establish an official commentary legislative institution, professional partner for the Ministry of Finance for preparation of the accounting legislation, commentary procedure, as well as other standards related to accounting, taxes, and audit. Professional accounting body, National Accounting Board (NAB), was established as a common decision of professional chambers in accounting. What is supposed to be unusual is that accounting professional body was based also on agreement with the chamber of tax advisors which demonstrates the interconnectedness of accounting and the tax system.

Until now, the Ministry of Finance has never delegated any professional accounting body by setting accounting standards. Separating the standard-setting process from practical processes in the real life of companies caused difficulties in understanding rules prepared by the Ministry of Finance and caused difficulties in treatment of practical events. This brought the NAB to the decision to start to elaborate on interpretations of the Czech accounting regulations as a professional help to accounting public. As it is declared in the preface to Interpretations, "interpretations of the National Accounting Board consider accounting issues in the Czech legislation that are likely to receive divergent or unacceptable treatment in the absence of authoritative guidance." Even though this professional accounting body has not been nominated by the Ministry of Finance as a standard setter, the work of the NAB has over more than two decades an impact on the accounting profession and accounting entities. NAB became a respected authority by the accounting public because of the high level of professional responsibility. Companies use the Interpretations as recommendation, or they use the published Interpretations as guidelines even though those Interpretations are not legally enforceable. The work of the NAB is important as it has a strong influence on the development of the accounting profession and responsibility for accounting in companies.

Acknowledgments This chapter has been prepared within the research project: Institutional Support of Research Activities IP100040.

References

Benston, G. J. (1980). The establishment and enforcement of accounting standards: Methods, benefits and costs. *Accounting and Business Research, 11*, 51–60.

Bromwich, M. (1985). *The economics of accounting standards setting*. Prentice-Hall.

Camfferman, K. (2020). International accounting standard setting and geopolitics. *Accounting in Europe, 17*(3), 243–263. https://doi.org/10.1080/17449480.2020.1795214

Dennis, I. (2014). *The nature of accounting regulation*. Routledge.

Di Pietra, R., McLeay, S., & Ronen, J. (2014). *Accounting and regulation. New insight on governance, markets and institutions*. Springer.

Flower, J., & Ebbers, G. (2002). *Global financial reporting*. Palgrave.

Hartmann, B., Jan, M., & Andersson, S. J. (2020). IFRS in National Regulatory Space: Insights from Sweden. *Accounting in Europe, 17*(3), 367–387. https://doi.org/10.1080/17449480.2020.1824073

Horngren, C. T. (1985). Institutional alternatives for regulative financial reporting. *Journal of Comparative Business and Capital Market Law, 7*, 267–289.

Jönsson, S. (1991). Role making for accounting while the state is watching. *Accounting, Organizations and Society, 16*(5), 521–546.

Klumpes, P. J. (1994). The politics of rule development: A case study of Australien pension fund accounting rule-making. *Abacus, 30*, 140–159.

Königsgruber, R. (2007). An economic analysis of cross-listing decisions. *Working Paper.*

Königsgruber, R. (2014). Accounting standard setting in two political contexts. In *Accounting and regulation* (pp. 59–78). Springer.

McLeay, S., Ordelheide, D., & Young, S. (2000). Constituent lobbying and its impact on the development of financial reporting regulations: Evidence from Germany. *Accounting, Organizations and Society, 25*, 79–98.

Mejzlík, L. (2008). Národní účetní rada a její interpretace českých účetních předpisů [National Accounting Board and its interpretations of Czech accounting regulations.]. *Bulletin Komory daňových poradců., 16*, 29–35.

Mejzlík, L. (2011). Interpretace Národní účetní rady jako „best practice" v ČR? [Interpretation of the National Accounting Board as "best practice" in the Czech Republic?]. *Český finanční a účetní časopis, 6*, 4–6.

Mejzlík, L., Arltová, M., Procházka, D., & Vítek, L. (2015). Implementace mezinárodních standardů účetníhovýkaznictví v České republice a její vliv na zdanění podniků. Politická ekonomie, 2015(7), 811–832.

Mitchell, A., & Sikka, P. (1993). Accounting for change: Institutions of accountancy. *Critical Perspectives on Accounting, 4*, 29–52.

Müllerová, L. (2012). Historie Národní účetní rady a její interpretace. [History of the National Accounting Board and its interpretations]. *Auditor, 19*, 5–7.
NAB (2012). Interpretace Národní účetní rady. Wolters Kluwer, 304 pp, ISBN 978-80-7357-968-5
Nobes, C., & Parker, R. H. (2012). *Comparative international accounting*. Pearson Education.
Procházka, D. (2015). *Ekonomické dopady implementace IFRS v Evropě* [Economic impact of IFRS implementation] (pp. 154). Vysoká škola ekonomická – Oeconomica.
Robson, K. (1993). Accounting policy making and "interests": accounting for research and development. *Critical Perspectives on Accounting, 4*(1), 1-27.
Sanada, M. (2020). Legitimacy of private accounting standard setters: Literature review and suggestions for future research. *Accounting in Europe, 17*(3), 264–302. https://doi.org/10.1080/17449480.2020.1837889
Schmidt, M., & Kirchner, C. (2005). Private law-making: IFRS – Problems of hybrid standard setting. In P. Nobel (Hg.), *International standards and the law* (pp. 67–82). *Stämpfli*.
Schroll, R. (1995). The new accounting system in the Czech Republic. *The European Accounting Review, 4*(4), 827–832. https://doi.org/10.1080/09638189500000052
Tandy, P. R., & Wilburn, N. L. (1996). The academic community's participation in standard setting: Submission of comment letters on SFAS nos. 1-117. *Accounting Horizons, 10*, 92.
Veron, N. (2007). *The global accounting experiment* (Bruegel blueprint series, Vol. 2).
Walker, R. G., & Robinson, P. (1993). A critical assessment of the literature on political activity and accounting regulation. *Research in Accounting Regulation, 7*(1), 3–40.
Walker, R. G., & Robinson, S. P. (1994). Competing regulatory agencies with conflicting agendas: Setting standards for cash flow reporting in Australia. *Abacus, 30*(2), 119–139.
Walton, P. (2020). Accounting and politics in Europe: Influencing the standard. *Accounting in Europe, 17*(3), 303–313. https://doi.org/10.1080/17449480.2020.1714065
Watts, R. L., & Zimmerman, J. L. (1978). Towards a positive theory of the determination of accounting standards. *Accounting Review, 53*, 112–134.
Žárová, M. (2011). Impact of international financial reporting standards on development of accounting regulatory system in the Czech Republic. In *Trends in international business* (pp. 253–261). IAE Lyon.
Žárová, M. (2016). Changes in accounting regulation in the Czech Republic over past twenty five years. In *Účetnictví a auditing v procesu světové harmonizace* (Vranov nad Dyjí, 13.09.2016–15.09.2016, s. 205–211). Oeconomica. ISBN 978-80-245-2157-2.
Žárová, M., & Mejzlík, L. (2018). Vývoj a regulace účetnictví a účetního výkaznictví po roce 1989. In *Sto let financí a účetnictví na území České republiky* (s. 168–179, 304 s.). Oeconomica. ISBN 978-80-245-2286-9. Kapitola 11.
Zeff, S. A. (2005). The evolution of US GAAP: The political forces behind professional standards. *The CPA Journal, 75*(2), 18.

Chapter 28
Audit Committee Composition and Corporate Risk Disclosure in Emerging Country

Musa Uba Adamu

Abstract This study examines the effect of audit committee structure on the amount of risk information disclosed by banks in the emerging country. The sample of the study comprises eight banks listed on the Nigeria Stock Exchange. The data was collected from 72 annual reports for the year 2010–2018. The manual content analysis and regression methods were the analytical tools employed for the analysis of our panel data. The content analysis outcomes demonstrate that the frequency of operational risk disclosure is substantially greater than strategic and environmental risk disclosures. It is also discovered that good news, non-monetary, and backward-looking risk information are perceived to be less relevant to stakeholders' decisions and nevertheless have considerably outweighed the most relevant information concerning bad news, monetary, and forward-looking risk information. Meanwhile, the number of independent directors in the audit committee, the presence of an independent chairperson in the audit committee, and the frequency of audit committee meetings have a significant positive effect on the quantity of risk information to disclose. However, the audit committee size and the existence of non-executive members in the audit committee are statistically insignificant; hence they do not influence the movement of risk information disclosure. The overall risk disclosure practice involving Nigerian banks is inadequate as the general statements and risk definitions and other irrelevant risk information are the most common practices adopted by banks. This disclosure behavior tends to promote agency costs between management and various corporate stakeholders.

Key words Corporate risk disclosure · Risk management · Corporate governance · Audit committee · Content analysis

M. U. Adamu (✉)
School of Finance, National Research University Higher School of Economics, Moscow, Russia

D. Procházka (ed.), *Regulation of Finance and Accounting*, Springer Proceedings in Business and Economics, https://doi.org/10.1007/978-3-030-99873-8_28

28.1 Introduction

The Company and Allied Matters Acts (CAMA) have required corporate shareholders to appoint an independent auditor to revisit the financial statements and express their professional opinion on the state of company affairs. The rationale behind seeking the auditors' opinion is to ensure the quality of the financial statement that might boost investors' confidence. However, the increase in devastating corporate failure that is recurrently connected with management malpractice has raised questions on the auditors' opinion as well as the quality of financial statements. In their effort to address the problem, the Institute of Chartered Accountants in England and Wales has released a discussion paper in 1998 that pinpointed the importance of risk disclosure (Grassa et al., 2020). This discussion paper was the first that recommended corporate entities to report their risk profile in their annual report (Grassa et al., 2020), and the title of the paper was Financial Reporting of Risk Proposals for a statement of business risk. Moreover, the 2007–2009 financial crisis that occasioned economic slowdown across the globe has motivated many stakeholders to intensify the advocacy of effective corporate governance (Ivashkovskaya & Nadezhda, 2009; Al-maghzom et al., 2016) and risk disclosure. Internal control system and effective risk management transparency have turned out to be an essential part of corporate governance (Vergauwen et al., 2009). Moreove, risk disclosure is currently a crucial trait of business risks (Beretta & Bozzolan, 2004; Linsley et al., 2006), and risk management signifies a key aspect of corporate economic stability, financial health, and resilience (Lajili et al., 2020) as greater information disclosure improves corporate transparency and investors' confidence. The regulatory reforms (BASEL II and IFRS 7) that require greater measures on risk transparency and disclosure (Al-maghzom et al., 2016) and an effective corporate governance system are the power that facilitates the economic recovery (Ivashkovskaya & Nadezhda, 2009).

Meanwhile, many scholars from diverse jurisdictions have indicated greater interest in risk disclosure research. For example, the studies (Solomon et al., 2000; Deumes & Knechel, 2008; Rajab & Handley-Schachler, 2009; Oliveira et al., 2011; Barakat & Hussainey, 2013; Elshandidy et al., 2013, 2015; Elamer et al., 2017; Netti, 2018) have explored risk disclosure practice involving advanced economies. Equally, the other studies employed the emerging countries datasets (Adamu, 2013; Al-maghzom et al., 2016; Elamer et al., 2017; Neifar & Jarboui, 2018; Elghaffar et al., 2019; Khlif & Hussainey, 2016; Abdallah et al., 2015; Viljoen & Enslin, 2016; Ishtiaq et al., 2017; Seta & Setyaningrum, 2018; Mazaya & Fuad, 2018; Habtoor et al., 2018; Grassa et al., 2020; Adamu, 2021; Adamu & Ivashkovskaya, 2021; Albitar, 2015) and tested different economic theories that explain corporate risk disclosure behavior. Meanwhile, the relevance of risk disclosure cannot be overemphasized as the previous studies provide evidence that risk disclosure is associated with the improvement of corporate risk management (ICAEW, 2002), the reduction of information asymmetry and agency costs (Rajab and Handley-

Schachler 2009), the protection of the investors (Linsley & Shrives, 2007), and the enhancement of the company's reputation (Yang, 2018).

Moreover, the literature has identified several factors that influence the extent of risk disclosure practice. Many corporate governance attributes such as ownership structure, board composition, and audit quality were found very relevant in explaining the extent of risk disclosed by firms. Nevertheless, the code of corporate governance has identified the audit committee as one of the monitoring mechanisms, and the practicing firms tend to lower their agency cost due to greater disclosure quality (Forker, 1992). Notwithstanding this argument, there are limited studies that have investigated the connection between the features of the audit committee and corporate disclosure (Albitar, 2015). This linearity was initially suggested by Forker (1992), in which he believes the audit committee traits might enhance voluntary corporate disclosure practice. In recent years, scholars (Al-maghzom et al., 2016) found the audit committee as one of the factors that influence the risk to be disclosed by firms. These audit committee variables are yet to be tested in the Nigeria banking sector. This study makes an essential contribution to the governance and risk disclosure literature by examining the risk disclosure practices of eight banks operating in Africa's emerging economies, especially Nigeria, over a period of 9 years (from 2010 to 2018). Concerning the real-world implications of our research, we attempt to evaluate the risk disclosure behavior involving the listed banks in Nigeria and also ascertain the effect of audit committee characteristics on corporate risk disclosure. It appears to be valuable to policy-makers, regulators, preparers, and users of corporate reporting. The study raises the spirits of regulators (CBN, NNDC, NSE, etc.) to promote corporate risk disclosure transparency by ensuring strict compliance with effective corporate governance through auditing committee mechanisms. The paper is organized as follows: The first section is introduction; relevant literature and hypotheses are developed in Sect. 28.2. Sample, data and measurement of the variables are described in Sect. 28.3. Results are discussed in the fourth section. Conclusion, limitation, and suggestion for future research are provided in Sect. 28.5.

28.2 Literature Review

28.2.1 Risk and Risk Disclosure

The extent of growth experienced by the business environments in the last couple of decades has exposed many firms and banks to risk. The major factors attributed to business growth are globalization and technological advancement (Adamu, 2021). Banks are exposed to both systematic and unsystematic risk. The increasing number of corporate failures, which were usually connected with management malpractice, and the 2008 global financial crisis have shaken the investors and other stakeholders' confidence, and therefore, the advocacy to disclose business risk has emerged (Adamu, 2021). This action could help the users of the annual report read and understand the nature of risk the business is exposed to. The earlier perceptions of many stakeholders about the risk were linked to the occurrence of a bad event (Linsley et al., 2006). However, this perception was considered as the pre-modern idea of risk as to the company's present, and prospects were incorporated in the modern idea of risk (Adamu & Ivashkovskaya, 2021). Risk disclosure is considered adequate, "if the reader is informed of any opportunity or prospect, or of any hazard, danger, harm, threat or exposure, that has already impacted upon the company or may impact upon the company in the future or of the management of any such opportunity, prospect, hazard, harm, threat or exposure (Linsley et al., 2006)." The disclosure of these kinds of information will give the readers more insight into the risk profile of the firm, and the strategy would be adapted by corporate managers in risk management. Despite several motivations for corporate risk disclosure, nevertheless, many corporate managers are reluctant to reveal their risk information. This is not unconnected with the adverse effect associated with corporate risk disclosure. It appears that many countries across the globe do not regulate the disclosure of risk information in the annual report. Consequently, there is no uniformity and clarity in the manner in which firms communicate their risk information (Lajili et al., 2012).

However, most of the previous research developed the risk disclosure index based on the framework proposed by ICAEW in 1999. Researchers usually modify the framework to suit the country of the study characteristics (culture, religion, risk, etc.), rules, and regulation. Moreover, the application of content analysis on annual report narratives has become a common methodology adopted by researchers. Despite the element of subjectivity identified in the process of capturing risk information, however, content analysis remains the most appropriate procedure for risk disclosure research. It permits scholars to analyze the strategy which firms adopt to disclose their information. The prior studies appear unsatisfactory in the manner in which the risk information is divulged in many jurisdictions. For example, previous studies (Linsley et al., 2006; Adamu & Ivashkovskaya, 2021) discovered that the frequency of good news always dominated that of bad news. The investors and other stakeholders prefer the disclosure of bad news as it would substantially influence their decision. Also, the previous studies (Adamu, 2013) identify biases on the time horizon on which backward (past) risk information substantially dominates forward-looking (future) risk information.

Furthermore, the relevance of the information could be very high, especially where stakeholders access the quantitative (monetary) risk information. Nonetheless, the previous studies conducted by Lajili (2009) and Lajili et al. (2012) have found that most of the disclosure is qualitative (non-monetary) rather than qualitative. The dominance of bad news, non-monetary, backward-looking risk information is the major factor that scholars render current risk disclosure practice as not satisfactory.

28.2.2 The Nigerian Stocks Exchange

The Nigerian Stock Exchange (NSE) was created on September 15, 1960, as the Lagos Stock Exchange. Official operations began on August 25, 1961, with the listing of 19 stocks for trading. August 1961 volume was approximately 80,500 pounds, and it increased to approximately 250,000 pounds in September of the same year, with the majority of investments in government securities. In December 1977, it was renamed the NSE, with branches created in several of the country's major commercial centers. Since April 27, 1999, the NSE has operated an automated trading system (ATS), in which dealers trade over a computer network. The NSE unveiled its next-generation trading platform, X-Gen, in 2013, with the goal of enabling electronic trading for both retail and institutional investors. Monday through Friday, the exchange's trading hours are 9.30 a.m. to 2.30 p.m. The Nigerian Securities and Exchange Commission (SEC) regulates the NSE. The SEC and The Federal Ministry of Finance are the primary regulatory bodies for the Nigeria's capital market. Although the NSE is privately owned and self-regulating, the SEC monitors it with the objective of maintaining orderly and equitable securities transactions and safeguarding the market against insider trading abuses. As of November 2019, it featured 161 businesses, including 8 domestic companies on the premium board, 144 on the main board, and 4 on the Alternative Securities Market (ASeM) board. The NSE currently lists 84 FGN bonds, 21 state bonds, 27 corporate bonds, 1 supranational bond, and 53 memorandum listings in the fixed-income market.

28.2.3 Auditing and Audit Committee Regulations in Nigeria

The Company and Allied Matters Act (CAMA), 2004, is the fundamental regulatory framework in Nigeria for company operations. Additionally, it is the primary piece of legislation overseeing financial reporting for publicly traded corporations. Part X1-Financial Statements and Audit contains the fundamental requirement for business financial reporting. The Sections 331–356 of CAMA 2004 deal with financial statements, while parts 357–369 deal with audits. Along with the CAMA, corporate reporting must adhere to additional rules, such as the local statement of accounting standards (SAS) and the International Accounting Standard (IAS). The accounting standards are largely concerned with ensuring financial reporting uniformity and comparability. Prior to the proclamation of CAMA 1990, which has become a statute under the civilian rule in Nigeria, conformity with accounting standards was persuasive. However, with the passage of CAMA 1990, financial disclosure by businesses has become a primary necessity. The Financial Reporting Council of Nigeria (formerly NASB) is also actively engaged in attempts to improve and promote financial disclosure. The Nigeria Accounting Standard Board (NASB) was founded in 1982 with the authority to define and issue accounting standards that must be followed while compiling financial accounts. Nigeria adopted International Financial Reporting Standards (IFRS) on January 1, 2012 and renamed its national standards-setting organization the Financial Reporting Council of Nigeria from the Nigerian Accounting Standards Board. The motivation for adopting IFRS was to improve financial reporting quality by providing information relevant to varied stakeholders' decision-making. Corporate governance standards enforced by authorities in Nigeria have also aided in the improvement of the corporate reporting environment. This is specified under section 359 of the CAMA.

Additionally, the Nigerian Securities and Exchange Commission (SEC) issued a code of best corporate governance practices in 2003, and Section 11 (a) of that code requires public corporations in Nigeria to create an audit committee. Additionally, it requires that the audit committee's members be primarily non-executive directors. Section 12 (a) of the SEC code of 2003 prohibits the appointment of more than one executive director to the audit committee (Gabriel, 2012). Moreover, following the 2005 financial consolidation, the Nigerian central bank (CBN) issued a post-consolidation code of best practices that became active in April 2006. Section 5.3.12 requires all banks to establish an audit committee as a standing committee of their board of directors. It is crucial to note that Section 8.1.4 of this code requires the establishment of an audit committee composed of non-executive members and representatives of ordinary shareholders elected at the annual general meeting. Nonetheless, this code is silent on the committee's maximum membership size. It is valuable to note that the banking industry plays a critical role in the overall economic development of a country, which is why the authorities concerned have implemented numerous rules to ensure its transparency.

28.2.4 Theoretical Background

Agency and institutional theories are among the essential theoretical lenses by which corporate risk disclosure can be examined (Lajili et al., 2020). The company law has directed the principal (shareholders and other stakeholders) of the publicly listed companies to appoint the agents (corporate managers) to run the day-to-day affairs of the business. This directive signifies the separation of ownership from control. The relationship between owners and their agents has been extensively explained by agency theory. The conflict of interest is inevitable in almost every corporate setting as each stakeholder group is trying to protect its interest. Managers might promote unnecessary agency costs by concealing valuable information from investors and other stakeholders. Therefore, corporate managers are often encouraged to divulge the pertinent risk information as it tends to lower the potential agency cost associated with information asymmetry. It also serves as a monitoring mechanism that helps align all the stakeholders with managerial incentives which could exploit additional firm value as well as decrease the cost of capital (Lajili et al., 2020).

Moreover, institutional theory and sociopolitical research may perhaps explain risk disclosure variations through national borders, legal as well as institutional contexts (Lajili et al., 2020). The social pressures to comply with the standard and search for instituting and/or preserving legitimacy can be explained by institutional theory as this theoretical approach emphasizes to explain factors attributed to organizational behaviors (e.g., risk disclosure practice). For instance, the CBN directives that mandated all listed banks in Nigeria to maintain a uniform calendar (31st December) for the preparation of their financial statements as well as the International Financial Reporting Standards (IFRS) adoption effective from the year 2012 represents a fascinating institutional change context. Before the observance of the common calendar among the listed banks, the CBN uncovered some irregularities whereby the reporting bank could borrow money from non-reporting banks to cover up certain loopholes. The adoption of IFRS and uniform calendars has substantially improved stakeholders' confidence. In this study, we explicitly consider the risk disclosure trend after IFRS was adopted by banks.

28.2.5 *Prior Empirical Studies*

The lack of specific regulations that mandated firms to disclose their risk profile motivated scholars to search the major factors that influence firms to reveal their risk information. For instance, company-specific characteristics and corporate governance attributes were the major factors that determine the extent of corporate risk disclosure. Moreover, the audit committee is one of the important corporate governance mechanisms that are responsible to ensure a sound internal control system and risk management in the firm. The nature of their duties has motivated scholars to test the audit committee composition variables as one of the factors that explained corporate risk disclosure. For example, the study conducted by Vandemaele et al. (2009) sampled 46 films listed on Euronext for the year 2006 and assesses the influence of risk committee/manager on corporate risk disclosure. Based on the information included in the disclosure index developed, the content analysis and regression analysis discovered that the presence of risk committee/manager is not statistically significant and therefore does not influence the extent of risk disclosure. In a similar study, Al-maghzom et al. (2016) sampled 12 listed banks in Saudi Arabia and examined the effect of audit committee structure on risk disclosure. They employed content analysis on 60 annual reports for the years 2009–2013. The regression results reveal a positive significant audit committee meetings and corporate risk disclosure, whereas independent directors in the audit committee and the size of the audit committee are not statistically significant.

Moreover, a study conducted by Ishtiaq et al. (2017) analyzes the impact of audit committee variables on corporate risk disclosure in Pakistan. The study samples 85 annual reports for the year 2011–2016 and performs content analysis on risk disclosure. The GLS regression results discovered that the audit committee meeting is positively statistically significant in driving risk disclosure upward. Furthermore, a similar study conducted by Seta and Setyaningrum (2018) assesses the role played by the risk committee on corporate risk disclosure. They sample 365 annual reports of the firms listed in Indonesia for the year 2015. The result identifies that the presence of a risk committee has a positive significant effect on the extent of risk divulged by firms. In South Africa, Viljoen et al. (2019) sampled 40 annual reports of the top companies listed in JSE for the year 2011 and examined the influence of audit committee characteristics on risk information disclosure. It is discovered that the presence of risk officers and the frequency of audit committee meetings have a positive effect, while the independent director and his experience in the audit committee as well as size are not statistically significant in commanding the amount of risk information to reveal by firms.

28.3 Development of Hypothesis

28.3.1 Audit Committee Size

The audit committee is one of the corporate governance mechanisms that are typically used to ensure the existence of a concrete internal control system in the firm. The manner in which the committee is constituted appears to be one of the recent risk disclosure research questions. The earlier studies (Forker, 1992) have argued that the firm can use the audit committee as a monitoring mechanism; thus, the potential agency cost could be minimized by improving the corporate disclosure quality. The presence, size, and composition of the audit committee are highly relevant to the amount of information to be divulged by firms. The literature has identified the size of the audit committee as one of the contributing factors of corporate disclosure practice. For example, the findings of the study conducted by Achmad et al. (2017) have revealed a positive association between the audit committee size and corporate risk disclosure. Grounded on this empirical conclusion, the following hypothesis was developed:

H1: There is a positive association between corporate risk disclosure and audit committee size.

28.3.2 Independent Director in the Audit Committee

The code of corporate governance has identified the audit committee as one of the monitoring mechanisms that could improve corporate transparency and lessen the potential agency cost (Forker, 1992). Firms have to assign an audit committee to gain an effective internal control system and governance (Al-maghzom et al., 2016), and the existence of that committee tends to substantially influence the firm's disclosure behavior (Ho & Wong, 2001). The members of the committee have to delegate the board and also have a duty to protect shareholders' interests. Investors and other stakeholders could experience further corporate transparency provided the major audit committee members are independent directors as they have the power to moderate the quantity of information withheld. The audit committee tends to be autonomous, provided the independent directors are included in the committee. According to the argument suggested by Agency theory, the independence of the audit committee from the top management has greater implication in reducing information asymmetry problems because the committee has to consider investors' interest in the process of discharging their responsibilities (Al-maghzom et al., 2016). However, the previous empirical studies provided a mixed finding on the position of independent directors in driving corporate disclosures. For example, the findings (Oliveira et al., 2011) have shown a positive association between risk disclosure and audit committee independence. In contrast, Viljoen et al. (2019) discovered an insignificant relationship. However, consistent with agency theory, the hypothesis is formulated as follows:

H2: There is a positive association between an independent director in the audit committee and corporate risk disclosure.

28.3.3 Independent Chairperson in the Audit Committee

Firms have to assign an audit committee to gain an effective internal control system and governance (Al-maghzom et al., 2016), and the existence of that committee tends to substantially influence the firms' disclosure behavior (Ho & Wong, 2001). The members of the committee are delegated by the board and responsible to work on their behalf and also have a duty to protect shareholders' interests. Investors and other stakeholders could experience further corporate transparency provided the major audit committee members are nonexecutives as they have the power to moderate the quantity of information withheld (Ho & Wong, 2001). According to the argument suggested by Agency theory, the independence of the audit committee from the top management has greater implications in plummeting information asymmetry problems because the committee has to consider investors interested in the process of discharging their responsibilities. The audit committee's crucial duty is to ensure the presence of effective internal control, risk management, and the truthfulness of the information disclosed in the financial statement (Al-maghzom et al., 2016). However, the previous empirical studies on audit committee independence and corporate disclosure have reported mixed findings. For example, the findings (Oliveira et al., 2011) have shown a positive association between risk disclosure and independent chairperson in the audit committee. Hence, the hypothesis is formulated as follows:

H3: The presence of an independent chairperson in the audit committee influences the banks to reveal greater risk information.

28.3.4 Nonexecutive Member in the Audit Committee

The extent of corporate disclosure is substantially influenced by the audit committee's presence (Ho & Wong, 2001). However, the manner in which the committee is constituted is also very important because if the firm appointed higher nonexecutive members in the audit committee, they will use their influence to moderate the withheld information due to improve corporate transparency (Ho & Wong, 2001). Furthermore, scholars (Al-maghzom et al., 2016) motivated the firms to include a higher number of directors in the audit committee composition due to boost in their disclosure policy; this practice could reduce the potential information asymmetry of information problems. The committee of nonexecutive directors is term to be independent. However, the previous empirical studies on audit committee independence and corporate disclosure have reported mixed findings. For example, the findings (Oliveira et al., 2011) have shown a positive association between risk disclosure and audit committee independence. Hence, the hypothesis is formulated as follows:

H4: There is a positive association between a nonexecutive member in the audit committee and the quantity of risk disclosure.

28.3.5 Audit Committee Meetings

It is generally believed that the major corporate strategic decisions are taken at the board room meeting. In compliance with the provision of corporate governance that required the board to constitute an audit committee mainly to establish a sound internal control system and risk management strategy, the inclusion of nonexecutive members is motivated in the audit committee composition as their presence could moderate the influence of the management in the meetings. The literature delivers experiential evidence that the directors exercise their monitoring activities by influencing the extent of corporate disclosure based on the number of meetings held by the committee (Allegrini & Greco, 2013). The importance of regular meetings cannot be overemphasized as Cheng and Courtenay (2006) asserted that firms could minimize fraud risk by conducting regular meetings. We test the hypothesis that the board and the audit committee's diligence in delivering monitoring activity positively affect the level of information voluntarily disclosed. The prior studies (Al-maghzom et al., 2016) have reported positive linearity between corporate disclosure and the frequency of audit committee meetings. So, the hypothesis is coined as follows:

H5: There is a positive association between the risk disclosure and the number of audit committee meetings.

Table 28.1 Sample

Criteria	N
Total number of listed banks	15
Number of banks without complete data	7
Final sample	8

28.4 Methodology

28.4.1 Sample and Data

The study selected all the banks listed on the Nigerian Stock Exchange as our sample. However, any bank that has no relevant data for variables of interest (audit committee data) from 2014 to 2018 was excluded from the sample. Table 28.1 provides the total number of the study sample. Nonetheless, the data on Risk Disclosure (RD) which serves as our dependent variable was collected from the annual reports of the sample banks that were downloaded from their respective websites. We explore all the narratives sections including notes to the accounts to collect RD data. Moreover, the data peculiar with independent and control variables were collected from the Bloomberg database. To meet the research objectives, we employed content analysis and the descriptive statistics to analyze the risk disclosure behavior among the listed banks in Nigeria. Furthermore, we employ a multivariate regression analysis to examine the effect of the explanatory factors on the explained variable. This analysis would enable us to understand the direction of the relationship among our variables and also to measure the extent of their connection or otherwise.

28.4.2 Content Analysis

Content analysis is the major analytical tool employed by prior risk disclosure studies. The procedure involves the analysis of annual reports narratives such as management discussion and analysis, chairman statements, directors' review, etc. This study uses the analysis instrument (checklist) that was adopted for previous studies (Rajab & Handley-Schachler, 2009; Linsley et al., 2006) to explore and code the extent of risk disclosure reported in the listed banks' annual report. Table 28.1 of the appendix shows the checklist with little modification. The main target is to identify and count the number of risks disclosed based on a variable measurement a researcher considers more appropriate. The use of words and sentences are the two common measurement approaches adopted by risk disclosure researches. Each of these approaches has its advantages and drawbacks. In the word approach, a researcher can count the number of risk-related words with reasonable accuracy; however, the coder cannot classify the risk into diverse risk disclosure categories. In contrast, the sentence approach as a measurement tool has the advantage of coding the risk information into a diverse risk disclosure category.

However, we cannot code the whole risk sentence with reasonable certainty compared to the word approach. Despite the existing argument, this study is consistent with previous studies (Rajab & Handley-Schachler, 2009; Linsley et al., 2006) and selected the sentence approach because the procedure will enable us to analyze the risk into a diverse category. We adopted the style in which prior study (Rajab & Handley-Schachler, 2009) classifies the risk disclosure into four different categories. The first category classifies the risk disclosure into strategic, operational, and environmental risk disclosure. The second category classifies risk disclosure into future (forward-looking) information and past (backward-looking) information. The third category classifies risk disclosure into qualitative (monetary) and non-qualitative (nonmonetary). The fourth category classifies risk disclosure into good news, bad news, and neutral information. Moreover, to minimize the sentence approach drawbacks and subjectivity element inherited in the content analysis, we adopted the decision rule developed by prior studies. Thus:

- To identify the risk-related disclosure, the definition that considers good, bad, and uncertainty has to be considered "if the reader is informed of any opportunity or prospect, or of any hazard, danger, harm, threat or exposure, that has already impacted upon the company or may impact upon the company in the future or of the management of any such opportunity, prospect, hazard, harm, threat or exposure (Linsley et al., 2006)."
- The statement cannot be implied but rather must be unambiguously specified.
- Table 28.1 of the appendix will be maintained as a term of reference for identification and classification of risk disclosures.
- Sentences related to general policy statements vis-à-vis corporate governance, statements of risk management policy, risk management systems, internal control, employee health and safety, and general policy about financial risk management shall be categorized as nonmonetary/neutral/non-time.
- The sentence is considered monetary risk disclosures if the statement either acknowledges the precise financial impact of a risk or they have provided the information that is enough for the readers to compute the financial implication of the risk involved.
- If the statement has two or more likely classifications, the disclosure is suggested to be coded in the category that is best emphasized in the sentence.
- Tables (qualitative and quantitative) that report risk-related information should be construed as each line equals one sentence and be categorized accordingly.
- Any risk disclosure statement that is repeated shall be considered as a new risk sentence whenever it is discussed. Besides, the disclosure shall not be coded as risk disclosure provided it is too ambiguous in its reference to risk.

Table 28.2 Variable description and measurement

Variable	Variable definition	Measurement of the variable
RD	Risk disclosure	Number of risk sentences
SAC	Size of the audit committee (AC)	Number of people in the AC
IDAC	Independent director in the AC	Number of independent member in the AC
ICPAC	Independent chairperson in the AC	1 if the audit committee has an independent chairperson and 0 otherwise
NEDAC	Nonexecutive in audit committee	Number of independent member in the AC
ACM	Audit committee meetings	Number of audit committee meetings

28.4.3 Measurement of Variables

Table 28.2 presents the study variables, definitions, and the procedure by which we measure our dependent and independent variables. This could permit us to run the regression and test the hypotheses developed in the previous section.

In developing the study model, the total risk disclosure (RD) is our explained variable, while the size of the audit committee (SAC), an independent member in the audit committee (IDAC), presence of an independent chairperson in the audit committee (ICPAC), the nonexecutive member in the audit committee (NEDAC), and the audit committee meeting (ACM) are the five explanatory factors included in the model. This will permit us to know to what extent the covariates explain the model developed. The following is our regression equation:

$$\begin{aligned}\mathrm{RD} = \beta_{0it} + \beta_{1it}\,(\mathrm{SAC}) + (\mathrm{IDAC}) + \beta_{3it}(\mathrm{ICPAC}) + \beta_{4it}(\mathrm{NEDAC}) \\ + \beta_{5it}(\mathrm{ACM}) + \varepsilon_{it}\end{aligned}$$

28.5 Result and Discussion

This sector presents and discusses the descriptive statistics, diagnosis test, as well as regression result. The results of the content analysis are presented based on the procedures described in the methodology. The summary statistics provide the number of observations used in the study, the mean, standard deviation, and minimum and maximum number of risks disclosed by banks from the entire category described in the checklist (appendix 1). Table 28.3 shows the summary statistics of the different categories of the risk disclosed by banks. The mean, standard deviation, and minimum and maximum number of total risk disclosure are 2290.47, 640.08, 852, and 3499, respectively. To have broad insight into risk disclosure behavior

Table 28.3 Descriptive statistics

Variable	Obs.	Mean	Std. dev.	Min	Max
Risk disclosure	72	2290.47	640.08	852	3499
Environmental risk	72	787.72	297.89	177	1498
Operational risk	72	1010.21	370.58	318	1860
Strategic risk	72	496.74	203.52	110	998
Quantitative risk info	72	388.90	19,813	140	975
Qualitative risk info	72	1905.76	628.41	639	3201
Good news	72	838.28	238.07	340	1380
Bad news	72	268.29	101.69	69	467
Neutral news	72	1188.03	358.07	434	1902
Future risk information	72	403.47	106.28	170	671
Past risk information	72	910.49	352.74	269	1766
Non-time risk information	72	980.78	263.01	384	1456

involving the listed banks in Nigeria, the disclosure is categorized into four diverse groups.

The first group classifies risk disclosure into environmental, operational, and strategic. The average risk disclosure under operational risk disclosure (1010.21) substantially dominates both environmental (787.72) and strategic (496.74) risk information. Despite the IFRS 7 and other macroeconomics problems being required to be coded under environmental risk, however, their frequency is less relative to operational risk disclosure. The above results were highly anticipated as the general statement about the internal control system, corporate governance, and risk definition, were all required by the checklist to report them in the operational risk disclosure category. This finding is consistent with prior studies (Rajab & Handley-Schachler, 2009; Lajili et al., 2012) that reported operational risk disclosure as the most regular risk information divulged by firms.

Meanwhile, the second group analyzes risk disclosure into quantitative (monetary) and qualitative risk information. The result reported in Table 28.3 shows that the monetary-related risk information accounted for about 388.90 disclosures, while 1905 disclosures are attributed to nonmonetary risk information. The nature of this disclosure practice has impaired the relevance of risk disclosure for the informed decision as many stakeholders such as analysts consider quantitative risk information more appropriate in the stock valuation as well as earning forecast. Our finding provides support for the earlier empirical studies (Adamu, 2013) that discovered monetary risk information is rarely unveiled.

Moreover, the checklist analyzed the risk disclosure into good news, bad news, and neutral risk information. This analysis will give the readers to understand the status of their investment. Table 28.3 shows that about 838.28, 268.29, and 1188.03 are associated with good news, bad news, and neutral risk information, respectively. It appears that the corporate managers are keen to divulge more good news perhaps due to impressing their shareholders. The new approach to risk has recognized the occurrences of good events as a risk. This would give the investors and other stakeholders to evaluate the business prospect that could create additional value to the firm. Nevertheless, many stakeholders remain too conservative for their preference to see bad news that linked risk to the occurrences of bad events. Nonetheless, the higher appearances of neutral information and good news have raised the question about the quality of risk disclosure practice among the banks in Nigeria. This finding is consistent with previous studies (Adamu, 2013) that discovered bad news is less frequently divulged.

Furthermore, group four of the checklist considered the time horizon on which the risk information is disclosed. This could permit us to know if the risk-related information is past information (backward-looking), future information (forward-looking), or has no specific time (non-time) to relate the disclosure. Table 28.3 shows about 403.47 future risk information, 910.49 backward-looking information, and 980.78 non-time risk information. The dominance of non-time and past risk information is highly alarming about the quality of risk information disclosure. The forward-looking information is more pertinent to investors and other stakeholders because they might estimate and accumulate the magnitude of the risks in their decision-making process. Even so, the greater appearances of non-time and past in our result are consistent with prior studies' findings (Adamu, 2013).

28.5.1 *Pearson's Correlation*

Table 28.4 presents Pearson's correlations results that will help us have an intuition about the linearity of our otherwise among our study variables. To know the significant factors, the correlations were computed at the 5% level of significance.

The result found that total risk disclosure is associated with audit committee size, independent director, and the independent audit committee. These correlation results (independent director, nonexecutive director, and the independent audit committee) are similar to our regression outcome, except for audit committee size and audit committee meetings. In our regression, the audit committee size was not significant, while an audit committee meeting was statistically significant.

Meanwhile, for the OLS to be more appropriate, we used the correlation results depicted in Table 28.4 results due to knowing the relationship position of our

Table 28.4 Pairwise correlations

Variables	RD	SAC	IDAC	ICPAC	NEDAC	ACM
RD	1.000					
SAC	−0.267*	1.000				
IDAC	0352*	0.139	1.000			
ICPAC	0.520*	−0.020	0.599*	1.000		
NEDAC	−0.071	0.533*	0.527*	0.435*	1.000	
ACM	0.106	−0.098	0.326*	0.031	0.085	1.000

*Shows significance at the 0.05 level

independent variables. This would enable us to understand if the multicollinearity assumption was satisfied. The results show that the size of an audit committee is significant and positively associated with the nonexecutive directors in the audit committee (0.533). However, the coefficient of the independent audit committee (0.599), a nonexecutive director in the audit committee (0.527), and audit committee meetings (0.326) are significant and positively related to independent directors in the audit committee. Nonexecutive director in the audit committee (0.435) reveals the significant coefficient and positively connected with independent audit committee chairperson. Nevertheless, it is obvious that all the linearity vis-à-vis our explanatory factors are extensively underneath the threshold of 0.80. Consequently, the model is free from potential multicollinearity problems.

Likewise, to authenticate this particular finding, we compute the variance inflation factor (VIF) for the robustness of the multicollinearity assumption. The VIF results have authenticated our pairwise correlation results which suggest the nonexistence of multicollinearity in the model. This can be justified by the values demonstrated by all the explanatory factors as none of them reached the threshold of 10.

28.5.2 *Heteroskedasticity*

We computed the Breusch-Pagan LM test to ascertain if the variance of our error term is homoscedastic or otherwise. The outcome reveals 2.94 and 0.0866 for the chi-square and p-value, respectively. The higher p-value above 5% is an indication that our error term is homoscedastic. However, to solidify our result, we perform the White test for homoscedasticity of the error term. The result was statistically significant at the 5% level of significance because the chi-square and p-value reveal 30.76 and 0.0429, respectively. Consequently, we used the white standard error to address the heteroskedasticity problem in our model.

28.5.3 *Regression Result*

The study applied OLS regression analysis to examine the effect of the audit committee on the total risk disclosure. The regression outcome is presented in Table 28.5 after the total risk disclosure (dependent variable) was regressed against five explanatory factors of the audit committee. These factors include the size of the audit committee, the number of independent directors in the audit committee composition, the presence of an independent chairperson in the audit committee, the nonexecutive member in the audit committee, and the number of meetings held by the audit committee. The overall *P*-value (0.000) of the model is statistically significant at a 1% level of significance. Moreover, the value of F-statistics is 9.516, while the R-squared figure is 0.502. Grounded on the R-square value, the explanatory factors incorporated in the model have explained the variation of total

Table 28.5 Variance inflation factor

Variables	VIF	1/VIF
NEDAC	1.831	.546
IDAC	1.792	.558
ICPAC	1.603	.624
SAC	1.29	.775
ACM	1.191	.84
Mean VIF	1.541	.

Table 28.6 Regression result

RD	Coefficient	Std. error	*t*-value	*p*-value	Sig
SAC	−74.705	87.966	−0.85	0.402	
IDAC	260.529	128.241	2.03	0.051	*
ICPAC	605.776	276.262	2.19	0.036	**
NEDAC	−150.950	129.413	−1.17	0.253	
ACM	164.840	71.893	2.29	0.029	**
Constant	1805.287	474.15	3.81	0.001	***

***$P < 0.01$, **$p < 0.05$, *$p < 0.1$

risk disclosure by 50.2%. Meanwhile, the number of independent members reveals a positive coefficient which is statistically significant at the 10% level of significance. This signifies that greater independent members in the audit committee will influence the firm to disclose the higher level of risk information. This assertion provides considerable support for the H1 that predicts that RD is influenced by the independent member in the audit committee. The finding is in line with the previous studies (Oliveira et al., 2011).

Moreover, the existence of an audit committee chairperson is very important because there is a tendency for the committee to discharge their duties effectively. The audit committee appears to be autonomous, provided there is a person who is responsible to chair and preside over the committee meetings. If the committee is responsible for corporate risk management, it means that the chairperson is considered a risk committee chairperson. The result presented in Table 28.6 shows the existence of a relationship between audit committee chairperson and corporate risk disclosure. The results reveal a positive coefficient which is statistically significant at the 5% level of significance. This result provides strong statistical evidence to support H2. Our finding is also consistent with prior empirical studies by Viljoen et al. (2019). Meanwhile, the number of the audit committee meeting is very essential as the crucial issues are presented for the critical deliberations in the committee meetings. One of the rationales behind the setting up of the audit committee is to ensure the existence of a solid internal control system and effective risk management procedures in the organization.

The regression results presented in Table 28.6 have indicated the positive linkage between the number of audit committee meetings and the extent of risk divulged by banks. This can be justified by the positive coefficient which is statistically significant at a 5% level of significance. Hence, the predicted H5 is accepted. This finding is consistent with prior studies by Viljoen et al. (2019). Nevertheless, the other variables (audit committee size and nonexecutive member) included in the model are not statistically significant. The results reported in Table 28.6 have revealed an insignificant coefficient for the audit committee size. This is a strong indication that constituting too many people in the audit committee would not improve the quality or quantity of the risk information the banks decided to unveil. This led us to reject the H1 which postulated the positive linearity between total risk disclosure and audit committee size. This result authenticates the prior studies' findings (Al-maghzom et al., 2016).

Likewise, the coefficient of the nonexecutive director reported in Table 28.6 appears insignificant. Despite the role of nonexecutive director suggested by the code of corporate governance in many countries, nevertheless, it was found to have less influence in the audit committee, especially on the amount of risk to divulge by banks. It appears there is no statistical evidence to support the H4, thus rejected.

28.6 Conclusion

The study examines the influence of audit committee structure on corporate risk disclosure in the Nigerian banking sector. The independent member in the audit committee, the presence of an independent audit committee chairperson, and the frequency of audit committee meetings are the important factors that influence banks to disclose greater risk information. However, audit committee size and the presence of nonexecutive members in the audit committee are not among the factors that determine the extent of risk to divulge by banks. Also, the study provides evidence that the banks are willing to disclose risk-related information. The frequency of operational risk disclosure is higher than that of environmental and strategic risk information categories. Nonetheless, most of the risk informtion reported were qualitative, neutral, and non-time. It is important to note that investors and other stakeholders often prefer greater disclosure on monetary, bad news, and forward-looking information; nevertheless, they are less frequently disclosed by banks. The higher disclosures of backward-looking information, good news, nonmonetary information, risk definitions, and the general statements have decreased the relevance of the risk information disclosed to the users of annual reports. The present practice is not adequate to meet the demand of many stakeholders especially in their decision-making process. Moreover, there is a lack of uniformity in the styles employed by banks to disclose their risk. This is not unconnected with the unavailability of a comprehensive framework about how risk will be disclosed from the regulators, as the disclosure of this nature is still voluntary in Nigeria. However, the risk disclosure is annually advancing; hence there is a tendency that the quality of risk disclosure could increase in the near future especially if the audit committee remains active in discharging their duties judiciously. The banks that institute their audit committee with many independent members, an independent chairperson, and adopt the spirit of meeting consistently tend to improve the quality and quantity of their risk confession. These study findings have implications for investors, regulators, banks, and other stakeholders in the emerging economy. Consistent with prior studies, the risk disclosure coding process is one of the major limitations identified in this study. The subjectivity element in coding risk disclosure sentences in the annual narratives is unavoidable. However, the decision criteria we adopted from Linsley et al., (2006) has reduced the element of risk sentence coding bias. The second limitation is the lack of data concerning variables of interest in the Bloomberg data stream; this problem has mandated us to reduce our sample size. Nonetheless, future studies are advised to explore other databases if data is available.

References

Abdallah, A. A., Mcclelland, P., & Hassan, M. K. (2015). Islamic financial institutions, corporate governance, and corporate risk disclosure in Gulf Cooperation Council countries. *Journal of Multinational Financial Management, 31*, 63–82. https://doi.org/10.1016/j.mulfin.2015.02.003

Achmad, T., Faisal, F., & Oktarina, M. (2017). Factors influencing voluntary corporate risk disclosure practices by Indonesian companies. *Corporate Ownership and Control, 14*(3–2), 286–292. https://doi.org/10.22495/cocv14i3c2art2

Adamu, M. U. (2013). Risk reporting: A study of risk disclosures in the annual reports of listed companies in Nigeria. *Research Journal of Finance and Accounting, 4*(16), 140–148. Retrieved from www.iiste.org

Adamu, M. U. (2021). Organisational characteristics corporate governance and corporate risk disclosure: An overview. *Journal of Corporate Finance Research / Корпоративные Финансы | ISSN: 2073-0438, 15*(1), 77–92. https://doi.org/10.17323/j.jcfr.2073-0438.15.1.2021.77-92

Adamu, M. U. & Ivashkovskaya, I. (2021). Corporate governance and risk disclosure in emerging countries. *Journal of Corporate Finance Research/Корпоративные Финансы | ISSN: 2073-0438, 15*(4), 5–17. https://doi.org/10.17323/j.jcfr.2073 0438.15.4.2021.5 17

Albitar, K. (2015). Firm characteristics, governance attributes and corporate voluntary disclosure: A study of Jordanian listed companies. *International Business Research, 8*(3), 1–10. https://doi.org/10.5539/ibr.v8n3p1

Allegrini, M., & Greco, G. (2013). Corporate boards, audit committees and voluntary disclosure: Evidence from Italian listed companies. *Journal of Management and Governance, 17*, 187–216. https://doi.org/10.1007/s10997-011-9168-3

Al-maghzom, A., Hussainey, K., & Aly, D. (2016). Corporate governance and risk disclosure: Evidence from Saudi Arabia. *Corporate Ownership and Control, 13*(2), 145–166. https://doi.org/10.22495/cocv13i2p14

Barakat, A., & Hussainey, K. (2013). Bank governance, regulation, supervision, and risk reporting: Evidence from operational risk disclosures in European banks. *International Review of Financial Analysis, 30*, 254–256. https://doi.org/10.1016/j.irfa.2013.07.002

Beretta, S., & Bozzolan, S. (2004). Framework for the analysis of firm risk communication. *The International Journal of Accounting, 39*, 265–288. https://doi.org/10.1016/j.intacc.2004.06.006

Cheng, E. C. M., & Courtenay, S. M. (2006). Board composition, regulatory regime and voluntary disclosure. *The International Journal of Accounting, 14*(3), 262–289. https://doi.org/10.1016/j.intacc.2006.07.001

Deumes, R., & Knechel, W. R. (2008). Economic incentives for voluntary reporting on internal risk management and control systems. *A Journal of Practice and Theory, 27*(1), 35–66. https://doi.org/10.2308/aud.2008.27.1.35

Elamer, A. A., Ntim, C. G., & Abdou, H. A. (2017). Islamic governance, national governance and bank risk management and disclosure in MENA countries. *Business and Society, 00*(0), 1–42. https://doi.org/10.1177/0007650317746108

Elghaffar, E. S. A., Abotalib, A. M., Azeem, M. A., & Khalil, M. (2019). Determining factors that affect risk disclosure level in Egyptian banks. *Banks and Bank Systems, 14*(1), 159–171. https://doi.org/10.21511/bbs.14(1).2019.14

Elshandidy, T., Fraser, I., & Hussainey, K. (2013). Aggregated, voluntary and mandatory risk disclosure incentives: Evidence from UK FTSE all share companies. *International Review of Financial Analysis, 30*, 320–333. https://doi.org/10.1016/j.irfa.2013.07.010

Elshandidy, T., Fraser, I., & Hussainey, K. (2015). What drives mandatory and voluntary risk reporting variations across Germany, UK and US ? *The British Accounting Review, 47*(4), 376–394. https://doi.org/10.1016/j.bar.2014.06.001

Forker, J. (1992). Corporate governance and disclosure quality corporate governance and disclosure quality. *Accounting and Business Research, 22*(86), 111–124. https://doi.org/10.1080/00014788.1992.9729426

Grassa, R., Moumen, N., & Hussainey, K. (2020). Do ownership structures affect risk disclosure in Islamic banks? International evidence. *Journal of Financial Reporting and Accounting*, 1985–2517. https://doi.org/10.1108/JFRA-02-2020-0036

Habtoor, O. S., Ahmad, N., Baabbad, M. A., Masood, A., Raihan, N., Hassan, M., & Haat, C. (2018). Corporate risk disclosure practice in Saudi Arabia: Secrecy versus transparency. *International Journal of Advanced and Applied Sciences, 5*(12), 42–58. https://doi.org/10.21833/ijaas.2018.12.007

Ho, S. S. M., & Wong, K. S. (2001). A study of the relationship between corporate governance structures and the extent of voluntary disclosure. *Journal of International Accounting, Auditing and Taxation, 10*, 139–156. https://doi.org/10.1016/S1061-9518(01)00041-6

ICAEW (2002). No surprises: the case for better risk reporting. *Balance Sheet, 10*(4), 18–21.

Ishtiaq, M., Latif, K., Ashraf, A., & Akram, M. A. (2017). Determinants of risk disclosure in Pakistan: Evidence from textile firms listed at Pakistan stock exchange. *Journal of Managerial Sciences, XI*(03), 534–552. Available at https://qurtuba.edu.pk/jms/EIEF.htm. Accessed 20 Nov 2020.

Ivashkovskaya, I., & Nadezhda, Z. (2009). The relationship between corporate governance and company performance in concentrated ownership systems: The case of Germany. *Journal of Corporate Finance, 4*(12), 34–56. https://doi.org/10.17323/j.jcfr.2073-0438.3.4.2009.34-56

Khlif, H., & Hussainey, K. (2016). The association between risk disclosure and firm characteristics: A meta-analysis. *Journal of Risk Research, 19*(2), 181–211. https://doi.org/10.1080/13669877.2014.961514

Lajili, K. (2009). Corporate risk disclosure and corporate governance. *Journal of Risk and Financial Management, 2*, 94–117. https://doi.org/10.3390/jrfm2010094

Lajili, K., Dobler, M., & Zéghal, D. (2012). An empirical investigation of business and operational risk disclosures. *International Journal of Management and Business, 3*, 53–71. Retrieved from https://www.researchgate.net/publication/267327503

Lajili, K., Dobler, M., Zeghal, D., & Bryan, M. J. (2020). Risk reporting in financial crises: A tale of two countries. *International Journal of Accounting and Information Management.* https://doi.org/10.1108/IJAIM-03-2020-0034

Linsley, P. M., & Shrives, P. J. (2007). Transparency and the disclosure of risk information in the banking sector. *Journal of Financial Regulation and Compliance, 13*(3), 205–214. https://doi.org/10.1108/13581980510622063

Linsley, P. M., Shrives, P. J., & Crumpton, I. (2006). Risk disclosure: An exploratory study of UK and Canadian banks. *Journal of Banking Regulation, 7*(3/4), 268–282. https://doi.org/10.1057/palgrave.jbr.2350032

Mazaya, N., & Fuad, F. (2018). Business strategy, corporate governance, firm characteristics and risk disclosure in the Indonesian stock exchange. *Jurnal Keuangan Dan Perbankan | Finance, 22*(3), 381–394. https://doi.org/10.26905/jkdp.v22i3.2167

Neifar, S., & Jarboui, A. (2018). Corporate governance and operational risk voluntary disclosure: Evidence from Islamic banks. *Research in International Business and Finance, 46*, 43–54. https://doi.org/10.1016/j.ribaf.2017.09.006

Netti, A. (2018). Firm determinants of risk disclosure: Evidence from Italian listed companies. *Corporate Ownership and Control, 16*(1), 168–177. https://doi.org/10.22495/cocv16i1c1art

Oliveira, J., Rodrigues, L. L., & Craig, R. (2011). Voluntary risk reporting to enhance institutional and organizational legitimacy: Evidence from Portuguese banks. *Journal of Financial Regulation and Compliance, 19*, 271–289. https://doi.org/10.1108/13581981111147892

Rajab, B., & Handley-Schachler, M. (2009). Corporate risk disclosure by UK firms: Trends and determinants. *World Review of Entrepreneurship Management and Sustainable Development, 5*(3), 224–243. https://doi.org/10.1504/WREMSD.2009.026801

Seta, A. T., & Setyaningrum, D. (2018). Corporate governance and risk disclosure: Indonesian evidence. In *Advances in economics, business and management research, 6th international accounting conference* (Vol. 55, pp. 37–41). Retrieved from http://creativecommons.org/licenses/by-nc/4.0/

Solomon, J. F., Solomon, A., Norton, S. D., & Joseph, N. L. (2000). A conceptual framework for corporate risk disclosure emerging from the agenda for corporate governance reform. *The British Accounting Review, 32*, 447–478. https://doi.org/10.1006/bare.2000.0145

Vandemaele, S., Vergauwen, P., & Michiels, A. (2009). *Management risk reporting practices and their determinants*. Retrieved from https://uhdspace.uhasselt.be/dspace/bitstream/1942/9392/2/CorporateriskB.pdf

Vergauwen, P., Dao, M., & Brüggen, A. (2009). Determinants of intellectual capital disclosure: Evidence from Australia. *Management Decision, 47*(2), 233–245. https://doi.org/10.1108/00251740910938894

Viljoen, C., & Enslin, Z. (2016). Determinants of enhanced risk disclosure of JSE top 40 companies: The board risk committee composition, frequency of meetings and the chief risk officer. *Southern African Business Review, 20*(May), 208–312. https://doi.org/10.25159/1998-8125/6050

Viljoen, C., Bruwer, B. W., & Enslin, Z. (2019). Determinants of enhanced risk disclosure of JSE Top 40 Companies: the board risk committee composition frequency of meetings and the chief risk officer. *Southern African Business Review, 20*(1), 208–235. https://doi.org/10.25159/1998-8125/6050

Yang, Songling, Ishtiaq, M., & Anwar, M. (2018). Enterprise risk management practices and firm performance the mediating role of competitive advantage and the moderating role of financial literacy. *Journal of Risk and Financial Management, 11*(3), 35–10. https://doi.org/10.3390/jrfm11030035

Chapter 29
The Supervisory Authorities' View on Audit Quality in the Czech Republic

Michal Šindelář and Libuše Müllerová

Abstract The aim of the chapter is to analyze the audit quality from the point of view of supervisory authorities in the Czech Republic based on publicly available sources. Users of financial statements must be assured that the auditor has performed his work in accordance with the standards and that the result is a high-quality audit. The analysis is processed on the basis of reports of Supervisory Board of the Chamber of Auditors of Czech Republic and reports of Public Audit Oversight Board. Based on the analysis, we found that audit quality control has come to the forefront of supervisory priorities in recent years, both in terms of the number of inspections performed and the number of findings themselves. We can conclude that the audit firm will be subject to PAOB supervision approximately once every 3 years. Moreover, in 2019, the percentage of findings led to proposals to initiate disciplinary proceedings increased significantly.

Key words Audit quality · Supervisory Board of the Chamber of Auditors of the Czech Republic · Public Audit Oversight Board · Auditors of Public Interest Entities

29.1 Introduction

An audit of financial statements is a process of verification of these statements by an independent expert – auditor. The result of this process is an expression of auditor's opinion whether the audited financial statements give a true and fair view at the date when the financial statements are prepared.

Audited financial statements should be a reliable source of information for decision-making by all users of this information, not only owners but also potential investors, banks, business partners, etc. The general objective of the audit is to increase assurance of the accounting information of the companies that are required

M. Šindelář (✉) · L. Müllerová
Department of Financial Accounting and Auditing, Prague University of Economics and Business, Prague, Czech Republic
e-mail: michal.sindelar@vse.cz; libuse.mullerova@vse.cz

D. Procházka (ed.), *Regulation of Finance and Accounting*, Springer Proceedings in Business and Economics, https://doi.org/10.1007/978-3-030-99873-8_29

to publish financial statements and annual reports. The greatest attention must be paid to companies that are important to the whole society, the so-called public interest entities. There are many ways that lead the scientific research, e.g., the influence of the economic structure of the audit market (Asthana et al., 2019; Ciconte et al., 2015; Gigler & Penno, 1995; Sindelar & Mullerova, 2016), or the determinants of audit fees and the influence of Big4 firms (Afesha, 2015; Felix Jr. et al., 2001; Super & Shil, 2019), or the quality of audit (Cassell et al., 2020; Cho et al., 2017; Ernstberger et al., 2020; Srikandhi & Suryandari, 2020; Tepalagul & Lin, 2015). The main goal of this chapter is to analyze the audit quality in the Czech Republic from the point of view of the supervisory authorities.

The chapter is structured as follows. After the introduction, which briefly describes the meaning of the audit and the main ways of research in the audit, follows the literature review containing the audit quality research. The next section contains the data and methodology on which this research is based. The results discuss findings, and the conclusion of the chapter summarizes the major findings.

29.2 Literature Review

Users of information from financial statements must be assured that the auditor has performed his or her work in accordance with the standards and that the result is a high-quality audit. For this reason, the International Auditing and Assurance Standards Board (IAASB) has developed an Audit Quality Assessment System (Framework), which describes the input and output factors that support the improvement of audit quality at audit firm level, at audited company level, and from the perspective of the whole society. The basic features of this Framework are (IAASB, 2014):

- Encourage national audit firms, international networks of audit firms, and professional accountancy organizations to reflect on how to improve audit quality and better communicate information about audit quality.
- Raise the level of awareness and understanding among stakeholders of the important elements of audit quality.
- Enable stakeholders to recognize those factors that may deserve priority attention to enhance audit quality.
- Assist standard setting, both internationally and at a national level.
- Facilitate dialogue and closer working relationships between the IAASB and key stakeholders as well as among these key stakeholders themselves.
- Stimulate academic research on the topic.
- Assist students of auditing to more fully understand the fundamentals of the profession they are aspiring to join.

The quality management system for auditors and audit firms is then managed by the International Standard on Quality Control (ISQC1), which entered into force on 15 December 2017. This standard requires the audit firm to have a quality management system that provides reasonable assurance that the audit firm and its employees comply with professional and legal requirements and that the reports issued by the firm are appropriate to the circumstances. Regulation of the quality of audit work is a natural reflection of the fact that auditors' work is provided in the public interest and must therefore be credible. For this reason, compliance with the established rules is also monitored by national professional organizations (Chamber of Auditors of the Czech Republic) and national supervisory authorities (Public Audit Oversight Board).

Currently, Quality Management Projects are underway at the IAASB level. As a result of these project, a new standard dealing with audit quality has been published, namely, the International Standard on Quality Management 1 (ISQM 1). This standard will replace the ISQC 1 standard from 15 December 2022. By that date, audit firms must bring their internal regulations in line with the requirements of this standard (with selected requirements having another year for full implementation). Along with this standard, the International Standard on Quality Management 2 (ISQM 2), which deals with Engagement Quality Reviews, has also been issued. The main proposed change embodied in ISQM 1 is the need for an eight-component system of quality management. Much of what that system comprises will already be there, but thinking about it as a system will be new. The effectiveness of this new regulation will certainly be the subject of many scientific analyses.

In international research, there are many ways and studies that analyze the audit quality. Many of them analyze the indicators of audit quality. Ernstberger et al. (2020) examine how compensation policies of audit firms are associated with audit quality. They use detailed mandatory disclosure of the compensation policies in German audit firms and find some evidence suggesting that audit quality may be most at risk in cases in which partners rely more heavily on variable compensation to divide a relatively small profit pool. International standard setters have sponsored initiatives to develop a reliable portfolio of audit quality indicators (AQIs). Brown and Popova (2019) examine how investors respond to receiving auditor-disclosed AQIs. They find that investors experience a stronger negative affective reaction toward the auditors when receiving a negative-trending AQI portfolio compared to receiving a positive trend of AQIs or when no AQIs are disclosed. In turn, investors receiving a negative-trending AQI portfolio are less likely to support auditor ratification and choose to voluntarily decrease their investment in the company. Albersmann and Quick (2020) investigate whether goodwill impairments are perceived as timely and whether specific auditor characteristics affect the perceived timeliness. Based on a sample of German listed firms for the period 2006–2013, their results indicate that goodwill impairments are not recognized in a timely manner and delayed by at least 1–2 years. Alareeni (2019) aims to investigate the associations between audit firm attributes (i.e., audit firm size, non-audit services, auditor industry specialization, and auditor-client tenure) and specific indicators of audit quality. In this study are significant positive relationships between all audit firm attributes and audit quality. Additionally, the associations between all audit firm attributes and audit quality are moderated by proxies for audit quality. Willekens et al. (2020) examine whether auditor market power is associated with audit quality. Their results indicate that industry market shares distance is positively associated with audit quality, but we do not find an association between market concentration and audit quality.

Another direction of research in the field of audit quality is the analysis of internal rules of audit firms or the corporate governance system of the audited company and their impact on audit quality. Cassell et al. (2020) focus on the first year of the auditor-client relationship and investigate whether audit quality varies with the timing of the new auditor's appointment. They find that audit quality is not lower for companies that engage new auditors before the end of the third fiscal quarter than for companies that do not change auditors. However, companies that engage new auditors during or after the fourth fiscal quarter are more likely to misstate their audited financial statements than companies that engage new auditors earlier in the year and companies that do not change auditors. Srikandhi and Suryandari (2020) aim to analyze the moderation effect of audit quality on the relationship of independent commissioners, audit committee, and whistleblowing system on the integrity of financial statements. Their results showed that independent commissioners and whistleblowing systems do not influence the integrity of financial statements. On the other hand, find a significant positive effect of the audit committee. Kuang et al. (2020) analyze a sample of mandatory partner rotation events hand collected from SEC filings to investigate the relation between mandatory audit partner rotation and audit quality in the United States. Across a variety of control groups and audit quality proxies, they do not find evidence consistent with rotation materially improving audit quality.

The most important research related to this chapter is the research in the field of analyses of supervisory authorities on audit quality. These studies are primarily held in the United States. Mendiratta (2019) examines whether mandated introduction of Public Company Accounting Oversight Board in the United States improves the audit quality for listed companies. Johnson et al. (2020) investigate the coinciding effects of the implementation of Auditing Standard No. 5, the change in the Public Company Accounting Oversight Board's (PCAOB) inspection regime, and the Great Recession on the audit fees and audit quality of accelerated filers. They find that, following the three events, audit fees decreased and quality increased for accelerated filers. Lennox (2016) analyzes the PCAOB imposed restrictions on auditors' tax services in order to strengthen auditor independence and improve audit quality. The result of this study is that there is no change in audit quality. Based on this literature review, we decide to analyze the publicly available data from quality control of audit services in the Czech Republic.

29.3 Data

The subject of quality control of audit firms and statutory auditors is not only the management and control system they have established but also compliance with the Act on Auditors, the Code of Ethics for Auditors and Accountants, and auditing standards issued by the Chamber. The quality control of audit files is focused on meeting the requirements of ISA during the implementation of a specific audit, starting with the acceptance of the contract, risk assessment, planning, performance of tests, and their documentation, to the issuance of the auditor's report. The control team also assesses the auditor's internal organization and procedures, evaluates the auditor's internal quality management system, assesses the amount and quality of resources expended, meets continuing education requirements, and assesses the area of remuneration for auditing, internal regulations, or auditor's methodology. The Act on Auditors requires that quality control of auditors performing auditing activities in public interest entities be performed at least once every 3 years, as required by European law. The person performing the quality control shall prepare a report stating the identified deficiencies and recommending the method and deadline for their elimination. If the auditor does not eliminate the identified deficiencies within the recommended period, disciplinary proceedings are initiated against him.

In the Czech Republic, there are two main authorities performing audit quality controls – the Supervisory Board of the Chamber of Auditors of Czech Republic and the Public Audit Oversight Board (PAOB). The inspections organized by the PAOB focus not only on the quality of audits of public interest entities (PIE) but also on the quality of audits and audit activities performed by the PIE auditor at non-PIE entities. If the audit firm does not have a PIE in its portfolio, it is subject to quality control by the Supervisory Board of the Chamber of Auditors of Czech Republic. For the purposes of this chapter, we analyzed both reports on the control activities of the Supervisory board of the Chamber of Auditors of the Czech Republic and reports on the activities of the Public Audit Oversight Board.

29.4 Results and Discussion

In Table 29.1, there are stated the inspections performed by the Supervisory Board of the Chamber of Auditors of Czech Republic in 2014–2019. Table 29.1 shows the stable number of planned inspections, but there is a gradual growth in the last years. Only in the years 2017 and 2018, there was a slight decrease in the planned inspections. In the last analyzed year (2019), there was a huge increase in the number of performed inspections compared to the 6-year average. Based on the approved protocols from the performed inspections (including the possible settlement of objections), a total of 221 inspections were completed in 2019 at individual meetings

Table 29.1 Number of inspections by Supervisory Board of the Chamber of Auditors of Czech Republic

Year	2014	2015	2016	2017	2018	2019	6-years average
Planned	230	256	250	222	231	266	243
Performed	209	225	231	201	194	241	217
Not performed	21	31	19	21	37	5	22

Source: KAČR, 2020, authorial computation

of the Supervisory Board. Out of the total number of 221 completed inspections, the next inspection was approved for 33 inspected entities within the statutory period of 6 years. Due to the findings of less serious deficiencies, a follow-up inspection was approved for 92 inspected entities in a slightly shortened periodicity, and for 96 inspected entities, a repeat inspection was planned in a shortened period of 2–3 years due to the identified deficiencies (KAČR, 2020).

Out of the total number of 221 inspections completed in 2019, 60 inspections were completed by filing a petition for the initiation of disciplinary proceedings. This is 31% of the checks completed during this period (Table 29.2).

This table shows the development of proposals to initiate disciplinary proceedings and there is a significant growth in the last year. This can be caused by two influences. The first is that in 2019, the inspections carried out by the Supervisory Board of the Chamber of Auditors of the Czech Republic were generally tightened. This trend can also be observed in international comparisons (CEAOB, 2020), and this trend is likely to continue. The second may be that the inspections carried out are more targeted and thus lead to the detection of problematic ones. Additionally, the data shows that the most common disciplinary measure is the imposition of a fine.

The second institution that performs quality controls of the audit profession is the Public Audit Oversight Board (PAOB). Table 29.3 shows the number of inspections performed by PAOB.

The PAOB performs quality controls on auditors who have a public interest entity in their portfolio. The number of these auditors is currently 38. When comparing the number of quality controls per year and the number of audit firms, it can be concluded that the audit firm will be subject to PAOB supervision approximately

Table 29.2 Proposals to initiate disciplinary proceedings out of the total number of closed inspections in 2014–2019

Year	2014	2015	2016	2017	2018	2019
Proposals to initiate disciplinary proceeding	15	37	50	28	24	60
Closed quality inspections	193	232	246	203	193	221
Percentage (%)	7.8	15.9	20.3	13.8	12.4	31.1

Source: KAČR, 2020, authorial computation

Table 29.3 Number of inspections Public Audit Oversight Board

Year	2017	2018	2019
Inspections carried over from the previous year	0	1	0
Inspections initiated in the previous year	X[a]	4	4
Planned inspections	14	17	17
Completed inspections	8	18	14
Inspections in progress and completed in the following year	4	4	7

Source: PAOB, 2017, 2018, 2020, authorial computation

Note: [a]From 1 October 2016, effective date of the amendment to the Act on Auditors, the PAOB started to perform inspections of auditors that have public interest entities in their portfolios (previously the Supervisory Board of the Chamber of Auditors of Czech Republic carried out these inspections) once every 3 years. Moreover, all inspections were closed with findings and corrective actions imposed. A total of 284 findings were identified during the inspections concluded in 2019, of which 58 findings were in the area of the management and control system and 211 findings that resulted from the inspection of individual auditor's files (PAOB, 2020). For half of the auditors, 20 or more findings were identified which indicate deficiencies in the internal control system (PAOB, 2020). Based on 2 analyzed years, no overall conclusions can be drawn regarding the quality of audit services. To evaluate the quality of audit services of PIE auditors in the Czech Republic, it will be necessary to obtain relevant data for a longer period of time. Audit quality is also one of the main areas of interest for the CEAOB.

29.5 Conclusion

In recent years, audit quality has come to the forefront of the interest of supervisory authorities over the audit profession in the Czech Republic. This follows both from the growing number of inspections carried out and from the number of individual disciplinary proceedings. In 2016, Public Audit Oversight Board took over the supervision of auditors of public interest entities, to ensure compliance with a large number of requirements arising from both the Act on Auditors and the EU Directive and EU Regulation specifically applicable to auditors of public-interest entities. Reports from supervisory authorities show that sanctions are in place, which most auditors apply effectively. However, as the above statistics also show, there is no significant reduction in the number of findings. The chapter presents an overview of the audit obtained from publicly available reports of supervisory authorities. It can be assumed that the quality of the audit will be the subject of further research in the Czech Republic toward comparison in relation to the market concentration or from the point of view of the audit firms themselves.

Acknowledgment The chapter is processed as an output of a research project IGA VŠE F1/25/2019 (Market failures and their impact on audit quality in the Czech Republic).

References

Afesha, T. (2015). Audit fee determinants and audit quality in Ethiopian commercial banks. *Ethiopian Journal of Business and Economics, 5*, 159–186. https://doi.org/10.4314/ejbe.v5i2.1

Alareeni, B. A. (2019). The associations between audit firm attributes and audit quality-specific indicators. *Managerial Auditing Journal, 34*, 6–43. https://doi.org/10.1108/MAJ-05-2017-1559

Albersmann, B. T., & Quick, R. (2020). The impact of audit quality indicators on the timeliness of goodwill impairments: Evidence from the German setting. *Abacus, 56*, 66–103. https://doi.org/10.1111/abac.12184

Asthana, S., Khurana, I., & Raman, K. K. (2019). Fee competition among big 4 auditors and audit quality. *Review of Quantitative Finance and Accounting, 52*, 403–438.

Brown, J. O., & Popova, V. K. (2019). How do Investors respond to disclosure of audit quality indicators? *Auditing: A Journal of Practice & Theory, 38*, 31–53. https://doi.org/10.2308/ajpt-52417

Cassell, C. A., Hansen, J. C., Myers, L. A., & Seidel, T. A. (2020). Does the timing of auditor changes affect audit quality? Evidence from the initial year of the audit engagement. *Journal of Accounting, Auditing & Finance, 35*, 263–289. https://doi.org/10.1177/0148558X17726241

CEAOB. (2020). *Report on the 2020 CEAOB enforcement questionnaire*. Committee of European Auditing Oversight Bodies.

Cho, M., Ki, E., & Kwon, S. Y. (2017). The effects of accruals quality on audit hours and audit fees. *Journal of Accounting, Auditing & Finance, 32*, 372–400. https://doi.org/10.1177/0148558X15611323

Ciconte, W., Knechel, W. R., Schelleman, C., & Monroe, G. (2015). An examination of the relation between market structure and the profitability of audit engagements. *Accounting and Finance, 55*, 749–781. https://doi.org/10.1111/acfi.12078

Ernstberger, J., Koch, C., Schreiber, E. M., & Trompeter, G. (2020). Are audit firms' compensation policies associated with audit quality? *Contemporary Accounting Research, 37*, 218–244. https://doi.org/10.1111/1911-3846.12528

Felix, W. L., Jr., Gramling, A. A., & Maletta, M. J. (2001). The contribution of internal audit as a determinant of external audit fees and factors influencing this contribution. *Journal of Accounting Research Wiley-Blackwell, 39*, 513–534. https://doi.org/10.1111/1475-679x.00026

Gigler, F., & Penno, M. (1995). Imperfect competition in audit markets and its effect on the demand for audit-related services. *The Accounting Review, 70*, 317–336.

IAASB. (2014). *A framework for audit quality: Key elements that create an environment for audit quality*. International Auditing and Assurance Standards Board.

Johnson, E. S., Reichelt, K. J., & Soileau, J. S. (2020). The impact of PCAOB auditing standard no. 5, the PCAOB inspection regime, and the great recession on audit fees and audit quality. *Journal of Accounting, Auditing & Finance*, 1. https://doi.org/10.1177/0148558x20982207

KAČR. (2020). *Report on the control activities of the supervisory Board of the Chamber of auditors of the Czech Republic for 2019*. The Chamber of Auditors of the Czech Republic.

Kuang, H., Li, H., Sherwood, M. G., & Whited, R. L. (2020). Mandatory audit partner rotations and audit quality in the United States. *Auditing: A Journal of Practice & Theory, 39*, 161–184. https://doi.org/10.2308/ajpt-18-152

Lennox, C. S. (2016). Did the PCAOB's restrictions on auditors' tax services improve audit quality? *The Accounting Review, 91*, 1493–1512. https://doi.org/10.2308/accr-51356

Mendiratta, A. (2019). Abnormal audit fees and audit quality post Pcaob. *Journal of Commerce and Accounting Research, 8*, 47–63.

PAOB. (2017). *Report on the activities of the Public Audit Oversight Board 2016*. Public Audit Oversight Board.

PAOB. (2018). *Report on the activities of the Public Audit Oversight Board 2017*. Public Audit Oversight Board.

PAOB. (2020). *Report on the activities of the Public Audit Oversight Board 2019*. Public Audit Oversight Board.

Sindelar, M., & Mullerova, L. (2016). Auditorske sluzby v Ceske republice pohledem analyzy trzni koncentrace. (Market Concentration of Audit Services in the Czech Republic: Empirical Evidence [Focusing on Auditors of Public Interest Entities]. With English summary.). *Polit Ekon, 64*, 730–746.

Srikandhi, M. F., & Suryandari, D. (2020). Audit quality moderates the effect of independent commissioners, audit committee, and whistleblowing system on the integrity of financial statement. *AAJ Account Analysts Journal, 9*, 186–192. https://doi.org/10.15294/aaj.v9i2.x

Super, S. O., & Shil, N. C. (2019). Determinants of audit fee in the manufacturing sector in Nigeria. *IUP Journal of Accounting Research and Audit Practices, 18*, 62–75.

Tepalagul, N., & Lin, L. (2015). Auditor Independence and audit quality: A literature review. *Journal of Accounting, Auditing & Finance, 30*, 101–121. https://doi.org/10.1177/0148558X14544505

Willekens, M., Dekeyser, S., Bruynseels, L., & Numan, W. (2020). Auditor market power and audit quality revisited: Effects of market concentration, market share distance, and leadership. *Journal of Accounting, Auditing & Finance, 1*. https://doi.org/10.1177/0148558x20966249

Chapter 30
Shadow Economy in the Regions of Russia: Spatial Aspects

Ekaterina Nevzorova and Anna Kireenko

Abstract The chapter provides a spatial analysis of the scale of the shadow economy of the regions of the Russian Federation. The values of the local and global Moran index were calculated, and the Moran diagrams were also constructed. To identify how accurately the data of the shadow economy are reflected in the indicators of criminal statistics by regions, a correlation analysis was carried out. Based on estimates of the shadow economy based on Rosstat data on the extent of the shadow economy and the sectoral structure of the gross product, spatial autocorrelation indicators of the shadow economy in the Russian regions were calculated. A significant positive spatial autocorrelation of this indicator was found. Also revealed is a variation in spatial interdependence across regions. Differences in the spatial distribution of the centers of the shadow economy are revealed. The conclusions are formulated on the configuration of the spatial distribution patterns of shadow economic activity in Russia: the area of the greatest prevalence of shadow activity in the western part of the country; the "transitional" zone surrounding it (not free from the risk of the spread of shadow economic activity); isolated centers of shadow activity in Siberia and the Far East; and zones of relative well-being.

Key words Shadow economy · Spatial econometrics · Spatial autocorrelation · Tax evasion

30.1 Introduction

The shadow economy creates obstacles to economic development, since the implementation of the economic activity partly in the shadow sector affects the structure of the national economy and changes its growth trends. In this regard, the need to assess

E. Nevzorova (✉)
Baikal International Business School, Irkutsk State University, Irkutsk, Russian Federation

A. Kireenko
Baikal School of BRICS, Irkutsk National Research Technological University, Irkutsk, Russian Federation

D. Procházka (ed.), *Regulation of Finance and Accounting*, Springer Proceedings in Business and Economics, https://doi.org/10.1007/978-3-030-99873-8_30

the extent of the shadow economy, its distribution, and dynamics is not only of academic but also political interest. Tanzi (1999) points out that the results of evaluating the shadow economy affect the volume of the gross product and, thus, influence a number of political decisions.

Our earlier studies of the shadow economy showed that the shadow economy in our country has regional specifics (Kireenko et al., 2017, 2019). A logical question arises: If there are regional differences in the differentiation of the shadow economy, then is there a relationship or spatial correlation between them?

A study on the spatial aspects of the shadow economy will answer the questions: Is it possible to change (improve) the situation in a single region? How independent are the regions in solving the shadow economy problem, or is the general situation and the state of affairs in neighboring regions and the geographical position of the region influencing this?

A spatial analysis of the shadow economy data has been presented in several recent studies.

Goel and Saunoris (2014) based on an analysis of data from 106 countries (averaged over the period 1999–2008) obtained evidence in support of their hypotheses of "infection" and "contagion" of the shadow economy. The essence of this phenomenon is as follows. In the process of activity, shadow firms sell products, including to other companies, partly during cross-border trade, including with neighboring countries. This can contribute to the spread of the shadow economy (abroad) in the following ways: (1) shadow firms export products manufactured without complying with official environmental standards, which are then to be sold, as can be assumed, also by the shadow method; (2) business units can "learn" from neighboring countries how to "evade the system" to conduct shady activities.

The same authors (Goel & Saunoris, 2016) obtained results that show that the development of the shadow economy is "contagious" for neighboring regions, and this conclusion is sustainable taking into account international borders, alternative methods of spatial weighting, and various dimensions of the shadow economy. The study is based on the use of annual observations for the period 1997–2008 for 48 contiguous states of the USA, i.e., without taking into account Alaska and Hawaii, as these states do not border on other states of the USA).

Carfora, Pansini, and Pisani (2018a, b) based on data from 20 regions of Italy (NUTS 2) for 2001–2011 revealed a significant positive spatial correlation of the tax gap indicator. The results show that proximity to a region with a high (low) share of the tax gap is an important factor determining the high or, respectively, low share of the tax gap in the neighboring region.

Similar results were obtained by Alm and Yunus (2009). According to the data of US states for 1979–1997, it was revealed that tax evasion for individuals' income is characterized by positive spatial correlation.

García et al. (2018) analyzed the spatial factor in the behavior of taxpayers. The data used for the analysis are the results of the European Values Survey (EVS), which was conducted in 2008 (43 European countries). The level of rejection of tax evasion is measured by the number of participants who stated that they would never justify tax evasion. Moran diagram showed a positive spatial correlation of the analyzed data: countries where were a high level of rejection of tax evasion and per capita tax evasion, bordering on countries where the levels of rejection of tax evasion and per capita tax evasion were also high. However, we are not aware of similar studies in the context of regions on Russian data.

In this chapter, we conduct a spatial analysis of the shadow economy scale. If the spatial autocorrelation of the shadow economy scale in the regions is significant, this will allow us to conclude that measures aimed at reducing it in certain regions without similar actions in other regions will have a weak effect.

30.2 Data and Methodology

The empirical analysis carried out in this work covers the period from 2004 to 2016. The number of regions in the sample is 82; the Chechen Republic is not included in the sample due to the lack of an estimate of the shadow economy for the analyzed period, the Republic of Crimea, and the city of Sevastopol, since a portion of the analyzed period (until 2014) they had not been federal subjects of the Russian Federation.

The evaluation of the shadow economy scale in the Russian regions was made by the authors according to Russian Statistic Agency (Rosstat) data: GRP by constituent entities of the Russian Federation (gross value added at current basic prices – total) (1998–2018);[1] GRP structure by industry according to the Russian Classification of Economic Activities (at current prices; as a percentage of the total), 2004–2016;[2] adjustment of gross value added for economic transactions that are not observed by direct statistical methods (data for 2002–2018 are available, but due to limitations related to the availability of data by previous indicator we used data for 2004–2016).[3]

We proceeded from the assumption that the level of the shadow economy in the industry sectors is the same in all regions of the country. Based on this assumption, we made calculations to estimate the shadow economy in the regions of the Russian Federation.

At the first stage of the analysis, we calculate the global Moran's index (Moran's I) (Moran, 1950) and the criteria that determine its significance. The global Moran's index measures spatial autocorrelation using data on the location of objects and the values of the analyzed indicator:

[1] http://www.gks.ru/free_doc/new_site/vvp/vrp98-17.xlsx (accessed 28.02.2020).

[2] http://www.gks.ru/free_doc/new_site/vvp/tab-vrp2.htm (accessed 13.03.2019).

[3] http://www.gks.ru/free_doc/new_site/vvp/vvp-god/tab14-19.htm (accessed 13.03.2019).

$$I = \frac{N}{\sum_{i=1}^{n}\sum_{j=1}^{n} W_{ij}} \frac{\sum_{i=1}^{n}\sum_{j=1}^{n} W_{ij}(Y_i - \bar{Y})(Y_j - \bar{Y})}{\sum_{i=1}^{n}(Y_i - \bar{Y})^2} \quad (30.1)$$

where N is the number of spatial units (regions) indexed by i and j; Y is the variable of interest; and Wij is a matrix of spatial weights with zeroes on the diagonal (i.e., wii = 0). The spatial weights matrix is square matrix. Thus, the matrix takes into account the influence of territories on each other but excludes the influence of territories on itself. A review of the literature shows that various modifications of the reciprocal distance matrix are used in studies: a matrix of reciprocal geographical distances; matrix of reciprocal shortest railway distances). In this paper, we use the matrix of the shortest distances between the administrative centers of the Russian regions (presented by Abramov & Gluschenko, 2000). Recommendations on this subject are contained in research by Vakulenko (2015).

The expected value of Moran's I is

$$E(I) = -\frac{1}{(N-1)} \quad (30.2)$$

Moran I value for normally distributed data ranges from -1 to +1. If $I > E(I)$, it denotes positive spatial autocorrelation, which means that similar values, either high values or low values are spatially clustered (neighboring regions have similar values of the analyzed indicator). If $I < E(I)$, it denotes negative spatial autocorrelation, which means that neighboring values are dissimilar (neighboring regions have dissimilar characteristics). If $I \approx E(I)$, the observations are mutually independent and randomly distributed.

The inverse distance weighting is a method based on the so-called first law of geography, which, according to *W.* Tobler, states that "everything is related to everything else, but near things are more related than distant things" (Tobler, 1970). This law is the basis of the fundamental concepts of spatial dependence and spatial autocorrelation.

To evaluate the significance of Moran's I, we calculated the z-score.

$$z = \frac{I - E(I)}{SD(I)} \quad (30.3)$$

If the null hypothesis is rejected, p-value <0.05, then $Z > 0$ indicates a positive spatial autocorrelation, while $Z < 0$ indicates a negative one.

At the second stage, we construct a spatial scatter diagram (spatial Moran diagram, Moran scatterplot) and identify regional clusters with its help. The spatial scatterplot allows to visualize the belonging of each unit (the value of the variable of interest) to a certain type of autocorrelation, and the dependence of the variable Y on the spatial lag. The X-axis shows the values of the vector Z, where Z is the variable

WZ

LH (2)	HH (1)	Z
LL (3)	HL (4)	

Fig. 30.1 Designations of the quadrants on the Moran scatterplot (numbers of the quadrant are according to the Cartesian coordinate system)

Y in a standardized form. The *Y*-axis displays the values of the spatial lag vector WZ. To obtain the values of the spatial lag vector, it is necessary to multiply the matrix of spatial weights by the vector of standardized values of the variable. The regression line WZ on *Z* in the spatial scatterplot diagram has an inclination angle corresponding to the value of the global Moran's *I*. Moran scatterplot is an illustration of the relationship between the values of variable at each location and the average value of the same variable at neighboring locations. Moran scatterplot has four quadrants, which match four types of local spatial relationship between regional unit and its neighbors (Fig. 30.1).

H is for high value; *L* is for low value. The HH and LL quadrants indicate clustering of high values and low values, respectively. The LH and HL quadrants indicate spatial outliers. HH (1), units with a high value of the variable are neighboring to units with high values of the variable; LL (3), units with a low value of the variable are neighboring to units with low values of the variable; LH (2), units with a low value of the variable are neighboring to units with a high value of the variable; and HL (4), units with a high value of the variable are neighboring to units with a low value of the variable. Positive spatial autocorrelation is observed for objects located in HH and LL quadrants, where spatially close objects are displayed that have a close value of the analyzed feature. Here there is a territorial grouping (clustering) by similar values of the indicator. Negative spatial autocorrelation is observed for objects located in LH and HL quadrants, where spatially distant objects with a close value of the analyzed feature are displayed. By visual analysis of the spatial Moran diagram, it is possible to visually identify atypical objects (concentrated in LH and HL quadrants).

At the third stage, we calculate the local Moran index (LISA, Local Indicator of Spatial Association) (Anselin, 1995) for each region, and based on its values, we formulate conclusions about the territorial specifics of the spread of shadow economic activity in the Russian Federation. The local Moran index measures the degree of similarity of each object with neighboring objects by the values of the analyzed variable. This index is calculated by the formula:

$$I_i = \frac{z_i}{m} \sum_{j=1}^{n} w_{ij} z_j \tag{30.4}$$

where *zi* – normalized variable *Y*:

$$z_i = \frac{Y_i - \overline{Y}}{SD_Y} \tag{30.5}$$

$$m = \frac{\sum_i Z_i^2}{N} \tag{30.6}$$

wij – spatial weights.

Moran's indices are interconnected as follows:

$$I = \sum_i \frac{I_i}{N} \tag{30.7}$$

where *I*, global Moran's *I*; Ii, local Moran's indices (LISA).

A positive LISA value indicates that the object has neighboring objects with the same high or low variable values. This object is part of a cluster. A negative LISA value indicates that the object has neighboring objects with dissimilar variable values. This object is an outlier. LISA values are compared by federal district.

30.3 Results and Discussion

For a sample of 82 subjects, the expected value of the global Moran index is −0.012. The obtained actual values of the Moran indices (global and local) are significant for all years except 2005 (according to p-value). Table 30.1 presents the information resulting from the calculations.

The dynamics of the Moran's *I* shows that, in general, there is a tendency to strengthen the role of spatial mutual influence of regions. The Moran's *I* is positive, which indicates the interconnections of regional "shadow economies." When comparing with the data on the shadow economy scale in Russia as a whole, with a visual analysis, it can be noticed that with a decrease in the shadow economy, spatial interaction tended to increase, and when it grew, it decreased.

The actual values of the Fechner signs correlation coefficient for the upper and lower boundaries for estimates of the shadow economy scale are −0.538, for an average value of −0.692. The tightness of the variables' relationship on the Cheddock scale is notable. The direction of the relationship is negative: the signs in deviations of the shadow economy scale and the calculated global Moran's I from the average value for the most part do not coincide. Then we analyzed the distribution of regions according to the LISA value by the intervals:

LISA < E(I)	negative spatial autocorrelation
E(I)< LISA <0	positive spatial autocorrelation (weak)
0 < LISA < Moran I	positive spatial autocorrelation (below the average)
LISA > Moran I	positive spatial autocorrelation (above the average)

Table 30.1 Moran *I* for shadow economy scale

	2004	2006	2008	2009	2010	2011	2012	2013	2014	2015	2016
Constant	0,114	0,164	0,166	0,180	0,148	0,153	0,173	0,174	0,199	0,173	0,190
Zi	0,046	0,054	0,068	0,092	0,051	0,070	0,088	0,092	0,132	0,081	0,117
Significance	0,014	0,026	0,006	0,000	0,014	0,002	0,001	0,001	0,000	0,002	0,000
p-value	0,014	0,026	0,006	0,000	0,014	0,002	0,001	0,001	0,000	0,002	0,000

Source: Authorial computation

Regions with negative LISA values have a small share in the total number of regions (29.3% of the analyzed), and their share among the federal districts (FD) is the largest in Ural FD and Northwestern FD. Other regions have more similar values of the scale of the shadow economy.

Then we compared the data on the scale of the shadow economy and actually obtained LISA values by FDs (Fig. 30.2).

This diagram indicates that in 2016, the relatively high scale of the shadow economy in the Central FD, Volga FD, the Northwestern FD, and the Southern FD corresponded to positive spatial autocorrelation of this indicator.

It must be taken into account that the comparison by FDs may not coincide with the actual distribution of shadow activity in the country, and the interaction of the entities employed in it. The economy within the boundaries of one FD may be characterized by a high degree of heterogeneity due to the uneven distribution of economic resources. The interaction of certain regions with the regions of another FD may be stronger than the interaction with the regions of this FD. Therefore, we also analyze spatial interactions through the use of a scatterplot (Fig. 30.3). The X-axis displays standardized estimates of the shadow economy (Z, by average values), along the Y-axis, spatial lag estimates (WZ). Units are not available. The slope of the regression line corresponds to the value of the coefficient of the global Moran index.

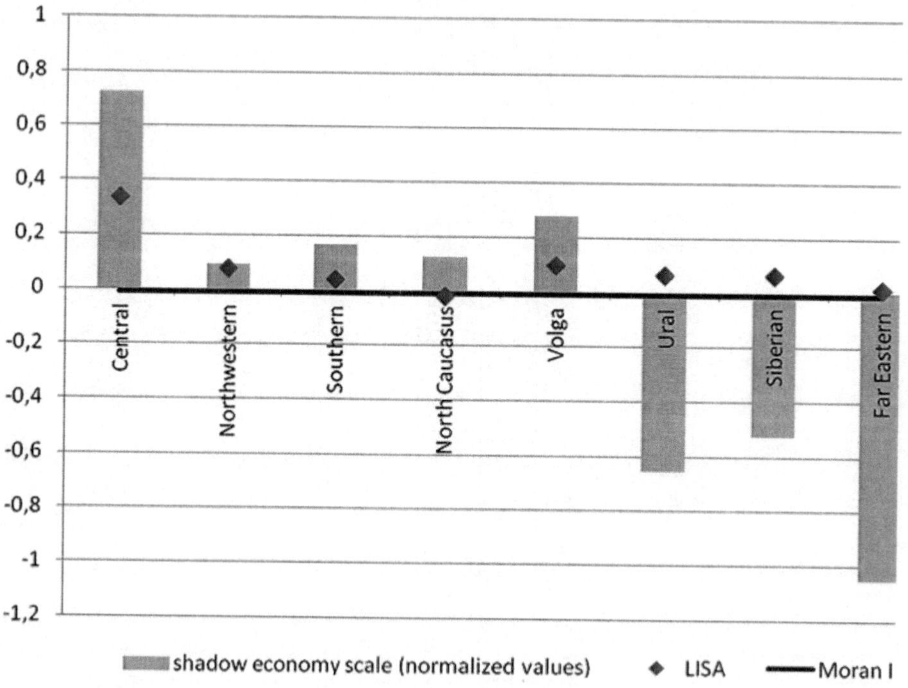

Fig. 30.2 The shadow economy scale (normalized values) and the Moran's I by federal districts (2016). (Source: Authorial computation)

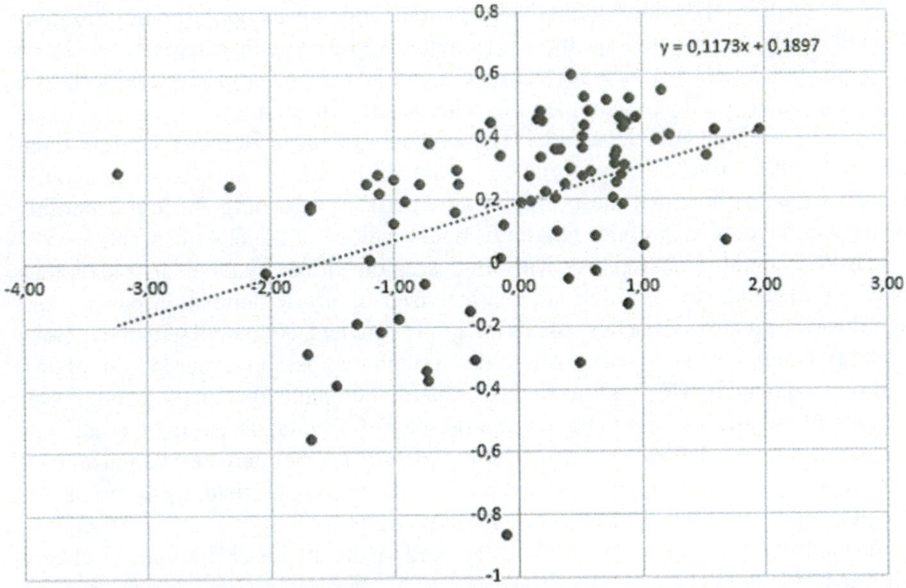

Fig. 30.3 Moran scatterplot – the shadow economy scale in regions of Russia (2016). (Source: Authorial computation)

Table 30.2 Distribution of regions on the Moran scatterplot (numbering of quadrants according to the Cartesian coordinate system)

Federal districts	Number of regions					%			
	1 – HH	2 – LH	3 – LL	4 – HL	Total	1 – HH	2 – LH	3 – LL	4 – HL
Central	17	1	0	0	18	94,4	5,6	0,0	0,0
Northwest	7	4	0	0	11	63,6	36,4	0,0	0,0
Southern	4	2	0	0	6	66,7	33,3	0,0	0,0
North Caucasus	3	3	0	0	6	50,0	50,0	0,0	0,0
Volga	11	3	0	0	14	78,6	21,4	0,0	0,0
Ural	2	3	1	0	6	33,3	50,0	16,7	0,0
Siberian	0	2	7	3	12	0,0	16,7	58,3	25,0
Far eastern	1	2	5	1	9	11,1	22,2	55,6	11,1
Total	45	20	13	4	82	54,9	24,4	15,9	4,9

Source: Authorial computation

The analysis of regions' distribution by quadrants on the Moran scatterplot allows to spot the spatial features of Russia's shadow economic activity (Table 30.2). Results are grouped by federal district.

First quadrant (HH, high-high). This quadrant contains the largest part of regions (45 out of 82). In these regions, there is a relatively low unemployment rate and share of population with cash incomes below the regional subsistence level, as well as a high migration coefficient compared to other Russian territories.

Second quadrant (LH, low-high). This quadrant includes 20 regions. All of them favorably differ from their territorial environment in terms of the shadow economy. However, we believe that these regions are at risk of spreading shadow economic activity in the course of contacts with business entities of the HH quadrant.

Third quadrant (LL, low-low). Most of the regions of this quadrant are the regions of Siberia and Far East, which are characterized by a low population density and significantly greater remoteness of administrative centers, compared with the regions of the HH quadrant. This quadrant included a small number of regions (13 out of 82).

Fourth quadrant (HL, high-low). This quadrant contains the smallest number of regions (4 out of 82), and these are the regions of Siberia. These regions are less prosperous in the shadow economy in comparison with their territorial environment (i.e., it is possible to assume the presence of factors that are particularly favorable for the development of the shadow economy in them).

Visualization of the data on the map will make it possible to more clearly represent the process of spatial interaction of shadow activity in the regions (Fig. 30.4).

Here can be noticed the area of the most widespread shadow economy in the western part of the country; the "transitional" zone surrounding it, then – a significant part of Siberia and Far East, more prosperous in the shadow economy (based on estimates of the structure of gross value added and estimates of the shadow economy of Rosstat); and two centers of a relatively higher level of the shadow economy compared with the territorial environment (the port zone of Vladivostok and the commercial and business center in Siberia – Novosibirsk Region and regions bordering it).

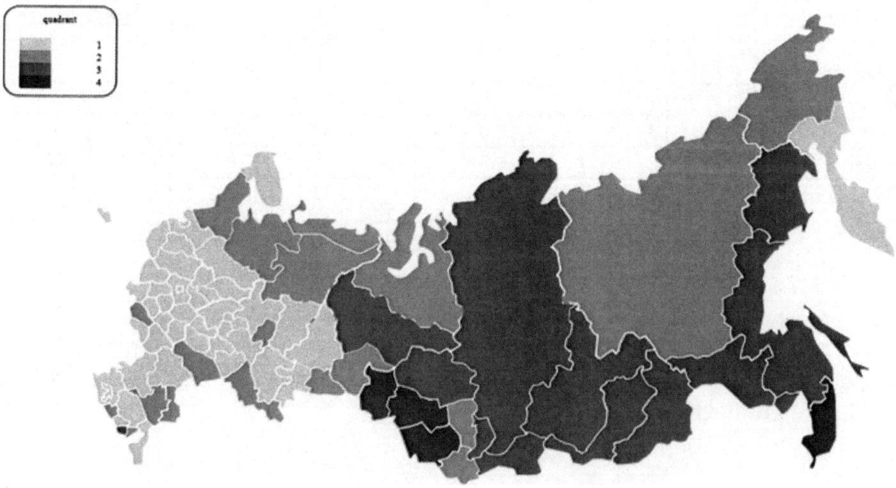

Fig. 30.4 Distribution of regions on the Moran scatterplot (numbering of quadrants according to the Cartesian coordinate system). (Source: Authorial computation)

The greatest homogeneity in 2016 is shown by the shadow economy of Central FD, followed by Volga FD. The regions of Far Eastern FD are most heterogeneous. We believe that this is due both to the territorial vastness of the latter and the sectoral differentiation of its economy.

30.4 Conclusion

As a result of the analysis, we revealed the presence of spatial interdependence and interconnectedness of the Russian regions on the shadow economy scale. This means that regions characterized by a relatively high scale of the shadow economy tend to neighbor with regions with similar indicators. This phenomenon is more common than it would be if the data were distributed randomly. Since this is so, each region should not be considered as an independent observation, but only in conjunction with other regions. In our opinion, this, on the one hand, complicates the estimation of the extent of the shadow economy using indirect and model approaches, because a researcher cannot rule out the influence of regions on each other. At the same time, this necessitates the development of a targeted approach in the process of shaping policies aimed at reducing the size of the shadow economy in the regions.

Acknowledgments The research was supported by the grant of the Russian Foundation for Basic Research (project http://search.rfbr.ru/ №19-010-00365A "Shadow economy and its sector-specific characteristics as a factor impeding technological development").

References

Abramov A., & Gluschenko, K. (2000). *The matrix of the shortest distances between capital cities of Russian regions*. [WWW Document]. Novosibirsk; Novosibirsk State University. http://pub.econom.nsu.ru/staff/chair_et/gluschenko/Research/Data/Distances.xls. Accessed 13 Mar 2019

Alm, J., & Yunus, M. (2009). Spatiality and persistence in US individual income tax compliance. *National Tax Journal, 62*(1), 101–124. https://doi.org/10.17310/ntj.2009.1.05

Anselin, L. (1995). Local indicators of spatial association – LISA. *Geographical Analysis, 27*(2), 93–115. https://doi.org/10.1111/j.1538-4632.1995.tb00338.x

Carfora, A., Pansini, R. V., & Pisani, S. (2018a). Regional tax evasion and audit enforcement. *Regional Studies, 52*(3), 362–373. https://doi.org/10.1080/00343404.2017.1299934

Carfora, A., Pansini, R. V., & Pisani, S. (2018b). Spatial dynamic modelling of tax gap: The case of Italy. *European Spatial Research and Policy, 25*(1), 7–28. https://doi.org/10.18778/1231-1952.25.1.02

García, G. A., Azorín, J. D. B., del Mar, M., & de la Vega, S. (2018). Tax evasion in Europe: An analysis based on spatial dependence. *Social Science Quarterly, 99*(1), 7–23. https://doi.org/10.1111/ssqu.12382

Goel, R. K., & Saunoris, J. W. (2014). Global corruption and the shadow economy: Spatial aspects. *Public Choice, 161*(1–2), 119–139. https://doi.org/10.1007/s11127-013-0135-1

Goel, R. K., & Saunoris, J. W. (2016). Casting a long shadow? Cross-border spillovers of shadow economy across American states. *Public Finance Review, 44*(5), 610–634. https://doi.org/10.1177/1091142115584815

Kireenko, A. P., Nevzorova, E. N., Orlova, E. N., Olga, Y., & Polyakova. (2017). Shadow economy in Russian regions: An estimation with the MIMIC model. *Region: Economics & Sociology, 1*(93), 164–189. https://doi.org/10.15372/REG20170108. (In Russ.).

Kireenko, A. P., Nevzorova, E. N., Dmitry, Y., & Fedotov. (2019). Sector-specific characteristics of tax crime in Russia. *Journal of Tax Reform, 5*(3), 249–264. https://doi.org/10.15826/jtr.2019.5.3.071

Moran, P. A. P. (1950). Notes on continuous stochastic phenomena. *Biometrika, 37*(1/2), 17–23. https://doi.org/10.2307/2332142

Tanzi, V. (1999). Uses and abuses of estimates of the underground economy. *The Economic Journal, 109*(456), 338–347. https://doi.org/10.1111/1468-0297.00437

Tobler, W. R. (1970). A computer movie simulating urban growth in the Detroit region. *Economic Geography, 46*, 234–240. https://doi.org/10.2307/143141

Vakulenko, E. S. (2015). Analysis of the relationship between regional labour markets in Russia using Okun's model. *Applied Econometrics, 40*(4), 28–48. (In Russ.).

Chapter 31
State-Owned Enterprises in the Era of Peter the Great

Ekaterina Zuga and Svetlana Karelskaia

Abstract The chapter describes the history of the creation of state-owned enterprises in Russia in the late seventeenth – early eighteenth centuries, discloses the main types of activities in which they functioned more than three centuries ago, and methods of transferring ownership of state-owned enterprises, etc. The research shows that the economic policy of the Russian government was based on the doctrine of mercantilism, and the impact of existing reality on its implementation.

Key words State-owned enterprise · State · Russia

31.1 Introduction

State enterprise is a special type of state activity that exists in most countries. In some countries, it does not matter. However, in some countries during a certain period, it turns out to organize some types of activities only in this form, as it was in Russia at the turn of the eighteenth century. From the historiographic point of view, Russia is a geographical region for which there is a shortage of research. There are a very limited number of publications in Russia devoted to the period stated in the title of the chapter.

The era of the reign of Peter the Great (years of life. 1672–1725; years of reign, 1682–1725; together with co-ruler – his brother Ivan until 1696, hereinafter – single-handedly) arouses the interest of researchers primarily because this period of Russian history has become a key one in the development of the country. It was in this era that large-scale reform aimed at shaping and stimulating the development of industry was first undertaken. The economic reforms of Peter the Great were described by Leshkov (1872), Milyukov (1905), Strumilin (1966), and others; his state and control and accounting reforms, Kuter and Sokolov (2012), Lvova (2012), Nazarov and Sidorova (2020), and Platonova (2009); his foreign policy, Cracraft

E. Zuga (✉) · S. Karelskaia
St Petersburg State University, St Petersburg, Russia
e-mail: e.zuga@spbu.ru; s.karelskaya@spbu.ru

D. Procházka (ed.), *Regulation of Finance and Accounting*, Springer Proceedings in Business and Economics, https://doi.org/10.1007/978-3-030-99873-8_31

(2010), Macgregor (2004), Matveev (2000), Piirimae (2007); his military reforms, Paul (2004); and others.

At the same time, researchers more often studied private industry, while the public industry paid much less attention. However, the role of state-owned enterprises in the development of the country was quite noticeable. This type of enterprises was studied by Bogatyrev (2009), Doinikov (2009), Larina (2009), Sokolov et al. (2019); and others.

The main purpose of this chapter was to analyze the history of the creation of state-owned enterprises at the end of the seventeenth to early eighteenth century in Russia and their significance in the development of the country's economy.

The chapter describes state-owned enterprises, the dynamics of its foundation, and the principles of transformation of state-owned enterprises into private ones.

31.2 Data and Methodology

The research is based on the following methodological principles: a combination of historical and modern approaches to research; the use of a systematic approach to the study of legal acts of the era of Peter the Great reign concerning regulation of the activities of state-owned enterprises; application of comparative analysis methods; etc. The most important approach is an interdisciplinary methodological synthesis: the study of public administration, as well as the development of state business in the context of economic theory, general and economic history, institutional and cultural-historical approaches.

One of the important sources of research is the regulatory documents contained in the complete collection of laws of the Russian Empire (hereafter – CCLRE). Many of them are devoted to the regulation of state-owned enterprises, the basis of which was created by Peter the Great.

31.3 Results and Discussion

31.3.1 Mercantilism as the Basis of Peter the Great's State Policy

In Russia, the state has traditionally played a dominant role in the economic life of society. In the seventeenth century, Russia was a state whose economic basis was the land and labor of the peasants assigned to it. Industrial production was not developed, and existed enterprises worked to supply the state needs. Peter the Great was the first ruler who recognized Russia's backwardness from other countries and attempted to correct this situation.

Back in the nineteenth century, Milyukov (1905) and Leshkov (1872) identified the state policy of Peter the Great as based on the doctrine of mercantilism. It was common in Europe in the seventeenth and eighteenth centuries. The main provisions of the mercantilism were the following: prohibitions of the export of coins, the establishment of the high customs tariff, favor of the development of domestic trade and industry, and introduction of monopolies and privileges. Peter the Great was not the first in this issue. In Russia, Alexey Mikhailovich Romanov (years of life 1629–1676, years of reign: 1645–1676) followed the mercantilism. In 1667, he adopted the new Trade Charter, which included duties on the sale and exchange of foreign goods in Russia, as well as bans on the export of Russian goods to other countries (CCLRE, 1667, Vol. 1, pp. 677–691). However, in pre-Peter times, the trade could not form the basis of the Western doctrine of mercantilism.

According to the Russian historian S.M. Solovyov (1820–1879), Peter the Great announced the beginning of a new economic policy in the Manifesto "On calling foreigners to Russia, with the promise of freedom of religion" (1702) (Solovyov, 2020, p. 97). In this document, Peter the Great approved the priority of the new policy to ensure the security of the country through the development of trade and attracting foreigners, useful to the state (CCLRE, 1702, Vol. 4, pp. 192–195). His reforms always began with changes in the army and navy or intended to strengthen them.

Peter the Great made several decisions to encourage the development of trade and industry exactly to provide the army. First, it aimed at overcoming dependence on foreign goods (supplying the army as well) and the outflow of money from the country. Great privileges were given to those who organized factories and manufactories: the loans from the Treasury, exemption from duties, the right to attract foreign masters, as well as guarantees for the purchase of products at the state expense (Lvova, 2012, p. 233). According to the mercantilism, a ban was imposed on the export of raw materials needed for domestic production and significant import duties on those goods that could be produced in Russia. Peter the Great encouraged foreign trade by assisting in the export of goods. He provided merchants with ships belonging to the Treasury for the delivery of their goods abroad. He established trade agencies abroad – consulates, signed up trade agreements with foreign countries, and built new harbors. In 1719, he ordered the elimination of state trade (with the exception of two goods – *potash* and *smolchug*) (CCLRE, 1711, Vol. 5, pp. 734–735). According to European sources, by the end of Peter's reign, the export of goods outside the state exceeded the import, which, according to the doctrine of mercantilism, served as a measure of the success of the reform (Lvova, 2012, p. 233).

The success of Peter's mercantilist policy was achieved by peculiar methods: using the status and capabilities of the autocratic ruler, he forcibly demanded that private entrepreneurs create industrial enterprises or take them under their control, as well as through state pricing and the introduction of increased duties on imported goods.

31.3.2 State-Owned Enterprises in Russia at the End of the Seventeenth to Early Eighteenth Centuries: Industry Affiliation

By the beginning of the era of Peter the Great, there were only 25 large industrial enterprises in Russia. During his reign, the number of plants and factories increased to 233[1] (Solovyov, 2020, pp. 133–134). Most of them were created as state-owned enterprises. There is some terminological uncertainty in the understanding of the definition of "state-owned enterprises." In Russia, in the seventeenth and early eighteenth centuries, state enterprises were usually called state-owned (in Russian – *kazennyj*) enterprises, including large industrial enterprises and state monopolies. They got this name from the word "Treasury (in Russian – *kazna*)," which was interpreted as a set of assets belonging to the state. Russian civil lawyers D.I. Meyer (1819–1856) and G F. Shershenevich (1863–1912) used this approach from the end of the nineteenth century (Meyer, 1861, p. 153; Shershenevich, 2017, p. 78).

It is possible to identify certain industry specifics for state-owned enterprises. Several key industries Peter the Great paid special attention to and accelerated their development. First, he focused on the security of the country, so the emphasis was the military industry (Table 31.1).

Table 31.1 State-owned enterprises in the military industry

State-owned enterprise	Number	Location (Employees)
Admiralty shipyard	3	St. Petersburg (3441), Kronstadt (1156), Astrakhan (186)
Arsenal	2	St. Petersburg (218), Moscow (131)
Gunpowder factory	2	St. Petersburg (85, 64)
Printing House	3	St. Petersburg (75, 21, 15)
Sailing factory	1	Moscow (1162)
Saw mill	1	St. Petersburg (135)
Spinning yard	1	St. Petersburg (451)
Weapons factory	1	Sestroretsk (677)
Total	14	

Compiled by Strumilin (1966, p. 333)

[1]Many manufacturers turned out to be "false" during calibration in 1730. In 1744, 44 factories were closed due to poor product quality; many enterprises closed by themselves (Kulisher, 2019, p. 84). However, the successful industry development and the entire Peter the Great economic policy are obvious. In the seventeenth century, Russia exported exclusively raw materials and agricultural products, and in 1726, manufactures accounted for 52% of exports mainly iron and canvas (Konotopov, 2019, p. 107).

During the reign of Peter the Great, 14 large state-owned enterprises in the military industry were created. In total, these enterprises employed about 8000 employees. Geographically, they were extremely concentrated and were mostly located in or near the capital of the country, Saint Petersburg,[2] as well as in Moscow. Especially large factories served the needs of the Navy and belonged to the Admiralty.

Iron, copper, and silver plants were also built at state expense. Twelve of the 25 (or 48%) iron plants belonged to the Treasury by the end of Peter the Great's reign. These plants were founded mainly in the early eighteenth century (Table 31.2).

Table 31.2 State-owned enterprises – iron plants

Year of foundation	State	Private	Name and location	Employees
1653		1	Kashirsky on the Skniga river	62
1666–1705		1	Ugodsky, Borovsky and Menshowsky	156
1693–1695		1	Borinsky	–
1701	1	1	Kamensky in the Urals/Tulitsky on the river Tulitsa	92/40
1701–1702	1		Nevyansky in the Urals	380
1702	2		Verhne and Nizhne Lipsky; Petrovsky on the river Lososinka	– ; 303
1702–1703	2		Kozminsky; Ustyuzhensky-Izhinsky on the Izhina river	– ; –
1702–1704	2		Belozersky-Tyrpitsky on the river Shogde; Uktussky in the Urals	41; 119
1703	1		Povenetsky on the river Poventsy	37
1704	1		Alapaevsky in the Urals	108
1704–1707	1		Konchezersky	24
1707		1	Dugnensky on the river Dugna	56
1713–1716		1	Istyinskie on the Istye river	16
1716		1	Shuralinsky	54
1716–1717		1	Tulitsky on the river Tulitsa	24
1717		1	Istyinsky – Gulynsky	18
1718		1	Byngowsky in the Urals	180
1718–1720		1	Tagilsky in the Urals	112
1719		1	Tulitsky on the river Tulitsa	36
1719–1722		1	Ryabkinsky on the river Ryabka	24
1723–1724	1		Yekaterinburgsky in the Urals	409
Total	12	13		

Compiled by Strumilin (1966, pp. 334–335)

[2]In 1712–1714, the capital of Russia was moved from Moscow to St. Petersburg, which remained the capital until 1918.

As can be seen from Table 31.2, the first iron plants were built with private capital. It should be noted that the first iron plants (Kashirsky on the Skniga river; Ugodsky, Borovsky and Menshovsky) were founded with the participation of foreigners. Thus, one of the features of the state policy of Peter the Great – the involvement of foreign specialists, officially announced in the Manifesto dated 1702, was demonstrated in this industry. Later Peter the Great began to actively build iron plants at the state expense, and in a short time – about 7 years – 11 state-owned iron plants were built out of 12 (more than 90%). This haste was due to the outbreak of the war with Sweden (the Northern war of 1700–1721), which had previously been the main supplier of metal to Russia. The beginning of the war required a sharp increase in the consumption of metal for military needs, but its supplies stopped. A few years later, this industry continued to develop again at the expense of private investors. Within 9 years (1713–1722), eight plants were built by private investment. At the same time, about half of all private iron plants or almost a quarter of their total number (six plants) belonged to one person – Nikita Demidov.[3]

Such an indicator indirectly evidenced the significant role of state-owned enterprises in the development of industry and the economy of the country as a whole as the number of employees: their number in state-owned enterprises was more than twice much than in private enterprises.

Copper and silver plants were built mainly later than the iron ones, already closer to the end of the Northern war or even after it (Table 31.3).

As can be seen in Table 31.3, five of six (or 83%) copper and silver plants were state-owned enterprises. There was only one private plant (Vyisky copper plant in the Urals) built by Nikita Demidov. All the copper plants (five plants) were built in a very short time, as well as iron plants, for 4 years (1720–1724). The plant built earlier in 1704 was silver (Nerchinsky silver plant in Siberia).

Table 31.3 State-owned enterprises – copper and silver plants

Year of foundation	State	Private	Name and location	Employees
1704	1		Nerchinsky silver plant in Siberia	47
1720–1724	1		Pyskorski copper plant on the river Kamgorka	111
1722		1	Vyisky copper plant in the Urals	60
1724	3		Lyalinsky on the Kamenka river; Polevskoy on the river Polevoy; Yagushihinsky on the river Yagushiha	25; 40; 31
Total	5	1		

Compiled by Strumilin (1966, p. 335)

[3] Demidov (Antufiev) Nikita Demidovich (1656–1725) – a large Russian industrialist. He started as a gunsmith, owned many iron plants in the Urals, covered the need for metal by 2/3 in the domestic market, and exported iron abroad. He delivered iron and weapons to the state.

Table 31.4 State-owned manufactories

Year of foundation	Number	Type of activity	Employees
1704	1	Cloth	730
1706	1; 1	Linen; Hosiery	851; 33
1713/15	1	Cloth	118
1714	1	Cloth	742
1718	1; 1	Kalaminkovskaya; Tobacco plant	69; 43
1722	1	Paper	117
Total	8		

Compiled by Strumilin (1966, pp. 330–331)

The state-owned shipyards, iron and other military enterprises, etc. and also the largest Peter's manufactories were originally state-owned (Table 31.4). They worked mainly to satisfy state interests too.

Only 8 of the 40 manufactories (or 20%) belonged to the state. The share of state-owned enterprises among manufactories was very low. In the first years of their appearance, they were founded at the state expense, but for a long period of 10 years (1704–1714), only five manufactories were founded. Starting 1714, manufactories were founded at the expense of private capitals. In almost the same period of 11 years, 32 private manufactories appeared. At the same time, the state stopped spending money on the development of manufactories. Only in some years, three manufactories were founded: tobacco factory, paper, and kalaminkovskaya manufactories.

Manufactories were opened in various industries, but mostly they were related to consumer industry. The largest of them were linen manufactory in Moscow (851 employees), cloth manufactories in Kazan (742 employees), and Moscow (730 employees). All three of them were state-owned and founded at the dawn of the development of this type of business. These enterprises also worked primarily for state military needs, since they provided fabrics (canvas, cloth) for the army and navy. Only six industries were represented among state-owned manufactories, while in the private sector – 16. A distinctive feature was that the hosiery and tobacco factory (two of the six state-owned industries) belonged to the state and had no competitors in the private sector. The first tobacco factory in Russia, built in 1718 in the city of Akhtyrka, was state-owned. However, 15 years later, it was transferred to private sector. The rest of the state-owned manufactories (except for paper one) were transferred to the merchants, foreigners, and palace servants in 10–16 years after their foundation. Among the iron plants, Nevyansky in the Urals[4] was built at the state expense and then was given to Nikita Demidov by a letter of March 4, 1702.

[4]The Nevyansky plant in the Urals is an iron and smelting and iron-making plant, based on the Neiva River, that was built in 1699–1701. In December 1701, it produced products for the first time. In 1702, it was transferred from the state to N. Demidov. It has survived to the present as the Nevyansky Engineering Plant.

State-owned enterprises also included those operated for the production and sale of alcohol. Peter paid special attention to the regulation of this industry. During his reign, more than 65 regulations were issued to regulate its operation. He created a lot of preferences for state-owned plants, limiting private entrepreneurship (e.g., "On the construction of a state-owned distillery plant in Siberia and on the destruction of private distilleries built in villages and settlements" (CCLRE, 1698, Vol. 3, p. 489), "On the existence of state-owned distilleries in grass-roots cities" (CCLRE, 1715, Vol. 5, p. 152)).

31.3.3 State-Owned Enterprises in Russia at the End of the Seventeenth to Early Eighteenth Centuries: Transition to Private Sector

Due to various circumstances, many state-owned enterprises were transferred to private sector (Table 31.5). For example, in the first years of its existence, the tobacco factory was unprofitable. This was facilitated not so much by the novelty of the case and its initial poor staging, but by the remoteness of the factory from the places where tobacco products were sold. Transportation of tobacco to St. Petersburg is cheaper when delivered by sea from abroad than transported by dry road from Akhtyrka. In 1722, it was decided to give the plant to private sector, and if no one takes it, sell the building, and distribute tobacco seeds to the population. In the absence of other candidates, the factory was given without bidding to merchant Maslov, and after his death, it was given to the Akhtyrsky regiment (1733) (Russian tobacco factory, 1933).

According to the results of the analysis of the transfer of state-owned enterprises, most of the manufactories were alienated from the Treasury in favor of merchants (six out of eight (or 75%)), but only 2 iron factories out of 12 (or 17%).

Table 31.5 State-owned enterprises that became private

State-owned enterprise	Year of foundation	Year of transfer to private sector	"State-owned" period
Borinsky plant (iron)	1693/95	1721	26
Cloth manufactory			
	1704	1720	16
	1714	1724	10
	1713/15	1726	13
Hosiery manufactory	1706	1722	16
Linen manufactory	1706	1718	12
Nevyansky plant in the Urals (iron)	1701	1702	1
Tobacco plant	1718	1733	15

Compiled by Strumilin (1966, pp. 330–331, 334–335)

Sometimes the transfer was the initiative of the future "owner," but often it was carried out in a compulsory manner. For example, Nikita Demidov asked the Tsar about iron plants in the Ural. In the letter of surrender of the iron plants in Verkhotursky uyezd on the Neiva river dated March 11, 1702, it stated: "We, the Great Sovereign, ordered to give Verkhotursky plants to Nikita, because careless attitude to his duties and quarrels parole officers had led to a halt of this rewarding business and a significant burden for local residents, as well as additional expenditures on payments to employees, downtime and additional costs, and in some places things were done carelessly or without adequate knowledge, and thus has caused not only losses, but also spent a lot of time because of long distances and unwarranted requests of the supervising officers, in this connection, there was a risk of complete ruin, because they began to talk about the need to move the dam to another place, which required new costs and expenses, as well as the postponement of terms..." (after Chumakov, 2011). Examples of the compulsory manner, which ensured the success of the state policy of Peter the Great, and based on the doctrine of mercantilism, are presented below.

February 28, 1711, was issued a decree "On the transferring the plain, featuring tablecloth and napkin plants to the commercial people, Andrew Turke and Tzimbalistov": While in the Ambassadorial order (in Russian – *prikaz*), the Great Sovereign ordered to list everything in plain, featuring tablecloth and napkin plants, factories and buildings acquired to Novonemetskoy settlement, which are run by Ambassadorial order, as well as foreign experts working there on the basis of contracts and those Russian people who were there in the training, and send them to the merchants engaged in trade in Moscow: Andrew Turke, Stepan Tsimbalistov and others; they must increase these enterprises at their own expense, and they are allowed to sell their products at a margin at their own discretion; if they increase this enterprise as a result of their actions and get a profit, they will receive the favor of the Great Sovereign; if they do not increase it and reduce it by careless attitude, then a fine of one thousand rubles per person will be imposed on them and those who will be their partners (CCLRE, 1711, Vol. 4, p. 640).

In 1711, the Senate issued a decree: "The existing practice of transferring state-owned enterprises to private individuals is evidenced by the Senate decree of April 13, 1711, which ordered to submit to Moscow the statements on fulfilled monetary and natural obligations and existing debts for goods, plants, crafts and wine contracts that were transferred to the farming or sale and implementation of production activities" (CCLRE, 1711, Vol. 4, p. 662).

On January 18, 1715, a personal decree "On the propagation of cloth manufactories..." was issued: "It is necessary to increase the number of cloth manufactories in different places in order not to buy foreign uniforms in five years; established manufactories should be given to the merchants, combining them into the company, even if they don't want it, and transferred the plant to take payment for several years in such amount that it does not interfere with the operations" (CCLRE, 1715, Vol. 5, p. 137).

Later this approach to state-owned enterprises was captured in the legislation. The rules of the Manufactories College (in Russian – *kollegia*) "On the content of the manufactories and factories at the expense of His Majesty" dated December 3, 1723, provided that "the Manufactories College should strive to manufactories and factories that were opened or will be opened the Treasury of His Majesty, was brought into good condition and were given to individuals" (CCLRE, 1723, Vol. 7, p. 171).

In conclusion, it is possible to identify three ways to transfer of state-owned enterprises to private sector at the end of the seventeenth to early eighteenth century in Russia:

1. By way of the transfer of the company's products to the treasury in full within a certain period (e.g., "On the return of the cloth factory in Moscow to the company of merchant Shchegolin and others" (CCLRE, 1719, Vol. 5, p. 667))
2. By way of the transfer of only part of the company's products to the treasury for a certain period (e.g., "On the return to Gregory Stroganov consisting in great Perm state-owned Zyriansky salt plants with farmers and land possession with the annual delivery to the Treasury 100 thousand poods of salt free of charge and on sell the rest of the salt according to the rules of the payment of the fee" (CCLRE, 1697, Vol. 3, p. 305))
3. By way of the monetary contributions to the treasury for a certain period (e.g., "On giving a foreigner Timerman mills with land for 15 years in the maintenance and permission to start him linen manufactories" (CCLRE, 1714, Vol. 5, p. 113); "On the producing all kinds of artillery supplies by Demidov at iron plants and his possession of those plants with volosts assigned to them" (CCLRE, 1713, Vol. 5, p. 73))

Often, the form of "payment" for the transfer of a state-owned enterprise from the treasury to private sector was established individually through a personal decree of the Great Sovereign.

31.4 Conclusion

In the late seventeenth and early eighteenth centuries, Peter the Great based his state policy on the doctrine of mercantilism. At the same time, mercantilism was followed by the leading countries in Europe, which made Peter want to follow their models in many areas – economic, social, cultural, etc.

In the first years of his single-handed reign (since 1696), Peter the Great began to develop Russian industry, primarily military. He founded quite large state-owned enterprises that provided the army and navy, including shipyards, sailing factories, weapons and gunpowder factories, and others. First manufactories were built by the state, and it gave them an impetus to their further development. And later manufactories were founded and financed by private capital. At the same time, the state gave them tangible preferences in the form of tax incentives, subsidies with money, materials, etc.

Peter the Great began to build state-owned military and iron enterprises first, a little later – silver plants and manufactories, and then – copper plants. The time gap between the beginnings of this construction boom was more than 20 years. By the time the copper factories began to open, many state-owned manufactories had already become private ones.

After a short period of active investment of state funds in the industry, Peter the Great gradually began transferring state-owned enterprises to the private sector. He considered it necessary to "get rid" mainly of state-owned manufactories. While the iron and copper plants, with a few exceptions, remained in the treasury, at the same time, the transfer of state-owned enterprises was carried out more often by force, i.e., there were situations when there were no people willing to run a state-owned enterprise, even despite quite serious preferences.

Another important feature of industrial development in Russia was the participation of foreigners.

Comparative analysis of the size of state-owned and private companies operating at the end of the seventeenth to early eighteenth century showed that state-owned enterprises were usually larger than private ones.

Acknowledgments The reported study was funded by RFBR, project number 20-010-42004.

References

Bogatyrev, E. D. (2009). Export-oriented state-owned industry in Russia in the context of modernization processes of the late XVII – The first half of the XVIII century. *Vestnik RUDN. Series History of Russia, 3*, 65–75. Богатырев Э.Д. Экспортоориентированная казенная промышленность России в условиях модернизационных процессов конца XVII – первой половины XVIII в. Вестник РУДН. Серия История России.

Chumakov, V. Y. (2011). *Demidov. Five generations of metallurgists in Russia*. Busineskom. Чумаков В.Ю. Демидовы. Пять поколений металлургов России. Москва: Бизнеском.

Cracraft, J. (2010). The Russian Empire as Cultural Construct. *The Journal of the Historical Society x, 2*, 167–188. https://doi.org/10.1111/j.1540-5923.2010.00297.x

Doinikov, P. I. (2009). Management of treasury industry in Russia in the XVII – early XIX centuries. *Proceedings of MGIU, 5*, 70–76. Дойников П. И. Управление казенной промышленностью в России в XVII –начале XIX в. Известия МГИУ.

Konotopov, M. V. (2019). In M. V. Konotopov, S. I. Smetanin, & A. V. Tebekin (Eds.), *Economic history: A textbook for bachelors* (12th ed.). Yurayt Publishing House. Конотопов, М.В. Экономическая история: учебник для бакалавров/М.В. Конотопов, С.И. Сметанин, А.В. Тебекин. 12-е изд. Москва: Издательство Юрайт.

Kulisher, I. M. (2019). *An essay on the history of Russian industry*. Yurayt Publishing House. Кулишер, И.М. Очерк истории русской промышленности. Москва: Издательство Юрайт.

Kuter, M., & Sokolov, V. (2012). Russia. In *Global history of accounting, financial reporting and public policy: Eurasia, the Middle East and Africa* (pp. 75–107). Emerald Group Publishing Limited.

Larina, O. G. (2009). State regulation of the system of state-owned enterprises in Russia in XVII – early XIX centuries. *Actual problems of Russian law, 4*(13), 54–60. Ларина О.Г. Государственное регулирование системы казенных предприятий в России XVII – начале XIX вв. Актуальные проблемы российского права.

Leshkov, V. N. (1872). Peter the Great in his decrees on people's industry. *Legal Bulletin* 10, 11 and 12. Лешков В.Н. Петр Великий в его указах о народной промышленности. Юридический вестник.

Lvova, D. A. (2012). Admiralty regulations of Peter the Great as a monument of accounting of the era of mercantilism. *Finance and Business, 4*, 229–241. Львова Д. А. Адмиралтейский регламент Петра Великого как памятник учета эпохи меркантилизма. Финансы и бизнес.

Macgregor, A. (2004). The Tsar in England: Peter the Great's visit to London in 1698. *The Seventeenth Century, 19*, 116–147.

Matveev, V. (2000). Summit diplomacy of the seventeenth century: William III and Peter I in Utrecht and London, 1697–98. *Dyplomacy and Statecraft, 11*, 29–48. https://doi.org/10.1080/09592290008406168

Meyer, D. I. (1861). *Russian civil law: Readings by D.I. Meyer, published according to notes of students under the edit. [and with a preface] by A. Vitsyn* (Vol. 1). N. Tiblen. Мейер Д. И. Русское гражданское право: Чтения ДИ Мейера, изданные по запискам слушателей под редакцией [и с предисловием] А. Вицына. СПб.: Н. Тиблен.

Milyukov, P. N. (1905). *State economy of Russia in the first quarter of the XVIII century and the reform of Peter the Great* (2nd ed.). Милюков П.Н. Государственное хозяйство России в первой четверти XVIII столетия и реформа Петра Великого. Изд. 2-е. СПб.

Nazarov, D. V., & Sidorova, M. I. (2020). *At the origins of the profession of an accountant in Russia – People and events of the 18th century*. Scientific Technologies Publishing House. Назаров Д. В., Сидорова М. И. У истоков профессии бухгалтера в России – люди и события XVIII века: Монография. Москва: Издательство «научные технологии».

Paul, M. C. (2004). The Military Revolution in Russia, 1550–1682. *The Journal of Military History, 68*(1), 9–45. https://doi.org/10.1353/jmh.2003.0401

Piirimae, P. (2007). Russia, The Turks and Europe: Legitimations of War and the formation of European identity in the early modern period. *Journal of Early Modern History, 11*(1–2), 63–86. https://doi.org/10.1163/157006507780385017

Platonova, N. V. (2009). Peter the Great's government reforms and accounting practice in Russia. *Accounting History, 14*(4), 437–464. https://doi.org/10.1177/1032373209342476

Russian tobacco factory *in the XVIII and XIX centuries*/M.V. Dzhervis; Acad. sciences of the USSR. 1933. Leningrad: publishing and printing house of Academy of Sciences of the USSR. Русская табачная фабрика в XVIII и XIX веках/М. В. Джервис; Акад. наук СССР. Ленинград: изд. и тип. изд-ва Акад. наук СССР.

Shershenevich, G. V. (2017). *Selected writings*: in 6 vol. vol. 2 including the Civil Law Course/ Entry. word, comp.: P.V. Krasheninnikov. Statute. Шершеневич Г.В. Избранное: в 6 т. Т. 2 включая Курс гражданского права/Вступ. слово, сост.: П.В. Крашенинников. Москва: Статут.

Sokolov, V., Karelskaia, S., & Zuga, E. (2019). Accounting in state-owned companies operated for the production and sale of alcohol in Russia in the fifteenth-seventeenth centuries. *Accounting History, 24*(3), 425–443. https://doi.org/10.1177/1032373219846663

Solovyov, S. M. (2020). *Readings and stories on the history of Russia in 2 parts* (Part 2. From the history of the XVII-XVIII centuries). Yurayt Publishing House. Соловьев С.М. Чтения и рассказы по истории России в 2 ч. Часть 2. Из истории XVII-XVIII веков. Москва: Издательство Юрайт.

Strumilin, S. G. (1966). *Essays on the economic history of Russia and the USSR*. Nauka. Струмилин С.Г. Очерки экономической истории России и СССР. Москва: Наука.

Chapter 32
Examining the Impact of Socioeconomic Factors on Crime Rates: A Panel Study

Korhan K. Gokmenoglu, Bünyamin Fuat Yıldız, and Mohamad Kaakeh

Abstract Understanding the underlying causes of crime is vital for economies to prosper. Previous attempts to understand crime drivers from an economic perspective are limited by a country-based approach and variable diversity. Therefore, it is necessary to use a cross-country dataset that considers demographic, economic, and institutional perspectives to reveal common factors affecting crime rates. This study examines the socioeconomic determinants of crime with a panel consisting of 17 countries using the fully modified least squares regression and Dumitrescu and Hurlin causality test. The obtained empirical findings indicate that rapid urbanization and high-rate unemployment are influential factors in increasing crime rates. Besides, real GDP growth and progress in the rule of law reduce crime rates. Empirical results also reveal that real GDP and urbanization Granger cause crime rates, while a bidirectional causal relationship exists between crime rates and the rule of law. The policy implications of these findings are discussed in the conclusion section.

Key words Crime rates · Rule of law · Urbanization · Unemployment

32.1 Introduction

Security is the primary factor for humanity to live in prosperity. High levels of crime rates can lead to anger among the members of the society, weaken the belief in the state and law enforcement agencies, reduce the willingness of the residents to work with the police, and cause social destruction (Kochel, 2013; Kochel & Weisburd,

---

K. K. Gokmenoglu (✉)
Department of Banking and Finance, Eastern Mediterranean University, Famagusta, Cyprus

Department of Finance and Banking, Ankara HBV University, Ankara, Turkey
e-mail: korhan.gokmenoglu@hbv.edu.tr

B. F. Yıldız · M. Kaakeh
Department of Banking and Finance, Eastern Mediterranean University, Famagusta, Cyprus
e-mail: mohamad.kaakeh@emu.edu.tr

D. Procházka (ed.), *Regulation of Finance and Accounting*, Springer Proceedings in Business and Economics, https://doi.org/10.1007/978-3-030-99873-8_32

2017; Schuck, 2020). Hence, understanding the causes of crime and taking preventive measures in this direction is one of the main goals of governments. Crime rates, economic performance, and social factors are closely linked (World Bank, 2007). The recent global increase in crime rates despite the increase in global economic growth (Chioda, 2017) has brought the attention of the international community (UN-ECOSOC, 2017). Although there is extensive literature on this subject, to date, researchers have conducted single-country studies considering mostly economic factors. This study aims to provide a more comprehensive understanding of determinants of crime rates by considering economic, demographic, and institutional factors for a panel of 17 selected countries.

Since the factors that cause individuals to commit crimes are multifaceted, studies examining the determinants of crime rates consider many different factors (Aaltonen et al., 2011; Bennett & Flavin, 1994; Brown, 2001; Buonanno & Montolio, 2008; Cahill & Mulligan, 2003; Fajnzylber et al., 2002a, b; Howsen & Jarrell, 1987; İmrohoroĝlu et al., 2006; Levitt & Lochner, 2001; Manzoni et al., 2006; Masih & Masih, 1996; Omotor, 2009; Rickman & Witt, 2007). Beirne (1987) approached the issue from a sociological perspective and claimed that crime is created by external factors produced by society. From an economic point of view, income-related variables are emphasized as vital determinants of the crime rates (Levitt, 1999; Narayan & Smyth, 2004). Goulas and Zervoyianni (2015) reported a link between economic growth and homicides. Dávila and Pardo-Montaño (2019) investigated crime rates using unemployment, economic growth, and poverty variables. Saleemi and Amir-ud-Din (2019) included institutional factors in their models and showed that these factors significantly affect various crime categories (Saleemi & Amir-ud-Din, 2019). Although the specified perspectives provide essential information on the determinants of crime rates, economic, institutional, and demographic factors should be discussed together to provide a more comprehensive understanding.

Our research aims to evaluate the factors affecting crime rates using economic, demographic, and institutional variables. In this respect, for a panel of 17 countries, we examined the relationship between crime rates, real GDP, unemployment, urbanization, and the rule of law by using the fully modified least squares (FMOLS) regression. Granger causality analysis was carried out to determine the direction of the relationship between these variables. Our study contributes to the literature in several aspects. Firstly, we use "prisoners per 100.000 people" as a proxy for the crime rates. This proxy is more inclusive than the proxies that represent a single type of crime (e.g., homicide rates, robbery, etc.) used by the previous studies. Secondly, our study employs social, economic, and demographic factors to explain changes in crime rates; therefore, it approaches our research question from a broader perspective. Thirdly, Dumitrescu and Hurlin's (2012) causality test hasn't been employed in previous studies to examine the direction of the relationship between the variables. This method considers the heterogeneity of causal relationships and hence provides robust results.

The overall structure of this paper takes the form of five sections. The purpose of Sect. 32.2 is to provide a brief review of the relevant literature. Section 32.3 provides information about the dataset and the methodology. Section 32.4 presents and discusses the empirical findings, and finally, Sect. 32.5 is the conclusion.

32.2 Literature Review

Following Becker (1968), who noted that income reductions unfavorably influence society, the role of economic factors on crime rates has been extensively examined. Studies investigating the economic determinants of crime rates frequently employ a proxy for economic growth or income growth in their model. Marvell and Moody (1988) explored a potential link between metropolitan crime and territorial economic growth and found a negative relationship. More recently, Peri (2004) indicated a nonlinear relationship between economic growth and crime rates for Italy. The literature on the economic growth-crime rates nexus has been dominated by single-country studies (Adekoya & Razak, 2016; Ahmad et al., 2014; Ajide, 2019; Baysan et al., 2019; Clancey et al., 2017; Enamorado et al., 2014; Mulok et al., 2017). However, the literature also includes studies that analyze a group of countries. For example, Nayebyazdi (2017) examined this nexus for the European Union countries with a panel vector autoregressions approach, however, couldn't find sufficient evidence to indicate the effect of growth on crime rates.

Many empirical studies reveal that unemployment is one of the most critical factors affecting crime rates (Altindag, 2012; Britt, 1994; Duster, 1987; Guza et al., 2019; Narayan & Smyth, 2004; Nordin & Almén, 2017; Öster & Agell, 2007; Smith et al., 1992; Tabar & Noghani, 2019). Freeman (1996) showed that criminal activity is more intense in regions with high unemployment. Raphael and Winter-Ebmer (2001) argued that households would not attempt to commit crimes when the unemployment rate falls because of increased legal earnings opportunities. Burdett et al. (2003) drew attention to the strong link between unemployment and youth crime. Mehlum et al. (2005) found that an increase in job vacancies resulted in a decrease in criminal activity. The positive relationship between unemployment and crime rates is also supported by recent empirical studies (Gao et al., 2017; Ha & Andresen, 2017; Jawadi et al., 2021; Nordin & Almén, 2017; Siwach, 2018). Although there are studies in the literature that do not support the positive relationship stated, their number is quite limited. For example, Machin and Meghir (2004) could not find any evidence to support a statistically significant relationship between unemployment and crime in the UK.

Demographic variables are also used in the investigation of crime rates. The most commonly used of such variables is urbanization. Although urbanization creates a positive perception as a symbol of modernization at first glance, it can bring many problems with it. Uncontrolled and rapid urbanization, which occurs without the necessary infrastructure, may cause an increase in crime rates. Mills and Price (1984) revealed that urbanization is a factor that increases crime rates. In their study on Germany, Entorf and Spengler (2000) found evidence that there is a positive relationship between urbanization and crime rates. Blackmore (2003) obtained similar results in his extensive study on South Africa. Neumayer (2003) conducted a fixed-effect analysis and found that urbanization leads to violent crimes. Most single-country studies investigating urbanization-crime rates nexus have found a positive relationship among these variables (Haider & Badami, 2010; Hassan et al., 2016; Owusu et al., 2016).

Studies examining the determinants of crime rates have used many other variables in their empirical models, such as institutional structure, law enforcement, and the establishment of the rule of law. The fact that law enforcement is one of the main tools used in the fight against crime causes researchers to use a proxy to represent this variable in their models. Ehrlich (1973) showed that the presence of law enforcement has a strong influence on crime rates. Soares (2004) emphasized the importance of institutional development in reducing crime rates. Chatterjee and Ray (2014) reported that institutional quality is as effective as economic factors in fighting crime. Ott (2010) cited the rule of law as one of the main tools for developing a welfare state that reduces criminal activity. Haggard and Tiede (2011) emphasized that the rule of law not only reduces crime but also increases economic growth.

Although many empirical studies examine the determinants of crime rates, our study differs from them in terms of perspective, proxies used, or methodology (Buonanno et al., 2018; Butkus et al., 2019; Kızılgöl & Selim, 2017; Piatkowska et al., 2016; Sandner & Wassmann, 2018). Our study contributes to the literature by measuring crime in a broader sense (using the number of prisoners instead of a given crime to represent total crime) and explaining heterogeneous causality using the Dumitrescu and Hurlin (2012) causality test.

32.3 Data and Methodology

The panel dataset used in the study covers 17 countries: Brazil, Chile, Colombia, Czechia, Estonia, France, Greece, Hungary, Italy, Ireland, Latvia, Lithuania, Poland, Portugal, Slovakia, Slovenia, and Turkey for the years between 2003 and 2017. Following Rodríguez-Menés and López-Riba (2019), we use "the prisoner rate per 100.000 people" as a proxy for our dependent variable. This data was obtained from United Nations Office on Drugs and Crime (UNODC, 2020). The real GDP with constant prices and unemployment series were compiled from OECD (2019). We retrieved the urbanization rate from the population division of the United Nations (UN, 2018). Rule of law focuses on how citizens adhere to society's rules, including compliance of contracts, the effectiveness of the judiciary system, and the perception of crime and violence (Kaufmann et al., 2003). This series was obtained from the Worldwide Governance Indicators dataset from World Bank (WGI, 2020).

Our empirical methodology consists of several steps. First, Maddala and Wu (1999) and Choi (2001) unit root tests were applied to assess whether the series are stationary. Since each unit root test has its advantages and drawbacks, the application of more than one test is necessary for confirmatory purposes. Secondly, the Engle-Granger-based cointegration test of Pedroni (2004) was employed to determine whether there is any long-run relationship between the variables. In the third step, we examined how the independent variables affect crime rates by applying fully modified least squares (FMOLS) (Pedroni, 2001; Phillips & Hansen, 1990).

The weighted FMOLS approach is selected for this investigation as it provides more efficient estimates where there are heterogeneous panels. The model is presented by Eq. 32.1:

$$\text{lpris}_{it} = \beta_1 \text{lune}_{it} + \beta_2 \text{lgdp}_{it} + \beta_2 \text{rlaw}_{it} + \beta_1 \text{lurb}_{it} + \varepsilon_{it} \qquad (32.1)$$

where lpris is the dependent variable, represented by prisoner rate per 100.000 people; lune is unemployment rates, lgdp is real GDP in constant prices, lurb is urbanization, and rlaw represents the rule of law as an indicator of institutional factors. Aside from rlaw all variables are in their logarithmic forms.

Lastly, we examined the causal relationship among the variables using the method developed by Dumitrescu and Hurlin (2012). The ability to avoid the heterogeneity problem is a notable advantage of this causality test. Another advantage of using the aforementioned method is that the standardized statistics of Dumitrescu and Hurlin (2012) hold powerful small sample properties compared to previous causality methods.

32.4 Empirical Findings

32.4.1 Preliminary Test Results

Table 32.1 provides an overview of the descriptive statistics of the variables included in our empirical model. As can be seen in Table 32.1, GDP has the highest mean value of 13.71, followed by crime proxy (5.43), urbanization (4,22), unemployment (2.22), and the rule of law (0.73). In addition, we conclude that there is no outlier in our dataset since the interval between the minimum and maximum values is moderate compared to the mean values of the variables. Moreover, the null hypothesis of normality is rejected for all variables but unemployment rates.

Unit root tests were conducted to determine the stationarity of the variables, and obtained results are summarized in Table 32.2. The majority of the results indicate the existence of unit root at the level for all variables. However, the first differences of the series become stationary. Hence, we concluded that variables in the dataset are all integrated of order I(1).

Table 32.1 Descriptive statistics

	rlw	lurb	lune	lpris	lgdp
Mean	0.73	4.22	2.22	5.43	13.71
Maximum	1.77	4.47	3.31	11.69	20.54
Minimum	−0.70	3.93	1.06	3.98	9.63
Std. Dev.	0.56	0.13	0.36	1.56	2.99
Jarque-Bera	10.16	5.46	3.71	1377.39	17.02
Probability	0.00	0.06	0.15	0.00	0.00

Source: Authors' analysis

Table 32.2 Unit root tests results

Lvl	Fisher ADF					Fisher PP				
Var	Lpris	lgdp	lune	rlw	lurb	lpris	lgdp	lune	rlw	lurb
τ_T	51.7**	44.4	38.4	38.7	18.4	29.1	19.3	9.79	62.8*	38.9
τ_μ	38.4	41.9	44.4	55.1**	21.9	39.1	41.0	18.6	45.3	21.9
τ	27	3.7	29.4	35.9	14.3	40	3.2	34.3*	38.0	14.3
First difference										
τ_T	64.1*	46.7**	43.1	115*	44.2*	94.1*	34.9	34.0	155*	28.0
τ_μ	85.1*	69.2*	66.0*	116*	35.3	101*	63.1*	52.9**	164*	111*
τ	133*	109*	129*	189*	112*	137*	94.6*	115*	207*	122*

Source: Authors' analysis
Note: *, **, *** denote significance at 1%, 5%, 10%, respectively

Table 32.3 Panel cointegration tests results

Test	τ_T	τ_μ	τ
Panel *v-statistic*	−0.77	−0.28	0.39
Panel *rho-statistic*	3.50	2.36	1.49
Panel *t-statistic: (nonparametric)*	−4.41*	−1.62**	−1.82*
Panel *t-statistic (adf): (parametric)*	−5.68*	−3.16*	−3.57**
Group *rho-statistic*	4.89	4.09	3.26
Group *t-statistic: (nonparametric)*	−16.62*	−3.70*	−3.62**
Group *t-statistic (adf): (parametric)*	−9.28*	−4.04*	−5.23*

Source: Authors' analysis
Note: *, **, *** denote significance at 1%, 5%, 10%, respectively

After confirming that the variables are I(1), cointegration analysis was utilized to investigate the long-run relationship between the variables. In Table 32.3, we present Pedroni Cointegration test results. A majority of the test statistics indicate cointegration, which means the existence of a long-term relationship between the variables.

32.4.2 FMOLS and Causality Test Results

Then we applied the FMOLS regression to estimate the coefficients of our empirical model, and the findings are presented in Table 32.4. Results reveal a significant positive impact of unemployment on crime rates, which is supported by recent studies (Gao et al., 2017; Jawadi et al., 2021). As unemployment rises, people who cannot obtain legal income tend to engage in illegal activities (e.g., robbery, theft, and burglary), resulting in an increase in crime rates. Findings also confirm that the relationship between crime rates and real economic growth is significant and negative. As economic growth accelerates, new employment opportunities will emerge, per capita income will increase, and citizens' increasing welfare will

Table 32.4 Fully modified OLS (FMOLS) results

Dependent variable: lpris			
Variable	Coefficient	Std. error	t-Statistic
Lune	1.02*	0.04	24.6
Lgdp	−0.22*	0.01	−15.7
Rlaw	−0.41*	0.02	−15.3
Lurb	2.87*	0.00	346

Source: Authors analysis
Note: * denotes significance at 1%

decrease crime rates (Fajnzylber et al., 2002a). This finding is consistent with the results of many previous studies (Fajnzylber et al., 2002b; Islam, 2014; Lederman et al., 2002). The rule of law has a significant negative relationship with crime rates. Strengthening the rule of law will make the fight of law enforcement officers against criminals more effective, and thus, a deterrent environment will be created for committing crimes (Ott, 2010). Finally, 1% increase in urbanization results in a 2.8% increase in crime rates. Concentration of the population in urban areas facilitates certain types of crime and increases crime rates (Hassan et al., 2016). The positive relationship between urbanization and crime rates is also supported by the literature (Hassan et al., 2016; Owusu et al., 2016).

The results of the Dumitrescu and Hurlin (2012) causality test are presented in Table 32.5. The rule of law has a bidirectional relationship with all the other variables, but the relationship is unidirectional from unemployment to the rule of law for unemployment. In addition, unemployment has a bidirectional causal relationship with real GDP and urbanization. Moreover, unidirectional causalities were found running from urbanization to crime rate, real GDP to the crime rate, and from crime rates to unemployment.

32.5 Conclusion

Because of its direct and indirect costs and harmful consequences, such as widespread disturbances in society, loss of human capital, expansion of prisons, and recruitment of new prison staff, the fight against crime has been a vital issue for creating a sustainable welfare society. Although many studies have examined the determinants of crime rates, they have limitations in terms of modeling, methodology, sample selection, or proxy selection. Our study differs from many previous studies with its choice of proxy for the dependent variable, its large panel dataset consisting of 17 countries, and usage of the Dumitrescu and Hurlin (2012) test to investigate the causal relationship. Obtained findings confirm that the increase in unemployment and intense urbanization tend to increase the crime rates, while the growth of the real economy and enhancement of the rule of law have a decreasing effect on the crime rates.

Table 32.5 Dumitrescu and Hurlin (2012) causality test results

Null hypothesis:	W-Stat.	Prob.
Urbanization → rule of law	8.01	0.00
Rule of law → urbanization	4.62	0.03
Unemployment → rule of law	4.65	0.02
Crime → rule of law	4.93	0.01
Rule of law → crime	8.52	0.00
Real GDP → rule of law	6.19	0.00
Unemployment → urbanization	7.87	0.00
Urbanization → unemployment	6.30	0.00
Urbanization → crime	9.05	0.00
Urbanization → real GDP	6.39	0.00
Crime → unemployment	4.67	0.02
Real GDP → unemployment	4.37	0.06
Unemployment → real GDP	4.41	0.05
Real GDP → crime	4.57	0.03

Source: Authors' analysis

These results imply some policy implications. First, sustainable economic growth and lower rates of unemployment are the most fundamental weapons in preventing crime. This result points to the principle that providing legal means of earning income to individuals will reduce the marginal return of committing a crime. Improving the institutions that serve the social order, establishing a well-functioning legal order, and effective law enforcement will significantly support the fight against crime. Although it is not possible to prevent urbanization, it is vital to take necessary precautions by considering the dynamics of urbanization that cause increased criminal activity. Uncontrolled migration from rural areas to cities and structural problems such as insufficient infrastructures and shelter are the factors that create a suitable environment for crime. In this respect, it will be beneficial to give importance to social state policies and increase the support given to disadvantaged groups to strengthen the social fabric.

References

Aaltonen, M., Kivivuori, J., & Martikainen, P. (2011). Social determinants of crime in a welfare state: Do they still matter? *Acta Sociologica, 54*(2), 161–181.

Adekoya, A. F., & Razak, N. A. A. (2016). Crime dependency on punishment: Evidence on economic growth in Nigeria. *Journal of Economics, 4*(2), 219–228.

Ahmad, A., Ali, S., & Ahmad, N. (2014). Crime and economic growth in developing countries: Evidence from Pakistan. *Journal of Basic and Applied Scientific Research, 4*(4), 31–41.

Ajide, F. M. (2019). Institutional quality, economic misery and crime rate in Nigeria. *Economics and Business, 33*(1), 170–182.

Altindag, D. T. (2012). Crime and unemployment: Evidence from Europe. *International Review of Law and Economics, 32*(1), 145–157.

Baysan, C., Burke, M., González, F., Hsiang, S., & Miguel, E. (2019). Non-economic factors in violence: Evidence from organized crime, suicides and climate in Mexico. *Journal of Economic Behavior & Organization, 168*, 434–452.

Becker, G. S. (1968). Crime and punishment: An economic approach. *Journal of Political Economy, 76*(2), 169–217.

Beirne, P. (1987). Adolphe Quetelet and the origins of positivist criminology. *American Journal of Sociology, 92*(5), 1140–1169.

Bennett, R. R., & Flavin, J. M. (1994). Determinants of fear of crime: The effect of cultural setting. *Justice Quarterly, 11*(3), 357–381.

Blackmore, F. L. E. (2003). A panel data analysis of crime in South Africa. *South African Journal of Economic and Management Sciences, 6*(3), 439–458.

Britt, C. L. (1994). Crime and unemployment among youths in the United States, 1958-1990: A time series analysis. *American Journal of Economics and Sociology, 53*(1), 99–109.

Brown, K. V. (2001). The determinants of crime in South Africa. *South African Journal of Economics, 69*(2), 269–298.

Buonanno, P., & Montolio, D. (2008). Identifying the socioeconomic and demographic determinants of crime across Spanish provinces. *International Review of Law and Economics, 28*(2), 89–97.

Buonanno, P., Drago, F., Galbiati, R., & Vertova, P. (2018). How much should we trust crime statistics? A comparison between EU and US. *European Journal of Law and Economics, 46*(3), 343–357.

Burdett, K., Lagos, R., & Wright, R. (2003). Crime, inequality, and unemployment. *American Economic Review, 93*(5), 1764–1777.

Butkus, M., Matuzevičiutė, K., & Mačiulytė-Šniukienė, A. (2019). Do economic conditions still cause crime? Some comforting empirical evidences from EU Panel. *Zbornik Radova Ekonomski Fakultet u Rijeka, 37*(2), 603–628.

Cahill, M. E., & Mulligan, G. F. (2003). The determinants of crime in Tucson, Arizona. *Urban Geography, 24*(7), 582–610.

Chatterjee, I., & Ray, R. (2014). Crime, corruption and the role of institutions. *Indian Growth and Development Review, 7*(1), 73–95.

Chioda, L. (2017). *Stop the violence in Latin America: A look at prevention from cradle to adulthood*. The World Bank. Available via https://openknowledge.worldbank.org/bitstream/handle/10986/25920/9781464806643.pdf?sequence=7. Accessed 15 Apr 2020

Choi, I. (2001). Unit root tests for panel data. *Journal of International Money and Finance, 20*(2), 249–272.

Clancey, G., Kent, J., Lyons, A., & Westcott, H. (2017). Crime and crime prevention in an Australian growth centre. *Crime Prevention and Community Safety, 19*(1), 17–30.

Dávila, C. A., & Pardo-Montaño, A. M. (2019). Factores socioeconómicos asociados con la mortalidad por homicidios en Colombia, 2000-2014. *Ciência & Saúde Coletiva, 24*, 2793–2804.

Dumitrescu, E. I., & Hurlin, C. (2012). Testing for Granger non-causality in heterogeneous panels. *Economic Modelling, 29*(4), 1450–1460.

Duster, T. (1987). Crime, youth unemployment, and the black urban underclass. *Crime & Delinquency, 33*(2), 300–316.

Ehrlich, I. (1973). Participation in illegitimate activities: A theoretical and empirical investigation. *Journal of Political Economy, 81*(3), 521–565.

Enamorado, T., López-Calva, L. F., & Rodríguez-Castelán, C. (2014). Crime and growth convergence: Evidence from Mexico. *Economics Letters, 125*(1), 9–13.

Entorf, H., & Spengler, H. (2000). Socioeconomic and demographic factors of crime in Germany: Evidence from panel data of the German states. *International Review of Law and Economics, 20*(1), 75–106.

Fajnzylber, P., Lederman, D., & Loayza, N. (2002a). Inequality and violent crime. *The Journal of Law and Economics, 45*(1), 1–39.

Fajnzylber, P., Lederman, D., & Loayza, N. (2002b). What causes violent crime? *European Economic Review, 46*(7), 1323–1357.
Freeman, R. B. (1996). Why do so many young American men commit crimes and what might we do about it? *Journal of Economic Perspectives, 10*(1), 25–42.
Gao, G., Liu, B., & Kouassi, I. (2017). The contemporaneous effect of unemployment on crime rates: The case of Indiana. *Southwestern Economic Review, 44*, 99–107.
Goulas, E., & Zervoyianni, A. (2015). Economic growth and crime: Is there an asymmetric relationship? *Economic Modelling, 49*, 286–295.
Guza, G. M., Musa, A. B., & Elijah, S. (2019). Violent crime and unemployment in Nigeria: An ARDL bounds test cointegration. *Journal of Economic Info, 6*(4), 21–24.
Ha, O. K., & Andresen, M. A. (2017). Unemployment and the specialization of criminal activity: A neighborhood analysis. *Journal of Criminal Justice, 48*, 1–8.
Haggard, S., & Tiede, L. (2011). The rule of law and economic growth: Where are we? *World Development, 39*(5), 673–685.
Haider, M., & Badami, M. G. (2010). Urbanization and local governance challenges in Pakistan. *Environment and Urbanization ASIA, 1*(1), 81–96.
Hassan, M. S., Akbar, M. S., Wajid, A., & Arshed, N. (2016). Poverty, urbanization and crime: Are they related in Pakistan. *International Journal of Economics and Empirical Research, 4*(9), 483–492.
Howsen, R. M., & Jarrell, S. B. (1987). Some determinants of property crime: Economic factors influence criminal behavior but cannot completely explain the syndrome. *American Journal of Economics and Sociology, 46*(4), 445–457.
İmrohoroĝlu, A., Merlo, A., & Rupert, P. (2006). Understanding the determinants of crime. *Journal of Economics and Finance, 30*(2), 270–284.
Islam, A. (2014). Economic growth and crime against small and medium-sized enterprises in developing economies. *Small Business Economics, 43*(3), 677–695.
Jawadi, F., Mallick, S. K., Idi Cheffou, A., & Augustine, A. (2021). Does higher unemployment lead to greater criminality? Revisiting the debate over the business cycle. *Journal of Economic Behavior & Organization, 182*, 448–471.
Kaufmann, D., Kraay, A., & Mastruzzi, M. (2003). *Governance Matters III: Governance Indicators for 1996–2002*. Available via http://papers.ssrn.com/sol3/papers.cfm?abstract_id=405841. Accessed 15 Apr 2020.
Kızılgöl, O., & Selim, S. (2017). Socioeconomic and demographic determinants of crime by panel count data analysis: The case of EU28 and Turkey. *Journal of Business Economics and Finance, 6*(1), 31–41.
Kochel, T. R. (2013). Robustness of collective efficacy on crime in a developing nation: Association with crime reduction compared to police services. *Journal of Crime and Justice, 36*(3), 334–352.
Kochel, T. R., & Weisburd, D. (2017). Assessing community consequences of implementing hot spots policing in residential areas: Findings from a randomized field trial. *Journal of Experimental Criminology, 13*(2), 143–170.
Lederman, D., Loayza, N., & Menendez, A. M. (2002). Violent crime; Does social capital matter? *Economic Development and Cultural Change, 50*(3), 509–539.
Levitt, S. D. (1999). The changing relationship between income and crime victimization. *Economic Policy Review, 5*(3), 87–98.
Levitt, S. D., & Lochner, L. (2001). The determinants of juvenile crime. NBER chapters. In *Risky behavior among youths: An economic analysis* (pp. 327–374). University of Chicago Press.
Machin, S., & Meghir, C. (2004). Crime and economic incentives. *Journal of Human Resources, 39*(4), 958–979.
Maddala, G. S., & Wu, S. (1999). A comparative study of unit root tests with panel data and a new simple test. *Oxford Bulletin of Economics and Statistics, 61*, 631–652.
Manzoni, P., Brochu, S., Fischer, B., & Rehm, J. (2006). Determinants of property crime among illicit opiate users outside of treatment across Canada. *Deviant Behavior, 27*(3), 351–376.

Marvell, T. B., & Moody, C. E. (1988). *Crime and economic trends*. US Department of Justice, National Institute of Justice. Available via https://www.ojp.gov/ncjrs/virtual-library/abstracts/crime-and-economic-trends. Accessed 15 Apr 2020
Masih, A. M., & Masih, R. (1996). Temporal causality and the dynamics of different categories of crime and their socioeconomic determinants: Evidence from Australia. *Applied Economics, 28*(9), 1093–1104.
Mehlum, H., Moene, K., & Torvik, R. (2005). Crime-induced poverty traps. *Journal of Development Economics, 77*(2), 325–340.
Mills, E. S., & Price, R. (1984). Metropolitan suburbanization and central city problems. *Journal of Urban Economics, 15*(1), 1–17.
Mulok, D., Kogid, M., Lily, J., & Asid, R. (2017). The relationship between crime and economic growth in Malaysia: Re-examine using bound test approach. *Malaysian Journal of Business and Economics, 3*(1), 15–26.
Narayan, P. K., & Smyth, R. (2004). Crime rates, male youth unemployment and real income in Australia: Evidence from Granger causality tests. *Applied Economics, 36*(18), 2079–2095.
Nayebyazdi, A. (2017). The relationship between occurrence of crime and economic growth in the European Union: Panel VAR Approach. *International Journal of Contemporary Economics and Administrative Sciences, 7*(1–2), 57–80.
Neumayer, E. (2003). Good policy can lower violent crime: Evidence from a cross-national panel of homicide rates, 1980–97. *Journal of Peace Research, 40*(6), 619–640.
Nordin, M., & Almén, D. (2017). Long-term unemployment and violent crime. *Empirical Economics, 52*(1), 1–29.
OECD. (2019). *Main economic indicators – Complete database*. Available via https://doi.org/10.1787/data-00052-en. Accessed 15 Apr 2020.
Omotor, D. G. (2009). Socioeconomic determinants of crime in Nigeria. *Pakistan Journal of Social Sciences, 6*(2), 54–59.
Öster, A., & Agell, J. (2007). Crime and unemployment in turbulent times. *Journal of the European Economic Association, 5*(4), 752–775.
Ott, J. C. (2010). Good governance and happiness in nations: Technical quality precedes democracy and quality beats size. *Journal of Happiness Studies, 11*(3), 353–368.
Owusu, G., Owusu, A. Y., Oteng-Ababio, M., Wrigley-Asante, C., & Agyapong, I. (2016). An assessment of households' perceptions of private security companies and crime in urban Ghana. *Crime Science, 1*(5), 1–11.
Pedroni, P. (2001). Fully modified OLS for heterogeneous cointegrated panels. In *Nonstationary panels, panel Cointegration, and dynamic panels*. Emerald Group Publishing Limited.
Pedroni, P. (2004). Panel cointegration: Asymptotic and finite sample properties of pooled time series tests with an application to the PPP hypothesis. *Econometric Theory, 20*(3), 597–625.
Peri, G. (2004). Socio-cultural variables and economic success: Evidence from Italian provinces 1951-1991. *Topics in Macroeconomics, 4*(1), 1–36.
Phillips, P. C., & Hansen, B. E. (1990). Statistical inference in instrumental variables regression with I(1) processes. *The Review of Economic Studies, 57*(1), 99–125.
Piatkowska, S. J., Messner, S. F., & Raffalovich, L. E. (2016). The impact of accession to the European Union on homicide rates in Eastern Europe. *European Sociological Review, 32*(1), 151–161.
Raphael, S., & Winter-Ebmer, R. (2001). Identifying the effect of unemployment on crime. *The Journal of Law and Economics, 44*(1), 259–283.
Rickman, N., & Witt, R. (2007). The determinants of employee crime in the UK. *Economica, 74*(293), 161–175.
Rodríguez-Menés, J., & López-Riba, J. M. (2019). The impact of the 2008 economic crisis on imprisonment in Europe. *European Journal of Criminology, 1*, 1–32.
Saleemi, M. W., & Amir-ud-Din, R. (2019). *How does quality of governance influence occurrence of crime? A longitudinal analysis of Asian countries* (Germany paper no. 94142). University

Library of Munich. Available via https://mpra.ub.uni-muenchen.de/94142/1/MPRA_paper_94142.pdf. Accessed 15 Apr 2020

Sandner, M., & Wassmann, P. (2018). The effect of changes in border regimes on border regions crime rates: Evidence from the Schengen treaty. *Kyklos, 71*(3), 482–506.

Schuck, A. M. (2020). Examining the community consequences of arrests for low-level criminal activity. *Journal of Community Psychology, 48*(1), 86–103.

Siwach, G. (2018). Unemployment shocks for individuals on the margin: Exploring recidivism effects. *Labour Economics, 52*, 231–244.

Smith, M. D., Devine, J. A., & Sheley, J. F. (1992). Crime and unemployment: Effects across age and race categories. *Sociological Perspectives, 35*(4), 551–572.

Soares, R. R. (2004). Crime reporting as a measure of institutional development. *Economic Development and Cultural Change, 52*(4), 851–871.

Tabar, S. A. M. M., & Noghani, M. (2019). Unemployment and crime in developing countries: A meta-analysis in Iran. *Crime, Law and Social Change, 72*(3), 327–338.

UN-ECOSOC (2017). World crime trends and emerging issues and responses in the field of crime prevention and criminal justice. Available via https://www.unodc.org/documents/data-and-analysis/statistics/crime/ccpj/World_crime_trends_emerging_issues_E.pdf. Accessed 15 Apr 2020.

UN (2018). World Urbanization Prospects - Population Division. Available via https://population.un.org/wup/Download/. Accessed 15 Apr 2020.

UNODC. (2020). *United Nations office on drugs and crime*. Available via https://www.unodc.org. Accessed 15 Apr 2020.

WGI. (2020). *World Governance indicators*. Available via https://databank.worldbank.org/source/worldwide-governance-indicators. Accessed 15 Apr 2020.

World Bank (2007). Crime, violence, and development: trends, costs and policy options in the Caribbean. Report No. 37820. Available via https://www.unodc.org/pdf/research/Cr_and_Vio_Car_E.pdf. Accessed 15 April 2020.

Chapter 33
Tax Avoidance and Companies' Opacity: A Theoretical Approach

Cristina Sá and Helena Alves

Abstract The problem of companies' opacity is related to the existence of asymmetric information, which is the extent to which the amount of information regarding the company varies from one group to another. Tax avoidance can be considered as the art of avoiding tax without violating the law, for example, by exploiting the loopholes in the legal text. The call for greater transparency from companies is seen as a way to help reduce tax avoidance. This study presents a theoretical reflection on the relation between companies' opacity and tax avoidance practices. Financial disclosure quality and tax planning can be a source of conflict for managers. Some authors argue that the board represents a means to promote the dissemination of higher-quality disclosure, which decreases information asymmetry and resulting agency problems. The discussion of whether information disclosure policy is influenced by tax activities is under discussion. The added value of this work relies on the analysis of empirical literature about information asymmetry and tax planning activities, providing a more extensive overview of this relation, that can be used to better understand compliance behavior and reduce tax fraud.

Key words Tax avoidance · Asymmetric information · Theory of agency · Disclosure

33.1 Introduction

The need for mechanisms of decision-making within companies is evident and lacks no additional considerations. Without these mechanisms, the companies simply would not work. It is necessary to take decisions and promote their realization:

C. Sá (✉)
CARME, ESTG, Polytechnic Institute of Leiria, Leiria, Portugal
e-mail: cristina.sa@ipleiria.pt

H. Alves
School of Technology and Management of Leiria, Polytechnic Institute of Leiria, Leiria, Portugal
e-mail: helena.alves@ipleiria.pt

D. Procházka (ed.), *Regulation of Finance and Accounting*, Springer Proceedings in Business and Economics, https://doi.org/10.1007/978-3-030-99873-8_33

This is the task of the mechanisms for controlling agency costs. Similarly, it becomes apparent how important it is that these mechanisms function effectively, for only in this manner will the business optimally achieve its goals. In this context, companies possess a set of external and internal mechanisms to face the costs associated with the agency problem.[1] According to Vitolla et al. (2020), control by the board represents a means to promote the dissemination of higher-quality disclosure, which decreases information asymmetry and resulting agency problems.

According to Wan (2009: 15), "the selective disclosure allows managers the opportunity to act in their own interest against the interest of ordinary shareholders, creating the possibility of an agency problem."

The information asymmetry is the extent to which the amount of information regarding the company varies from one group of investors to another and, thus, provides the differentiation between the informed and uninformed investors. Otherwise, the information asymmetry between administration and new shareholders can affect the investment decisions of the company because of the sub- or underevaluation of the shares in the market. Information differences across investors (or groups of investors) have been a long-standing concern to securities regulators (Lambert et al., 2007). To Bergh et al. (2019), the information asymmetry concept underlies some of the management field's most important theories and topics. To the authors, limited information may be one of the most common problems surrounding human and organizational interactions of any kind. According to Cheyney and Levine (2020), voluntary disclosures lead to higher ex ante information asymmetry.

Kerr (2012) concludes positively on the influence of information asymmetry on tax avoidance. On the contrary, there are several evidences that aggressive tax planning influences earnings quality and information asymmetry (e.g., Hanlon, 2005; Ayers et al., 2009; Comprix et al., 2011; Balakrishnan et al., 2012). According to Chen and Lin (2017), the question of whether the information disclosure policy is affected by tax activities is under discussion because the relation between these two concepts is not yet clearly defined.

33.2 The Conflict Between Agents and Principals

The major conflict analyzed in the context of corporate governance is the one between shareholders and managers. This conflict was the main issue of the theoretical analysis of the agency problem. In fact, the agency problem is an essential element of the so-called contractual view of the firm, developed by Coase (1937), Jensen and Meckling (1976), and Fama and Jensen (1983).

[1] This paper in based on PhD Thesis of the author Helena Alves available on: https://estudogeral.sib.uc.pt/handle/10316/20365

Hart (1995: 678) states that "corporate governance issues arise in an organization whenever (. . .) there is an agency problem (. . .)." An agency problem arises within a firm whenever managers have incentives to pursue their own interest at shareholder expense (Agrawal & Knoeber, 1996). So, there are agency costs. Basically, Hart (1995: 678) explains why corporate governance does not matter in the absence of agency costs. He states that in the absence of agency problems, "all individuals associated with an organization can be instructed to maximize profit or net market value or to minimize costs (. . .). Also, no governance structure is required to resolve disagreements, since there are none."

The theoretical motives for agency problems are analyzed by Jensen and Meckling (1976: 9), who developed a theory of the ownership structure of a firm. The basis for their analysis is the perspective that a corporation is "a legal fiction which serves as a nexus for contracting relationships and which is also characterized by the existence of divisible residual claims on the assets and cash-flows of the organization which can generally be sold without the permission of the other contracting individuals." In this sense, the particular focus of the Jensen and Meckling (1976) model is the contract of an agency relationship between a principal (the external owner of the firm) and an agent (the owner-manager or entrepreneur). They demonstrate that as the owner-manager's fraction of the equity falls (as more equity is sold to outside investors), the agent has the incentive to appropriate a large amount of the corporations' resources and to exert less than full effort to create value for shareholders. The principal can limit the effects of this divergence of interests by incurring monitoring costs to restrain the agent's self-serving behavior. Monitoring expenditures potentially include those related to payments to auditors to inspect the company's accounts, costs of providing information to financial analysts, rating agencies, or independent directors on the board.

The difference of interests between the principal intervenient and the agent creates some problems, among which, the "adverse selection" and "moral hazard." The problem of "adverse selection" [2] (Akerlof, 1970) arises when one party of the relationship has information that reveals in a selective manner for their benefit and in detriment of the other party. So, by hiding part of the information possessed, one deliberately harms the interests of another party. Managers have inside information about the position of their businesses and have an interest in disclosing such information when they realize that their company is not having a proper valuation in the markets. The problem of "moral hazard" appears when the principal and the agent have different objectives. The principal cannot easily determine if the information and the actions of the agents pursue his goals, or instead, respond only to self-interest. In fact, according to Jensen and Meckling (1976), if both relationship parties have the same objective to maximize its utility, there are good reasons to believe that

[2] Akerlof (1970) identifies and analyzes the problem of asymmetric information in the context of used cars, in which the sellers (agents) know better than the buyers (principal) the quality of the cars they sell. The consequence is that sellers have the advantage in terms of information on the buyers, and they may sell low-quality cars at the same price as high-quality cars, as long as the buyers cannot distinguish the good car from the bad.

the agent did not always act in the interests of the principal. The fact that there is some freedom allowing for the choice by the manager may lead to procedures that fit more to their personal interests, being this usually called moral hazard.

A further problem is associated with the managers having a different horizon than shareholders. In fact, while firms have an indefinite life, the manager's horizon is usually limited to the cash flows received during the employment relation. This problem is naturally aggravated as managers approach retirement. This can lead managers to have a short-term perspective on investments, with a preference for projects with faster cash-flow returns.

An additional source is related to different risk preferences. Shareholders eliminate unsystematic risk by diversifying their portfolios, so they are not concerned with company-specific risk but only with market risk. In contrast, managers are typically not well diversified as a large portion of their wealth is tied to their company's fortunes. This is not just because of direct cash flows received from the firm but also because their future employment prospects are dependent on the survival of the firm (Farinha, 2003).

Another problem associated with agency costs is the dispersion of capital which is common to most large listed firms. With a large dispersion of capital, individual external shareholders have no incentive to engage in managerial monitoring. According to Farinha (2003), although it may be in the interests of the collective group of external owners to employ in actions aimed at disciplining management, no single rational individual shareholder will undertake such actions.

Also the free cash-flow theory, proposed by Jensen (1986: 323), considers preponderant the conflicts arising from the prevailing theory of agency. The free cash flow is "cash flow in excess of that required to fund all projects that have positive net present values when discounted at the relevant cost of capital." When a company generates substantial amounts of free cash flow, conflicts of interest between shareholders and managers arise over the payout policies. These companies run the risk, by the lack of good investment opportunities, to see those funds spent by managers on projects with no added value. The restriction of the problem of free cash flow will depend on the effectiveness of corporate governance mechanisms, meaning on mechanisms that ensure that managers do not apply the funds available in potential organizational inefficiencies.

According to Shleifer and Vishny (1997: 741), the essence of the agency problem also relays on the separation of the management and finance. The manager needs the financiers' funds. The financiers need the manager's specialized human capital to generate returns on their funds. "But how can financiers be sure that, once they sink their funds, they get anything but a worthless piece of paper back from the managers?" The agency problem in this context refers to the difficulties financiers have in assuring that their funds are not expropriated or wasted on unattractive projects. In most general terms, the financiers and the managers sign a contract that specifies what the manager does with the funds, and how the returns are divided. Ideally, they would sign a complete contract that specifies exactly what the manager does and how the profits are allocated. The problem is that most of the future contingencies are hard to describe and foresee, and as a result, complete contracts are technologically infeasible (Shleifer & Vishny, 1997). Because of these problems in designing their contract, the manager and the financier have to allocate residual control rights, the rights to make decisions in circumstances not fully foreseen by the contract (Grossman & Hart, 1986; Hart & Moore, 1990).

33.3 Companies' Opacity

The asymmetric information arises when, in the context of market transactions, the two sides that deal with the subject or content of information, in terms of quantity and quality, are not equal (Watts & Zimmerman, 1986). According to Ranaldo (2002), the information asymmetry refers to information not yet embodied in the fundamental asset value. To Brown and Hillegeist (2007: 444), information asymmetry in the stock market occurs when "one or more investors possess private information about the firm while other investors are uninformed (e.g., have access only to public information)." As stated previously, the separation of ownership and control in publicly listed companies gives rise to information asymmetries between managers and investors because managers have superior information on the firm's current and future performance than outside investors (Jensen & Meckling, 1976; Myers & Majluf, 1984). The literature recognizes that firms might find it advantageous to give additional pieces of information to outsiders, through the annual report or other communication channels. The information asymmetry between firms and potential investors, due to a low level of disclosure, increases the cost of capital by introducing the adverse selection between buyers and sellers of the firm's shares (Petersen & Plenborg, 2006).

According to Welker (1995), considerable resources are devoted to establishing and enforcing regulations that improve public perceptions of corporate disclosure practices. Despite these regulatory efforts, firms still have considerable discretion in determining the timeless, scope, content, and form of disclosure provided to equity market participants, among others. According to Welker (1995: 802), "this diversity in disclosure practices produces variation in the level of information asymmetry characterizing trade in equity market." Welker (1995) also speaks about one persistent component of the adverse selection problem that is the possibility that material firm-specific information exists and has not been publicly disclosed by the firm. According to the author, this "withheld" information may be privately available to select traders who invest in costly information acquisition, creating an adverse selection problem when uncertainty about the occurrence of information events exists and firms follow a policy of providing incomplete disclosures with respect to such events.

Past literature has pointed out the adverse effects that information asymmetries have on the functioning of markets (Akerlof, 1970). Information asymmetry is thought to promote reluctance to trade and increase the cost of capital as investors "price protect" against potential losses from trading with better informed market participants (Bhattacharya & Spiegel, 1991). The study of market microstructures formalized this notion of price protection and suggested that observable measures of market liquidity can be used to identify the perceived level of information asymmetry facing (uninformed) participants in equity markets (Lev, 1988).

To Kanagaretnam et al. (2007), investors possess varying degrees of information about the companies in which they invest, and this may lead to the existence of informed traders, which transact with the advantage of superior information. Kim and Verrecchia (1994) suggest that earnings releases will reduce information asymmetry as they disseminate information to all market participants. However, the same authors also recognized that information asymmetry may remain at an elevated level following the earnings release because some traders are better able to process the information than others.

Analytically, Barry and Brown (1985), Diamond (1985), Diamond and Verrecchia (1991), and Kim and Verrecchia (1994) argue that more information generally reduces information risk on prices. Likewise, voluntary disclosure serves to reduce information asymmetry among traders. Empirically, Leuz and Verrecchia (2000) and Welker (1995), among others, investigate links between voluntary disclosure and stock liquidity. They found that firms with better quality disclosure have lower bid-ask spreads. In addition, Botosan and Plumlee (2002) test the capital market effect of voluntary disclosure on the cost of capital, and they found that the cost of capital decreases with more disclosure. Trabelsi et al. (2004) and Trabelsi et al. (2008) study the incentives of internet financial reporting and found that internet disclosure helps to reduce analysts' forecasting error.

Most of the above evidences are consistent with the idea that public voluntary disclosure serves to reduce information asymmetry. Furthermore, the previous disclosure research also demonstrated that the corporate governance quality has a significant impact on both the quantity and quality of these corporate information disclosures (e.g., Ho & Wong, 2001; Chau & Gray, 2002; Eng & Mak, 2003; Kanagaretnam et al., 2007).

33.4 Tax Avoidance

Flesch (1968) defined tax avoidance as the art of avoiding tax without actually breaking the law. Oats (2005) considered this definition wide, and it does not allow to understand the degrees and the distinctions between acceptable and unacceptable tax avoidance. Other authors considered tax avoidance a legal activity (Sikka & Haslam, 2007). Halon and Heitzman (2010) state tax avoidance as the reduction of explicit cash taxes, which includes all transactions from investing in a municipal bond to engaging in tax shelters. Tax avoidance concept is not always use with the same meaning which difficult the comparison between empirical studies results. Minnick and Noga (2010: 708) define tax management "as the ability to pay a low amount of taxes over a long period of time."

Also the concept of tax planning is difficult to define. Literature presents us with a large set of definitions with similar meanings. One evidence of that difficulty is the set of different expressions present in empirical literature to refer to these activities, for example, tax planning (Halon & Heitzman, 2010), tax management (Minnick & Toga, 2010), tax avoidance (Anouar & Houria, 2017), among others.

Tax planning activities often involve a large number of monetary resources. Fees related to tax and legal areas represent around 30% of the revenues of International Accountancy firms (Accountancy Age, 2016). There are several factors firms take into account before implementing tax planning activities. Some firms limit those practices depending on reputational effects. They fear being considered poor corporate citizens for having low tax rates (Hanlon & Slemrod, 2009). Other companies implement tax planning activities in order to increase financial accounting results. Firms engage in tax planning activities with the purpose to improve accounting results. Graham et al. (2014) state that it's important that tax planning activities do not harm earnings per share. Also firms attend to generally accepted accounting principles effective tax rate (GAAP ETR) and paid cash taxes before defining tax planning strategies.

McBarnet (1992: 334) refers that a large corporation compliance strategy tends to "If successful, it allows taxpayers to escape tax. But at the same time, whether successful in that first goal or not, it allows them to escape any risk of stigma or penalty." Companies' tax avoidance is, in most situations, possible due to the various interpretations of the tax law letter (Sikka & Haslam, 2007). It depends on the use of preferential provisions in the tax code, such as exclusions, exemptions, deductions, credits, preferential rate, and deferral of tax liability. In this context, companies with good tax planning strategies are able to legally avoid a high amount of taxes. These savings have enormous possibilities through the use of foreign direct investment (FDI) options. Some researchers state tax planning as a key factor for competitiveness in a competitive environment (Anouar & Houria, 2017). Nowadays, international institutions like OEDC and European Commission have been made efforts to fight illegal tax avoidance. For example, according to news published on 4th October 2017, the European Commission has ruled that Amazon must pay €250 m in back taxes to Luxembourg. European Commission is developing efforts to crack down on tax avoidance by tech giants (COM, 2017). Close to a third of the growth of the overall industrial output in Europe is already due to the uptake of digital technologies. In 2017, 9 out of the top 20 companies by market capitalization were technology companies, accounting for 54% of the total top 20 market capitalization (PWC, 2017b).

Walker (2006) refers to several possible actions to improve corporate tax compliance, namely, simplifying the tax code, obtaining better data on noncompliance, continuing to oversee the effectiveness of Internal Revenue Service (IRS) enforcement, leveraging technology, and sending sound compliance signals through increased collections of taxes owed. The IRS has estimated the amount of clear noncompliance to total $32 billion for tax year 2001 in the USA (Walker, 2006).

Considering small companies and entrepreneurs, Kirchler (1999, p. 133) refers that "especially entrepreneurs who take the risk of establishing an enterprise perceive taxes as severe reduction of their profit and possibilities for reinvestment."

Legal tax rules influence a large spectrum of corporative decisions in particular multinational corporations. In respect to finance theory, it influences capital structure decisions, including the choice of debt, equity, leasing, and other financing instruments. The relationship between tax administration and corporative taxpayers plays a role in corporate risk management, dividend, and share repurchase policies. Also taxes can shape the form and timing of compensation and pension policies. Sometimes they influence the choice of organizational form (corporate versus partnership). Finally, the complexity and richness of the international tax code provide a variety of incentives that affect corporate decisions.

There are several instruments of corporation tax fraud. As examples, we can consider not declaring income, unlawfully claiming or overclaiming investment tax credit and expenses, unlawfully, providing false information on a company's place of establishment or hiding money from the government through laundering or illegal accounting schemes. Taylor and Richardson (2012) examined tax management practices within corporate groups and found that transfer pricing and the use of intragroup debt are the most widely used techniques to reduce the tax liabilities on groups. World economy development and technologic advances create conditions for the appearing of new ways of developing business activities. COM (2017) outlines some examples: online retailer model (business model of Amazon, Zalando, Alibaba); social media model (business model of Facebook, Xing, Qzone); subscription model (Netflix, Spotify, iQiyi); and collaborative platform model (Airbnb, Blablacar, Didi Chuxing). According to PWC (2017a, p. 6), "the effective tax rate for digital business models lies between −10% and 25%." On average, digital business models are taxed at a rate of 10.20% which is 11.73% percentage point lower than traditional business models. The reason for this is an assumed higher portion of costs that do not require capitalization in the investment structure (in particular software developed in-house and intangible assets) as well as more favorable depreciation rules for digital capital goods and the applicability of special tax incentives for research, development, and innovation (PWC, 2017b).

33.5 Relation Between Disclosure Practices and Corporate Tax Strategies

According to Bergh et al. (2019), information asymmetry is a condition wherein one party in a relationship has more or better information than another. To Johnson and So (2018), the severity and content of asymmetric information influence most interactions between economic agents, particularly in cases of adverse selection or moral hazard.

Literature provides, essentially, two potential mechanisms through which disclosure quality was expected to reduce information asymmetry: by altering the trading incentives of informed and uninformed investors so that there is relatively less trading by privately informed investors and by reducing the likelihood that investors discover and trade on private information (Brown & Hillegeist, 2007).

In relation to the first mechanism, Merton (1987) argues that investors are more likely to invest and trade in firms that are well known or that they judge favorably. If higher disclosure quality increases a firm's visibility and/or reduces the costs of processing firm-specific public information, then higher disclosure quality will induce more trading in the firm's stock by uninformed investors. Also Fishman and Hagerty (1989) use a similar argument. So, quality will be associated with relatively less informed trading, which in turn will reduce information asymmetry. To Brown and Hillegeist (2007: 444), the presence of information asymmetry creates "an adverse selection problem in the market when privately informed investors trade on the basis of their private information." In this sense, there is the risk that an uninformed investor will trade against a privately informed investor. For the authors, a firm's choice of disclosure quality affects this information risk by altering the distribution of public and private information among investors.

In relation to the second mechanism, Verrecchia (1982) examines a setting where public information disclosed by the firm is a perfect substitute for private information. He shows that the amount of costly private information that investors choose to acquire is generally decreasing in the amount of firm-disclosed public information. Diamond (1985) also finds that the incentives for investors to acquire private information are reduced when firms disclose information publicly. Gelb and Zarowin (2002) and Lundholm and Myers (2002) find that current stock returns reflect more information about future earnings when disclosure quality is higher. Also Brown and Hillegeist (2007) state that firms with high disclosure quality are more likely to publicly release material information promptly and provide forward-looking information. As such, the authors argue that higher disclosure quality reduces private information search incentives and that more informativeness disclosures reduce the total set of information about future earnings that can be privately discovered about a firm. Since there is less information available to be discovered, in addition to the reduced search incentives, the authors expect that the frequency of private information events will be declining in disclosure quality. Admati (1985), Wang (1993), Dow and Gorton (1995), and Easley and O'Hara (2004) all model the activities of informed and uninformed traders, and they found that, because of the different degree of available information, informed traders and uninformed traders invest in different portfolios. Specifically, informed traders construct their portfolios on the efficient frontier associated with their superior information. Since uninformed traders have inferior information, they cannot "replicate" the informed traders' portfolios; thus, their portfolios will always locate below the informed traders' efficient frontier. As selective disclosure causes information asymmetry, it makes informed traders better at the expense of uninformed traders.

The framework developed by Easley and O'Hara (2004) consider both public information and private information together. They provide an analytical model to demonstrate how a firm's information structure affects its capital market behavior. Their findings suggest that for stocks with more private information and less public information, uninformed investors require a higher rate of return as compensation because more private information increases information asymmetry and the information risk uninformed investors face.

In addition to disclosure's effect on information asymmetry, the previous arguments also show that the level of information asymmetry is likely to influence the firm's choice of disclosure quality, because the firm may choose a higher level of disclosure quality when the current level of information asymmetry is high.

Tax planning by firms is a highly significant activity. Also the engagement of those activities by firms is of wider public interest since it can affect the level of provision of public goods which can then contribute to social issues (Slemrod, 2004). Although traditionally tax planning has been viewed as benefiting shareholders via increased after tax earnings, more recently, the underlying motivation has been questioned. Desai and Dharmapala (2006) argue that when an information asymmetry exists between managers and shareholders with respect to tax planning, it can facilitate managers acting in their own interests resulting in a negative association between tax planning and firm value.

According to Hanlon and Heitzman (2010), tax avoidance is considered as the reduction of explicit cash taxes and considers different operations since simple investments to complex corporation restructuration's or tax shelters.

Kerr (2012) finds that information asymmetry leads to tax avoidance. According to Chen and Lin (2017), the research interrogation of information environment is different due to the existence of tax avoidance or if tax avoidance influences information environment. Furthermore, both concepts can be influenced by other factors. These authors found that firms avoid tax more aggressively after a reduction in analyst coverage. This effect is mainly driven by firms with higher existing tax-planning capacity, smaller initial analyst coverage, and a smaller number of peer firms. Moreover, the effect is more pronounced in industries where reputation matters more and in firms subject to less monitoring from tax authorities.

The authors also argue that financial analysts pay attention to corporate tax strategies because a firm's tax shield is associated with capital budgeting, cost of capital, and even firm valuation. Financial analysts have simultaneously the skills and incentives to produce and distribute tax-related information and hence reduce information asymmetry. When that happens, it may be harder for a firm to hide earnings through tax sheltering or complicated financial structures because the transaction costs for tax avoidance will tend to be higher.

Chen and Lin (2017) found that firms with low initial analyst coverage are associated with an increase in tax avoidance behavior. This result enforces the hypothesis that information asymmetry materially affects corporate, including both direct and indirect costs. Direct costs are related to the risk of detection by tax authorities, and indirect costs include reputational and financial costs. Also, the strong effects of analyst coverage on tax avoidance are verified in consumer-oriented industries. A possible justification lies in the fact that customer perception of a firm is more important in those industries (also see Hanlon and Slemrod (2009) and Graham et al. (2014). Graham et al. (2014) empirical study showed that if a firm's reputation is affected by its tax avoidance practices, then tax planning behavior will be more careful in the future. According to Chen and Lin (2017), a reduction in analyst coverage effect on tax avoidance is more visible in firms with less direct competitors and less controlled by tax authorities.

33.6 Conclusion

This paper examines the relation between companies' opacity and tax avoidance in the context of agency problems. The added value of this work relies on the analysis of empirical literature results about the relation between information asymmetry, disclosure policy, and tax planning activities, providing a more extensive overview of this relation. The information asymmetry results from the fact that managers have more and much better information, than the general investors, about the present situation and future perspectives of the company. The expression tax planning was applied to refer to all the activities designed to have a positive effect on effective tax rate. From an economic perspective, it is rational behaviour that a company uses legal loopholes in order to reduce the amount of taxes to pay.

Academic research points financial analysts as a way to reduce the information asymmetry between firms and investors, and as a consequence, they reduce corporate tax avoidance.

Some authors argue that if shareholders want to monitor firms' tax-related decision, disclosure policies and tax regulatory bodies should consider requiring increased tax-related disclosures by firms. Increased disclosure reduces "illegitimate" activity, and so shareholders and tax administrators would benefit.

However, other authors argue that with increased tax-related disclosure, managers are discouraged from pursuing "legitimate" tax planning activities. So, it's difficult to determine the extent and form of additional disclosures and the boundary between "legitimate" and "illegitimate" tax planning.

This study provides insights that tax authorities and politicians can use to better focus their strategies and actions in order to increase compliance, reduce tax evasion, fight underground economy, and increase the country's competitiveness.

References

Accountancy Age. (2016). *The top 40 networks & associations 2016: The survey*. 2016. Available at https://www.accountancyage.com/aa/analysis/1776670/top-35-networks-2013-the-survey. Accessed 19 Oct 2017.

Admati, A. (1985). A noisy rational expectations equilibrium for multi-asset securities markets. *Econometrica*, May, 629–657.

Agrawal, A., & Knoeber, C. (1996). Firm performance and mechanisms to control agency problems between managers and shareholders. *Journal of Financial and Quantitative Analysis, 31*, 377–397.

Akerlof, G. (1970). The Market for Lemons: Quality uncertainty and the market mechanism. *The Quarterly Journal of Economics, 84*(3), 488–500.

Anouar, D., & Houria, Z. (2017). The determinants of tax avoidance within corporate groups: Evidence from Moroccan Groups, International Journal of Economics. *Finance and Management Sciences, 5*(1), 57–65.

Ayers, B. C., Jiang, J., & Laplante, S. K. (2009). Taxable income as a performance measure: The effects of tax planning and earnings quality. *Contemporary Accounting Research, 26*, 15–54.

Balakrishnan, K., Blouin, J. L., & Guay, W. R. (2012). *Does tax aggressiveness reduce corporate transparency?* (Working paper). London Business School.

Barry, B., & Brown, S. (1985). Differential information and security market equilibrium. *The Journal of Financial and Quantitative Analysis, 20*(4), 407–422.

Bergh, D. D., Ketchen, D. J., Jr., Orlandi, I., Heugens, P. P., & Boyd, B. K. (2019). Information asymmetry in management research: Past accomplishments and future opportunities. *Journal of management, 45*(1), 122–158.

Bhattacharya, U., & Spiegel, M. (1991). Insiders, outsiders and markets breakdowns. *The Review of Financial Studies, 4*(2), 255–282.

Botosan, C., & Plumlee, M. (2002). A re-examination of disclosure level and expected cost of equity capital. *Journal of Accounting Research, 40*(1), 2–40.

Brown, S., & Hillegeist, S. (2007). How disclosure quality affects the level of information asymmetry. *Review of Accounting Studies, 12*, 443–477.

Chau, G., & Gray, S. (2002). Ownership structure and corporate voluntary disclosure in Hong Kong and Singapore. *The International Journal of Accounting, 37*(2), 247–265.

Chen, & Lin. (2017). Does information asymmetry affect corporate tax aggressiveness? *Journal of Financial and Quantitative Analysis, 52*(5), 2053–2081.

Cheyney and Levine. (2020). Public Disclosures and Information Asymmetry: A Theory of the Mosaic. *The Accounting Review, 95*(1), 79–99.

Coase, R. (1937). The nature of the firm. *Economica, 4*, 386–405.

COM. (2017). 547 final. 2017. A fair and efficient tax system in the European Union for the digital single market.

Comprix, J., Graham, R. C., & Moore, J. A. (2011). Empirical evidence on the impact of book-tax differences on divergence of opinion among investors. *Journal of the American Taxation Association, 33*, 51–78.

Desai, M. A., & Dharmapala, D. (2006). Corporate tax avoidance and high-powered incentives. *Journal of Financial Economics, 79*, 145–179.

Diamond, D. (1985). Optimal release of information by firms. *Journal of Finance, 40*(4), 1071–1094.

Diamond, D., & Verrecchia, R. (1991). Disclosure, liquidity and the cost of capital. *Journal of Finance, 46*, 1325–1359.

Dow, J., & Gorton, G. (1995). Profitable informed trading in a simple general equilibrium model of asset pricing. *Journal of Economic Theory, 67*, 327–369.

Easley, D., & O'Hara, M. (2004). Information and the cost of capital. *Journal of Finance, 59*, 1553–1583.

Eng, L., & Mak, Y. (2003). Corporate Governance and voluntary disclosure. *Journal of Accounting and Public Policy, 22*(4), 325–345.

Fama, E., & Jensen, M. (1983). Separation of ownership and control. *Journal of Law and Economics, 26*(2), 301–325.

Farinha, J. 2003. *Corporate governance: A review of the literature*. Centro de Estudos de Economia Industrial, do Trabalho e da Empresa, Working paper. Faculdade de Economia, Universidade do Porto.

Fishman, M., & Hagerty, K. (1989). Disclosure decisions by firms and the competition for price efficiency. *Journal of Finance, 44*, 633–646.

Flesch, M. C. (1968). Tax avoidance: The attitude of the courts and the legislature. *Current Legal Problems, 21*, 215–238.

Gelb, D., & Zarowin, P. (2002). Corporate disclosure policy and the informativeness of stock prices. *Review of Accounting Studies, 7*(1), 33–52.

Graham, J. R., Hanlon, M., Shevlin, T., & Shroff, N. (2014). Incentives for tax planning and avoidance: Evidence from the field. *Accounting Review, 89*, 991–1023.

Grossman, S., & Hart, O. (1986). The costs and benefits of ownership: A theory of vertical and lateral integration. *Journal of Political Economy, 94*, 691–719.

Hanlon, M. (2005). The persistence and pricing of earnings, accruals, and cash flows when firms have large book-tax differences. *Accounting Review, 80*, 137–166.
Hanlon, M., & Heitzman, S. (2010). A review of tax research. *Journal of Accounting and Economics, 50*, 127–178.
Hanlon, M., & Slemrod, J. (2009). What does tax aggressiveness signal? Evidence from stock price reactions to news about tax shelter involvement. *Journal of Public Economics, 93*, 126–141.
Hart, O. (1995). Corporate governance, some theory and applications. *The Economic Journal., 105*, 678–689.
Hart, O., & Moore, J. (1990). Property rights and the nature of the firm. *Journal of Political Economy, 98*, 1119–1158.
Ho, S., & Wong, K. (2001). A study of the relationship between corporate governance structure and the extent of voluntary disclosure. *Journal of International Accounting, Auditing and Taxation, 10*(1), 139–156.
Jensen, M. (1986). Agency costs of free cash flow, Corporate Finance and Takeovers. *The American Economic Review, 76*, 323–329.
Jensen, M., & Meckling, W. (1976). Theory of the firm: Managerial behaviour, agency costs and ownership structure. *Journal of Financial Economics, 3*(4), 305–360. Electronic version available at http://ssrn.com/abstract=94043, 1–77
Johnson, T., & So, E. (2018). A simple multimarket measure of information asymmetry. *Management Science, Articles in Advance*, 1–26.
Kanagaretnam, K., Lobo, G.J., & Whalen, D. (2007). Does good corporate governance reduce information asymmetry around quarterly earnings announcements? *Journal of Accounting and Public Policy, 26*(4), 497–522.
Kerr, J. (2012). *The real effects of asymmetry: Evidence from tax avoidance* (Working paper). Columbia Business School.
Kim, O., & Verrecchia, R. (1994). Market liquidity and volume around earnings announcements. *Journal of Accounting and Economics, 17*, 41–68.
Kirchler, E. (1999). Reactance to taxation: Employers´ attitudes towards taxes. *Journal of Social-Economics, 28*, 131–138.
Lambert, R. A., Leuz, C., & Verrecchia, R. E. (2007). Accounting information, disclosure, and the cost of capital. *Journal of Accounting Research, 45*, 385–420.
Leuz, C., & Verrecchia, R. (2000). The economic consequences of increased disclosure. *Journal of Accounting Research, 38*, 91–124.
Lev, B. (1988). Toward a theory of equitable and efficient accounting policy. *The Accounting Review, 63*(1), 1–22.
Lundholm, R., & Myers, L. (2002). Bringing the future forward: The effect of disclosure on the return-earnings Relation. *Journal of Accounting Research, 40*(3), 809–839.
McBarnet, D. (1992). The construction of compliance and the challenge of control: The limits of noncompliance research. In J. Slemrod (Ed.), *Why people pay taxes: Tax compliance and enforcement* (pp. 333–345). University of Michigan Press.
Merton, R. (1987). A simple model of capital market equilibrium with incomplete information. *Journal of Finance, 42*(3), 483–510.
Minnick, K., & Noga, T. (2010). Do corporate governance characteristics influence tax management? *Journal of Corporate Finance, 16*(5), 703–718.
Myers, S., & Majluf, N. (1984). Corporate financing and investment decisions when firms have information that investors do not have. *Journal of Financial Economics, 13*(2), 187–221.
Oats, L. (2005). Distinguishing closely held companies for taxation purposes: the Australian experience 1930–1972. *Accounting, Business and Financial History, 15*(1), 335–361.
Petersen, C., & Plenborg, T. (2006). Voluntary disclosure and information asymmetry in Denmark. *Journal of international Accounting, Auditing and Taxation, 15*, 127–149.
PWC. (2017a). *Digital Tax Index 2017: Location tax attractiveness for digital business models.* http://www.pwc.de/digitalisierungsindex2017

PWC. (2017b). Global Top 100 Companies by market capitalisation. In M. S. Scholes, M. A. Wolfson, M. Erickson, E. L. Maydew, T. Shevlin (2005), *Taxes and business strategy: A planning approach* (3rd ed.). Prentice-Hall.

Ranaldo, A. (2002). Transaction costs on the Swiss stock. *Financial Markets and Portfolio Managemnet, 16*, 53–63.

Shleifer, A., & Vishny, R. (1997). A survey of corporate governance. *Journal of Finance, 52*, 737–783.

Sikka, P., & Haslam, C. (2007). *Transfer pricing and its role in tax avoidance and flight of capital: Some theory and evidence*. Centre for global accountability, seminar series University of Essex.

Slemrod, J. (2004). The economics of corporate tax selfishness. *National Tax Journal, 57*(4), 877–899.

Taylor, G., & Richardson, G. (2012). International corporate tax avoidance practices: Evidence from Australian firms. *International Journal Accounting, 47*, 469–496.

Trabelsi, S., Laurin, C. & Labelle R. (2004). The management of financial disclosure on corporate websites: A conceptual model. *Canadian Accounting Perspectives, 3*(2), 235–259.

Trabelsi, S., Lábel, R. & Dumontier, P. (2008). Incremental voluntary disclosure on corporate websites, determinants and consequences. *Journal of Contemporary Accounting and Economics, 4*(2), 120–155.

Verrecchia, R. (1982). Information acquisition in a noisy rational expectations economy. *Econometrica*. November, 1415–1430.

Vitolla, F., Raimo, N., & Rubino, M. (2020). Board characteristics and integrated reporting quality: an agency theory perspective. *Corporate Social Responsibility and Environmental Management, 27*(2), 1152–1163.

Walker, D. M. (2006). *Challenges to corporate tax enforcement and options to improve securities basis reporting*. Statement to United States Government Accountability Office.

Wan, Y. (2009). *Corporate governance, disclosure malhod and information asymmetry*. Master thesis. Edwards School of Business, University of Saskatchewan.

Wang, J. (1993). A model of intertemporal asset prices under asymmetric information. *Review and Economic Studies, 60*, 249–282.

Watts, R., & Zimmerman, J. (1986). *Positive accounting theory*. Prentice-Hall.

Welker, M. (1995). Disclosure policy, information asymmetry and liquidity in equity markets. *Contemporary Accounting Research, 11*(2), 801–827.

Chapter 34
Testing the Validity of Wagner's Law in the Czech Republic

Žaneta Tesařová

Abstract This chapter analyses the relationship between nominal gross domestic product and nominal public expenditures in the Czech Republic and the direction of the connection to investigate if the Keynesian relationship holds or Wagner's law holds. The estimate uses the standard Peacock-Wiseman specification of Wagner's law and provides the results for the Czech Republic. Our main aim is to identify a long- and/or short-term relationship between the nominal GDP and nominal government expenditures (both current and capital expenditures). We employ a VAR model, Johansen Cointegration test, and VEC model to address this question. The studied period starts in the first quarter of 1999 and ends in the second quarter of 2019. The results support Wagner's law validity in the long and the Keynesian theory in the short run in the Czech Republic.

Key words Development · Expenditures · Public finance · Wagner's law · Keynes · Cointegration

34.1 Introduction

The connection and direction of the relationship between public expenditures and gross domestic product (GDP) started to be investigated by economic theorists three centuries ago. Classical economists were the first to investigate the relationship in the eighteenth century. They expected the negative impact of public expenditure on economic growth as increasing public spending and public debt decreased economic growth and destabilised the economies. They were followed by Adolph Wagner in the nineteenth century, who had an idea of a positive relationship from GDP to public expenditure, while the reasoning is explained in detail below. Similarly, John Maynard Keynes anticipated a positive relationship, but, on the contrary, in the opposite direction.

Ž. Tesařová (✉)
Department of Monetary Theory and Policy, Prague University of Economics and Business, Prague, Czech Republic
e-mail: xtesz00@vse.cz

D. Procházka (ed.), *Regulation of Finance and Accounting*, Springer Proceedings in Business and Economics, https://doi.org/10.1007/978-3-030-99873-8_34

This topic receives the interest of public policymakers as the knowledge of the relationship between government expenditure and the gross domestic product is necessary for implementing a public policy. The key is to know the impact of public policy, e.g., increasing or decreasing public spending effect on GDP that closely relates to the exogeneity or endogeneity of public spending. Exogeneity of public expenditures inherently means that increase in spending is a tool that can be used to boost economic growth. Keynesian economists expected this boosting effect. Under this assumption, it is possible to increase the growth of the economy in the short term by increasing spending. However, if the reverse direction holds, government spending is ineffective in this sense, and unnecessary expenditures should be reduced.

For these reasons, the relationship was tested in several countries worldwide, and there are several publications devoted to the empirical analysis of the connection for different countries. This short chapter is the initial analysis of a data sample for the Czech Republic from 1Q 1999 to 2Q 2019. It contributes to the extended article Tesařová (2020) that investigates the relationship by similar econometrics methods for the sample of Visegrád four countries. The extended article has additionally explained the differences in otherwise related economies.

We aim to investigate the equilibrial relationship between total nominal (both current and capital expenditures) government spending and GDP with the focus to find support for Wagner's or Keynesians theory of validity. Similarly, as in other empirical papers, we use stationarity tests, VAR (vector autoregression) model, Johansen test of cointegration, and VEC (vector error correction) model. Our main findings confirm the Keynesian hypothesis validity in the short term. However, this hypothesis does not hold in the long term, and there is support for Wagner's law validity.

In the following section, we briefly review the relevant literature and compare the topic's current state of the art. The second section examines the empirical framework and data. The third section explains the results, and the last section concludes.

34.2 Theoretical Background

As mentioned in the introductory part of the chapter, the main difference between the economists that investigated the connection between GDP and public spending is twofold. The first question is if the relationship is positive (Keynesians/Wagnerians) or negative (classical economists). The second connects to the positive connection, whereas the variable of public expenditure can be exogenous and used as a tool (Keynesians) or endogenous (Wagnerians). Based on the empirical findings, it is possible to decide on the expected effects of expansive public policy on economic growth. At least in the short term, it could then be possible to stabilise the economic development by the public policy without possible adverse economic effects, e.g. without adverse impact on investments.

Regarding classical economists, it is necessary to mention the critical publication of Adam Smith written in 1776 *Wealth of Nations*, which is a reaction to Mercantilism and their view on wealth and international trade. The book mentions the designation "invisible hand" for a free-market force, characterising that economic agents enforce public interest through their own economic choices. Smith promoted "laissez-faire", an arrangement where the government does not influence or regulate private transactions (Musgrave & Peacock, 1958). In his view, the only governmental functions are maintaining internal peace and order, defence against foreign aggression, and public development (Akrani, 2011). Any other activities are assumed to be useless with negative effects on economic growth. Based on this fact, the link between government spending and GDP is rather negative, and fiscal policy cannot be viewed as a tool to boost economic growth.

Wagner's law of increasing state activity was formulated in the late nineteenth century by the German economist Adolph Wagner. The theory stipulates that the relationship between government spending and GDP is positive and heading from gross domestic product to government expenditure. In other words, as the GDP increases, the share of public spending to GDP tends to increase (Magazzino et al., 2015), and this direction has also its explanation. As the economy becomes more complex, it requires higher government intervention. Industrialisation, and continuing urbanisation further leads to stricter governmental regulation. Higher expenditures are then needed to ensure law and order (Pistoresi et al., 2017). In other words, as the economy develops socially, technically, and economically, it requires a still higher share of public expenditures on GDP to ensure the current public need.

After the Great Depression that paralysed the global economy, economic theorists and practises sought a tool or any practical approach to help the economies recover from the devastating depression and prevent a recurrence of the crisis. British economist John Maynard Keynes offered the possible answer on pulling the economies out of the trouble. In 1936, he published his approach in *The General Theory of Employment, Interest and Money*. The book significantly contradicted neoclassical economics and was considered a revolution in economic thinking. Like Wagner, Keynes expected a positive relationship between economic growth and public expenditures. On the contrary, the variable of public spending is exogenous, and it is possible to boost the economy by the expansionary fiscal policy during the economic depression. On the other hand, the government should spend less during economic expansion to prevent increasing public debt and thus behave countercyclically (Musgrave & Peacock, 1958).

Peacock A. T. and Wiseman J. offered a further extension of Wagner's law theory in their publication published in 1961 (Gemmel, 1993). Based on their findings, Wagner's law holds and follows a specific pattern of "displacement effect", where public expenditures crowd out household expenditures. Public spending follows a stepwise pattern coinciding with social upheavals and wars. It is politically challenging to enforce higher taxes during peaceful times, and the growth of a share of public spending to GDP is slow. On the contrary, it is easier to increase taxes due to the necessary increase in war expenditures. As the public is grateful for peace, the taxes can remain the same after the war, and thus, the share of public spending to GDP does not decrease. However, as household expenditures decrease when taxes increase, the higher public spending displaced the household expenditures. The displacement effect during the war is another explanation of the increasing share of the public sector on total GDP with the economic growth.

34.2.1 *Wagner's Law Validity Testing in Developing Countries*

The original analysis provided by Adolph Wagner analysed a long-run, equilibrial link between real public sector spending and real gross domestic product for Germany. Based on the results, the law was formulated and published in 1883.

Wagner's law was then tested by many authors who also used different relationship specifications. The specification uses a logarithmic transformation as the coefficients then express elasticities. It is currently possible to use one of six specifications (Andrei et al., 2009; Richter & Dimitrios, 2012). A coefficient value higher than 1 indicates Wagner's law validity (for specifications 1, 2, 3, and 4). For the last two specifications 5 and 6, the coefficients should be higher to 0 to confirm the law validity. The authors use real and nominal variables (see Kuckuck, 2012).

1. **Peacock-Wiseman** (1967): G = public expenditure

$$\ln G_t = \alpha_1 + \beta_1 \ln \mathrm{GDP}_t + \varepsilon_{1t} \tag{34.1}$$

2. **Gupta** (1967): G/N = public expenditure per capita

$$\ln \left(\frac{G}{N}\right)_t = \alpha_1 + \beta_1 \ln \left(\frac{\mathrm{GDP}}{N}\right)_t + \varepsilon_{3t} \tag{34.2}$$

3. **Pryor** (1968): C = consumption

$$\ln C_t = \alpha_1 + \beta_1 \ln \mathrm{GDP}_t + \varepsilon_{2t} \tag{34.3}$$

4. **Goffman** (1968): G = public expenditure

$$\ln G_t = \alpha_1 + \beta_1 \ln \left(\frac{\mathrm{GDP}}{N}\right)_t + \varepsilon_{4t} \tag{34.4}$$

5. **Musgrave** (1969): G/GDP = share of public expenditure on GDP

$$\ln \left(\frac{G}{\mathrm{GDP}}\right)_t = \alpha_1 + \beta_1 \ln \left(\frac{\mathrm{GDP}}{N}\right)_t + \varepsilon_{5t} \tag{34.5}$$

6. **Mann** (1980): G/GDP = public expenditure to GDP

$$\ln\left(\frac{G}{\text{GDP}}\right)_t = \alpha_1 + \beta_1 \ln\text{GDP}_t + \varepsilon_{6t} \quad (34.6)$$

For our purposes, we reviewed analyses for developing countries.

Wagner's law for Iran was studied in Pohlavani et al. (2011) on a sample starting in 1960 and lasting to 2008. The analysis uses a Pesaran et al. (2001) cointegration test and Granger causality test based on the Error Correction (EC) model and Toda and Yamamoto (1995) causality test. The authors use the last specification, i.e. the link between GDP and share of public spending to gross domestic product. The results support Wagner's law validity. For Iran, the Keynesian hypothesis is not valid in the short term. Thus, it is also impossible to boost the economy by increasing public expenditure. Now we jump to the different continents. Wagner's law for Bolivia was examined by Bojanic (2013). The author uses a time sample starting in 1940 and lasting to 2010. The author uses the nine different law specifications compared to the previously mentioned publication. The extension lies in the fact that he tests the link between gross domestic product and different items of government spending (i.e. infrastructural, health care, or defence). The cointegration is tested by Johansen (1988) and Johansen and Juselius (1990) test. Causality is tested by Error Correction (EC) model and the Granger causality test. The author finds the relationship in six specifications in both directions and points to the stronger causality directed from gross domestic product to government spending. In the discussion part, the author emphasises a need for strict supervision over government spending on services. For Pakistan, Wagner's law testing was done by Ali et al. (2016). The authors test the total public expenditure and their components on a sample starting from 1976 and lasting to 2015 using the same methods as mentioned for previous analyses. A long-run relationship to GDP was identified for economic, education, and social services. Wagner's law was found as valid for current subsidies, defence, current expenditures, and development. On the other hand, this analysis confirms the Keynesian hypothesis for expenditure on social, education, and economic services in the short term.

Several publications also test the law on the larger set of countries. The sample of post-Soviet countries was tested by Abbasov et al. (2018). The authors analyse the long- and short-run link between real GDP per capita and real government spending per capita. In the short run, the results find a relationship in both directions for all tested countries except Lithuania and Kyrgyz Rep. An equilibrial (long) relationship in the Wagnerian sense was confirmed for Lithuania, Uzbekistan, Georgia, Kyrgyz Rep., Ukraine, and Latvia. Beyond, a long-run link validating the Keynesian theory was also confirmed for Estonia, Uzbekistan, Azerbaijan, Kyrgyz Rep., and Moldova.

The validity of Wagner's law in specific items of government expenditures may be explained by Baumol's cost disease that explains the rise of wage costs in job positions without the productivity rise. This effect may explain the increase in health, justice, culture, defence, or education expenditures. Based on the literature review, we may expect a bidirectional relationship, whereas in the short term, the Keynesian theory might hold, and in the long run, Wagner's law.

34.3 Empirical Framework

The following part of the chapter focuses solely on the empirical analyses of the Czech data between 1Q 1999 and 2Q 2019. We aim to analyse the long- and short-term link between the nominal gross domestic product and nominal government spending (current and capital expenditures by ESA2010). Methodologically, we start with the unit-root test of the series and build a vector autoregression model and test cointegration (Johansen Cointegration test). Finally, we estimate a vector error correction model that separates short- and long-term relationships.

34.3.1 Methodology

In the previous section, we described the specifications that are used for Wagner's law testing. This chapter tests the Peacock and Wiseman specification, where the elasticity of government spending to the gross domestic product should be above 1 to confirm the law's validity. Regarding the Keynesian hypothesis, the exact specification is used, but heading from government expenditure to GDP, the elasticity should be above 0. We use logarithmically transformed[1] time series to estimate the elasticities. We can write the relationship by the following equation, where y and x stand for logarithms of GDP and public expenditures (GOV):

$$x_t = \alpha_1 + \beta_1 y_t + \varepsilon_{1t} \tag{34.7}$$

As the initial step of the analysis, we test the stationarity of the time series (order of integration) by the augmented Dickey-Fuller test (Dickey & Fuller, 1979) and Phillips-Perron test. The series with the integration of the first order must be tested to cointegration, a long-term joint movement. Regarding the literature review, we expect a bidirectional relationship. Therefore, the VEC model (Arlt & Arltová, 2009) and Johansen cointegration test (Greene, 2003) is further used. As mentioned above, the VEC model separates the long- and short-run relationships, whereas the short-term link is tested by Wald test and the long term by the weak exogeneity test imposing restrictions on the VEC model. These tests are situated in Appendix.

34.3.2 Data

Time series for this analysis were downloaded from the ECB statistical data warehouse. We use data starting from 1Q 1999 to 2Q 2019, altogether 82 quarters.

[1]Further, log-normally distribution of the economic time series requires work with logarithmically transformed data to receive normal distribution of the series.

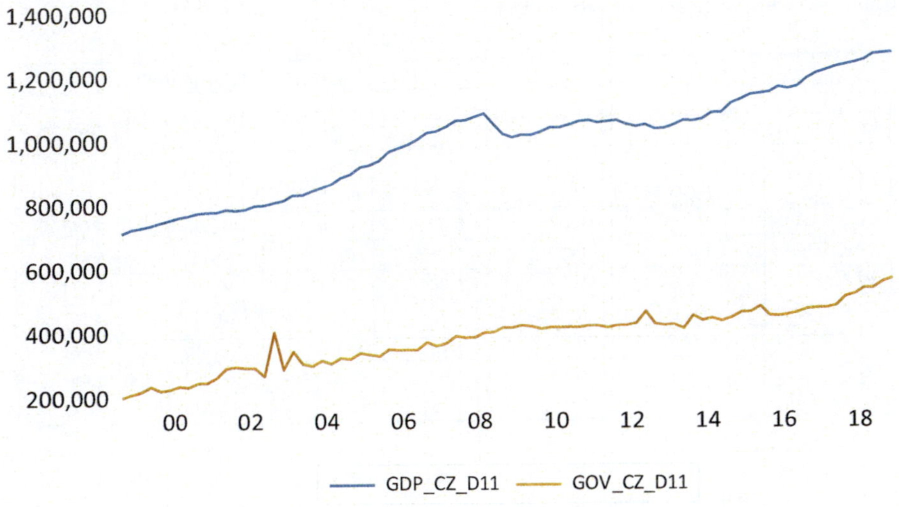

Fig. 34.1 The Czech Republic series seasonally adjusted (in CZK million). (Source: Author's estimate, Eviews 11)

As the data includes a seasonality, we must test it and adjust the series by Census X13 (Fig. 34.1). The stationarity tests results can be found in Table 34.2 Appendix. The results indicate that the time series are non-stationary and integrated the first order I(1). The first differences of the times series are integrated of zero order.

34.4 Empirical Results and Discussion

The following subsections summarise the results of the described process and interpret them.

34.4.1 VEC Model Construction and Testing

The construction of a suitable VAR model requires performing the test of the appropriate number of lags and the residual diagnostic of the model. The VAR model for the Czech Republic and the residual diagnosis are in the Appendix.

The suitable lag's number is four, and by the residual diagnosis, dummies' inclusion to smooth the series' shocks is unnecessary. The estimated VAR (4) model (see Table 34.4. in Appendix) is further tested by the Johansen test (see Table 34.3 in Appendix). Based on the results, deterministic trend specification with the intercept and no trend is used in the co-integrating equation. We further estimate the VEC model (see Table 34.1 and model diagnosis in Appendix).

Table 34.1 Vector error correction model (3)

				Co-integrating Equation		
LGOV^{CZ} (-1)				1.000		
LGDP^{CZ} (-1)				-1.29	(0.13)	[-9.88]
C				4.82	(1.81)	[2.67]
	d(LGDP^{CZ})			d(LGOV^{CZ})		
CointEq1	-0.01	(0.02)	[-0.31]	-0.30	(0.08)	[-3.66]
d(LGOV^{CZ} (-1))	-0.02	(0.02)	[-1.08]	-0.64	(0.11)	[-5.88]
d(LGOV^{CZ} (-2))	0.03	(0.02)	[1.20]	-0.16	(0.13)	[-1.21]
d(LGOV^{CZ} (-3))	-0.01	(0.02)	[-0.33]	0.02	(0.11)	[0.21]
d(LGDP^{CZ} (-1))	0.46	(0.12)	[3.94]	-0.58	(0.66)	[-0.88]
d(LGDP^{CZ} (-2))	-0.06	(0.13)	[-0.43]	-0.32	(0.71)	[-0.46]
d(LGDP^{CZ} (-3))	0.35	(0.12)	[2.85]	0.05	(0.68)	[0.08]

Source: Eviews, author's estimate. First column, the estimated coefficient; second column, standard error; and third column, the t-statistic

As shown in Table 34.1, the results indicate that Wagner's law is valid in the long term (the elasticity is higher to 1 and statistically significant), and the Keynesian theory is valid only in the short run. The weak exogeneity test indicates that the co-integrating equation (co-integrating equation, long-term relationship) is significant in the Wagnerian direction, and the Wald test suggests the validity only of the Keynesian theory in the short term (for both find Table 34.5 Appendix, on the left of the grey area). Further, the loading coefficient is relatively high (−0.3; the return speed to the long-term equilibrium).

34.4.2 Discussion

We identified several shortages during this analysis that are usually not mentioned in the literature and should be considered. Firstly, the estimates may suffer from omitted variables bias. Though this problem is addressed by some authors who add in the estimated equations other regressors. For example, Maggazzino (2010) estimates both the standard and augmented equation, whereas the augmented version includes the public deficit variable. The author concludes that omitted variables may hide or overstate the long-run relations between GDP and government spending.

Further, we do not consider the possible presence and effects of the structural breaks in the empirical analysis. To address this problem, we estimate the CUSUM stability test (see Figure 34.2 in Appendix). The co-integrating relationship is stable for the Czech Republic estimate and within the 5% interval.

We can see that there is still space for further research in this area, but it is beyond the scope of the research chapter (for other estimates in Visegrád four countries, see Tesařová (2020).

34.5 Conclusion

In the literature review, we mentioned studies and their results of testing Wagner's law validity. A number of the estimates confirmed the law's validity, but there are also cases where the bidirectional relationship was found (Wagnerian theory in the long run and Keynesian theory in the short run).

The empirical part estimates the standard model to test Wagner's law and Keynesian hypothesis validity for the Czech Republic for data starting in 1Q 1999 and lasting to 2Q 2019. Our findings support the validity of Wagner's law in the long term (the elasticity is 1.29), which shows that the adjustment tendency to this equilibrial relationship is quite high (−0.3, meaning that 30% of the difference between the current values and the long-term equilibrium adjusts during the previous period to the equilibrium). Therefore, any short-term relationship relatively quickly expires. In the short term, the results support the Keynesian hypothesis validity. It is possible to use the fiscal policy as a stabiliser and boost economic growth in the economic depression in the short run. However, this effect expires, and the system returns to the long-term steady state.

The results validating Wagner's law are usually explained by the validity of the Baumol cost disease. This effect explains the growth of wage costs for job positions that did not experience the increase in productivity by an increase in prices and salaries in other jobs. This effect may be sound reasoning for the rise in health, culture, justice, education, or defence expenditures in response to the private sector's increase in salaries.

Acknowledgements This chapter has been prepared within the research project F1/03/2020 "Dynamika finančních a ekonomických veličin v kontextu vnější rovnováhy".

Appendix

Data

Table 34.2 Stationarity tests – seasonally adjusted and logarithmically transformed series

Augmented Dickey-Fuller Test									
I/1999 – II/2019	**Seas. adjusted time series**			**Seas. adjusted time series**			**First diff.**		
	Spec.	**t ADF**	**Prob.**	**Spec.**	**t ADF**	**Prob.**	**Spec.**	**t ADF**	**Prob.**
LGDP ^{CZ}	I	−1.17	0.68	I, T	−1.58	0.79	I	−6.09	0.00
LGOV ^{CZ}	I	−1.82	0.37	I, T	−2.97	0.15	I	−9.70	0.00
Phillips-Perron Test									
I/1999 – II/2019	**Seas. adjusted time series**			**Seas. adjusted time series**			**First diff.**		
	Spec.	**t PP**	**Prob.**	**Spec.**	**t PP**	**Prob.**	**Spec.**	**t PP**	**Prob.**
LGDP ^{CZ}	I	−1.32	0.62	I, T	−1.72	0.73	I	−6.29	0.00
LGOV ^{CZ}	I	−1.85	0.35	I, T	−4.82	0.001	I	−22.57	0.00

Source: EViews, author's estimate; Note: *I* intercept, *T* trend. For levels, we test specification with intercept and intercept and trend to find out the source of the non-stationarity (stochastic or deterministic trend)

Test of Cointegration (Johansen)

Table 34.3 Summary of the cointegration test

Czech Republic					
Lags interval: 1–4					
Selected (0.05 level[a]) number of cointegrating relations by model					
Data trend:	None	None	Linear	Linear	Quadratic
Test type	No intercept	Intercept	Intercept	Intercept	Intercept
	No trend	No trend	No trend	Trend	Trend
Trace	1	1	0	0	0
Max-Eig	1	1	0	0	0

Source: EViews, author's estimate

[a]Critical values based on MacKinnon, Haug, Michelis (1999)

VAR Model

Table 34.4 Czech Republic – VAR (4)

	$LGDP^{CZ}$			$LGOV^{CZ}$		
$LGOV^{CZ}$ (−1)	−0.02	(0.02)	[−1.17]	0.06	(0.12)	[0.47]
$LGOV^{CZ}$ (−2)	0.05	(0.02)	[2.51]	0.48	(0.12)	[4.04]
$LGOV^{CZ}$ (−3)	−0.02	(0.02)	[−1.00]	0.18	(0.12)	[1.47]
$LGOV^{CZ}$ (−4)	0.02	(0.02)	[1.17]	0.03	(0.12)	[−0.25]
$LGDP^{CZ}$ (−1)	1.37	(0.11)	[12.18]	0.16	(0.67)	[−0.24]
$LGDP^{CZ}$ (−2)	−0.49	(0.19)	[−2.54]	0.24	(1.14)	[0.21]
$LGDP^{CZ}$ (−3)	0.43	(0.19)	[2.25]	0.37	(1.13)	[0.32]
$LGDP^{CZ}$ (−4)	−0.36	(0.12)	[−3.13]	0.05	(0.69)	[−0.07]
C	0.30	(0.15)	[2.03]	1.56	(0.88)	[−1.78]
Adj. R-Sq.	0.997			0.945		
F-Stat.	2848.37			165.14		
Prob. (F-Stat.)	0.000			0.000		
DW stat.	1.958			1.941		

Source: Eviews, author's estimate. First column, the estimated coefficient; second column, standard errors; and third column, the t-statistic

VECM Test of Coefficients

Table 34.5 VECM (3) – coefficients tests

WALD test – coefficient restrictions							
Coefficient c(5), c(6), c(7) = equal to 0 (lagged d($LGDP^{CZ}$))				**Coefficient c(9), c(10), c(11) = equal to 0 (lagged d($LGOV^{CZ}$))**			
Test stat.	**Value**	**df**	**Prob.**	**Test stat.**	**Value**	**df**	**Prob.**
F-stat.	0.49	(3, 71)	0.69	F-stat.	2.90	(3, 71)	0.04
Chi-square	1.46	3	0.69	Chi-square	8.69	3	0.03
VEC restrictions – Cointegration equation parameter test							
Cointegration restrictions: $LGOV^{CZ}$				Cointegration restrictions: $LGDP^{CZ}$			
A(1,1) = 0				A(2,1) = 0			
Convergence achieved after five iterations				Convergence achieved after five iterations			
Not all cointegrating vectors are identified LR test for binding restrictions (rank = 1):				Not all cointegrating vectors are identified LR test for binding restrictions (rank = 1):			
Chi-square(1)	4.58			Chi-square(1)	0.04		
Probability	0.03			Probability	0.85		

Source: EViews, author's estimate

Stability Testing: CUSUM Stability Test Results

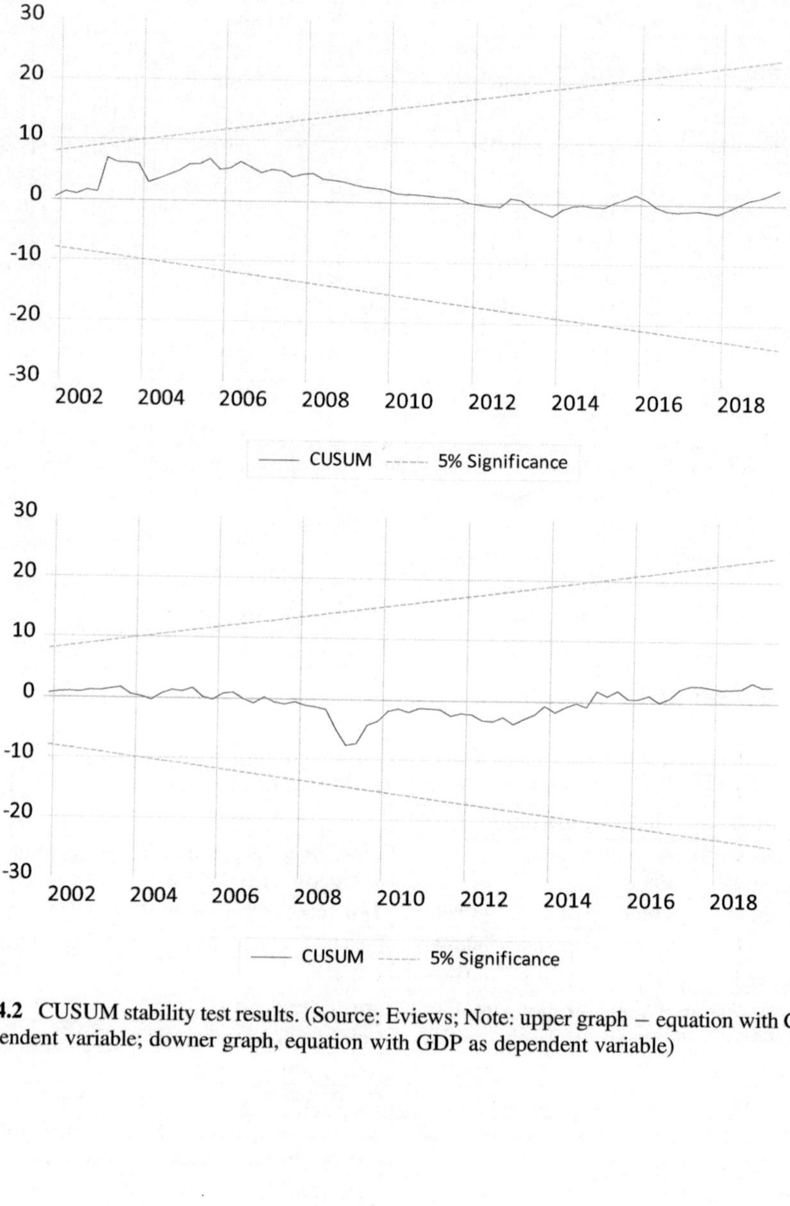

Fig. 34.2 CUSUM stability test results. (Source: Eviews; Note: upper graph – equation with GOV as dependent variable; downer graph, equation with GDP as dependent variable)

References

Abbasov, J. A., & Aliyev, K. (2018). Testing Wagner's law and Keynesian hypothesis in selected post-soviet countries. *Acta Universitatis Agriculturae et Silviculturae Mendelianae Brunensis, 66*(5), 1227–1237. https://doi.org/10.11118/actaun201866051227

Ali, W., & Munir, K. (2016). Testing Wagner versus Keynesian Hypothesis for Pakistan: The Role of Aggregate and Disaggregate Expenditure. MPRA Paper 74570, University Library of Munich, Germany. Retrieved from: https://ideas.repec.org/p/pra/mprapa/74570.html

Akrani, G. (2011). Wagner law of increasing state activity – Public expenditures. Retrieved from: https://kalyan-city.blogspot.com/2011/02/wagner-law-of-increasing-state-activity.html

Arlt, J., & Arltová, M. (2009). Ekonomické časové řady. Professional Publishing. ISBN 978-80-86946-85-6.

Andrei, T., Stancu, S., Iacob, A. I., & Herteliu, C. (2009). Testing Wagner's law for Romania. Retrieved from: www.eco.u-szeged.hu/download.php?docID=40380.

Bojanic, A. N. (2013). Testing the validity of Wagner's law in Bolivia: A cointegration and causality analysis with disaggregated data. *Revista de análisis económico, 28*(1), 25–45. https://doi.org/10.4067/S0718-88702013000100002

Dickey, D.A., & Fuller, W. A. (1979). Distribution of estimators for autoregressive time series with a unit root. *Journal of American Statistical Association, 74*(366), 427–431. https://doi.org/10.2307/2286348

Gemmel, N. (1993). The growth of the public sector: Theories and international evidence, edited by Norman Gemmell. Edward Elgar Publishing. ISBN: 978 1 85278 525 3.

Greene, W. (2003). Econometric analysis (5th ed., p. 2003). Prentice Hall. ISBN:0-13-066189-9.

Goffman, I. J. (1968). On the Empirical Testing of Wagner's Law: A Technical Note. *Public Finance, 23*(3), 359–364.

Gupta, S. P. (1967). Public Expenditure and Economics Growth: A TimeSeries Analysis. *Public Finance, 22*, 423–461.

Johansen, S. (1988). Statistical analysis of cointegration vectors. *Journal of Economic Dynamics and Control, 12*(2–3), 231–254, https://doi.org/10.1016/0165-1889(88)90041-3

Johansen, S., & Juselius, K. (1990). Maximum likelihood estimation and inference on cointegration with applications to demand for money. *Oxford Bulletin of Economics and Statistics*, 52, 169–210, https://doi.org/10.1111/j.1468-0084.1990.mp52002003.x

Kuckuck, J. (2012). Testing Wagner's Law at Different Stages of Economic Development - A Historical Analysis of Five Western European Countries. IEER Working Papers 91, Institute of Empirical Economic Research, Osnabrueck University.

Magazzino, C., Giolli, L., & Mele, M. (2015). Wagner's law and Peacock and Wiseman's displacement effect in European Union countries: A panel data study. *International Journal of Economics and Financial Issues, 5*(3), 812–819. ISSN: 2146-4138.

Magazzino, C. (2010). Wagner's law and augmented Wagner's law in EU-27. A time-series analysis on stationarity, cointegration and causality. MPRA paper no. 26668. Retrieved from: https://core.ac.uk/download/pdf/6564538.pdf.

Musgrave, R. A., & Peacock, A. T. (1958) Classics in the theory of public finance. Palgrave Macmillan. ISBN: 978-1-349-23426-4.

MacKinnon, J. G., Haug, A. A., & Michelis, L. (1999). Numerical distribution functions of likelihood ratio tests for cointegration. *Journal of Applied Econometrics, 14*, 563–577. https://doi.org/10.1002/(SICI)1099-1255(199909/10)14:53.0.CO;2-R

Mann, A. J. (1980). Wagner's law: An econometric test for Mexico, 1925–1976. *National Tax Journal, 33*(2), 189–201, https://doi.org/10.1086/NTJ41862301

Musgrave, R. A. (1969). Fiscal Systems. New Haven and London: Yale University Press

Pahlavani, M., Abed, D., & Pourshabi, F. (2011). Investigating the Keynesian view and Wagner's law on the size of government and economic growth in Iran. *International Journal of Business and Social Science, 2*(13), 170–175.

Pistoresi, B., Rinaldi, A., & Salsano, F. (2017). Government spending and its components in Italy, 1862–2009: Drivers and policy implications. *Journal of Policy Modeling, 39*(6), 1117–1140. https://doi.org/10.1016/j.jpolmod.2017.05.003

Peacock, A. T., & Wiseman, J. (1967). The growth of public expenditure in the United Kingdom. 2nd edn, London: George Allen & Unwin.

Pesaran, M. H., Shin, Y., Smith, R. (2001). Bounds testing approaches to the analysis of level relationships. *Journal of Applied Econometrics, 16*, 289–326.

Pryor, F. L. (1968). Public expenditures in communist and capitalist nations. London: George Allen and Unwin

Richter, C., & Dimitrios, P., (2012). The validity of Wagner's law in the United Kingdom for the period 1850–2010. INFER working papers 2012.9. Retrieved from: https://repository.uel.ac.uk/item/85y74.

Tesařová, Ž. (2020). The Wagner's law testing in the Visegrád four countries. *Review of Economic Perspectives, Sciendo, 20*(4), 409–430.

Toda, H. Y., & Yamamoto, T. (1995). Statistical inference in vector autoregressions with possibly integrated processes. *Journal of Econometrics, 66*(1–2), 225–250, https://doi.org/10.1016/0304-4076(94)01616-8

Chapter 35
Developing a Business Model for an Oil Company by Integrating Sustainable Development Goals

Zhanna Chistopolova and Roza Kaspina

Abstract Today, no one has any questions about the importance of sustainable development of the world including business. There are still issues related to effective management of sustainable business development. Integrated reporting is becoming a trend of best practices. It can help to attract additional investment and manage the business better. The chapter considers the issues of managing the sustainable development of an oil company on the basis of integrated reporting, specifically the development of a business model integrated with the Sustainable Development Goals (SDGs) and Key performance indicators (KPIs), to assess the achievement of these goals. KPIs are offered to companies for each of the 17 goals and it is recommended to monitor KPIs in order to be able to take stock of progress and compare their results with those of other companies in the same industry. For analysis, 13 member companies of the Oil and Gas Climate Initiative (OGCI) were taken. A qualitative analysis of their activities in alternative energy was carried out and their activities in combating climate change were evaluated.

Keywords Business model · Key performance indicators · Integrated reporting · Capitals · Accounting · Management accounting · Sustainable development

35.1 Introduction

Greta Thunberg, a 16-year-old activist from Sweden who gave a speech about global warming at the UN General Assembly, has been named *Time* Magazine's Person of the Year for 2019. The Nobel Prize in Economic Sciences 2019 was awarded jointly to scientists "for their experimental approach to alleviating global poverty." More than 11,000 scientists have declared a "World Scientists Warning of a Climate Emergency" in the journal *BioScience*.

The last edition of The World Economic Forum was held in Davos from 21 to 24 January 2020. The theme of the 50th anniversary meeting is Stakeholders for a

Z. Chistopolova (✉) · R. Kaspina
High School of Business, Kazan Federal University, Kazan, Russia

D. Procházka (ed.), *Regulation of Finance and Accounting*, Springer Proceedings in Business and Economics, https://doi.org/10.1007/978-3-030-99873-8_35

Source: United Nations Sustainable Development Goals web site: https://www.un.org/sustainabledevelopment/

Fig. 35.1 Sustainable development goals (The content of this publication has not been approved by the United Nations and does not reflect the views of the United Nations or its officials or the Member States). (Source: United Nations Sustainable Development Goals web site: https://www.un.org/sustainabledevelopment/)

Cohesive and Sustainable World. The Annual Meeting was among the most sustainable international summits ever held. It focused on the Forum's founding principle – Stakeholder Capitalism – and defines ways in which companies can update their purpose and key performance indicators in this new era. The Meeting was also champion metrics governments and international organizations can use to track and improve our global progress on climate change and meaningful economic growth.

The SDGs (Fig. 35.1) were set in 2015 by the United Nations General Assembly (UN) which today is known as the international agenda, and business is one of the main drivers for achieving global goals until the year 2030.

Focusing on SDGs can be useful for businesses to make investment decisions in research and development (R&D) of new types of products to help organizations navigate the current environmental, social, and economic problems of the modern world.

Therefore, today's relevant issues are how to use financial and non-financial indicators to reflect the desire of companies to achieve the SDGs and how to represent in accounting and reporting to management decisions. An integrated reporting (IR) format is best suited for these purposes.

Integrated financial reporting plays to existing management accounting strengths in addition to fulfilling a clear and growing need within the market. Quantifying and reporting information to end user groups, communicating such information to internal and external functional groups, and leveraging technology to improve efficiency in information analysis represent trends situated to become increasingly important for organizations and individuals (Petera et al., 2016). Management accounting professionals, in addition to being situated squarely within these emerging areas of growth, also have the opportunity to address broader strategic needs of business decision-making through an IR template and a multiple capital model. Financial information and reporting continues to evolve. Management accounting professionals willing to embrace new ideas, concepts, and opportunities appear to be well positioned for future success in a rapidly shifting and dynamic marketplace. When data is measured, it is managed. Improved management allows decision makers to make better results, and IR provides accounting professionals a platform to advocate and effectuate strategic change within organizations and the profession at large (Dr. Sean Stein Smith, 2017).

35.2 Data and Methodology

Thirteen member companies of the OGCI were taken for analysis. The OGCI aims to increase the ambition, speed, and scale of the initiatives undertaken by its individual companies to help reduce manmade greenhouse gas emissions, in particular from the production and use of oil and gas in power, heating, industry, and transport. It is more than a $1 billion investment. OGCI Climate Investments supports the development, deployment, and scale-up of low emissions technology and business models. Launched in 2014, OGCI is now made up of 13 oil and gas companies: BP, Chevron, CNPC, Eni, Equinor, ExxonMobil, Occidental, Pemex, Petrobras, Repsol, Saudi Aramco, Shell, and Total.

OGCI members now represent around 30% of global oil and gas production and supply close to 20% of global primary energy consumption. The 13 member companies represent regions including China, the Middle East, Latin America, Europe, and now the United States, widening OGCI's global reach and making its members' collaborative effort in support of the Paris Agreement, a significant global action.

The data for the analysis was taken from the OGCI annual report and the sustainability reports of OGCI member companies.

We adapted Balanced Scorecard (Kaplan and Norton 1996) to assess the achievement of sustainable development goals.

The information disclosed in the corporate reporting is the results of the analysis of various aspects of the company's activities under the actual conditions established in the reporting year. The analysis' key financial and non-financial indicators can form the basis of their balanced system as the basis for the company's strategy (Kaspina & Trofimova, 2016).

KPI should ensure continuous monitoring of objectives and improving the efficiency of the company (Kaspina & Sabirzyanova, 2017).

35.3 Results and Discussion

Oil and gas companies have a negative impact on the environment and climate, so it is important that they focus on the SDGs in their business strategies. We consider that the main directions of sustainable development for oil companies are innovations, renewable energy sources, and a business model integrated with the SDGs (Stevens, 2016; Tanțau & Khorshidi, 2016). An increasing number of oil and gas corporations are involved in alternative energy and are implementing projects in solar, wind, and biofuel production. Table 35.1 presents a qualitative analysis of companies' activities in alternative energy.

The largest oil companies are supporting the transition to a low-carbon development paradigm and are increasingly investing in alternative energy, R&D, and innovation. All these changes are directly reflected in the structure of the company's business model.

Business model: An organization's system of transforming inputs through its business activities into outputs and outcomes that aim to fulfil the organization's strategic purposes and create value over the short, medium and long term (IIRC, 2013).

An important point is the correlation of the company's strategy with the business model. The relationship between a business model and a strategy can be explained by the fact that value for consumers and other stakeholders is created as a result of implementing a business strategy based on a business model that is specifically designed to meet the set strategic goals. The business model and strategy are closely related and can be considered as value creation factors (Kaspina & Sabirzyanova, 2017).

Table 35.1 Qualitative results of analysis of leading oil and gas companies in alternative energy

	Solar energy	Wind energy	Hydropower	Biofuels	Hydrogen energy	Geothermal energy	Others
BP	+	+		+			
Chevron	+	+		+		+	
CNPC	+	+		+	+	+	+
Eni	+	+		+			
Equinor		+					
ExxonMobil				+	+		
Occidental Petroleum	+	+	+	+			
Pemex							
Petrobras	+	+	+	+			+
Repsol	+	+	+	+			
Saudi Aramco	+						
SHELL	+	+		+	+		
TOTAL	+			+			

Source: The Oil and Gas Climate Initiative, Companies' webpages, annual reports, sustainability reports

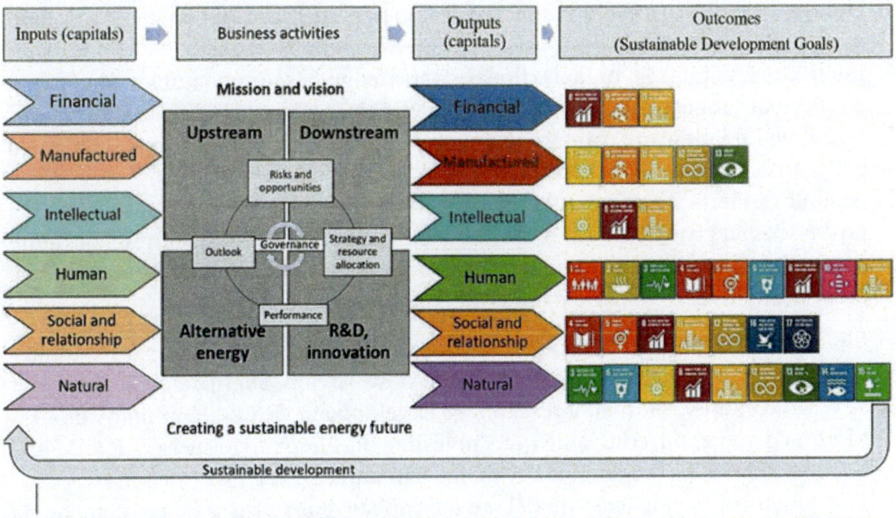

Source: adapted from Adams (2017b) which is adapted from a diagram in International Framework (IIRC, 2013), United Nations Sustainable Development Goals web site: https://www.un.org/sustainabledevelopment/

Fig. 35.2 Oil company's business model aligned with the SDGs in the value creation process (The content of this publication has not been approved by the United Nations and does not reflect the views of the United Nations or its officials or the Member States). (Source: adapted from Adams (2017) which is adapted from a diagram in International Framework (IIRC, 2013), United Nations Sustainable Development Goals web site: https://www.un.org/sustainabledevelopment/)

In the course of an enterprise's activity, the value chain consists of mutually influencing elements (external influences, inputs, and outputs) that are subordinating to business processes.

The business model is a strategic analysis tool. Through its formation, the use of all types of capital (financial, industrial, human, intellectual, natural, social) in the company's value chain becomes transparent.

Structure of business model affects information disclosed in management reporting. The company can describe such an element of business model as a financial component using selected management methods (Kaspina & Khapugina, 2017).

Figure 35.2 shows a business model for an oil company integrated with the SDGs.

The inputs to this model are capital, which has a significant impact on a company's ability to create value in the short, medium, and long term:

1. Financial capital – the pool of funds that is available to an organization for use in the production of goods or the provision of services, obtained through financing, such as debt, equity or grants, or generated through operations or investments.
2. Manufactured capital including buildings, equipment, infrastructure (such as roads, ports, bridges, and waste and water treatment plants).

3. Human capital – people's competencies, capabilities and experience, and their motivations to innovate.
4. Intellectual capital – organizational, knowledge-based intangibles, including intellectual property, such as patents, copyrights, software, rights, and licenses.
5. Social and relationship capital – the institutions and the relationships within and between communities, groups of stakeholders, and other networks.
6. Natural capital – all renewable and nonrenewable environmental resources and processes that provide goods or services which support the past, current, or future prosperity of an organization. It includes: air, water, land, minerals and forests, biodiversity & eco-system health (IIRC, 2013).

It is possible to identify the main business processes in the oil company's future-oriented business model structure: upstream, downstream, alternative energy (solar energy, wind energy, biofuels), research & development (R&D), and innovation.

More and more oil companies are investing in alternative energy, R&D, and innovation to have a competitive advantage and attract more investor funds.

The outputs of the business model are the capitals transformed by the company's business processes, aligned with the 17 Global Goals (Fig. 35.1).

Financial capital may be related to three of the goals. Manufactured capital may be related to five of the goals. Intellectual capital may be related to three of the goals, human capital may be related to nine of the goals, social and relationship capital may be related to seven of the goals, and natural capital may be related to nine of the goals.

Consider how capital can be transformed as a result of the activities of oil companies.

When a company is successful, its financial capital increases, shareholders receive their dividends, taxes are paid, and employees are paid a decent salary.

Manufactured capital is transformed into extracted resources, high-quality petroleum products, and developed infrastructure.

The introduction of innovative technologies allows growth of oil recovery factor in brownfields, production in the challenging environment, increasing the conversion rate, and producing innovative products that reduce the environmental impact of products consumed by clients. All these transformations are possible with the development of intellectual capital.

High-quality jobs, stable and decent pay, social support, training and career development programs, safe working conditions, medical care programs and support for a healthy lifestyle increase and transform human capital in a positive way.

The contribution of oil companies to the socio-economic stability of regions and their development, improving the quality of life of local communities, promoting social activity, implementing best social practices, and developing cooperation with stakeholders increases the social and relationship capital.

Oil companies have a huge impact on natural capital. In this regard, in the interests of sustainable development, it is necessary to reduce technogenic impact on environment, prevent environmental damage, rational use, restoration, and protection of natural resources, preserve biodiversity, and implement the best world ecological safety practices, energy conservation, and efficiency.

The business model is a key element of integrated reporting and connected to other content elements (Kaspina & Shneydman, 2013), such as strategy, risks and opportunities, and performance (including KPIs).

Table 35.2 shows KPIs for assessment toward the global goals through the oil company's business model. Indicators measure the degree of achievement of a strategic goal; they should be used to make the SDGs measurable.

Using Table 35.3, we evaluated OGCI's activities in achieving SDG 13. Climate action.

In 2018, carbon intensity fell 4%, upstream flaring intensity fell 10%, greenhouse gas emissions from flaring fell by about 9%, total operated greenhouse gas emissions from all sectors (Scope 1) fell 3%, total operated methane emissions from all sectors fell 15%, total upstream methane emissions fell 12%. Upstream operated greenhouse gas emissions (Scope 2) rose 14% as several companies decreased their own power and steam generation in favor of imports. Methane intensity fell by 9% in 2018, dropping to 0.29% over the year. That provides confidence that the actions on track to reach our target of 0.25% by 2025. In 2018, OGCI companies invested $5.5 billion in low carbon energy technologies. Significant areas of spending were energy efficiency, renewable energy, carbon capture, utilization and storage (CCUS), hydrogen and storage. In addition to investment, R&D spending in lower carbon energy rose by 38% to more than $1 billion in 2018 – amounting to 15% of total R&D spend for those companies. Over a quarter of low carbon, R&D focuses on renewable technologies (OGCI, 2019).

The data in Table 35.2 demonstrate that the OGCI companies are successfully working together to achieve SDG 13. They reduce greenhouse gas emissions, methane emissions, and flaring and increase investment in low carbon energy technologies. This provides confidence that joint actions will lead to the achievement of the goal by 2025.

35.4 Conclusion

The proposed business model focuses on short- and long-term sustainable development. The main priorities in sustainable development are safe production, reduction of environmental stress, developing personnel, promote regional development and responsiveness to stakeholders. These priorities are consistent with world trends and the SDGs.

The development of the company's business model integrated with the SDGs and the implementation of the KPI to achieve the Global goals would allow to objectively assess the contribution of each company to sustainable development, ensure comparability of results, allow to constantly monitor the set goals, and compare the company's strategic goals with the SDGs, as well as improving the company's effective activities and their competitive advantage.

Table 35.2 KPI for achieving SDGs through the implementation of oil company business model

SDG	KPI
1. No poverty	Social investments
2. No hunger	Social investments, free and subsidized meals
3. Good health and well-being	Social investments, health insurance costs, total recordable injury frequency (TRIF), total serious incident frequency (SIF), total fatalities, work-related illness frequency (WRI), psychosocial working environment, sporting and cultural events
4. Quality education	Investment in development and training, class room course training days per employee-learning training days per employee
5. Gender equality	Female:male earnings ratio, percentage of permanent employees: women, percentage of women in leadership positions
6. Clean water and sanitation	Total water consumption, number of hydrocarbon spills, total volume of hydrocarbon spills, environmental investment, environmental impact fees
7. Affordable and clean energy	Renewable energy production, oil and gas production, investments in new energy solutions
8. Decent work and economic growth	Number of employees, turnover rate, average monthly salary, employee's commitment rate, cost of social guarantees and benefits, payments to governments, dividends declared, personnel costs
9. Industry innovation and infrastructure	R&D investment, investment in innovation, and infrastructure
10. Reduced inequalities	Social investments sponsorships and donations, purchase of goods and services
11. Sustainable cities and communities	Social investments, investments in social projects
12. Responsible consumption and production	Customers' satisfaction, human rights verifications, total waste generation, waste recovered, waste disposal, energy consumption, energy savings
13. Climate action	Greenhouse gas (GHG) emissions, methane (CH_4) emissions, flaring, total investment in low carbon energy technologies
14. Life under water	Environmental investment, environmental impact fees, oil spills
15. Life on land	Environmental investment, environmental impact fees, reclamation of oil contaminated land, reclamation of sludge pits, ratio of the area of contaminated land at the end of the year vs. at the start of the year, specific amount of spilled oil, condensate, and petroleum products as a result of accidents and leaks, kg/t of extracted hydrocarbons
16. Peace, justice, and strong institutions	Permanent employees' membership of trade unions, average overall zero tolerance for discrimination and harassment score, supplier human rights (HR) verifications conducted
17. Partnerships for the goals	Partnership agreements

Source: companies' webpages, annual reports, sustainability reports

Table 35.3 The relationship of KPI with the SDG13

Category of indicators	Indicator name	Unit	KPI	2017	2018	Dynamics, abs.	Dynamics, %	"+"/ "–" *	"+"/ "–" **
Greenhouse gas emission	Upstream Carbon intensity[a]	kgCO2e/ boe[b]	Dynamics	23,70	22,70	−1,00	−4	+	+
	Total operated greenhouse gas emissions – all sectors (Scope1)[c]	MtCO2e[d]	Dynamics	749	724	−25,00	−3	+	+
	Upstream greenhouse gas emissions (Scope2)	MtCO2e	Dynamics	41,5	47,4	5,90	14	–	–
Methane emission	Upstream Methane Intensity[e]	%	0,25	0,32	0,29	−0,03	−9	+	–
	Total operated methane emission – all sectors[f]	MtCH4[g]	Dynamics	2,42	2,06	−0,36	−15	+	+
	Total operated methane emissions – upstream	MtCH4	Dynamics	2,20	1,93	−0,27	−12	+	+
Flaring	Upstream Flaring Intensity[h]	Mm3/Mtoe	Dynamics	10,00	9,00	−1,00	−10	+	+
	Total natural gas flared- upstream	Mm3[i]	Dynamics	25,89	23,52	−2,37	−9	+	+
	Flaring greenhouse gas emissions-upstream	MtCO2 e	Dynamics	70,00	64,00	−6,00	−9	+	+
Investment in low carbon energy	Total investment in low carbon energy technologies[j]	$ million	Dynamics	4706	5518	812	17	+	+
	R&D expenditures on low carbon technologies[k]	$ million	Dynamics	737	1019	282	38	+	+

[a]Upstream Carbon Intensity is calculated on the basis of upstream carbon dioxide and methane emissions, both Scope 1 and 2, on an operated basis
[b]kgCO2e per barrel of oil equivalent
[c]This figure includes direct (Scope 1) emissions of carbon dioxide, methane, and nitrogen oxide from all operated activities (upstream, as well as downstream, which includes refineries and petrochemicals)
[d]Million tons of carbon dioxide
[e]This is the KPI for OGCI's 2025 upstream methane target. It includes total upstream methane emissions from all operated gas and oil assets. Emissions intensity is calculated as a share of marketed gas

(continued)

[f]This figure includes relevant operated activities (upstream, refineries, petrochemical, power generation etc., where these are operated by the company). Since the share of non-upstream activities varies strongly from company to company, we aim to separate out upstream and downstream data

[g]Million tons of methane

[h]Upstream Flaring Intensity is calculated on the basis of the volume of gas flared per million tons of oil equivalent produced on an operated basis

[i]Million cubic meters

[j]Low carbon energy technologies include but are not limited to: energy efficiency, wind, solar and other renewables, CCUS, hydrogen, biofuels, energy storage, and sustainable mobility

[k]R&D spending is additional to investment

Source: The Oil and Gas Climate Initiative webpages, annual report

Note: * "+"positive/"–" negative dynamics, ** "+" reached/"–" target value not reached, "+"/"–" dynamics

Organizations that adopt the concept of responsible business integrate sustainable development goals into their strategies, take better positions, and gain a competitive advantage, as this will no longer be a matter of choice in the future, but will be a responsibility that affects how the organization operates.

Focusing the business model on the SDGs will open up new business opportunities and have a positive impact on financial results. This is especially true for large business players such as oil companies.

References

A report from the Oil and Gas Climate Initiative September 2019. URL: https://oilandgasclimateinitiative.com/wp-content/uploads/2019/10/OGCI-Annual-Report-2019.pdf, pp 49–61.

Adams, C. A. (2017). *The Sustainable Development Goals, integrated thinking and the integrated report*. IIRC and ICAS. ISBN 978-1-909883-41-3. URL: https://www.icas.com/data/assets/pdf_file/0010/336475/SDGs-and-the-integratedreport_full17.pdf

Dr. Sean Stein Smith Integrated Financial Reporting & Management Accounting An Opportunity for Strategic Leadership Rutgers University School of Business- Camden United States. *Journal of Business & Economic Policy, 4*(1), 2017. https://doi.org/10.30845/jbep. ISSN 2375-0766 (Print), 2375-0774 (Online).

International Integrated Reporting Council (IIRC). (2013). *International framework*. URL: http://integratedreporting.org/resource/international-ir-framework/

Kaplan, R., & Norton, D. (1996). Linking the balanced scorecard to strategy. *California Management Review, 39*(1). https://doi.org/10.2307/41165876

Kaspina, R. G., & Khapugina, L. S. (2017). *Use of management accounting information for the formation of the business model of a public company. New trends in finance and accounting*. In Proceedings of the 17th annual conference on finance and accounting, pp. 581–586. https://doi.org/10.1007/978-3-319-49559-0_53

Kaspina, R. G., & Sabirzyanova, R. (2017). Analysis of the best practice of disclosing information about key performance indicators and business models in the integrated reporting of an oil company. *Kazan Social and Humanitarian Bulletin, 4*, 40–44. https://doi.org/10.24153/2079-5912-2017-8-4-40-44

Kaspina, R. G., & Shneydman, L. Z. (2013). New approach to the oil companies' corporate reporting. *Oil Industry, 9*, 14–17.

Kaspina R. G., & Trofimova, D. A. (2016). Formation of indicators of the corporate reporting according to information expectations of the interested users. *Kazan Social and Humanitarian Bulletin, 5*, 21–27. https://doi.org/10.24153/2079-5912-2016-7-5-21-27

Petera, P., Wagner, J., & Knorová, K. (2016). Perception and interpretation of sustainability among the largest corporations established in the Czech Republic. *Acta Universitatis Agriculturae et Silviculturae Mendelianae Brunensis, 64*, 1053–1065. https://doi.org/10.11118/actaun201664031053

Resolution adopted by the General Assembly on 25 September 2015. URL: https://www.un.org/en/development/desa/population/publications/2030_Agenda_en.pdf

Stevens, P. (2016, May). *International oil companies: The death of the old business model*. London: The Royal Institute of International Affairs. Chatham House. URL: https://www.chathamhouse.org/sites/files/chathamhouse/publications/research/2016-05-05-international-oil-companies-stevens.pdf

Tanţău, A. D., & Khorshidi, M. (2016). New business models for state companies in the oil industry. *Management & Marketing Challenges for the Knowledge Society, 11*(3), 484–497. https://doi.org/10.1515/mmcks-2016-0011

The official website of The Oil and Gas Climate Initiative (OGCI). URL: https://oilandgasclimateinitiative.com/

The official website of the United Nations. URL: https://www.un.org/sustainabledevelopment/

The official website of the World Economic Forum. URL: https://www.weforum.org/events/world-economic-forum-annual-meeting-2020

Index

D. Procházka (ed.), *Regulation of Finance and Accounting*, Springer Proceedings in Business and Economics, https://doi.org/10.1007/978-3-030-99873-8

B

C

D

E

F